DATE DUE

MAY 0 7 2002	

Health and well-being during adolescence depend largely on the fit between the young person's developmental needs and desires and the opportunities provided by the changing context. In *Health Risks and Developmental Transitions During Adolescence*, prominent researchers in the adolescent field examine how various developmental transitions associated with the passage from childhood to adulthood present risks and opportunities for adolescents' mental and physical health.

Given the importance of adolescence in determining the course of health and well-being across the life span, efforts to ease the various transitions into and out of adolescence will yield long-term health benefits. By focusing on the link between health risks and developmental transitions, and particularly on the individual and contextual conditions and planned interventions that moderate the link, this interdisciplinary book offers a foundation for a unifying framework for research and application in health and human development.

**Health Risks and Developmental Transitions
During Adolescence**

Health Risks and Developmental Transitions During Adolescence

Edited by

JOHN SCHULENBERG
University of Michigan

JENNIFER L. MAGGS
University of Arizona

KLAUS HURRELMANN
University of Bielefeld

CAMBRIDGE
UNIVERSITY PRESS

PUBLISHED BY THE PRESS SYNDICATE OF THE UNIVERSITY
OF CAMBRIDGE
The Pitt Building, Trumpington Street, Cambridge, CB2 1RP,
United Kingdom

CAMBRIDGE UNIVERSITY PRESS
The Edinburgh Building, Cambridge CB2 2RU, United Kingdom
40 West 20th Street, New York, NY 10011-4211, USA
10 Stamford Road, Oakleigh, Melbourne 3166, Australia

© Cambridge University Press 1997

First published 1997

Printed in the United States of America

Typeset in Times Roman

Library of Congress Cataloging-in-Publication Data
Health risks and developmental transitions during adolescence / edited
by John Schulenberg, Jennifer L. Maggs, Klaus Hurrelmann.
p.   cm.
Includes index.
ISBN 0-521-48053-1
1. Health behavior in adolescence.   2. Adolescent psychology.
3. Risk-taking (Psychology) in adolescence.   4. Teenagers – Health
and hygiene.   I. Schulenberg, John.   II. Maggs, Jennifer L.
III. Hurrelmann, Klaus.
RJ47.53.H435   1997
613′.0433 – dc20   96-7839
                                                           CIP

A catalog record for this book is available from the British Library.

ISBN 0-521-48053-1 hardback

Contents

Contributors

Jan Alwin
Institute for Child Development
University of Minnesota
Minneapolis, Minnesota, USA

Toni C. Antonucci
Institute for Social Research, and
Department of Psychology
University of Michigan
Ann Arbor, Michigan, USA

Jerald G. Bachman
Institute for Social Research
University of Michigan
Ann Arbor, Michigan, USA

Bonnie L. Barber
School of Family and Consumer
   Resources
University of Arizona
Tucson, Arizona, USA

Ruth Beyth-Marom
Department of Psychology
Open University of Israel
Tel Aviv, Israel

Jeanne Brooks-Gunn
Center for the Study of Youth,
   Children, and Families
Teachers College, Columbia
   University
New York, New York, USA

B. Bradford Brown
Department of Educational
   Psychology
University of Wisconsin
Madison, Wisconsin, USA

Cleopatra Howard Caldwell
Institute for Social Research
University of Michigan
Ann Arbor, Michigan, USA

Laurie Chassin
Psychology Department
Arizona State University
Tempe, Arizona, USA

Lisa J. Crockett
Department of Psychology
University of Nebraska
Lincoln, Nebraska, USA

Shuai Ding
Institute for Child Development
University of Minnesota
Minneapolis, Minnesota, USA

M. Margaret Dolcini
Prevention Sciences Group
University of California–San
   Francisco
San Francisco, California, USA

Jacquelynne S. Eccles
Department of Psychology,
School of Education, and

Institute for Social Research
University of Michigan
Ann Arbor, Michigan, USA

Marion F. Ehrenberg
Department of Psychology
University of Victoria
Victoria, British Columbia, Canada

Michael D. Finch
Institute for Health Services
  Research and Policy
University of Minnesota
Minneapolis, Minnesota, USA

Baruch Fischhoff
Department of Social and Decision
  Sciences
Carnegie-Mellon University
Pittsburgh, Pennsylvania, USA

Melissa A. Freel
Institute for Children, Youth, and
  Families
Michigan State University
East Lansing, Michigan, USA

Nancy L. Galambos
Department of Psychology
University of Victoria
Victoria, British Columbia, Canada

Barbara Graham
Institute for Child Development
University of Minnesota
Minneapolis, Minnesota, USA

Klaus Hurrelmann
School of Public Health and Special
  Research Center 227: Prevention
  and Intervention in Childhood
  and Adolescence
University of Bielefeld
Bielefeld, Germany

Lloyd D. Johnston
Institute for Social Research
University of Michigan
Ann Arbor, Michigan, USA

Debra M. Hernandez Jozefowicz
Institute for Social Research
University of Michigan
Ann Arbor, Michigan, USA

Eric L. Kohatsu
Department of Psychology
California State University
Los Angeles, California, USA

Bärbel Kracke
Department of Education
University of Mannheim
Mannheim, Germany

Nancy Leffert
Institute for Child Development
University of Minnesota
Minneapolis, Minnesota, USA

Richard M. Lerner
Institute for Children, Youth, and
  Families
Michigan State University
East Lansing, Michigan, USA

Amy Leventhal
Department of Educational
  Psychology
University of Wisconsin–Madison
Madison, Wisconsin, USA

Sarah E. Lord
Institute for Social Research
University of Michigan
Ann Arbor, Michigan, USA

Jennifer L. Maggs
School of Family and Consumer
  Resources
University of Arizona
Tucson, Arizona, USA

Eduard Matt
Special Research Center 186: Status
  Changes and Risk-Taking in the
  Life Course
University of Bremen
Breman, Germany

Jeylan T. Mortimer
The Life Course Center, and
Department of Sociology
University of Minnesota
Minneapolis, Minnesota, USA

Peter Noack
Department of Education
University of Mannheim
Mannheim, Germany

Jari-Erik Nurmi
Department of Psychology
University of Jyvaskyla
Jyvaskyla, Finland

Patrick M. O'Malley
Institute for Social Research
University of Michigan
Ann Arbor, Michigan, USA

Charles W. Ostrom
Institute for Children, Youth, and
  Families
Michigan State University
East Lansing, Michigan, USA

Roberta Paikoff
Department of Psychiatry
University of Illinois, Chicago
Chicago, Illinois, USA

Anne C. Petersen
National Science Foundation,
Arlington, Virginia, USA, and
Institute for Child Development
University of Minnesota
Minneapolis, Minnesota, USA

Jean S. Phinney
Department of Psychology
California State University
Los Angeles, California, USA

Robert W. Roeser
School of Education
University of Michigan
Ann Arbor, Michigan, USA

Seongryeol Ryu
The Life Course Center
University of Minnesota
Minneapolis, Minnesota, USA

John Schulenberg
Institute for Social Research, and
Department of Psychology
University of Michigan
Ann Arbor, Michigan, USA

Karl F. Schumann
Special Research Center 186: Status
  Changes and Risk-Taking in the
  Life Course
University of Breman
Bremen, Germany

Lydia Seus
Special Research Center 186: Status
  Changes and Risk-Taking in the
  Life Course
University of Breman
Bremen, Germany

Rainer K. Silbereisen
Department of Developmental
  Psychology

Friedrich Schiller University of Jena
Jena, Germany

Katherine N. Wadsworth
Institute for Social Research
University of Michigan
Ann Arbor, Michigan, USA

John M. Wallace, Jr.
School of Social Work, and

Institute for Social Research
University of Michigan
Ann Arbor, Michigan, USA

David R. Williams
Department of Sociology, and
Institute for Social Research
University of Michigan
Ann Arbor, Michigan, USA

Foreword

Laurie Chassin

In the last 20 years there has been an explosion of scientific interest in the adolescent years, and adolescence is assuming a more prominent place both in developmental research and in national public policy (Takanishi, 1993). The field of adolescent health is no exception to this trend and, in fact, has provided much of the impetus for the heightened interest in adolescent research. Long-standing views of adolescence as a period of optimal physical health and therefore a topic undeserving of research attention have been challenged by recent empirical reports and expanded definitions of health (which include mental health indicators as well as health risk behaviors, rather than focusing strictly on mortality rates; Dougherty, 1993). Applying such an expanded definition, recent estimates are that one in five adolescents aged 10–18 have at least one serious health problem (Dougherty, 1993). This high prevalence, along with several recent highly publicized reviews (including the Office of Technology Assessment's 1991 report to Congress), have made the health needs of adolescents more salient.

Adolescents' health risks are also of particular importance to social scientists because the major threats to health in this age period are largely behaviorally based (e.g., suicide, homicide, teen pregnancy, delinquency, alcohol and drug abuse, and human immunodeficiency virus infection). Because of the pressing public health importance of adolescent health risks and the behavioral bases of these risks, the adolescent health arena offers a challenge to behavioral and social scientists to apply recent innovations in theory and methodology to develop an understanding of adolescents' health outcomes, and to design and evaluate appropriate interventions to optimize these outcomes. This volume is an exciting response to this challenge, and the research reported here exemplifies important new directions for the field of adolescent health.

First, research in adolescent health must adopt a more differentiated view of adolescence as involving a series of multiple transitions rather than combining samples of diverse ages. One important transition (which is rarely studied) involves the move from adolescence to young adulthood. Epidemiological data on age-related trends in risk behaviors suggest that many of these behaviors peak in the period from late adolescence to early adulthood and then decline. An understanding of these age patterns requires a research focus on the transition from adolescence to young adulthood such as the one seen in this volume. For example, research presented here describes the ways in which taking on (and losing) marital and parental roles, establishing occupational roles, building a sense of personal identity and ethnic identity, and setting and implementing life plans and goals relate to health outcomes during this transition. Other important transitions within the adolescent age period are also well represented here, including the transition to middle school and transitions in pubertal status. Thus, this volume illustrates the utility of considering multiple transitions that occur during adolescence, and the health risks and opportunities associated with each.

Another important direction for research in adolescent health is to apply recent theory and data that challenge conventional wisdom about the nature of adolescence. This volume exemplifies such a direction by recasting the way we view adolescent health risk behaviors. Rather than portray health risk behaviors as irrational aberrations adopted by adolescents who are deficient in cognitive abilities, research presented here suggests that these behaviors represent subjectively rational decisions and examples of purposeful, goal-directed behaviors. This theme, echoed in many chapters, is critical for the design of effective interventions because unless their functions are challenged or replaced, it is unlikely that health risk behaviors can be altered. Moreover, research in this volume challenges the conventional wisdom that adolescents are victims of monolithic, antisocial peer influences by describing the transformations of peer relationships in adolescence and their implications for health risk behaviors. Given the prominence accorded to peer influences in current preventive interventions aimed at adolescents, a better understanding of these influences is of critical importance for improving the outcomes of these interventions.

An emerging trend in adolescent developmental research is the renewed attention to context and the need to embed behavior in multiple interacting contexts (Jessor, 1993). This trend is advanced in the current volume by the consideration of multiple levels of analysis and the recognition that adolescent outcomes are influenced by multiple contexts, including biological developmental processes, families, neighborhoods, schools, subcultures, ethnic and racial groups, and historical contexts. The book includes a rare look at how processes of large-scale societal change may be reflected in family processes and in individual health outcomes. Most important, the book illustrates the interplay among levels of analysis that both allow for new directions for intervention research and transcend simplistic arguments about which level of analysis is most useful.

Adolescent health researchers must also be mindful of the fact that adolescents are active construers, choosers, and shapers of their environments rather than simply passive recipients of environmental influences. As adolescents make health-relevant behavioral decisions, these decisions will be considered in the context of their values, goals, life plans, and self-definitions. Interventions designed to influence adolescents' health behaviors will have to consider these contexts. Research presented in this volume highlights this perspective.

Finally, previous research in adolescent health has been overly focused on negative health outcomes and behaviors. However, as this volume illustrates, important opportunities for health promotion occur during adolescence. Adolescents' cognitive abilities, abilities for self-regulation, and increasing autonomy offer the potential for positive health behaviors and for effective mastery of threats to health. As this volume repeatedly reminds us, such conditions as work roles, peer influences, cognitive development, and even family adversity also offer opportunities for growth, even as they convey risk for negative outcomes.

Of course, the challenge for the future is to build on the generative data base that is being developed and that is advanced by this volume, and to apply these data to the design and evaluation of preventive interventions to reduce adolescents' health risks. Converging trends in the fields of physical and mental health have come together in the newly emerging discipline of prevention science (Coie ct al. 1993) and, as evidenced in recent reports by the Institute of Medicine (1994a, 1994b), adolescents are an important target audience for these preventive interventions. However, to develop effective interventions for adolescents requires a knowledge of their unique characteristics and of the processes that impact their health-relevant decisions. More specifically, researchers must learn to develop interventions (1) that are capable of reaching high-risk adolescents within the general population, (2) that deal with the co-occurrence of multiple adolescent health risk behaviors (Takanishi, 1993), (3) that appropriately address the multiple social contexts within which adolescent health behaviors are embedded, and (4) that effectively translate knowledge about adolescent development and processes of risk and resilience into powerful interventions.

References

Coie, J., Watt, N., West, S., Hawkins, J. D. Asarnow, J. R., Markman, H. J., Ramey, S. L., Shure, M. B., & Long, B. (1993). The science of prevention: A conceptual framework and some directions for a national research program. *American Psychologist, 48*, 1013–1022.

Dougherty, D. M. (1993). Adolescent health: Reflections on a report to the U.S. Congress. *American Psychologist, 48*, 193–201.

Institute of Medicine. (1994a). *Growing up tobacco free: Preventing nicotine addiction in children and youths.* Washington, DC: National Academy Press.

Institute of Medicine. (1994b). *Reducing risks for mental disorders: Frontiers for preventive intervention research.* Washington, DC: National Academy Press.

Jessor, R. (1993). Successful adolescent development among youth in high-risk settings. *American Psychologist, 48*, 117–126.

Takanishi, R. (1993). The opportunities of adolescence – Research, interventions, and policy. *American Psychologist, 48*, 85–87.

U.S. Congress, Office of Technology Assessment. (1991). *Adolescent health: Volume 1. Summary and policy options* (Pub. No. OTA-H-468). Washington, DC: U.S. Government Printing Office.

Preface

Until about three decades ago there was relatively little empirical research on adolescents, and most of the scientific and popular views were based on the notion that adolescence is necessarily a time of "storm and stress." Over the past few decades, the situation has changed dramatically. Simplistic conceptual perspectives have given way to ones that more adequately embrace the complexity and multidimensionality of adolescence. Historically, interest in the study of adolescence has spanned several disciplines (e.g., psychology, sociology, public health, education, anthropology, psychiatry). Recently, however, there has been a trend toward interdisciplinary efforts and a blending of multiple levels of analysis (e.g., biological, psychological, social, cultural). In terms of empirical research, both the number and the quality of studies have increased steadily over the years. Contextually sensitive and cross-cultural studies have become much more common, and cross-sectional studies have given way to longitudinal ones. Yet, at this time, we can say that the study of adolescence, like the study of human development in general, is still in its "childhood." There are few facts – only occasional glimpses of what makes for optimal health and development during adolescence. We hope that this book can offer more than the occasional glimpse.

The idea for this edited volume grew out of our mutual interest in the nexus between developmental transitions and health risks during adolescence, and more generally between developmental psychology and public health. There is substantial evidence that health risks increase dramatically during adolescence. Yet, health risks do not accrue automatically as part of the maturation process, but instead as a function of the multiple social, psychological, and physical transitions that occur during adolescence. At the same time, developmental transitions may have salutary effects by offering opportunities for increased mental and physical health. Our purpose in editing this volume was to bring together some of the leading developmental scientists who represent a variety of disciplines to consider the research, theory, and practice that relate developmental transitions during adolescence with health risks and opportunities. The perspective offered in this volume is not comprehensive, but rather is illustrative of the type of research suggested as well as the nature of insights that may be gained by focusing on the link between health risks and developmental transitions. This link, and especially the individual and contextual conditions that moderate it, provide a basis for a unifying framework for research and intervention in health and human development.

We first wish to acknowledge the authors. Our strong enthusiasm for the book was matched in each case by theirs, and we especially appreciated their patience with our active editing. For many authors, their efforts here represent new directions in their research programs, and we wish to thank them sincerely for their willingness to share these new ventures in this book.

John Schulenberg wishes to acknowledge with gratitude the support and intellectual challenge provided by the Survey Research Center in the Institute for Social Research. Jennifer Maggs would like to acknowledge the support of the Social Sciences and Humanities Research Council of Canada throughout all phases of this endeavor.

We developed ideas for this book at various international conferences in Germany and the United States. Some of these conferences were sponsored in part by the Johann Jacobs Foundation, the Pennsylvania State University Center for the Study of Child and Adolescent Development, the International Society for the Study of Behavioral Development, and the German Research Association. We extend our gratitude to these organizations for their indirect support in this international collaboration.

We wish to acknowledge the assistance of several individuals at the University of Michigan. Terry Sawyer helped with the editing of the chapters, making valuable suggestions to improve the clarity and continuity of the entire manuscript. Hadley Dynak was very helpful in the early phases of this project by conducting literature searches and providing overviews of relevant literature. The editorial and logistical assistance provided by Joyce Buchanan and Elaine Cousino is much appreciated.

We would like to thank Julia Hough, our editor at Cambridge University Press. Her professionalism, enthusiasm, and guidance were very important in moving this book from an interesting idea to a reality.

Finally, we each wish to express our deep gratitude to our spouses, Cathleen Connell, David Almeida, and Bettina Hurrelmann. It is difficult to imagine how or why we would have completed this project without them.

John Schulenberg, Jennifer L. Maggs, and Klaus Hurrelmann

1   Negotiating Developmental Transitions During Adolescence and Young Adulthood: Health Risks and Opportunities

*John Schulenberg, Jennifer L. Maggs,
and Klaus Hurrelmann*

Developmental transitions are the paths that connect us to transformed physical, mental, and social selves. Puberty represents an obvious developmental transition, and the same is true for moving from elementary school to junior high, from school to work, and from being single to getting married. There are many other developmental transitions that are more subtle yet still distinct, such as a young adolescent who usually does what she is told beginning to argue persuasively against her parents' directives; a small same-sex group of friends becoming folded into a larger group made up of boys and girls, which in turn is replaced by individual friendships and dating relationships; and a concrete and typically unquestioned self-definition becoming more abstract and tentative, and eventually more hierarchic and future oriented. Together, these and the many other developmental transitions during the second and third decades of life provide the structure that transforms children into adolescents and adolescents into young adults.

Common to all developmental transitions is the element of discontinuity. Although the discontinuity is neither necessarily abrupt nor unequivocal, it is clear that each transition involves some change in how we experience ourselves and our world, as well as in how others experience us. And change involves risk. On our way to transformed selves, we may stumble. Experiencing a transition, regardless of the type of transition or the extent of our past experience, is likely to disrupt our sense of balance and well-being, if only momentarily. Such disruption is particularly likely to occur when one experiences multiple and simultaneous transitions, which is typical for most adolescents (Coleman, 1978). In addition to the risks to health and well-being that may be associated with the stress of confronting and being confronted with a developmental transition, health risks can occur as adolescents make their way through developmental transitions and may even be part of the negotiation process. For example, in negotiating increased autonomy from parents and

John Schulenberg and Jennifer Maggs would like to acknowledge that their efforts in preparing this chapter were supported in part by grants from the National Institute on Alcohol Abuse and Alcoholism (AA06324) and the Social Sciences and Humanities Research Council of Canada.

1

increased intimacy with peers, smoking a cigarette may seem like a great idea if our valued and adventurous friends are likewise indulging. Yet the health risks of this transition-inspired behavior could be substantial.

Change also involves opportunity. Developmental transitions can be salutary. For example, moving from the relatively monolithic role of high school student to the diversity of post–high school experiences is associated with increased self-esteem (e.g., Aseltine & Gore, 1993; Bachman, O'Malley, & Johnston, 1978). Gaining a better understanding of how the world works, a firmer grasp of logic and cause–effect relationships, broader access to social support, and greater control over one's social context will likely increase one's ability to avoid or alter behaviors detrimental to one's health. Although identity exploration is associated with instability in well-being, as well as with experimentation and risk taking that has the potential to compromise one's health, subsequent identity achievement is associated with higher levels of well-being and a lower incidence of health-compromising behaviors (e.g., Jones, 1992; Marcia, 1994). When opportunities for increased responsibility and freedom match the young person's desire and readiness for such – that is, a developmental "match" (cf. Eccles et al., 1993; Eccles, Lord, Roeser, Barber, & Jozefowicz, chapter 11, this volume) or "good fit" (cf. Lerner, 1982; Lerner, Ostrum, & Freel, chapter 19, this volume) – it is likely that health and well-being will be enhanced. In short, developmental transitions sometimes do, and perhaps with appropriate intervention more often could, serve to diminish health risks and promote well-being.

In addition to discontinuity, developmental transitions are characterized by continuity. Indeed, it is this blend of continuity and discontinuity that makes a developmental transition a unique vantage point for examining developmental processes (Petersen, 1993; Schulenberg, Wadsworth, O'Malley, Bachman, & Johnston, 1996). Continuity in functioning and adjustment across developmental transitions occurs for numerous reasons, including the stability of physical, temperamental, and personality characteristics, as well as stability of many features of one's context. One of the best predictors of future adjustment is past adjustment, and health over the life span tends to follow a specific trajectory reflecting continuity (e.g., Susman, Dorn, Feagans, & Ray, 1992). Obviously, this continuity can be either salutary or detrimental to health. The challenge is how to influence developmental transitions such that there is continuity in health-enhancing behaviors and discontinuity in health-compromising behaviors.

In this book, we examine how various developmental transitions associated with the passage from childhood to adulthood provide risks and opportunities for adolescents' mental and physical health. More specifically, our purpose is to provide a showcase for research, theory, and practice that relates normative and nonnormative transitions during adolescence to health-compromising and health-enhancing behaviors. Although there is a wealth of literature regarding normative and nonnormative tasks and transitions during adolescence, and likewise a wealth of literature on health risks during adolescence, there have been few systematic attempts to integrate these perspectives to highlight the link between developmental transitions and health (some important exceptions are included in Millstein, Petersen, & Nightingale, 1993; Rutter, 1995a; Susman, Feagans, & Ray, 1992). This link, and especially the individual and contextual conditions that moderate the link, provide the basis for a unifying framework for research and intervention in health and human development. In this introductory chapter, we discuss some of the issues involved in building such a framework. First, we provide a brief and selective overview of the study of adolescent development. We then briefly discuss developmental transitions during adolescence, health and well-being during adolescence, and the different ways in which health risks and developmental transitions may be related. Finally, we summarize the plan and organization of the book.

Selected Issues in the Study of Adolescent Development

G. Stanley Hall, considered to be the founder of the scientific study of adolescence (Muuss, 1988), gave us the lasting image of adolescence as a time of unavoidable "storm and stress." According to Hall's biologically based theory, individual development (ontogeny) recapitulates the development of the species (phylogeny), with the stage of adolescence reflecting the turbulent transition in the history of the human race from savagery to civilization (Hall, 1904). Thus, by definition, adolescence is a turbulent stage in the life course. The adolescent that the field inherited from Hall is a troubled and troubling soul, fickle in the extreme, desperate for a leader yet reactive against all authority, and constantly torn between such desires as passion and fidelity, conceit and humility, and so on. Nothing can be done to ease adolescents' pain or the pain they cause others, Hall tells us, because development is a maturational process controlled completely by biological factors and thus unaffected by sociocultural factors. That is, adolescence is "just a stage," and when it passes, health and well-being will return. Approaching a century later, this mythical image we inherited from Hall is still difficult to shake.

Of course, Hall was not alone in his beliefs on this subject. Most prominently, Sigmund Freud's psychoanalytic theory made it exceedingly clear that turmoil is an essential and unavoidable component of adolescence. According to Freud, puberty brings on the genital stage of psychosexual development, and the re-emergence of sexual desire topples the delicate balance between the id, ego, and superego achieved during the previous latency stage. At the same time, in order eventually to form healthy sexual relations and to function independently as an adult, it is essential that the adolescent sever his or her emotional dependence on parents, which is likely to take the form of hostility and conflict (A. Freud, 1958). Although other psychoanalytic theorists disagreed with Freud with respect to the causes of turmoil during adolescence (e.g., Blos, 1970; Sullivan, 1947), they did not disagree with the inevitability of turmoil. Even Erik Erikson (1950), whose theory includes a strong emphasis on the healthy personality as well as on the importance of historical and cultural contexts, considered the physiological changes of puberty as prompting a psychological crisis during adolescence.

In addition to these organismic and psychoanalytic roots of the current image of adolescence, there are mechanistic and contextual roots as well (cf. Pepper, 1942). In particular, based partly on the work of Margaret Mead (1950), Ruth Benedict (1950) argued that storm and stress is more a cultural phenomenon due to the discontinuity in roles and responsibilities between childhood, adolescence, and adulthood in modern societies. Likewise, Kurt Lewin (1939) made it clear that difficulties during adolescence were as much attributable to the ambiguous life space that adolescents are placed in as they were to any individual characteristics. Finally, Robert Havighurst (1952) delineated the several culturally defined developmental tasks that individuals need to accomplish during certain age ranges in order to realize successful adaptation. Difficulties that arose during adolescence were thought of in terms of inability or unwillingness to accomplish the necessary tasks.

The current image of adolescence in the scientific literature is harder to pinpoint, in part because modern theories and models tend to be more variable centered than person centered (cf. Cairns & Cairns, 1994; Magnusson, 1988). Furthermore, notions of stages and developmental determinism have given way to probabilistic conceptualizations focused on person–context interactions (e.g., Jessor, 1993; Lerner, 1985; Lerner et al., chapter 19, this volume; Sameroff, 1987). Consistent with life span and ecological perspectives (e.g., Baltes, Cornelius, & Nesselroade, 1979; Bronfenbrenner & Crouter, 1982; Elder, 1974; Featherman, 1983; Lerner, 1985; Schaie, 1965), today's portrayal of the adolescent is historically and culturally bound. Increasingly, the answer to any question about the impact of some characteristic or event on a young person's development typically is "it depends." With regard to difficulties during adolescence, a common view now is that "adolescence is characterized by change, and is challenging, but it need not be tumultuous and problematic unless societal conditions prompt it" (Petersen & Leffert, 1995, p. 3).

This strong focus on context in the study of adolescence has been associated with the field becoming more interdisciplinary, international, and sensitive to diversity. Taking seriously the focus on development in context and person–context interactions necessitates an interdisciplinary emphasis. This emphasis permits explication of how causal forces move across traditionally discipline-bound domains, such as how social structure influences and is influenced by parent–child relationships and parenting goals and practices (e.g., Kohn & Schooler, 1983; McLoyd, 1990; Mortimer, 1976; Ogbu, 1981). Likewise, interdisciplinary efforts are necessary to delineate the multilevel influences on behavior, such as how social context and biological factors interact to influence adolescent difficulties (e.g., Cairns & Cairns, 1994; Caspi, Lynam, Moffitt, & Silva, 1993; Silbereisen & Kracke, chapter 4, this volume; Simmons & Blyth, 1987; Stattin & Magnusson, 1990; Udry, 1988). The international emphasis draws from and permits further consideration of person–context interactions, and specifically the cultural embeddedness of adolescent development. Through this emphasis, it is possible to begin to understand the diversity and similarity in experience across cultures (e.g., Feldman & Rosenthal, 1994; Hamilton, 1994; Silbereisen, Noack, & Schoenpflug, 1994). Likewise, there has been increasing emphasis on diversity of experience within cultures, particularly with understanding the embeddedness of social class, ethnicity, and gender within the larger sociocultural context, and how these can shape health and development during adolescence (e.g., Dryfoos, 1990; Earls, 1993; Elliott, 1993; Lerner et al., chapter 19, and Phinney & Kohatsu, chapter 16, this volume; Spencer & Dornbusch, 1990). This attention to diversity and similarity of the adolescent experience between and within cultures not only will offer greater understanding of person–context interactions, but will also provide the knowledge base necessary to promote optimal development and health for all adolescents.

Developmental Transitions During Adolescence

The transformation from childhood to adulthood involves many smaller transitions through which individuals move toward greater freedom and responsibility in many domains of life. In addition to the pubertal and cognitive transitions that occur during adolescence, other developmental transitions can be grouped into affiliation transitions (e.g., changes in relationships associated with parents, peers, romantic partners, and offspring), achievement transitions (e.g., school and work transitions), and identity transitions (e.g., changes in self-definition, ethnic identity formation). This categorization is used in organizing the present volume.

The nature of developmental transitions originates in the interaction of physical maturational processes, cultural influences and expectations, and personal values and goals. Individuals shape their own developmental transitions as their physical and psychological selves act on and are acted upon by the social and physical environment (e.g., Gottlieb, 1991; Lerner, 1982; Scarr & McCartney, 1983). Like other developmental processes, these transitions are embedded in a sociocultural context, and therefore are likely to vary with gender, class, culture, and historical period. Culturally based, age-related expectations shape developmental transitions by providing a normative social timetable for role transitions (e.g., employment, parenthood). There are also significant interindividual variations in the order and importance of the various transitions, depending on personal goals and life situations (e.g., Nurmi,

6   J. SCHULENBERG, J. L. MAGGS, AND K. HURRELMANN

1993). Thus, developmental transitions can be normative or nonnormative, depending on their prevalence within a given population, as well as on their timing. Leaving school is normative, but dropping out before high school graduation or graduating from college at age 18 is typically viewed as nonnormative. Likewise, becoming a parent is a normative transition, but doing so early in adolescence or late in adulthood is typically viewed as nonnormative. Health risks may be more likely to be associated with nonnormative transitions, but this is not always the case. Just as normative transitions can be associated with both health risks and opportunities, so can nonnormative transitions (e.g., Caldwell & Antonucci, chapter 9, this volume).

It is important to make a distinction between developmental transitions and developmental tasks. *Developmental tasks* (Havighurst, 1952; Oerter, 1986) are socially prescribed psychosocial tasks that should be accomplished during specific "sensitive periods" across the life span. Although tasks and transitions are clearly related and sometimes even overlapping (e.g., selecting a mate as a task versus the transition to marriage), we view *developmental transitions* as pertaining more to the actual changes than to the accomplishments that contribute to and result from the changes. Furthermore, some transitions are changes that one has little or no control over, such as puberty and school transitions. In this sense, we view developmental transitions as the larger category that encompasses developmental tasks. It is also important to distinguish developmental transitions from developmental pathways or trajectories (cf. Cairns & Cairns, 1994; Crockett & Crouter, 1995; Schulenberg, Wadsworth et al., 1996). *Developmental trajectories* refer to patterns of structured change over time and might incorporate several developmental transitions for a given individual or groups of individuals. An emphasis on trajectories represents a powerful approach to understanding the path of individual change over time, providing a needed alternative to more normative change approaches. Nevertheless, as Steinberg (1995) argues, an emphasis on developmental trajectories may serve to overestimate continuity in functioning over time. In contrast, a focus on individual developmental transitions permits the consideration of discontinuity in adjustment as a function of the transition.

Health Risks and Opportunities During Adolescence

Health is clearly more than the lack of illness. That is, in addition to surviving it also encompasses thriving. Increasingly, it is becoming recognized that the distinction between physical and mental health is often artificial and sometimes misleading (e.g., Cohen & Rodriguiz, 1995). Consistent with the World Health Organization's (1986) conception of health, Hurrelmann (1990) defines *health* as the objective and subjective state of well-being that is present when the physical, psychological, and social development of a person are in harmony with his or her own possibilities, goals, and prevailing living conditions. Just as the process of working through developmental transitions is shaped by biological, personal, and sociocultural influences, health and well-being are influenced by these factors as well. This definition is sufficiently broad to recognize the diversity of approaches to health extant in the adolescent development field and in the present volume.

The term *health risk* refers to any threat to one's immediate or future health and well-being. Health risk constitutes a broad category that can include both health risk factors (e.g., poverty, role strain, social isolation, hostile temperament) and health risk behaviors (e.g., substance abuse, violence, sedentary lifestyle or habits, unprotected sexual intercourse, poor eating habits). This distinction is not always useful, however (e.g., in the case of depression), and one could view health risk factors and behaviors as being reciprocally related (e.g., a past risk behavior becomes a risk factor for future risk behavior). Health opportunities include factors (e.g., supportive prosocial peers) and behaviors (e.g., physical exercise) that serve to promote or enhance health and should be viewed as referring to more than simply the absence of health risks. When attempting to understand health during adolescence, there is a need to appreciate the balance between health risks and opportunities. As we discuss in the next section, short-term health risks may become long-term health opportunities, and what may objectively appear as a health risk can be interpreted as a health opportunity from the adolescent's perspective.

Linking Developmental Transitions and Health Risks

In thinking about how developmental transitions may be linked with health risks and opportunities, we believe it is more productive to focus on "interactions" rather than "main effects" (cf. Bronfenbrenner, 1979). That is, rather than questioning whether a given developmental transition contributes to health risks or opportunities, a more illuminating question would be: What are the individual and contextual conditions under which a given developmental transition contributes to a given health risk or health opportunity? It is also important to recognize the dependency of the link between developmental transitions and health risks/opportunities on the overarching cultural context, and likewise to recognize that the link is subject to historical change. There have been important changes in the nature of developmental transitions during adolescence over the past several decades, changes that may have increased the possibility of accompanying health risks (e.g., Crockett, chapter 2, this volume; Dryfoos, 1990; Jessor, 1993; Lerner et al., chapter 19, and Noack & Kracke, chapter 3, this volume; Robins, 1995; Rutter, 1995b). In particular, the timing and patterns of developmental transitions associated with the transformation from childhood to adulthood have become more diverse and thus

less certain. For example, several important social trends have made the
transition to adulthood more variable and potentially more difficult, including
changes in the order, timing, and patterns of interpersonal relationships (e.g.,
cohabitation, parenthood); increased duration of vocational training; difficulty
entering uncertain labor markets; and increased pluralism of societal norms
and values (e.g., Hurrelmann, 1984). At the same time, however, it is essential
to recognize that the increased diversity in the timing and patterns of developmental transitions may well contribute to more fulfilling options and thus serve
to promote health and well-being.

There are at least four ways that we can view the relationship between
developmental transitions and health risks and opportunities. None is mutually exclusive of the others, and given the multiplicity of developmental transitions as well as of health risks and opportunities, all four models are likely to
operate across individuals in a given population and within individuals over
time. In the first three models, developmental transitions are viewed as tempo-
rally, and perhaps even as causally, preceding health risks and opportunities,
whereas in the fourth model, developmental transitions are viewed as moderating changes in health status over time. As we briefly discuss in this section,
each of these models has implications regarding interventions aimed at promoting optimal health and development (see also Maggs, Schulenberg, &
Hurrelmann, chapter 20, this volume).

Model 1. Health Risks as Consequences of Experiencing
Developmental Transitions: Storm and Stress Redux Part 1

In the first model, health risks are viewed as a result of experiencing developmental transitions, although health risks are not seen as inevitable outcomes.
To the extent that developmental transitions contribute to stress that exceeds
current coping capabilities, health and well-being are likely to suffer, and
health risk behaviors (e.g., substance use) may be used as an alternative way of
coping. Across the life span, it is the rare developmental transition that does
not contribute to stress, but in many cases, coping capacities are not overwhelmed and health is not adversely affected. Nevertheless, given the major
and multiple transitions that occur during adolescence, existing coping strategies may have difficulty in keeping up with the stress (Mechanic, 1983). This is
consistent with Coleman's Focal Theory (1978), which states that decrements
in well-being during adolescence result not from hormone-induced storm and
stress, but instead from the multiple and simultaneous transitions that occur in
a relatively short period of time. Furthermore, if it were possible to distribute
the transitions more evenly over time, decrements in well-being would be less
likely to occur. A classic empirical example of this is the work of Simmons and
Blyth (e.g., 1987). They found that it was not simply entering puberty or
making a school transition that adversely affected self-esteem, but rather the

simultaneous experience of the two along with other transitions such as the initiation of dating.

This first model represents the most straightforward and perhaps most common approach to examining the link between developmental transitions and health risks. Although it can be considered a main-effects model (e.g., with the number of transitions influencing health risks), it is more appropriately viewed as an interactive one in the sense that health risks depend on the co-occurrence of specific individual and contextual-based transitions, as well as on individual coping responses and other individual and contextual factors (e.g., Colten & Gore, 1991; Dryfoos, 1990; Ebata & Moos, 1994; Garmezy & Rutter, 1983; Mechanic, 1983). It is primarily a direct-effects approach, one that does not delineate specific indirect paths. Potential interventions based on this approach include attempting to increase adolescents' coping capacity (e.g., Compas, 1995; Nurmi, chapter 15, Petersen, Leffert, Graham, Alwin, & Ding, chapter 18, and Phinney & Kohatsu, chapter 16, this volume), as well as attempting to alter the timing of various transitions (e.g., Brooks-Gunn & Paikoff, chapter 8, and Eccles et al., chapter 11, this volume). In terms of understanding how developmental transitions can be directly related to *health opportunities*, this approach may be limited. Nevertheless, short-term health risks could be more than offset by the eventual long-term salutary effects of expanding one's coping repertoire and mastering a developmental transition.

Model 2. Developmental Transitions as Altering the Developmental Match between Individual Desires/Needs and Contextual Affordances: Storm and Stress Redux Part 2

In the second model, health risks and opportunities are viewed as a result of the impact of developmental transitions on the developmental match (e.g., Eccles et al., 1993; Eccles et al., chapter 11, this volume; Galambos & Ehrenberg, chapter 6, this volume) or goodness of fit (e.g., Lerner, 1982; Lerner et al., chapter 19, this volume) between individuals and their contexts. This model underscores one avenue of indirect effects between developmental transitions and health risks and opportunities. In conceptualizing the developing individual as embedded in his or her changing ecological niche, the match between the individual's developmental needs and desires and what is afforded by the context is itself dynamic. Developmental transitions could serve to improve the match and thus provide health opportunities, or they could serve to lessen the match and thus adversely affect health. For example, an important common (if not universal) feature of adolescence is the desire for increased freedom and responsibilities. To the extent that a developmental transition results in a new context that is appropriately responsive to this desire, it could result in salutary effects for the adolescent. In contrast, to the extent that opportunities for freedom and responsibility are blocked or even decreased as a result of the transition, then it is likely that health and well-being will be adversely affected.

Eccles and colleagues (1993 and chapter 11, this volume) and Galambos and Ehrenberg (chapter 6, this volume) emphasize this match with respect to school transitions and families, but the notion itself can be viewed in terms of any developmental transition. For example, Schulenberg and colleagues (Schulenberg, O'Malley, Bachman, Wadsworth, & Johnston, 1996; Schulenberg, Wadsworth et al., 1996) show that although binge drinking is associated with poor adaptation to high school, the transition out of high school is associated with a decrease in binge drinking for those who appear to be thriving in their post–high school achievement and affiliation contexts. This suggests that the post–high school developmental transitions serve to increase the match between the individual desires and contextual affordances, thus decreasing health risks. Health risks and opportunities could also occur when a developmental transition results in a decreased or increased concordance among the developing individual's several immediate contexts – that is, meso-system links (Bronfenbrenner, 1979). For example, the transition to part-time work could place the adolescent in a new work context that either competes with or enhances the goals of the school context, which may contribute to health risks or health opportunities, respectively (Finch, Mortimer, & Ryu, chapter 12, this volume).

The mechanism for this model could take many forms. For example, a developmental mismatch could cause the young person to become "turned off" to the current context (e.g., school) and then go elsewhere to seek fulfillment and challenge in a compensatory context (e.g., a deviant peer group) that ultimately may pose increased health risks. Likewise, a mismatch could contribute to frustration and rebellion, which in turn could contribute to engagement in problem behaviors as a form of coping or expression. By contrast, an increased match could provide the young person with developmentally appropriate challenges and experiences, feelings of competence, and increased well-being. These are all possibilities, of course, and there is a clear need to delineate empirically the complex pathways that connect developmental transitions and health risks suggested by this model.

This mismatch model stands in contrast to the first model in that it underscores the indirect paths between developmental transitions and health risks, it focuses more on the developing person–changing context interaction, and it can account for health opportunities just as easily as it can for health risks. The "agent" for storm and stress is the interaction between the developing adolescent and his or her changing context, specifically the increased developmental mismatch that may occur as a result of developmental transitions. Thus, as with the first model, storm and stress is by no means inherent. To the extent that we can increase the synchrony between developmental needs and contextual affordances, we should be able to diminish health risks associated with developmental transitions.

Model 3. Health Risk- and Health-Enhancing Behaviors as Components of Negotiating Developmental Transitions

According to the third model, health risk behaviors and risk taking in general can be viewed as important components of negotiating a developmental transition. The idea that a certain amount of adolescent and young adult risk taking is normative is supported by the high prevalence rates and by evidence that it often accompanies healthy personality development (e.g., Baumrind, 1987; Shedler & Block, 1990; Sibereisen, Eyferth, & Rudinger, 1986). According to Chassin, Presson, and Sherman (1989), risk taking and even deviance can serve constructive as well as destructive functions in adolescents' health and development (see also Jessor & Jessor, 1977; Maggs, Almeida, & Galambos, 1995; Sibereisen & Noack, 1988). For example, risk taking appears to be an important aspect of negotiating greater autonomy from parents (e.g., Irwin & Millstein, 1992). On the other hand, such autonomy-seeking behavior could be detrimental to one's health – for example, if it contributes to noncompliance with behavioral regimens prescribed to manage chronic illnesses (e.g., Kreipe & Strauss, 1989). Furthermore, as Maggs (chapter 13 this volume) demonstrates, alcohol use and binge drinking during the transition to college may help adolescents achieve valued social goals, such as making friends in a new environment. At the same time, however, binge drinking could be quite destructive in terms of one's safety and short- and long-term health and well-being.

According to the identity literature, experimentation with alternative identities may involve some increased risk taking. Given that failing to explore options may lead to premature identity foreclosure (Erikson, 1968; Marcia, 1994), some risk taking can be viewed as an important component of developmental transitions associated with identity formation. This highlights an important dilemma with this model with respect to intervention implications. To the extent that risk taking plays an essential role in identity formation, as well as in negotiating peer-related and other developmental transitions (e.g., Brown, Dolcini, & Leventhal, chapter 7, this volume; Chassin, Tetzloff, & Hershey, 1985), attempts to curb risk taking may, in turn, have adverse consequences for identity development and optimal development in general (e.g., Baumrind, 1987). It should be recognized, of course, that health-enhancing behaviors may also be components of negotiating developmental transitions. For example, as Bachman, Wadsworth, O'Malley, Schulenberg, and Johnston (chapter 10, this volume) demonstrate, health-enhancing behaviors (reducing or quitting substance use) are part of the transition to marriage and to parenthood.

Model 4. Developmental Transitions as Exacerbators of
Health Risk Status

In this model, developmental transitions are viewed as moderators of one's ongoing health risk status. Developmental transitions can serve to increase interindividual variability in functioning and adjustment, and in this way can be viewed as important junctures along one's health status trajectory. Evidence from a variety of studies indicates that divergence increases throughout adolescence between those who cope effectively with various stressors and those who do not (e.g., Kazdin, 1993; Petersen, 1993). For example, Eccles et al. (1993; chapter 11, this volume) provide evidence to suggest that the transition to junior high is worse for young people already experiencing behavior problems and difficulty with adjustment to school (see also Berndt & Mekos, 1995), and likewise that those who have difficulties with the transition are likely to have increasingly severe difficulties throughout junior high and high school. Evidence also indicates that psychological disturbances, including schizophrenia and major depression, manifest during adolescence and young adulthood. In taking a biopsychosocial perspective regarding the timing of the onset of these disturbances, one contributing factor is likely to be ongoing difficulties with negotiating developmental transitions (e.g., Kazdin, 1993; Petersen et al., 1993).

This "pathways" perspective (e.g., see Cairns & Cairns, 1994; Caspi, Elder, & Bem, 1988; Crockett & Crouter, 1995) is consistent with Erikson's (1950, 1968) psychosocial theory of life course development, in which the individual's resolution of the developmental crisis at a given stage (e.g., adolescent identity versus identity confusion) is dependent on how he or she resolved the previous crisis (preadolescent industry versus inferiority) and has implications for the resolution of the subsequent crisis (young adulthood intimacy versus isolation) (see also Havighurst, 1952). There are likely to be several mechanisms that exacerbate a trajectory of ongoing health risks. According to Nurmi (chapter 15, this volume), one mechanism is self-defeating cognitive styles. Another mechanism may be a lack of social support to alter, and an abundance of support to maintain, a trajectory of ongoing health risks (e.g., Brown et al., chapter 7, and Caldwell & Antonucci, chapter 9, this volume). The prevention implications of this model include, for example, altering self-defeating coping strategies and providing support to redirect a detrimental trajectory. Furthermore, as is true for the mismatch model discussed previously, interventions aimed at giving adolescents alternative contexts that provide challenging experiences and opportunities for success are likely to have long-term beneficial health effects.

These four models are not new, of course, but by conceptualizing them together, we can compare and contrast them in terms of their research and practical implications. Clearly, other models are possible. For illustrative purposes, we focused primarily on developmental transitions as influencing health risks and opportunities, but influence also flows the other way. For example, Kreipe and Strauss (1989) argue that chronic illnesses can interfere with accomplishing developmental tasks and delay developmental transitions into and out of adolescence. Similarly, Barkely, Anastopoulos, Guevremont, and Fletcher (1991) discuss the difficulties that adolescents with attention deficit and hyperactivity disorder have in making peer-relevant transitions and how these difficulties, in turn, adversely affect self-esteem and contribute to increased risk taking. Brown et al. (chapter 7, this volume) consider reciprocal models between developmental transitions and health risks (see also Caldwell & Antonucci, chapter 9, this volume) and indicate that the links between health risks and developmental transitions themselves change with age. It is our hope that the four models presented here will stimulate discussion and debate concerning alternative ways of conceptualizing the link between developmental transitions and health risks and opportunities across the life span.

Plan and Organization of the Book

This edited volume examines how various developmental transitions associated with the passage from childhood to adulthood provide risks and opportunities for adolescents' mental and physical health. In planning this volume, we had several goals that guided the selection of contributors, as well as the requests of and suggestions to the contributors. As discussed previously, the study of adolescence is becoming increasingly interdisciplinary, international, and sensitive to diversity of experience. These three characteristics derive, in part, from the increasing emphasis on contextual influences on adolescent development. We wanted these characteristics to be reflected in the present volume. Our focus on health and developmental transitions is clearly interdisciplinary, and the contributors bring a strong interdisciplinary emphasis to their writing and research. The disciplines represented in this volume include psychology (especially developmental, social, personality, and cognitive), sociology, public health, education, nursing, and psychiatry. Yet, like the editors, the contributors can be described as developmental scientists interested in stability and change over time during adolescence. The contributors are from Western societies, including the United States, Germany, Canada, Finland, and Israel, thus permitting some consideration of both diversity and similarity of experience across cultures. Similarly, within and across the chapters there is an emphasis on within-culture diversity and similarity of experience, particularly according to social class, ethnicity, and gender.

The chapters that follow provide a selective and in-depth discussion of current knowledge about how adolescents' and young adults' developmental transitions are related to their health and well-being. In our efforts to examine a broad framework and to span several disciplines, it was not possible to be comprehensive in this single edited volume, either in terms of developmental transitions or health risks and opportunities. Contributors were selected based on their having a long-standing research program pertaining to a given developmental transition, and it was important that their chapters emphasize as much as possible their relevant program of research. We therefore requested that they provide a balance between existing literature relating health risks to the particular developmental transition and their own original research. Authors were encouraged to provide sufficient methodological details to permit insight into the process of their research. We also suggested that they highlight new findings from their research. This "selective depth" and focus on new findings are most useful in providing heuristic illustrations of the link between developmental transitions and health risks, as well as structure and direction for future research on this link.

The book is organized around major adolescent developmental transitions. Rather than organizing the book according to different health risks and opportunities, perhaps the more typical strategy in the literature that delineates multiple causes of specific health-relevant outcomes, we believed that an explicit developmental perspective was needed. We therefore decided to emphasize the various developmental transitions and to illustrate how they may relate to different aspects of health and well-being. Beyond this introductory chapter, the volume includes 5 major sections and 19 chapters.

Part I focuses on the sociocultural, historical, physical, and cognitive foundations of adolescent transitions and includes four chapters. The first two chapters provide a broad overview of historical and contextual influences. Crockett (chapter 2) discusses historical changes in, and cultural and subcultural influences on, adolescent development and health. Noack and Kracke (chapter 3) examine the impact of social change, specifically the reunification of Germany, on the health and well-being of former East and West German adolescents. The next two chapters in this part focus on puberty and cognitive transitions during adolescence, two transitions that can be considered universal, and their associations with health risks. Silbereisen and Kracke (chapter 4) examine the impact of pubertal transitions, specifically maturational timing, on mental health and risky behaviors. Beyth-Marom and Fischhoff (chapter 5) consider a cognitive perspective on decision making about risk taking during adolescence.

Part II focuses on affiliation transitions and includes five chapters regarding transitions in family, peer, and romantic relationships. Galambos and Ehrenberg (chapter 6) consider family transitions as providing health risks and opportunities, highlighting the impact of divorce and working parents on adolescent development and health. Brown et al. (chapter 7) discuss the ongoing transformations in peer relations during adolescence and how they relate to health risks and opportunities. Brooks-Gunn and Paikoff (chapter 8) focus on sexual transitions during adolescence, emphasizing the potentially positive effects of healthy sexual identities on health and well-being. Caldwell and Antonucci (chapter 9) consider the mental health risks and opportunities that can follow from bearing a child during adolescence. Finally, Bachman et al. (chapter 10) examine the impact of normative transitions to marriage and parenthood during young adulthood, as well as the nonnormative transition out of marriage (e.g., divorce) on cigarette, alcohol, and illicit drug use.

Part III focuses on achievement transitions and includes four chapters on school and work transitions. Eccles et al. (chapter 11) examine the increased developmental mismatch that typically accompanies the transition to middle or junior high school and the short- and long-term health risks that can result from this mismatch. Finch et al. (chapter 12) consider the transition to part-time work during the school year and its impact on health and well-being, underscoring the importance of examining person–context interactions. Maggs (chapter 13) examines the impact of the transition to college on alcohol use, focusing on the subjectively positive aspects of alcohol use and binge drinking. Matt, Seus, and Schumann (chapter 14) examine the transition from school to work and how difficulties with this transition can be related to deviancy and problem behaviors.

Part IV focuses on identity tasks and transitions and includes three chapters. Nurmi (chapter 15) considers the importance of self-definition during adolescence and its impact on coping and mental health, focusing especially on individuals having difficulties with the transition to young adulthood. Phinney and Kohatsu (chapter 16) discuss ethnic identity development during adolescence and emphasize the importance of negotiating a positive ethnic identity for optimal mental health. Wallace and Williams (chapter 17) focus on religious identity and consider how health-compromising behaviors are inversely related to religious beliefs and participation.

Part V includes three chapters on health promotion policy and interventions. Petersen et al. (chapter 18) discuss risk and protective factors for adolescent depression, and present findings from an evaluation of their comprehensive intervention effort aimed at easing the transition to adolescence and preventing depression. Lerner et al. (chapter 19) discuss the health and prospects of American youth, and argue that the most effective and lasting strategy for preventing health-compromising behaviors is to provide opportunities for positive development among adolescents. Finally, Maggs et al. (chapter 20) consider the prevention implications of the material covered in this volume, highlight the issues involved in viewing health promotion from a developmental perspective, and emphasize school and community prevention efforts. This final part makes explicit a theme that runs throughout the volume: Efforts to facilitate developmental transitions into and out of adolescence can serve to promote health and well-being.

References

Aseltine, R. H., Jr., & Gore, S. (1993). Mental health and social adaptation following the transition from high school. *Journal of Research on Adolescence, 3*, 247–270.

Bachman, J. G., O'Malley, P. M., & Johnston, J. (1978). *Adolescence to adulthood: Change and stability in the lives of young men.* Ann Arbor, MI: Institute for Social Research.

Baltes, P. B., Cornelius, S. W., & Nesselroade, J. R. (1979). Cohort effects in developmental psychology. In J. R. Nesselroade & P. B. Baltes (Eds.), *Longitudinal research in the study of behavior and development* (pp. 61–88). New York: Academic Press.

Barkely, R., Anastopoulos, A., Guevremont, D., & Fletcher, K. (1991). Adolescents with ADHD: Patterns of behavioral adjustment, academic functioning, and treatment utilization. *Journal of American Academy of Child and Adolescent Psychiatry, 30*, 752–761.

Baumrind, D. (1987). A developmental perspective on adolescent risk taking in contemporary America. In C. E. Irwin, Jr. (Ed.), *Adolescent social behavior and health* (pp. 93–125). San Francisco: Jossey-Bass.

Benedict, R. (1950). *Patterns of culture.* New York: New American Library.

Berndt, T. J., & Mekos, D. (1995). Adolescents' perceptions of the stressful and desirable aspects of the transition to junior high school. *Journal of Research on Adolescence, 5*, 123–142.

Blos, P. (1970). *The young adolescent: Clinical studies.* New York: Free Press.

Bronfenbrenner, U. (1979). *The ecology of human development: Experiments by nature and design.* Cambridge, MA: Harvard University Press.

Bronfenbrenner, U., & Crouter, A. C. (1982). Work and family through time and space. In S. B. Kamerman & C. D. Hayes (Eds.), *Families that work: Children in a changing world* (pp. 39–83). Washington, DC: National Academy of Sciences.

Cairns, R. B., & Cairns, B. D. (1994). *Lifelines and risks: Pathways of youth in our time.* New York: Cambridge University Press.

Caspi, A., Elder, G. H., Jr., & Bem, D. J. (1988). Moving away from the world: Life-course patterns of shy children. *Developmental Psychology, 24*, 824–831.

Caspi, A., Lynam, D., Moffitt, T. E., & Silva, P. A. (1993). Unraveling girls' delinquency: Biological, dispositional, and contextual contributions to adolescent misbehavior. *Developmental Psychology, 29*, 19–30.

Chassin, L., Presson, C. C., & Sherman, S. J. (1989). "Constructive" vs. "destructive" deviance in adolescent health-related behaviors. *Journal of Youth and Adolescence, 18*, 245–262.

Chassin, L., Tetzloff, C., & Hershey, M. (1985). Self-image and social-image factors in adolescent alcohol use. *Journal of Studies on Alcohol, 46*, 39–47.

Cohen, S., & Rodriguez, M. S. (1995). Pathways linking affective disturbances and physical disorders. *Health Psychology, 14*, 374–380.

Coleman, J. (1978). Current contradictions in adolescent theory. *Journal of Youth and Adolescence, 7*, 1–11.

Colten, M. E., & Gore, S. (Eds.). (1991). *Adolescent stress: Causes and consequences.* New York: Walter de Gruyter.

Compas, B. E. (1995). Promoting successful competence during adolescence. In M. Rutter (Ed.), *Psychosocial disturbances in young people: Challenges for prevention* (pp. 247–273). New York: Cambridge University Press.

Crockett, L. J., & Crouter, A. C. (Eds.). (1995). *Pathways through adolescence: Individual development in relation to social contexts.* Mahwah, NJ: Erlbaum.

Dryfoos, J. G. (1990). *Adolescents at risk: Prevalence and prevention.* New York: Oxford University Press.

Earls, F. (1993). Health promotion for minority adolescents: Cultural considerations. In S. G. Millstein, A. C. Petersen, & E. O. Nightingale (Eds.), *Promoting the health of adolescents: New directions for the twenty-first century* (pp. 58–72). New York: Oxford University Press.

Ebata, A. T., & Moos, R. H. (1994). Personal, situational, and contextual correlates of coping in adolescence. *Journal of Research on Adolescence, 4*, 99–126.

Eccles, J. S., Midgley, C., Wigfield, A., Buchanan, C. M., Reuman, D., Flanagan, C., & MacIver, D. (1993). Development during adolescence: The impact of stage–environment fit on young adolescents' experiences in schools and in families. *American Psychologist, 48*, 90–101.

Elder, G. H., Jr. (1974). *Children of the Great Depression: Social change in life experience.* Chicago: University of Chicago Press.

Elliott, D. (1993). Health-enhancing and health-compromising lifestyles. In S. G. Millstein, A. C. Petersen, & E. O. Nightingale (Eds.), *Promoting the health of adolescents: New directions for the twenty-first century* (pp. 119–145). New York: Oxford University Press.

Erikson, E. H. (1950). *Childhood and society.* New York: Norton.

Erikson, E. H. (1968). *Identity: Youth and crisis.* New York: Norton.

Featherman, D. L. (1983). Life-span perspectives in social science research. In P. B. Baltes & O. G. Brim, Jr. (Eds.), *Life-span development and behavior* (Vol. 5, pp. 1–59). New York: Academic Press.

Feldman, S. S., & Rosenthal, D. A. (1994). Culture makes a difference ... or does it? In R. K. Sibereisen & E. Todt (Eds.), *Adolescence in context: The interplay of family, school, peers, and work in adjustment* (pp. 99–124). New York: Springer-Verlag.

Freud, A. (1958). Adolescence. *Psychoanalytic Study of the Child, 13*, 255–278.

Garmezy, N., & Rutter, M. (Eds.). (1983). *Stress, coping, and development in children.* New York: McGraw-Hill.

Gottlieb, G. (1991). Experiential canalization of behavioral development: Theory. *Development Psychology, 27*, 4–13.

Hall, G. S. (1904). *Adolescence.* New York: Appleton.

Hamilton, S. F. (1994). Employment prospects as motivation for school achievement: Links and gaps between school and work in seven countries. In R. K. Silbereisen & E. Todt (Eds.), *Adolescence in context: The interplay of family, school, peers, and work in adjustment* (pp. 267–283). New York: Springer-Verlag.

Havighurst, R. (1952). *Developmental tasks and education.* New York: McKay.

Hurrelmann, K. (1984). Societal and organizational factors of stress on students in school. *European Journal of Teacher Education, 7*, 181–190.

Hurrelmann, K. (1990). Health promotion for adolescents: Preventive and corrective strategies against problem behavior. *Journal of Adolescence, 13*, 231–250.

Irwin, C. F., Jr., & Millstein, S. G. (1992). Risk-taking behaviors and biopsychosocial development during adolescence. In E. J. Susman, L. V. Feagans, & W. J. Ray (Eds.), *Emotion, cognition, health, and development in children and adolescents* (pp. 75–102). Hillsdale, NJ: Erlbaum.

Jessor, R. (1993). Successful adolescent development among youth in high risk settings. *American Psychologist, 48*, 117–126.

Jessor, R., & Jessor, S. L. (1977). *Problem behavior and psychological development: A longitudinal study of youth.* New York: Academic Press.

Jones, R. M. (1992). Ego identity and adolescent problem behavior. In G. R. Adams, T. P. Gullotta, & R. Montemayor (Eds.), *Adolescent identity formation* (pp. 216–233). Newbury Park, CA: Sage.

Kazdin, A. E. (1993). Adolescent mental health: Prevention and treatment programs. *American Psychologist, 48*, 127–141.

Kohn, M. L., & Schooler, C. (1983). *Work and personality: An inquiry into the impact of social stratification.* Norwood, NJ: Ablex.

Kreipe, R. E., & Strauss, J. (1989). Adolescent medical disorders, behavior, and development. In G. R. Adams, R. Montemayor, & T. P. Gullotta (Eds.), *Biology of adolescent behavior and development* (pp. 98–140). Newbury Park, CA: Sage.

Lerner, R. M. (1982). Children and adolescents as producers of their own development. *Developmental Review, 2*, 342–370.

Lerner, R. M. (1985). Individual and context in developmental psychology: Conceptual and theoretical issues. In J. R. Nesselroade & A. von Eye (Eds.), *Individual development and social change: Explanatory analysis* (pp. 155–187). New York: Academic Press.

18   J. SCHULENBERG, J. L. MAGGS, AND K. HURRELMANN

Lewin, K. (1939). The field theory approach to adolescence. *American Journal of Sociology, 44,* 868–897.

Maggs, J. L., Almeida, D. M., & Galambos, N. L. (1995). Risky business: The paradoxical meaning of problem behavior for young adolescents. *Journal of Early Adolescence, 15,* 339–357.

Magnusson, D. (1988). *Individual development from an interactional perspective.* Hillsdale, NJ: Erlbaum.

Marcia, J. (1994). Identity and psychotherapy. In S. L. Archer (Ed.), *Interventions for adolescent identity development* (pp. 29–46). Thousand Oaks, CA: Sage.

McLoyd, V. C. (1990). The impact of economic hardship on black families and children: Psychological distress, parenting, and socioemotional development. *Child Development, 61,* 311–346.

Mead, M. (1950). *Coming of age in Samoa.* New York: New American Library.

Mechanic, D. (1983). Adolescent health and illness behavior: Review of the literature and a new hypothesis for the study of stress. *Journal of Human Stress, 9,* 4–13.

Millstein, S. G., Petersen, A. C., & Nightingale, E. O. (Eds.). (1993). *Promoting the health of adolescents: New directions for the twenty-first century.* New York: Oxford University Press.

Mortimer, J. T. (1976). Social class, work and family: Some implications of the father's occupation for family relationships and son's career decisions. *Journal of Marriage and the Family, 38,* 241–254.

Muuss, R. E. (1988). *Theories of adolescence* (5th ed.). New York: Random House.

Nurmi, J. E. (1993). Adolescent development in an age-graded context: The role of personal beliefs, goals, and strategies in the tackling of developmental tasks and standards. *International Journal of Behavioral Development, 16,* 169–189.

Oerter, R. (1986). Developmental tasks through the life span: A new approach to an old concept. In P. B. Baltes, D. L. Featherman, & R. M. Lerner (Eds.), *Life span development and behavior* (Vol. 7, pp. 233–271). Hillsdale, NJ: Erlbaum.

Ogbu, J. V. (1981). Origins of human competence: A cultural-ecological perspective. *Child Development, 52,* 413–429.

Pepper, S. C. (1942). *World hypotheses: A study of evidence.* Berkeley: University of California Press.

Petersen, A. C. (1993). Creating adolescents: The role of context and process in developmental trajectories. *Journal of Research on Adolescence, 3,* 1–18.

Petersen, A. C., Compas, B. E., Brooks-Gunn, J., Stemmler, M., Ey, S., & Grant, K. E. (1993). Depression in adolescence. *American Psychologist, 48,* 155–168.

Petersen, A. C., & Leffert, N. (1995). What is special about adolescence. In M. Rutter (Ed.), *Psychosocial disturbances in young people: Challenges for prevention* (pp. 3–36). New York: Cambridge University Press.

Robins, L. N. (1995). Sociocultural trends affecting the prevalence of adolescent problems. In M. Rutter (Ed.), *Psychosocial disturbances in young people: Challenges for prevention* (pp. 367–384). New York: Cambridge University Press.

Rutter, M. (Ed.). (1995a). *Psychosocial disturbances in young people: Challenges for prevention.* New York: Cambridge University Press.

Rutter, M. (1995b). Preface. In M. Rutter (Ed.), *Psychosocial disturbances in young people: Challenges for prevention* (pp. ix–xvi). New York: Cambridge University Press.

Sameroff, A. J. (1987). The social context of development. In N. Eisenberg (Ed.), *Contemporary topics in developmental psychology* (pp. 273–291). New York: Wiley.

Scarr, S., & McCartney, K. (1983). How people make their own environment: A theory of genotype–environment effects. *Child Development, 54,* 424–435.

Schaie, K. W. (1965). A general model for the study of developmental problems. *Psychological Bulletin, 64,* 92–107.

Schulenberg, J., O'Malley, P. M., Bachman, J. G., Wadsworth, K. N., & Johnston, L. D. (1996). Getting drunk and growing up: Trajectories of frequent binge drinking during the transition to young adulthood. *Journal of Studies on Alcohol, 57,* 289–304.

Schulenberg, J., Wadsworth, K. N., O'Malley, P. M., Bachman, J. G., & Johnston, L. D. (1996). Adolescent risk factors for binge drinking during the transition to young adulthood: Variable- and pattern-centered approaches to change. *Developmental Psychology, 32*, 659–674.

Shedler, J., & Block, J. (1990). Adolescent drug use and psychological health: A longitudinal inquiry. *American Psychologist, 45*, 612–630.

Silbereisen, R. K., Eyferth, K., & Rudinger, G. (Eds.). (1986). *Development as action in context: Problem behavior and normal youth development.* New York: Springer-Verlag.

Silbereisen, R. K., & Noack, P. (1988). On the constructive role of problem behavior in adolescence. In N. Bolger, A. Caspi, G. Downey, & M. Moorehouse (Eds.), *Persons in context: Developmental processes* (pp. 152–180). Cambridge: Cambridge University Press.

Silbereisen, R. K., Noack, P., & Schoenpflug, U. (1994). Comparative analyses and beliefs, leisure contexts, and substance use in West Berlin and Warsaw. In R. K. Silbereisen & E. Todt (Eds.), *Adolescence in context: The interplay of family, school, peers, and work in adjustment* (pp. 176–198). New York: Springer-Verlag.

Simmons, R. G., & Blyth, D. A. (1987). *Moving into adolescence: The impact of pubertal change and school context.* Hawthorne, NY: Aldine.

Spencer, M. B., & Dornbusch, S. M. (1990). Challenges in studying minority youth. In S. G. Millstein, A. C. Petersen, & E. O. Nightingale (Eds.), *Promoting the health of adolescents: New directions for the twenty-first century* (pp. 123–146). New York: Oxford University Press.

Stattin, H., & Magnusson, D. (1990). *Pubertal maturation in female development.* Hillsdale, NJ: Erlbaum.

Steinberg, L. (1995). Commentary: On developmental pathways and social contexts in adolescence. In L. J. Crockett & A. C. Crouter (Eds.), *Pathways through adolescence: Individual development in relation to social contexts* (pp. 245–253). Mahwah, NJ: Erlbaum.

Sullivan, H. S. (1947). *Conceptions of modern psychiatry.* New York: Norton.

Susman, E. J., Dorn, L. D., Feagans, L. V., & Ray, W. J. (1992). Historical and theoretical perspectives on behavioral health in children and adolescents: An introduction. In E. J. Susman, L. V. Feagans, & W. J. Ray (Eds.), *Emotion, cognition, health, and development in children and adolescents* (pp. 1–8). Hillsdale, NJ: Erlbaum.

Susman, E. J., Feagans, L. V., & Ray, W. J. (Eds.). (1992). *Emotion, cognition, health, and development in children and adolescents.* Hillsdale, NJ: Erlbaum.

Udry, J. R. (1988). Biological predispositions and social control in adolescent sexual behavior. *American Sociological Review, 53*, 709–722.

World Health Organization. (1986). *Charter der I. Internationalen Konferenz für Gesundheitsförderung.* Ottawa: Author.

Part I

Sociocultural, Physical, and Cognitive Foundations of Adolescent Transitions

2 Cultural, Historical, and Subcultural Contexts of Adolescence: Implications for Health and Development

Lisa J. Crockett

Although clearly influenced by biological and psychological growth, adolescent development is also molded by the social and cultural context in which it occurs. As the transition from childhood to adulthood, adolescence is closely tied to the structure of adult society, and the expectations for youth during this period reflect, in important ways, the skills and qualities deemed important for success in adult roles (Benedict, 1937; Havighurst, 1948/1972). Furthermore, prevailing demographic, economic, and political conditions determine the adult occupational and social roles to which young people can aspire, as well as the access to and competition for those roles (Elder, 1975). The integral connection between adolescence and the societal context means that, despite universals such as puberty and cognitive development, adolescents' experiences will vary across cultures and over history. The settings in which young people develop, the skills they are expected to acquire, and the ways in which their progress toward adulthood is marked and celebrated depend on the cultural and historical contexts.

Within stratified, heterogeneous societies, the experience of adolescence also differs among subgroups of youth. Economic and social resources, as well as access to valued adult roles, may differ for youth from distinct racial-ethnic groups, social classes, and geographic regions. Lack of resources and opportunities in some settings may profoundly shape the course of adolescent development by influencing the timing of key developmental transitions and the supports available for coping with these transitions. Moreover, to the extent that anticipated adult lives differ for youth from distinct social subgroups, differences in socialization patterns and goals would be expected (Ogbu, 1985). In heterogeneous societies, therefore, local ecological conditions may alter considerably the normative template of adolescent development, with important implications for adolescents' current health and future life course.

Thus, both macrolevel, societal arrangements and local conditions help shape adolescents' experiences and the course of their development. Both kinds of influences may also have consequences for adolescent health. In particular, they affect the health risks to which young people are exposed before and during adolescence, as well as the protective factors that may shield them from these risks. In this chapter, I examine the impact of both societal and local contexts, highlighting some of their implications for adolescent health. Essentially, the chapter addresses two questions: First, how has adolescent health and development been affected by changing social and economic conditions in the United States? Second, how does the health and development of adolescents in the contemporary United States vary as a function of the local ecology? Before turning to these issues, however, an overview of sociocultural influences on adolescent development will be presented.

The Cultural Context of Adolescent Development

Whether or not adolescence is formally recognized as a distinct stage of life, virtually all cultures distinguish between young people and adults. Furthermore, most cultures institutionalize a period of preparation for adulthood that may be analogous to adolescence as we know it. Despite some uniformities, however, the structure and content of the adolescent period varies markedly from culture to culture in ways that reflect broader social and institutional patterns (Benedict, 1937). In other words, the "cultural structuring" of adolescence differs among societies. Although a comprehensive review of cross-cultural differences is beyond the scope of this chapter, a few examples will serve to illustrate the ways in which cultural arrangements shape the adolescent period and the course of adolescent development. These include the selection of developmental milestones, practices affecting the clarity of adolescence as a phase of life, and the provision of social roles, settings, and activities that shape the "content" of adolescence.

Critical Developmental Markers

Worthman (1986) suggests that cultures structure the adolescent experience in part by ascribing social significance to particular developmental cues such as menarche, physical size, or acquired skills. These perceptible cues serve as "index" variables or social markers to which the acquisition of privileges and responsibilities is attached. The selected markers have social significance and, consequently, become psychologically meaningful as well. In a sense, cultures co-opt developmental cues, imbue them with social significance, and in this way create social milestones around which young people's activities and expectations are organized. These milestones serve as landmarks along the path to adulthood, defining the normative course of adolescent development. They become developmental goals to be attained and celebrated.

The developmental markers selected for cultural emphasis vary cross-culturally and appear to be linked to the social and economic organization of society. Biological markers of maturation such as menarche are more frequently celebrated in settings where puberty is linked to marriage and where marriage, in turn, has important political and economic functions (Brooks-Gunn & Reiter, 1990). For example, in some societies, marriage is used politically to cement interfamilial ties. Further, in labor-intensive agrarian economies, in which large numbers of children are desirable, menarche, which is associated with fertility, may increase a daughter's value in the marriage market. Paige (1983) suggests that practices such as chaperonage, seclusion, and residence with the bridegroom's family prior to puberty are all ways of ensuring a daughter's economic value to her family. Thus, puberty is celebrated where it constitutes a political or economic asset.

Puberty may also receive greater emphasis in societies with simple technology and less differentiated economies. In such societies, young people learn adult skills and tasks gradually over the course of childhood and, by the time of puberty, have acquired many of the competencies needed to function successfully as adults. In contrast, in industrialized societies with complex occupational structures and a focus on achieved rather than ascribed social status, puberty occurs long before the requisite level of social and technical competence is reached. Hence, the emphasis on puberty is replaced by a focus on other events (e.g., school completion) that more accurately index readiness for adulthood. Puberty is not celebrated by the community and, in fact, is viewed as a private issue (Brooks-Gunn & Reiter, 1990).

Other events reflecting social maturation may also receive differential cultural emphasis. In most societies, marriage marks the end of adolescence and the beginning of adulthood (Schlegel & Barry, 1991). In industrialized societies, the completion of formal schooling, entry into full-time employment, moving out of the parental household, and becoming financially independent also may serve as markers of entry into adulthood (Elliott & Feldman, 1990). A recent study of American college students indicated that living apart from parents and financial independence were particularly salient milestones for these youth (Arnett, 1994).

The choice of key developmental markers and the age at which particular milestones can be attained affect the temporal boundaries of adolescence. Thus, the social transition from childhood to adolescence may be initiated at different ages in different cultures (Cohen, 1964), and the formal phase of preparation for adulthood may last several months, as in some traditional societies, or many years, as is common in modern industrialized societies. The interdependence of particular milestones may also affect the length and timing of adolescence: For example, the right to marry may be tied to biological maturity; similarly, in Western industrialized societies, entry into full-time employment may depend on the completion of formal schooling.

Importantly, the timing and contingency of developmental milestones are determined by institutional arrangements. In industrialized societies, the transition from school to work is shaped by the educational system and the labor market. The nature and timing of the school-to-work transition differs, even among modern industrialized societies, due to differences in the degree of alignment between these key institutions (Hamilton, 1994; Petersen, Hurrelmann, & Leffert, 1993).

In summary, both the choice of developmental markers and the timing of these markers are embedded in cultural arrangements. One example of this embeddedness comes from cross-cultural data on the regulation of *maidenhood*, defined as the period between menarche and marriage. Examining data from contemporary nations as well as from ethnographic cross-cultural files, Whiting, Burbank, and Ratner (1986) show that societies differ in both the length of maidenhood and the degree of permissiveness concerning premarital sex. One strategy involves extended maidenhood (5 years or more) combined with restrictive rules governing premarital sex: this approach is common among modern European and Asian societies. It can be contrasted with strategies that involve a shorter maidenhood (combined with either encouragement of or restrictions on premarital sex) or with arrangements in which maidenhood is virtually nonexistent because marriage occurs before or immediately after menarche. The type of arrangement depends, in part, on what characteristics are desired in a bride (e.g., virginity or sexual competence), but it is also related to cultural values concerning family size, which, in turn, depend on population density, the social class system, and the type of economic activity (agricultural, herding, foraging, industrial) (Whiting et al., 1986). In this example, both the length of the maidenhood period and the treatment of female adolescents during this period appear to depend on broader social and economic patterns.

Clarity of Adolescence

Cultures also differ in the clarity of adolescence as a stage of life. Clarity is enhanced by culturally shared milestones that mark the entrance into and exit from adolescence, as well as by consistency in the treatment of young people during that phase of life. In some traditional societies, public ceremonies and physical alteration (e.g., through the use of particular clothing or scarification) accompany the change from child to adult (or preadult) social status (Ford & Beach, 1951). In small communities, and in larger ones in which the physical alterations are commonly recognized, the change in social status is followed by consistent social treatment confirming the young person's new status. In contrast, modern industrialized societies have few publicly celebrated or consistently recognized indicators of the status transition; typically, there are multiple milestones (e.g., completion of secondary schooling, age of legal majority, entry into the labor force, marriage, and parenthood) that are reached at different ages. The abundance of social markers and their spread in timing are thought to increase the ambiguity of the transition to adulthood because young people are treated inconsistently: on some occasions as adults, on other occasions as juveniles (Steinberg, 1993). In support of this perspective, a recent study of college students in a midwestern university revealed that less than one-quarter of the sample felt they had reached adulthood, whereas almost two-thirds felt they had attained adulthood in some respects but not in others (Arnett, 1994).

The clarity of adolescence may derive in part from institutional arrangements. Hurrelmann (1989) links the ambiguity of adolescence in Western industrialized societies to the ongoing process of institutional differentiation within these societies. Increasingly, social functions related to economics, social control, education, and religion, which were initially carried out within the family unit, have been relegated to specialized institutions (e.g., schools, churches, courts). These institutions have distinct rules, procedures, and reward structures; thus they may place inconsistent demands on young people and permit differing degrees of participation and autonomy. Such inconsistency may lead to confusion among youth about their social status and expected behavior; it may also produce frustration because autonomy is supported in some settings but denied in others. Moreover, inconsistent expectations are thought to impede the formation of a healthy identity (Ianni, 1989) and may also lead young people to engage in "adult" behaviors such as sex and drinking as a way of affirming adult status (Jessor, 1984).

Social Roles and Settings

Institutional arrangements within a society also shape the content of adolescence – the social roles and prescribed activities of youth. First, institutional arrangements and cultural patterns influence the sequencing of important social roles (Hogan & Astone, 1986). In the United States, for example, the preferred sequence of role transitions during late adolescence and early adulthood is from student to worker to spouse/partner to parent. Studies of adolescents' goals and plans confirm that this normative role sequence influences their thinking about their future lives (Greene, Wheatley, & Aldava, 1992; Hogan, 1982; Nurmi, 1989, this volume). Moreover, data on the average ages of school completion, job entry, marriage, and parenthood support the normative sequence, although it is also clear that many individuals do not follow it (Marini, 1987; Rindfuss, Swicegood, & Rosenfeld, 1987).

In addition, cultural theories of the normal or ideal life course, in conjunction with institutional arrangements, prescribe the typical sequence of settings through which a young person passes en route to adulthood, as well as the ideal timing of the transition from one setting to the next. The normative educational sequence in Western societies, for example, specifies a sequence of elementary school, secondary school, and postsecondary education, although the last is not required. This sequence of settings is in marked contrast to that of agrarian or foraging societies, in which children help with adult tasks and have economic responsibilities from an early age. Not only are the activities different, but so are the companions. In school settings, adolescents tend to be segregated with age-mates, which reduces contact with adults and enables the emergence of peer cultures with distinct values and reward structures. Such outcomes are less likely in societies where children work alongside adults and are more fully integrated into the adult community.

In summary, the experiences of adolescents are integrally tied to prevailing cultural, institutional, and economic patterns. These cultural arrangements define the roles, settings, and activities of youth and determine the temporal boundaries of adolescence. In combination, they also affect the clarity of adolescence as a developmental status.

Adolescence in Contemporary Western Society

In contemporary Western society, the phase of adolescence has taken a particular form as a consequence of economic and social changes associated with the process of industrialization. The length and timing of adolescence, its distinctness as a phase of life, and the ambiguities that currently characterize this period are rooted in the institutional arrangements of industrialized society. The critical role of social conditions in molding contemporary adolescence is best understood in historical perspective. In the following sections, the historical foundations of adolescence are reviewed, followed by a discussion of recent societal changes that have affected the nature of adolescence. Finally, recent trends in adolescent health are examined in relation to social change.

Historical Foundations of Contemporary Adolescence

Preindustrial Era. Prior to industrialization, young people played an important economic role in the family and community. In the relatively undifferentiated agarian economy of the 16th and 17th centuries, children's labor contributed directly to the economic well-being of the family. Thus, children were recognized as an economic asset (Modell & Goodman, 1990); they were brought into economic activity at an early age and often worked alongside adults. In this sense, young people appeared to be more fully integrated into adult society than is true today.

In determining social status, the focus in the preindustrial era was on capability (Modell & Goodman, 1990). In colonial America, developmental status was linked to economic standing. *Youth* was used to describe the period during which young people were no longer fully dependent on parents but were not yet in a position to set up their own households (Kett, 1977). Until the early 19th century, this period was associated with the practice of *fostering out*, in which children from the age of 12 were often sent to live with other families in the community to serve as domestics and apprentices (Katz, 1975; Kett, 1977). This practice created a situation in which youngsters were away from home but still under adult supervision. For this reason, the status of youth has been described as one of "semi-independence" (Kett, 1977).

The focus on capability was accompanied by a relative lack of emphasis on chronological age as an indicator of developmental status. General life stage distinctions were made, as indicated by the use of such terms as *childhood* and *youth*, but these distinctions were less elaborated and less tied to age than they would be in later eras. For example, the term *youth* could be applied to someone as young as 12 or as old as 24 (Modell & Goodman, 1990). Thus, age-based distinctions between young people and adults appear to have been less salient than they are today. (For an alternative perspective, however, see Hanawalt, 1993.)

Youth in Industrialized Society. The relation of youth to adult society changed in the late 19th and early 20th centuries as a function of three interrelated trends: a decline in the demand for child labor, an increased emphasis on education, and a transformation in the cultural view of children. The declining demand for youth labor derived in part from changes in the occupational structure brought on by industrialization. Although rapid industrialization in the 19th century created new occupations for children in the United States (e.g., in the southern textile mills), improvements in technology eventually reduced the demand for unskilled labor and made many "children's" jobs obsolete (Fasick, 1994; Zelizer, 1985). In addition, immigration at the turn of the century provided an alternative source of unskilled labor. Thus, by the early 20th century, industry no longer required child and adolescent labor, and youth employment declined.

The reduction in employment among youth was offset, in part, by an increased emphasis on schooling. Greater family affluence in the late 19th and early 20th century meant that more families could afford to keep their children in school (Fasick, 1994; Zelizer, 1985). In addition, schooling came to be seen as a route to occupational success. As opportunities in farming decreased, many families encouraged their sons to pursue formal education in order to prepare for alternative careers in business or the professions. Although formal schooling was initially a middle-class strategy, American working-class youth also began to pursue formal education as a means to upward mobility (Modell & Goodman, 1990). By the end of the 19th century, an increasing number of American youth attended secondary school, at least temporarily, rather than being immediately absorbed into the adult work force.

A third factor affecting children and adolescents was a cultural change in the view of children (Zelizer, 1985). In 18th-century rural America, children were seen as economic assets as well as objects of sentiment. Among working-class families, this view persisted through the end of the 19th century. Between the 1870s and the 1930s, however, children were increasingly defined in exclusively sentimental terms. The sentimental view of children made their use for economic gain morally suspect. According to Zelizer (1985), this cultural transformation in the normative view of children gave momentum to child labor movements that progressively excluded children under 14 from most kinds of paid work. Children and young adolescents were recast as emotionally priceless but economically useless.

Implications for Adolescents' Social Role. These historical trends profoundly altered the social roles and daily contexts of children and adolescents. The declining value of youth labor and the increased utility of formal schooling shifted the center of adolescent activity from work to school and the primary social role from worker to student. The progressive exclusion of children from adult work created separate institutional bases for young people and adults and effectively segregated adolescents from adult society. The young adolescent's status in the family also changed. Rather than contributing economically to the family, young adolescents became an economic liability.

The sentimentalized view of children also led to increased public concern about child health and safety. The perceived need to protect children from the hazards (moral and physical) of street life led to a progressive restriction of children's activities to the school and the home (Zelizer, 1985). Similarly, among urban middle-class families, the response to urban dangers was to shift adolescents from semi-independent to fully dependent status in order to protect them (Modell & Goodman, 1990). Although working-class youth continued to work alongside adults and to participate in street life, middle- and upper-class youth increasingly stayed home. Thus, rather than experiencing a period of semiautonomy, middle-class adolescents moved increasingly into a fully dependent status within the family.

Over the course of the 20th century, economic and educational trends in the United States have further differentiated the role of adolescents from that of adults. The emergence of the comprehensive high school in the 1920s and the extension of compulsory schooling through age 16 underscored the importance of school as a primary institutional setting for adolescents. Between 1920 and 1960 the proportion of 14- to 16-year-olds in school rose from about 30% to 90% (Tanner, 1972). In addition, the refinement and extension of child labor laws have largely excluded adolescents under age 16 from full-time work. These twin developments have reinforced the distinct institutional bases of adolescents and adults and the distinct cultural expectations for them regarding activities, orientation, and behavior. Even the increasing prevalence of part-time employment among high school students has not altered this basic pattern: At least among mainstream, middle-class youth, part-time work is viewed as a secondary activity (the primary activity being school), not as part of the youth's economic responsibility to the family. Earnings tend to be spent on leisure activities and on discretionary items (e.g., stereos) rather than on basic necessities. Thus, developments in the 20th century have tended to reinforce both economic marginality and frivolity as key features of the adolescent role. Exceptions to this rule include farm youth, whose labor contributes directly to the family's economic enterprise, and poor youth, whose earnings may be used for basic necessities.

Timing of Developmental Transitions. Recent changes in the labor market have further extended the length of adolescence for many young people. The past several decades have witnessed a continued decline in employment within the primary sector (especially farming), a sharp drop in manufacturing, and prolonged growth in the service sector (Polk, 1987). Much of the growth is concentrated in high-status service professions, which require a university degree, and in technology, which requires specific training. Growth has also occurred in low-level service jobs (e.g., restaurant work), but these jobs are typically part-time and poorly paid. Thus, the need for postsecondary education has increased. In response to these labor market conditions, college enrollments rose precipitously in the second half of the 20th century (Church, 1976). Increasingly, youth are extending their education into the third decade of life, thereby prolonging their "adolescent" period of economic dependence.

The postponement of key role transitions marking the entry into adulthood is documented in historical studies. A comparison of data from 1880 and 1970 (Modell, Furstenberg, & Hershberg, 1976) indicates that the ages of school completion and entrance into the labor force rose over that period, with the change being especially pronounced for school completion. However, over the same period, the median ages of family transitions (departure from the family home, marriage, and establishment of an independent household) decreased. Thus, the postponement of career-related role transitions co-occurred with an acceleration of family transitions, resulting in a temporal convergence of these distinct role changes.

More recent data indicate that the median ages of first marriage and entering parenthood have been increasing since 1960 (Modell, 1989), suggesting that the trend toward convergence has ceased. Nonetheless, the initial temporal compression of family and nonfamily transitions has increased the potential for these two types of transitions to overlap. Because some of these role transitions are contingent on others (e.g., full-time employment and marriage are supposed to follow completion of full-time schooling), careful orchestration of these transitions may be required (Modell et al., 1976). Thus, the temporal compression has increased the complexity of the transition to adulthood.

Implications of Historical Changes for Adolescent Health

The more sentimentalized view of children that emerged in the early 20th century had clear benefits for the health of children and young adolescents. In the United States, a nationwide compaign for child health resulted in reduced infant and child mortality. In some states, mass inoculation and vaccination campaigns virtually eliminated major communicable diseases among school-children (Zelizer, 1985). Similarly, public efforts in the 1920s successfully reduced traffic fatalities among school-age children at a time when fatalities among older age groups continued to rise (Zelizer, 1985). Although older adolescents were not the focus of these public health campaigns, they probably also benefitted from improved public health and safety.

Some other historical changes, however, may have had less positive conse-quences for adolescents. In particular, the increasing economic marginality of youth may have negatively affected adolescent psychological well-being. Some scholars have suggested that the contemporary experience of extended eco-nomic dependence and exclusion from valued economic and social roles is alienating for youth (Nightingale & Wolverton, 1993). Frustration may lead to a preoccupation with the superficial symbols of adulthood such as alcohol use, sex, and material goods, and possibly to health-risking behaviors such as drug use, unprotected sexual activity, and delinquency (Jessor, 1984).

In addition, the progressive segregation of adolescents from adults has sharpened the discontinuity between adolescence and adulthood. Rather than learning economic roles by observing adults at work, young people are encour-aged to focus on learning abstract skills in school. Hamilton (1987) has argued that present institutional arrangements in the United States do not entail strong connections between school work, adolescent jobs, and adult occupa-tional careers. The abstract skills learned in school typically are not utilized in the unskilled part-time jobs most adolescents hold today (Greenberger & Steinberg, 1986); moreover, school achievement does not lead necessarily to adult occupational success. Under these circumstances, school work may seem irrelevant to adolescents, reducing their motivation to achieve in school (Ham-ilton, 1994). Furthermore, lack of a perceived connection between school achievement and future success may reduce adolescents' commitment to the social order and increase the likelihood of problem behaviors such as sub-stance use and delinquency (Hamilton, 1987).

The historical changes in the organization of adolescence also have implica-tions for the conditions under which some developmental transitions are nego-tiated. Modell and Goodman (1990) speculate that the practice of fostering out in the preindustrial period reduced tensions in the family by removing adolescents to semi-independent living arrangements. Today, the young per-son's growing need for autonomy is more likely to be negotiated within the family unit. Moreover, these negotiations are carried out in the closer, more emotionally charged climate of the modern nuclear family, in which children are viewed as precious and in need of protection. Thus, the negotiation of autonomy today may involve more family tension and conflict than in earlier eras. In addition, the temporal compression of young adult role transitions may have implications for adolescent health. Although the temporal convergence of familial and nonfamilial transitions may have clarified the boundary between adolescence and adulthood, it has also increased the need to coordinate multiple role changes, potentially exacerbating the stressfulness of late adolescence (Modell et al., 1976).

Historical Changes in Adolescent Health and Health Risks

In addition to shaping the adolescent social role, societal changes in the 20th century have directly affected the health risks to which young people are exposed. On the positive side, the present century has seen dramatic improvements in nutrition, public health practices, and medical technology. These advances have significantly reduced mortality among adolescents. By 1985, the mortality rate for adolescents between the ages of 10 and 19 years was only one-third of what it had been in the 1930s (Fingerhut & Kleinman, 1989). Between 1985 and 1990, youth mortality trends differed by race and gender. Death rates declined slightly for white males and females aged 15–24, increased slightly for black females in this age range, and increased sharply for black males (National Center for Education Statistics, 1993).

Illness and Disease. The overall reduction in adolescent mortality during this century is primarily attributable to a decline in adolescent deaths due to natural causes, which dropped 90% between the 1930s and 1985 (Fingerhut & Kleinman, 1989). (See Figure 2.1.) Improved public health practices reduced the incidence of infectious diseases in the United States and the mortality rate associated with these diseases. The reduction in infectious disease can be observed in several youth-related diseases. For example, the incidence of polio in the general population dropped to nearly zero by 1960, and that of measles dropped sharply between 1955 and 1970 (National Center for Education Statistics, 1993). Improved medical technology has also reduced mortality from some noninfectious diseases. For example, the death rate from cancer among youth aged 15–24 declined gradually from 1960 to 1990 (National Center for Education Statistics, 1993).

Against this backdrop of improved physical health, however, are health risks associated with violence, injury, drug use, and sexually transmitted diseases. These risks appear to affect adolescents disproportionately and may account for the rise in adolescent mortality between 1960 and 1980, a period when all other age groups experienced a decline in mortality rates (Shafer & Moscicki, 1991).

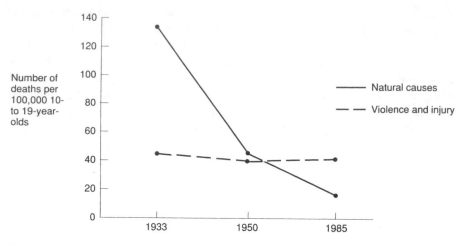

Figure 2.1. Trends in death rates among adolescents. *Source*: Fingerhut, L. A., & Kleinman, J. C. (1989). *Trends and current status in childhood mortality, United States, 1900–85*. Vital and Health Statistics, Series 3, No. 26 (DHHS Pub. No. PHS 89-1410). Hyattsville, MD: National Center for Health Statistics.

Violence and Injury. In contrast to the steep decline in adolescent death rates related to natural causes, death rates related to injury and violence remained stable from the 1930s to the 1980s, accounting for an ever-increasing proportion of adolescent mortality (Figure 2.1). In 1990, motor vehicle accidents were the single leading cause of adolescent death, followed by homicide and suicide (National Center for Education Statistics, 1993). Suicide and homicide rates have increased dramatically in recent decades. Suicide rates for teenagers more than doubled between 1968 and 1985; homicide rates nearly doubled for younger adolescents and increased by 20% for older adolescents (Fingerhut & Kleinman, 1989). Between 1985 and 1990 homicide rates continued to rise among youth aged 15 to 24, whereas suicide rates remained fairly stable (National Center for Education Statistics, 1993). Nonwhite males aged 15–24 have experienced the largest increase in homicide rates in recent decades; in 1990, homicide rates for these males were seven times those of other race-gender groups. In contrast, white males aged 15–24 have the highest suicide rates among youth.

The trend toward increased violence is also seen in victimization rates among adolescents. For youth aged 12 to 19, the rate of victimization from violent crimes (robbery, assault, rape) rose between 1988 and 1991. In 1991, 16- to 19-year-olds experienced higher rates of victimization than either younger adolescents or people aged 20 and older. Victimization rates were higher for males than for females and higher for blacks than for whites (National Center for Education Statistics, 1993).

Adolescents are also perpetrators of violent crimes. In the 1980s, youth under age 18 accounted for roughly one-half of all property crimes, and youth between the ages of 18 and 24 accounted for over one-third of all violent crimes (U.S. Bureau of the Census, 1985). In both cases, the amount of youth crime was disproportionately high, considering the size of the adolescent population. Moreover, a study of age patterns in crime between 1940 and 1980 suggests a shift toward committing offenses at younger ages (Steffensmeier, Allan, Harer, & Streifel, 1989). In line with these trends, arrest rates for adolescents aged 14–17 and for youth aged 18–24 increased dramatically from 1950 to 1990 (National Center for Educational Statistics, 1993).

Substance Use. The 20th century has witnessed a major shift in public attitudes toward drugs, from the official intolerance of the Prohibition years to the relative indulgence of the late 1960s and the 1970s. The shift in public attitudes and in the availability of drugs have been accompanied by changes in adolescent use patterns. Data from representative samples of high school seniors indicate that the prevalence of illicit drug use increased from 1975 to the late 1970s but then declined appreciably in the 1980s (Johnston, O'Malley, & Bachman, 1994). The decline during the 1980s may reflect increased awareness of the risks associated with drug use because the perceived harmfulness of some illicit drugs increased over the same period. Data from the 1990s, however, indicate a reversal of this trend: In 1993, reported use of illicit drugs rose sharply among 8th, 10th, and 12th graders, and negative attitudes toward many drugs declined (Johnston et al., 1994). Although current usage rates are still well below the peak rates observed in the late 1970s and early 1980s, the apparent turnaround is cause for concern. It is also noteworthy that the level of illicit drug use reported by adolescents in the United States is higher than that documented in other industrialized countries (Johnston et al., 1994).

Sexual Activity. Public attitudes about sex also changed in the 20th-century United States, becoming more permissive. Between the 1960s and 1980s, tolerance of nonmarital sex and childbearing increased among adults, along with the acceptance of divorce and cohabitation (Chilman, 1986). As with substance use, adolescent behavior patterns appear to mirror these broader societal trends. Estimates indicate that the rate of premarital intercourse among adolescents increased sharply between the mid-1960s and the 1980s, particularly among white females (Chilman, 1986). During the 1970s, the percentage of metropolitan teenage girls aged 15 to 19 who had experienced sexual intercourse rose from 30% to 50% (Zelnick & Kantner, 1980). Most of this increase occurred among white girls; for black adolescent girls, rates of premarital sexual intercourse rose from 54% in 1971 to 66% in 1976 but then leveled off. Retrospective data from multiple birth cohorts suggest that for white girls the rate of sexual activity began to level off in the early 1980s, whereas for black girls it declined slightly (Hofferth, Kahn, & Baldwin, 1987). Between 1982 and 1988 the proportion of sexually active adolescent girls increased again – from 47% to 53% – with the largest increase occurring among white girls (Forrest & Singh, 1990).

The increase in adolescent sexual activity in the United States has been accompanied by an increased incidence of sexually transmitted diseases and pregnancy. Cases of gonorrhea among 15- to 19-year-old girls quadrupled between 1940 and 1980 (Shafer, Irwin, & Sweet, 1982). From 1980 to 1990, the number of gonorrhea cases among adolescents aged 15 to 19 dropped, at it did in the general population (National Center for Education Statistics, 1993). Nonetheless, data from the 1980s indicate that approximately 2.5 million adolescents contracted a sexually transmitted disease each year (Moore, 1989). Moreover, it is estimated that one in four sexually active adolescents will contract a sexually transmitted disease before they graduate from high school (Shafer & Moscicki, 1990). In addition, human immunodeficiency virus (HIV) infection has become a serious threat. Adolescents are believed to be at particular risk because acquired immunodeficiency syndrome (AIDS) often appears in young adults who presumably contracted the virus as adolescents. Furthermore, reported cases of AIDS among adolescents between the ages of 15 and 19 quintupled between 1985 and 1990, although the numbers are still small (National Center for Education Statistics, 1993).

The increased prevalence of adolescent sexual activity is also reflected in pregnancy rates. Among 15- to 19-year-old adolescent girls in the United States, the pregnancy rate increased during the 1970s but then stabilized at about 11% a year (Hayes, 1987; Henshaw, Kenney, Somberg, & Van Vort, 1992). An estimated 1 million teenage girls become pregnant each year, most premaritally (Dryfoos, 1990). Birth rates for 15- to 19-year-old girls actually declined between 1960 and 1985 (due in part to the legalization of abortion) but then increased somewhat in the late 1980s; in contrast, *nonmarital* birth rates have been increasing since the 1950s for teenage girls and for women in general (National Center for Education Statistics, 1993). Thus, a larger proportion of births to teenagers now occur outside of marriage.

A comparative study of 30 nations conducted in the early 1980s indicated that rates of adolescent pregnancy and childbearing are considerably higher in the United States than in other Western industrialized nations (Jones et al., 1986). Several explanations have been offered to account for the high rates, including inadequate sex education, lack of easy access to contraceptives, mixed messages about the appropriateness of sex for adolescents, and lack of educational and occupational opportunities that would serve as deterrents to early childbearing (e.g., Brooks-Gunn & Furstenberg, 1989; Crockett & Chopak, 1993; Dryfoos, 1990).

Changing Social Contexts and Adolescent Health. Given the evidence that social change affects adolescent development in part by shaping the nature of key developmental contexts, it is important to evaluate the present constellation of health risks in light of recent changes in adolescent social contexts. For example, societal trends in family structure and the rising prevalence of part-time work among teenagers may increase adolescents' exposure to some risks. Adolescents in nonintact families and adolescents whose mothers are employed outside the home are more likely to be sexually active (Billy, Brewster, & Grady, 1994; Crockett & Bingham, 1995; Newcomer & Udry, 1987), perhaps because these conditions are associated with reduced parental supervision and control. These adolescents are potentially at increased risk for sexually transmitted diseases and early pregnancy. Similarly, extensive participation in part-time work is associated with lower participation in such healthy behaviors as eating breakfast, exercising, and getting enough sleep (Bachman & Schulenberg, 1993); it is also associated with potentially harmful behaviors such as delinquency, drug use, and disengagement from school (Steinberg, Fegley, & Dornbusch, 1993). Whether these associations reflect negative effects of work or simply the characteristics of adolescents who choose to work long hours is a matter of ongoing debate (see Finch, Mortimer, & Ryu, chapter 12, this volume); nonetheless, such patterns have generated concern (Greenberger & Steinberg, 1986).

At the same time, nontraditional family patterns and adolescent part-time work may have certain benefits. Adolescents in families with divorced mothers appear to take on more responsibilities and develop more egalitarian gender role attitudes (Barber & Eccles, 1992), and adolescents with working mothers benefit from increased family income. Similarly, part-time work is associated with increased self-reliance among high school students (Greenberger & Steinberg, 1986), and low-intensity work is positively related to some aspects of behavioral and psychological adjustment for 10th graders (Mortimer, Shanahan, & Ryu, 1994). Thus, it is important to recognize that changes in key contexts may enhance growth as well as risk and may have different implications for adolescent health, depending on other circumstances. In particular, preexisting characteristics of the adolescent may influence both the response to new or changed social contexts and subsequent health and well-being.

Implications for Adolescent Health. Adolescents in the United States today come of age in a society in which violence, drug use, sexually transmitted diseases, and AIDS present ongoing threats to health. These pervasive health risks, in conjunction with our ambivalent treatment of adolescents, which involves inconsistent autonomy and inconsistent messages about sex and substance use, may have increased the likelihood of some negative outcomes.

The current pattern of adolescent health risks needs to be considered in the context of ongoing societal changes in the family and other important developmental contexts. Such contextual changes may either mitigate or exacerbate the health risks to which young people are exposed. Given that most adolescent health risks are linked to behavioral choices (e.g., sex and substance use) or to violence, inadequate adult guidance and supervision might be expected to increase the likelihood of negative health outcomes, particularly for younger adolescents (Carnegie Council on Adolescent Development, 1989). In fact, recent studies attest to the importance of parental supervision and monitoring throughout the secondary school years (Brown, Mounts, Lamborn, & Steinberg, 1993; Jacobson & Crockett, 1995; Small, 1995). Trends in adolescent health should also be considered in the context of broader societal changes such as the economic recession of the 1980s, the economic decline of many urban centers and rural counties, and the growth of urban problems.

Subgroup Differences in Adolescent Transitions and Health

Although national patterns are useful for understanding the general template of adolescent development, they are insufficient for capturing the diversity of young people's experiences in heterogeneous societies. As Elder and his colleagues have noted, "Adolescents do not come of age in society as a whole, but rather in a particular community, school, and family" (Elder, Hagell, Rudkin, & Conger, 1994, p. 261). Rather than operating directly and uniformly, societal influences are filtered through local social contexts and conditioned by opportunities and risks in the immediate social environment (Ianni, 1989). This is especially true in an ethnically heterogeneous and socially stratified society such as the United States, in which local variations in racial and ethnic mix, educational institutions, economic resources, and employment opportunities create distinct ecological niches for developing youth. Across these niches, variations may occur in many of the cultural features of adolescence, such as the timing and sequencing of role transitions, the length of adolescence, and socialization goals; health risks also may vary across ecological niches. Two cases will serve to illustrate these differences: that of inner-city African American adolescents and that of disadvantaged rural youth. These subgroups experience an adolescence that appears to differ from the mainstream pattern in important ways. Further, both of these groups are believed to be at risk for poor psychological and social outcomes (William T. Grant Foundation, 1988).

Inner-City African American Youth

One distinctive ecological niche is that of African American youth growing up in poor inner-city neighborhoods. Although African Americans represent only one-third of the adolescents aged 10–17 living in cities, they constitute one-half of all impoverished adolescents in these areas (U.S. Bureau of the Census, 1990). Moreover, poor African Americans are more likely than their white counterparts to live in *ghetto* neighborhoods, defined as urban areas with poverty rates of at least 40% (Wilson, 1991). In 1980, 21% of poor blacks, 16% of poor Hispanics, and 2% of poor whites lived in ghettos (Jargowsky & Bane, 1990). In fact, the ghetto poor (poor people who live in ghetto neighborhoods) are disproportionately African American: In 1980, 65% of the ghetto poor were black (Jargowsky & Bane, 1990).

Inner-city neighborhoods are characterized by a scarcity of jobs, unstable, low-wage employment, and the presence of a street economy (Ogbu, 1985). These conditions increase the likelihood that individuals will engage in alternative or illegal activities in order to generate income (Wilson, 1991). Apart from low access to jobs and job networks, residents of inner-city neighborhoods may be constrained by poor-quality schools, a reduced pool of potential marriage partners, and lack of exposure to conventional role models (Wilson, 1987). In extreme cases, illicit drug trafficking makes the streets physically dangerous, particularly at certain times of the day (Burton, 1991).

Implications for Adolescent Development. Burton, Allison, and Obeidallah (1995) argue that adolescence is qualitatively different for African American youth in poor urban neighborhoods than for youth in mainstream contexts. One difference may be the amount of ambiguity concerning one's developmental status. Burton and her colleagues note that inner-city African American youth experience sharply divergent role expectations across school and family settings: At home they are given considerable autonomy and adult responsibilities, whereas at school they are expected to accept the typical subordinate status of high school students. These mixed messages may exacerbate the ambiguity of adolescence as a developmental stage.

In some families, the ambiguity is reinforced by a condensed family age structure in which generations are separated by only 13–17 years. The closeness in age between parents and children blurs generational boundaries and creates a situation in which parent–adolescent relationships are less hierarchical and more peerlike (Burton et al., 1995). This can weaken parental authority and create difficulties in disciplining adolescent children. Similarities between adolescents and their parents are further underscored by considerable overlap in the social worlds of teenagers and their parents, who share economic and child-care tasks and may compete for the same jobs and romantic partners. Such similarities make it difficult to differentiate between the developmental statuses of teenagers and their parents.

Finally, because of the dangers of life in inner-city neighborhoods, many adolescent boys share the expectation of a life cut short by early death. These young boys push to experience the privileges and autonomy of adulthood early because they believe their time is limited. They engage in adult behaviors at a young age and tend to view themselves as adults, thereby accelerating their transition to adulthood in some domains. A parallel acceleration can be seen among teenage girls, particularly with respect to early childbearing. Burton and her colleagues (1995) argue that adolescence may not exist for these youth; at the very least, it is foreshortened. In any case, the experience of these youth stands in marked contrast to the mainstream adolescent experience, characterized by prolonged dependence, lack of adult responsibilities, and economic uselessness.

Burton and colleagues also find that in these neighborhood settings, adults and adolescents alike have adopted an expanded view of successful developmental outcomes (Burton et al., 1995). Although they may recognize traditional milestones such as finishing high school and securing stable employment, additional markers of developmental success are also accepted. Such markers include dressing well, attaining financial independence (legally or illegally), fathering/giving birth to a child, physical survival, getting out of the neighborhood, spirituality, and contributing to the well-being of the family and community. These alternative conceptions of success appear to reflect adaptations to the physical dangers and limited economic opportunities of inner-city life. They may also reflect a shared knowledge of long-term discrimination and ongoing racial barriers to conventional (mainstream) success. Ogbu (1985) suggests that both current economic resources and a shared knowledge of the opportunity structure shape a population's definitions of the competencies required for success in adulthood. The unique situation of inner-city African Americans would thus be expected to result in the development of alternative developmental milestones and criteria for success.

Implications for Adolescent Health. The neighborhood environment of some inner-city African American youth appears to increase their exposure to some kinds of health-related risks. Apart from increased contact with drugs and street violence, youth in these neighborhoods are at increased risk for engaging in behaviors that have negative implications for their long-term well-being. For example, Brooks-Gunn and her colleagues found that the presence of middle-class neighbors was associated with a reduced risk of teenage childbearing even when family-level characteristics such as socioeconomic status were statistically controlled (Brooks-Gunn, Duncan, Kato & Sealand, 1994). In addition, the prevalence of female-headed families in the neighborhood was positively associated with both dropping out and teenage childbearing.

A decade ago, Hogan and Kitagawa (1985) reported an association between neighborhood quality and the risk of adolescent pregnancy in a black urban sample. More recently, Brewster (1994) showed that much of the racial difference in adolescent girls' sexual activity could be attributed to neighborhood differences in economic resources and the full-time employment rate for women. Her results indicate that nonmarital intercourse is more likely among girls living in neighborhoods where the costs of this activity appear to be low because opportunities are generally limited anyway. Because of residential segregation by race, African American teenagers are more likely than white teenagers to live in such neighborhoods. Such findings reinforce the notion that the local ecology outside the family has important implications for adolescent health and development.

Some neighborhood characteristics may affect adolescents' exposure to health risks indirectly by influencing the social networks and social integration of local adults. Residents of inner-city neighborhoods characterized by high population turnover, ethnic heterogeneity, and scarce resources may exhibit mutual mistrust and low social cohesion (Sampson, 1992). Parents in such neighborhoods tend to rely on individualistic rather than collective child-monitoring strategies (Furstenberg, 1993), which may reduce their ability to supervise teenage peer groups and control delinquency (Sampson, 1992). An adolescent's risk of exposure to violence is likely to be inflated in such neighborhoods.

In addition, it appears that the inconsistent expectations for behavior confronting some inner-city African American youth (Burton et al., 1995) may have implications for their identity formation and psychological well-being. Ianni (1989) argues that inconsistent messages about what constitutes appropriate behavior and future goals may impede the process of developing a coherent sense of self. Conflicting expectations from family, school, and peers, for example, may force adolescents to choose one set of expectations over another in defining their sense of self or may lead to a fragmented (situational) identity rather than a fully integrated sense of self.

Disadvantaged Rural Youth

A second distinctive ecological niche is that of disadvantaged rural youth. In 1990, 25% of adolescents aged 10–17 lived in rural areas (U.S. Bureau of the Census, 1990). Of these youth, 87% were white, 10% were African American, and 3% were from other racial groups. As in cities, poverty rates differ for distinct racial groups: Although the overall poverty rate among rural youth was 18% in 1990, approximately 15% of white rural adolescents were impoverished compared to 44% of African American and Native American rural youth and 5% of Asian/Pacific Islander youth. In contrast to cities, however, most impoverished rural adolescents are white.

In the United States, the economic health of rural communities has been affected by two distinct historical trends. First is the long-term decline in agricultural employment. The number of jobs in farming has decreased sharply since 1910, and the proportion of total jobs accounted for by farming has been declining since the early 1800s (Freudenberg, 1992). This historical trend, coupled with the farm crisis of the 1980s (e.g., Conger & Elder, 1994), has substantially reduced employment opportunities in agriculture. The second trend involves changes in extractive industries – another traditional mainstay of the rural economy. The proportion of jobs in mining and logging, for example, has been decreasing since the early 1900s (Freudenberg, 1992). The economic downturns in rural areas have been accompanied by increasing poverty; currently, poverty rates are often higher in rural areas than in metropolitan areas (Jensen & McLaughlin, 1992). Thus, downward trends in both farming and extractive industries have created a shrinking opportunity structure for rural youth.

Studies Comparing Rural and Suburban Youth. In several papers, my colleagues and I have explored the future plans and current adjustment of a sample of rural adolescents and a comparison sample of suburban adolescents. The rural adolescents came from a small community in the northeastern United States that has traditionally depended on coal mining and a few small factories. The comparison sample came from two suburban middle- to upper-middle-class communities located outside a large city in the Midwest. Both samples were studied intensively in the 1980s: The suburban study began in 1978 (Petersen, 1984), the rural study in 1985 (Vicary, 1991). Although the studies had somewhat different foci, they were both longitudinal studies of adolescent development and covered the years from junior high school through 12th grade. Importantly, they included identical measures of key developmental constructs.

Residents of all three communities were primarily white. The communities differed markedly, however, in social and economic resources. The rural community was considered disadvantaged: Although residents ranged in socioeconomic status from lower to middle class, school census data from 1980 indicated that the median family income was only $14,400 and that 12% of families lived below the poverty line. In contrast, the two suburban communities were relatively affluent: Median family incomes were $42,000 and $55,000, respectively. Similarly, educational attainment indicated a large community difference in human capital: Only 7% of adults in the rural community had completed college compared to over half of those in the suburban communities. Differential opportunity was also indicated by the employment situation. The rural community was undergoing economic decline at the time of the study, as evidenced by periodic shutdowns of the local coal mine and the closing of another major company (Sarigiani, Wilson, Petersen, & Vicary, 1990); in contrast, the suburban community was thriving.

Our analyses have focused on elucidating the impact of these two distinct community settings on young people's current behavior and expectations for the future. In one set of analyses, we examined the ages at which adolescents in each context expected to experience several role transitions reflecting the transition to adulthood: finishing their education, getting their first real job, getting married, and becoming a parent. Results indicated that adolescents from both community contexts subscribed to the normative sequence of adult role transitions: The youngest ages were anticipated for school completion and job entry, followed by marriage and parenting. For each of these transitions, however, the average age cited by rural youth was significantly lower than that for the suburban youth, indicating expectations of an earlier transition to adulthood among rural adolescents (Bingham, Crockett, Stemmler, & Petersen, 1994). Importantly, differences in family socioeconomic status did not entirely account for these differences: controlling for parental educational attainment diminished but did not remove the significant community differences.

A second set of analyses focused on rural–suburban differences in health-related behaviors. Rural males reported a higher frequency of drunkenness and minor delinquency than did suburban males; in addition, rural youth of both genders reported an earlier age at first sexual intercourse than suburban youth. Despite these differences in the levels of some problem behaviors, regression analyses revealed that family relationships and peer relationships were important predictors of these behaviors in both communities (Crockett, Stemmler, Bingham, & Petersen, 1991).

Rural youths' earlier involvement in adult behaviors may indicate greater "transition proneness" (Jessor, 1984) and an accelerated developmental timetable. This interpretation is supported by data on adolescent pregnancy and childbearing. In the rural community, 20% of the girls became pregnant as teenagers, and 12% were mothers before age 20. In the suburban community, there was virtually no adolescent childbearing, although a few girls became pregnant. Similar findings have been reported in other studies (Ianni, 1989). The higher rate of teenage childbearing among rural adolescents is consistent with an accelerated transition to adulthood in the rural community, although it could also reflect community differences in family socioeconomic status.

Finally, a comparison of three dimensions of self-image (emotional tone, peer relations, and family relations) indicated a lower self-image in the rural sample. In particular, rural males and females reported significantly poorer emotional well-being, peer relations, and family relations than their suburban counterparts of the same gender (Sarigiani et al., 1990). Interestingly, within-community analyses revealed only modest associations between parental educational attainment and self-image in the rural sample and no associations in the suburban sample.

Implications for Adolescent Development. The findings on projected timing of young adult role transitions suggest that some rural youth anticipate an early transition to adulthood. This expectation is in accord with data on the actual timing of young adult transitions. For example, rural youth tend to complete fewer years of education than their counterparts in metropolitan areas (Elder, 1963); moreover, rural women marry earlier than women in metropolitan areas (McLaughlin, Lichter, & Johnston, 1993).

Among rural youth, early entry into adult roles may represent a response to limited economic opportunities. For example, restricted job opportunities in rural Appalachia reduce the likely value of extended schooling as a route to occupational attainment and upward mobility (Wilson & Peterson, 1988). In such settings, educational attainment is not stressed, and few youth consider postsecondary education. In the absence of extended schooling, the transition to adult work and family roles proceeds at an accelerated pace.

The timing of adult role transitions may also be influenced by local norms. Rural communities are often characterized as supporting traditional gender role attitudes. Such attitudes encourage marriage and childbearing as an appropriate route to adulthood for women and would be expected to result in accelerated family transitions, especially for females. In addition, such traditional attitudes may combine with a comparative lack of educational and occupational opportunities for women in rural areas, making marriage (and earlier marriage in particular) more attractive for them.

The mingling of economic and cultural influences is also evident in other studies of rural youth. For example, Shanahan, Elder, Burchinal, and Conger (1995) found that working for pay was more common among rural than among urban adolescents. Furthermore, rural adolescents were more likely than urban adolescents to use their earnings to pay for school expenses and to contribute money to their families. Perhaps most interesting, such nonleisure spending was differentially related to parent–child relationships in the rural and urban contexts: The interaction between nonleisure spending and earnings was positively associated with parent–child relations among rural youth but negatively associated among urban youth. Shanahan et al. (1995) interpret this rural–urban difference as reflecting the differential meaning of adolescent work in rural versus urban settings. Adolescent work has traditionally been an acceptable part of rural life; thus, it may be welcomed as a positive sign of maturity and a commitment to the communal good. In the urban setting, however, nonleisure spending by adolescents may be viewed as threatening because it signifies an inability of parents to fill the provider role adequately. Such findings suggest that the expectations of rural adolescents need to be considered within the framework of rural cultural and economic traditions.

Implications for Adolescent Health. Like inner-city African American youth, disadvantaged rural adolescents may experience an accelerated transition to adulthood. Early school completion, marriage, and childbearing may, in turn, limit future educational and occupational attainment among these youth, although at present we cannot say to what extent later disadvantage is a consequence of premature role transitions per se or of preexisting resource limitations and personal characteristics that spurred an accelerated transition in the first place.

Nonetheless, the limited opportunity structure of many rural communities poses a dilemma for rural youth, especially those with high aspirations. Donaldson (1986) suggests that for many rural youth, the pull to remain close to family and friends is pitted against the need to seek economic opportunities elsewhere. This conflict may increase the psychological stress associated with the transition to adulthood (Schonert-Reichl & Elliott, 1994).

The fact that several studies have found rural youth to have poorer self-images than their metropolitan counterparts (Petersen, Offer, & Kaplan, 1979; Sarigiani et al., 1990) also indicates that some aspects of rural residence may be psychologically debilitating. Given that self-image is positively associated with educational and occupational aspirations (Lee, 1984; Sarigiani et al., 1990), the poorer self-image of rural youth may be a consequence of family and community variables (e.g., lack of resources) that operate to constrain opportunities and reduce aspirations.

In any case, the greater involvement of rural youth in such adult behaviors as drinking and sex may have implications for current and subsequent health. To the extent that rural youth initiate these behaviors at younger ages, they may be at increased risk for negative outcomes. For example, contraception and condom use are less common among younger than older adolescents; thus, adolescents who begin to have intercourse at younger ages may be at increased risk of pregnancy and sexually transmitted diseases. Early initiation of drinking may also increase the risk of some negative outcomes.

Future Directions in the Study of Subgroup Differences

As illustrated by these two cases, adolescence may differ for subgroups of youth in the United States, depending on features of the family and the community ecology. Both inner-city African American youth and disadvantaged white rural youth appear to experience a truncated adolescence, although the foreshortening is more dramatic for the African American sample when it is also combined with other adaptations to the conditions of inner-city life. For disadvantaged rural youth, adolescence appears to follow the mainstream template but may be foreshortened by early school completion and early entry into adult family roles. In both subgroups, the foreshortening is likely to reflect a lack of educational and employment opportunities that may be a function both of family economic resources and of depressed economic conditions in the surrounding community. Cultural and historical traditions may also play a role. For example, the alternative construction of developmental success among African American youth may reflect responses to the long-term economic oppression of African Americans (Ogbu, 1985), as well as the isolation of inner-city youth from mainstream role models and norms (Wilson, 1987). Similarly, the early transition to adulthood among rural adolescents may be encouraged by traditional sex role attitudes and traditional routes to economic success within rural communities. The health-related risks of the local context appear more pressing for inner-city youth. However, both inner-city youth and rural youth who accelerate the transition to adulthood are likely to be disadvantaged in terms of future earnings and occupational attainment (William T. Grant Foundation, 1988).

Despite the intriguing possibility that community-level cultural and economic variables play an important role in shaping adolescent development, the study of community effects on adolescent development is just beginning. Currently, it is impossible to draw firm conclusions about the extent of these effects and the mechanisms through which they operate. One ongoing problem concerns selection effects (e.g., Tienda, 1991). If certain kinds of people gravitate toward certain kinds of neighborhoods or communities, it is hard to disentangle community effects from person effects. Longitudinal studies in which personal characteristics are assessed before residents move into a particular community or neighborhood would help to disentangle selection effects from socialization effects.

A second issue involves the need to distinguish among the multiple factors that create a particular ecological niche. In most studies, place of residence is confounded with either race or socioeconomic status. Although to some extent this reflects the complexity of ecological niches, which are defined by multiple characteristics, it is important to determine whether community effects depend primarily on one of these factors as opposed to a combination of factors. Thus, we need studies of samples that differ on key dimensions (e.g., white inner-city youth, black middle-class urban youth, well-to-do rural white youth). Large national samples allow us to control statistically on various dimensions and determine the unique variance due to others. However, if such dimensions are truly confounded, this approach may be misleading; thus, studies of multiple naturally occurring subgroups may be more fruitful.

It is also important to recognize the heterogeneity within chosen subgroups. For example, Elder and his colleagues (Elder et al., 1994) have made an important distinction between youth whose families are engaged in farming and nonfarm youth whose families earn their livings through other means. These authors found stronger rural orientations among farm youth than among small-town youth whose fathers were not involved in farming. More important, the meaning of rural ties differed for farm and nonfarm youth: Among farm youth, wanting to live in a rural area was associated with positive psychological adjustment, whereas among nonfarm youth it was associated with conduct disorder and low self-esteem. Variability undoubtedly exists among inner-city minority youth as well.

A fourth critical need is to identify the mechanisms through which presumed community effects operate. Initially, this involves distinguishing community effects from family influences. It also requires identifying which features of the community are active in producing a particular outcome. Finally, it involves testing hypothesized processes and pathways through which community-level influences operate to affect adolescent behavior and exposure to health risks. For example, some ecological variables appear to operate by affecting parenting processes: Economic stress affects parent–child interaction (Conger & Elder, 1994) and may also lead to ineffective parental monitoring and discipline (Patterson, deBaryshe, & Ramsey, 1989; Sampson & Laub, 1994). Similarly, some neighborhood characteristics appear to affect parenting strategies; for example, high levels of mistrust and low mutual investment among neighbors appear to encourage individualistic parenting strategies rather than collective strategies (Furstenberg, 1993). These strategies may, in turn, have implications for the community's ability to control teenagers (Sampson, 1992).

Equally important, community characteristics may interact with parenting competence in ways that affect both adolescents' opportunities for social mobility and their exposure to health risks (Furstenberg, 1993). Community characteristics would also be expected to interact with characteristics of the adolescent in affecting exposure to health risks. Thus, studies that include measurement at each of these levels (community, family, individual) would be useful. Unfortunately, studies have tended to focus on one or at most two of these levels; data sets with rich measures on all three are rare.

Finally, many studies examine adolescent development in distinct family and community contexts but fail to measure a broad array of health outcomes. Inclusion of more comprehensive health measures within studies of neighborhood and community effects will be needed to understand the role of local conditions in the etiology of health-related behavior and health outcomes.

Conclusions

The primary purpose of this chapter was to explore the connection between adolescents' experiences and dimensions of the broader societal context, showing how adolescent development is embedded in and defined by cultural and institutional arrangements. This connection can be seen on all three levels examined here – cross-cultural, historical, and intrasocietal. Anthropological studies have documented cross-cultural differences in the structuring of adolescence and have demonstrated a connection between this structuring and the social and economic organization of societies. In addition, historical accounts of the development of contemporary adolescence in Western societies have documented a correspondence between changes in economic and social organization and changes in the conceptions and treatment of youth. Finally, studies of particular subgroups within contemporary U.S. society illustrate the variations in developmental patterns that arise in response to distinct economic and social conditions.

A second goal of the chapter was to examine the implications of societal conditions for adolescent health. An examination of historical changes in adolescent health suggested general improvements in the health of American adolescents during the 20th century. A number of health risks remain, however, and the incidence of some kinds of health problems (e.g., sexually transmitted diseases) has increased. The current array of health risks is worrisome in part because risks are not evenly distributed throughout the population but rather are often concentrated in areas already plagued by a lack of social and economic resources. Therefore, some adolescents are exposed to multiple risks on a continuing basis, with potentially disastrous consequences. In addition, the contemporary pattern of health risks is characterized by a preponderance of risks that involve voluntary participation by the adolescent (e.g., smoking, other substance use, sexual activity, some forms of violence). Thus, the issue of adequate education and guidance for youth is critical, as well as the need to provide educational and occupational opportunities that increase young people's motivation to avoid health-risking behavior. The current demographic picture, which includes increases in single-parent families, increasing poverty within female-headed families, and ongoing residential segregation that isolates some youths from mainstream resources and role models, suggests that enhanced efforts will be needed to meet these important goals.

References

Arnett, J. J. (1994). Are college students adults? Their conceptions of the transition to adulthood. *Journal of Adult Development, 1*, 213–224.

Bachman, J. G., & Schulenberg, J. (1993). How part-time work intensity relates to drug use, problem behavior, time use, and satisfaction among high school seniors: Are these consequences or merely correlates? *Developmental Psychology, 29*, 220–235.

Barber, B. L., & Eccles, J. S. (1992). Long-term influence of divorce and single parenting on adolescent family- and work-related values, behaviors, and aspirations. *Psychological Bulletin, 111*, 108–126.

Benedict, R. (1937). *Patterns of culture*. Boston: Houghton Mifflin.

Billy, J. O. G., Brewster, K. L., & Grady, W. R. (1994). Contextual effects on the sexual behavior of adolescent behavior. *Journal of Marriage and the Family, 56*, 387–404.

Bingham, C. R., Crockett, L. J., Stemmler, M., & Petersen, A. C. (1994). *Community–contextual differences in adolescents' expectations for the timing of adulthood transitions*. Unpublished manuscript.

Brewster, K. L. (1994). Race differences in sexual activity among adolescent women: The role of neighborhood characteristics. *American Sociological Review, 59*, 408–424.

Brooks-Gunn, J., Duncan, G. J., Kato, P., & Sealand, N. (1994). Do neighborhoods affect child and adolescent development? *American Journal of Sociology, 99*, 353–395.

Brooks-Gunn, J., & Furstenberg, F. F. (1989). Adolescent sexual behavior. *American Psychologist, 44*, 249–257.

Brooks-Gunn, J., & Reiter, E. (1990). The role of pubertal processes. In S. S. Feldman & G. R. Elliott (Eds.), *At the threshold: The developing adolescent* (pp. 16–53). Cambridge, MA: Harvard University Press.

Brown, B. B., Mounts, N., Lamborn, S. D., & Steinberg, L. (1993). Parenting practices and peer group affiliation in adolescence. *Child Development, 64*, 467–482.

Burton, L. (1991, May–June). Caring for children in high-risk neighborhoods. *The American Enterprise*, 34–37.

Burton, L., Allison, K., & Obeidallah, D. (1995). Social context and adolescence: Perspectives on development among inner-city African American teens. In L. J. Crockett & A. C. Crouter (Eds.), *Pathways through adolescence: Individual development in relation to social contexts* (pp. 119–138). Hillsdale NJ: Erlbaum.

Carnegie Council on Adolescent Development. (1989). *Turning points: Preparing American youth for the 21st century*. Washington, DC: Carnegie Corporation.

Chilman, C. S. (1986). Some psychological aspects of adolescent sexual and contraceptive behaviors in a changing American Society. In J. B. Lancaster & B. A. Hamburg (Eds.), *School-age pregnancy and parenthood: Biosocial dimensions* (pp. 191–217). New York: Aldine de Gruyter.

Church, R. (1976). *Education in the United States*. New York: Free Press.

Cohen, Y. (1964). *The transition from childhood to adolescence*. Chicago: Aldine.

Conger, R. D., & Elder, G. H., Jr. (1994). *Families in troubled times: Adapting to change in rural America*. New York: Aldine de Gruyter.

Crockett, L. J., & Bingham, C. R. (1995). *Family influences on girls' sexual experience and pregnancy risk*. Manuscript submitted for publication.

Crockett, L. J., & Chopak, J. (1993). Pregnancy prevention in early adolescence: A developmental perspective. In R. M. Lerner (Ed.), *Early adolescence: Perspectives on research, policy, and intervention* (pp. 315–333). Hillsdale, NJ: Erlbaum.

Crockett, L. J., Stemmler, M., Bingham, C. R., & Petersen, A. C. (1991, July). *Subcultural variation in the development of adolescent problem behaviors*. Poster presentation at the meeting of the International Society for the Study of Behavioral Development, Minneapolis.

Donaldson, G. A., Jr. (1986). Do you need to leave home to grow up? The rural adolescents dilemma. *Research on Rural Education, 3*, 121–125.

Dryfoos, J. (1990). *Adolescents at risk: Prevalence and prevention*. New York: Oxford University Press.

Elder, G. H., Jr. (1963). Achievement orientations and career patterns of rural youth. *Sociology of Education, 37*, 30–58.

Elder, G. H., Jr. (1975). Adolescence in the life cycle: An introduction. In S. E. Dragastin & G. H. Elder, Jr. (Eds.), *Adolescence in the life cycle: Psychological change and social context* (pp. 1–22). Washington, DC: Hemisphere.

Elder, G. H., Jr., Hagell, A., Rudkin, K., & Conger, R. D. (1994). Looking forward in troubled times: The influence of social context on adolescent plans and orientations. In R. K. Silbereisen & E. Todt (Eds.), *Adolescence in context: The interplay of family, school, peers, and work in adjustment* (pp. 244–264). New York: Springer-Verlag.

Elliott, G., & Feldman, S. S. (1990). Capturing the adolescent experience. In S. S. Feldman & G. R. Elliott (Eds.), *At the threshold: The developing adolescent* (pp. 1–13). Cambridge, MA: Harvard University Press.

Fasick, F. A. (1994). On the "invention" of adolescence. *Journal of Adolescent Research, 14*, 6–23.

Fingerhut, L. A., & Kleinman, J. C. (1989). *Trends and current status in childhood mortality, United States, 1900–85*. Vital and Health Statistics, Series 3, No. 26 (DHHS Pub. No. PHS 89–1410). Hyattsville, MD: National Center for Health Statistics.

Ford, C., & Beach, F. (1951). *Patterns of sexual behavior*. New York: Harper & Row.

Forrest, J. D., & Singh, S. (1990). The sexual and reproductive behavior of American women, 1982–1988. *Family Planning Perspectives, 22*, 206–214.

Freudenberg, W. R. (1992). Addictive economies: Extractive industries and vulnerable localities in a changing world economy. *Rural Sociology, 57*, 305–332.

Furstenberg, F. F., Jr. (1993). How families manage risk and opportunity in dangerous neighborhoods. In W. J. Wilson (Ed.), *Sociology and the public agenda* (pp. 231–258). Newbury Park, CA: Sage.

Greenberger, E., & Steinberg, L. (1986). *When teenagers work: The psychological and social costs of adolescent employment*. New York: Basic Books.

Greene, A. L., Wheatley, S. M., & Aldava, J. F. (1992). Stages on life's way: Adolescents' implicit theories of the life course. *Journal of Adolescent Research, 7*, 364–381.

Hamilton, S. F. (1987). Adolescent problem behavior in the United States and West Germany: Implications for prevention. In K. Hurrelmann, F. X. Kaufmann, & F. Lösel (Eds.), *Social intervention: Chances and constraints* (pp. 185–204). Berlin: Walter de Gruyter.

Hamilton, S. F. (1994). Employment prospects as motivation for school achievement: Links and gaps between school and work in seven countries. In R. K. Silbereisen & E. Todt (Eds.), *Adolescence in context: The interplay of family, school, peers, and work in adjustment* (pp. 267–283). New York: Springer-Verlag.

Hanawalt, B. A. (1993). *Growing up in medieval London: The experience of childhood in history*. New York: Oxford University Press.

Havighurst, R. J. (1948/1972). *Developmental tasks and education* (3rd ed.). New York: David McKay.

Hayes, C. D. (Ed.). (1987). *Risking the future: Adolescent sexuality, pregnancy, and childbearing* (Vol. 1). Washington, DC: National Academy Press.

Henshaw, S. K., Kenney, A. M., Somberg, D., & Van Vort, J. (1992). *U.S. teenage pregnancy statistics*. New York: Alan Guttmacher Institute.

Hofferth, S. L., Kahn, J. R., & Baldwin, W. (1987). Premarital sexual activity among U.S. women over the past three decades. *Family Planning Perspectives, 19*, 46–53.

Hogan, D. P. (1982). *Adolescent expectations about the sequencing of early life transitions*. Unpublished manuscript, University of Chicago.

Hogan, D. P., & Astone, N. M. (1986). The transition to adulthood. *Annual Review of Sociology, 12*, 109–130.

Hogan, D. P., & Kitagawa, E. (1985). The impact of social status, family structure, and neighborhood on the fertility of black adolescents. *American Journal of Sociology, 90*, 825–855.

Hurrelmann, K. (1989). The social world of adolescents: A sociological perspective. In K. Hurrelman & U. Engel (Eds.), *The social world of adolescents: International perspectives* (pp. 3–26). Berlin: Walter de Gruyter.

Ianni, F. A. J. (1989). *The search for structure: A report on American youth today*. New York: Free Press.

Jacobson, K., & Crockett, L J. (1995). *Parental monitoring and adolescent adjustment: An ecological approach*. Manuscript Submitted for publication.

Jargowsky, P. A., & Bane, M. J. (1990). *Neighborhood poverty: Basic questions*. Discussion Paper Series, #H-90-3. Cambridge, MA: Malcolm Weiner Center for Social Policy, John F. Kennedy School of Government, Harvard University.

Jensen, L., & McLaughlin, D. K. (1992). Human capital and nonmetropolitan poverty. In L. J. Beaulieu & D. Mulkey (Eds.), *Investing in people: The human capital needs of rural America* (pp. 111–138). Boulder, CO: Westview Press.

Jessor, R. (1984). Adolescent development and behavioral health. In J. Matarazzo, S. Weiss, J. Herd, N. Miller, & J. M. Weiss (Eds.), *Behavioral health: A handbook of health enhancement and disease prevention* (pp. 69–90). New York: Wiley.

Johnston, L. D., O'Malley, P. M., & Bachman, J. G. (1994). *National survey results on drug use from the Monitoring the Future Study, 1975–1993* (Vol. 1). National Institute on Drug Abuse (NIH Pub. No. 94-3809). Washington, DC: U.S. Government Printing Office.

Jones, E., Forrest, J., Goldman, N., Henshaw, S., Lincoln, R., Rosoff, J., Westoff, C., & Wulf, D. (1986). *Teenage pregnancy in industrialized countries.* New Haven, CT: Yale University Press.

Katz, M. (1975). *The people of Hamilton, Canada West: Family and class in a mid-nineteenth-century city.* Cambridge, MA: Harvard University Press.

Kett, J. (1977). *Rites of passage: Adolescence in America, 1790 to the present.* New York: Basic Books.

Lee, C. C. (1984). An investigation of the psychosocial variables in the occupational aspirations and expectations of rural black and white adolescents: Implications for vocational education. *Journal of Research and Development in Education, 17,* 28–34.

Marini, M. M. (1987). Measuring the process of role change during the transition to adulthood. *Social Science Research, 16,* 1–38.

McLaughlin, D. K., Lichter, D. T., & Johnston, G. M. (1993). *Journal of Marriage and the Family, 55,* 827–838.

Modell, J. (1989). *Into one's own: From youth to adulthood in the United States, 1920–1975.* Berkeley: University of California Press.

Modell, J., Furstenberg, F. F., Jr., & Hershberg, T. (1976). Social change and transitions to adulthood in historical perspective. *Journal of Family History, 1,* 7–32.

Modell, J., & Goodman, M. (1990). Historical perspectives. In S. S. Feldman & G. R. Elliott (Eds.), *At the threshold: The developing adolescent* (pp. 93–122). Cambridge, MA: Harvard University Press.

Moore, K. A. (1989). *Facts at a glance.* Washington, DC: Child Trends, Inc.

Mortimer, J. T., Shanahan, M., & Ryu, S. (1994). The effects of adolescent employment on school-related orientation and behavior. In R. K. Silbereisen & E. Todt (Eds.), *Adolescence in context: The interplay of family, school, peers, and work in adjustment* (pp. 304–326). New York: Springer-Verlag.

National Center for Education Statistics. (1993). *Youth indicators 1993: Trends in the well-being of American youth.* Department of Education. Washington, DC: U.S. Government Printing Office.

Newcomer, S., & Udry, J. R. (1987). Parental marital status effects on adolescent sexual behavior. *Journal of Marriage and the Family, 49,* 235–240.

Nightingale, E. O., & Wolverton, L. (1993). Adolescent rolelessness in modern society. *Teachers College Record, 94,* 472–486.

Nurmi, J. (1989). Development of orientation to the future during early adolescence: A four-year longitudinal study and two cross-sectional comparisons. *International Journal of Psychology, 24,* 195–214.

Ogbu, J. U. (1985). A cultural ecology of competence among inner-city blacks. In M. B. Spencer, G. K. Brookins, & W. R. Allen (Eds.), *Beginnings: Social and effective development of black children* (pp. 45–66). Hillsdale, NJ: Erlbaum.

Paige, K. (1983). A bargaining theory of menarcheal responses in preindustrialized cultures. In J. Brooks-Gunn & A. C. Petersen (Eds.), *Girls at puberty: Biological and psychological perspectives* (pp. 301–322). New York: Plenum.

Patterson, G., deBaryshe, B., & Ramsey, E. (1989). A developmental perspective on antisocial behavior. *American Psychologist, 44,* 329–335.

Petersen, A. C. (1984). The Early Adolescence Study: An overview. *Journal of Early Adolescence, 4,* 103–106.

Petersen, A. C., Hurrelmann, K., & Leffert, N. (1993). Adolescence and schooling in Germany and the United States: A comparison of peer socialization to adulthood. *Teachers College Record, 94,* 611–628.

Petersen, A. C., Offer, D., & Kaplan, E. (1979). The self-image of rural adolescent girls. In M. Sugar (Ed.), *Female adolescent development* (pp. 141–155). New York: Brunner/Mazel.

Polk, K. (1987). The new marginal youth. *Crime and Delinquency, 30,* 482–480.

Rindfuss, R. R., Swicegood, C. G., & Rosenfeld, R. A. (1987). Disorder in the lifecourse: How common and does it matter? *American Sociological Review, 52*, 785–801.

Sampson, R. J. (1992). Family management and child development: Insights from social disorganization theory. In J. McCord (Ed.), *Advances in criminological theory* (Vol. 3, pp. 63–93). New Brunswick, NJ: Transaction.

Sampson, R. J., & Laub, J. H. (1994). Urban poverty and the family context of delinquency: A new look at structure and process in a classic study. *Child Development, 65*, 523–540.

Sarigiani, P. A., Wilson, J. L., Petersen, A. C., & Vicary, J. R. (1990). Self-image and educational plans of adolescents from two contrasting communities. *Journal of Early Adolescence, 10*, 37–55.

Schlegel, A., & Barry, H., III. (1991). *Adolescence: An anthropological inquiry*. New York: Free Press.

Schonert-Reichl, K. A., & Elliott, J. P. (1994, February). *Rural pathways: Stability and change during the transition to young adulthood*. Paper presented at the biennial meeting of the Society for Research on Adolescence, San Diego, CA.

Shafer, M. A., Irwin, C. E., & Sweet, R. L., (1982). Acute salpingitis in the adolescent female. *Journal of Pediatrics, 100*, 339–350.

Shafer, M. A., & Moscicki, A. B. (1991). Sexually transmitted diseases in adolescents. In W. R. Hendee (Ed.), *The health of adolescents* (pp. 211–249). San Francisco: Jossey-Bass.

Shanahan, M. J., Elder, G. H., Jr., Burchinal, M., & Conger, R. D. (1995). *Adolescent earnings and relationships with parents: The work–family nexus in urban and rural ecologies*. Unpublished manuscript.

Small, S. (1995). Enhancing contexts of adolescent development: The role of community-based action research. In L. J. Crockett & A. C. Crockett (Eds.), *Pathways through adolescence: Individual development in relation to social contexts* (pp. 211–233). Hillsdale, NJ: Erlbaum.

Steffensmeier, D. J., Allan, E. A., Harer, M. D., & Streifel, C. (1989). Age and the distribution of crime. *American Journal of Sociology, 94*, 803–831.

Steinberg, L. (1993). *Adolescence* (3rd ed.). New York: McGraw-Hill.

Steinberg, L., Fegley, S., & Dornbusch, S. M. (1993). Negative impact of part-time work on adolescent adjustment: Evidence from a longitudinal study. *Developmental Psychology, 29*, 171–180.

Tanner, D. (1972). *Secondary education*. New York: Macmillan.

Tienda, M. (1991). Poor people and poor places: Deciphering neighborhood effects on poverty outcomes. In J. Huber (Ed.), *Macro–micro linkages in sociology* (pp. 244–262). Newbury Park, CA: Sage.

U.S. Bureau of the Census. (1985). *Statistical abstract of the United States*. Washington, DC: U.S. Government Printing Office.

U.S. Bureau of the Census. (1990). *1990 current population survey*. Washington, DC: U.S. Government Printing Office.

Vicary, J. R. (1991). *Psychological impact of pregnancy on rural adolescents*. Final report to the Office of Adolescent Pregnancy Programs. University Park, PA: Author.

Whiting, J. W. M., Burbank, V. K., & Ratner, M. S. (1986). The duration of maidenhood across cultures. In J. B. Lancaster & B. A. Hamburg (Eds.), *School-age pregnancy and parenthood: Biosocial dimensions* (pp. 273–302). New York: Aldine de Gruyter.

William T. Grant Foundation, Commission on Work, Family and Citizenship. (1988). *The forgotten half: Pathways to success for America's youth and young families*. Washington, DC: Author.

Wilson, S. M., & Peterson, G. W. (1988). Life satisfaction among young adults from rural families. *Family Relations, 37*, 84–91.

Wilson, W. J. (1987). *The truly disadvantaged: The inner city, the underclass, and public policy*. Chicago: University of Chicago Press.

Wilson, W. J. (1991). Studying inner-city social dislocations: The challenge of public agenda research. *American Sociological Review, 56*, 1–14.

Worthman, C. M. (1986). Developmental dyssynchrony as normative experience: Kikuyu adolescents. In J. B. Lancaster & B. A. Hamburg (Eds.), *School-age pregnancy and parenthood:
Biosocial dimensions* (pp. 95–112). New York: Aldine de Gruyter.

Zelizer, V. A. (1985). *Pricing the priceless child: The changing social value of children.* New York:
Basic Books.

Zelnick, M., & Kantner, J. F. (1980). Sexual activity, contraceptive use, and pregnancy among
metropolitan area teenagers: 1971–1979. *Family Planning Perspectives, 12,* 230–237.

3 Social Change and Adolescent Well-Being: Healthy Country, Healthy Teens

Peter Noack and Bärbel Kracke

Introduction

Most conceptualizations of adolescence converge in understanding this period of the life span as a phase of multiple transitions – biological, cognitive, and social (Steinberg, 1993). A major mechanism of development is seen in mutual influences operating between individuals and their contexts, which themselves undergo changes (Hurrelmann, 1994; Silbereisen & Eyferth, 1986). In disentangling developmental processes, developmentalists have so far mainly studied adolescents' interactions within microsystems (Bronfenbrenner, 1989) such as family and friendship relationships, whereas comparably little attention has been paid to macrosocial contexts of the transition to adulthood. Cross-cultural psychology, as well as migration studies that have increasingly broadened the scope of developmental research, are major exceptions. Recent investigations into adaptational processes of adolescent immigrants and their families, for example, have identified strong effects of core cultural values on adolescent development, whereas more distant cultural values are less influential and subject to faster processes of assimilation (e.g., Feldman, Mont-Reynaud, & Rosenthal, 1991; Silbereisen & Schmitt-Rodermund, 1995). Clearly, less is known concerning the influence of challenges and risks young people must master while growing up in a changing society.

Even though a static society may generally be the exception rather than the rule, there is reason to assume that present youth cohorts, in particular, have to master their transition to adulthood in times of accelerated social change. A trend toward modernization and individualization of life (Beck, 1986), the transition from manufacturing to service-based economies, the increase in intercultural contacts due to improved opportunities for travel and communication, the growing international involvement of businesses, and worldwide migrational movements are but a few examples of changes characterizing at least industrial democracies. Citizens of Western European countries

Portions of the chapter are based on the ongoing study "Individuation and Social Change" funded by the German Research Council. The study is conducted in collaboration with Manfred Hofer, Elke-Klein-Allermann, Klaus Udo Ettrich, and Hanns Ullrich Jahn.

54

experience effects of the European Union integration despite – or possibly because of – the numerous problems and drawbacks involved. Moreover, for many countries, the recent collapse of the Eastern bloc has markedly affected the larger context of life. In a certain sense, Germany in the process of unification could be considered as experiencing the combined impact of these developments.

Adolescents may be particularly sensitive to social change. Seemingly far away from immediate consequences of the end of the Soviet empire, U.S. adolescents, for instance, responded to the events at the beginning of the 1990s by a spontaneous increase in their feeling of political self-efficacy, which then returned to normal at a similarly fast pace (Schulenberg, Bachman, Johnston, & O'Malley, 1993). East German youth who experienced these macrosocial changes more directly showed parallel reactions. Palentien, Pollmer, and Hurrelmann (1993) studied East German adolescents' optimism regarding the efficacy of various political activities such as political rallies or citizens' action. Whereas in 1990, the year of Germany's unification, the majority of these young people believed that such activities would influence political decisions, in 1992, after two years in united Germany, the experience of having limited influence on political decisions led to less enthusiastic interpretations.

Public as well as scholarly interest in associations between individual development and social change have focused so far mainly on the emergence of problems negatively affecting society. The search for reasons to explain increased adolescent violence – namely, verbal and physical attacks on foreigners, minorities, and groups with different orientations and lifestyles – is a recent case in point. Youth researchers have argued that the loss of traditional social bonds, as well as a decrease in the certainty and predictability of life during times of rapid change, strongly contribute to political intolerance and violence among young people (e.g., Heitmeyer, 1987).

In this chapter, we draw attention to effects that changes in the macrocontext may exert on adolescent somatic and psychological well-being that are likely to be overlooked because of their less obvious repercussions on society. The extent of risks and problems related to teenagers' physical health, in particular, is not well recognized by the general public. First, we discuss the prevalence of health-related problems during adolescence and their possible explanations. Then we turn to investigations of macrocontextual influences on young people's development. In this section, we report on experiences of social change at both the individual and family levels. Earlier empirical research has focused particularly on the consequences of economic strains. Major findings from these studies and related work are summarized. Next, we introduce our own analyses of social change and well-being in adolescence. After presenting some data on the distribution of different aspects of adolescent health, we report on the effects of change on well-being in a sample of

East and West German teenagers. Given the scarcity of available research, the final section provides tentative conclusions and delineates directions for future research.

Adolescence as a Period of Elevated Health Risks

Paralleling popular notions, "storm and stress" conceptualizations of adolescent individual and relationship development heavily influenced youth research for a considerable period of time. Meanwhile, empirical evidence has forced the field to revise this view. This does not imply, however, that adolescents smoothly turn into adults without experiencing conflict or distress. The prevalence of a variety of problem behaviors, for instance, reaches its peak during adolescence. Many of these behaviors constitute immediate or long-term health risks.

When discussing adolescent health, we address psychological and somatic well-being as well as health-compromising behaviors. Our main focus is on physical health in adolescence, which developmental research has only recently recognized as a potential problem requiring systematic investigation (Millstein & Litt, 1990).

Cross-sectional and longitudinal studies on adolescents' *psychological well-being* have contributed importantly to the disappearance of "storm and stress" notions. Findings addressing evaluative aspects of young people's self-concept, in particular, suggest a high degree of (normative) stability across time, as well as an increase rather than a decrease in, for example, self-esteem with age (Alsaker & Olweus, 1992; Dusek & Flaherty, 1981). General trends, however, mask substantial interindividual variability. Thus, Hirsch and DuBois (1991) observed chronically low or declining trajectories of self-esteem in about one-third of the early adolescents they studied longitudinally. Moreover, many studies reveal gender differences, with female adolescents faring more poorly than their male age-mates (Petersen, Silbereisen, & Sorensen, 1992).

Depressive mood, depression, and suicidal ideation or suicide attempts are particularly serious indications of psychosocial problems that also increase during adolescence (e.g., Millstein & Litt, 1990; Rutter, 1986). Although girls are at greater risk for depressive symptomatology (Gore, Aseltine, & Colten, 1993; Stiffman, Chueh, & Early, 1992), suicidal ideation, and suicidal attempts (Windle, Miller-Tutzauer, & Domenico, 1992), boys are more likely to commit suicide (Millstein & Litt, 1990; Windle et al., 1992).

At the same time, adolescence is characterized by a high prevalence and high intensity of a wide range of *problem behaviors*. The prevalence of substance use and delinquency is particularly well documented. Despite some decline in alcohol consumption from the 1970s through the mid-1980s observed in adolescent cohorts (Silbereisen, Robins, & Rutter, 1995), absolute rates remain high. A recent European Community survey (Commission of the

European Communities, 1991), for instance, reports a rate of 7–27% of heavy drinking among 11- to 15-year-olds in the European countries studied. Johnston, O'Malley, and Bachman (1991) found that about one-third of their late adolescent U.S. subjects engaged in heavy drinking. Caution is necessary, however, when comparing figures from different studies that employ varying modes of assessment (e.g., five or more drinks on at least one occasion during the last 2 weeks) and strategies of sample selection. More important for our line of argumentation than mere levels of intake is the fact that for most substances, consumption sharply increases during the teenage years, reaching a peak in late adolescence or early adulthood, followed by a substantial decline in the course of adulthood (Bachman, Wadsworth, O'Malley, Schulenberg, & Johnston, chapter 10, this volume; Fillmore et al., 1991).

Involvement in various delinquent behaviors follows a similar pattern. Police statistics identify petty theft, vandalism, and physical violence as law-breaking acts that are particularly widespread among youth. In Germany, for instance, the proportion of 14- to 21-year-olds suspected of perpetrating physical violence resulting in bodily injuries is about 30%, even though this group makes up less than 10% of the population (Bundeskriminalamt, 1994). Several of the criminal behaviors adolescents engage in, such as violent fights, involve serious health risks for the young delinquents as well as their often same-age victims. Along the same line, 15- to 20-year-olds account for about 7% of U.S. drivers, yet they are involved in almost 15% of the registered driver fatalities (National Transportation Safety Board, 1993). Deviating from the pattern observed for internalizing problems, the prevalence of most types of delinquent behaviors as well as substance use (except for cigarette smoking) is substantially higher among male adolescents than among females (e.g., Hurrelmann, 1994).

Unlike substance use and delinquency, young people's *health problems* have remained largely unnoticed. Teenage physical problems, as Hurrelmann (1994) points out, do not fit the popular image, which portrays youth and health as synonymous. Furthermore, the underestimation of adolescents' health problems may result from the fact that not all somatic or psychosomatic problems of adolescents are treated by professionals. Often parents cure their teenagers' minor illnesses (Millstein & Litt, 1990).

Recent developments such as increasing morbidity rates among 10- to 25-year-olds (despite decreasing morbidity rates in other age groups) and prevalence rates of about 20% of diffuse psychosomatic complaints such as headaches, stomachaches, and sleeping difficulties have alerted researchers to pay attention to adolescents' health conditions (Hurrelmann, 1994). Eating disorders such as anorexia nervosa and bulimia nervosa have a prevalence of 1% and 5–18% respectively, among adolescents (Millstein & Litt, 1990). In Germany, Marschall and Zenz (1989) observed rates of somatic complaints among adolescents clearly exceeding those typical of 18- to 30-year-olds.

Survey data unanimously document that girls are generally more affected by somatic symptoms than boys. This gender-specific distribution of complaints seems to be an almost universal characteristic of adolescence (Crystal et al., 1994). On the one hand, this finding could result from a higher sensitivity to and awareness of body processes among female adolescents, as well as from a greater willingness to talk about these problems. On the other hand, many studies suggest a higher psychological and physical vulnerability of females during adolescence, whereas adverse conditions seem to be more harmful to males in the childhood years. Processes of pubertal maturation, in particular, often have been assumed to be related to somatic problems in girls (e.g., Aro & Taipale, 1987; Wehner, 1986). Another reason for the higher vulnerability of girls in adolescence is seen in the complex and partly contradictory role expectations they have to cope with (Millstein & Litt, 1990).

Before we turn to the antecedents of adolescents' psychosocial adjustment, we briefly present data on adolescent health from two additional perspectives relevant for our own empirical analyses: school track and regional differences between East and West Germany. In Germany, the school system is divided into institutionalized tracks after fourth or sixth grade, with the highest track (*Gymnasium*) leading to the final exam (*Abitur*) after 12 to 13 years of school-ing – a mandatory prerequisite for studying at universities. The lower track (*Hauptschule*; 9 to 10 years of schooling) leads to apprenticeships mainly in skilled trades or unskilled jobs. The middle track (*Realschule*; 10 years of schooling) mostly prepares students for apprenticeships aimed at employment in the service economy. In several states of East Germany, the two lower tracks are not differentiated. School tracks in Germany not only represent different starting positions for status and employment opportunities in voca-tional life but are also associated with numerous social variables influencing adolescent development, such as socialization goals of teachers and parents, adolescents' cultural preferences, and life values. Therefore, it could be as-sumed that health-related behaviors and health status also vary by school track. In particular, frequent cigarette smoking – a behavior associated with earlier transitions to adult roles and lower educational background – is more prevalent in the lower school track, as shown by several studies (Engel & Hurrelmann, 1989; Semmer et al., 1987; Silbereisen, Boehnke, & Crockett, 1991). With respect to the relationship between alcohol use and school track, empirical findings are less unanimous. Silbereisen et al. (1991) reported no differences in the prevalence and frequency of alcohol use among 14- to 15-year-olds related to school milieus, mainly characterized by tracks. Engel and Hurrelmann (1989), however, observed lower rates of beer/wine or hard liq-uor consumption among 12- to 16-year-old adolescents from the highest track than among their age-mates in *Hauptschule* or *Realschule*.

Studies have rarely addressed health problems in different school tracks. The few studies focusing on this question showed that school track was not a determinant of health status. Rather, health was influenced by the specific negative experiences of being overloaded by achievement demands that could occur at different grades, varying with school track. In particular, times before transitions (e.g., to the secondary schooling system after 4th grade or to apprenticeship after 9th or 10th grade) are very stressful for those adolescents who have to fear not reaching the expected educational goals (Hurrelmann, Holler, & Nordlohne, 1988; Marschall & Zenz, 1989). In general, school failure is strongly associated with adolescent health problems (Engel & Hurrelmann, 1989).

Adolescent problem behaviors summarized under the label *delinquency*, such as vandalism, truancy, or stealing, are found to be most prevalent in the lowest track and least prevalent in the highest track of the German school system (e.g., Engel & Hurrelmann, 1991).

Regional differences concerning adolescent psychosocial adjustment have just begun to be an objective of empirical study. Silbereisen, Kracke, and Nowak (1992) reported that 13- to 16-year-old East Germans had more experience drinking alcohol than young West Germans. They started to drink at younger ages, and showed higher annual prevalences and higher frequencies of consumption. Similar findings were reported by Simon, Bühringer, and Wiblishäuser (1991). In contrast, Kolip, Nordlohne, and Hurrelmann (1995) found no differences in the prevalence and frequency of alcohol use between 12- to 16-year-old East and West German adolescents. In the case of cigarette smoking, they found higher frequencies among West German adolescents than among East Germans. West German adolescents also showed a higher prevalence in the use of illicit drugs.

When studying the health status of East and West German adolescents, Kolip et al. (1995) found no differences in subjective well-being between the two groups. About 70% of the 12- to 16-year-old adolescents reported at least a good state of health. When prevalences of various symptoms and illnesses were analyzed, however, significant differences were found in 7 of 29 symptoms under examination. West German adolescents showed a higher prevalence of allergic symptoms, circulatory disturbances, fractures, and physical handicaps that the authors interpreted as consequences of accidents. Psychosomatic symptoms such as stomachaches, sickness, or constipation were also more prevalent among West German adolescents. These adolescents also showed more anger, aggression, and irritation than the East Germans, whereas the latter more often experienced symptoms of stress, such as fatigue or exhaustion.

Antecedents of Adolescents' Psychosocial Adjustment:
Strains and Protective Factors

So far, the reported data on adolescents' psychosocial adjustment portray adolescence as a period of increased risk for adjustment problems without consideration of possible reasons. Although genetic influences, parental models, and inadequate parenting practices have been rightly pointed out as important factors in the emergence of problem behaviors (e.g., Kandel, 1986; Rowe & Gully, 1992; Steinberg, Mounts, Lamborn, & Dornbusch, 1991), these explanations only partially account for the peak in prevalence during adolescence. This age-graded pattern has drawn attention to conditions fostering the emergence of problem behaviors related to normative transitions of adolescence. Silbereisen and colleagues (Silbereisen & Eyferth, 1986; Silbereisen & Noack, 1988; Silbereisen & Reitzle, 1992), studying links between problem behavior and normal youth development, for instance, have suggested that substance use may occur as a side effect of efforts to master age-specific developmental challenges or may itself be instrumental in the pursuit of developmental goals.

Whereas the previously mentioned research draws on normative transitions, in particular, research more commonly links adolescents' adjustment problems to strains that are nonnormative aspects of adolescent development such as divorce, parental unemployment, or strained family relationships (e.g., Dubois, Felner, Brand, Adan, & Evans, 1992; Masten, Neemann, & Andenas, 1994). This research shows that negative life events, especially when they are cumulative in nature, negatively affect adolescents' adjustment in various ways. More recent research not only focuses on the negative effects of life stressors but also takes potentially protective factors into account. Because the concept of *protective variables* is still evolving, at present different approaches to the conceptualization of protectors exist. Rutter (1990), for instance, views protective factors as exerting influence only in the presence of stress and becoming more important with greater stress. Another point of view acknowledges the importance of protectors for mental health even if there are no salient risks (e.g., Perry & Shapiro, 1986; Stiffman et al., 1992). So far, studies on protective factors have revealed positive effects of supportive relationships with family members and friends for adolescent adjustment (e.g., Dubois et al., 1992; Stiffman et al., 1992).

The stressors affecting adolescents' well-being range from distinct life events such as the death of a family member or a move to another home to a chronically negative home environment due to ongoing quarreling between family members. Masten et al. (1994) classify life events according to two criteria: (1) whether or not there is a distinct beginning of the problem, such as when fathers or mothers lose their jobs, and (2) whether the stressor is dependent on or independent of the adjustment problems under study. School failure, for instance, is usually linked to behavior problems, whereas a parent's loss of a job does not depend on how the adolescent behaves.

In summary, psychological and somatic health problems affect substantial groups of adolescents. These problems are seen as responses to difficulties in mastering the multiple challenges and burdens related to the age-specific normative transitions and nonnormative problems young people face. Drawing on conceptualizations of adolescent development as a goal-directed process of self-regulation (e.g., Silbereisen & Eyferth, 1986), mismatches between future expectations, on the one hand, and teenagers' factual abilities and opportunities, on the other hand, are suggested as being particularly harmful to adolescent well-being. Individual resources such as coping capacities and social support provided in close relationships – namely, the quality of family and peer bonds – operate as protective factors buffering the impact of stressful conditions.

Following this line of thought, rapid social change is likely to impact adolescent well-being. On the one hand, societal development may directly affect the mastery of transitions. Change can result in alterations of age-specific demands as well as in new challenges, and ways to meet them may no longer be provided. Macro-contextual conditions could also influence teenagers' access to resources. Uncertainty among young people and lack of confidence in their control over their own lives, as well as a lack of orientation and a preoccupation with their own situation on the part of their parents, are examples of possible indirect effects. Following the taxonomy suggested by Masten et al. (1994), changes on the macro level (and their reflections, such as in the family budget and in difficulties at work) can be classified as negative strains of a chronic and independent nature because they are not under the control of the families studied and because they exert their effects over longer periods of time.

Macro Context and Adolescent Well-Being

Because industrialization has led to the separation of the family and the work context and because education has become institutionalized, alienation between the generations has increased and adolescence has been identified as a social problem that must be studied empirically (Gillis, 1974). Especially since the late 1960s, adolescents' value orientations have attracted much research interest. Adolescents were said to have lax work values, to be materialistic and hedonistic, and to be unwilling to think about their future. A generation gap was assumed. Empirical research did not confirm this picture. Rather, more similarities than differences between the generations regarding work values and family orientation were observed (Bengston & Troll, 1978; Schulenberg, Bachman, Johnston, & O'Malley, 1995). Even though adolescents of each generation do not seem to be particularly different from their parents' generation, they must still face new societal demands for which they are not sufficiently prepared by parents or schools in times of rapid societal change. This might lead to a lack of orientation and put adolescents without secure and adequate resources at particular risk (Heitmeyer, 1987).

Ideas about influences of social change on adolescent well-being are drawn primarily from aggregate-level data. Secular trends in the prevalence of problem behaviors are, for instance, interpreted in the light of figures on the

economic development in a given society or on changes in the distribution of
different family structures. One problem with this approach is the lack of
reliable data on secular trends in well-being. Studies employing (quasi-)iden-
tical measures in assessments of successive cohorts across a sufficient period of
time are scarce. The well-charted trends in substance use (e.g., Johnston et al.,
1991) or crime registered by the police are the exception. A more typical
example is the open question of whether the public perception of growing
violence in German schools is correct or is a media-created artifact. A second
problem with the aggregate-change approach is that interpretations of secular
trends in terms of changes in other characteristics of a society are often
speculative given the confounds between a host of variables on the macro
level. Thus, in their search for the origins of secular trends in substance use,
Silbereisen et al. (1995) point out the necessity of studies including a sufficient
number of subsamples representing variations in the factors assumed to be of
influence.

A second approach in contrast to the aggregate-level approach targets social
change in terms of its manifestations on the micro level and explores influences on well-being. It implicitly spells out part of the processes linking
macrosocial conditions and individual psychosocial adaptation, as called for by
Silbereisen et al. (1995). Variations in adolescents' microsystems are assumed
to reflect macrolevel change. Accordingly, parental unemployment could be
interpreted as a microsystem reflection of a national economic depression.
Likewise, parents' and adolescents' feelings of uncertainty are possible consequences of increasing anomie in society. Experiences of change on the mi-
crosystemic level may, in turn, directly influence family members' well-being,
such as unemployment resulting in a depressive mood, or they may operate on
the individual through an impairment of family relationships. Because the
extent to which families and their members experience change varies throughout society, a major problem of aggregate-level approaches – namely, the
confounding of possible sources of influence – can be avoided. Moreover,
effects of changes experienced as real should be more strongly related to well-
being than objective indices of change (Thomas & Thomas, 1973).

In the following discussion, we confine ourselves to the second approach,
that is, analyses of experiences of social change and its consequences. This is
not meant to suggest the superiority of the second approach. A proper understanding of the processes in focus requires both types of investigation. An
important step toward an integration is to explore to what extent micro-level
experiences actually reflect macrosocial change. To do this, we will first report
some earlier findings from our own research conducted in East and West
Germany. We consider the situation in Germany after unification as particularly instructive, as it approximates a large-scale natural experiment with the
pace of change systematically varying in both parts of the country, whereas
(many) other conditions are at least quite similar. Then we discuss empirical

research on the effects of experiences of societal conditions – namely, economic depression – on adolescent well-being.

Experiences of Macrocontextual Changes on the Family and
Individual Levels

As part of a more extensive study of 15-year-olds and their parents living in Mannheim, West Germany, and Leipzig, East Germany, we explored family members' experiences of social change (for a more detailed report, see Noack, Hofer, Kracke, & Klein-Allermann, 1995). Assessments focused on changes in economic as well as sociopolitical conditions. Increase, stability, or decline of families' purchasing power was measured to tap reflections of economic trends (cf. Conger et al., 1991). Both parents were asked to indicate changes in their ability to pay for a variety of goods, comparing their actual situation to their purchasing power 5 years prior to our 1992 assessment, that is, the time period around the East–West unification. In our measurements, we distinguished purchasing power concerning rent, child care, and cultural/leisure activities that were highly subsidized in the former German Democratic Republic (GDR), on the one hand, and purchasing power concerning a variety of consumer goods such as stereo sets/VCRs and household machines in short supply in the GDR, on the other hand. Addressing changes in sociopolitical conditions, we assessed perceptions of the state of the social welfare system, uncertainty, competition and lack of solidarity in public life, technological progress, opportunities for political participation, and nepotism. Each aspect was measured by summary scales of adolescents', fathers', and mothers' perceptions of change during the previous 5 years.

Parental reports of families' purchasing power resulted in a highly differentiated picture closely paralleling changes in the economic system. On average, West German parents experienced virtually no change at all. East German families, however, found it far more difficult to pay their rent and other formerly subsidized items. Conversely, mothers and fathers from East Germany reported a considerable improvement in their purchasing power for a variety of consumer goods. Further systematic variations in this measure point to a more privileged financial pattern among families of higher social status. Moreover, mothers (who can be assumed to have more knowledge of the prices for different goods) provided less optimistic reports than their husbands.

Other aspects of social change also seemed to be closely reflected by family members' perceptions. In line with the general trend toward modernization in industrialized countries (Beck, 1986), East and West Germans indicated increases in competition, uncertainty, the state of technology, and nepotism, as well as improved opportunities for political participation. Reports from the two parts of the country, however, varied markedly. Except for nepotism, subjects in the East perceived more rapid change concerning each aspect of sociopolitical conditions. This was true for changes for the worse, such as growing uncertainty, as well as for improvements, such as in political participation. In most instances, parental judgments were more pessimistic than teenagers' reports.

In summary, the findings suggest a high correspondence between macrolevel processes and family members' experiences of social change. Even though the data base does not allow for a statistical test of this association, the highly differentiated pattern of family members' experiences paralleling a complex and dynamic macrosocial situation favors our interpretation. It should to be noted, however, that the differences in the pace of social change between East and West Germany are extreme. It is thus open to question whether family experiences would also reflect more subtle variations on the macro level. Clearly, research going beyond this initial step is needed to further the understanding of this important link between social change and individual well-being.

Economic Deprivation and Unemployment

Although theoretical assumptions about the disastrous impact of rapid social change on adolescents' well-being are numerous, few empirical investigations have been undertaken to explore their validity. More thoroughly studied are the effects of economic strain on families and of parental unemployment on adolescents' psychosocial functioning. Starting with the seminal study of Jahoda, Lazarsfeld, and Zeisel (1933), who observed the psychological impact of mass unemployment in a whole village after a factory had closed down, research has shown that economic deprivation negatively affected adolescents' self-esteem, activity level, and future time perspective. Elder and colleagues, studying U.S. families during the Great Depression of the 1930s, pointed to the importance of intrafamily processes mediating the impact of economic loss on adolescents' well-being (e.g., Elder, van Nguyen, & Caspi, 1985). These findings were replicated with West German data collected during the economic recession of the early 1980s by Walper (1988). Recent research on the impact of the U.S. farm crisis on families with adolescent children once more underscored the importance of the family's economic situation for parental well-being, which, in turn, affects adolescents' adjustment (e.g., Conger et al., 1984, 1991).

Due to variations in the operationalization of strains, family processes, and psychosocial outcomes employed in these different studies, a comprehensive and at the same time differentiated picture of the effects of short-term economic trends has emerged. Income loss (e.g., Elder et al., 1985), financial strain (e.g., Conger et al., 1991), and parental unemployment (e.g., Flanagan & Eccles, 1993; McLoyd, 1989) were addressed when assessing the economic condition of families. Insufficient discipline and monitoring (Larzelere &

Patterson, 1990), rejection, exploitation, and emotional support of or indifference toward children (Elder et al., 1985), as well as hostility to children and spouse (Conger et al., 1990), were measured to tap family processes either by questionnaire or observations. Adolescents' depression (Lempers, Clark-Lempers, & Simons, 1989), low self-esteem (Isralowitz & Singer, 1986; Walper, 1988), delinquency (Larzelere & Patterson, 1990), social competence and goal orientation (Elder et al., 1985), antisocial behaviors and alcohol use (Conger et al., 1991), school adjustment (Flanagan & Eccles, 1993) and physical health (see McLoyd, 1989, for an overview) are psychosocial outcomes linked to economic hardship. Although bivariate associations between economy-related variables and adolescent outcomes were generally substantial, the majority of studies showed that economic strain often affects teenagers' well-being indirectly, mediated by the quality of parental behaviors. Thus, efforts to model adequately the impact of economic strain on adolescents' development should consider the quality of family processes as potential mediators.

Reflections of social change other than economic deprivation and employment-related problems have rarely been studied by developmental and educational researchers. Although Schröder and Melzer (1992) also focused on the consequences of macroeconomic processes, they targeted teenagers' perceptions of economic threats rather than considering variations in family finances. Examining the impact of these factors on German adolescents' extremist political orientations, which could be considered a type of problem behavior (cf. Noack, 1994a), Schröder and Melzer observed that West German youth clearly reacted to economic risks by becoming more extreme. Young East Germans, however, seemed to be unaffected by their perceptions. The authors interpreted the West German findings as an instance of the "normal pathology of modern societies." In contrast, authoritarian orientations among East German youth were suggested to depend more strongly on earlier socialization influences than on short-term historical development. Bochnke (1992) studied the effects of macrosocial stress by considering a broader range of perceived risks including, for instance, threats of nuclear war and environmental destruction. Their findings confirm systematic associations linking adolescents' feelings of being threatened and their psychological well-being. Although the directions of the effects operating between perceptions of the macro context and psychosocial adaptation are clearly in need of further investigation, these studies delineate important areas of future research.

The Empirical Study

As part of our research on youth and their families in Germany after unification, we analyzed adolescent health-related risks and problems. In the study, we examined different aspects of young people's health. A particular emphasis was on somatic symptoms that have often been neglected in previous research. Our *major objective* was to investigate influences that experiences of social change might exert on well-being. In addition to the comparably well-documented effects of macroeconomic variations, we wanted to study the impact of changes in other areas of life. We expected both aspects to affect adolescents' successful adaptation. A *second objective* of our analyses was to shed light on the role the family plays in teenagers' reactions to social change. Earlier research suggests that associations between the dynamics of the family's material situation and adolescent well-being are mediated by the quality of parent–child relationships. Families' economic losses are assumed to result in a deterioration of the quality of relationships between family members, which, in turn, impairs adolescents' psychosocial adaptation. At the same time, it seems plausible to expect a possible moderating role of the family, such as buffering effects of sound relationships. This buffering hypothesis would predict no substantial effects of financial problems on adolescents in families characterized by harmony and connectedness, whereas adolescent well-being would be so affected if family relationships are poor. In our study, we wanted to explore both hypotheses.

Our first set of analyses examines the distribution of different aspects of adolescent psychological and physical well-being. These analyses address variations by gender, school track, and place in Germany (West versus East). As reported earlier, recent social changes in East Germany are affecting more facets of everyday life and are taking place at a much faster pace than changes in the West. Possible differences between the East and West could thus be considered a first indication of the effects of social change on young people's well-being. Given the character of the East–West dichotomy as a social address variable (Bronfenbrenner & Crouter, 1983), however, the confounding of social change and a host of other variables prohibits straightforward interpretations. To solve this problem, we directly studied relations between families' experiences of change and teenagers' well-being in the second step of our investigation.

In the following discussion, we first introduce the study and give a brief description of the sample characteristics and measures included in our analyses. The first section of the results provides information on the distribution of different indices of psychological and physical well-being, as well as of health-compromising behaviors among adolescent boys and girls in East and West Germany. Finally, we report findings from regression analyses exploring the effects of experiences of change on well-being.

Method

Sample and Measures

Sample. The overall study of mutual influences linking experiences of social change, family relationships, and adolescent development (Hofer & Noack,

1992) was initiated in late 1992, that is, about 3 years after the Berlin Wall separating East and West Germany had come down. Following a longitudinal design, main data collections in East and West Germany were conducted at 1-year intervals bridged by a short telephone interview midway between these annual assessments. The total *sample* includes about 500 adolescents who were 15 years old at the time of the first assessment, as well as a little more than 300 mothers and 300 fathers. All teenagers and parents completed standardized questionnaires. In addition, a smaller group of 80 families participated in more extensive assessments, including audio recordings of family interactions.

The two subsamples were recruited in Leipzig (East) and Mannheim (West), respectively. Because the urban study sites were chosen partly for pragmatic reasons, the subjects cannot be considered fully representative of East and West German families with adolescent offspring. The cities, however, provide a sound basis for comparison, with parallel population sizes of about 500,000 in both Leipzig and the twin city of Mannheim–Ludwigshafen and their mixture of heavy industry, as well as mid-sized and small companies involved in production and services. More important, both cities are located close to Germany's eastern and western borders, thus, yielding a more typical portrayal of German cities than, for example, East and West Berlin, which are frequently chosen sites for comparative studies.

In Mannheim, most subjects were contacted by telephone, employing a random procedure. Official birth announcements were used to spot families with adolescents around age 15, who were then called and asked to particpate. It was necessary to contact about 25% of them directly in their schools. In Leipzig, only school-based recruitment was possible because of the then poorly developed telephone system. Adolescent subjects were enrolled in the major school tracks in Mannheim and Leipzig. In the German institutionalized tracking system, school tracks are roughly indicative of socioeconomic background.

The following analyses are based on data from our first measurement conducted in winter 1992–1993. The 503 participating 15-year-olds were about evenly distributed by gender (45% female, 55% male) and place in Germany (46% from Mannheim, 54% from Leipzig). About one third attended high-track schools (*Gymnasium*) in both cities; the others attended middle- and low-track schools (Mannheim: *Realschule, Hauptschule*; Leipzig: *Mittelschule*, i.e., schools combining both lower tracks). Due to the lower rates of parental participation as well as missing data, our regression analyses, including information from adolescents, mothers, and fathers, are based on a group of 222 families. Statistical comparisons, however, yielded only a few significant differences between included and missing subjects. Among the former, West German adolescents and high-track students are slightly more numerous. Moreover, adolescents included in the analyses reported being less prone to violence as well as alcohol use. With other adolescent health measures, as well as parental reports on experiences of social change, both groups can be considered equivalent.

Physical and Psychological Health. In order to arrive at a comprehensive picture of *adolescents' physical and psychological well-being*, six measures were considered to address several aspects of well-being as well as health-compromising behaviors. *Physical health* was captured by a list of nine symptoms such as cough/cold and headache (for a complete list, see Table 3.1). In each case, adolescents indicated the number of times they had experienced each symptom during the 12 months prior to assessment (0 = never; 4 = more than five times). Besides the single items, we used a sum scale of eight items (alpha: .75; excluding rash/pimples, which showed the lowest incidence rates) in our analyses.

Sum scales of *self-esteem* (six items, alpha: .76; Schwarzer, 1986) and *depressive mood* (four items; alpha: .75, Goldberg, 1972) assessed psychological well-being. Sample items are "I am satisfied with myself" (*self-esteem*) and "Lately, I often feel like it's not worthwhile living" (*depressive mood*). Finally, *proneness to use violence* (four items; alpha: .71, own development; e.g., "Sometimes you have to use violence to get your way"), frequency of *alcohol consumption* (one item, 1 = not at all, 5 = almost daily), and *cigarette smoking* (prevalence: 0 = no, 1 = yes; frequency: 1 = less than 8; 2 = 8–20; 3 = more than 20 cigarettes per day) were examined as variables indicating health risks. Moreover, proneness to violence can also be considered an indicator of externalizing problems.

Social Change. Our major interest was in variations of adolescent health depending on social change. As described previously, we aimed to capture *social change* in terms of its impact at the family level. According to Elder (e.g., Elder et al., 1985), economic development in the larger context is a particularly powerful and potentially disruptive source of influence on the family, operating through effects on the family budget as well as on family members' employment status. In our analyses, we included both a measure of change in the family budget (*purchasing power*) and a measure of recent parental *employment problems*.

Changes in purchasing power were assessed with reference to the preceding 5 years, that is, an interval that had started before unification. On 5-point scales, mothers and fathers rated whether it had become much easier (1), had remained the same (3), or had become much more difficult (5) to cover the costs for three items, namely, rent, leisure/cultural activities, and child care (i.e., high scores indicating a decrease in purchasing power; alphas: .75/.80) for mothers and for fathers. Parental *employment problems* were captured by a measure indicating whether mothers or fathers had experienced regular or "hidden" unemployment (partial layoff/part-time work, retraining schemes, work schemes offered by labor offices) during the preceding 2 years.

In an attempt to overcome the reduction of short-term historical development to changes in the local or national economy, we also asked our subjects to report their perceptions of changes affecting other aspects of social life, such as relations between people, social welfare and security, and technological development. In the following discussion, we confine ourselves to the exploration of the effects of changes in *social welfare*, on the one hand, and perceptions of unpredictability and lack of control concerning life in society (*uncertainty*), on the other hand.

Perceptions of *changes in social welfare* were measured by a sum scale of items such as "Old people are financially and socially secure." As with purchasing power, parents rated change or stability during the preceding 5-year time period (1 = much less, 3 = the same, 5 = much more; high scores indicating changes for the worse; four items, alphas: .77/.61). Feelings of decreasing or increasing *uncertainty* (lack of control, unpredictability) were assessed on the basis of responses to statements such as "Everything is so uncertain that anything may happen" using the same response formats used for social welfare (i.e., high scores indicating changes for the worse; six items; alphas: .79/.71). As already suggested by objective differences in life circumstances, parental experiences of change vary markedly between regions, with East Germans reporting a faster pace of societal development and economic problems in each respect (see the earlier discussion for a more extensive report).

In our examination of effects on adolescent well-being, we only employed social change variables based on parental reports to ensure independent measures of both sets of variables. Moreover, we used averaged measures of mothers' and fathers' reports that were mostly highly correlated (e.g., *purchasing power*: $r = .66, p < .001$; *social welfare*: $r = .68, p < .001$) and, at the same time, yield a more intersubjective account of change than individual responses.

Family Relationships. One objective of our investigation was to explore the role of family relationships with regard to processes linking social change and adolescent health. Therefore, in our analyses we included *connectedness* in the family, which has been pointed out as a focal aspect of parent–child relationships during the adolescent years (Grotevant & Cooper, 1985; Youniss & Smollar, 1985). Connectedness was measured by adolescents' responses to a six-item sum scale (e.g., "I openly tell my parents what I think and how I feel"; "Much of what my parents say is not right" [reverse coded]; alpha: .73).

Results

Physical Symptoms and Well-Being as a Function of Place, Gender, and School Track

So far, developmental research has paid comparably little attention to adolescents' physical health. Thus, we first report in some detail on the prevalence and intensity of individual symptoms before turning to analyses of our collapsed measure. Overall, our findings confirm earlier observations pointing to considerable health problems during the adolescent years (e.g., Marschall & Zenz, 1989). More than two-thirds of our adolescent subjects indicated one or more incidents of nausea/vomiting, cough/cold, aching limbs, headache, tiredness, and stomachache in the course of the preceding 12 months. Over 40% of these 15-year-olds reported on circulatory debility (e.g., instances of lowered blood pressure and related symptoms) and sleeping problems. The picture provided by the mean values may be even more alarming than the prevalence rates. Several of these symptoms, including headache, stomachache, and aching limbs, had occurred more than two times on average during the 1-year period in focus. Table 3.1 shows prevalences and means for male and female adolescents in East (Leipzig) and West Germany (Mannheim).

A multivariate analysis of variance with gender, place (East versus West), and school track (low/middle versus high), and type of symptom (within-subject factor) as the independent variables and intensity of the somatic symptoms as dependent variables point to gender as a major source of variation [$F(1, 476) = 25.38, p < .001$]. Gender-specific differences vary, however, depending on the symptom in focus [Gender × Symptom interaction; $F(8, 3808) = 7.50, p < .001$]: In seven of the nine symptoms, female adolescents indicated more frequent problems than did their male age-mates. Although this pattern corresponds to the results reported by, for instance, Pollmer and Hurrelmann (1992), we could only partly confirm the few findings available from comparisons of health among East and West German adolescents. In line with observations of Kolip et al. (1995), there was almost no systematic variation, as evidenced by the lack of a multivariate effect of place. A significant Place × Symptom interaction effect [$F(8, 3808) = 4.02, p < .001$] resulted from substantial differences between East and West German adolescents (tiredness and circulatory debility). In each instance, adolescents from Leipzig reported higher frequencies than did those from Mannheim. Variations depending on school track were confined to four symptoms [School Track × Symptom interaction: $F(8, 3808) = 2.32, p < .05$] and were mostly small in size. High-track students complained of headaches slightly less often than middle/low-track students. Differences concerning circulatory debility were in the reverse direction and occurred mainly among male adolescents. Additional

Table 3.1. *Adolescents' somatic symptoms as a function of gender, place (West/East Germany), and school track:[a] means, standard deviations, and annual prevalences*

Symptom	West German		East German		Effects[b,c]		
	Male	Female	Male	Female	Gender	Place	Track
Nausea/vomiting	1.87	2.08	1.68	2.05	***	ns	ns
	(.76)	(.89)	(.67)	(.95)			
	66.9%	73.4%	58.7%	68.3%	+	ns	ns
Cough/cold	2.60	2.82	2.55	2.88	***	ns	ns
	(.85)	(.80)	(.91)	(.88)			
	95.8%	98.2%	89.4%	96.4%	*	+	*
Aching limbs	2.32	2.44	2.41	2.48	ns	ns	ns
	(1.14)	(1.07)	(1.06)	(1.09)			
	70.0%	78.0%	78.4%	78.0%	ns	ns	ns
Headache	2.39	2.73	2.41	2.98	***	ns	+d
	(1.10)	(1.11)	(1.07)	(1.06)			
	75.0%	82.6%	77.7%	90.2%	**	+	ns
Rash/pimples	1.35	1.66	1.30	1.62	***	ns	ns
	(.73)	(1.05)	(.74)	(.96)			
	24.2%	35.8%	17.5%	37.6%	***	ns	ns
Tiredness	2.61	2.79	3.07	3.21	ns	***	ns
	(1.18)	(1.16)	(1.15)	(1.02)			
	78.3%	83.5%	83.5%	93.3%	**	**	+
Circulatory deb.	1.58	2.04	1.50	1.81	***	+	*e
	(.97)	(1.15)	(.93)	(1.03)			
	32.8%	56.0%	28.2%	47.3%	***	ns	ns
Troubled sleep	1.56	1.83	1.61	1.87	**	ns	ns
	(.89)	(.97)	(.82)	(1.07)			
	35.3%	51.9%	42.2%	49.7%	**	ns	+
Stomach trouble	1.82	2.68	1.83	2.64	***	ns	ns
	(.81)	(1.09)	(.87)	(1.03)			
	61.3%	82.6%	58.3%	85.3%	***	ns	ns

Note: $N = 484$; self-ratings on 4-point scales: 1 = never; 4 = more than five times during the 12 months before assessment (standard deviations in parentheses); annual prevalence indicating one or more occurrences of a symptom (%).
[a] School track: high (*Gymnasium*) vs. middle/low (*Realschule/Hauptschule*).
[b] Only univariate main effects in three-way ANOVAs; additional interaction effects: Aching Limbs (Gender × School Track: male, high > middle/low track; female, high < middle/low track; $F(1, 476) = 11.17, p < .001$); Rash/Pimples (Place × School Track: West, high < middle/low track; East, high > middle/low track, $F(1, 476), p < .05$); Tiredness: male, high > middle/low track; female, high = middle/low track; $F(1, 476), p < .10$); comparisons of prevalences by chi^2 tests.
[c] Significant multivariate effects: Gender: $F(1, 476) = 25.38$ $p < .001$, Symptom × Gender: $F(8, 3808) = 7.50, p < .001$, Symptom × Place: $F(8, 3808) = 4.02, p < .001$, Symptom × School Track: $F(8, 3808) = 2.32, p < .05$, Gender × School Track: $F(1, 476) = 4.15, p < .05$.
[d] High < middle/low track.
[e] High > middle/low track.
$+p < .10$, $*p < .05$, $**p < .01$, $***p < .001$.

tests based on prevalence rates largely confirmed the pattern observed for the frequencies.

Means for *self-esteem* (M = 2.76, SD = .55) as well as *depressive mood* (M = 1.91, SD = .67) on scales ranging from 1 to 4 indicated that on average adolescents' psychological well-being was not impaired. Analyses corroborated well-known gender-specific variations favoring male adolescents (cf. Petersen et al., 1992). Moreover, self-esteem among East German teenagers was somewhat lower than in the West German subsample. Finally, West German low/middle-track students indicated higher levels of depressive mood than high-track students, whereas the opposite pattern was observed in the East.

Our last set of health-related variables provided information on behaviors posing risks to teenagers' health and, in the case of proneness to violence, indicating externalizing problems. Although *proneness to violence* was only slightly denied by our subjects (M = 2.25, SD = .48), substantial effects depending on gender and school track suggest considerable interindividual variation. Not surprisingly, female adolescents rejected the use of violence far more strongly than did males, as did high-track students compared to their lower-track age-mates. Average *alcohol consumption* was reported to be slightly less than once a week, with slightly higher levels of drinking among boys than among girls. The strongest effect, however, concerns the East–West dichotomy. Subjects from Leipzig indicated more frequent drinking than did those from Mannheim. A total of 16% of the adolescent sample identified themselves as *cigarette smokers*, a more frequent finding in low/middle-track students. The daily consumption among these 77 smokers averaged about half a pack per day. Their consumption pattern did not vary with gender, place, or school track.

*Relations between Social Change and Physical
and Psychological Health*

In a preliminary step, we inspected the *intercorrelations* of the variables in focus. The pattern of associations provides tentative support for our assumptions. Although the correlations between experiences of social change and adolescent well-being were moderate to small, they mostly suggest negative effects of change. That is, parental reports of growing uncertainty in society, in particular, were negatively associated with teenagers' physical health and self-esteem and positively associated with teenagers' substance use. Moreover, indicators of adolescent psychological well-being were related to a perceived decline of the welfare system, as well as to losses in family purchasing power and parental employment problems. Across all indicators of adolescent well-being, correlations with family connectedess corresponded to our assumption that the quality of family relationships fosters adolescent health. Table 3.2 shows the matrix of zero-order correlations.

Table 3.2. *Intercorrelations of place, gender, experiences of social change, family connectedness, and aspects of adolescent well-being*

Variables[a]	2	3	4	5	6	7	8	9	10	11	12	13
1 Place	.07	.44 ***	.56 ***	.46 ***	.66 *	−.14 +	.09	−.06	.04	−.06	.13 *	−.03
2 Gender	—	.04	.04	.14 *	.10 +	.07	.34 ***	−.23 ***	.25 ***	−.25 ***	−.06	−.01
3 Purch. power		—	.32 ***	.35 ***	.42 ***	−.04 +	.11 *	−.14	.08	.01	.06	.05
4 Empl. probl.			—	.20 ***	.43 ***	−.13 *	.03 *	−.11 +	.09 +	−.01	.09 +	−.06
5 Uncert.				—	.39 ***	−.05	.23* ***	−.09 +	.06	−.06	.22 ***	.15 *
6 Decline					—	−.02	.00	−.07	.12 *	−.08	.01	−.05
7 Connected						—	−.09 +	.33 ***	−.34 ***	−.23 ***	−.11 *	−.12 *
8 Somatic health							—	−.29 ***	.33 ***	.16 *	.21 ***	.12 *
9 Self-esteem								—	−.67 ***	−.15 *	.06	−.07
10 Depr. mood									—	.20 **	.09 +	.04
11 Viol. prone										—	.20 **	.15 *
12 Alcohol											—	.24 ***
13 Cigarettes												—

[a] Purch. power = purchasing power; Empl. probl. = employment problems; Uncert. = uncertainty; Decline = decline of the welfare system; Connected = family connectedness; Depr. mood = depressive mood; Viol. prone = proneness to violence.
$^+p < .10$, $^*p < .05$, $^{**}p < .01$, $^{***}p < .001$.

In order to test our first hypothesis postulating *social change effects on adolescent well-being*, we conducted multiple regression analyses separately for each of the six health-related measures. In each analysis, gender and place were considered first as control variables. In a second step, we entered purchasing power, employment problems, experiences of uncertainty, and perceptions of a decline of the welfare system as more distal predictors into the regression equation. Then we entered family connectedness, which we consider to be a more proximal predictor. Finally, we wanted to examine whether the same processes hold for East and West German families. To assess this, we tested whether the Place × Social Change and Place × Connectedness interaction terms significantly added to the explanation of the criterion variables.

Our second research question addressed the possible *moderating and mediational role of family connectedness*. A *moderation* of social change effects was again examined by testing the interactions of change variables and connectedness. A significant increase in explained variance by an interaction term entered in the last step would indicate differences in change effects as a function of family connectedness. In order to analyze the *mediational role* of the quality of family relationships, we compared the increase in explained variance when social change variables were entered into the equation directly after controls, on the one hand, and after controls as well as family connectedness, on the other hand. Smaller increases in the latter model would suggest that change effects on adolescent well-being (at least partly) operate through connectedness as a mediating link.

The set of predictors considered in our regression analyses explained a substantial amount of variance in most of the health-related measures. Whereas gender, experiences of social change, and family connectedness accounted for only 8% to 10% of the variation in drinking and cigarette smoking, the proportion of explained variance in physical health, psychological well-being, and violence proneness ranged from 16% to 26%. Gender proved to be a particularly powerful predictor of different aspects of somatic as well as psychological health, confirming female adolescents' particular vulnerability to somatic problems, reduced self-esteem, and depressive mood, as well as males' proneness to violence. Likewise, family connectedness added considerably to the prediction of well-being. In the total sample, positive family relationships were related to lower levels of depressive mood and violence, as well as to a more positive self-concept.

Our major interest was in the influences of social change. Even though the effects of family experiences of change were modest to small, change variables had an impact on most aspects of adolescent well-being above and beyond the effects of gender and connectedness. The strongest effects of change concerned somatic health (6% increase in explained variance) and alcohol consumption (7% increase). Parental uncertainty, in particular, was linked to higher levels of health complaints and drinking. Moreover, decreases in family purchasing power were associated with lower self-esteem among adolescents. Curiously, parental perceptions of a decline in social welfare were negatively related to health complaints.

Tests of interaction terms indicate that the pattern of associations described for the total sample mostly holds for East and West German families. Due to significant interactions observed for depressive mood (Place × Employment Problems), violence proneness (Place × Purchasing Power; Place × Uncertainty), and cigarette smoking (Place × Connectedness), however, we inspect

Table 3.3. *East and West German adolescents' well-being depending on gender, experiences of social change, and family connectedness; standardized regression coefficients and explained variance*

Predictor	Somatic health		Self-esteem		Depressive mood	
	West	East	West	East	West	East
Gender	.30**	.36**	−.24**	−.27**	.31**	.21*
Purchasing power	.18*	−.02	−.12+	−.11	.07	.02
Employment problems	.01	.01	−.01	−.11	.14	−.01[a]
Uncertainty	.17+	.17+	−.04	−.04	−.03	.07
Decline of welfare	−.23*	−.07	−.07	.03	.16+	.09
Connectedness	−.18*	−.02	.35**	.34**	−.33**	−.41**
R^2	.23***	.16**	.20**	.20**	.26**	.21**
R^2cha Interactions[b]	ns	ns	PP × C* EP × C+	EP × C*	U × C+	ns

Predictor	Violence proneness		Alcohol consumption		Cigarette smoking	
	West	East	West	East	West	East
Gender	−.29**	−.17+	−.03	−.11	.04	−.06
Purch. power	.25**	−.13[a]	.09	−.09	.10	.03
Empl. prob.	.04	−.01	−.07	.11	−.06	−.07
Uncertainty	.20*	−.21*[a]	.26**	.18+	.23*	.13
Decline	.03	.00	−.08	−.12	.02	−.07
Connectedness	−.25**	−.22*	−.05	−.11	−.01	−.25*[a]
R^2	.26**	.17**	.10+	.08	.08	.10*
R^2cha Interactions[b]	ns	PP × C* EP × C+	PP × C+	ns	ns	ns

Note: N = 222; coefficients from regression analyses conducted separately for aspect of adolescent health and place (East–West).
[a] Significant Predictor × Place interactions identified in preliminary regression analyses based on the total sample.
[b] Change × Connectedness interaction terms significantly adding to the explanation of variance when entered in the final step; PP = purchasing power; EP = employment problems; U = uncertainty; C = connectedness.
+ $p < .10$, * $p < .05$, ** $p < .01$, *** $p < .001$.

the findings for the regional subsamples more closely in the following. In Table 3.3, standardized regression coefficients and explained variance of the final regression model are presented separately for the different outcome variables and for both German subsamples.

In each case of significant Place × Change interactions, it appeared that West German youths responded more negatively to changes for the worse. Adolescents from Mannheim evidenced higher levels of depressive mood when their parents reported employment problems; they were more prone to use violence when their fathers and mothers experienced losses in purchasing power and an increase in uncertainty. Among East German adolescents, no association (depressive mood) or even the opposite relationships (violence proneness) can be observed. This finding is underscored by parallel East–West differences in several other associations, which, however, are not substantial (e.g., decline of social welfare, decreased somatic health, increased depressive mood). Analyses on connectedness yield only one substantial difference between the regional subsamples: Whereas cigarette smoking is negatively related to connectedness among the young East Germans, there is no such relationship for their West German age-mates.

Finally, we further examined the role of family connectedness. So far, we have seen that good family relationships foster adolescent health and could thus compensate for negative effects of, for instance, parental uncertainty. In a first step, we investigated the possible *moderation* of change effects by connectedness. Several significant Connectedness × Change interaction terms indeed suggested connectedness as a moderating variable (see Table 3.3). Additional analyses conducted to explore these interactions point to stronger social change effects in West German families characterized by lower levels of connectedness compared to those who are highly connected. This pattern also holds for the associations between adolescent self-esteem and losses in purchasing power as well as unemployment problems. Likewise, parental uncertainty was related to depressive mood among young West Germans when family connectedness is low. In the Eastern subsample, the unexpected negative effect of losses in purchasing power on adolescent proneness to use violence is mainly due to high levels of family connectedness. Self-esteem among East German youth is also more strongly affected by parental experiences of change when the quality of family relationships is high. Interestingly, in this case connectedness accentuates a negative effect. With West German families, the latter pattern can only be observed in the association of purchasing power and alcohol consumption. Given the small size of the interaction effects, caution is necessary when interpreting these findings. Still, in the Mannheim subsample, connectedness among family members seems to operate mainly as a buffer, protecting adolescents against potentially dangerous effects of social change. By contrast, in the Leipzig subsample, processes such as adolescents' more intensive identification with parents in highly connected families may result in more marked adjustment problems.

In the last step, we examined the possible *mediational role* of connectedness. The findings can be briefly summarized. In general, there was little evidence that experiences of social change affected adolescent well-being by loosening family bonds. In the East German subsample only, change effects on self-esteem and drinking were partly mediated by family connectedness. In absolute terms, however, the mediation was negligible (self-esteem: 1.5% out of 4%; alcohol: 1.1% out of 6%). Given the pattern of correlations (see Table 3.2), this result does not come as a surprise. Among the four change variables analyzed, only parental employment problems were significantly related to family connectedness.

Discussion

In this chapter, we set out to investigate links between social change and adolescent health. A variety of evidence has identified adolescence as a period of elevated problems of somatic and psychological health that are seen to be related to the multiple challenges and strains experienced in the transition to adulthood. We suggested that rapid changes on the societal level might set adolescents at particular risk by making developmental transitions more difficult or by placing additional burdens on young people already attempting to accomplish multiple age-typical tasks. Macrosocial developments such as economic recessions or trends toward modernization could directly affect adolescent well-being or else operate through effects on, for example, family relationships.

From our point of view, however, changes in the macrosystem can be effective on the individual level only when they are reflected in adolescents' more immediate contexts. Financial problems of families or parental unemployment during economic recession, as studied by Elder and colleagues (e.g., Conger & Elder, 1994; Elder, 1974), are cases in point. Data that we collected in Germany shortly after unification show that societal transformations are indeed closely reflected on the family level. This is not only true for the economic situation. In general, there seems to be a great deal of sensitivity to changes in various areas of life, such as competition among people and technological progress.

In line with earlier findings (e.g., Hurrelmann et al., 1988; Marschall & Zenz, 1989), our own analyses revealed considerable health problems among young people in midadolescence. With somatic health, for instance, symptoms caused by a cold or influenza are highly prevalent, as are feelings of general tiredness. Our results also confirmed the particular vulnerability of female adolescents.

Following our general hypothesis, we had expected the faster pace of social change in East Germany to result in higher levels of somatic and psychological problems compared to the situation in West Germany. This was not the case. Except for feelings of tiredness, which were more frequent among East German teenagers, regional differences favoring young people in West Germany proved to be negligible, similar to the findings of Kolip et al. (1995). Evidence of the opposite pattern provided by this earlier study were also absent in our data. It has to be noted, however, that Kolip et al. observed higher rates of problems among West German adolescents mainly in regard to allergic symptoms and injuries, which we did not directly address in our symptom lists. Moreover, we cannot claim representativeness for our sample of East and West German youths. Unfortunately, the lack of representative studies on adolescent health in Germany does not allow us to settle this point. National surveys such as those conducted in the United States are badly needed in the future.

Although we could not identify general effects when comparing East and West German adolescents, variations in social change as experienced at the family level were systematically related to adolescent health. Overall, reflections of changes for the worse were linked to higher levels of health problems as well as health-compromising behaviors. This association was particularly evident for parental feelings of uncertainty concerning future life in German society. When interpreting these effects, it should be kept in mind that they are small in absolute terms, accounting for only 1–7% of the explained variance. Moreover, the analyses were based on cross-sectional data that did not allow us to specify the direction of effects. Even though it seems more plausible to assume that losses in family purchasing power influence adolescent self-esteem than to claim influences in the reverse direction, matters are more complex when it comes to, for instance, the association of parental uncertainty and adolescent somatic health. The longitudinal nature of the overall study will allow us to address this issue in future analyses.

Another question is raised by differences in findings for the East and West German subsamples. Whereas the pattern of associations was mostly parallel, some systematic variations suggest a higher vulnerability of young West Germans to experiences of change for the worse compared to East German teenagers. At first glance this may come as a surprise, considering the generally higher levels of change in the East. Encouraged by a couple of other unexpected findings, we would like to suggest that it might be useful to recollect an old lesson from social psychology pointing out the importance of social comparison processes (cf. Hofer et al., 1995). Whereas families in Leipzig share the experience of rapid changes with many of their neighbors, relatives, and friends, for many West Germans, namely those living far away from the former FRG–GDR borders, the parallel situation is exceptional. They may thus respond more strongly, for example, to declining purchasing power. So far, this interpretation is quite speculative. East Germans might not compare themselves primarily to their immediate environment, but rather to West Germans or to the situation in other formerly socialist countries. Depending on the chosen frame of reference, the meaning of financial shortages or of a decline of the social welfare system could be quite different. Based on a recent pilot study conducted in Mannheim (Noack, 1994b), we have developed an instrument that will allow us to examine criteria for social comparisons in further research and to test to what extent the adoption of different criteria influences psychosocial adaptation.

Our study also confirmed the powerful role that the quality of family relationships plays in adolescent health. Higher levels of connectedness among family members were associated with fewer problems concerning self-esteem, depressive mood, and proneness to violence. In addition, West German adolescents who reported high-quality family relationships complained less about somatic symptoms. Finally, the prevalence of cigarette smoking was lower among young East Germans from highly connected families. Nevertheless, we found virtually no evidence to suggest that experiences of social change impact on adolescent health through a deterioration of family connectedness as the mediating link. Indeed, family connectedness seems to remain largely unaffected by the various social change variables.

We thus failed to replicate the mediational model suggested by several earlier studies (Conger & Elder, 1994; Elder et al., 1985; Walper, 1988). One reason for this unexpected finding could be our focus on connectedness when assessing the quality of family relationships. On the one hand, connectedness is pointed out as a major family characteristic by conceptualizations of relationship development during adolescence, namely, individuation theory (Grotevant & Cooper, 1985; Youniss & Smollar, 1985). On the other hand, connectedness may be a fundamental quality of family relationships, showing little variation due to temporary contextual strain. A different picture might emerge when, for instance, the amount of conflict among family members is analyzed.

There was, however, some evidence that family connectedness moderates influences of social change, even though the pattern of findings was more complex than expected. First, moderating effects were mostly confined to experiences of change related to the family economy (losses in purchasing power; parental employment problems). Second, connectedness operating as a buffer (i.e., change mainly affecting adolescents in families with lower levels of connectedness) was observed only in the West German subsample. Among East German families, the opposite was true. In Leipzig, there was little association between, for instance, parental employment problems and adolescent self-esteem when connectedness was low, whereas young East Germans who reported close family bonds responded strongly to their parents' work situation. In these cases, the quality of family relationships obviously did not provide a resource in attempting to cope with strain. Rather, connectedness seemed to indicate adolescents' identification with their parents' fate or else their lack of opportunities to evade the consequences of financial and employment problems in the family. In this sense, close family relationships could also be a risk factor instead of protecting adolescent well-being in situations of strain. We do not know yet, however, under which conditions connectedness assumes these different moderating roles. Again, the prevalence of, for instance, economic problems in the larger family context could be decisive. If financial shortages are more common and, consequently, cannot readily be attributed to individual failure, adolescents should be more willing to empathize with their parents. Strong family bonds could accentuate this tendency. Conversely, if a tightened family budget is interpreted as the problem of a given family, connectedness between family members may prevent adolescents from blaming their own family. Instead, a sound family system could be experienced as a solid basis for attempts to overcome temporary difficulties. Lacking further empirical evidence, however, at present we can only speculate about the underlying processes.

In summary, our study provides some empirical indication of influences that social change has on adolescents' somatic and psychological health. At the same time, our findings have raised a host of questions that call for further research on the workings of macrocontextual conditions in times of rapid transformations of our societies.

References

Alsaker, F. D., & Olweus, D. (1992). Stability of self evaluations in early adolescence: A cohort-longitudinal study. *Journal of Research on Adolescence, 2,* 123–145.

Aro, H., & Taipale, V. (1987). The impact of timing of puberty on psychosomatic symptoms among 14- to 16-year-old Finnish girls. *Child Development, 58,* 261–268.

Beck, U. (1986). *Risikogesellschaft [Risk society].* Frankfurt: Suhrkamp.

Bengston, V. L., & Troll, L. (1978). Youth and their parents: Feedback and intergenerational influence in socialization. In R. M. Lerner & G. B. Spanier (Eds.), *Children's influences on family and marital interaction* (pp. 215–240). New York: Academic Press.

Boehnke, K. (1992). Auswirkungen von makrosozialem Stress auf die psychische Gesundheit. Ein Beitrag zur Theoriebildung [Effects of macrosocial stress on psychological health]. In J. Mansel (Ed.), *Reaktionen Jugendlicher auf gesellschaftliche Bedrohung [Adolescents' responses to societal threat]* (pp. 24–37). Weinheim: Juventa.

Bronfenbrenner, U. (1989). Ecological systems theory. In R. Vasta (Ed.), *Six theories of child development* (pp. 185–246). Greenwich, CT: JAI Press.

Bronfenbrenner, U., & Crouter, A. (1983). Environmental models in developmental research. In P. H. Mussen (Ed.), *Handbook of child psychology* (Vol. 1, pp. 357–414). New York: Wiley.

Bundeskriminalamt (1994). *Polizeiliche Kriminalstatistik Bundesrepublik Deutschland. Berichtsjahr 1993 [Police criminal statistics FRG].* Wiesbaden: Bundeskriminalamt (BKA).

Commission of the European Communities. (Ed.). (1991). Young Europeans of 11 to 15 and alcohol. Survey conducted in the European Community by the European Omnibus Survey. Luxembourg: Health and Safety Directorate of the Commission of the European Communities.

Conger, R. D., & Elder, G. H. (1994). *Families in troubled times.* New York: Aldine De Gruyter.

Conger, R. D., Elder, G., Lorenz, F., Conger, K., Simons, R., Whitbeck, L., Huck, S., & Melby, J. (1990). Linking economic hardship to marital quality and instability. *Journal of Marriage and the Family, 52,* 643–656.

Conger, R. D., Lorenz, F. O., Elder, G. H., Melby, J. N., Simons, R. L., & Conger, K. J. (1991). A process model of family economic pressure and early adolescent alcohol use. *Journal of Early Adolescence, 11,* 430–449.

Conger, R. D., McCarty, J. A., Yang, R. K., Lahey, B. B., & Kropp, J. P. (1984). Perception of child, child-rearing values, and emotional distress as mediating links between environmental stressors and observed maternal behavior. *Child Development, 55*, 2234–2247.

Crystal, D. S., Chen, C., Fuligni, A. J., Stevenson, H. W., Hsu, C.-C., Ko, H.-J., Kitamura, S., & Kimura, S. (1994). Psychological maladjustment and academic achievement: A cross-cultural study of Japanese, Chinese, and American high school students. *Child Development, 65*, 738–753.

Dubois, D. L., Felner, R. D., Brand, S., Adan, A. M., & Evans, E. G. (1992). A prospective study of life stress, social support, and adaptation in early adolescence. *Child Development, 63*, 542–557.

Dusek, J. B., & Flaherty, J. F. (1981). The development of the self-concept during the adolescent years. *Monographs of the Society for Research in Child Development*, vol. 46.

Elder, G. H. (1974). *Children of the Great Depression*. Chicago: University of Chicago Press.

Elder, G. H., van Nguyen, T., & Caspi, A. (1985). Linking family hardship to children's lives. *Child Development, 56*, 361–375.

Engel, U., & Hurrelmann, K. (1989). *Psychosoziale Belastung im Jugendalter [Psychosocial strain in adolescence]*. Berlin: Aldine De Gruyter.

Feldman, S. S., Mont-Reynaud, R., & Rosenthal, D. A. (1991). When East moves West: The acculturation of values of Chinese adolescents in the United States and Australia. *Journal of Research on Adolescence, 1*, 109–134.

Fillmore, K. M., Hartka, E., Johnstone, B. M., Leino, V., Motoyoshi, M., & Temple, M. T. (1991). The collaborative alcohol-related longitudinal project. A meta-analysis of life course variation in drinking. *British Journal of Addiction, 86*, 1221–1268.

Flanagan, C. A., & Eccles, J. S. (1993). Changes in parents' work status and adolescents' adjustment at school. *Child Development, 64*, 246–257.

Gillis, J. R. (1974). *Youth and history: Tradition and change in European age relations 1770–present*. New York: Academic Press.

Goldberg, W. (1972). *The detection of psychiatric illness by questionnaire*. London: Oxford University Press.

Gore, S., Aseltine, R. H., & Colten, M. E. (1993). Gender, social-relational involvement, and depression. *Journal of Research on Adolescence, 3*, 101–125.

Grotevant, H. D., & Cooper, C. R. (1985). Patterns of interaction in family relationships and the development of identity exploration in adolescence. *Child Development, 56*, 415–428.

Heitmeyer, W. (1987). *Rechtsextremistische Orientierungen bei Jugendlichen [Rightist orientations among adolescents]*. Weinheim: Juventa.

Hirsch, B., & DuBois, D. (1991). Self-esteem in early adolescence: The identification and prediction of contrasting longitudinal trajectories. *Journal of Youth and Adolescence, 20*, 53–72.

Hofer, M., Kracke, B., Noack, P., Klein-Allermann, E., Kessel, W., Jahn, H. U., & Ettrich, K. U. (1995). Der soziale Wandel aus Sicht ost- und westdeutscher Familien, psychisches Wohlbefinden und autoritäre Vorstellungen [East and West German families' perceptions of social change, psychological well-being, and authoritarian orientations]. In B. Nauck, N. Schneider & A. Toelle (Eds.), *Familie und Lebensverlauf im gesellschaftlichen Umbruch [Family and life course in times of social transformation]* (pp. 154–171). Stuttgart: Enke.

Hofer, M., & Noack, P. (1992). Jugendliche und ihre Eltern unter Bedingungen des sozialen Wandels: Individuation in den alten und neuen Bundesländern [Adolescents and their parents under conditions of social change]. Grant proposal to the German Research Council. Mannheim: University of Mannheim.

Hurrelmann, K. (1986). Das Modell des produktiv realitätsverarbeitenden Subjekts in der Sozialisationsforschung [The productive reality processing subject as a model of socialization research]. In K. Hurrelmann (Ed.), *Lebenslage, Lebensalter, Lebenszeit [Social situation, age, biography]*. (pp. 11–23). Weinheim: Beltz.

Hurrelmann, K. (1994). *Lebensphase Jugend [The adolescent life phase]*. Weinheim: Juventa.

Hurrelmann, K., Holler, B., & Nordlohne, E. (1988). Die psychosozialen Kosten verunsicherter Statuserwartungen im Jugendalter [Psychosocial costs of adolescents' uncertain status expectations]. *Zeitschrift für Pädagogik, 34*, 25–44.

Isralowitz, R., & Singer, M. (1986). Unemployment and its impact on adolescent work values. *Adolescence, 21*, 145–158.

Jahoda, M., Lazarsfeld, P. F., & Zeisel, H. (1993). *Die Arbeitslosen von Marienthal. Ein soziographischer Versuch [The unemployed of Marienthal]*. Leipzig: Hirzel.

Johnston, L. D., O'Malley, P. M., & Bachman, J. G. (1991). *Drug use among American high school students, college students, and other young adults, 1975–1990*. Rockville, MA: National Institute on Drug Abuse.

Kandel, D. B. (1986). Processes of peer influences in adolescence. In R. K. Silbereisen, K. Eyferth, & G. Rudinger (Eds.), *Development as action in context* (pp. 203–227). Berlin: Springer.

Kolip, P., Nordlohne, E., & Hurrelmann, K. (1995). Der Jugendgesundheitssurvey 1993 [Adolescent health survey 1993]. In P. Kolip, K. Hurrelmann & P.-E. Schnabel (Eds.), *Jugend und Gesundheit [Adolescents and health]* (pp. 25–48). Weinheim: Juventa.

Larzelere, R. E., & Patterson, G. R. (1990). Parental management: Mediator of the effect of socioeconomic status on early delinquency. *Criminology, 28*, 301–323.

Lempers, J., Clark-Lempers, D., & Simons, R. (1989). Economic hardship, parenting practices, and adolescent distress. *Child Development, 60*, 25–39.

Marschall, P., & Zenz, H. (1989). Psychophysiologische Befunde in der Schule und das Beschwerdebild von Kindern und Jugendlichen [Psychophysiological findings in schools and health complaints among children and adolescents]. *Zeitschrift für Sozialisationsforschung und Erziehungssoziologie, 4*, 305–320.

Masten, A. S., Neemann, J., & Andenas, S. (1994). Life events and adjustment in adolescence: The significance of event independence, desirability, and chronicity. *Journal of Research on Adolescence, 4*, 71–97.

McLoyd, V. (1989). Socialization and development in a changing economy. *American Psychologist, 44*, 293–302.

Millstein, S. G., & Litt, I. F. (1990). Adolescent health. In S. S. Feldman & G. R. Elliott (Eds.), *At the threshold* (pp. 431–456). Cambridge, MA: Harvard University Press.

National Transportation Safety Board (1993). *Safety recommendation*. Washington, DC: Author.

Noack, P. (1994a, May). *What is "normal" about authoritarian orientations in adolescence? The case of East and West German teenagers*. Paper presented at the Fourth Biennial Conference of the European Association for Research on Adolescence, Stockholm, Sweden.

Noack, P. (1994b). *Gesellschaftlicher Wandel, soziale Vergleichsprozesse und autoritäre Einstellungen bei Studenten [Societal change, social comparison, and authoritarian orientations among university students]*. Unpublished manuscript, University of Mannheim.

Noack, P., Hofer, M., Kracke, B., & Klein-Allermann, E. (1995). Adolescents and their parents facing social change: Families in East and West Germany after unification. In P. Noack, M. Hofer, & J. Youniss (Eds.), *Psychological responses to social change* (pp. 129–148). Berlin: Aldine De Gruyter.

Palentien, C., Pollmer, K., & Hurrelmann, K. (1993). Ausbildungs- und Zukunftsperspektiven ostdeutscher Jugendlicher nach der politischen Vereinigung Deutschlands [East German adolescents' perspectives on education and their future after the political unification of Germany]. *Aus Politik und Zeitgeschichte, B24/93*, 3–13.

Perry, G., & Shapiro, D. A. (1986). Social support and life events in working class women: Stress buffering or independent effects. *Archives of General Psychiatry, 43*, 315–323.

Petersen, A. C., Silbereisen, R. K., & Sorensen, S. (1992). Adolescent development: A global perspective. In W. Meeus, M. de Goede, W. Kox & K. Hurrelmann (Eds.), *Adolescence, careers, cultures* (pp. 1–34). Berlin: Aldine De Gruyter.

Pollmer, K., & Hurrelmann, K. (1992). Neue Chancen oder neue Risiken für Jugendliche in Ostdeutschland? – Eine vergleichende Studie zur Stressbelastung sächsischer und nordrhein-westfälischer Schülerinnen und Schüler [New opportunities or new risks for adolescents in East Germany]. *Zeitschrift für Sozialisationsforschung und Erziehungssoziologie, 12*, 2–29.

Rowe, D. C., & Gully, B. (1992). Sibling effects on substance use and delinquency. *Criminology, 30*, 217–233.

Rutter, M. (1986). The developmental psychopathology of depression: Issues and perspectives. In M. Rutter, C. Izard, & P. Read (Eds.), *Depression in young people: Developmental and clinical perspectives* (pp. 3–30). New York: Guilford Press.

Rutter, M. (1990). Psychosocial resilience and protective mechanisms. In J. Rolf, A. Masten, D. Cicchetti, K. H. Neuchterlein, & S. Weintraub (Eds.), *Risk and protective factors in the development of psychopathology* (pp. 181–214). New York: Cambridge University Press.

Schröder, H., & Melzer, W. (1992). Ökonomische Risiken und Verunsicherungspotentiale Jugendlicher in Ost- und Westdeutschland. Vergleichende Befunde aus dem Jahr nach der Wende [Economic risks and uncertainty among adolescents in East and West Germany]. In J. Mansel (Ed.), *Reaktionen Jugendlicher auf gesellschaftliche Bedrohung [Adolescents' responses to societal threats]* (pp. 163–184). Weinheim: Juventa.

Schulenberg, J., Bachman, J. G., Johnston, L. D., & O'Malley, P. M. (1993, June). *Historical trends in perceptions and preferences regarding family and work among American adolescents: National data from 1976 through 1992*. Paper presented at a symposium on "Macrosocial Variations, Families, and Adolescent Development," Reisensburg, Germany.

Schulenberg, J., Bachman, J. G., Johnston, L. D., & O'Malley, P. M. (1995). American adolescents' views on family and work: Historical trends from 1976–1992. In P. Noack, M. Hofer, & J. Youniss (Eds.), *Psychological responses to social change* (pp. 37–64). Berlin: Aldine De Gruyter.

Schwarzer, R. (Ed.). (1986). *Skalen zur Befindlichkeit und Persönlichkeit [Scales of well-being and personality characteristics]*. Berlin: Forschungsbericht 5, Institut für Psychologie, Freie Universität Berlin.

Semmer, N. K., Dwyer, J. H., Lippert, P., Fuchs, R., Cleary, P. D., & Schindler, A. (1987). Adolescent smoking from a functional perspective: The Berlin-Bremen Study. *European Journal of Psychology of Education, 2*, 387–402.

Silbereisen, R. K., Boehnke, K., & Crockett, L. (1991). Zum Einfluss von Schulmilieu und elterlicher Erziehungshaltung auf Rauchen und Trinken im mittleren Jugendalter [The impact of school milieu and parenting behaviors on smoking and drinking in middle adolescence]. In R. Pekrun & H. Fend (Eds.), *Schule und Persönlichkeitsentwicklung [School and personality development]* (pp. 272–293). Stuttgart: Enke.

Silbereisen, R. K., & Eyferth, K. (1986). Development as action in context. In R. K. Silbereisen, K. Eyferth, & G. Rudinger (Eds.), *Development as action in context* (pp. 1–25). Berlin: Springer.

Silbereisen, R. K., Kracke, B., & Nowak, M. (1992). Körperliches Entwicklungstempo und jugendtypische Übergänge [Maturational timing and adolescent transitions]. In Jugendwerk der Deutschen Shell (Ed.), *Jugend '92* (Vol. 2, pp. 171–196). Opladen: Leske & Budrich.

Silbereisen, R. K., & Noack, P. (1988). On the constructive role of problem behavior in adolescence. In N. Bolger, A. Caspi, G. Downey, & M. Moorehouse (Eds.), *Persons in context* (pp. 152–180). Cambridge: Cambridge University Press.

Silbereisen, R. K., & Reitzle, M. (1992). On the constructive role of problem behavior in adolescence: Further evidence on alcohol use. In L. P. Lipsitt & L. L. Midnick (Eds.), *Self-regulation, impulsivity, and risk-taking behavior: Causes and consequences* (pp. 199–217). Norwood, NJ: Ablex.

Silbereisen, R. K., Robins, L., & Rutter, M. (1995). Secular trends in substance use: Concepts and data on the impact of social change on alcohol and drug use. In M. Rutter & D. J. Smith (Eds.), *Psychosocial disorders in young people* (pp. 490–543). Chichester, U.K.: Wiley.

Silbereisen, R. K., & Schmitt-Rodermund, E. (1995). German immigrants in Germany: Adaptation of adolescents' timetables for autonomy. In: P. Noack, M. Hofer, & J. Youniss (Eds.), *Psychological responses to social change* (pp. 105–125). Berlin: Aldine De Gruyter.

Simon, R., Bühringer, G., & Wiblishäuser, P. M. (1991). *Repräsentativerhebung 1990 zum Konsum und Missbrauch von illegalen Drogen, alkoholischen Getränken, Medikamenten und Tabakwaren (Grundauswertung für die alten und neuen Bundesländer)* [*Consumption and abuse of illicit drugs, alcoholic beverages, medicine, and tobacco – Representative survey 1990*]. Munich: Deutsches Jugendinstitut (German Youth Institute).

Steinberg, L. (1993). *Adolescence* (3rd ed.). New York: McGraw-Hill.

Steinberg, L., Mounts, N. S., Lamborn, S. D., & Dornbusch, S. M. (1991). Authoritative parenting and adolescent adjustment across various ecological niches. *Journal of Research on Adolescence, 1*, 19–36.

Stiffman, A. R., Chueh, H.-J., & Early, F. (1992). Predictive modeling of change in depressive disorder and counts of depressive symptoms in urban youth. *Journal of Research on Adolescence, 2*, 295–316.

Thomas, W. I., & Thomas, D. S. (1973). Die Definition der Situation [The definition of the situation]. In H. Steinert (Ed.), *Symbolische Interaktion* [*Symbolic interactions*] (pp. 333–335). Stuttgart: Klett.

Walper, S. (1988). *Familiäre Konsequenzen ökonomischer Deprivation* [*Consequences of economic deprivation on the family*]. Munich: Psychologie Verlags Union.

Wehner, C. (1986). *Das Körperbeschwerdebild bei Jugendlichen in Abhängigkeit vom körperlichen Reifegrad und anamnestischen Faktoren* [*Adolescents' somatic symptoms as a function of physical maturation and anamnestic factors*]. Unpublished doctoral dissertation, University of Ulm, Germany.

Windle, M., Miller-Tutzauer, C., & Domenico, D. (1992). Alcohol use, suicidal behavior, and risky activities among adolescents. *Journal of Research on Adolescence, 2*, 317–330.

Youniss, J. & Smollar, J. (1985). *Adolescent relations with mothers, fathers, and friends*. Chicago: University of Chicago Press.

4 Self-Reported Maturational Timing and Adaptation in Adolescence

Rainer K. Silbereisen and Bärbel Kracke

Introduction

Pubertal processes present a major challenge to adolescents. Young people need to integrate into their self-concepts their changing bodily appearance, their unprecedented feelings, and the as yet unknown reactions by people in their surroundings. These changes take place at a time in adolescents' development when being "like among likes" is an important impetus in peer relations. In this regard, the fact that the age of onset of puberty varies greatly presents a particular problem. Menarche in girls, for instance, may happen as early as age 10 or as late as age 15, with about 5% of the population reporting even earlier or later onset.

Adolescents' capacity to adapt to the changes related to puberty may be challenged to varying degrees, depending on pubertal timing. Being in synchrony and on time with the majority of age-mates can be seen as an advantage relative to the adaptive problems faced by early or late maturers.

Until a decade ago, most investigations on adolescence tended to overlook puberty and its associated biological processes. Their effects were likely to be confounded with the aspects of socialization that were being investigated. By not distinguishing among subjects according to pubertal status, for instance, a study on the effect of parental socialization on adolescents' achievement motivation may actually aggregate across rather different types of parent–adolescent relations, shaped as a consequence of the attempts to adapt mutually to the adolescent's pubertal development. Thus, the interactive effects between puberty and other dimensions of development – seen by many as more important than the respective main effects – are masked (Brooks-Gunn & Reiter, 1990).

The authors' research reported in this chapter is based on German Research Council grants Si 296/1-6 and Si 296/14-1 (Principal Investigator: R. K. Silbereisen). We want to thank all the young people who participated in the studies. Parts of the work were accomplished while the first author was on the faculty at the Department of Human Development and Family Studies, Pennsylvania State University. Special thanks go to Helmut Bludszuweit and Alexander von Eye for their statistical help and expertise and to Verona Christmas.

85

In two earlier works (Kracke & Silbereisen, 1994; Silbereisen & Kracke, 1993), we reviewed recent research on the assessment, antecedents, and consequences of differences in adolescents' maturational timing. The focus of the present chapter is on some selected consequences of maturational timing on adolescent adjustment. The emphasis on individual variation in maturational timing is justified by the fact that differences in timing are likely to be more relevant for psychosocial adaptation than are differences in maturational status per se (Petersen & Crockett, 1985; Petersen, Graber, & Sullivan, 1990).

Concerning the relation between being off time relative to the majority of age-mates and psychosocial functioning, two basic conceptualizations have been proposed and have guided the interpretation of empirical results (Brooks-Gunn, Petersen, & Eichhorn, 1985). First, the deviance hypothesis claims that any deviation from the norm, whether toward earlier or later timing of maturation, provokes difficulties in adolescents' adaptation. Second, the stage termination hypothesis presumes early rather than late maturers to be at particular risk for developmental problems because, relative to the rest of their age-mates, they have less time to adapt to the new challenges associated with their more "grown-up" status.

There are a number of qualifications to these two general conceptualizations. For instance, some cultures and contexts may be more tolerant than others in regard to deviations from the typical pace of maturation (Lerner, 1985). For example, girls may be more affected in general than boys because of stricter social norms concerning their appearance and behavior (Zakin, Blyth, & Simmons, 1984), and the effects may be restricted to a short period of time until the majority of the age group has caught up with an individual's advanced developmental status (Magnusson, Stattin, & Allen, 1986).

Nevertheless, the basic juxtaposition here is between symmetry in off-time effects versus asymmetry, with early timing representing a more serious case of adaptational problems. Testing these two competing conceptualizations has been a primary purpose of our recent research on the impact of maturational timing on biopsychosocial adaptation. More specifically, we hoped to determine whether being off time or being earlier than age-mates is the more decisive experience.

Because we refer to several different studies in this chapter, we begin with a brief description of the design of each study. The first data set is from the Berlin Youth Longitudinal Study (Silbereisen, Noack, & Schoenpflug, 1994). At the initial assessment, a stratified random sample was drawn from more than 70 schools in Berlin (West Germany), representative with respect to socioeconomic status and educational track. The results discussed in this chapter are based on two cohorts, born in 1973–1974 and 1970–1971. Their data were gathered in three annual waves when the adolescents were between 11.5 and 13.5 ("younger cohort"; $n = 206$ to 222, depending on the wave) and 13.5

and 16.5 years of age ("older cohort"; n = 377 to 519). The analyses reported refer to two kinds of data: (1) survey data provided by all subjects in both cohorts, based on self-administered questionnaires, and (2) qualitative data gathered during the last wave of assessment, based on interviews conducted with a small subsample (28 males, 16 females) drawn from both cohorts that was selected to represent groups of adolescents who were characterized as fast, on-time, and slow maturers during the survey assessments. Boys were interviewed individually (Kracke, 1993), whereas the interviews with girls were held in groups of two or three (Kracke, 1988).

The second data set originates from the Shell Youth Study 1992 (Jugendwerk der Deutschen Shell, 1992) a nationwide survey reporting on multiple aspects of life and the development of young people in Germany. Extensive questionnaire data were gathered in 1990, provided by a sample of 4,000 adolescents and young adults (aged 13 to 29) representative of youth in both parts of Germany. Results reported in this chapter concern groups in early (ages 13–14, n = 513) and middle adolescence (ages 15–16, n = 440).

Concerning the assessment of maturational timing, our key variable, we relied on adolescents' self-reports, using two different approaches. First, in the Berlin Youth Longitudinal Study, adolescents were asked to categorize the pace of their maturational timing relative to that of peers at the time of assessment, judged overall without reference to a specific physical attribute. In the Shell Youth Study '92, the same basic procedure was applied, but with a variation as to the time of reference. Specifically, respondents rated their perceived maturational timing at age periods 11/12, 13/14, and, if old enough, 15/16. Thus, depending on their age, ratings of concurrent as well as previous timing were available. Second, for the Shell Youth Study '92 only, self-report data were available on girls' age at menarche and boys' age at peak height velocity. We use these data occasionally in supplementary analyses.

Whenever the distinction is important, differences in perceived maturational timing are characterized for clarification by the terms *fast* and *slow*, whereas differences in maturational timing based on self-reported pubertal events are denoted as *early* and *late*.

In the remainder of this chapter, we first address assessment issues, specifically the relation between perceived maturational timing and the change in physical attributes during puberty. We then deal with two main consequences of differences in maturational timing. Under the heading of internalizing aspects of adolescent adjustment, differences concerning satisfaction with one's appearance, global self-esteem, and emotional difficulties are discussed. Externalizing behaviors are represented by smoking and drinking, and their relation to variation in maturational timing is shown. Next, we provide evidence concerning how interpersonal relations are associated with maturational timing. Throughout the report of empirical results, quantitative survey data are supplemented by quotations from the qualitative interviews with selected adolescents who represent prototypes of the categories of maturational timing. In the concluding discussion, we return to the question of how best to conceptualize the role of variation in maturational timing in psychosocial adjustment.

Analyses of Self-Rated Maturational Timing

In regard to the impact of pubertal changes on adolescents' psychosocial development, researchers have studied two different aspects: maturational status and maturational timing. Whereas *maturational status* refers to the current level of physical development relative to the overall process of pubertal change, *maturational timing* refers to whether the pubertal process occurs early, on time, or late relative to a reference group, such as age-mates or classmates in school (Dubas, Graber, & Petersen, 1991). Each of these aspects can be assessed in various ways, including objective measures, self-ratings, and retrospective accounts.

Previous research has demonstrated that retrospective assessments of certain pubertal events, particularly age at menarche, appear to be highly valid. Bean, Leeper, Wallace, Sherman, and Jagger (1979) reported concordance rates of 90% between adults' recall of the year of their menarche and medical information gathered up to 33 years earlier. Further, results of Stattin and Magnusson and our own data (Kracke, Nowak, Thiele, & Silbereisen, 1992) suggest that the time span since puberty does not systematically interfere with the reported age at menarche.

Relation to Physical Attributes

Adolescence is a period of the life span when social comparisons play a critical role (Silbereisen & Noack, 1988). Against this backdrop, it makes sense to assume that individual differences in maturational timing are more relevant for psychosocial functioning than one's status in pubertal development per se. The various assessment approaches that are used reflect this comparative aspect to different degrees.

One approach to assessing timing effects is to define groups of early, on-time, and late maturers according to the distribution of a given pubertal characteristic in a reference group. Examples are estimates of age at peak height velocity (Petersen & Crockett, 1985) or the age of accomplishment of pubertal stages or individual markers such as menarche (Alsaker, 1990). Obviously, the choice of the reference group is crucial. If the assessment is based on population norms, timing groups formed accordingly may not represent the visible differences in appearance that are prevalent in a specific environment such as one's classroom.

At least conceptually, a second approach better represents the comparative aspect. Rather than relying on computed measurements, the adolescents themselves can be requested to rate their overall maturational timing relative to age-mates in general or to a specific group, such as their classmates (Dubas et al., 1991). When compared to the previously mentioned computed measures, adolescents show a slight tendency to rate themselves as not deviating from the majority (Alsaker, 1992).

A better understanding of the basis for such self-categorizations should be gained by investigating their association with physical characteristics of pubertal development. Using data from the Berlin Youth Longitudinal Study, Silbereisen and Kracke (1993) examined age differences in the relation of self-reported body height and weight with perceived maturational timing, comparing several age groups between 11.5 and 16.5 years. The variation in perceived timing was assessed by using adolescents' responses to the item "Compared to my age-mates, I develop slower (faster, as fast)," which was placed in a section of the questionnaire concerning physical development.

Slow and fast maturers of both genders differed significantly in height. Whereas for girls this difference between the timing groups gradually diminished from 12.5 years on, for boys the difference remained significant up to 15.5 years. Repeated measurements after 1 year also revealed differential change in height among the timing groups. Slow maturers gained more height across 1 year than on-time or fast maturers. Corresponding analyses on weight revealed even more distinct cross-sectional differences and longitudinal changes among the timing groups, particularly in early adolescence.

Taken together, the results seem to indicate that the adolescents use height and weight as markers for their self-categorization of maturational timing. More direct evidence is also available. In the Shell Youth Study '92, the adolescents and young adults had first indicated their perceived maturational timing using a procedure similar to the one applied in the Berlin Youth Longitudinal Study. Then they were shown a list of physical characteristics and asked to which they referred when they categorized themselves as fast, on time, or slow maturers compared to classmates. Multiple responses were possible. Table 4.1 gives the percentage of respondents who endorsed the respective categories.

When we tabulated the frequencies of all possible combinations of the physical characteristics (not shown in the table) and ordered them according to magnitude from most to least frequent, a few stood out. In boys, about 40% of the responses included height, either alone or in combination with other aspects, particularly with muscle development, facial hair, and voice deepening, or a combination thereof. The rest were distributed across a large number of other combinations. In girls, the same procedure resulted in 50% comprised of breast development, menarche, and height, or combinations thereof. All other characteristics, single or in combination, were rarely mentioned. Al-

Table 4.1. *Physical characteristics relevant in perceived maturational timing: percentages of agreement*

Physical Characteristic	Male			Female		
	13–14	15–16	17–29	13–14	15–16	17–29
Facial hair	19.0%	44.6%	63.6%			
Breast				70.0%	81.2%	81.5%
Height	74.8	73.4	67.6	57.1	50.5	49.0
Skin changes	33.2	32.4	30.9	33.1	31.7	25.4
Pubic hair	28.8	42.8	36.6	42.2	34.4	37.1
Axillary hair	24.3	28.4	26.4	27.9	21.6	25.4
Voice deepening	42.9	59.9	52.6			
Menarche				64.8	71.1	70.8
Muscle development	45.6	54.1	52.5			
n	226	222	1510	287	218	1505

Note: Multiple responses were possible. Thus, the base for the percentages is the number of responses, not the number of individuals.

though there was some variation in the most frequent patterns across age groups, the basic structure remained the same.

Nevertheless, the relative frequencies of some physical characteristics show age trends consistent with what is known about developmental change during the age period studied (Marshall & Tanner, 1969, 1970). The development of facial hair represents a rather late development during puberty. Using the Pfanzagl test for monotonic trends (Pfanzagl, 1966; with Bonferroni's correction), an increasing trend across age groups was revealed for those males who endorsed facial hair as relevant for their perceived maturational timing ($z = 12.81$, $p < .0001$). In girls, the percentage of responses concerning breast development showed an increasing trend ($z = 3.52$, $p < .001$), and those concerning skin changes showed a decreasing trend ($z = -3.57$, $p < .001$). Again, both trends seem to be consistent with the concept of reflecting the course of developmental change in respective physical attributes.

Stability of Perceived Timing

Given that we know at least part of the experiential basis for perceived maturational timing, the next question is: How stable are such judgments across time? In the previously described study of Dubas et al. (1991), nearly half of the adolescents revealed no change in the three assessments between 7th and 12th grades. Most of these adolescents were on-time maturers, with only about 4% consistently judging themselves as faster or slower than their age-mates. The other half reported the same categorization two out of three times. Among the latter, between 10% and 15% rated themselves as faster on two occasions. Likewise, about 10% to 15% of the girls rated themselves as slower on two occasions, but none of the boys did so.

The data of the Berlin Youth Longitudinal Study provided an opportunity to investigate the generalizability of the Dubas et al. (1991) results. Kracke (1993) examined the stability of the self-categorization as being an on-time or off-time maturer in two cohorts of boys (11.5 and 13.5 years of age at first assessment) across three consecutive years. For the younger cohort, degrees of stability similar to those in the previous study were found. The older cohort, however, showed higher stability of self-categorizations in the off-time groups. About 8% of these boys judged themselves as slow maturers across three measurements and about 12% as fast maturers (compared to 4% as reported by Dubas et al.).

The present and previous results taken together reveal rather low stabilities of the off-time categorizations, particularly in early adolescence. In this sense, then, deviating from the majority of the age-mates seems to be a rather transitional experience for most off-time maturers; consequently, its psychosocial correlates and sequelae are also likely to be time bound. Indeed, this is what researchers have found in regard to various aspects of psychosocial adjustment (e.g., Magnusson et al., 1986). Additional examples of the time-bound role of maturational timing are discussed in later sections of this chapter.

The results presented thus far leave open the question of why particular adolescents changed their self-categorizations. Even if the physical attributes discussed earlier represented the only basis for the self-ratings, the fact that more than one attribute may change at a time gives rise to various possibilities. In our view, there are three, not mutually exclusive, possible reasons for changes in self-reported maturational timing across time: (1) adolescents may indeed undergo change in their tempo relative to others, that is, catch up or slow down; (2) other adolescents may change (or the reference group may change), thereby changing the adolescent's relative position; and (3) the salience of particular physical attributes may change in the adolescent's view.

The interview study with a subsample of 28 male participants of the Berlin Youth Longitudinal Study, aged 15 and 18 (Kracke, 1993), provided examples of all three cases. Concerning (1), the following quote from an interview illustrates a situation where an adolescent boy caught up in height (which he deemed an important aspect) with classmates.

M25 (14.3 years; self-categorization as slow maturer at age 11; at ages 12, 13, and 14 self-rated as on-time maturer)
A: Most important for me was growing, because formerly I was rather short.
I: Compared to your classmates you were rather short?

A: Yes, at that time. There were some who were unnaturally tall.

I: And what would you say . . . are you one of the slower growing in your class? Or one of the faster growing? Or one of the middle group?

A: I would say of the middle group.

I: And formerly?

A: Regarding body height, I was one of the slower growing.

A case in point for (2) is represented by the experience reported by a boy who had to repeat a year in school. In the new context, he perceived himself as faster maturing than his new classmates, whereas compared to his old classmates he regarded himself as an on-time maturer. Finally, (3) is characterized by adolescents who perceived themselves as off time because of a perceived delay in a number of physical attributes, especially height. If some attributes showed progress, they recategorized their status as on time, irrespective of the fact that there was no change in the other attributes, such as voice.

Consequences of Variation in Maturational Timing

It is well known that age-graded expectations or "developmental timetables" play a prominent role in shaping the course of adolescent development (Feldman & Quatman, 1988; Greene, Wheatley, & Aldava, 1992). The age at which adolescents are expected to act responsibly, for instance, also determines when opportunities conducive to such behaviors are offered. Thus, bodily characteristics that lead partners in social interaction to believe that the age of an adolescent is different from the actual age increase the risk of inappropriate demands and experiences. For instance, Johnson and Collins (1988) found that when teachers and parents rated adolescents whom they knew, physical and social maturity were highly correlated. The researchers also found that adults who were not previously acquainted with the adolescents gave even higher estimates of the age of those who were more mature looking. Similar findings were reported by Kossakowski (1965) in a study of adolescents in East Germany. In general, teachers assumed that early-maturing girls were more psychologically mature, and parents granted their early-maturing daughters more autonomy. Furthermore, parents of early-maturing daughters assumed them to be more interested in romantic relationships.

In contrast, adolescents who appear younger than their chronological age because of their shorter stature are regarded by adults as being less emotionally independent (Brackbill & Navill, 1981). Furthermore, teachers tend to view late maturers as being less capable concerning school achievement (Duke et al., 1982).

Internalizing Aspects of Psychosocial Adjustment

In the following, we discuss some of the consequences of being off time for adolescents' view of themselves.

Satisfaction with One's Appearance. Studies have shown that early-maturing boys tend to be more satisfied with their bodily appearance than late or on-time maturers. This effect is particularly pronounced among those whose advanced body height is accompanied by an athletic body type (Blyth et al., 1982).

Dorn, Crockett, and Petersen (1988) found that more physically mature male seventh graders reported less desire to change their appearance compared to less mature age-mates. Petersen and Crockett (1985), studying male adolescents between sixth and eighth grades, found a better body image in early maturers compared to late maturers only in seventh grade, a time when differences in height spurt are most obvious. This was also reported by Alsaker (1992).

In contrast to early-maturing boys, early-maturing girls are less satisfied with their bodies. Petersen and Crockett (1985) found that early-maturing girls develop an increasingly negative body image between sixth and eighth grades. This seems to be especially due to their lower satisfaction with their weight, as demonstrated by Dorn et al. (1988). Another reason that girls have a temporarily lower satisfaction with their bodies, as reported by Brooks-Gunn (1984), could be their experiences of being teased by peers, and sometimes even by parents, at the beginning of their breast development.

Paper-and-pencil measures of adolescents' satisfaction with their physical appearance tell researchers relatively little about the nature of everyday situations in which being off time contributed to adolescents' dissatisfaction with their appearance. In this regard, qualitative interviews provide worthwhile information. The following is an illustration of gender differences in the everyday meaning of being fast or slow relative to others' maturational pace. Participants of the Berlin Youth Longitudinal Study who rated themselves as fast (slow) in at least one out of three consecutive assessments, and who never categorized themselves as slow (fast), were deemed fast (slow). All others were scored as on time.

Boys. In her interviews with boys, Kracke (1993) found that they had positive attitudes toward the pubertal changes, particularly regarding height, muscle development, voice deepening, and growth of facial hair. In their view, these changes were associated with the experience of being regarded as more grown up by adults and peers and feeling more equal in social relationships, particularly with parents and teachers.

Specific attitudes toward the relative timing in height development were expressed by 17 of the 28 boys interviewed. Off-time maturers reported extensively about their experiences, whereas on-time maturers rarely discussed how it felt to be like the others. The three on-time maturers who referred explicitly to height development underscored the importance of being "normal" because of their observation that slow maturers were put down by age-mates due to their shortness.

M02 (17.8 years; on-time maturer)
A: For me it was most important not to stay so short.
I: Why was that important for you?
A: Hm . . . when somebody is so short . . . then people call you "dwarf." We had one
     who we put down a lot because he was so short. Because of that, I found it
     important to grow along with the others.

Nine of 11 fast maturers described their experiences regarding height
development. They all shared positive or neutral attitudes, and none felt
negative about being faster than age-mates in height development. The most
common positive attitudes centered on advantages in sports and in social
relationships.

M07 (15.0 years; fast maturer)
I: How did you like it to be taller than the others?
A: Not a disadvantage.
I: And did you sometimes experience it as an advantage?
A: No disadvantage is an advantage, isn't it?
I: Advantage in what respect?
A: For example in sports, when I play basketball it's not bad to be that tall.

Five of seven slow maturers talked about their attitudes and experiences
with regard to being slower in height development. Although they did not
explicitly express negative feelings toward their slower height development,
they mentioned the waiting and hoping for growth that would allow them to
catch up with the majority of their age-mates.

M08 (15.0 years; slow maturer)
I: And concerning height development, were the others earlier . . . than you?
A: Yes, they were.
I: You were one of the shorter kids?
A: Yes.
I: And how was this?
A: I don't know. (. . .)
I: It was a little irritating for you that you were not as tall as the others?
A: Yes . . . not really irritating. I was astonished (. . .) I was waiting.

      Girls. According to Kracke's (1988) interviews with 16 girls, height
was a less important issue than it was for boys. In contrast to slow-maturing
boys, only two of the six slow-maturing girls mentioned waiting and hoping for
height growth as an issue. These short girls, however, received the same kind
of comments reported for boys. Thus, they felt ridiculed because of their short
build, particularly by boys.

F19 (14.0 years; slow maturer)
I: What about height development?
A: In 5th grade, all classmates were growing . . . I always thought, "shit, they are
     already tall, you have to grow yourself." There was a time when I found it demean-
     ing to be so short . . . always to look up.

Breast development was mentioned by virtually all girls interviewed and was characterized as favorable because of the associated higher prestige among age-mates, especially male peers. Nevertheless, the timing of breast development seems to be crucial.

All six on-time maturers expressed satisfaction with experiencing breast development at the same time as the majority of girls. They were aware of the teasing that fast and slow developers received from boys.

Two of the four fast maturers described negative attitudes toward their early maturation. They were particularly dissatisfied because they experienced problems that their age-mates did not yet encounter, such as the already mentioned teasing by boys or the necessity of wearing a brassiere. In addition, at least at the beginning, they felt stress because they had nobody with whom to share their thoughts and feelings. Later, however, once the other girls had caught up and boys were showing a real interest, the fast maturers seemed to recover quickly.

F07 (17.2 years; fast maturer)
I: You said you had suffered. Can you describe it?
A: Yes. More in practical situations. I mean, when your bosom develops early . . . you need a bra at sports . . . I had to think about such things when I was 12, 13, while the others had another two years of time. And it is awkward if you have to think about these problems and others don't. You don't have people of your age with whom you can talk about it.

Four of the six slow maturers also expressed rather negative attitudes in regard to breast development. They felt less attractive to boys and saw themselves in competition with more physically mature girls.

F19 (14.0 years; slow maturer)
I: And the others, do they comment on your development? The boys?
A: Yes, they always want to grab you, and then they say "my god, you don't have anything." Sometimes you could get mad . . .

In contrast to breast development, menarche seems to be a more private pubertal issue that is not openly discussed even among girls. The majority of the girls interviewed were prepared for the onset of menstruation and did not express specifically negative attitudes. Nevertheless, most girls felt that menstruation had changed their life by imposing more constraints. Explicitly negative attitudes, however, were mentioned only by the fast maturers. They felt unprepared for the issues of personal hygiene and did not know how to behave in sports.

F10 (17.0 years; fast maturer)
I: How did you experience puberty?
A: When it started, I was completely unsatisfied with myself . . . everything was disturbing me. For instance, I was in a sports club. When I had my period, it was stupid, I didn't know whether to participate in sports or not. I worried that someone might notice it. I was totally alone with it . . . nobody to talk to.

Taken together, the results on attitudes toward perceived maturational timing show a commonality across gender. Boys and girls found those pubertal events that are publicly visible and socially significant as more relevant for their satisfaction than more private events. In everyday terms, being slow in height development among boys or in breast development among girls implies particularly negative situations, such as being teased by peers. The major difference between the genders is that girls are influenced by reactions of their male and female peers, whereas boys are more concerned about being accepted by other boys.

Global Self-Esteem. Several studies found that early maturation in girls is negatively related to self-esteem (e.g., Simmons, Blyth, van Claeve, & Bush, 1979). According to Alsaker (1992), this seems to be particularly true during early adolescence. In comparing early-maturing girls to their classmates in Grades 6 through 8, only those in Grades 6 and 7 were found to be less satisfied with themselves than their classmates. Regression analyses revealed that this relationship between early maturation and negative self-esteem was mediated by the girls being overweight in seventh grade. Thus, only the lower self-esteem among the sixth graders seemed to be influenced by early maturation per se.

Utilizing the data of the Berlin Youth Longitudinal Study, Silbereisen, Petersen, Albrecht, and Kracke (1989) examined relations between perceived maturational timing and negative self-evaluations ("I would like to change a lot concerning myself"; Kaplan, 1978) among groups of 11.5- and 14.5-year-old girls. In the younger age group, no differences in self-evaluation were found in relation to adolescents' perceived pace of maturation. Among the 14.5-year-olds, however, who mainly attended Grade 8, as in Alsaker's study, fast maturers reported less pronounced negative self-evaluations compared to their classmates. Although a lack of negative self-evaluations does not necessarily reflect positive self-esteem, the results point to a potential advantage of fast maturers in midadolescence, when a more feminine appearance is appreciated by females' social environment.

This finding should sensitize researchers to the possibility of cultural influences on the link between self-evaluation and early maturation. In contrast to what is common in the United States, for instance, German adolescents routinely receive more information on sexual development within the school curriculum, suggesting that early-maturing German girls are more accepting of their bodily changes than their American counterparts.

Although early-maturing boys have higher satisfaction with their bodily appearance compared to their classmates, they report no particular advantage in regard to self-esteem (Simmons, Blyth, & Bulcroft, 1987). By contrast, late maturers tend to be less satisfied with themselves compared to on-time and early maturers (Alsaker, 1992; Brack, Orr, & Ingersoll, 1988). The disadvantage of late maturers was also confirmed in analyses of the Berlin Youth Longitudinal Study. From age 13.5 to age 16.5, adolescents who perceived their rate of maturation as slow compared to that of age-mates reported higher levels of self-derogation than the other two timing groups (Kracke, 1993).

Emotional Difficulties. There is some empirical evidence that early-maturing boys and girls exhibit more emotional difficulties than on-time and late maturers. Petersen and Crockett (1985), for instance, reported that early maturers of both genders in sixth, seventh, and eighth grades showed the highest levels of adjustment problems such as anxiety. Alsaker (1992) also found more depressive tendencies in early-maturing girls of the same grades compared to their classmates. In boys, however, the effect was confined to Grade 7. Other studies found either no relation between maturational timing and depressive mood (Simmons et al., 1987) or more emotional difficulties among late maturers, particularly boys (Nottelmann et al., 1987).

Our own explorations of the relation between maturational timing and emotional difficulties were based on data from the Shell Youth Study '92. In 13- to 14-year-olds and in 15- to 16-year-olds, anxiety and depressive tendencies were assessed utilizing short scales adopted from Goldberg's General Health Questionnaire (1972). Anxiety was measured by three items addressing nervousness and sleeping difficulties (e.g., "I am feeling irritated, nervous, and bad-tempered"). Depressive tendencies were measured by three items describing hopelessness and feelings of worthlessness (e.g., "Life seems completely hopeless to me").

For girls and boys there were no systematic differences in depression between groups in perceived maturational timing, and in regard to anxiety only the younger off-time boys showed higher scores than the rest. These findings were consistent with those reported by Stattin and Magnusson (1990). However, although they also found no relation between emotional difficulties and perceived maturational timing, their data revealed a clear relation between emotional difficulties and objectively determined timing. This supported their assumption that there is a direct link between timing and emotional difficulties rather than, as in many of the other behaviors they studied, a pathway mediated through perceived timing differences.

These findings prompted us to reanalyze the data using our measure of self-reported pubertal events, and we found results compatible with those of Stattin and Magnusson (1990). Maturational timing in girls referred to their self-reported age at menarche (early = age 11 or earlier, on time = age 12 or 13, late = age 14 or later; among 13-year-olds only, late = not yet occurred). Table 4.2 shows the means. The data were analyzed by ANOVAs; significant overall effects were followed by Scheffé tests ($p < .05$).

First, as one might have expected for a random sample of noninstitutional

Table 4.2. *Anxiety and depressive tendencies by maturational timing: means and standard deviations*

	Male			Female		
Variables	Early	On Time	Late	Early	On Time	Late
13- to 14-year-olds						
Anxiety	1.46	1.45	1.35	1.62	1.52	1.37
	(.48)	(.47)	(.48)	(.65)	(.51)	(.45)
Depression	1.16	1.30	1.18	1.34	1.31	1.19
	(.28)	(.41)	(.26)	(.44)	(.40)	(.33)
n	44	124	56	39	173	74
15- to 16-year-olds						
Anxiety	1.63	1.32	1.40	1.52	1.57	1.56
	(.46)	(.43)	(.51)	(53)	(.51)	(.50)
Depression	1.43	1.19	1.27	1.25	1.36	1.31
	(.57)	(.36)	(.35)	(.48)	(.48)	(.47)
n	31	149	42	21	144	53

adolescents, the levels on both aspects of emotional difficulties were very low. In the younger female group, the effect of maturational timing on anxiety was significant ($F = 3.61$, $p < .05$). Early and late maturers, showing the highest and lowest anxiety scores, respectively, differed according to the Scheffé tests. Concerning depressive symptoms, there was a nonsignificant tendency among both early and on-time maturers for higher levels ($F = 2.86, p < .10$). Neither depression nor anxiety differed among the groups of girls in the older group, a finding consistent with the earlier mentioned prediction that in the absence of other risk factors, most effects of maturational timing are rather circumscribed and short-lived.

Concerning boys, the equivalent in assessment to menarche was the reported age of the growth spurt. We acknowledge that in all likelihood this is a less valid marker than the reported age at menarche. In regard to anxiety, timing-related differences were revealed only in the older group ($F = 6.20, p < .05$). The early maturers, reporting the highest scores, differed significantly from the on-time maturers. The same was true for depressive symptoms among the older boys ($F = 4.77, p < .05$). The timing groups among the younger adolescents differed in depression as well ($F = 3.81$, $p < .05$). The results of the Scheffé tests were not significant, however.

In line with some of the earlier research, our results indicate that early maturers of both genders tend to report higher levels of emotional difficulties compared to their classmates. Note that this conclusion holds true only when early maturation is considered in terms of pubertal events, not when it is considered in terms of perceived maturational tempo relative to classmates. In our view, a plausible interpretation of this difference can refer to Brooks-Gunn and Warren's (1988) finding that negative feelings, such as anxiety and depressive tendencies, correlate higher with girls' hormonal changes during puberty than with changes in the physical secondary sex characteristics. As the latter play a role in perceived timing, the lower levels of emotional difficulties we found among late maturers may be rooted in less hormonal changes. Certainly this view remains speculative because we have no hormonal data. Furthermore, the similar results on males may need other biological explanations (note that these effects were observed only among the older boys).

To summarize our findings and those of previous researchers regarding the association between various internalizing behaviors and maturational timing, it is fair to say that any deviation in maturational timing increases the potential for adjustment problems in girls. Similarly, boys seem to share the potential for some negative side effects of early maturation. Although early-maturing boys tend to be much more satisfied with their bodily appearance than early-maturing girls, they are still at increased risk for emotional difficulties.

Externalizing Behaviors

Many externalizing behaviors are not deviant per se but deviant only due to their early timing. For instance, sexuality as such is not problematic, but sexual activity that cannot yet build on adequately developed social skills and responsibility is likely to be viewed as problematic. In other words, the core of some externalizing behaviors is the fact that they challenge adult privileges and norms of appropriate behavior.

Seen against this backdrop, it is not surprising that early maturation has been shown to relate primarily to age-inappropriate behaviors. Cigarette smoking and alcohol drinking, for instance, are more prevalent among early maturers compared to on-time or late-maturing age-mates. Furthermore, among early-maturing adolescents, those who use cigarettes and alcohol report comparatively high frequencies of consumption (Aro & Taipale, 1987; Petersen et al., 1990; Stattin & Magnusson, 1990). These differences in the prevalence and frequency of substance use are observed particularly in early adolescence, whereas later in adolescence the differences diminish. Thus, the early maturers show an advanced transition to these adultlike behaviors. Silbereisen and Kracke (1993) confirmed these results for self-reported differences (fast versus slow) in the pace of maturation.

Because cigarette and alcohol use are strongly influenced by peers who provide behavioral models (e.g., Gerber & Newman, 1989; Hundleby &

Mercer, 1987), an important question is whether peers play a mediating role in the effect of variation in maturational timing on smoking and drinking. According to Magnusson et al. (1986), this is the case particularly for peers who are more advanced in regard to psychosocial transitions to adulthood. More specifically, the researchers demonstrated that early-maturing girls who socialized with older friends (or peers who had already left school) consumed alcohol and marijuana more frequently than did age-mates.

Utilizing data from the Berlin Youth Longitudinal Study, Silbereisen and Kracke (1993) attempted to replicate this finding. The data did not confirm the mediational influence of peers. Rather, we found that contacts with adolescents who oppose adult norms, and socializing regularly with the same group of friends represented additional, independent risk factors for more frequent substance use among early maturers. Although the different results may be attributed to different measurements, it is safe to say that the actual process by which peers provoke problem behaviors among early maturers is not yet fully understood.

In line with results on the interplay between early maturation and peer influence as reported by Stattin and Magnusson (1990), we want to emphasize the active role that the adolescents themselves may play. An early-maturing girl has to master a mismatch between her actual social maturity and the expectations of others, the latter being provoked by her advanced physical development. According to this notion, socializing with older friends and following their behaviors helps to overcome the mismatch, albeit at the price of being perceived as deviant by adults (Silbereisen, Noack, & von Eye, 1992b). As long as there is no interference by other risk factors such as school failure (Stattin & Magnusson, 1990), the attempts to eliminate the asynchrony in the pace of social and physical maturation are unlikely to contribute to long-term negative effects.

Thus far, we have focused on the role of problem behaviors for early maturers. What about late maturers? Andersson and Magnusson (1990) found excessive drinking among late maturers, which they interpreted as stemming from late-maturing boys' attempts to gain prestige among age-mates. Compatible with this view, Silbereisen and Kracke (1993) reported a closer association between drinking and drunkenness in off-time maturers.

The interviews conducted by Kracke (1993) provide additional insight into the functional value of excessive drinking for late maturers. In the group of the older boys, the three slow maturers reported periods of excessive drinking when they were about 16 years of age. Reasons for this behavior included the need to feel more relaxed and to appear stronger in social situations. None of the boys in the other timing groups reported such excessive behavior.

M13 (17.0 years; slow maturer)
A: When I was almost 16, I had a wild time. I got drunk frequently. My parents took it badly.

I: Why did you get drunk so often?
A: Somehow one was tempted, one wanted to try it ... and you felt strong.
I: Did this feeling make it easier to talk to people?
A: Yes, but not aggressively. You were more sociable ... you talked to people more easily.

In summary, drinking alcohol is related to the attainment of adult status for male adolescents, regardless of maturational timing. Its particular function, however, seems to differ between fast and slow maturers. Whereas late maturers use alcohol to catch others' attention, thus giving them a chance to become recognized, fast maturers drink as part of their advanced peer activities. Similar analyses for female adolescents, particularly slow maturers, are lacking.

Interpersonal Relations

Maturational timing does not seem to have a differential impact on the onset of activities with same-sex peers. When comparing fast, on-time, and slow maturers at age 14, Kracke and Silbereisen (1990) found no difference in the proportion of adolescents who belonged to a clique of peers ("Do you belong to a group of youths who meet regularly?").

Again drawing on the Shell Youth Study '92, Silbereisen, Kracke, and Nowak (1992a) found that fast maturers reported more advanced experiences with romantic friendships between 13 and 16 years of age compared to their age-mates. Specifically, about 80% of the females aged 15 to 16 years who had rated themselves at ages 11/12 or 13/14 as developing faster than age-mates already had a steady boyfriend, whereas only about 50% of the slow maturers reported this experience. Note that the concurrent timing at age 15/16 was not relevant in this regard, and there was no difference in friendship experiences among the timing groups in the younger females aged 13 to 14 years. In boys, fast maturers in the entire age range between 13 and 16 showed this pattern or even more advanced experiences with heterosexual relations. The proportion of fast- to slow-maturing boys who had a steady girlfriend was 50% to 15% at ages 13/14 and 70% to 40% at ages 15/16.

Along with showing the higher prevalence of romantic friendships among early maturers, previous research has also shown that these adolescents are more involved in sexual activities such as kissing, petting, and sexual intercourse (Ahrendt, 1985; Aro & Taipale, 1987; Magnusson et al., 1986). This association was confirmed for self-reported maturational timing by Crockett and Bingham (1990) and by Silbereisen et al. (1992a).

The relation between the timing of maturation and sexual activities appears to be influenced by other mediating and moderating factors. Of course, one major moderating factor is gender. Concerning girls, Stattin and Magnusson (1990) described the role of older boyfriends in mediating the relationship between early timing and more advanced sexual activities. Above and beyond the immediate setting, more remote contextual conditions also are important, such as societal norms. Thus, Udry (1988) found boys' sexual behavior to be strongly influenced by individual differences in levels of sex hormones, whereas girls' sexual activities were predominantly influenced by permissive attitudes toward sexuality and other social factors (sexual fantasies, however, did not differ across genders in the role of hormonal influences).

Other evidence supporting the gender-differential role of social norms comes from Dornbusch et al. (1981), who reported that for girls' dating behavior chronological age (a proxy for developmental timetables) was a decisive factor, whereas boys' dating was influenced most strongly by maturational timing. In the same vein, Starke (1984) found that the early-maturing girls in his East German sample experienced the longest, and the late maturers experienced the shortest, time span between menarche and first sexual intercourse, indicating that maturational timing is less critical for girls' sexual experiences.

It is unclear whether the mediating role of older boyfriends, as reported for girls, also applies to boys in relation to their girlfriends. Unfortunately, none of our data sets allows us to address this issue directly. However, information on peers who violate age norms ("My friends often are in trouble with adults") gathered in the Berlin Youth Longitudinal Study can shed some light on the nature of this gender differential. In comparing age groups cross-sectionally, from age 13.5 on, fast-maturing girls reported more frequent contacts with norm-violating peers compared to their female age-mates. Among boys, at age 14.5 both fast and slow maturers had such contacts (Silbereisen & Kracke, 1993).

Results of the Shell Youth Study '92 help to describe further the specific quality of the peer contacts. The adolescents were asked whether their friends would approve of alcohol drinking and truancy. Using ANOVAs, no effects of perceived timing were found except for the concurrently judged pace of maturation among the 15- to 16-year-old females ($F = 5.69$, $p < .01$). As revealed by Scheffé tests, both fast and slow maturers had significantly ($p < .05$) more such contacts than on-time maturers. However, when assessed by their reported age at menarche, the maturational groups differed among the 13- to 14-year-old girls ($F = 7.52$, $p < .001$). Specifically, the peers of early-maturing girls approved more of drinking and truancy than did the peers of the other two groups ($p < .05$). Among males, none of the effects of maturational timing, (measured either way) were significant (except for a tendency toward more negative peer contacts among 13- to 14-year-old boys who perceived themselves as developing faster than others at the time of assessment).

In summarizing all the results reported in this section on interpersonal relations thus far, it is fair to say that older peers (or peers who engage in behaviors appropriate for older ages) seem to play an important role, particularly in early adolescence and especially among girls.

Concerning gender differences, Kracke's qualitative interviews (1988, 1993) point to a more basic distinction. For girls in middle adolescence (13- to 15-year-olds) in general, older boys are more attractive because same-age boys are perceived as socially less mature – "They want to appear cool but they are mentally childish," as one of the girls stated. For fast-maturing girls, this impression appears even stronger and the search for a person with whom one can exchange intimate experiences becomes crucial. As exemplified in the following quote from a fast-maturing girl, the relation with older peers is seen as an opportunity for psychosocial development and identity search.

F06 (17.0 years; fast maturer)
A: I got into contact with a group of adolescents who were two, three, four years older than me. I was the youngest. I have made great progress in my development . . . in my behavior. I was always more fascinated by older people because you could talk to them about things. They provided much more understanding for me. During that time among my classmates nobody really understood me or was interested in me.

In contrast, the interviews with fast-maturing boys revealed a different role of older peers. For them it was important to have better opportunities for hanging out at discotheques and sports clubs. Gaining insight into one's developing identity and exchange of views, by contrast, was emphasized much less often.

M27 (15.3 years; fast maturer)
I: Did you just begin going to parties and spending much time with friends?
A: No, I did this before. But now I am going more often, very often.
I: And what about drinking alcohol, beer, wine?
A: Yes, I drink alcohol (. . .) when I am with friends or at parties.
I: Are your friends from your 9th grade classroom?
A: Yes, and from the 10th grade.

Based on our findings, one could speculate that males who mature faster see older friends as supportive in terms of providing more access to more mature leisure settings, whereas faster-maturing females expect help and support in terms of understanding heterosexual relations.

Discussion

The purpose of this chapter was to emphasize the role of the often neglected biological factors in adolescents' psychosocial adaptation. The behavioral aspects studied clearly could cover only a fraction of the range of health outcomes possibly related to individual differences in puberty. For instance, one important facet of health we did not address is eating problems. The role of potentially mediating factors, such as maturational timing, dating experiences, and modeling by media, peers, and parents, needs clarification in further research (Halpern & Udry, 1994).

The results of our analyses, both previous ones and those conducted for this chapter, relied on adolescents' self-reports of maturational timing, gathered from two independent, rather large samples. With few exceptions, the focal variable was perceived maturational timing, that is, a self-categorization on the pace of one's physical development relative to classmates.

The data showed consistent and plausible relations to adolescents' reports on bodily changes. The fact that breast development in girls or height gain in boys was mentioned by a majority as salient sources for their self-categorizations points to the validity of perceived maturational timing. Moreover, the qualitative interviews revealed that it was exactly the attributes identified in the survey that distinguished the experience of adolescents who judged themselves to be faster, as fast, or slower in maturational timing than their classmates.

In line with others (e.g., Dubas et al., 1991), we believe that the measure of perceived maturational timing reflects real differences in pubertal timing. Nevertheless, it is clear that differences vis-à-vis more objective and/or more specific measures of pubertal processes remain, especially in regard to associations with measures of psychosocial adjustment. This is primarily the case because perceived maturational timing represents a complex self-attribution based on, but not restricted to, variation in the change of physical attributes relative to age-mates (rather than population norms).

Assuming adequate validity, the consistency of the results across a number of aspects of internalizing and externalizing adjustment problems is remarkable. In our efforts, which were always guided by previous research on the impact of maturational timing that used less subjective measures, we attempted to shed light on a basic question, conceptualized in the literature as the juxtaposition between two hypotheses. According to the deviance hypothesis, being off time (faster or slower) relative to the majority of age-mates should imply similar risks for psychosocial adjustment (or, in a more specific version, fast-maturing girls and slow-maturing boys ranking highest in risk). In contrast, according to the stage termination hypothesis, those adolescents who mature faster than the majority should be at greater risk for psychosocial adjustment difficulties (Brooks-Gunn et al., 1985).

In light of the results presented in this chapter, the impact of variations in maturational timing seems to depend on whether the outcomes are internalizing or externalizing behaviors. Concerning the latter, alcohol consumption was the only behavior we studied. Those who matured faster reported more frequent drinking than other same-age adolescents. As the data on interpersonal relations showed, this is presumably due to the fact that a greater proportion of the fast-maturing girls and boys were already involved in their first romantic friendships. Such relations correspond to leisure activities that imply more opportunities for substance use, such as dancing in a discotheque. The additional data concerning peer approval of drinking and other mild norm violations point in the same direction (Silbereisen et al., 1992b).

In spite of the fact that fast-maturing girls and boys revealed a higher propensity for status offenses such as drinking, the interviews revealed that the actual role of the accompanying peer activities differed remarkably across genders. Whereas older peers helped boys gain access to more grown-up leisure locales, older peers provided emotional support to early-maturing girls and helped the girls in their identity search.

Also, as shown by the interviews, alcohol consumption played a role for late-maturing boys, particularly as a means to attract attention. Nevertheless, the stage termination hypothesis, with its emphasis on a faster than usual pace of maturation as antecedent to adjustment problems, seems to capture more effectively the role of perceived maturational timing in regard to drinking (although the levels of drinking presumably are not problematic in the long term).

In regard to the internalizing behaviors studied, however, the deviance hypothesis finds more support in parts of our data. Although fast-maturing boys reported more satisfaction with their own bodies than did their age-mates, early- and late-maturing girls reported challenges to their self-esteem, particularly due to teasing from boys. Furthermore, late-maturing boys had a hard time because they could not succeed in pertinent social comparisons among age-mates. The fact that fast-maturing girls seemed not to be really satisfied – as indicated by their complaining about many daily problems – does not rule out the fact that at least some young females actually liked the feeling of attraction expressed by boys.

Regarding anxiety, maturation-related differences were found at different points in time in girls' compared to boys' adolescence. Being earlier than others corresponded to higher scores only for the younger girls and the older boys. In our view, this result still fits the irritation-by-novelty notion just mentioned. Due to the gender-differential pace of maturation, females are not only confronted with social expectations and competition among peers earlier than males, but they also undergo the physiological changes of puberty earlier. In short, the mild irritation and confusion related to pubertal timing are repeated at different times during adolescence, and this is likely to be due in part to the experiences of new situations and companions.

In summary, the results do not support a simple formula that would link the two models with different types of adjustment problems. Obviously, other conditions play a role, among them gender and the particular type of problem behavior. Presumably, any further clarification would require more specific hypotheses about the processes mediating puberty and behavioral adjustments.

In the concluding paragraphs we illustrate these topics, beginning with our results on emotional difficulties. Viewing oneself as maturing faster than most age-mates in one's social environment means playing the role of forerunner, whether this is what an adolescent wants or not. Exploring (or being forced to explore by interested peers) new expectations by others is likely to induce at least some temporary uneasiness. Consequently, one might expect this uneasiness to be reflected in elevated scores on the depression and anxiety measures.

Recently, building on earlier conceptualizations, Brooks-Gunn, Graber, and Paikoff (1994) have discussed a number of models in the link between hormonal change and negative affect during puberty. In the most elaborated model, three potential mediating processes are delineated: internal states such as arousal, status and timing of maturation, and the perception of puberty.

Interestingly enough, our measure of perceived timing did not correspond to differences in emotional difficulties. However, the timing of the onset of menarche and the growth spurt in boys did correspond. Seen against the backdrop of the aforementioned three-pathways model, it would appear that the perception of puberty is not a mediator with regard to negative affect, as suggested by this model. Indeed, as reported in previous sections, there is a substantial amount of research demonstrating a link between physical maturation and negative affect, whereas neither Stattin and Magnusson (1990) nor we in the present study found evidence for the role of perceived maturational timing vis-à-vis negative affect.

Further research is needed to clarify these findings. This work will profit from the present results on perceived maturational timing, but assessing the other groups of variables mentioned by Brooks-Gunn et al. (1994), including measures of hormonal change, and thus incorporating perceived maturational timing into an ensemble of multiple pathways to adolescent behavior seems mandatory.

The model proposed would require further elaboration with regard to well-known mediators of the relation between puberty and externalizing behaviors. Among them, according to Stattin and Magnusson (1990) and our own work, peer affiliations stand out.

References

Ahrendt, J. F. (1985). *Geschlechtliche Entwicklung, Sexualverhalten und Kontrazeption 15- bis 17-jähriger weiblicher Jugendlicher* [*Sexual development, sexual behavior, and contraception among 15- to 17-year-old female adolescents*]. Unpublished thesis. (Habilitation): Magdeburg: Medizinische Akademie.

Alsaker, F. D. (1990). *Global negative self-evaluations in early adolescence.* Doctoral dissertation, University of Bergen, Norway.

Alsaker, F. D. (1992). Pubertal timing, overweight, and psychological adjustment. *Journal of Early Adolescence, 12,* 396–419.

Andersson, T. A., & Magnusson, D. (1990). Biological maturation in adolescence and the development of drinking habits and alcohol abuse among young males: A prospective longitudinal study. *Journal of Youth and Adolescence, 19*, 33–41.

Aro, H., & Taipale, V. (1987). The impact of timing of puberty on psychosomatic symptoms among fourteen- to sixteen-year-old Finnish girls. *Child Development, 58*, 261–268.

Bean, J. A., Leeper, J. D., Wallace, R. B., Sherman, B. M., & Jagger, H. J. (1979). Variations in the reporting of menstrual histories. *American Journal of Epidemiology, 109*, 181–185.

Blyth, D. A., Simmons, R. G., Bulcroft, R., Felt, D., van Claeve, E. F., & Bush, D. M. (1982). The effects of physical development on self-image and satisfaction with body-image for early adolescent males. *Research in Community and Mental Health, 2*, 43–73.

Brack, C. J., Orr, D. A., & Ingersoll, G. (1988). Pubertal maturation and adolescent self-esteem. *Journal of Adolescent Health Care, 9*, 280–285.

Brackbill, Y., & Navill, D. D. (1981). Parental expectations of achievement as expected by children's height. *Merrill-Palmer Quarterly, 27*, 429–441.

Brooks-Gunn, J. (1984). The psychological significance of different pubertal events to young girls. *Journal of Early Adolescence, 4*, 315–327.

Brooks-Gunn, J., Graber, J. A., & Paikoff, R. L. (1994). Studying links between hormones and negative affect: Models and measures. *Journal of Research on Adolescence, 4*, 469–486.

Brooks-Gunn, J., Petersen, A. C., & Eichhorn, D. (1985). The study of maturational timing effects in adolescence. *Journal of Youth and Adolescence, 14*, 149–161.

Brooks-Gunn, J., & Reiter, E. O. (1990). The role of pubertal processes. In S. S. Feldman & G. R. Elliot (Eds.), *At the threshold. The developing adolescent* (pp. 16–53). Cambridge, MA: Harvard University Press.

Brooks-Gunn, J., & Warren, M. P. (1988). Biological and social contributions to negative affect in young adolescent girls. *Child Development, 60*, 40–55.

Crockett, L. J., & Bingham, R. (1990, March). *Pubertal timing, social class, and problem behaviors among rural adolescents.* Paper presented at the third Biennial Meetings of the Society for Research on Adolescence, Atlanta, Georgia.

Dorn, L. D., Crockett, L. J., & Petersen, A. C. (1988). The relations of pubertal status to intrapersonal changes in young adolescents. *Journal of Early Adolescence, 8*, 405–419.

Dornbusch, S. M., Carlsmith, J. M., Gross, R. T., Martin, J. A., Jennings, D., Rosenberg, A., & Duke, P. (1981). Sexual development, age and dating; A comparison of biological and social influences upon one set of behaviors. *Child Development, 52*, 179–185.

Dubas, J. S., Graber, J. A., & Petersen, A. C. (1991). A longitudinal investigation of adolescents' changing perceptions of pubertal timing. *Developmental Psychology, 27*, 580–586.

Duke, P. M., Carlsmith, J. M., Jennings, D., Martin, J. A., Dornbusch, S. M., Gross, R. T., & Siegel-Gorelick, B. (1982). Educational correlates of early and late sexual maturation in adolescence. *Adolescent Medicine, 100*, 633–637.

Feldman, S. S., & Quatman, T. (1988). Factors influencing age expectations for adolescent autonomy: A study of early adolescents and parents. *Journal of Early Adolescence, 8*, 325–343.

Gerber, R. W., & Newman, I. M. (1989). Predicting future experimental smoking of adolescents. *Journal of Youth and Adolescence, 18*, 191–201.

Goldberg, W. (1972). *The detection of psychiatric illness by questionnaire.* London: Oxford University Press.

Greene, A. L., Wheatley, S. M., & Aldava, J. F., IV. (1992). Stages on life's way. Adolescents' implicit theories of the life course. *Journal of Adolescent Research, 7*, 364–381.

Halpern, C. T., & Udry, J. R. (1994). *Pubertal increases in body fat and implications for dieting, dating and sexual behavior among Black and White females.* Paper presented at the Fifth Biennial Meeting of the Society for Research on Adolescence, San Diego, California, February 10–13.

Hundleby, J. D., & Mercer, G. W. (1987). Family and friends as social environments and their relationship to young adolescents' use of alcohol, tobacco, and marijuana. *Journal of Marriage and the Family, 49*, 151–164.

Johnson, B. M., & Collins, W. A. (1988). Perceived maturity as a function of appearance cues in early adolescence: Ratings by unacquainted adults, parents and teachers. *Journal of Early Adolescence, 8*, 357–372.

Jugendwerk der Deutschen Shell (Ed.). (1992). *Jugend 1992.* Opladen: Leske & Budrich.

Kaplan, H. B. (1978). Deviant behavior and self-enhancement in adolescence. *Journal of Youth and Adolescence, 7*, 253–277.

Kossakowski, A. (1965). *Ueber die psychischen Veraenderungen in der Pubertaet* [*On psychosocial change during puberty*]. Berlin: Volk und Wissen.

Kracke, B. (1988). *Pubertaet und Problemverhalten bei Maedchen* [*Puberty and problem behavior among girls*]. Unpublished master's thesis, Technical University Berlin, Germany.

Kracke, B. (1993). *Pubertaet und Problemverhalten bei Jungen* [*Puberty and problem behavior among boys*]. Weinheim: Psychologie Verlags Union.

Kracke, B., Nowak, M., Thiele, G., & Silbereisen, R. K. (1992). Gedaechtniseffekte und Antworttendenzen in der Shell Jugendstudie [Memory effects and response tendencies in the Shell Youth Study]. In Jugendwerk der Deutschen Shell (Eds.), *Jugend '92* (Vol. 4, pp. 55–58). Opladen: Leske & Budrich.

Kracke, B., & Silbereisen, R. K. (1990, April). *On the interaction between maturational timing and social factors in the development of problem behavior.* Paper presented at the Second European Workshop on Adolescence, Groningen, The Netherlands.

Kracke, B., & Silbereisen, R. K. (1994). Koerperliches Entwicklungstempo und psychosoziale Anpassung im Jugendalter: Ein Ueberblick zur neueren Forschung [Maturational timing and psychosocial adjustment in adolescence]. *Zeitschrift für Entwicklungspsychologie und Paedagogische Psychologie, 4*, 293–330.

Lerner, R. M. (1985). Adolescent maturational changes and psychosocial development: A dynamic interactional perspective. *Journal of Youth and Adolescence, 14*, 355–372.

Magnusson, D., Stattin, H., & Allen, V. A. (1986). Differential maturation among girls and its relevance to social adjustment: A longitudinal perspective. In D. L. Featherman & R. M. Lerner (Eds.), *Life-span Development and Behavior* (Vol. 7, pp. 135–172). New York: Academic Press.

Marshall, W. A., & Tanner, J. M. (1969). Variations in the pattern of pubertal changes in girls. *Archives of Disease in Childhood, 44*, 291–303.

Marshall, W. A., & Tanner, J. M. (1970). Variations in the pattern of pubertal changes in boys. *Archives of Disease in Childhood, 45*, 13–23.

Nottelmann, E. D., Susman, E. J., Dorn, L. D., Inoff-Germain, G., Loriaux, D. L., Cutler, G. B., Jr., & Chrousos, G. P. (1987). Relationships among chronological age, pubertal stage, height, weight, and serum levels of gonadotropins, sex steroids, and adrenal androgens. *Journal of Adolescent Health Care, 8*, 35–48.

Petersen, A. C., & Crockett, L. J. (1985). Pubertal timing and grade effects on adjustment. *Journal of Youth and Adolescence, 14*, 191–206.

Petersen, A. C., Graber, J. A., & Sullivan, P. (1990, March). *Pubertal timing and problem behavior: Variations in effects.* Paper presented at the Third Biennial Meetings of the Society for Research on Adolescence, Atlanta, Georgia.

Pfanzagl, J. (1966). *Allgemeine Methodenlehre der Statistik* [*Statistical methods*] (Vol. 2). Berlin: Goeschen.

Silbereisen, R. K., & Kracke, B. (1993). Variation in maturational timing and adjustment in adolescence. In S. Jackson & H. Rodriguez-Tome (Eds.), *The social worlds of adolescence* (pp. 67–94). East Sussex, U.K.: Erlbaum.

Silbereisen, R. K., Kracke, B., & Nowak, M. (1992a). Koerperliches Entwicklungstempo und jugendtypische Uebergaenge [Maturational timing and transitions in adolescence]. In Jugendwerk der Deutschen Shell (Ed.), *Jugend '92* (pp. 171–196). Opladen: Leske & Budrich.

Silbereisen, R. K., & Noack, P. (1988). On the constructive role of problem behavior in adolescence. In N. Bolger, A. Caspi, G. Downey, & M. Moorehouse (Eds.), *Person and context. Developmental processes* (pp. 152–180). Cambridge: Cambridge University Press.

Silbereisen, R. K., Noack, P., & Schoenpflug, U. (1994). Comparative analyses of beliefs, leisure contexts, and substance use in West Berlin and Warsaw. In R. K. Silbereisen & E. Todt (Eds.), *Adolescence in context. The interplay of family, school, peers and work in adjustment* (pp. 176–198). New York: Springer-Verlag.

Silbereisen, R. K., Noack, P., & von Eye, A. (1992b). Adolescents' development of romantic friendship and change in favorite leisure contexts. *Journal of Adolescent Research, 7*, 80–93.

Silbereisen, R. K., Petersen, A. C., Albrecht, H. T., & Kracke, B. (1989). Maturational timing and the development of problem behavior: Longitudinal studies in adolescence. *Journal of Early Adolescence, 9*, 247–268.

Simmons, R. G., Blyth, D. A., & Bulcroft, R. A. (1987). The social-psychological effects of puberty on white males. In R. G. Simmons & D. A. Blyth (Eds.), *Moving into adolescence. The impact of pubertal change and school context* (pp. 171–199). Hawthorne, NY: de Gruyter.

Simmons, R. G., Blyth, D. A., van Claeve, E. F., & Bush, D. E. (1979). Entry into early adolescence: The impact of school structure, puberty and early dating on self-esteem. *American Sociological Review, 44*, 948–967.

Starke, K. (1984). Geschlechtsreife und Beginn des Sexuallebens Jugendlicher [Sexual maturity and the beginning of adolescents' sexual life]. In K. Starke & W. Friedrich (Eds.), *Liebe und Sexualitaet bis 30 [Love and sexuality up to 30]*. (pp. 115–139). Berlin: Deutscher Verlag der Wissenschaften.

Stattin, H., & Magnusson, D. (1990). *Pubertal maturation in female development*. Hillsdale, NJ: Erlbaum.

Udry, J. R. (1988). Biological predisposition and social control in adolescent sexual behavior. *American Sociological Review, 53*, 709–722.

Zakin, D. F., Blyth, D. A., & Simmons, R. G. (1984). Physical attractiveness as a mediator of the impact of early pubertal changes for girls. *Journal of Youth and Adolescence, 13*, 439–450.

5   Adolescents' Decisions About Risks: A Cognitive Perspective

Ruth Beyth-Marom and Baruch Fischhoff

In 1993, one in five high school seniors reported using some illicit drug within the preceding 30 days, and almost one in three did so for the last year. Over 10% reported having used a hallucinogen at some time in their lives, and 6% had tried cocaine at least once. One-quarter reported having had five or more drinks at one time during the past two weeks; 20% reported smoking daily (Johnston, O'Malley, & Bachman, 1994). Although many adults engage in *problem behaviors*, adolescents perform them more frequently (Jessor & Jessor, 1977): Use of alcohol, marijuana, and cocaine increases from early to midadolescence and declines sharply only after the early 20s (Gans, Blyth, Elster, & Gaveras, 1990). Furthermore, adolescents experience the negative consequences of such behaviors to a disproportionately high degree (Dryfoos, 1990; Hechinger, 1992). For example, young people aged 16–20 comprise 21% of all licensed drivers in Canada but account for 58% of the traffic accidents (Jonah, 1986). Young women aged 15–24 have both the highest abortion rate (Tietze, 1983) and the highest rate of births to unmarried women (U.S. Department of Education, 1988).

Such *problem behavior* (e.g., Jessor, Donovan, & Costa, 1992) or *reckless behavior* (e.g., Arnett, 1992) or *risk-taking behavior* (e.g., Furby & Beyth-Marom, 1992) has been explained in several ways. Some authors have suggested that adolescents tend to be especially high in sensation seeking (Zuckerman, Eysenck, & Eysenck, 1978). Jessor (1987) argues that "the most salient function of problem behavior in adolescence is as a transition marker, a way of placing a claim on a more mature status" (p. 335). Elkind (1985) attributed adolescents' risk behaviors to heightened egocentrism. Many authors (e.g., Arnett, 1992; Jessor, 1987) see these developmental changes as predispositions whose expression depends on social and environmental factors, such as family, peers, school, community, the legal system, cultural belief systems, and the media.

The present chapter looks at adolescents' risk behaviors from a cognitive perspective. It attempts to account for behaviors that are the result of deliber-

Preparation of this chapter was supported by the National Institute of Alcohol Abuse and Alcoholism. The opinions expressed are those of the authors.

110

ate choices among alternative courses of action. One focus of this account is how seemingly unthinking behavior can be interpreted in cognitive terms. A second focus is how a detailed analysis of decisions is needed to reveal the structure of the tasks facing individuals and the opportunities they have to make successful choices.

Adolescence is a time of choices. It involves gaining autonomy, assuming responsibility, and making choices about health, family, career, peers, and school. The ability to confront these decisions effectively is essential to teens' well-being. This chapter examines that ability.

Definitions

Risk refers to a chance of loss. A *risk behavior* is an action (e.g., driving after drinking) or a nonaction (e.g., not using a condom during sex) that entails a chance of loss to the actor. Engaging in a risk behavior is *risk taking*. A *risky decision* involves a choice in which at least one of the options entails a chance of loss.

Normative decision theory specifies the steps that decision makers should take in order to act in their own best interests (e.g., Raiffa, 1968; von Winterfeldt & Edwards, 1986). In their simplest form, those steps are as follows:

1. Identify the possible options.
2. Identify the possible consequences of each option.
3. Evaluate the desirability of each consequence.
4. Assess the likelihood of each consequence, should each action be taken.
5. Combine everything according to a logically defensible "decision rule."

Behavioral decision theory describes people's actual decision processes, often in terms of their adherence to or departure from this normative standard (e.g., Fischhoff, 1988; Kahneman, Slovic, & Tversky, 1982; Yates, 1989).

As an example of a normative analysis, imagine a teenager at a party where marijuana is being passed around. That situation presents a decision with two possible options – accept the offer to smoke or decline it (step 1), each with several possible variants (e.g., different ways to decline). Each option can lead to several consequences (step 2), whose desirability (step 3) and likelihood (step 4) will depend on the individual. Smoking might be very likely to cause a teen to feel high, sick, and guilty; refusing to smoke may be certain to increase self-respect but is also likely to incur some teasing. The typical normative decision rule (step 5) calculates the expected value of each option, namely, the sum of the values or utilities of the consequences, weighted by their probabilities.

The descriptive analysis of such decisions involves comparing actual behavior with each element in the ideal represented by a thorough normative analysis. That analysis can have value in its own right by clarifying the nature of the situations facing people. In this case, for example, it shows all options to be risky in the sense of entailing a chance of loss. Smoking marijuana risks a "bad trip" and getting caught; not smoking risks peer rejection. Thus, the question for research is not why people take risks but why they choose particular risks. This analysis supports Jessor and Jessor's (1977) proposal to replace the term *risk behaviors* with *problem behaviors*, namely, "behavior that is socially defined as a problem, a source of concern, or as undesirable by the norms of conventional society" (p. 33).

Normative analyses can also clarify the difficulty of a decision and the criticality of its different components. For example, does it have too many options for each to be explored thoroughly? How available are the most critical pieces of information? What difficult trade-offs would remain even with complete information (Fischhoff, 1991, 1992a; Simon, 1957; von Winterfeldt & Edwards, 1986)?

The cognitive side of decision making can be divided into three parts:

1. Cognitions: What do people believe?
2. Cognitive processes: How do people think while making choices?
3. Metacognitions: What do they think about their knowledge and thought?

The next three sections examine, in turn, the roles of each of these three elements in explaining and predicting adolescents' decision making. They are followed by a section considering the methodological, educational, and political implications of this research. The concluding section discusses the role of cognitions in decision making.

Cognitions: What Do Adolescents Believe?

Any good/wise/efficient/rational choice should take into account all available and relevant information. This section considers, in turn, each component of knowledge in the decision-making model: the possible options, the possible consequences, the desirability of each consequence, and its probability (given each option). Knowing what adolescents know about each component is essential to understanding their existing behavior, predicting their future choices, and increasing the chance of informed decisions (e.g., by creating pertinent educational messages).

Options

People cannot take appropriate actions if they do not even think of them. Many interventions with teens are designed to expand their repertoire of actions. These range from general campaigns like "Just Say No" (which ignore the details of the option and its consequences) to social skills training programs teaching specific response strategies (Botvin, 1986; Schinke & Gilchrist, 1984). How people generate options has rarely been studied for teens or adults. One exception is Rogel, Zuehlke, Petersen, Tobin-Richards, and Shelton (1980), who interviewed 120 young women (aged 12–19) in three clinics about their sexual and obstetric history, as well as their contraceptive and sexual knowledge, attitudes, and practices. They concluded that "The perceived costs of contraception are inflated by the fact that the girls equate 'birth control' and 'the pill.' They have almost no knowledge of or experience with other methods of birth control. Therefore, their options are severely limited" (p. 504).

As an example of how option production might be studied, Furby, Fischhoff, and Morgan (1990) posed a series of open-ended questions, asking what a woman could do to protect herself from the threat of sexual assault. Their subjects included 43–45 women drawn from each of three populations: students, middle-aged alumna of the same university, and working-class young mothers. Subjects produced 26 different options on average.[1] Although this is a large number of strategies for an individual to write, it is still less than a tenth of the options produced by each group as a whole. To these lists we added options produced by a group of men and a national sample of sexual assault experts, as well as ones culled from a sample of 50 publications written for lay or professional audiences. The total of over 1,100 different options is a bewildering number of possibilities for women or researchers to consider in any detail. Gettys, Pliske, Manning, and Casey (1987) also found that people could produce many decision options if pressed to do so, especially when asked to use goals as prompts.

The array of options revealed by these open-ended studies is markedly different from the few (perhaps one or two) options offered in many structured studies. A normative analysis would show the challenges created by option spaces of different sizes.

Consequences

Having generated options, one must then envision their potential consequences. Few investigators have studied the consequence-production process. A more common strategy has been to have teens evaluate the consequences on investigator-provided lists. For example, Bauman (1980) had seventh graders evaluate 54 possible consequences of using marijuana in terms of valence, importance, and likelihood. A "utility structure index" computed from these three judgments predicted about 20% of the variance in his subjects' reported marijuana usage. Such expectancy-value models assume, in effect, that people adopt something like the decision theory calculus described earlier.

The same general paradigm has been used to study cigarette smoking by Bauman, Fisher, Bryan, and Chenoweth (1984) and Urberg and Robbins (1981); drinking behavior by Barnes (1981), Bauman and Bryan (1983), and Bauman, Fisher, and Koch (1988); and sexual intercourse by Bauman and

Udry (1981) and Gilbert, Bauman, and Udry (1986). Here, too, teens reported engaging in behaviors that they described as more likely to bring consequences that they perceived as positive and less likely to bring consequences that they perceived as negative. Adults may not always like the consequences that teens value. However, if teens pursue their goals in an orderly fashion, then one cannot dismiss them with a blanket charge of "irrationality."

The experience of these studies resembles that of earlier studies of clinical judgment, which successfully modeled decision making with multiple regression. Initially, investigators interpreted the regression coefficients as reflecting the weights that people give to different concerns (Goldberg, 1968; Hammond, Hursch, & Todd, 1964; Hoffman, 1960). However, formal analyses eventually showed that many weighting schemes would produce similar predictions, as long as they contained the same variables (or highly correlated surrogates) (Dawes & Corrigan, 1974; Wilks, 1938). The good news in this result is that any linear combination of relevant variables will have some predictive success. The bad news is that it can be very difficult to distinguish alternative strategies. Thus, linear models can have considerable practical value at the same time that they have limited ability to illuminate decision-making processes (Camerer, 1981; Dawes, Faust, & Meehl, 1989). As a result, linear models provide a sort of cognitive task analysis, identifying the factors that might be involved in people's choices. Other procedures are needed to clarify the finer structure of how decisions are made.

One such procedure was used by Beyth-Marom, Austin, Fischhoff, Palmgren, and Jacobs-Quadrel (1993), who asked teens drawn from low-risk settings (e.g., sports teams, service clubs) and their parents to produce possible consequences of several decisions (e.g., you decided to smoke marijuana which was passed around at a party). Different subjects considered the acts of accepting the offer and of rejecting it in order to see whether these formally complementary options would elicit complementary consequences. In almost all respects, the teens and parents reponded quite similarly. On average, they produced four to seven consequences, with a somewhat higher number for accepting the risky offer (suggesting that doing something is more evocative than not doing it). They produced many more bad than good consequences of doing the focal behavior but fairly equal numbers for *not* doing it, so that avoidance was not as attractive as acceptance was unattractive. Most of the consequences mentioned were social reactions and personal effects. The social reactions of peers were particularly salient as a consequence of rejecting the risk behavior (e.g., more subjects said "they will laugh at me if I decline the offer" than "they will like me if I accept"). Doing a behavior once versus regularly evoked somewhat different consequences. For example, the social reactions of peers were mentioned more frequently for "accepting an offer to smoke marijuana at a party," whereas decreased mental function was mentioned more frequently for "using marijuana." These open-ended questions produced quite different consequences than appeared in the fixed lists of earlier studies (e.g., the proportion of positive consequences was lower here).

One of the few developmental differences was that the parents more frequently mentioned risk-amplifying behaviors like "go on to harder drugs," "lead to crimes," and "go to wilder and wilder parties." Possibly, parents have a longer time horizon or a fuller understanding of how one thing can lead to another (Greene, 1986; Nurmi, 1991). Such differences might tip the scales for individuals who otherwise view decisions quite similarly.

Probabilities

Of course, decisions should depend on probability, not just possibility. It is uncommon, however, for investigators to elicit quantitative estimates of likelihood. Rather, one finds verbal quantifiers ("risky," "highly probable") that are known to be ambiguous (Beyth-Marom, 1982; Budescu & Wallsten, 1995): The same term can mean different things to different people in the same context or to a single individual across contexts.

One study with quantitative estimates was Quadrel, Fischhoff, and Davis's (1993a) examination of the *invulnerability hypothesis*: the presumed tendency of adolescents to take risks because they underestimate the probability of bad consequences happening to them (Burger & Burns, 1988; Rotheram-Borus & Koopman, 1990; Whitely & Hern, 1991). Elkind (1967) postulated that adolescents held such beliefs because of their special egocentrism and "personal fable" of their indestructibility. However, little empirical evidence supports these constructs (Dolcini et al., 1989; Enright, Lapsley, & Shukla, 1979; Lapsley, Milstead, Quintana, Flannery, & Buss, 1986), whereas there is an extensive literature demonstrating adult perceptions of invulnerability (Weinstein, 1980, 1987).

Quadrel et al. (1993a) used a response scale that was linear for probabilities from 1% to 100% and log for probabilities from 10^{-2} to 10^{-6} in order to facilitate the expression of very small probabilities. Subjects were trained in its use, with examples drawn from nonrisky topics. They were drawn from populations of low-risk teens, their parents, and high-risk teens (in group homes and juvenile centers). They evaluated the probability that each of eight possible adverse events would occur to themselves, an acquaintance, a close friend, and their parent or child (as appropriate). Four events were relatively high in perceived controllability (e.g., unplanned pregnancy), and four were relatively low (e.g., sickness from air pollution).

No group showed much *absolute* invulnerability in the sense of assessing a personal probability of risk as at or near zero. In terms of *relative* invulnerability, subjects typically assigned the same probability to themselves and to others. Where they did make a distinction, respondents were almost twice as likely to assign lower risk probabilities to themselves than to the targets (36.8% versus 20%). This tendency was strongest among the adults, primarily because they viewed their own risk to be less than that of their children, a belief that the children shared – and that may well have been accurate. In most respects, the thought processes of teens were not dramatically different from those of adults.

Quadrel et al.'s study did not allow evaluation of the absolute accuracy of these beliefs – a task that few investigators have attempted (e.g., Jonah & Dawson, 1982; Namerow, Lawton, & Philiber, 1987). Other studies have shown the limits of adults' quantitative risk estimates. For example, the estimated frequencies of various causes of death are biased in ways that reflect their frequency in newspapers reports (Combs & Slovic, 1979). The overestimation of overreported causes of death is an example of a general tendency to assess frequency or probability by the availability of the relevant instances (Tversky & Kahneman, 1973).

Eliciting quantitative estimates requires attention to methodological details, especially when subjects are inexperienced with the task (Fischhoff, Furby, & Morgan, 1987; Linville, Fischer, & Fischhoff, 1993; Poulton, 1988). One cannot just ask people to guess at a risk estimate in whatever unit statisticians happen to have reported it. For example, Fischhoff and MacGregor (1983) found that different response modes produced 100-fold differences in estimates of the probability of dying from a disease (e.g., tuberculosis) once afflicted by it.[2] After having drivers estimate the frequency and the probability of traffic accidents, injuries, and fatalities, Finn and Bragg (1986) concluded that "Generalized questions about the number of persons killed or injured . . . produce highly erroneous estimates. Estimates of the percentage of drivers involved in an accident per annum produce less erroneous overestimates" (p. 293). Precise questions, possibly using multiple methods, are needed to determine the role of risk beliefs in decisions about risk behaviors.

Values

Unlike probability estimates, for which relatively objective comparison values can often be computed, the value of consequences is inherently subjective. Adults may disapprove of teens' values. However, that is a very different kind of criticism than faulting teens for not knowing the frequencies recorded in public health statistics. Few studies have elicited quantitative assessments of values, using any of decision theory's normatively acceptable procedures. Surveys sometimes ask about the "importance" of different decision criteria (e.g., pay versus benefits versus fulfillment – in choosing a job; style versus performance versus safety – in buying a car). However, importance depends on context: Pay matters to the extent that jobs vary on that dimension. Investigators can only guess at how respondents interpreted that context. People are often described in terms of one particular kind of importance judgment: their degree of *risk aversion*. However, that term is ill-defined when all options entail some degree of some kind of risk. People might show a relative aversion to one kind of risk (e.g., the chance of physical harm) over another kind (e.g., the chance of social censure). However, more complex procedures are needed to measure importance and risk aversion (e.g., Keeney & Raiffa, 1976; von Winterfeldt & Edwards, 1986).

Unlike a public health perspective, which presumes to know what is right for people, decision theory asks first what values individuals are attempting to realize. For example, teen pregnancy and parenthood are socially undesirable phenomena. They reflect the outcomes of decisions such as whether to become sexually active, whether to use contraceptives, and whether to maintain a relationship. Adolescents who particularly value children might (rationally) be more accepting of sexual intercourse and childbirth outside of marriage, as might those who do not value the career and educational opportunities that might be foregone (Furstenberg, 1987; Johnson, Lay, & Wilbrandt, 1988; Ortiz & Nuttall, 1987). In cases where consequences are valued differently by adolescents and their society, more rational decisions might produce more deviant results.

Cognitive Processes: How Do Adolescents Think?

Determining whether beliefs and values are combined rationally requires a shift from knowledge to processes. The research focus moves from "Do adolescents know as much as adults, or as much as they should know about the risks of . . .?" to "Do they reason logically?" and "Can they think about abstract possibilities?"

Piaget held that cognitive development involved a series of stages, culminating in the formal operational stage, allowing deductive reasoning about the form of an argument rather just its substance (Piaget & Inhelder, 1969). Piaget believed that this transition occurs gradually between ages 12 and 16. Even if the details of this claim are controversial (e.g., Arlin, 1977; Basseches, 1984; Commons, Richards, & Armon, 1984; Neimark, 1979; Ward & Overton, 1990), the final stage involves mastery of four skills germane to effective decision making (Flavell, 1985; Keating, 1980).

> *Complexity*: The ability to consider many elements simultaneously, systematically, and exhaustively – allowing one to integrate the diverse components of a decision.
> *Thinking about possibilities*: The ability to imagine abstract possibilities – allowing one to think further into the future and consider long-term consequences.
> *Solving problems*: The ability to generate possible solutions to problems – allowing one to produce and evaluate decision options.[3]

Perspective-taking ability or relativistic thinking: The ability to recognize
others' perspectives – allowing one to consider and anticipate their actions
and values.

Overton and Byrnes (1991) added a fifth skill, claiming that adolescents
learn a "third-order level of abstraction," the ability to think logically about
thought and even systems of thought – allowing one to reflect on one's
decision-making processes.

Scholars adopting this general perspective still disagree over the time period
during which formal operations develop (e.g., Martorano, 1977). For example,
whereas early studies found that relativistic thinking developed late in
adolescence, recent research has found it in the majority of high school
students (Leadbeater, 1991). On the other hand, Keating (1980) holds that
only about 50–60% of 18- to 20-year-olds in Western countries use formal
operations at all. Others argue that most adolescents can use formal operations with familiar topics and tasks (Overton, Ward, Noverck, Black, &
O'Brien, 1987).

Information-processing theories provide an alternative view of cognitive
change between childhood and adolescence (Case, 1985; Sternberg & Powell,
1983). They picture the human mind as a complex system for taking in, storing,
and using information. As children mature into adolescents, the capacity of
this system appears to increase along with increased knowledge (Brown,
Bransford, Ferrara, & Campione, 1983), more sophisticated control processes
(Butterfield & Belmont, 1977), and more rapid, automatic processing (Flavell,
1985).

Relatively little research has examined these thought processes in decision
making. In one notable exception, Klayman (1985) had 12-year-olds solve a
multiattribute decision problem, selecting among bicycles varying on several
features. He found that they adopted systematic procedures, showing such
processes as compensation, contingency elimination, and multipass searches.
They also adapted their strategies to task complexity. Their general approach
and strategies resembled those of adults.

In another empirical study, Ross (1981) had adolescents make decisions
about six different issues (e.g., drinking and smoking). Ross found constancy
across the early adolescent years in the skills of identifying alternative courses
of action, selecting appropriate consequences, evaluating alternatives, and
summarizing information. Adolescents were not compared to adults. Reyna,
Woodruff, and Brainerd (1987) found that adolescents may be more im-
pressed by single-case histories than adults when estimating probabilities
(Nisbett & Ross, 1980).

These studies give a mixed picture of adolescent decision-making competence. Generally speaking, from midadolescence, teens seem capable of the
imperfect performance observed in adults subjected to similar cognitive tasks.
Further research is needed on how well adolescents have mastered the cogni-

tive skills involved in decision making and how well they perform to their cognitive capacity.

Metacognition: What Do Adolescents Think About Their Beliefs and Thought?

Knowing the extent of one's knowledge is essential to using it effectively. It tells one when to take confident action, when to hedge one's bets, and when to look for help. Younger children have been found to think primarily in terms of the objects and events that they have experienced, with gradually increasing reflection on thought itself (Flavell, 1985; Keating, 1980; Miller, Kessel, & Flavell, 1970). The metacognitions of adolescents have seldom been studied, especially in ways with direct connection to decision making.

In decision theory, a standard measure of the appropriateness of confidence in knowledge is *calibration* (Lichtenstein, Fischhoff, & Phillips, 1982; Winkler & Murphy, 1968; Yates, 1989). Formally, beliefs are well calibrated if, over the long run, people are correct xx% (e.g., 90%) of the time when they believe that they have a .xx probability (e.g., .90) of being correct.

The most common task in calibration studies uses two-alternative questions (e.g., Rome is (1) north of New York or (2) south of New York). Respondents first choose the more likely answer and then assess the probability that their choice is correct. Responses are grouped into the ranges .5–.59, .6–.69, . . . , .9–.99, 1.0. The proportion of correct choices is calculated for each range. Many studies have found that people are moderately sensitive to how much they know, with an overall tendency toward overconfidence with difficult tasks and underconfidence with easy ones (Lichtenstein et al., 1982). The notable exception is experts who have the conditions needed to learn this skill (i.e., repeated practice with prompt, unambiguous feedback), like weather forecasters and bridge players.

Quadrel, Fischhoff, Fischhoff, and Halpern (1993b) applied this methodology to confidence in beliefs about risks, using 100 two-alternative questions about risk behaviors (e.g., cocaine affects the user more quickly when it is (1) injected or (2) smoked). Middle-class young teens and parents responded similarly to one another and to earlier results (i.e., they showed moderate sensitivity and tended toward overconfidence on moderately difficult items). Thus, these particular metacognitive capabilities seem to have been consolidated by early adolescence.

A group of at-risk youths (recruited from treatment centers and group homes) had many fewer correct answers, despite their much greater direct experience with risk behaviors as well as recent participation in courses on the topic. As would be expected with a more difficult task, they were also more overconfident. For example, only 45% of the at-risk teens knew that having a beer would affect their driving as much as drinking a shot of vodka. However, their mean judged probability of having answered this question correctly was 84%. People who exaggerate how much they know may unwittingly expose themselves to risks. One possible explanation of the group differences is that high-risk teens have poorer metacognitive skills, in the sense of less ability to think critically about the bases of their beliefs. They may also differ in their willingness to think critically. Their personal experiences may create an illusion of understanding, leading them to feel inappropriately like experts, as they misinterpret what they see on the street and learn in class. An artifactual explanation is that the high-risk teens in the Quadrel et al. (1993b) study were more likely to have interpreted questions differently than the (middle-class) investigators, leading the high-risk teens' responses to be scored inappropriately more often. The following section considers more thoroughly the possibility of miscommunication by middle-class adult educators and investigators.

Implications

Methodology

In principle, each component of the decision process can be investigated with either open-ended or structured measurement procedures (e.g., "What are the possible decision options?" versus "Circle the possible decision options available to you"). Open-ended approaches allow a broader range of perspectives to emerge and reduce the risk of formulating issues in ways that are at odds with respondents' intuitive representations. Arguably, they come closer to simulating the circumstances of actual decisions. As a result, open-ended studies might be necessary precursors to more structured ones, identifying the issues and formulations to be used in them.

For example, the National Adolescent Student Health Survey (American School Health Association, 1988) contained the following structured question: "How much do you think people risk harming themselves (physically or in other ways) if they drink alcoholic beverages occasionally?" Each term in this question is potentially ambiguous. Subjects must decide what *harm, alcoholic beverages, drink,* and *occasionally* mean. Unless, fortuitously, all subjects resolve these ambiguities in the same way, any variance in their answers may reflect differing interpretations rather than differing beliefs. Moreover, even if subjects agreed, investigators would still have to guess what those consensual interpretations are. Table 5.1 shows one question from a large-sample survey sponsored by the National Center for Health Statistics. Following it are alternative definitions of the quantity and intensity of this risk behavior. If one believed that this behavior posed any risk at all, one's risk estimate would depend on what one inferred regarding quantity and intensity (among other features). The numbers in parentheses indicate the percentages of subjects, in a relatively homogeneous population (juniors at an Ivy League college), who

Table 5.1. *Interpretations of AIDS risk questions*

How likely do you think it is that a person would get AIDS or the AIDS virus from sharing plates, forks, or glasses with someone who has AIDS?

How did you interpret "sharing plates, forks, or glasses with someone who has AIDS?"

_____ Sharing utensils during a meal (e.g., passing them around, eating off one another's plates). (81.8%)
_____ Using the same utensils after they have been washed. (10.9%)
_____ I was uncertain about the interpretation. (5.8%)
_____ Multiple interpretations. (1.5%)

Did you interpret "sharing plates, forks, or glasses with someone who has AIDS" as

_____ Occurring on a single occasion? (39.1%)
_____ Occurring on several occasions? (19.6%)
_____ Occurring routinely? (27.5%)
_____ I was uncertain about the interpretation. (12.3%)
_____ Multiple interpretations. (1.4%)

How likely do you think it is that a person would get AIDS or the AIDS virus from having sex with a person who has AIDS?

How did you interpret "having sex with a person who has AIDS?"

_____ Having vaginal intercourse without a condom. (72.5%)
_____ Having vaginal intercourse with a condom. (4.3%)
_____ Having other kinds of sex. (6.5%)
_____ I was uncertain about the interpretation. (6.7%)
_____ Multiple interpretations. (8.0%)

Did you interpret "having sex with a person who has AIDS" as

_____ Occurring on a single occasion? (61.6%)
_____ Occurring on several occasions? (22.5%)
_____ Occurring on many occasions? (7.2%)
_____ I was uncertain about the interpretation. (5.1%)
_____ Multiple interpretations. (3.6%)

Note: Entries are the percentage of subjects (in a sample of 135 students at an Ivy League college) who reported having inferred each definition of the phrase when they had answered a question about the risk that it entailed. The response mode comprised five verbal quantifiers: definitely not possible, very unlikely, somewhat unlikely, somewhat likely, and very likely.

Source: *International Journal of Forecasting*, Vol. 10, B. Fischhoff, what forecasts (seem to) mean, pp. 387–403, copyright © 1994, with kind permission from Elsevier Science B.V., Amsterdam, the Netherlands.

endorsed each alternative after having answered the question on a previous page. The range of opinion precludes a unitary interpretation of their pooled risk estimates.

The options in Table 5.1 were the investigators' invention. They might have neglected other possibilities or suggested alternatives that never would have occurred to subjects. Quadrel, Fischhoff, and Palmgren (1994) adopted a more open-ended strategy: Teens thought aloud as they answered risk-estimation questions that were deliberately ambiguous (at the level of a typical survey), for example, "What is the probability that a person will have an accident while drinking and driving?" or "What is the probability that a person will get AIDS from having sex with someone who has AIDS?" The teens were drawn from both low-risk and high-risk settings (as defined earlier).

Table 5.2 shows the framework for coding the factors that subjects produced, illustrated with examples from the drinking-and-driving question. There was considerable variation in the assumptions that individual subjects made about unstated elements of these risks (e.g., how much driving, what kind of driving, how serious an accident). As a result, they were, in effect, answering different questions from one another and from any investigator's expectations. Their assumptions revealed something about their implicit theories of risk. For example, most subjects spontaneously asked about the frequency of most risk behaviors. However, teens did not ask about the frequency of sex as a determinant of the risks of pregnancy and of AIDS. A follow-up study varied individual factors within highly specified risk questions. Subjects were most responsive to those factors that had been cited most frequently as relevant in the open-ended study. Thus, they seemed to have consistent underlying theories of risk, which emerged in different tasks.

Even clear, specific terms can bias responses. For example, the following question was posed to college students: "Will you be willing to allow a condom to be labeled effective if . . ." For half the students, the sentence ended with "it had a 95 percent success rate in stopping transmission of the AIDS virus," whereas the other half was presented with "it had a 5 percent failure rate in stopping transmission of the AIDS virus." In the first sample, 88% allowed the condom to be labeled effective, compared to 42% in the second sample (Linville et al., 1993). An extensive literature documents the changes in expressed values accompanying subtle variations in how questions are framed (Dawes, 1988; Fischhoff, 1991; Hogarth, 1982; Tversky & Kahneman, 1981).

Once open-ended responses have been collected, they must be coded. That process depends on the investigator's theoretical orientation. Much behavioral decision-making research examines behavior in terms of the five normative stages listed earlier. This strategy was followed, for example, in Beyth-Marom et al.'s (1993) study of the perceived consequences of risky behaviors and Quadrel et al.'s (1994) study of the interpretation of probability statements.[4]

Any normative model is, however, mute regarding the substance of the thinking at each stage. Table 5.2 offers one conceptualization of the domain of content for probability statements about risk behaviors. Its overall structure reflects a logical analysis of the causal elements that could affect risk levels. Its implementation involved coding all responses, regardless of whether they found any support in the scientific literatures. This strategy allows characteriz-

Table 5.2. *Coding framework*

Framework element	Variable categories	Example variables
Behavior	Dose	Amount of alcohol consumed
	Amount	
	Potency	
	Method	
Other behaviors	Risk buffers	Amount of food eaten
	Risk amplifiers	Other drugs consumed
	Time related	Night or day; day of the week
	Place related	Where alcohol was consumed
Actor	Physical	Tolerance of alcohol
	Cognitive	Awareness of effects of alcohol
	Social-psychological	Mood
	Material	Wealth
	Spiritual	Faith
	Skill	Driving skill
	Character	Responsible; mature
	Age	
	Gender	
	Genetic history	
	Status	
	Luck	
	Motivation	
	Self, other	
Context	Social	
	General, cultural	Drinking norms
	Family	Family approval
	Peers, others	Peer approval
	Environmental	Road conditions
Risk outcome	Social reactions	Get in trouble
	Personal effects	
	Physical	Injury
	Psychological	Worry, guilt
	Cognitive-physiological	Kill brain cells
	Cognitive-psychological	Can't think
	Material	Lose car, lose license
	Accidents	Get in a wreck while high
	Lifestyle	Become a bum
	Complex	Get high
	Effects on others	Hurt your friends, family
	Behaviors	Use more, do heavier drugs
	Severity	

Source: Quadrel, Fischhoff, and Palmgren (1994).

ing lay beliefs in terms of their consistency with expert beliefs. It has been used to describe people's *mental models* of many domains (Bostrom, Fischhoff, & Morgan, 1992; Chi, 1992; Ericsson & Simon, 1984; Gentner & Stevens, 1983; Reason, 1990). It assumes that people have pieces of relevant knowledge on a topic, which they apply when thinking about it. Mental models with many correct items can still contain latent problems that emerge when actions are taken (e.g., failure to realize that the risks of sexuality are amplified by the frequency of sexual acts). Or they may be undermined by "peripheral" beliefs (e.g., the small residual risk of AIDS in the blood supply), which, although accurate, detract attention from more critical issues (e.g., the illusion of being able to determine someone's AIDS risk status).

Mental-model descriptions of the processes controlling risks address several elements of decision-making processes. They can illuminate which options seem possible, what consequences might follow, and how likely they seem. They do not consider how consequences are weighted or how beliefs and desires are combined.

In an effort to get a fuller description, Fischhoff, Furby, Jacobs-Qudrel, and Richardson (1991; Fischhoff, 1996) asked 105 girls aged 13–17 to talk at length about recent difficult decisions in their lives. Responses were coded in terms of the content, structure, and process. For example, in terms of content, none of the 1,700-plus decisions that the teens mentioned dealt with drinking and driving, and very few dealt with sex. Many concerned relations with friends or parents, creating the conditions under which risk decisions are made (but without having the risks in focus). Options that are not mentioned may not be analyzed as thoroughly – as seen in the neglect of opportunity costs (benefits foregone by not adopting an option). In terms of structure, most decisions were described by a single option (whether to go to a party where alcohol would be served) rather than by the two or more options that the normative model prescribes. In terms of process, teens were much more likely to report listening to music than reading health communications (or anything else) as an aid to difficult decisions.

Understanding what teens know, how they think, and how they evaluate their own knowledge requires a variety of methods, with full knowledge of their respective strengths and pitfalls. An incomplete or biased picture will reduce the ability to deal effectively with the issues of adolescence, whether at the level of the individual – with educational interventions – or of the society – when determining the role of teens in it. The next two sections discuss the implications of this partial picture for these domains.

Education

Two strategies have been adopted to improving adolescents' risk decisions: (1) communicating information and (2) teaching higher-order thinking skills.

Communication. The first step in designing communications is selecting their content. That process should begin with a descriptive account of current beliefs and a normative analysis of what is worth knowing. Unfortunately, the choice of information in many communications seems less deliberate, reflecting some experts' intuitive notion of what people do and should know.

Value-of-information analysis is the general term for techniques that determine the sensitivity of decisions to different information (Raiffa, 1968). For example, Merz, Fischhoff, Mazur, and Fischbeck (1993) examined one medical decision, whether to undergo carotid endarterectomy. Both this procedure, which involves scraping out an artery leading to the head, and its alternatives have a variety of possible effects. These effects have been studied extensively, providing quantitative risk estimates. The value-of-information analysis showed that a few, but only a few, of the possible side effects should affect the preferred decision for any significant proportion of patients. Arguably, communications focused on these few side effects would make better use of patients' attention than laundry lists of undifferentiated possibilities. Focused on teens, such analyses might help compose messages with risk estimates about contraceptives or driving.

At times, though, people do not face explicit decisions. Rather, they are in a predecisional state, just trying to understand the processes involved in creating and controlling risks. In such cases, communications should be directed at those issues that are most important to science and least understood by individuals, as determined by mental-models studies of their beliefs. Bridging the gap between lay mental models and expert models could require adding missing concepts, correcting erroneous beliefs, strengthening correct beliefs, and deemphasizing peripheral ones (Morgan, Fischhoff, Bostrom, Lave, & Atman, 1992). Particular attention should be paid to the critical "bugs" in people's beliefs: cases where they confidently hold incorrect beliefs that could lead to inappropriate actions – or lack enough confidence in correct beliefs.

The specific approach would depend on, among other things, how much time is available for communication, how well the decisions are formulated, and what scientific risk information exists. For example, "bugs" in mental models might be focal facts for brief public service announcements. Such surprising facts (e.g., the dependence of pregnancy risk on frequency of sex, the equivalence of different forms of alcohol, the addictiveness of cigarettes) might grab recipients' attention and change their behavior. Contrasting lay and expert perceptions of the full set of processes governing risks might be better suited to preparing explanatory brochures or health curricula. Value-of-information analysis might suit recurrent decisions with well-characterized options and consequences (e.g., in medicine). In all cases, it is important to remember the imperfections in expert knowledge. Claiming undue certitude can undermine one's credibility.

Education in Reasoning and Decision Making. A focal topic in instructional psychology is cognitive competence (Glaser, 1982; Lochhead & Clement, 1979). The perception of a fast-changing modern world, where facts are rapidly outdated by new developments, has made decision-making skills a key competence (Fletcher & Wooddell, 1981; Gelatt, 1962). The transitions of adolescence create a special decision-making load, in addition to the general challenges of living in a modern society. Decisions regarding risk-taking behaviors are part of this growth in autonomy.

This need has prompted a proliferation of curricula for improving young people's decision-making skills (Baron & Brown, 1991). Beyth-Marom, Fischhoff, Quadrel, and Furby (1991) reviewed all curricula with some empirical evaluation. These curricula were divided into four categories along two dichotomous dimensions: (1) their focus (social or cognitive skills) and (2) their scope (general or specific). General social programs teach skills for solving interpersonal problems, such as coping strategies and assertiveness techniques. Specific social programs focus on particular problems, such as smoking and sexuality. In cognitive programs, thinking skills are the focus of interest and not just mediating variables. General cognitive programs teach decision making as one of many thinking skills; specific cognitive programs teach decision making per se.

Unfortunately, the evaluation studies all seemed flawed in ways that precluded reaching firm conclusions regarding their effect on decision making. Many of the curricula were produced with great care and imagination (and sometimes considerable expense). Typically, they provided training in the main steps of the normative process of decision making. However, most ignored the descriptive literatures regarding adolescent decision making. Exploiting that literature, under the guidance of focused evaluations, might make a general contribution to reducing adolescents' risk behaviors.

Politics

Until recently, few writers focused on adolescents' rights. However, two review chapters appeared in the 1991 *Encyclopedia of Adolescence* (Langer, 1991; Melton, 1991). Melton (1991) attributed the previous lack of interest to the fact that adolescence was a concept foreign to law. A 17-year-old, like a 17-day-old, was a legal "infant." Indeed, the U.S. Supreme Court had not considered minors persons under the Constitution until the landmark case of *In re* Gault (1967), which guaranteed juveniles the procedural rights necessary for "fundamental fairness."

More recent court decisions create an inconsistent picture (Moshman, 1993). For example, in *Hazelwood School District v. Kuhlmeier* (1988), the U.S. Supreme Court ruled 5-3 that a public high school may censor articles written by students for the school newspaper, arguing that students are immature and hence must be protected from one another. In contrast, in *Board of Education of Westside Community Schools v. Mergens* (1990), the U.S. Supreme Court ruled 8–1 that a public high school permitting any noncurriculum student group to meet on its premises must permit all such groups, including religiously oriented ones. Here the Court argued that students are mature enough to understand that permitting use on a nondiscriminatory basis does not constitute endorsement. "If one is thinking in terms of freedom of expression or religious liberty, one is likely to invoke the rights of the individuals involved and thus emphasize their maturity. If one is thinking in terms of shielding immature minds from controversy or from religious inculcation, one tends to invoke the need to protect students from each other and thus to stress their immaturity" (Moshman, 1993; see also Weithorn & Campbell, 1982).

These decisions reflect empirical assertions regarding the nature of adolescents' cognitive processes. As such, they should be informed by the full body of relevant research (Gardner, Scherer, & Tester, 1989; Lewis, 1981). According to Moshman (1993), the differences between adolescents and adults are modest compared to the differences among adolescents or among adults of any given age (see also Overton, 1990; Schauble & Glaser, 1990). Our review of decision-making competence also found small differences between adolescents and adults, at least under the conditions of research tasks.

A recurrent theme in this chapter is that poor measurement and incomplete conceptualization can blur the role of cognitive processes in teens' decision making. As a result, their behavior seems less orderly, less related to their beliefs, and less responsive to health communications. Inadequate attention to these issues does more than just impede the progress of science. Poorly documented claims about the incompetence of adolescents encourage frustration with their behavior and paternalistic solutions for dealing with it. If teens are seen as impervious to information, it may be easier to deny them the right to govern their own actions, to view them as a problem (rather than as a resource), and to interfere with the experimentation that is part of the business of adolescence. Such claims make teens, rather than society, responsible for teens' problems. They also place adults in the flattering position of knowing what is right (Baumrind, 1968; Fischhoff, 1992b; Gardner et al., 1989). They short-circuit the detailed research and conversation needed to understand teens' predicament and help them through it.

Conclusion

A full cognitive account of teen decisions must consider how its components are perceived, how those perceptions are processed, and how those processes are themselves understood. If teens' choices are ill advised, the failings may lie in any (or all) of these tasks, each subject to somewhat different interventions. For example, teens might overlook options that reduce the penalties for refusing risk behaviors. That might explain the success of life-skills training programs that teach the "refusal skills" needed to devise socially adroit ways to avoid taking risks (e.g., Botvin, 1986; Schinke & Gilchrist, 1984). Or teens might have faulty beliefs about the consequences of the options they consider; that would suggest communications focused on the "bugs" in their mental models – misconceptions that have escaped correction despite the many communications directed at teens. Or adolescents might reject the values leading to adult-approved behaviors; if so, interventions should promote other values, either in general or regarding particular decisions. For example, agreeing to drive teens home from parties, with no questions asked, changes the trade-offs in those specific decisions; over some period of time, it might change broader trade-offs (e.g., parent–teen relationships).

Or adolescents may just have difficulty making sense of complex decisions and keeping track of their details. As a result, they may resort to quicker, less thoughtful solutions. At the margin, such last-minute decision making may be disproportionately influenced by transient, visceral incentives (e.g., sexual drives). In that case, poor decision making might lead to impulsive decisions, adding to any general tendency toward impulsivity. Suitable interventions might attempt either to teach decision making as a general cognitive skill (Baron & Brown, 1991) or to preprogram choices, so that teens would not have to make decisions under real-time pressures.

The theoretical and policy implications of these studies depend on the generality of the phenomena that they document. Ultimately, that is a matter for future research. In the meantime, one might look for features that might induce unrepresentative behavior. For example, the research settings might encourage subjects to impress the investigators by considering issues that they might otherwise ignore; the settings might insulate subjects from social pressures and isolate them from social support. The studies may create time pressures that are greater or less than those of real life.

There is considerable debate among decision theorists about whether these conditions enhance or impair performance (Arkes & Hammond, 1986, pt. IX; Kahneman et al., 1982, pts. VIII and X). One critical developmental question is whether these factors affect adults and adolescents differently. If so, then similar performance in experiments might still mask differences in everyday life. Many speculations are possible (Fischhoff, 1992b). Research is needed to discipline them with fact.

A second critical developmental question is whether similar performance deficits have similar consequences for adults and adolescents. Generally speaking, a problem can cause more damage when decisions have irreversible consequences, when stakes are large, when decision makers lack the resources needed to recover from failures, when the domain is unfamiliar (requiring heavier reliance on judgment), and when decision makers lack structural protections (shielding them from the opportunity to make decisions that place them at risk). For example, the same degree of perceived invulnerability should create more actual vulnerability for those who rely on more such judgments. The same rate of poor decisions will create more problems for those who make more decisions. Those might be teens, who are determining what to do about many aspects of their lives. By contrast, adults often run much of their lives by routine, choosing among modest variations on habitual responses acquired through trial and error, where they cannot go too far wrong. Yet, they, too, sometimes work without a net, as when they ponder their first equity investment, extramarital liaison, power tool, or independent presidential candidate.

As with other conceptual frameworks, decision theory has limitations. One is a temptation to assume, without adequate evidence, that people follow the model of optimal decision making (leading to the choice in their own self-defined best interests). Although that assumption is not made in the account presented here, it can be found in theories falling closer to the economic roots of decision theory.[5] With its cognitive focus, the decision theoretic approach pays less attention to the roles of emotion (Fiske & Taylor, 1990; Janis & Mann, 1979), self-control (Thaler & Shefrin, 1981), and social forces (Bronfenbrenner, 1986; Majoribanks, 1979). Those factors can, in principle, be given cognitive representations. For example, parental pressure can be treated as a consequence of a decision, namely, the censure or approval that would follow from it (Beyth-Marom et al., 1993). Nonetheless, a verbal summary is not the same as the thing itself. Clearly, multimethod approaches are necessary, including open-ended ones that allow the discovery of decision variables not anticipated by investigators.

The methodological challenges to applying a cognitive perspective include specifying the consequence and the behavioral options, measuring the perceived probabilities and values, and identifying the information-processing strategies in combining these elements. These suggest limits to the perspective, as well as the complex reality facing teens. One potential complication that is largely missing in this literature is individual differences. One reason is that persistent efforts have seldom found individual difference measures with cross-situational validity (Bromiley & Curley, 1992). A second reason is cognitive psychologists' tendency to assume similarity in *how* people think while acknowledging differences in *what* people believe. A third reason is a predisposition to look for differences in the circumstances of people's decisions, within which similar cognitive processes are applied.

One cannot study everything at once. Behavioral decision theory examines some dimensions of difference while ignoring others. It tries to study the cognitive portion of decision making as clearly as possible. That is a necessary condition for determining how big – or small – a role cognitions play in those decisions and perhaps for expanding that role and helping teens make more effective decisions.

Notes

1 Two options were considered different if there were plausible reasons why women would view them as having different probabilities of producing relevant consequences. Those consequences were identified in another study, asking similar women to list important ones (Furby, Fischhoff, & Morgan, 1991).
2 Specifically, the estimates were much larger when people were asked, for example, "For each person who dies of mumps, how many have it and survive?" than when asked "Of each 100,000 people who had mumps, how many died?" As in other studies, the relative risk from different sources was largely independent of response mode.
3 "The generation of hypotheses out of sets of possibilities, the capacity to reason deductively from universal possibilities to particular realities, and the ability to compute systematically and exhaustively the relationships in any system, all constitute [adolescent] problem solving" (Overton & Byrnes, 1991, p. 154).
4 Fischhoff (1992a) summarizes a research program that looks at each component regarding decisions about reducing the risk of sexual assault.
5 A slavish commitment to rationality is often imputed to the field of decision making by people who have but a passing familiarity with it. Such a caricature provides an easy basis for dismissing the approach as implausible.

References

American School Health Association, Association for the Advancement of Health Education, and the Society for Public Health Education. (1988). *National Adolescent Student Health Survey: A report on the health of America's youth.* Oakland, CA: Third Party.
Arkes, H. R., & Hammond, K. R. (Eds.). (1986). *Judgment and decision making: An interdisciplinary reader.* New York: Cambridge University Press.
Arlin, P. K. (1977). Piagetian operations in problem finding. *Developmental Psychology, 13,* 297–298.
Arnett, J. (1992). Reckless behavior in adolescence: A developmental perspective. *Developmental Review, 12,* 339–373.
Barnes, G. M. (1981). Drinking among adolescents: A subculture phenomenon or a model of adult behaviors? *Adolescence, 16,* 211–229.
Baron, J., & Brown, R. (Eds.). (1991). *Teaching decision making to adolescents.* Hillsdale, NJ: Erlbaum.
Basseches, M. (1984). *Dialectical thinking and adult development.* Norwood, NJ: Ablex.
Bauman, K. E. (1980). *Predicting adolescent drug use: Utility structure and marijuana.* New York: Praeger.
Bauman, K. E., & Bryan, E. S. (1983). Adolescent beer drinking: Subjective expected utility and gender differences. *Youth & Society, 15,* 157–170.
Bauman, K. E., Fisher, L. A., Bryan, E. S., & Chenoweth, R. L. (1984). Relationship between subjective expected utility and behavior: A panel study of adolescent cigarette smoking. *Addictive Behaviors, 9,* 121–136.
Bauman, K. E., Fisher, L. A., & Koch, G. G. (1988). External variables, subjective expected utility, and adolescent behavior with alcohol and cigarettes. *Journal of Applied Social Psychology, 19,* 789–804.
Bauman, K. E., & Udry, J. R. (1981). Subjective expected utility and adolescent sexual behavior. *Adolescence, 16,* 527–535.
Baumrind, D. (1968). Authoritarian vs. authoritative control. *Adolescence, 3,* 255–272.

Beyth-Marom, R. (1982). How probable is probable? Numerical translation of verbal probability expressions. *Journal of Forecasting, 1*, 257–269.

Beyth-Marom, R., Austin, L., Fischhoff, B., Palmgren, C., & Jacobs-Quadrel, M. J. (1993). Perceived consequences of risky behaviors: Adults and adolescents. *Developmental Psychology, 29*, 549–563.

Beyth-Marom, R., Fischhoff, B., Quadrel, M. J., & Furby, L. (1991). Teaching adolescents decision making. In J. Baron & R. Brown (Eds.), *Teaching decision making to adolescents* (pp. 19–60). Hillsdale, NJ: Erlbaum.

Board of Education of Westside Community Schools v. Mergens, 110 S.O. 2356 (1990).

Bostrom, A., Fischhoff, B., & Morgan, M. G. (1992). Characterizing mental models of hazardous processes: A methodology and an application to radon. *Journal of Social Issues, 48*(4), 85–100.

Botvin, G. J. (1986). Substance abuse prevention research: Recent developments and future directions. *Journal of School Health, 56*, 369–374.

Bromiley, P., & Curley, S. P. (1992). Individual differences in risk taking. In J. F. Yates (Ed.), *Risk-taking behavior* (pp. 88–132). Chichester, U.K.: Wiley.

Bronfenbrenner, U. (1986). Ecology of the family as a context for human development: Research perspectives. *Developmental Psychology, 22*, 723–742.

Brown, A., Bransford, J., Ferrara, R., & Campione, J. (1983). Learning, remembering, and understanding. In P. Mussen, J. H. Flavell, & E. M. Markman (Eds.), *Handbook of child psychology: Vol. 3. Cognitive development* (4th ed., pp. 77–166). New York: Wiley.

Budescu, D. F., & Wallsten, T. S. (1995). Processing linguistic probabilities: General principles and empirical evidence. In J. R. Busemeyer, R. Hastie, & D. L. Medin (Eds.), *Decision making from the perspective of cognitive psychology* (pp. 275–318). New York: Academic Press.

Burger, J. M., & Burns, L. (1988). The illusion of unique invulnerability and the use of effective contraception. *Personality and Social Psychology Bulletin, 14*, 264–270.

Butterfield, E., & Belmont, J. (1977). Assessing and improving the executive cognitive functions of mentally retarded people. In I. Bialer & M. Sternlicht (Eds.), *Psychological issues in mental retardation* (pp. 21–34). Chicago: Aldine-Atherton.

Camerer, C. (1981). General conditions for the success of bootstrapping models. *Organizational Behavior and Human Performance, 27*, 411–422.

Case, R. (1985). *Intellectual development: Birth to adulthood.* New York: Academic Press.

Chi, M. T. (1992). Conceptual change within and across ontological categories: Examples from learning and discovery in science. In R. Giere (Ed.), *Cognitive models of science: Minnesota studies in the philosophy of science* (pp. 129–186). Minneapolis: University of Minnesota Press.

Combs, B., & Slovic, P. (1979). Newspaper coverage of causes of death. *Journalism Quarterly, 56*, 832–849.

Commons, M. L., Richards, F. A., & Armon, C. (Eds.). (1984). *Beyond formal operations: Late adolescent and adult cognitive development.* New York: Praeger.

Dawes, R. M. (1988). *Rational choice in an uncertain world.* San Diego: Harcourt Brace Jovanovich.

Dawes, R. M., & Corrigan, B. (1974). Linear models in decision making. *Psychological Bulletin, 81*, 95–106.

Dawes, R. M., Faust, D., & Meehl, P. (1989). Clinical versus actuarial judgment. *Science, 243*, 1668–1674.

Dolcini, M. M., Cohn, L. D., Adler, N. E., Millstein, S. G., Irwin, C. E., Kegeles, S. M., & Stone, G. C. (1989). Adolescent egocentrism and feelings of invulnerability: Are they related? *Journal of Early Adolescence, 9*, 409–418.

Dryfoos, J. G. (Ed.). (1990). *Adolescents at risk: Prevalence and prevention.* New York: Oxford University Press.

Elkind, D. (1967). Egocentrism in adolescence. *Child Development, 38*, 1025–1034.

Elkind, D. (1985). Egocentrism redux. *Developmental Review, 5*, 218–226.

Enright, R. D., Lapsley, D. K., & Shukla, D. G. (1979). Adolescent egocentrism in early and late adolescence. *Adolescence, 14,* 687–695.

Ericsson, K. A., & Simon, H. A. (1984). *Protocol analysis: Verbal reports as data.* Cambridge, MA: MIT Press.

Finn, P., & Bragg, B. W. E. (1986). Perception of the risk of an accident by young and older drivers. *Accident Analysis and Prevention, 18,* 289–298.

Fischhoff, B. (1988). Judgment and decision making. In R. J. Steinberg & E. E. Smith (Eds.), *The psychology of human thought* (pp. 153–187). New York: Cambridge University Press.

Fischhoff, B. (1991). Value elicitation: Is there anything in there? *American Psychologist, 46,* 835–847.

Fischhoff, B. (1992a). Giving advice: Decision theory perspectives on sexual assault. *American Psychologist, 47,* 577–588.

Fischhoff, B. (1992b). Risk taking: A developmental perspective. In J. F. Yates (Ed.), *Risk taking behavior* (pp. 133–162). Chichester, U.K.: Wiley.

Fischhoff, B. (1994). What forecasts (seem to) mean. *International Journal of Forecasting, 10,* 387–403.

Fischhoff, B. (1996). The real world: What good is it? *Organizational Behavior and Human Decision Processes, 65,* 232–248.

Fischhoff, B., Furby, L., Jacobs-Quadrel, M., & Richardson, E. (1991). *Adolescents' construal of choices: Are their decisions our "decisions?"* Unpublished manuscript, Carnegie Mellon University.

Fischhoff, B., Furby, L., & Morgan, M. (1987). Rape prevention: A typology and list of strategies. *Journal of Interpersonal Violence, 2,* 292–308.

Fischhoff, B., & MacGregor, D. (1983). Judged lethality: How much people seem to know depends upon how they are asked. *Risk Analysis, 3,* 229–236.

Fiske, S., & Taylor, S. (1990). *Social cognition* (2nd ed.). Reading, MA: Addison-Wesley.

Flavell, J. H. (1985). *Cognitive development* (2nd ed.). Englewood Cliffs, NJ: Prentice-Hall.

Fletcher, B. H., & Wooddell, G. (1981). Education for a changing world. *Journal of Thought, 16,* 21–32.

Furby, L., & Beyth-Marom, R. (1992). Risk taking in adolescence: A decision-making perspective. *Developmental Review, 12,* 1–44.

Furby, L., Fischhoff, B., & Morgan, M. (1990). Preventing rape: How people perceive the options for assault prevention. In E. Viano (Ed.), *The victimology research handbook* (pp. 227–259). New York: Garland.

Furby, L., Fischhoff, B., & Morgan, M. (1991). Rape prevention and self-defense: At what price? *Women's Studies International Forum, 14*(1/2), 49–62.

Furstenberg, F. (1987). Race differences in teenage sexuality, pregnancy, and adolescent child-bearing. *Milbank Quarterly, 65,* 381–403.

Gans, J., Blyth, D., Elster, A., & Gaveras, L. L. (1990). *America's adolescents: How healthy are they?* (Vol. 1). Chicago: American Medical Association.

Gardner, W., Scherer, D., & Tester, M. (1989). Asserting scientific authority: Cognitive development and adolescent legal rights. *American Psychologist, 44,* 895–902.

Gelatt, H. G. (1962). Decision making: A conceptual frame of reference for counseling. *Journal of Counseling Psychology, 9,* 240–242.

Gentner, D., & Stevens, A. L. (Eds.). (1983). *Mental models.* Hillsdale, NJ: Erlbaum.

Gettys, C. F., Pliske, R. M., Manning, C., & Casey, J. T. (1987). An evaluation of human act-generation performance. *Organizational Behavior and Human Decision Processes, 39,* 23–51.

Gilbert, M. A., Bauman, K. E., & Udry, J. R. (1986). A panel study of subjective expected utility for adolescent sexual behavior. *Journal of Applied Social Psychology, 16,* 745–756.

Glaser, R. (1982). Instructional psychology: Past, present and future. *American Psychologist, 37,* 292–305.

Goldberg, L. R. (1968). Simple models or simple processes? *American Psychologist, 23,* 483–496.

Greene, C. L. (1986). Future-time perspective in adolescence: The present of things future revisited. *Journal of Youth and Adolescence, 15,* 99–113.

Hammond, K. R., Hursch, C. J., & Todd, F. J. (1964). Analyzing the components of clinical inference. *Psychological Review, 71,* 438–456.

Hazelwood School District v. Kuhlmeier, 484 U.S. 260 (1988).

Hechinger, F. M. (1992). *Fateful choices.* New York: Carnegie Corporation of New York.

Hoffman, P. J. (1960). Paramorphic models representation of clinical judgment. *Psychological Bulletin, 57,* 116–131.

Hogarth, R. (Ed.). (1982). *New directions for methodology of social and behavioral science: Question framing and response consistency.* San Francisco: Jossey-Bass.

In re Gault, 387 U.S. 1 (1967).

Janis, I. L., & Mann, L. (1979). *Decision making: A psychological analysis of conflict, choice, and commitment.* New York: Free Press.

Jessor, R. (1987). Problem behavior theory, psychosocial development, and adolescent problem drinking. *British Journal of Addiction, 82,* 331–342.

Jessor, R., Donovan, J. E., & Costa, F. M. (1992). *Beyond adolescence.* New York: Cambridge University Press.

Jessor, R., & Jessor, S. L. (1977). *Problem behavior and psychosocial development: A longitudinal study of youth.* San Diego, CA: Academic Press.

Johnson, F., Lay, R., & Wilbrandt, M. (1988). Teenage pregnancy: Interventions and direction. *Journal of the American Medical Association, 80,* 145–152.

Johnston, L. D., O'Malley, P. M., & Bachman, J. G. (1994). *National survey results on drug use from Monitoring the Future Study, 1975–1993.* Washington, DC: U.S. Department of Health and Human Services.

Jonah, B. A. (1986). Accident risk and risk-taking behavior among young drivers. *Accident Analysis and Prevention, 16,* 255–271.

Jonah, B. A., & Dawson, N. E. (1982). *The National Vehicle Occupant Restraint Survey: Attitudes toward and use of restraints by Canadians* (Tech, Rep. TP3593E). Ottawa: Transport Canada, Road Safety Directorate.

Kahneman, D., Slovic, P., & Tversky, A. (Eds.). (1982). *Judgment under uncertainty: Heuristics and biases.* New York: Cambridge University Press.

Keating, D. P. (1980). Thinking processes in adolescence. In J. Adelson (Ed.), *Handbook of adolescent psychology* (pp. 211–246). New York: Wiley.

Keeney, R., & Raiffa, H. (1976). *Decisions with multiple objectives: Preferences and value trade offs.* New York: Wiley.

Klayman, J. (1985). Children's decision strategies and their adaptation to task characteristics. *Organizational Behavior and Human Decision Processes, 35,* 179–201.

Langer, D. H. (1991). Legal rights for adolescents as research subjects. In R. M. Lerner, A. C. Petersen, & J. Brooks-Gunn (Eds.), *Encyclopedia of adolescence* (pp. 591–593). New York: Garland.

Lapsley, D., Milstead, M., Quintana, S., Flannery, D., & Buss, R. (1986). Adolescent egocentrism and formal operations: Tests of a theoretical assumption. *Developmental Psychology, 22,* 800–807.

Leadbeater, B. (1991). Relativistic thinking in adolescence. In R. M. Lerner, A. C. Petersen, & J. Brooks-Gunn (Eds.), *Encyclopedia of adolescence* (Vol. 2, pp. 921–925). New York: Garland.

Lewis, C. C. (1991). How adolescents make decisions. *Child Development, 52,* 538–544.

Lichtenstein, S., Fischhoff, B., & Phillips, L. D. (1982). Calibration of probabilities: State of the art to 1980. In D. Kahneman, P. Slovic, & A. Tversky (Eds.), *Judgment under uncertainty: Heuristics and biases* (pp. 306–334). New York: Cambridge University Press.

Linville, P. W., Fischer, G. W., & Fischhoff, B. (1993). AIDS risk perceptions and decision biases. In J. B. Pryor & G. D. Reeder (Eds.), *The social psychology of HIV infection* (pp. 5–38). Hillsdale, NJ: Erlbaum.

Lochhead, J., & Clement, J. (Eds.). (1979). *Cognitive process instruction*. Philadelphia: Franklin Institute Press.

Majoribanks, L. (1979). *Families and their learning environments: An empirical analysis*. London: Routledge & Kegan Paul.

Martorano, S. C. (1977). A developmental analysis of performance on Piaget's formal operations tasks. *Developmental Psychology, 13*, 666–672.

Melton, G. B. (1991). Rights of adolescents. In R. M. Lerner, A. C. Petersen, & J. Brooks-Gunn (Eds.), *Encyclopedia of adolescence* (pp. 930–933). New York: Garland.

Merz, J., Fischhoff, B., Mazur, D. J., & Fischbeck, P. S. (1993). Decision-analytic approach to developing standards of disclosure for medical informed consent. *Journal of Toxics and Liability, 15*, 191–215.

Miller, P. H., Kessel, F. S., & Flavell, J. H. (1970). Thinking about people thinking about people thinking about . . . : A study of social cognitive development. *Child Development, 41*, 613–623.

Morgan, M. G., Fischhoff, B., Bostrom, A., Lave, L., & Atman, C. J. (1992). Communicating risk to the public. *Environmental Science and Technology, 26*, 2048–2056.

Moshman, D. (1993). Adolescent reasoning and adolescent rights. *Human Development, 36*, 27–40.

Namerow, P. B., Lawton, A. I., & Philiber, S. G. (1987). Teenagers' perceived and actual probabilities of pregnancy. *Adolescence, 22*, 475–485.

Neimark, E. D. (1979). Current status of formal operations research. *Human Development, 22*, 60–67.

Nisbett, R., & Ross, L. (1980). *Human inference: Strategies and shortcomings of social judgment*. Englewood Cliffs, NJ: Prentice-Hall.

Nurmi, J. E. (1991). How do adolescents see their future? *Developmental Review, 11*, 1–59.

Ortiz, C., & Nuttall, W. (1987). Adolescent pregancy: Effects of family support, education, and religion on the decision to carry or terminate among Puerto Rican teenagers. *Adolescence, 22*, 897–917.

Overton, W. F. (1990). Competence and procedures: Constraints on the development of logical reasoning. In W. F. Overton (Ed.), *Reasoning, necessity, and logic: Developmental perspectives* (pp. 1–32). Hillsdale, NJ: Erlbaum.

Overton, W. F., & Byrnes, J. P. (1991). Cognitive development. In R. M. Lerner, A. C. Petersen, & J. Brooks-Gunn (Eds.), *Encyclopedia of adolescence* (Vol. 1, pp. 151–156). New York: Garland Press.

Overton, W. F., Ward, S. L., Noverck, I. A., Black, J., & O'Brien, D. P. (1987). Form and content in the development of deductive reasoning. *Developmental Psychology, 23*, 22–30.

Piaget, J., & Inhelder, B. (1969). *The psychology of the child*. New York: Free Press.

Poulton, E. C. (1988). *Bias in quantifying judgment*. London: Erlbaum.

Quadrel, M. J., Fischhoff, B., & Davis, W. (1993a). Adolescent (in)vulnerability. *American Psychologist, 48*, 102–116.

Quadrel, M. J., Fischhoff, B., Fischhoff, M., & Halpern S. (1993b). *Calibration of adolescents' and adults' confidence judgments*. Unpublished manuscript.

Quadrel, M. J., Fischhoff, B., & Palmgren, C. (1994). Intuitive definitions of risk events. Unpublished manuscript.

Raiffa, H. (1968). *Decision analysis*. Reading, MA: Addison-Wesley.

Reason, J. (1990). *Human error*. Cambridge: Cambridge University Press.

Reyna, V. F., Woodruff, W. J., & Brainerd, C. (1987). *Attitude change in adults and adolescents: Moderation versus polarization, statistics versus case histories*. Unpublished manuscript.

Rogel, M. J., Zuehlke, M. E., Petersen, A. C., Tobin-Richards, M., & Shelton, M. (1980). Contraceptive behavior in adolescence: A decision-making perspective. *Journal of Youth and Adolescence, 9*, 491–501.

Ross, J. A. (1981). Improving adolescent decision-making skills. *Curriculum Inquiry, 11*, 279–295.

Rotheram-Borus, M. J., & Koopman, C. (1990). AIDS and adolescents. In R. Lerner, A. Peterson, & J. Brooks-Gunn (Eds.), *Encyclopedia of adolescence* (pp. 29–36). New York: Garland Press.

Schauble, L., & Glaser, R. (1990). Scientific thinking in children and adults. In D. Kuhn (Ed.), *Developmental perspectives on teaching and learning thinking skills* (Contribution to human development, Vol. 21, pp. 9–27). Basel: Karger.

Schinke, S. P., & Gilchrist, L. D. (1984). *Life skills counseling with adolescents*. Austin, TX: Pro-ed Publishers.

Simon, H. (1957). *Models of man: Social and rational*. New York: Wiley.

Sternberg, R. K., & Powell, J. (1983). The development of intelligence. In P. Mussen (Ed.), J. Flavell & E. Markman (Vol. Eds.), *Handbook of child psychology* (Vol. 3, pp. 341–419). New York: Wiley.

Thaler, R., & Shefrin, H. M. (1981). An economic theory of self-control. *Journal of Political Economy, 89*, 391–406.

Tietze, C. (1983). *Induced abortion: A world review*. New York: Population Council.

Tversky, A., & Kahneman, D. (1973). Availability: A heuristic for judging frequency and probability. *Cognitive Psychology, 4*, 207–232.

Tversky, A., & Kahneman, D. (1981). The framing of decisions and the psychology of choice. *Science, 21*, 453–458.

Urberg, K., & Robbins, R. L. (1981). Adolescents' perceptions of the costs and benefits associated with cigarette smoking: Sex differences and peer influences. *Journal of Youth and Adolescence, 10*, 353–361.

U.S. Department of Education. (1988). *Youth Indicators 1988: Trends in the well-being of American youth* (DE Pub. No. 065-000-00347-3). Washington, DC: U.S. Government Printing Office.

von Winterfeldt, D., & Edwards, W. (1986). *Decision analysis and behavioral research*. New York: Cambridge University Press.

Ward, S. L., & Overton, W. F. (1990). Semantic familiarity, relevance and the development of deductive reasoning. *Developmental Psychology, 26*, 488–493.

Weinstein, N. D. (1980). Unrealistic optimism about future life events. *Journal of Personality and Social Psychology, 39*, 806–820.

Weinstein, N. D. (Ed.). (1987). *Taking care: Understanding and encouraging self-protective behavior*. New York: Cambridge Unviersity Press.

Weithorn, L. A., & Campbell, S. B. (1982). The competence of children and adolescents to make informed treatment decisions. *Child Development, 53*, 1589–1598.

Whitely, B., & Hern, A. (1991). Perceptions of vulnerability to pregnancy and the use of effective contraception. *Personality and Social Psychology Bulletin, 17*, 104–110.

Wilks, S. S. (1938). Weighting systems for linear functions of correlated variables where there is no dependent variable. *Psychometrika, 8*, 23–40.

Winkler, R. L., & Murphy, A. H. (1968). "Good" probability assessors. *Journal of Applied Meteorology, 7*, 751–758.

Yates, J. F. (Ed.). (1989). *Judgment and decision making*. Chichester, U.K.: Wiley.

Zuckerman, M., Eysenck, S. B. G., & Eysenck, H. J. (1978). Sensation seeking in England and America: Cross-cultural, age, and sex comparisons. *Journal of Consulting and Clinical Psychology, 46*, 139–149.

Part II

Affiliation Transitions and Health

6   The Family as Health Risk and Opportunity: A Focus on Divorce and Working Families

Nancy L. Galambos and Marion F. Ehrenberg

As Dorothy Parker, the poet and writer, once commented, "The best way to keep children home is to make the home atmosphere pleasant – and let the air out of the tires" (Perspectives, 1990, p. 6). This quotation most aptly captures the major issues in the intricate dance between parents and children as they step through the period of adolescence – together and apart. For the young person, a successful transition through adolescence requires at the minimum a still-warm and protective nest, but at the same time there must be a gradual loosening of ties and the availability of opportunities to venture into a world where parents are not present. For the parent, the challenge is to maintain this delicate balance between appropriate supervision and the granting of autonomy within a pleasant and warm family atmosphere.

In this chapter we examine the role of the family in providing a context in which children can face and resolve the developmental tasks of adolescence. We begin by discussing the major broad goal of socialization: the achievement of psychosocial maturity. By understanding what adolescents must accomplish to move successfully into adulthood, we are able to consider the ways in which families can facilitate and hinder this process. What is optimal for the adolescent's development is a family context that is in synchrony with the adolescent's changing needs at particular points in development – a health-enhancing person–environment fit (Eccles et al., 1993). To this end, we will focus on family relationships that allow for separation and connectedness, the place that family conflict has in adolescents' lives, and the importance of parental monitoring of adolescents' activities. We then highlight two aspects of the family context – divorce and parents' work – that many adolescents experience today and that can present risks and opportunities to them in their search for psychosocial maturity. Some examples of research from our labora-

The Families in Motion Research and Information Centre is supported by research grants from the Social Sciences and Humanities Research Council of Canada (SSHRCC), the British Columbia Health Research Foundation, and the University of Victoria to M. Ehrenberg. The Two-Earner Family Study was supported by research grants from the SSHRCC and the University of Victoria to N. Galambos. Both authors wish to thank their research participants and research assistants for their contributions to this work.

139

tories will be used to illustrate these processes. Finally, this chapter concludes with a discussion of what we see as significant directions to follow in thinking about and conducting research on the family and its place in optimizing adolescent development.

Psychosocial Maturity: The Goal

When parents are asked what they want for their children, the most common response is: "To be healthy and happy." But what does this really mean? If we delve further into parents' ambitions for their children, we hear about the importance of attaining a sense of responsibility, having the ability to get along with others, giving and receiving love, doing well in school, pursuing work that is compatible with interests, and contributing to society. All of these aims fit under the rubric of a construct called *psychosocial maturity*. Psychosocial maturity, in turn, may be related to a variety of physical and behavioral health outcomes.

Psychosocial maturity, as defined by Greenberger and colleagues (Greenberger, Josselson, Knerr, & Knerr, 1975; Greenberger & Sorenson, 1974; Greenberger & Steinberg, 1986), encompasses three major domains of development: (1) autonomy, or the individual's ability to function independently; (2) interpersonal adequacy, or the individual's ability to communicate and interact well with others; and (3) social responsibility, or the individual's capacity for contributing to the well-being of society. Each of these key aspects of psychosocial maturity consists of multiple dimensions, all of which must be fostered if the child is to truly become an adult, complete with the ability to further his or her own goals as well as the goals of society.

According to Greenberger and Sorenson (1974), the achievement of *autonomy* encompasses the development of three dimensions: (1) self-reliance, which is the capacity to take initiative and to have a sense of control over one's life and activities; (2) identity, which involves the development of a coherent self-concept, complete with life goals and internalized values; and (3) work orientation, which comprises standards for competence and taking pleasure in work. These aspects of psychosocial maturity are important to the individual's functioning as a separate entity. The autonomous adolescent will be better equipped to pursue health-enhancing behaviors, such as physical exercise and getting enough sleep, and to decide against health-compromising activities, such as smoking and excessive dieting.

Interpersonal adequacy, the second component of psychosocial maturity, is important for the individual's activities as a social being. To be successful in a social sense, the individual requires effective communication skills, such as empathy and the ability to understand and receive messages. The individual also must develop a sense of trust (but not gullibility) in others, as well as a knowledge of role-appropriate behavior. As adolescents face issues of intimacy, well-developed interpersonal skills will aid them in exercising health-oriented options (e.g., regarding sexual behavior), whereas poor interpersonal skills may leave them with little confidence to deal assertively with social challenges (e.g., peer conflict or pressure).

With respect to *social responsibility*, the third dimension of psychosocial maturity, the adolescent must acquire a sense of social commitment to the good of the community, an openness to social and political change to achieve higher-order goals, and a tolerance and acceptance of individual and cultural differences (Greenberger & Sorenson, 1974). A sense of social responsibility may assist adolescents in joining with their peers to develop a social context in which health-compromising activities are seen as unacceptable (e.g., reckless or drunk driving).

To speak of opportunities in the family that might enhance the adolescent's health is to address those aspects of family life that increase the adolescent's chances for developing an all-around sense of psychosocial maturity. We believe that family relationships and parenting styles and practices are among the most significant influences on psychosocial maturity. To speak of risks in the family that might hinder healthy adolescent development is to zero in on threats to the development of psychosocial maturity – situations and relationships that will interfere with the adolescent's ability to function autonomously, interpersonally, and responsibly. These threats, if severe and long-lasting, may manifest themselves eventually in symptoms and behaviors that are not illustrative of psychosocial maturity, but rather the opposite. Thus, problems such as substance abuse, depression, eating disorders, externalizing and internalizing behaviors, sexual promiscuity, and school failure constitute evidence of psychosocial immaturity and suggest that the balance was more on the side of risks than on opportunities.

Of course, the picture is not so simple as a matter-of-fact weighing of the opportunities and risks (Rolf, Masten, Cicchetti, Nuechterlein, & Weintraub, 1990). All of us have had both. Some who have had many risks have almost breezed through adolescence to become fully functioning adults. And others who have had more opportunities than risks somehow never seemed to achieve full-fledged maturity. Any discussion of risks and opportunities must incorporate the notion of probability – which simply means that knowing about the relative balance of risks and opportunities only tells us about the likelihood that the goals of socialization will be met. As a result of individual differences in characteristics such as intelligence, personality (e.g., flexibility, assertiveness), responses to stress, and the ability to take different perspectives, the effect of the same opportunities and risks on different individuals will vary.

The Family: A Means to Psychosocial Maturity

The family is the most immediate and significant socialization influence on the child; it is the primary route to psychosocial maturity. In contemplating opportunities and risks presented by the family to the adolescent, it is possible to consider the family at different levels of analysis. For example, we might examine features of the family context such as family structure and size, socioeconomic status, ethnicity, and the employment status of parents. These are aspects of the family that tell us about the family's "social address" – whether they live in a divorced or two-parent household, for example, or in a wealthy or impoverished home (Bronfenbrenner, 1986). Or we might consider relationships within the family – the marital relationship, relations among siblings, and the parent–adolescent relationship. All of these qualities of family life deserve attention as potential purveyors of risk and opportunity. To truly understand the processes by which families influence adolescents, as many of these qualities as possible should be examined simultaneously to determine how they affect the adolescent in their interrelatedness.

A review of all the risks and opportunities in the family context is beyond the scope of this chapter. Instead, we focus on the parent–adolescent relationship because it assumes a special place in adolescent development. Indeed, family process models that attempt to describe how features of the family's social address (e.g., poverty, unemployment, divorce) influence the adolescent often posit parent–adolescent relations as a mediator between these features and adolescent development (Belsky, 1984; Conger et al., 1992; Galambos, Sears, Almeida, & Kolaric, 1995). That is, it is believed that many, but not all, risks and opportunities attributable to the family's economic, marital, or geographical situations are funneled down to adolescents through their influences on parent–adolescent relations (often via parents' levels of stress, their moods, or the existence of more general family conflict). Risks and opportunities posed by the parent–adolescent relationship, however, may derive from sources other than social address variables. Parent and adolescent personality and behavioral characteristics, for instance, will shape the course of parent–adolescent relations (Almeida, 1993). So, too, will the fit between parenting styles (e.g., whether the parent approaches the adolescent in an authoritarian or authoritative manner) and the autonomy-oriented needs of the adolescent (Baumrind, 1991; Eccles et al., 1993; Steinberg, Elmen, & Mounts, 1989). In any case, it is clear that one important source of risks and opportunities is the relations between parents and adolescents. Therefore, we consider next some aspects of the parent–adolescent relationship that we believe are most important in facilitating and hindering the adolescent's chances of achieving psychosocial maturity.

Separation and Connectedness

Earlier writings portrayed adolescence as a stage during which the individual establishes a sense of self as psychologically separate from parents (e.g., Blos, 1979). Cooper, Grotevant, and Condon (1983) drew on this notion to outline the importance of separation (or individuation) and connectedness as qualities that capture the ongoing interactions between parents and adolescents. Separation is defined in terms of behaviors that express a psychological sense of distinctiveness from parents (e.g., asserting one's own opinion or disagreement). Connectedness is conceptualized as behaviors that demonstrate sensitivity, responsiveness, and openness to the views of others (Grotevant & Cooper, 1985). Separation establishes the adolescent as a unique person who will have the capacity to move out into the world and make decisions, and connectedness ensures that the adolescent will remain close to his or her sources of support, guidance, and encouragement.

Families that are able to foster separation and connectedness in tandem present opportunities to their adolescents to develop competently and to behave in a mature fashion. Evidence suggests that when separation and connectedness are coupled, adolescents are likely to be psychosocially mature. Their identity development proceeds at a desirable pace (Grotevant & Cooper, 1985), they have a healthy respect for themselves (Allen, Hauser, Bell, & O'Connor, 1994), and they are self-reliant and less likely to engage in delinquent activities (Lamborn, Mounts, Steinberg, & Dornbusch, 1991; Steinberg, Lamborn, Dornbusch, & Darling, 1992). Where separation and connectedness do not occur together, there may be risks. Too much separation without connectedness, for instance, might lead to adolescents' detachment from parents, declining school achievement, problem behavior, and retreat into deviant peer subcultures (Eccles et al., 1991; Lamborn & Steinberg, 1993; Ryan & Lynch, 1989; Simmons & Blyth, 1987; Steinberg, 1990). Connectedness without separation, however, may not pose the risks that separation without connectedness docs. Research suggests that connectedness, even in the absence of separation from families, is associated with social and academic competence (Lamborn & Steinberg, 1993). Adolescents who are neither separated nor connected seem to be psychosocially immature (Allen et al., 1994; Lamborn & Steinberg, 1993).

An adolescent who does not resolve the conflict between continuing dependence on the family and the demands and privileges of independence will encounter difficulties in most other areas. With the achievement of a reasonable degree of separation in the context of connectedness, however, an adolescent will be able to form mature friendships and intimate relations, confidently pursue a vocation, and gain a clear sense of identity (Conger, 1991).

Family Conflict

Adolescence is often portrayed as a time during which children's conflict with parents is heightened. Although this assumption of an increase in conflict with parents in early to middle adolescence may yet prove to be unfounded

(Galambos & Almeida, 1992; Laursen & Ferreira, 1994), some conflict is a normal part of most families. The degree of conflict may range from no or mild conflict to severe conflict, but parent–adolescent conflict, for the most part, consists of "mild bickering, disagreements and conflicts over everyday issues" (Smetana, 1988, p. 79). Conflict that is severe, however, is harmful to both adolescents and parents (Steinberg, 1990).

In considering opportunities for growth that family relations present to adolescents, parent–adolescent conflict may be seen as serving an important psychological function. The existence of mild conflict may help to define the adolescent as separate from parents (Steinberg, 1990). In a study of the influence of parent–adolescent interactions on adolescent ego development, Allen et al. (1994) found that instances of father–adolescent conflict predicted increases in adolescents' ego development over a 2-year period (i.e., their views of themselves became more complex) as long as the conflict occurred in families characterized by both separation and connectedness. Smetana (1989) suggested that adolescent autonomy is a major concern underlying parent–adolescent conflict. Most issues over which conflict occurs are seen by adolescents (but not their parents) as under their own jurisdiction; therefore, they believe that parents should not interfere. When conflict gets out of hand, however, it no longer serves the purpose of helping to establish autonomy. Rather, it damages the relationship, thereby constituting a threat or a risk to adolescents' healthy development. High levels of parent–adolescent conflict are linked to increased levels of problem behavior, substance use, and school failure (Baer, Garmezy, McLaughlin, Pokorny, & Wernick, 1987; Forehand, Long, & Hendrick, 1987; Kandel, Kessler, & Margulies, 1978; Maggs & Galambos, 1993).

The ways in which family members resolve conflicts may be important for adolescents' interpersonal abilities. Exposure to poor conflict resolution strategies may pose a risk. Role modeling of effective conflict resolution strategies may be an opportunity, however, although this notion has only begun to be explored in the research literature, typically with reference to younger children (Easterbrooks, Cummings, & Emde, 1994).

Parental Monitoring

Research has pointed increasingly to the importance of parental monitoring of adolescents. *Monitoring* refers to the parent's knowledge of what the adolescent is doing, where the adolescent is, and with whom he or she is doing it (Steinberg, 1986). Whereas many of the interactions between parents and adolescents contribute to a sense of *psychological* separation or autonomy, parents' monitoring of adolescents' activities helps to regulate the adolescents' *behavioral* autonomy (Steinberg, 1990). An appropriate level of monitoring presents an opportunity for the adolescent to explore friendships and the surrounding environment alone, and is geared to what the adolescent can handle comfortably and wisely.

Where there is too little monitoring, the adolescent may have too much freedom and may very well make the wrong choices. Compared to adolescents in families where parents monitor their children's activities, adolescents whose parents are less effective monitors have more conduct problems and are more engaged in delinquent activities; they also perform more poorly in school and demonstrate lower levels of psychosocial competence (Barber, Olsen, & Shagle, 1994; Brown, Mounts, Lamborn, & Steinberg, 1993; Crouter, MacDermid, McHale, & Perry-Jenkins, 1990; Kurdek & Fine, 1994; Patterson & Stouthamer-Loeber, 1984). A lack of monitoring may be more likely to pose a problem in high-crime or impoverished neighborhoods where there are more opportunities to learn and engage in delinquent activities and where there is less access to health-enhancing social resources (e.g., recreational programs). From this perspective, the social address is important in maximizing the fit between parenting styles and the adolescents' health-related needs. We believe that there can be too much monitoring as well, where the parent becomes intrusive and controlling rather than guiding.

The Role of Family as Context

As adolescents navigate the risks and opportunities of their family lives, changes and diversity in family circumstances may color their strivings toward psychosocial maturity. Beyond negotiating the circumstances of their own family lives, today's adolescents are faced with a social fabric composed of increasing diversity in family forms and values. This growing complexity of family structures is apparent in the increasing number of common-law unions and single-parent families and in the incidence of divorce and remarriage over the past two decades (Statistics Canada, 1994a). Changes in the role of employment in families are evident from the large proportion of employed mothers in the paid work force at a time when the unemployment rate among family members is greater than during any year since the mid-1970s (Statistics Canada, 1994b). Challenges to existing notions of family values – for example, those presented by gay and lesbian lobbyists for the rights of homosexual families – are further evidence of today's diverse meanings and notions of "family life." For adolescents attempting to take control of their own family and work futures, pluralism of societal norms and values may present a window of alternatives, as exciting in the opportunities it may hold as it is overwhelming in the number and importance of choices required.

In striving toward psychosocial maturity and in developing their own orientations to family and work lives, adolescents face the challenge of integrating their immediate or proximal family experiences with the broader societal context of family values and diversity. Although this chapter focuses on parent–adolescent relations as the mediator of family risks and opportunities, consideration of the roles of proximal and distal family factors may prove useful for understanding these relations and their influence on adolescents' psychological and physical health. Perhaps of particular interest are adolescents whose immediate family circumstances are discrepant with notions of family communicated by peers, at school, and through media channels. Such discrepancies may surface in the parent–adolescent relationship, presenting a conflict that yields both opportunities and risks for the adolescent's psychosocial maturation. For example, a first-generation North American adolescent simultaneously faced with a culture that values autonomy in relationship choices, and with parents whose cultural values lean toward the selection of marriage partners by the family of origin, may feel caught between two worlds (cf. Silbereisen, Noack, & Schönpflug, 1994). Constructive resolutions of such conflicts, whereby adolescents are permitted to explore their cultural heritage and the meanings of family life conveyed through other socialization channels, may present opportunities for psychosocial growth that are not yet recognized in the empirical literature. Alternatively, destructive parent–adolescent conflict without possibility of negotiation, breakdown of communication, and eventual disengagement are already known to compromise the adolescent's psychosocial development and pose health risks (e.g., Eccles et al., 1991).

Specific features of the adolescent's immediate family context may bring into closer view aspects of family diversity that the adolescent would otherwise experience from a distance. By drawing on research in the areas of marital transitions and working families, we will examine how these two aspects of the family context may present opportunities and risks to the adolescent. As marital transitions and parents' employment will inevitably impact on parents and their relations with adolescents, they offer particularly rich examples of how family life may enhance or compromise psychosocial maturity. We turn now to a discussion of divorce, followed by an examination of working families.

Divorce and Family Transitions

The incidence of divorce increased fivefold between the late 1960s and the mid-1980s and has since been leveling off (Amato & Keith, 1991; Statistics Canada, 1994a). Of the 40% of North American children who will experience their parents' separation and divorce before they reach adulthood, most will reside in single-parent homes for at least 5 years, and a substantial proportion will experience the remarriages of their custodial parents as well as second divorces. Because children usually remain with their mothers after a divorce and because most parents tend to remarry, blended families headed by biological mothers and stepfathers are far more common than those involving biological fathers and stepmothers (Bray & Hetherington, 1993).

Not only are substantial proportions of North American adolescents likely to experience a series of family transitions in their immediate contexts, but for some groups of adolescents separation and divorce may be the normative conditions of family life. For example, 75% of African American children are likely to experience their parents' divorce or separation by age 16 and, in comparison with white children of divorce, they are also more likely to spend longer periods of time in a single-parent, mother-headed household or a household with a divorced mother and grandmother (Cherlin, 1992). Differences in the extent and type of marital transitions prevalent in specific subgroups of adolescents have only begun to be considered by divorce researchers, and may be of particular importance to those studying how adolescents develop a concept of marriage and family life by drawing on both their immediate family circumstances and their perceptions of family norms in their neighborhoods.

In contrast to early conceptualizations of single-parent and remarried families as atypical or pathogenic (e.g., Good, 1949), dramatic increases in the incidence of divorce and remarriage have prompted researchers to investigate the diversity of children's and parents' responses to marital transitions. The results of numerous investigations completed since the late 1970s have contributed to a dynamic picture of marital transitions as involving a series of economic, legal, social, and psychological implications for immediate and extended family members. In terms of their implications for children and adolescents, it has become clear that marital transitions can increase youths' risk for behavioral, social, emotional, and school adjustment problems (Bray & Hetherington, 1993; Wallerstein, 1991).

Current directions in divorce research include identifying developmentally specific risks that marital transitions may present for children and adolescents, illuminating the psychological processes underlying and mediating such negative outcomes, and looking for contexts and interventions that may minimize such risks (Barber & Eccles, 1992). Although the literature has moved far beyond its previously pessimistic view of divorce-related changes, the opportunities for psychosocial development that marital transitions may present to adolescents have not yet been considered. Because our interests lie in exploring the balance of risks and opportunities families may present for their adolescents' psychosocial development, we will follow our discussion of divorce-related risks and processes with examples of how this research may be reconceptualized and expanded to include notions of psychosocial health and opportunity.

The Risks

Recent reviews of the divorce literature demonstrate that marital transitions may have negative consequences for parents and children, although the size and significance of these effects continue to be disputed (e.g., Amato & Keith, 1991; Bray & Hetherington, 1993; Wallerstein, 1991). To understand these risks as they apply to adolescents, we must not only consider investigations of adolescents experiencing their parents' divorces, but must also take into account longitudinal studies of children's responses to marital transitions, in particular those suggesting the presence of "sleeper" effects as negative health outcomes that do not surface until the adolescent years (Hetherington, Stanley-Hagan, & Anderson, 1989). These studies taken together suggest that although the extent to which marital transitions may compromise psychosocial functioning is similar for children and adolescents, age and gender influence the form that such disturbances may take. Adolescents who have experienced their parents' divorces and remarriages may suffer more or less persistent difficulties in social, emotional, behavioral, cognitive, and school adjustment (Buchanan, Maccoby, & Dornbusch, 1991; Forehand et al., 1991; Hetherington, 1993; McCombs & Forehand, 1989). Although the negative effects of divorce on youths may be long-lasting, this view must be balanced with an understanding that the majority of children and adolescents in divorcing families achieve positive health outcomes in the long term. For example, one study revealed that 5 years after the family breakup, one-third of the affected youths seemed self-reliant and well adjusted; another one-third were coping reasonably well; and a substantial proportion, the remaining one-third, were experiencing significant psychological problems and actively longed for the lives they had enjoyed before their parents' divorce (Hetherington, 1991).

It is not surprising that a lack of parental monitoring has been offered as one explanation for the higher incidence of behavior problems among adolescents living in single-parent and remarried families compared with youths residing in intact families (Hetherington, 1993; Newcomer & Udry, 1987; Zimiles & Lee, 1991). Especially during the first 2 years following the marital separation, parents may be preoccupied with their own problems, and custodial mothers may be forced to return to work or to increase their working hours in order to offset the financial losses resulting from the divorce. Although these factors may indeed limit the time and energy single parents can devote to monitoring their adolescents' activities, research also suggests that parents' access to social support from other adults may improve their coping capacities and enhance their relationships with their children (Johnston, Gonzalez, & Campbell, 1987).

In addition to considering the relationship between divorce-related periods of diminished parenting and lack of parental monitoring, the negative effects of divorce for children and adolescents have been attributed to three conditions: (1) the absence of a second parent in the home, usually the father; (2) the economic disadvantages of single-parent families; and, (3) the level of interparental conflict. Although the first two conditions are consequential, interparental conflict is the most important predictor of children's and adolescents' postdivorce functioning (Amato & Keith, 1991). Even more detrimental than the level of interparental conflict to which adolescents are exposed during marital transitions is the extent to which adolescents are drawn into their parents' conflicts and asked to take sides, and how much they feel caught between their parents (Buchanan et al., 1991; Johnston, Campbell, & Mayes, 1985).

The fact that adolescents' involvement in their parents' conflicts dramatically increases their risk of psychosocial and behavioral difficulties, both before and after marital separation (Cherlin et al., 1991), suggests that the psychological processes underlying these effects are critical to our understanding of the more or less healthful roles that separating and divorced parents may play in their adolescents' lives. In one line of research at the University of Victoria's Families in Motion Research and Information Centre, we focus on the identification of psychological and interpersonal factors that predict cooperation and agreement between ex-spouses versus conflict and parenting disagreements. The first of this series of studies suggested that ex-couples who have difficulties negotiating and maintaining mutually agreeable shared parenting arrangements tend to be more narcissistic, more interpersonally vulnerable, less able to take another's perspective, less concerned about the feelings and needs of others, more self-oriented, and less child-centered in their parenting attitudes than divorcing parents who are able to maintain shared parenting agreements. Conversely, former couples who were able to maintain cooperative parenting arrangements after their marriages ended were more oriented toward the perspectives and feelings of others, and these tendencies were similarly reflected in more child-oriented parenting attitudes (Ehrenberg, Hunter, & Elterman, 1996). Compared with divorced mothers and fathers involved in parenting disputes, cooperative ex-spouses selected from a wider range of custody and parenting options and were more satisfied with several aspects of their lives, including their jobs, home life, and new relationships (Ehrenberg, 1996). Divorcing parents who are able to cooperate regarding parenting matters may not only be in a better position to protect their adolescents from the negative aspects of family transitions, but may also provide health-enhancing models of how conflict can be resolved and relationships renegotiated. A subsequent longitudinal study will investigate the pathways through which aspects of parents' child-centeredness hinder or support their children's and adolescents' adjustment to family transitions by considering health risks and opportunities simultaneously.

The Opportunities

Based on a definitive meta-analysis of the divorce literature, Amato and Keith (1991) alerted researchers to the possibility that the risks of marital transitions for children have been underestimated and effect sizes diluted because investigators have tended to look for the effects of divorce in the "wrong places." They suggest that the full effects of divorce will not be understood until specific, theory-informed aspects of adolescents' relationship, family, and work functioning rather than general adjustment per se are empirically targeted. To appreciate the long-term effects of divorce, researchers must consider more extensively the adolescent and young adult years as developmental periods when risks to relationship, family, and work functioning can be more reasonably assessed than during the childhood years alone.

Although Amato and Keith's (1991) intent is to encourage investigators to understand divorce-related risk factors more fully, we would argue that their advice applies also to a search for psychosocial opportunities for adolescents in divorcing families. To identify positive health outcomes, we will need to take a different look at the divorce process. Our best chance to look in the "right places" will likely depend on reformulating our research objectives to include a balance of risk and opportunity hypotheses and, more specifically, to look for points where the paths laid down by researchers of parent–adolescent relations cross with the paths of investigators who have led us to understand specific divorce-related health risks. For example, we might take a closer look at a recent finding that it was not the experience of conflict between divorcing parents per se that interfered with parent–adolescent relations and increased the risk of depression and anxiety in these youths, but rather the extent to which they felt "caught between their parents" (Buchanan et al., 1991). Adolescents who enjoyed close relationships with their divorcing parents were less likely to feel caught between them, suggesting that positive parent–adolescent relations may protect youths from being pulled into an inappropriate role vis-à-vis their parents' conflicts. The mere extrication of adolescents from a volatile and deeply conflictual marital relationship may be seen as an opportunity for the adolescent to develop psychosocial maturity unhindered by a distressed family situation. In other words, as adolescents strive toward psychosocial maturity, the renegotiation of relationships with their parents following divorce may create the risk of becoming entangled in their parents' conflicts at the expense of personal autonomy and well-being, but it may also present a unique opportunity for youths to clarify their roles appropriately as family members separate from their parents' conflicts yet closely connected and secure in their relationships with both parents. Similarly, we might draw on research suggesting that youths who are overburdened by increased family responsibilities following a family breakup may suffer adverse effects (Hetherington, 1989) and may translate this question about a divorce-related risk into a question about health opportunity. We might ask whether adolescents who are reasonably challenged by greater responsibilities within the divorcing family may benefit from this opportunity for greater self-reliance balanced with a sense of family connectedness derived from doing their fair share at home.

Divorce-related health opportunities may also be evident in approaches that consider adolescents' natural coping styles as a means of making the best of family transitions. For example, in another line of research at the Families in Motion Research and Information Centre, we are developing and evaluating a program that extends existing community-based services for divorcing families by further educating peer helpers already working in high schools to act as liaisons between adolescents experiencing family transitions and these divorce-related supports. This program emerged from an understanding that adolescents are more likely to seek support from their friends than from adults. Adolescents' needs for peer support may be especially important at times when their parents are themselves overwhelmed by divorce-related changes and unable to support their distressed adolescents. Interestingly, preliminary analyses of the first wave of data suggested that a substantial proportion of peer helpers responding to adolescents in separating families indicated that coming to terms with their own family histories of divorce helped them to help peers experiencing similar crises (Ehrenberg & Roche, 1995). This suggests that helping adolescents to access divorce-related information and community supports, through the developmentally natural means of peer helpers, may not only present a health opportunity for the adolescents currently experiencing marital transitions, but may also enhance the peer helpers' healthy adjustment to family changes. Adolescents who are able to help their peers by drawing on their own experiences will surely make gains toward psychosocial maturity.

By integrating our research and health-promotion efforts to enhance positive coping strategies among adolescents in divorcing families, we may expand our understanding of family transitions beyond the risks they may pose in order to take into account the psychosocial and health opportunities they may offer. We now turn from adolescents in divorcing families to consider another aspect of adolescents' family context – the parents' work.

Working Families

As a result of decades of women's increased participation in the labor force, the majority of adolescents now live in a family where the mother is working outside the home. In 1993, over three-fourths of Canadian women with children aged 6–15 years were in the labor force (Statistics Canada, 1994b). This transformation in women's family roles has led to a significant body of research on the relations between mothers' work (typically mothers' work status) and children's psychosocial adjustment (e.g., Frankel, 1993; Gottfried & Gottfried, 1988; Lerner & Galambos, 1991; Parcel & Menaghan, 1994).

Consideration of *both* parents' work situations within the larger family context is critical to understanding the risks and opportunities present in working families, but such research has been less than forthcoming (Barling, 1990; Crouter, Perry-Jenkins, Huston, & McHale, 1987; Galambos & Almeida, 1993). Relatively few, if any, studies have taken more than a cursory glance at parental employment in single-parent families.

The Risks

Much of the public discourse as well as the empirical literature on working families focuses on the costs that may accrue to family members from mothers' (and rarely fathers') employment. These potential costs have been discussed so often that it seems superfluous to do more than list them here. Specifically, families in which both parents are working (and especially those characterized by full-time work) are likely to experience a shortage of time, difficulties in providing adequate supervision for children and adolescents, at least occasional bouts of stress in the workplace, and fatigue. To the extent that these costs are experienced and interfere with the parent–adolescent relationship, they comprise sources of risk that may compromise the adolescent's psychosocial maturity.

As an example, consider the influence of a parent's work overload – or having more work than can be handled comfortably–on adolescent problem behavior (e.g., substance use, vandalism, cheating on a test). Using data from the Two-Earner Family Study – a longitudinal study of two-parent, two-earner families with adolescent children – we found that mothers who were more overloaded at work were less accepting of their adolescent children than were mothers who experienced less work overload (Galambos et al., 1995). Less acceptance in the mother–adolescent relationship was related, in turn, to increased levels of problem behavior among adolescents 6 months later. Higher work overload among fathers was linked to higher levels of conflict between parents and adolescents, which in turn predicted increased adolescent problem behavior. Furthermore, among mothers and fathers, feelings of stress (e.g., depression, anxiety) mediated the impact of work overload on parent–adolescent relations. That is, parental stress carried work overload into the parent–adolescent relationship. Additional analyses found that parent–adolescent conflict was highest among families in which *both* mothers and fathers experienced relatively high levels of stress.

Although this research illustrates how parents' employment may comprise a risk to adolescents' psychosocial maturity, it also demonstrates the complexity inherent in examining risks. Simply knowing that a parent is overloaded at work is not enough to allow us to say that the adolescent will engage in higher levels of problem behavior. The parent must experience the overload as stressful (e.g., feel depressed or anxious), and this stress must be translated into less than optimal parent–adolescent relations. Even then, because of personal strengths, coping strategies, and the availability of social support, not all adolescents experiencing distressed parent–adolescent relations will evidence higher levels of problem behavior. Indeed, in the preceding study we found that adolescents with high levels of parent–adolescent conflict were no more likely to engage in problem behavior than were adolescents in low-conflict families *as long as the mother–adolescent relationship was accepting* (Galambos et al., 1995). Thus, conflict was of no consequence if it occurred in the context of connectedness (i.e., acceptance).

Among the largest challenges for working families is to provide adequate parental monitoring of adolescents. We know that such monitoring is important, and that it is not easy to keep track of adolescents who are not in school ("latchkey adolescents") when parents are at work. Being a latchkey adolescent may be a risk, but again, there is evidence of the diversity of outcomes associated with this risk. In our research (Galambos & Maggs, 1991), we found that latchkey adolescents, especially girls, who spent their time away from home in the company of peers were more involved in problem behavior than were latchkey adolescents who stayed home alone after school. Among those girls most at risk, however, problem behavior was not elevated *if their parents were warm and accepting and provided consistent, firm control*. We suspect that, in a like manner, many of the risks present in working families may be offset by the maintenance of adequate parent–adolescent relations in the face of challenges. Where the risks are enduring, frequent, severe, and/or occur in a family or social context marked by stress (e.g., marital failure, poverty), we are more likely to see a breakdown in family functioning and the subsequent realization of threats to the adolescent's psychosocial maturity.

The Opportunities

Neither public discourse nor the empirical literature on working families has given much consideration to the benefits associated with parents' work. Some of these benefits are obvious. Children's material comforts and educational needs require a minimal level of family income. In many cases, both parents must work to provide this needed income. Even where the family *could* survive on one income, there are cash opportunities to the adolescent of both parents working (e.g., holidays, leisure and athletic pursuits, entertainment). A recent study found that the development of talent in teenagers required emotional and material support (e.g., lessons, musical instruments, sports equipment), and where this was not provided by parents, the teenager's talent was lost (Csikszentmihalyi, Rathunde, & Whalen, 1993). A higher family income provides necessary, though not sufficient, means to a lifestyle that may ultimately form a basis for the adolescent's emerging psychosocial maturity.

An opportunity that has been recognized in the empirical literature as potentially present in working families is the availability of a female role model who shares in the income production and wealth of the family. The supposition that the employed mother occupies a relatively powerful and instrumental role in the family and in the marital relationship has been used to explain why children in families where mothers are employed have more egalitarian sex-role attitudes and fewer sex stereotypes, and see more occupations as open to both men and women relative to children in single-earner families where the father is the only breadwinner (Galambos, Petersen, & Lenerz, 1988; Hoffman, 1980). This opportunity may be most critical for girls, as girls with employed mothers have higher academic and occupational aspirations than those with nonemployed mothers (Galambos et al., 1988).

Even some of the potential risks in working families (e.g., too little uncommitted time) may result in opportunities. Consider, for instance, the role of fathers in families where mothers work. There is accumulating evidence that fathers in two-earner families are more involved with their children than those in single-earner families. When mothers are employed or increase the number of hours they work outside of the home, fathers spend more time in child-care duties (Almeida, Maggs, & Galambos, 1993; Crouter et al., 1987). Moreover, results from the Two-Earner Family Study indicated that fathers who were initially more involved with their adolescents (spent more time with, took care of, or transported them) became more accepting of them in the following 6 months (Almeida & Galambos, 1991). Thus, in the best circumstances, the two-earner situation may pave the way to more connectedness between fathers and adolescents.

There are few situations in which there are all risks and no opportunities or vice versa. Again, we see that it is important to consider the relative balance. A parent might be periodically stressed by his or her job, for instance, but if the income allows the family to afford a regular vacation or to dine at a restaurant together, the risk may be offset. On the other hand, the self-esteem or prestige of working may enhance a parent's psychological well-being, but if the job allows little time for interacting with children, this opportunity for the parent may well be a risk for the child.

Conclusions

We began this chapter by focusing on psychosocial maturity as a critical goal for adolescents and on the importance of the family context in undermining or supporting the attainment of this goal. Judging from the literature on divorced and working families as contexts for the adolescent's development, it is clear that there is a considerable amount of research on risks, some research on the factors that buffer against risk, and very little research concerning diversity in family situations as health opportunities. In fact, a focus on opportunity often necessitates making inferences about the *presence* of opportunity by simply noting that adolescents are more psychosocially mature in the *absence* of risk. This leaves us, however, with a feeling of dissatisfaction – discomfort arising from a perspective on research that sees the glass as half empty rather than half full. Our first recommendation for future research, then, is to *actively conceptualize health opportunities arising from the family context.*

To accomplish this, we need to think hard about what *health opportunity* really means for adolescents. Maybe health opportunities stem from a moment in time or a series or accumulation of moments that can be seized on as they offer options or choices to adolescents in their search for autonomy, successful social relations, and social responsibility. Consider, for instance, how parents who are involved in and excited about their work present opportunities to adolescent children. Such excitement may benefit children through positive and warm parent–child interactions (which would contribute to a sense of connectedness), the modeling of a strong work ethic (which might contribute to the adolescent's developing work orientation), or involvement of the adolescent in a combined business–family trip (with all the benefits of traveling). Or consider that divorce may not only remove the adolescent from a tense and conflictual situation (thereby reducing risks) but may also lead some adolescents to consider their future spousal and family choices more carefully and wisely than they might have done otherwise (Barber & Eccles, 1992). It strikes us as peculiar that the very decisions that many parents make in order to better their children's futures have been seen by researchers not as opportunities but as risks. After all, if parents equated the process of divorce with a slate of disadvantages for their children, would so many ever initiate it? Would both parents work if they thought that two jobs carried only costs and no benefits? These questions lead to our second recommendation, namely, that researchers *ask if the apparent risks present in adolescents' lives can also be turned around and viewed as opportunities.*

For risks to be seen as opportunities, it is necessary to consider adolescents' needs – specifically, the fit between adolescents' needs and their environment (Eccles et al., 1993). It stands to reason that a risk may be an opportunity when it opens up the possibility that a previously unmet need may be satisfied. Imagine an adolescent daughter who has been overcontrolled and restricted at home; this adolescent may actually need more autonomy and less supervision. Living in a divorced family or one in which both parents work could provide a context in which she both learns and thrives on self-regulation. Our third recommendation is that future research *consider how the fit between the adolescent and the environment provides health opportunities.*

Defining and measuring opportunities is a challenging task, but one that is critical to understanding family processes and adolescent development. This is not to deny the importance of focusing on risks. Rather, a fuller picture of adolescent development will be gained by focusing on opportunities, combined with an assessment of risks. Equally important is the delineation of the type of adolescent outcome that ought to be observed. Research on family risks often focuses on negative outcomes – behaviors that we do not want to see in adolescents (e.g., depression or problem behavior). It is important to continue this line of research. But a consideration of opportunities should lead us also to an equivalent assessment of positive outcomes. Our fourth recommendation is to *define and measure positive health outcomes*. This would involve more than just measuring the absence of poor outcomes. It would also mean refocusing on those characteristics that we want to see develop, for example, strong self-esteem, a physically fit body, the ability to get along well with adults, or the many aspects of psychosocial maturity.

As indicated earlier in this chapter, we must strive to understand the balance of opportunities and risks for the adolescent in the family context. This is no easy task, given the presumed diversity in the number, intensity, and duration of opportunities and risks. It is complicated by the fact that the source of opportunity or risk may lie in multiple levels of analysis, such as family structure, family relations, the personality and/or behavioral characteristics of family members, or demographic features of the family (e.g., socioeconomic status). Moreover, an assessment of opportunities and risks requires investigation of the processes by which adolescents are so influenced – a focus, in many instances, on the parent–adolescent relationship as a mediator between the opportunities and risks, on the one hand, and adolescent development, on the other.

Our research will tell us only as much as we ask of it, and the path ahead is clear. We must begin by reframing our research and the research of others from the point of view of health risks *and* opportunities in the family context. By pursuing this goal, we will learn more about how families and parents set the stage for the critical developmental tasks of adolescence and how adolescents negotiate the route to adulthood.

References

Allen, J. P., Hauser, S. T., Bell, K. L., & O'Connor, T. G. (1994). Longitudinal assessment of autonomy and relatedness in adolescent–family interactions as predictors of adolescent ego development and self-esteem. *Child Development, 65,* 179–194.

Almeida, D. M. (1993). *A longitudinal examination of father-adolescent relations.* Unpublished doctoral dissertation, University of Victoria, Victoria, BC.

Almeida, D. M., & Galambos, N. L. (1991). Examining father involvement and the quality of father–adolescent relations. *Journal of Research on Adolescence, 1,* 155–172.

Almeida, D. M., Maggs, J. L., & Galambos, N. L. (1993). Wives' employment hours and spousal participation in family work. *Journal of Family Psychology, 7,* 233–244.

Amato, P. R., & Keith, B. (1991). Parental divorce and the well-being of children: A meta-analysis. *Psychological Bulletin, 110,* 26–46.

Baer, P. E., Garmezy, L. B., McLaughlin, R. J., Pokorny, A. D., & Wernick, M. J. (1987). Stress, coping, family conflict, and adolescent alcohol use. *Journal of Behavioral Medicine, 10,* 449–466.

Barber, B. L., & Eccles, J. S. (1992). Long-term influence of divorce and single parenting on adolescent family- and work-related values, behaviors, and aspirations. *Psychological Bulletin, 111*, 108–126.

Barber, B. K., Olsen, J. E., & Shagle, S. C. (1994). Associations between parental psychological and behavioral control and youth internalized and externalized behaviors. *Child Development, 65*, 1120–1136.

Barling, J. (1990). *Employment, stress and family functioning*. Chichester, U.K.: Wiley.

Baumrind, D. (1991). The influence of parenting style on adolescent competence and substance use. *Journal of Early Adolescence, 11*, 56–95.

Belsky, J. (1984). The determinants of parenting: A process model. *Child Development, 55*, 83–96.

Blos, P. (1979). *The adolescent passage*. New York: International Universities Press.

Bray, J. H., & Hetherington, E. M. (1993). Families in transition: Introduction and overview. *Journal of Family Psychology, 7*, 3–8.

Bronfenbrenner, U. (1986). Ecology of the family as a context for human development: Research perspectives. *Developmental Psychology, 22*, 723–742.

Brown, B. B., Mounts, N., Lamborn, S. D., & Steinberg, L. (1993). Parenting practices and peer group affiliation in adolescence. *Child Development, 64*, 467–482.

Buchanan, C. M., Maccoby, E. E., & Dornbush, S. M. (1991). Caught between parents: Adolescents' experience in divorced homes. *Child Development, 62*, 1008–1029.

Cherlin, A. J. (1992). *Marriage, divorce, remarriage* (rev. ed.). Cambridge, MA: Harvard University Press.

Cherlin, A. J., Furstenberg, F. F., Chase-Lansdale, P. L., Kiernan, K. E., Robins, P. K., Morrison, D. R., & Teitler, J. O. (1991). Longitudinal studies of effects of divorce on children in Great Britain and the United States. *Science, 252*, 1386–1389.

Conger, J. J. (1991). *Adolescence and youth* (4th ed.). New York: HarperCollins.

Conger, R. D., Conger, K. J., Elder, G. H., Jr., Lorenz, F. O., Simons, R. L., & Whitbeck, L. B. (1992). A family process model of economic hardship and adjustment of early adolescent boys. *Child Development, 63*, 526–541.

Cooper, C. R., Grotevant, H. D., & Condon, S. M. (1983). Individuality and connectedness in the family as a context for adolescent identity formation and role taking skill. In H. D. Grotevant & C. R. Cooper (Eds.), *Adolescent development in the family: New directions for child development* (pp. 43–59). San Francisco: Jossey-Bass.

Crouter, A. C., MacDermid, S. M., McHale, S. M., & Perry-Jenkins, M. (1990). Parental monitoring and perceptions of children's school performance and conduct in dual- and single-earner families. *Developmental Psychology, 26*, 649–657.

Crouter, A. C., Perry-Jenkins, M., Huston, T. L., & McHale, S. M. (1987). Processes underlying father involvement in dual and single career families. *Developmental Psychology, 23*, 431–440.

Csikszentmihalyi, M., Rathunde, K., & Whalen, S. (1993). *Talented teenagers: The roots of success and failure*. Cambridge: Cambridge University Press.

Easterbrooks, M. A., Cummings, E. M., & Emde, R. N. (1994). Young children's responses to constructive marital disputes. *Journal of Family Psychology, 8*, 160–169.

Eccles, J. S., Buchanan, C. M., Flanagan, C., Fuligni, A., Midgley, C., & Yee, D. (1991). Control versus autonomy during early adolescence. *Journal of Social Issues, 47*, 53–68.

Eccles, J. S., Midgley, C., Wigfield, A., Buchanan, C. M., Reuman, D., Flanagan, C., & MacIver, D. (1993). Development during adolescence: The impact stage–environment fit on young adolescents' experiences in schools and in families. *American Psychologist, 48*, 90–101.

Ehrenberg, M. F. (1996). Cooperative parenting arrangements after marital separation: Former couples who make it work. *Journal of Divorce and Remarriage, 24*.

Ehrenberg, M. F., Hunter, M. A., & Elterman, M. F. (1996). Parenting disagreements after marital separation: The roles of empathy and narcissism. *Journal of Consulting and Clinical Psychology, 64*, 808–818.

Ehrenberg, M. F., & Roche, D. (1995, June). *Adolescents coping with family transitions: The role of peer helpers.* Paper presented at the Family Research Consortium's Annual Summer Institute. Ogunquit, Maine.

Forehand, R., Long, N., & Hendrick, M. (1987). Family characteristics of adolescents who display overt and covert behavior problems. *Journal of Behavior Therapy and Experimental Psychiatry, 18,* 325–328.

Forehand, R., Wierson, M., Thomas, A., Fauber, R., Armistead, L., Kempton, T., & Long, N. (1991). A short-term longitudinal examination of young adolescent functioning following divorce: The role of family factors. *Journal of Abnormal Child Psychology, 19,* 97–111.

Frankel, J. (Ed.). (1993). *The employed mother and the family context.* New York: Springer.

Galambos, N. L., & Almeida, D. M. (1992). Does parent–adolescent conflict increase in early adolescence? *Journal of Marriage and the Family, 54,* 737–747.

Galambos, N. L., & Almeida, D. M. (1993). The two-earner family as a context for adolescent development. In R. K. Silbereisen & E. Todt (Eds.), *Adolescence in context: The interplay of family, school, peers, and work in adjustment* (pp. 222–243). New York: Springer.

Galambos, N. L., & Maggs, J. L. (1991). Out-of-school care of young adolescents and self-reported behavior. *Developmental Psychology, 27,* 644–655.

Galambos, N. L., Petersen, A. C., & Lenerz, K. (1988). Maternal employment and sex-typing in early adolescence: Contemporaneous and longitudinal relations. In A. E. Gottfried & A. Gottfried (Eds.), *Maternal employment and children's development: Longitudinal research* (pp. 155–189). New York: Plenum.

Galambos, N. L., Sears, H. A., Almeida, D. M., & Kolaric, G. C. (1995). Parents' work overload and problem behavior in young adolescents. *Journal of Research on Adolescence, 5,* 201–223.

Good, W. J. (1949). Problems in post-divorce adjustment. *American Sociological Review, 14,* 394–401.

Gottfried, A. E., & Gottfried, A. W. (Eds.). (1988). *Maternal employment and children's development.* New York: Plenum.

Greenberger, E., Josselson, R., Knerr, C., & Knerr, B. (1975). The measurement and structure of psychosocial maturity. *Journal of Youth and Adolescence, 4,* 127–143.

Greenberger, E., & Sorenson, A. B. (1974). Toward a concept of psychosocial maturity. *Journal of Youth and Adolescence, 3,* 329–358.

Greenberger, E., & Steinberg, L. (1986). *When teenagers work: The psychological and social costs of adolescent employment.* New York: Basic Books.

Grotevant, H. D., & Cooper, C. R. (1985). Patterns of interaction in family relationships and the development of identity exploration in adolescence. *Child Development, 56,* 415–428.

Hetherington, E. M. (1989). Coping with family transitions: Winners, losers, and survivors. *Child Development, 61,* 1–14.

Hetherington, E. M. (1991). Presidential address: Families, lies, and videotapes. *Journal of Research on Adolescence, 1,* 323–348.

Hetherington, E. M. (1993). An overview of the Virginia longitudinal study of divorce and remarriage with a focus on early adolescence. *Journal of Family Psychology, 7,* 39–56.

Hetherington, E. M., Stanley-Hagan, M., & Anderson, E. R. (1989). Marital transitions: A child's perspective. *American Psychologist, 44*(2), 303–312.

Hoffman, L. W. (1980). The effects of maternal employment on the academic attitudes and performance of school-aged children. *School Psychology Review, 9,* 319–335.

Johnston, J. R., Campbell, L. E. G., & Mayes, S. S. (1985). Latency children in post-separation and divorce disputes. *Journal of American Academy of Child Psychiatry, 25,* 563–574.

Johnston, J. R., Gonzalez, R., & Campbell, L. E. G. (1987). Ongoing postdivorce conflict and child disturbance. *Journal of Abnormal Child Psychology, 15,* 493–509.

Kandel, D. B., Kessler, R. C., & Margulies, R. Z. (1978). Antecedents of adolescent initiation into stages of drug use: A developmental analysis. In D. B. Kandel (Ed.), *Longitudinal research on drug use: Empirical findings and methodological issues* (pp. 73–99). New York: Wiley.

Kurdek, L. A., & Fine, M. A. (1994). Family acceptance and family control as predictors of adjustment in young adolescents: Linear, curvilinear, or interactive effects? *Child Development, 65*, 1137–1146.

Lamborn, S. D., Mounts, N. S., Steinberg, L., & Dornbusch, S. M. (1991). Patterns of competence and adjustment among adolescents from authoritative, authoritarian, indulgent, and neglectful families. *Child Development, 61*, 1049–1065.

Lamborn, S. D., & Steinberg, L. (1993). Emotional autonomy redux: Revisiting Ryan and Lynch. *Child Development, 64*, 483–499.

Laursen, B., & Ferreira, M. (1994, February). *Does parent–child conflict peak at mid-adolescence?* Paper presented at the Fifth Biennial Meetings of the Society for Research on Adolescence, San Diego.

Lerner, J. V., & Galambos, N. L. (Eds.). (1991). *Employed mothers and their children.* New York: Garland Press.

Maggs, J. L., & Galambos, N. L. (1993). Alternative structural models for understanding adolescent problem behavior in two-earner families. *Journal of Early Adolescence, 13*, 79–101.

McCombs, A., & Forehand, R. (1989). Adolescent school performance following parental divorce: Are there family factors that can enhance success? *Adolescence, 24*, 871–880.

Newcomer, S., & Udry, J. R. (1987). Parental marital status effects on adolescent sexual behavior. *Journal of Marriage and the Family, 49*, 235–240.

Parcel, T. L., & Menaghan, E. G. (1994). *Parents' jobs and children's lives.* New York: Aldine de Gruyter.

Patterson, G. R., & Stouthamer-Loeber, M. (1984). The correlation of family management practices and delinquency. *Child Development, 55*, 1299–1307.

Perspectives. (1990, summer-fall). The new teens [special issue]. *Newsweek*, p. 6.

Rolf, J., Masten, A. S., Cicchetti, D., Nuechterlein, K. H., & Weintraub, S. (Eds.). (1990). *Risk and protective factors in the development of psychopathology.* Cambridge: Cambridge University Press.

Ryan, R. M., & Lynch, J. H. (1989). Emotional autonomy versus detachment: Revisiting the vicissitudes of adolescence. *Child Development, 60*, 340–356.

Silbereisen, R. K., Noack, P., & Schönpflug, U. (1994). Comparative analyses of beliefs, leisure contexts, and substance use in West Berlin and Warsaw. In R. K. Silbereisen & E. Todt (Eds.), *Adolescence in context: The interplay of family, school, peers, and work in adjustment* (pp. 176–198). New York: Springer-Verlag.

Simmons, R. G., & Blyth, D. A. (1987). *Moving into adolescence: The impact of pubertal change and school context.* New York: Aldine de Gruyter.

Smetana, J. G. (1988). Concepts of self and social convention: Adolescents' and parents' reasoning about hypothetical and actual family conflicts. In M. R. Gunnar & W. A. Collins (Eds.), Minnesota symposium on child psychology (Vol. 21, pp. 79–122). Hillsdale, NJ: Erlbaum.

Smetana, J. G. (1989). Adolescents' and parents' reasoning about actual family conflict. *Child Development, 60*, 1052–1067.

Statistics Canada. (1994a). *A portrait of families in Canada: Target groups project* (Cat. 89-523E). Ottawa, Canada: Author.

Statistics Canada. (1994b). *Declining female labour force participation* (Cat. 75-001E). Ottawa: Minister of Industry, Science and Technology.

Steinberg, L. (1986). Latchkey children and susceptibility to peer pressure: An ecological analysis. *Development Psychology, 22*, 433–439.

Steinberg, L. (1990). Autonomy, conflict, and harmony in the family relationship. In S. S. Feldman & G. R. Elliott (Eds.), *At the threshold: The developing adolescent* (pp. 255–276). Cambridge, MA: Harvard University Press.

Steinberg, L., Elmen, J. D., & Mounts, N. S. (1989). Authoritative parenting, psychosocial maturity, and academic success among adolescents. *Child Development, 60*, 1424–1436.

Steinberg, L., Lamborn, S. D., Dornbusch, S. M., & Darling, N. (1992). Impact of parenting practices on adolescent achievement: Authoritative parenting, school involvement, and encouragement to succeed. *Child Development*, *63*, 1266–1281.

Wallerstein, J. S. (1991). The long-term effects of divorce on children: A review. *Journal of American Academy of Child and Adolescent Psychiatry*, *30*, 349–360.

Zimiles, H., & Lee, V. E. (1991). Adolescent family structure and educational progress. *Developmental Psychology*, *27*, 314–320.

7 Transformations in Peer Relationships at Adolescence: Implications for Health-Related Behavior

B. Bradford Brown, M. Margaret Dolcini, and Amy Leventhal

"Just say no!" Ten years ago, with that slogan, then First Lady Nancy Reagan championed a new prevention effort against adolescent drug use and abuse. There is no question about drug use being one of the major health-endangering behaviors among adolescents (Brown, Mott, & Stewart, 1992). What does seem more questionable to us are two assumptions implicit in this campaign. The first is that teenagers are goaded into health-diminishing behavior primarily by pressure from peers. The second is that, more generally, peers are a negative influence on adolescent health. In such prevention campaigns, as well as in much of the social scientific literature on adolescence, peers are routinely portrayed as a monolithic force guiding adolescents into unhealthy or undesirable behavior. In this chapter we will scrutinize that image of the peer group in light of studies of adolescent peer relations and health behavior.

As Hurrelmann (1990) noted, "health is both a personal and collective behavior" (p. 233). It exists only when physiological and personological forces within the individual combine with nurturing forces outside the individual. Similarly, poor health may be as much the result of a risk-laden or nonnurturing social environment as of poor personal habits. Thus, there is a natural linkage between adolescents' health-related behavior and their peer relationships. To appreciate the influence of peers on adolescent health, however, one must first understand three major transformations in peer relations that routinely occur in this stage of life. The first is a reorientation of friendships from the rather fluid, activity-based relationships of childhood to more stable, affectively oriented ties. Second is the growth of romantic and sexually oriented relationships that become institutionalized in the normative social fabric of teenage life. A third transformation is the emergence of peer "crowds," which are clusters of teenagers who appear to espouse various prototypic lifestyles and value systems.

After providing an overview of these transformations, we will consider each in more detail in terms of its linkage to adolescent health and implications for health-related behavior. In this discussion, *health* will refer to physical and emotional well-being; health-related behaviors involve actions of the individuals that either undermine health (health-compromising or risky behavior) or nurture it (health-enhancing or health-promoting behavior). The behaviors of particular interest are drug use, delinquency, poor nutrition, and sexual risk taking, on the one hand (health-compromising behaviors), and academic achievement and emotional well-being (health-promoting behaviors), on the other hand.

Three major themes will be emphasized. First, *causal connections between transformations in peer relations and health-related behavior go in both directions.* Whereas most research has focused on how peer relationships influence adolescent health, there is mounting evidence that adolescent health also affects peer relations or the way transformations in peer relations are negotiated. A second theme is that *connections between peer transformations and health-related behaviors change with age.* The magnitude of associations and the salience of a particular domain of peer relations or the type of health-related behavior may shift across adolescence. Finally, we suggest that *associations between peer relations and adolescent health may be indirect or interactive as well as direct.* For example, features of peer relations may moderate the influence of other agents or institutions, such as the family or schools; in addition, these agents and institutions may moderate the effects of peers.

The chapter concludes with comments on implications of the associations we have discussed for prevention/intervention programs as well as for future research in this area.

Transformations in Peer Relationships

Peers have long been regarded as one of the most salient forces in adolescents' lives (Hartup, 1993). They often compete with – and sometimes overpower – parents or schools in their influence over teenagers' attitudes and behavior (Brittain, 1963; Coleman, 1961; Kandel & Andrews, 1987). The salience of peers is heightened by transformations that broaden the peer networks, increase the depth of peer relationships, and increase their role in shaping individuals' self-concepts and interaction patterns. Three such transformations are of particular interest in this chapter: the stabilization of friendships, the initiation of romantic and sexually oriented relationships, and the emergence of peer crowds.

Stabilization of Friendships

Friends are a valued portion of young people's social networks long before adolescence (Hartup, 1983). Childhood friendships tend to be activity-based relationships that are easily severed when interests change or when proximity is lost. A friendship between two classmates is strained when the children end up in separate classrooms the following school year or when one child loses interest in an activity that has united the two friends.

By early adolescence, however, affective characteristics (loyalty, trust, willingness to share confidences) replace pragmatic ones (shared activities and interests) as the critical criteria for friendships (Bigelow, 1977). Trust and loyalty are developed only in long-term relationships. The quest for these features allows friendships to survive shifts in the activities or interests of one of the partners, or modest losses of proximity or contact, such as no longer sharing the same classes in school. With these features, friendships have a firm basis for the provision of emotional and instrumental support. As a result, friendships become more stable, more intimate, and more supportive relationships over the course of adolescence (Hartup, 1983; Berndt, 1982; Sharabany, Gershoni, & Hofman, 1981).

Another important qualitative change in friendships is in their autonomy from adult guidance or management. By adolescence, young people feel it is no longer legitimate for parents to control or restrain their selection or pursuit of friendships (Smetana & Asquith, 1994). Partially as a result of this, young people tend to spend an increasing amount of time with friends, and less time with family, over the course of adolescence (Csikszentmihalyi & Larson, 1984).

In sum, friendships are substantially transformed during adolescence. In contrast to the evanescent, activity-based relationships of childhood that are easily scuttled by shifts in partners' interests or access to each other, adolescent friendships emerge as more stable, intimate, affectively oriented attachments that occupy increasing amounts of a teenager's time and thrive relatively free of parental oversight or interference.

Initiation of Romantic Relationships

Qualitative shifts in friendships are accompanied by new orientations toward opposite-sex peers that focus on romance and sexual activity. Gender segregation in informal peer interactions reaches its height in late childhood (Maccoby, 1988). To some extent, this trend continues into adolescence. By an overwhelming margin, early adolescents still prefer same-sex to opposite-sex best friends (Blyth, Hill, & Thiel, 1982), and many peer activities (particularly sports teams) remain monosexual. Yet, particularly with the advent of puberty, there are both internal and external exigencies for reconsidering relationships with the opposite sex.

Puberty heightens interest in opposite-sex relationships as a means of exploring and gratifying sexual impulses. These interests are nurtured by the early adolescent's social world as well, as schools sponsor dances, parents allow or encourage mixed-sex parties, and the mass media tout images of "young teenagers in love." These external messages are so powerful and pervasive that even those who have not yet encountered puberty, or those who feel romantically and sexually attracted to members of the same sex, may still feel strong pressure to express an interest in dating or romantic liaisons (Cohen & Savin-Williams, 1996; Furman & Wehner, 1994). Health-related behaviors are implicated both in young people's ability to initiate such relationships and in their experiences within such relationships.

Emergence of Peer Crowds

For many people, the most curious transformation in adolescent peer relations involves young people's sudden penchant for labeling peers. In settings dominated by American youth of European heritage (European-Americans), labels tend to reflect individual abilities or interests: headbangers, jocks, populars, brains, skaters, nerds, and so on. In settings with large contingents of other ethnic groups, labels may also describe the ethnic background or ancestral origin of individuals (Brown & Mounts, 1989). Such labels provide a mechanism for adolescents to group peers into recognizable types, or "crowds" (Brown, 1990; Hartup, 1983), whose interests, activities, and values can be readily predicted. Early adolescents may identify only a small number of groups – the major ethnic divisions of their school or the anchor points of the social status hierarchy (e.g., populars, normals, and nerds) (Eder, 1985; Kinney, 1993). By the high school years, however, a much fuller range of crowds is usually articulated, including some hybrid groups such as jock-headbangers or smart populars (Kinney, 1993; Larkin, 1979).

Not all adolescents belong to a crowd (Brown & Lohr, 1987; Larkin, 1979). Yet even nonmembers may be influenced by crowds' capacity to restrict patterns of social interaction (Brown, Mory, & Kinney, 1994; Eder, 1985) or to establish behavioral norms for adolescents in a given social setting (Coleman, 1961; Eckert, 1989). In numerous ways, health-related behaviors are implicated in the dynamics of the peer crowd system.

Friendships and Health Behavior

Citing substantial correlations between adolescents and their close friends in delinquent activities, illicit drug use (tobacco, alcohol, marijuana, etc.), and sexual attitudes and behavior, many investigators argue that friendships are a primary source of health-compromising behavior among adolescents (Oeting & Beauvais, 1987). Others point out that the tendency to compare adolescents' behavior to their *perceptions* of friends' behavior, rather than the friends' self-reports, overstates peer influence (Kandel, 1994; Urberg, Shyu, & Liang, 1990); so does the common failure to control for "selection" effects, the tendency of adolescents to choose friends who already share their interests and activities (Cohen, 1977; Fisher & Bauman, 1988; Kandel, 1978).

Although it is important to determine the true magnitude of friends' influence on health-compromising behavior, other issues related to transformations in friendships at adolescence also deserve attention. We will discuss four such issues: First, to what extent does health-related behavior affect adolescents' ability to transform friendships into the close, stable, and trusting relationships expected at this stage of life? Second, how do friendships with these features enhance or endanger adolescent health? Third, are associations between friendship and health contingent on additional personal, interpersonal, or contextual factors (e.g., peer orientation or family relationships)? Finally, how do associations between friendship and health change across adolescence?

Health-Related Influences on Forming Adolescent Friendships

Do inclinations toward health-compromising behavior interfere with or enhance the transformations expected in friendships at adolescence? Data that bear directly on this issue are difficult to find, but evidence from studies of deviant youth suggests that the answer is equivocal. Cairns and Cairns (1992) found a marked instability in the friendships of their sample of aggressive preadolescents. By contrast, Giordano, Cernkovich, and Pugh (1986) found that although the friendships of delinquent youth featured more conflict than those of nondelinquents, the groups did not differ in the amount of time spent with friends, the stability of the relationships, or the levels of care and trust. Indeed, delinquents were more intimate with and more loyal to their friends.

These contradictory findings suggest that the link between health-related behaviors and the capacity to form close, stable friendships in adolescence may not be straightforward. Both type and level of health behavior may serve as contingent factors. Stable friendships may be disrupted more by poor emotional health than by drug use or poor eating habits. Moderate drug use may actually enhance friendship if adolescents rely on the loyalty and discreetness of friends to shield their deviant behavior from adults (Selnow & Crano, 1986). Heavy drug users, on the other hand, may be so preoccupied with drugs that they are thoroughly unreliable partners in relationships. There are simply not enough data to allow us to move beyond speculations about the effects of health-related behavior on adolescents' capacity to form close friendships.

Effects of Adolescent Friendships on Health-Related Behavior

As noted earlier, the transformation to a more mature relational style in adolescence is typified by three features of friendship: stability, intimacy, and supportiveness. A number of studies have traced the linkages between these characteristics and health-related behavior.

Stability. Although long-term effects of stable friendships in adolescence have not been studied, short-term consequences include improved school achievement and social status, both of which are associated with emotional health (Savin-Williams Berndt, 1990). Berndt and Keefe (1995) found that middle school youth (ages 12–14) who maintained their close friendships across a school year showed greater gains in school involvement and academic achievement, as well as lower increases in antisocial behavior, than those with unstable friendships. Curiously, however, Berndt and Hawkins (1991) reported that maintaining friendships across a school transition (elementary to middle school) was associated with health-enhancing behavior but that friendship stability across a school year had no such associations. Friendship stability may be particularly salient for adolescents confronting major life transitions, but more research is needed to verify this possibility.

Stability, however, can undermine as well as enhance adolescent health. Fisher and Bauman (1988) noted that teenagers are much less likely than children to end a relationship (or demote it to an acquaintanceship) when changes in a friend's attitudes or activities diminish the similarity between the pair. Thus, a friend who drifts into health-compromising activity patterns can "pull" an adolescent with her or him.

Intimacy. Intimacy in friendships has been associated with both behavioral and psychological health. For example, even though drug use is commonly perceived as a social activity (Smith, Koob, & Wirtz, 1985), Kandel (1978) reported that *low* levels of intimacy in friendship were one of the strongest predictors of adolescents' initiation into hard drugs (beyond alcohol, tobacco, and marijuana). With regard to emotional health, Buhrmester (1990) found that friendship intimacy was positively associated with self-esteem and negatively related to anxiety and depression; this was as true when intimacy scores were based on friend's ratings as on self-report.

Support. Because of the importance that adolescents accord to friends, supportive friendships seem crucial to emotional well-being. Cauce's (1986) work confirmed this among an ethnically diverse sample of American adolescents. Kirchler, Palmonari, and Pombeni (1993) found that Italian adolescents were more likely to talk to their best friend about a problem than to family members, the larger peer group, or even to no one at all! Respondents also reported that they were more likely to find a solution to their problem in conversations with their best friend than with other members of their support network.

Ironically, however, in American samples it is not uncommon to find significant associations between adolescents' reliance on friends (or peers in general) for support and *negative* health outcomes (e.g., Jessor & Jessor, 1977; Windle, 1992). Four explanations are possible for this counterintuitive finding. First, studies usually compare the amount of effort to access support from friends to the amount of emotional upset the adolescent feels. Such approaches do not measure the amount of support *obtained* from friends as much as the *need* for support; the latter is naturally associated with emotional dysfunction. Second, because studies are often correlational, investigators may make inappropriate causal attributions. Adolescents are likely to rely heavily on peers for support only when other support sources, especially parents and family members, are inadequate or unavailable, which in itself may exacerbate the stress. A third possibility is that in their measures of support, investigators fail to distinguish between assistance from close friends and assistance from peers in general. As Kirchler et al. (1993) indicated, the broader peer network may be less helpful than close friends. Finally, close friends (at least in the United States) may indeed promote less healthy coping strategies than adults do. Adolescents may suggest that the appropriate response to stress is to attack the provocateur or to employ escapist strategies (partying, drug use, reckless driving, etc.) that endanger physical health and provide only temporary relief from emotional concerns.

Obviously, these alternatives need to be systematically investigated. In doing so, researchers should also consider the possibility that the new features of adolescent peer relationships are a mixed blessing. In a study of Icelandic youth, for example, Vilhjalmsson (1994) found that although friends' support enhanced emotional health, it also exacerbated such health-compromising behaviors as tobacco use. It is also possible that friends are a "contingent" blessing – that they enhance health for some adolescents, or in some situations, more than others.

Moderating Factors

Results of several studies question the conclusion that all adolescents are adept at forming stable, intimate, and supportive peer relationships or that it is uniformly advisable to do so. DuBois and Hirsch (1990) reported that African-American youth disclose more to their friends than European-American youth do. The classic work of Sharabany et al. (1981) on Israeli youth suggests that the level of intimacy in adolescents' close friendships differs by sex, by the gender composition of the dyad, and by age.

Several ethnographers (Eckert, 1989; Eder, 1985; Kinney, 1993) have noted the tendency of youth in high-status peer crowds (jocks, populars, trendies) to form relatively superficial, instrumental friendships that contrast sharply with the intimate and enduring friendships typical of youth in more alienated or at-risk crowds (headbangers, burnouts). Eder and Kinney explain such differences in terms of the demands of the peer social system: Those on top need to maintain their competitive edge over peers who wish to supplant them as members of the social elite; they cannot afford to become too intimate because the "loose lips" of a friend could sink their reputation and thus their social standing. Eckert offers a more class-related explanation, suggesting that high-status youth emerge from the upper middle class with a more "corporate" mindset that regards friendships as cautious alliances with competitors for status and promotions. Lower-status crowds are populated by lower- and working-class youth who have learned from an early age to rely heavily on friends and to value honesty and loyalty in friendship above all else. Such different mindsets are bound to lead to different friendship patterns, which could have a profound impact on associations between friendship and health behavior.

Individual differences may affect not only the *capacity* to form stable, intimate, and supportive friendships but also the *outcomes* of such relationships for health-related behavior. For example, Moore and Rosenthal (1991) found sex differences in the effects of some forms of social support on sexual risk taking among Australian college students (casual relationships with multiple partners). Discussing precautions (e.g., use of contraceptives) with friends lowered risk taking among females but raised it among males.

It is also important to study linkages between friendship and health from the perspective of adolescents' broader social network. Barrera and Garrison-Jones (1992) reported that the influence of support from friends on adolescent depression was contingent on levels of support from parents. Friend support had little association with depression for those who were highly satisfied with support from their fathers, but friend support was inversely correlated with depression among those who were unsatisfied with support from their fathers. Satisfaction with mother support did not interact with friend support.

It is helpful, then, to differentiate the capacity to form close, enduring friendships from the advisability or necessity of doing so. Youths who *cannot* form close friendships should suffer greater health risks than those who avoid such relationships because of the norms of their peer group or the adequacies of other relationships (such as family ties).

Developmental Changes

Adolescent friendships are *dynamic* relationships. Across adolescence, they tend to grow more stable (Skorepa, Horrocks, & Thompson, 1963), more intimate (Hunter & Youniss, 1982), and more balanced in terms of partners' relative influence (Hartup, 1993). They also grow more salient among teenagers' network of relationships. We asked a sample of European-American teens in one midwestern school system to rate the importance of various relationships to their lives. The importance of one's best friend increased with age, especially relative to ratings for the mother and father. By the end of high school, both boys and girls rated their best friend as more important than any other category of relationship, including family members, romantic partners, and school adults (see Figure 7.1).

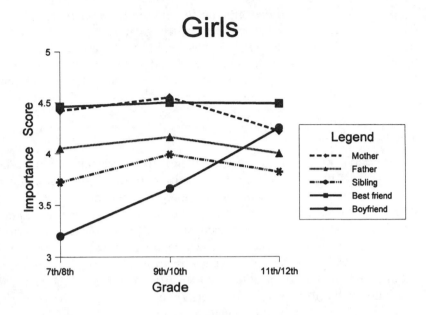

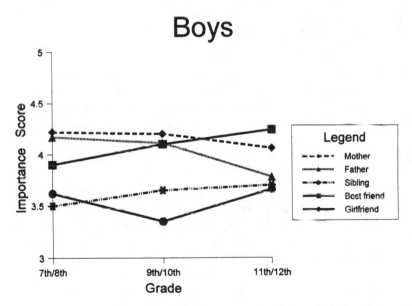

Figure 7.1. Age differences in mean ratings of the importance of each type of relationship to one's life. 1 = not at all important; 5 = extremely important. Scores for most significant teacher and coach/adviser are omitted because their means are well below those of other social network members.

As the character of friendship and its relation to other relationships shift during adolescence, it is reasonable to expect changes in the capacity of close friends to influence behavior that has health consequences for teenagers. Regrettably, there is virtually no research to date that approaches the associations between friendship and health in adolescence from a developmental view.

Summary

Glynn (1981) emphasized the reciprocal and interactive nature of the relationship between drug use and peer (especially friendship) influences. It is much better, he argued, to approach this area in terms of reciprocal causality than to study each causal direction separately. We believe this conclusion applies to associations between adolescent friendship and health-related behavior as a whole; but we would add the need to contextualize these reciprocal relationships by considering the moderating effects of three sets of variables: (1) enduring personality dispositions or background traits, (2) the character of relationships with other support givers (peers and, especially, family members), and (3) developmental changes in the quality of friendships.

Romantic Relationships and Health Behavior

The emergence of romantic relationships represents a second profound change in peer affiliations at adolescence. Understandably, most research on the health correlates of romantic ties have focused on sexual behavior. Because this topic is covered in detail in chapter 8, our comments will emphasize other linkages between romantic relationships and health-related behavior.

Initiation of Romantic Interests

Romantic relationships do not simply burst into prominence at the beginning of adolescence, but rather evolve slowly over this phase of life (Furman & Wehner, 1994). As a result, early adolescents are often preoccupied with being attractive to the opposite sex. In the United States, key features of such attractiveness are physical appearance, especially for girls, and athletic prowess, especially for boys (Coleman, 1961; Sebald, 1981). Efforts to acquire these features can prompt either health-enhancing or health-compromising behavior. On the one hand, to become more attractive or more athletic, adolescents may adopt good nutritional habits and engage in regular physical exercise. These can have positive effects on physical health. Moreover, when these efforts are successful, teenagers are typically rewarded with high peer status, which contributes to positive emotional health by bolstering self-esteem (Simmons & Blyth, 1987).

On the other hand, an interest in achieving the ideal figure prompts most adolescent girls to diet (Rosen & Gross, 1987), sometimes in cyclical dieting patterns that are harmful to long-term physical health and psychosocial development (French, Story, Downs, Resnich, & Blum, 1995). A small proportion of adolescents, primarily females, develop debilitating eating disorders, which can thwart the development of romantic ties (Mallick, Whipple, & Huerta, 1987; Stonehill & Crisp, 1977). Additionally, some adolescents (mostly boys) turn to steroids to give them a competitive edge in athletics (Tanner, Miller, & Alongi, 1995). Steroid use in this age group has been linked to a number of health-compromising behaviors (Burnett & Kleiman, 1994; DuRant, Rickert, Ashworth, Newman, & Slavens, 1993).

The timing of adolescents' entry into romantic relations also has implications for health. Because girls enter puberty at younger ages than boys, they often direct their romantic interests toward older males. Early-maturing girls, whose romantic inclinations are especially precocious, often become associated with deviantly oriented older males, who promote early entry into sexual activity with all its attendant health risks (Stattin & Magnussen, 1990). This tendency, however, can be reduced in social settings that shelter early maturers from contact with older boys, such as attending single-sex schools (Caspi, Lynam, Moffitt, & Silva, 1993).

Late-maturing boys, on the other hand, tend to have delayed physical development and heterosexual interests, both of which can diminish their attractiveness to the opposite sex and their status among peers. Merten (1996) found that these boys were routinely derided by peers for their small stature and "immature" interests. The lower self-esteem that resulted from peer derision, as well as the tendency to be the target of bullying behavior in middle school, represent genuine health risks to this group.

Pursuit of Romantic Relationships

As individuals move from the initiation phase to the pursuit of romantic relationships, sexual behavior becomes the chief health issue – so much so that few other facets of romantic relationships have been studied. Yet, there are other factors that may bear on health-related concerns. For example, there is some speculation that romantic relationships indirectly suppress risk-taking behavior, especially among boys. This conclusion is based on the assumption that health-compromising behaviors (apart from sexual activity) are enacted more often in the company of a same-sex clique than with an opposite-sex romantic partner. So, as an adolescent male devotes more time to his girlfriend and less time to "the guys," his risk taking should diminish. However, our study of predominantly European-American youth from two midwestern communities (see Brown, Clasen, & Eicher, 1986, for details of the sample) found little support for such speculations. From self-report surveys we derived

Table 7.1. *Differences on health-related outcomes of adolescents who have a romantic relationship and those who do not*

| | Early adolescents | | | | Older adolescents | | | |
| | Have romantic relationship | | No romantic relationship | | Have romantic relationship | | No romantic relationship | |
Variable	Mean	SD	Mean	SD	Mean	SD	Mean	SD
Drug use	1.66	.80	1.29	.56	1.69	.81	1.63	.81
Delinquency	1.82	.66	1.44	.52	1.62	.47	1.64	.50
Self-esteem	3.07	.52	3.01	.48	3.08	.52	3.13	.51
GPA	2.66	.88	2.89	.85	3.02	.72	3.12	.79
(*n*)	(127)		(188)		(153)		(114)	

Note: Early adolescents include 7th and 8th graders, and older adolescents include 11th and 12th graders; scores for 9th and 10th graders are omitted. Cronbach's alpha for drug use, delinquency, and self-esteem scales were .81, .74, and .85, respectively. Drug and delinquency scale scores range from 1 (never in past month) to 5 (almost every day); self-esteem scale scores range from 1 (low) to 4 (high esteem); grade point average scores range from 0 (F average) to 4 (A average).

scales measuring frequency of drug use and minor delinquency, along with academic achievement (self-reported grade point average) and global self-esteem, using Rosenberg's (1965) measure. Adolescents who had a romantic relationship (either ongoing or within the past year) reported significantly *higher* levels of drug use and delinquency – and, at best, only marginally higher levels of health-enhancing behaviors (academic achievement and self-esteem) – than those without such a relationship (see Table 7.1). This was as true for boys as for girls. Time spent with a romantic partner also varied significantly and positively with health-compromising behaviors. In both cases, however, the health-related deficits of those with romantic relationships were much greater among early adolescents (7th and 8th graders, *M* age = 13.1) than among older adolescents (11th and 12th graders, *M* age = 17.1).

Adolescent romances are usually short-lived but often intense. The dissolution of these relationships can be emotionally difficult. Possible outcomes include depressive symptoms, withdrawal from social relationships, unhealthy coping behaviors (such as heavy drinking), and disruption of the social network. Though probably temporary, these outcomes could pose health risks for individuals. More careful study of the course of romantic relationships, and adolescents' success in coping with their dissolution, is sorely needed. As with studies of friendship, this work must be attentive to individual and situational differences. For example, among Italian adolescents, Zani (1993) found that boys experienced an increase in status through dating, whereas girls experienced more conflict with peers.

Romantic Relationships in Homosexual Youth

Romantic attachments in adolescence are *typically* heterosexual but not always so (Remafedi, Resnick, Blum, & Harris, 1992). Associations between health and romantic relationships may be markedly different for homosexual or bisexual youth than for heterosexual teenagers. In the first place, feeling romantic and sexual attractions to persons of the same sex can be confusing and frightening for adolescents (Savin-Williams, 1994). The typical peer and cultural pressures toward opposite-sex social and sexual activities may be particularly stressful for these youths. Beyond this, those who act on their inclinations are vulnerable to ridicule and ostracism by peers and family alike (Cohen & Savin-Williams, 1996; Fricke 1981). These factors help account for the comparatively high rate of drug and alcohol abuse, depression and suicide attempts, and running away among gay teenagers (Remafedi, Farrow, & Deisher, 1991; Rotheram-Borus, Rosario, & Koopman, 1991).

Because of the strong peer and societal sanctions against homosexual activity and because adolescents have been socialized to believe that emotional intimacy is possible only in opposite-sex relationships (Savin-Williams, 1994), they may turn to a series of brief homosexual encounters to satisfy intimacy needs or even to prostitution (Coleman, 1989). These encounters are likely to involve young people in health-compromising sexual behavior. On the other hand, gay and lesbian youths who are successful in forming romantic attachments display comparatively good psychological health (self-acceptance and self-esteem) and find the social support necessary to fend off heterosexual pressures and prejudices from peers and adults (Savin-Williams, 1990). It is not clear, however, whether strong self-esteem is the cause or consequence of their capacity to form a supportive, same-sex romantic relationship (Savin-Williams, 1994).

Summary

Although information on the linkages between health and transformations in romantic relationships at adolescence is limited (except for studies of sexual behavior), the linkages again appear to be complex, reciprocal, shifting in content (the specific health behaviors involved) or magnitude across adolescence, and contingent on individual dispositions and social contexts. To better appreciate these linkages, however, researchers must move beyond their concern with sexual behavior as the only health-related issue in teenage romantic relations.

Peer Crowds and Health Behavior

In studying adolescent risk taking, it is not uncommon for researchers to divide adolescents into groups according to their level of risky behavior and then compare groups to discern characteristics that differentiate levels of risk taking (e.g., Chassin, Presson, Sherman, Montello, & McGrew, 1986; Downs, Flanagan, & Robertson, 1985–1986; Riester & Zucker, 1968). The same strategy has been employed for health-enhancing behaviors such as academic achievement (Steinberg, Mounts, Lamborn, & Dornbusch, 1991). It is ironic that young people do something similar on their own, creating a system of crowds into which to classify peers according to their appearance, attitudes, and/or behavior patterns. We argue that adolescents' own classification system is far more revealing than the artificial divisions of teenagers by social scientists. From this perspective we address three major questions in this section: How do crowd affiliations affect health-related behavior? Do these effects extend to adolescents who are not part of any crowd? Are crowd influences moderated by other forces in teenagers' lives, and can crowds moderate the influence of other social forces on adolescent health?

Crowd Differences in Health Behaviors: Reciprocal Influences

Health-related behaviors are among the central characteristics on which crowds are commonly differentiated (Brown, Lohr, & Trujillo, 1990). In fact, they are often important enough to figure in the name by which the group is commonly known: druggies, burnouts, gangbangers, granolas, brains, and so on. As a result, it is not surprising that investigators have found significant crowd differences on a variety of health-related behaviors, including smoking (Mosbach & Leventhal, 1988; Sussman, Dent, Stacy, & Burciaga, 1990; Urberg, 1992), drug and alcohol use (Dolcini & Adler, 1994; Downs & Rose, 1991), delinquent activity (Schwendinger & Schwendinger, 1985), sexual intercourse (Dolcini & Adler, 1994), academic achievement (Brown, Lamborn, Mounts, & Steinberg, 1993; Eckert, 1989), and emotional health (Brown & Lohr, 1987; Eder, 1985).

Dolcini and Adler's (1994) study of an ethnically diverse middle school in the San Francisco Bay Area serves as an example of crowd differences. Students who had been classified into crowds by peer nominations reported their sexual activity and levels of drug use. Even relatively early in adolescence, there were marked differences in alcohol and marijuana use and sexual experience among the three major crowds, as well as between students who "floated" among crowds and "outsiders" who were perceived as not belonging to any group (see Table 7.2). Health-compromising behavior was much more common in the two high-status groups (elites and popular blacks) than in the

Table 7.2. *Crowd differences in the percentage engaging in health-compromising behaviors*

Crowd	Cigarette use	Alcohol use	Marijuana use	Sexual intercourse
Elite ($n = 36$)	60	53	22	42
Popular black ($n = 16$)	44	38	25	43
Smart ($n = 32$)	28	16	9	6
Floaters ($n = 30$)	33	27	13	13
Outsiders ($n = 69$)	34	31	19	26

Source: Adapted from Dolcini and Adler (1994).

smart crowd, with outsiders and floaters manifesting intermediate rates of risky behavior.

Are health-related differences a cause or consequence of crowd affiliation? As with the similarity between close friends, the answer appears to be "both." For example, Dolcini and Adler (1994) found that associations between health-compromising behavior and crowd affiliation were attenuated when crowd differences in perceived competencies (elements of self-concept that probably predate crowd affiliation) are considered. At the same time, crowd differences in whether or not students had ever been offered drugs at school (an indicator of peer pressure) mirrored the differences in risky behaviors.

Effects of Health on Crowd Affiliation. Health behaviors can have direct influences on crowd affiliation. Drug use, deviant activity, and positive or negative self-concepts serve as "marker" behaviors that encourage peers to associate an adolescent with the crowd whose norms match those behaviors (Brown et al., 1993). If these behavior patterns change dramatically, so may the young person's crowd affiliation (Kinney, 1992). Yet, indirect linkages between health and crowd affiliations also have been observed. Gortmaker, Walker, Weitzman, and Sobol (1990) found comparatively high rates of peer conflict and social withdrawal among adolescents with one or more chronic health conditions. Such behaviors limit their chances of joining high-status crowds in which strong social skills are expected (Eder, 1985).

Effects of Crowd Affiliation on Health. Yet, it would be a mistake to presume that variations in health behaviors among crowds simply reflect preexisting individual differences. Indeed, one of the chief activities of crowds is to ensure that members conform to group norms and expectations and to sanction those who stray from norms (Cusick, 1973). Both ethnographic and survey studies have found significant differences among crowds in the types of peer pressures to which members are exposed – differences that reflect the norms of each crowd (Clasen & Brown, 1985; Eckert, 1989; Kinney, 1993). Ironically, however, adolescents may "buy into" the stereotype of their crowd rather than the actual (more moderate and variable) behavior of members. Their misperceptions of the prevalence of risky behavior among peers may lead them to feel pressure to engage in activities that are much less common than they presume (Hansen & Graham, 1991; Prentice & Miller, 1993).

Crowds as Barriers to Changing Health Behavior. Considering the role of peer pressure within crowds, an expedient way to promote adolescent health would be to shift young people's affiliations from crowds whose norms undermine health to those whose norms enhance it. As appealing as this strategy sounds, it is not realistic. Kinney (in Brown et al., 1994) mapped out the relationships between crowds in one midwestern high school, noting that the social boundaries between particular crowds were formidable. More often than not, barriers were constructed between crowds with markedly different health-related behavior patterns. Downs and Rose (1991) found that schools commonly feature one crowd whose members are not oriented to academics or school activities and are high in drug and alcohol use. This crowd appeared to be relatively isolated from interactions with other crowds. Even when adolescents labeled as heavy drinkers by peers reformed and became low or moderate drinkers, peers were disinclined to associate with them (Downs et al., 1985–1986).

Our most recent work with a sample of middle and high school youth in one midwestern American community helps to explain these dynamics. First, focus groups were conducted to identify the major crowds in each school. Then a sample of students rated how similar or different each possible pairing of major crowds was in their own minds. Applying multidimensional scaling techniques to these ratings, we constructed a two-dimensional map of the social relations among crowds (see Figure 7.2). It revealed several clusters of crowds that, on further interviewing, were found to differ on a number of behaviors, including health-related factors. For example, one crowd cluster in the high school included the black, gang member, and druggie crowds, all of which were described as alienated from school and prone to delinquent activity. The same was true of the skater/punker/gang crowd cluster in the middle school. A sharp contrast to these groups was the brain/nerd crowd cluster in each school, comprised of groups that embraced school achievement, eschewed drug use and delinquent activity, and suffered slightly from a modest reputation as social misfits.

All things considered, it would seem advantageous to encourage adolescents in the more alienated crowds to shift affiliations to the brains or the nerds – or at least to the preps or jocks, who featured more moderate levels of drug

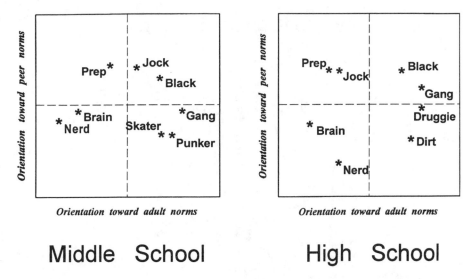

Figure 7.2. Perceptions of social distance among peer crowds in one midwestern sample.

use, delinquency, and other health-compromising behaviors. Our respondents, however, were not optimistic about this strategy. When asked if members of a particular crowd could shift into any of the other major crowds in their school, they reported that shifting would be easy among crowds within the sample cluster but moderately to very difficult across crowd clusters (see Figure 7.3). For example, middle school respondents felt that punkers would be fairly easily accepted by the skater or gang crowds but that acceptance by the brains or nerds would be very difficult.

These findings illustrate how the adolescent crowd system constructs channels and barriers to peer interaction. As *channels*, crowds bring together youths with similar orientations toward (among other things) health-related behaviors and create incentives to maintain these behaviors. The behaviors then become more than personal inclinations or habits. As Hurrelmann (1990) notes, "They provide a way of defining a public image and achieving social status" (p. 234). As a result, adolescents may be reluctant to relinquish such activities even if they compromise health and well-being. Behavioral changes are also likely to be resisted by peers within and beyond one's own crowd, who rely on them as stable markers of an individual's place within the crowd system. Adolescents then discover the *barriers* that crowd membership poses to shifting affiliations to other peer groups. Crowd affiliation becomes a protective factor for youth in groups that focus on health-enhancing behavior, but it exacerbates health risks for adolescents in crowds that embrace health-compromising activities.

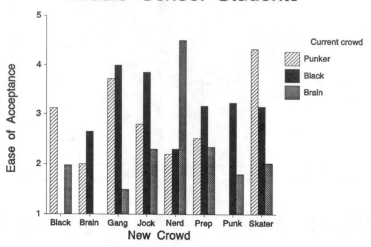

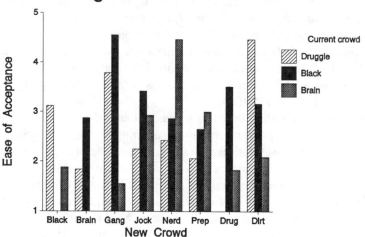

Figure 7.3. Perceptions of the ease with which members of specific crowds would be accepted by other crowds in one midwestern sample. Scores ranged from 1 (very difficult) to 5 (very easy).

Crowd Influences on Nonmembers

Not all adolescents are attached to a particular crowd. School-based studies indicate that up to half of the students either exist at the margins of two crowds, float among several groups, or are outside the crowd system altogether

(Brown, 1992; Dolcini & Adler, 1994; Eckert, 1989; Larkin, 1979). Ennet and Bauman (1994) suggested that such students, especially outsiders, are more likely to be smokers, and others have argued that their social skills are poorly developed, which could contribute to health-compromising behavior (Hurrelmann, 1990; Kirchler et al., 1993). Our own studies of teenagers in the American Midwest indicated that outsiders were not necessarily a cohesive group (Brown & Lohr, 1987). Their aspirations for crowd membership affected emotional health. Those who recognized that they were outsiders and wished to belong to a crowd fared as poorly in self-esteem and anxiety as members of low-status crowds; individuals who had little desire to be in a crowd seemed as psychologically healthy as members of high-status crowds.

Beyond aspirations for crowd affiliation, nonmembers can be affected by the climate that crowds create in a school. Tensions between major crowds can diminish emotional well-being for all students (Eckert, 1989); the leading crowd's emphasis on particular activities – partying, sexual experimentation, school achievement, or whatever – can create general normative pressures with which even nonmembers must cope (Coleman, 1961). Attempting to maintain a foothold in (or sustain friendships across) crowds with opposing norms can be both an exciting challenge and an emotional strain. Our understanding of how floaters and outsiders manage these indirect and/or competing pressures is remarkably limited.

Like crowd affiliation itself, then, escaping the crowd system is not necessarily a blessing or a curse for adolescents, but rather is contingent on the more specific features of one's noncrowd status and on the dynamics of intercrowd relationships.

Moderating Factors

Although crowds can be a formidable factor in adolescent health, their influence is moderated in several ways. First, crowds are less likely to redirect adolescent behavior than to sustain a preexisting trajectory. Brown et al. (1993) found that parents can influence their child's crowd affiliation through the specific behaviors that their parenting practices encourage. Even in preadolescence, entry into aggressive cliques (the forerunner of delinquent crowds in adolescence) is predicated on ineffective parenting behaviors (Dishion, Patterson, Stoolmiller, & Skinner, 1991). Parents continue to be a factor during the adolescent years. Brown and Huang (1995) reported that membership in antisocial or prosocial crowds may alter the effects of "facilitative" or "inhibitive" parenting, but it does not override these effects altogether.

Second, the norms and values, as well as the demography, of the community in which adolescents reside affect the types of crowds that exist in a school or at least the character of those crowds (Buff, 1970; Coleman, 1961; Larkin,

1979). Indeed, some have maintained that adolescent crowds are little more than adolescent labels for adult demographic clusters (Eckert, 1989; Ianni, 1989). In either case, crowd influences on adolescents are moderated by community influences on crowds.

Third, crowds are susceptible to the developmental mandates of adolescence. The importance of crowd affiliation declines across adolescence (Brown, Eicher, & Petrie, 1986; Coleman, 1974), and the barriers between crowds seem to weaken (Kinney, 1993). As this happens, the influence of crowds is probably supplanted by other peer relationships: close friendships and serious romantic ties. Urberg (1992), for example, reported that characteristics of close friends are better than crowd norms in predicting high school students' smoking behavior.

Fourth, ethnicity is an underexplored factor that may moderate crowd influences. Both Fordham (1988) and Kinney (1995) reported that youth from inner-city, predominantly African-American high schools worked assiduously to avoid crowd labels, preferring a reputation as a floater or as someone too complex or contradictory to pigeonhole in any crowd. Ethnicity itself supplants abilities or interests as the criterion for identifying crowds in ethnically diverse schools (Ianni, 1989), which may blur the connection between crowd affiliation and health behavior in these settings.

Of course, just as crowd influences on health may be moderated by other factors, crowd affiliation, in turn, may serve as a moderating variable. We have already mentioned evidence that crowd affiliation "filters" the effects of parenting practices on adolescents (Brown & Huang, 1995). It may also filter the effects of other peer relationships. Friendships are more stable and intimate in some crowds than in others (Eckert, 1989; Eder, 1985; Kinney, 1992; Peshkin, 1991). Romantic relationships display similar variability. In one midwestern sample of teenagers, the frequency of dating and the chances of having a romantic attachment were nearly twice as high among members of the druggie and popular crowds as among the brains and outcasts (Brown et al., 1994). By shaping romantic and friendship relationships, crowds may have a strong and as yet underappreciated *indirect* effect on adolescent health.

Summary

Especially in early adolescence, crowds are major organizing features of adolescents' social world. Health behaviors contribute to the personal image or reputation by which young people are channeled into particular crowds. Crowd norms and pressures, in turn, influence the degree to which adolescents are encouraged to pursue health-promoting or health-compromising behaviors. Over the course of adolescence, however, adolescents' allegiance to crowd norms deteriorates, as does the tendency of crowd affiliation to isolate young people from peers with divergent interests and health-related behaviors. As this happens, the influence of other peer associates – especially friends and romantic partners – on health-related activities is likely to increase. Crowd influences can be moderated by parental values and expectations, by community norms, and by the organization of the school or community. There is much more to be learned about how teenagers divide themselves into crowds (or scrupulously avoid crowd levels), and how these divisions affect and are affected by health-related behaviors.

Conclusion: Implications for Research and Intervention

New Emphases in Research

As researchers continue to explore connections between transformations in peer relations and adolescent health, three themes should be kept in mind. The first is that *associations between health and adolescent peer relationships are reciprocal and multidirectional.* The common assumption that peer relations alter health behavior must be complemented with more consideration of how health affects peer relations. The potential existence of vicious cycles in which, for example, predispositions toward risk taking groom adolescents for peer crowds that reinforce health-compromising behavior should be explored more carefully. At the same time, researchers must be more attentive to the capacity of peers to *improve* as well as diminish adolescent health. To what extent do friendships or romantic relationships improve emotional health? Under what conditions do crowd affiliations delimit health-compromising behavior?

A second theme is that *peer influences on adolescent health are embedded in a larger network of relationships and relational influences.* This is true both within and beyond peer relationships per se. Within such relationships, for example, the health consequences of engaging in romantic relationships are contingent on the norms of one's peer crowd – whether the crowd encourages shallow, short-lived "conquests" or more committed and intimate long-term relationships. Beyond peer relationships, there have been some attempts to understand how parental influences on adolescent health are altered by the rise in peer influences (Chassin et al., 1986; Glynn, 1981). Less has been done – and much more work is needed – on how parental relationships alter peer influences (Kandel & Andrews, 1987) or how peer affiliations alter parental influences (Brown & Huang, 1995). The consistency of norms across contexts (home, school, peer group) may also be a factor in how specific relationships affect physical and mental health (Phelan, Davidson, & Cao, 1991).

Third, more effort should be directed to understanding how *time and place alter associations between adolescent peer relationships and health behaviors.* Time may be a moderating factor in two separate ways. One is *historical time,* referring to how historical events or secular trends alter norms or behavior patterns in the wider society and how these changes affect peer relationships or health behaviors. For example, the growth of dual-career and single-parent households over the last two decades provides adolescents with more opportunities for unsupervised time at home, which makes it easier to add a sexual component to romantic relationships. At the same time, the spread of the acquired immunodeficiency syndrome (AIDS) in the heterosexual community in recent years could dissuade teenagers from taking full advantage of the available bedroom at home.

Time also can be measured in *individual, developmental terms*. A major point in this chapter is that the type and character of peer relationships – as well as their linkages to health – change appreciably over the course of adolescence. Berndt and Hoyle's (1985) study of the stability of friendships across school transitions, Kinney's (1993) assessment of transformations in crowd affiliations, and Furman and Wehner's (1994) outline of developmental changes in romantic relationships highlight the type of work that is needed in this area.

Beyond time is the issue of place – the degree to which community or subcultural factors alter associations between health and peer relationships. To date, most studies have relied on European or European-American samples from economically comfortable or advantaged backgrounds. Yet, there is evidence of socioeconomic and ethnic differences in the character of peer relationships (Eckert, 1989; Fordham, 1988; Kinney, 1992), as well as variability in the capacity of schools and communities to provide a peer climate that promotes healthy behavior (Coleman, 1961; Peshkin, 1991). These differences must be considered more seriously and systematically by researchers.

Implications for Intervention

Hopefully, these new themes in research studies will contribute to more sophisticated intervention efforts. Four recommendations can be highlighted. First and foremost, *practitioners must develop programs tailored to the subgroups of adolescents that emerge as a function of transformations in peer relationships*. In an ethnically diverse sample of seventh graders, Reardon, Sussman, and Flay (1989) found that the likelihood of resisting peer pressures and the specific strategies adolescents said they would use varied by their relationship to the peer giving pressure. For example, simple rejection was a more likely response with an acquaintance than a friend, in a group rather than a dyadic relationship, and in response to the first as opposed to subsequent instances of pressure by a peer. Based on these findings, the authors concluded that "teaching cross-situational strategies such as the widely advocated 'just say no' may be insufficient to the needs of adolescents in a variety of relationships and situations which they experience daily" (p. 320).

Prevention programs that feature peer leaders, although sometimes superior to those that feature adult leaders (Bangert-Drowns, 1988; Tobler, 1986), often are successful only with a specific group of students (Ellickson & Bell, 1990; Klepp, Halper, & Perry, 1986; Moskowitz, 1989). We suspect that this is because peer leaders typically are recruited from only one segment of the peer crowd system and have little credibility among members of many crowds. Drawing peer leaders from across the full range of crowds in the school or community should be far more effective. Better yet, practitioners can develop different prevention/intervention programs for specific peer crowds.

Second, *prevention and intervention programs cannot simply address health-compromising behaviors; they must also be concerned with adolescents' motivations to engage in such behavior.* Education about health risks is rarely sufficient to prevent or extinguish problematic behaviors. Adolescents may readily articulate the dangers of their health-compromising behavior, yet perform it anyway because of its importance to their loyalty to a friend, their attractiveness to the opposite sex, or their acceptance by a particular peer crowd. In promoting particular behaviors and discouraging others, practitioners must be more sensitive to adolescents' priorities (Leventhal & Keeshan, 1993). For example, asking some teenagers to give up smoking is tantamount to asking them to give up their identity (if smoking is the hallmark of the druggie crowd) or their credibility in a crowd that represents the only peer support system that they have. Compromising one's own health, especially when the consequences won't be manifest for years or decades, may be far less important to a teenager than compromising relationships with peers.

This raises a third point: *Health behaviors can be affected by indirect as well as direct intervention.* This is illustrated by programs designed to increase early adolescents' self-esteem in the hope that this will diminish susceptibility to health-compromising peer pressures. Such efforts should be expanded, but with more sensitivity to the dynamics of adolescent peer relationships. For example, Bierman and Furman (1985) found that to help rejected preadolescents forge a more positive image among peers, they not only had to improve rejected youths' social skills but also arrange social interactions that would alter peers' opinions of them. We suspect that one reason for high recidivism rates among adolescents after treatment for drug and alcohol abuse (Brown, Mott, & Myers, 1990; Catalano et al., 1991) is the inadequacy and insensitivity of posttreatment interventions. When teenagers return to the same school and community, the same peer system that fostered the drug use, their reputation precedes them. Peers are unwilling to "buy" the new "drug-free" image (Downs et al., 1985–1986), forcing the former abuser back into the same crowd under the influence of the same norms and pressures and, all too often, into the same pattern of unhealthy behavior. Interventions aimed at providing new social skills and new activity patterns that can help the teenager forge a new image among peers may be far more successful in preventing recidivism than current strategies.

Finally, *prevention and intervention programs must be more sensitive to developmental changes in peer relationships and peer influences.* The push to provide sex education at earlier ages, so as to catch youngsters at the initiation of sexual activities is all too often accompanied by the abandonment of sex education in the later high school years, when more stable romantic relationships spawn new forms of sexual risk taking. As the strong investment in conformity to crowd norms subsides in later adolescence, young people become receptive to messages and approaches in intervention programs that essentially fall on deaf ears in early adolescence.

Conclusion

Hurrelmann (1990) warned that "[i]f intervention concentrates only on the adolescent's individual attempts to cope with developmental tasks and thereby avoids contacts with the social basis of these attempts, it must remain ineffective" (p. 239). In this chapter we have charted some of the connections between health and transformations in peer relations at adolescence. Yet, studies to date constitute only a modest beginning toward an understanding of the complex linkages between health and peer relations. Forging a more sophisticated understanding of these linkages is a daunting task because of the complexities of reciprocal, multidirectional influences that are moderated by other social relationships and by individual, historical, and community factors. Yet, the exceptional capacity of peers to influence both health-enhancing and health-compromising behaviors makes it imperative that we take this research agenda very seriously. In so doing, we hope that researchers will dispel simplistic myths about peer influences on adolescent health and build a firmer basis for more effective health-related prevention and intervention programs for this age group.

References

Bangert-Drowns, R. L. (1988). The effects of school-based substance abuse education: A meta-analysis. *Journal of Drug Education, 18,* 243–264.
Barrera, M., & Garrison-Jones, C. (1992). Family and peer social support as specific correlates of adolescent depressive symptoms. *Journal of Abnormal Child Psychology, 20,* 1–16.
Berndt, T. J. (1982). The features and effects of friendship in early adolescence. *Child Development, 53,* 1447–1460.
Berndt, T. J., & Hawkins, J. A. (1991). *Effects of friendship on adolescents' adjustment to junior high school.* Unpublished manuscript, Purdue University.
Berndt, T. J., & Hoyle, S. G. (1985). Stability and change in childhood and adolescent friendships. *Developmental Psychology, 21,* 1007–1015.
Berndt, T. J., & Keefe, K, (1995). Friends' influence on adolescents' adjustment to school. *Child Development, 66,* 1312–1329.
Bierman, K., & Furman, W. (1985). The effects of social skills training and peer involvement on the social adjustment of preadolescents. *Child Development, 55,* 151–162.

Bigelow, B. J. (1977). Children's friendship expectations: A cognitive developmental study. *Child Development, 48,* 246–253.

Blyth, D. A., Hill, J. P., & Thiel, K. S. (1982). Early adolescents' significant others: Grade and gender differences in perceived relationships with familial and nonfamilial adults and young people. *Journal of Youth and Adolescence, 11,* 425–450.

Brittain, C. V. (1963). Adolescent choices and parent–peer cross-pressures. *American Sociological Review, 28,* 385–391.

Brown, B. B. (1990). Peer groups and peer cultures. In S. S. Feldman & G. R. Elliott (Eds.), *At the threshold: The developing adolescent* (pp. 171–196). Cambridge, MA: Harvard University Press.

Brown, B. B. (1992). The measurement and meaning of adolescent peer groups. *SRA Newsletter, 6,*(1). 6–8.

Brown, B. B., Clasen, D. R., & Eicher, S. A. (1986). Perceptions of peer pressure, peer conformity dispositions, and self-reported behavior among adolescents. *Developmental Psychology, 22,* 521–530.

Brown, B. B., Eicher, S. A., & Petrie, S. (1986). The importance of peer group ("crowd") affiliation in adolescence. *Journal of Adolescence, 9,* 73–96.

Brown, B. B., & Huang, B.-H. (1995). Examining parenting practices in different peer contexts: Implications for adolescent trajectories. In L. J. Crockett & A. C. Crouter (Eds.), *Pathways through adolescence: Individual development in relation to social contexts* (pp. 151–174). Hillsdale, NJ: Erlbaum.

Brown, B. B., Lamborn, S. D., Mounts, N. S., & Steinberg, L. (1993). Parenting practices and peer group affiliation in adolescence. *Child Development, 64,* 467–482.

Brown, B. B., & Lohr, M. J. (1987). Peer group affiliation and adolescent self-esteem: An integration of ego-identity and symbolic interaction theories. *Journal of Personality and Social Psychology, 52,* 47–55.

Brown, B. B., Lohr, M. J., & Trujillo, C. (1990). Multiple crowds and multiple life styles: Adolescents' perceptions of peer group stereotypes. In R. E. Muuss (Ed.), *Adolescent behavior and society* (4th ed., pp. 30–36). New York: McGraw-Hill.

Brown, B. B., Mory, M. S., & Kinney, D. (1994). Casting adolescent crowds in relational perspective: Caricature, channel, and context. In R. Montemayor, G. R. Adamas, & T. P. Gullotta (Eds.), *Personal relationships during adolescence* (pp. 123–167). Thousand Oaks, CA: Sage.

Brown, S. A., Mott, M. A., & Myers, M. G. (1990). Adolescent drug and alcohol treatment outcome. In R. R. Watson (Ed.), *Prevention and treatment of drug and alcohol abuse* (pp. 373–403). Clifton, NJ: Humana Press.

Brown, S. A., Mott, M. A., & Stewart, M. A. (1992). Adolescent alcohol and drug abuse. In C. E. Walker & M. C. Roberts (Eds.), *Handbook of clinical psychology* (2nd ed., pp. 677–693). New York: Wiley.

Brown, B. B., & Mounts, N. (1989). *Peer group structures in single versus multi-ethnic high schools.* Paper presented at the 1989 Biennial Meetings of the Society for Research in Child Development, Kansas City.

Buff, S. A. (1970). Greasers, dupers, and hippies: Three responses to the adult world. In L. Howe (Ed.), *The white majority* (pp. 60–77). New York: Random House.

Buhrmester, D. (1990). Intimacy of friendship, interpersonal competence, and adjustment during preadolescence and adolescence. *Child Development, 61,* 1101–1111.

Burnett, K. F., & Kleiman, M. E. (1994). Psychological characteristics of adolescent steroid users. *Adolescence, 29,* 81–89.

Cairns, R. B. & Cairns, B. D. (1992, March). The dynamics and fluidity of peer groups. In B. B. Brown (Chair), *Stability and change in adolescent peer relations: Characteristics and consequences.* Paper presented at a symposium conducted at the biennial meetings of the Society for Research on Adolescence, Washington, DC.

Caspi, A., Lynam, D., Moffitt, T. E., & Silva, P. A. (1993). Unraveling girls' delinquency: Biological, dispositional, and contextual contributions to adolescent misbehavior. *Developmental Psychology, 29,* 19–30.

Catalano, R. F., Wells, E. A., Hawkins, J. D., Miller, J., & Brewer, D. D. (1991). Evaluation of the effectiveness of adolescent drug abuse treatment, assessment of risks for relapse, and promising approaches for relapse prevention. *International Journal of the Addictions, 25,* 1085–1140.

Cauce, A.-M. (1986). Social networks and social competence: Exploring the effects of early adolescent friendships. *American Journal of Community Psychology, 14,* 607–628.

Chassin, L., Presson, C. C., Sherman, S. J., Montello, D., & McGrew, J. (1986). Changes in peer and parent influence during adolescence: Longitudinal versus cross-sectional perspectives on smoking initiation. *Developmental Psychology, 22,* 327–334.

Clasen, D. R., & Brown, B. B. (1985). The multidimensionality of peer pressure in adolescence. *Journal of Youth and Adolescence, 14,* 451–468.

Cohen, J. (1977). Sources of peer group homogeneity. *Sociology of Education, 50,* 227–241.

Cohen, K. M., & Savin-Williams, R. C. (1996). Developmental perspectives on coming out to self and others. In R. C. Savin-Wlliams & K. M. Cohen (Eds.), *The lives of lesbians, gays, and bisexuals: Children to adults* (pp. 113–151). Fort Worth, TX: Harcourt Brace.

Coleman, E. (1989). The development of male prostitution activity among gay and bisexual adolescents. *Journal of Homosexuality, 17,* 131–149.

Coleman, J. C. (1974). *Relationships in adolescence.* Boston: Routledge & Kegan Paul.

Coleman, J. S. (1961). *The adolescent society.* New York: Free Press.

Csikszentmihalyi, M., & Larson, R. (1984). *Being adolescent.* New York: Basic Books.

Cusick, P. A. (1973). *Inside high school.* New York: Holt, Rinehart, & Winston.

Dishion, T. J., Patterson, G. R., Stoolmiller, M., & Skinner, M. L. (1991). Family, school, and behavioral antecedents of early adolescent involvement with antisocial peers. *Developmental Psychology, 27,* 172–180.

Dolcini, M. M., & Adler, N. E. (1994). Perceived competencies, peer group affiliation, and risk behavior among early adolescents. *Health Psychology, 13,* 496–506.

Downs, W. R., Flanagan, J. C., & Robertson, J. F. (1985/1986). Labeling and rejection of adolescent heavy drinkers: Implications for treatment. *Journal of Applied Social Sciences, 10,* 1–19.

Downs, W. R., & Rose, S. R. (1991). The relationship of adolescent peer groups to the incidence of psychosocial problems. *Adolescence, 26,* 473–491.

DuBois, D. L., & Hirsch, B. J. (1990). School and neighborhood friendship patterns of blacks and whites in early adolescence. *Child Development, 61,* 524–536.

DuRant, R. H., Rickert, V. I., Ashworth, C. S., Newman, C., & Slavens, G. (1993). Use of multiple drugs among adolescents who use anabolic steroids. *New England Journal of Medicine, 328,* 922–926.

Eckert, P. (1989). *Jocks and burnouts: Social categories and identity in the high school.* New York: Teachers College Press.

Eder, D. (1985). The cycle of popularity: Interpersonal relations among female adolescents. *Sociology of Education, 58,* 154–165.

Ellickson, P. L., & Bell, R. M. (1990). Drug prevention in junior high: A multi-site longitudinal test. *Science, 247,* 1299–1305.

Ennet, S. T., & Bauman, K. E. (1994). Peer group structure and adolescent cigarette smoking: A social network analysis. *Journal of Health and Social Behavior, 34,* 226–236.

Fisher, L. A., & Bauman, K. E. (1988). Influence of selection and socialization in the friend–adolescent relationship: Findings from studies of adolescent smoking and drinking. *Journal of Applied Social Psychology, 18,* 289–314.

Fordham, S. (1988). Racelessness as a factor in black students' school success: Pragmatic strategy or pyrrhic victory? *Harvard Educational Review, 58,* 54–84.

French, S. A., Story, M., Downs, B., Resnich, M. D., & Blum, R. W. (1995). Frequent dieting among adolescents: Psychosocial and health behavior correlates. *American Journal of Public Health, 85,* 695–701.

Fricke, A. (1981). *Reflections of a rock lobster: A story about growing up gay.* Boston: Alyson.

Furman, W., & Wehner, E. A. (1994). Romantic views: Toward a theory of adolescent romantic relationships. In R. Montemayor, G. R. Adamas, & T. P. Gullotta (Eds.), *Personal relationships during adolescence* (pp. 168–195). Thousand Oaks, CA: Sage.

Giordano, P. C., Cernkovich, S. A., & Pugh, M. D. (1986). Friendships and delinquency. *American Journal of Sociology, 91*, 1170–1202.

Glynn, T. L. (1981). From family to peer: A review of transitions of influence among drug-using youth. *Journal of Youth and Adolescence, 10*, 363–383.

Gortmaker, S. L., Walker, D. L., Weitzman, M., & Sobol, A. (1990). Chronic conditions, socioeconomic risks, and behavioral problems in children and adolescents. *Pediatrics, 85*, 267–276.

Hansen, W. B., & Graham, J. W. (1991). Preventing alcohol, marijuana, and cigarette use among adolescents: Peer pressure resistance training versus establishing conservative norms. *Preventive Medicine, 20*, 414–430.

Hartup, W. W. (1983). Peer relations. In E. M. Hetherington (Ed.), *Handbook of child psychology* (Vol. 4, pp. 103–196). New York: Wiley.

Hartup, W. W. (1993). Adolescents and their friends. In B. Laursen (Ed.), *New directions for child development: Close friendships in adolescence* (pp. 3–22). San Francisco: Jossey-Bass.

Hunter, F., & Youniss, J. (1982). Changes in the functions of three relations during adolescence. *Developmental Psychology, 18*, 806–811.

Hurrelmann, K. (1990). Health promotion for adolescents: Preventive and corrective strategies against problem behavior. *Journal of Adolescence, 13*, 231–250.

Ianni, F. A. J. (1989). *The search for structure*. New York: Free Press.

Jessor, R., & Jessor, S. L. (1977). *Problem behavior and psychosocial development: A longitudinal study of youth*. San Diego, CA: Academic Press.

Kandel, D. B. (1978). Homophily, selection, and socialization in adolescent friendships. *American Journal of Sociology, 84*, 427–436.

Kandel, D. B. (1994, February). The interpersonal context of adolescent deviance: What we know, what we need to know. In B. Brown (Chair), *Family–peer linkages in adolescence: New directions for integrative research*. Symposium conducted at the biennial meetings of the Society for Research on Adolescence, San Diego.

Kandel, D. B., & Andrews, K. (1987). Processes of adolescent socialization by parents and peers. *International Journal of the Addictions, 22*, 319–342.

Kinney, D. A. (1992, March). Coming together and going your own way: Delineating diversity and change in adolescent crowd associations. In B. Brown (Chair), *Stability and change in adolescent peer relations: Characteristics and consequences*. Symposium conducted at the biennial meetings of the Society for Research in Adolescence, Washington, DC.

Kinney, D. A. (1993). From "nerds" to "normals": Adolescent identity recovery within a changing social system. *Sociology of Education, 66*, 21–40.

Kinney, D. A. (1995, April). From at-risk to resilient: Examining the role of extracurricular activities for urban high school students. In D. Mekos & G. H. Elder, Jr. (Chairs), *Developmental perspectives on adolescent extracurricular involvement*. Symposium conducted at the biennial meetings of the Society for Research in Child Development, Indianapolis.

Kirchler, E., Palmonari, A., & Pombeni, M. L. (1993). Developmental tasks and adolescents' relationships with their peers and their family. In S. Jackson & H. Rodriguez-Tome (Eds.), *Adolescence and its social worlds* (pp. 145–167). Hillsdale, NJ: Erlbaum.

Klepp, A., Halper, A., & Perry, C. (1986). The efficacy of peer leaders in drug abuse prevention. *Journal of School Health, 56*, 407–411.

Larkin, R. W. (1979). *Suburban youth in cultural crisis*. New York: Oxford University Press.

Leventhal, H. & Keeshan, P. (1993). Promoting healthy alternatives to substance abuse. In S. G. Millstein, A. C. Petersen, & E. O. Nightingale (Eds.), *Promoting the health of adolescents* (pp. 260–284). New York: Oxford University Press.

Maccoby, E. E. (1988). Gender as a social category. *Developmental Psychology, 24*, 755–765.

Mallick, M. J., Whipple, T. W., & Huerta, E. (1987). Behavioral and psychological traits of weight-conscious teenagers: A comparison of eating-disordered patients and high- and low-risk groups. *Adolescence, 22*, 157–168.

Merten, D. (1996). Visibility and vulnerability: Responses to rejection by nonaggressive junior high school boys. *Journal of Early Adolescence, 16,* 5–26.

Moore, S., & Rosenthal, D. (1991). Adolescents' perceptions of friends' and parents' attitudes to sex and sexual risk-taking. *Journal of Community and Applied Social Psychology, 1,* 189–200.

Mosbach, P., & Leventhal, H. (1988). Peer group identification and smoking: Implications for intervention. *Journal of Abnormal Psychology, 97,* 238–245.

Moskowitz, J. W. (1989). The primary prevention of alcohol problems: A critical review of the research literature. *Journal of Studies on Alcohol, 50,* 54–88.

Oeting, E. R., & Beauvais, F. (1987). Peer cluster theory, socialization characteristics, and adolescent drug use: A path analysis. *Journal of Counseling Psychology, 34,* 205–213.

Peshkin, A. (1991). *The color of strangers, the color of friends.* Chicago: University of Chicago Press.

Phelan, P., Davidson, A. L., & Cao, H. T. (1991). Students' multiple worlds: Negotiating the boundaries of family, peer, and school cultures. *Anthropology and Education Quarterly, 22,* 224–250.

Prentice, D. A., & Miller, D. T. (1993). Pluralistic ignorance and alcohol use on campus: Some consequences of misperceiving the social norm. *Journal of Personality and Social Psychology, 64,* 243–256.

Reardon, K. K., Sussman, S., & Flay, B. R. (1989). Are we marketing the right message: Can kids "just say 'no'" to smoking? *Communication Monographs, 56,* 307–324.

Remafedi, G., Farrow, J. A., & Deisher, R. W. (1991). Risk factors for attempted suicide in gay and bisexual youth. *Pediatrics, 87,* 869–875.

Remafedi, G., Resnick, M., Blum, R., & Harris, L. (1992). Demography of sexual orientation in adolescents. *Pediatrics, 79,* 331–337.

Riester, A. E., & Zucker, R. A. (1968). Adolescent social structure and drinking behavior. *Personnel and Guidance Journal, 47,* 304–312.

Rosen, J. C., & Gross, J. (1987). Prevalence of weight reducing and weight gaining in adolescent girls and boys. *Health Psychology, 6,* 131–147.

Rosenberg, M. O. (1965). *Society and the adolescent self-image.* New York: Princeton University Press.

Rotheram-Borus, M. J., Rosario, M., & Koopman, C. (1991). Minority youths at high risk: Gay males and runaways. In M. E. Colten & S. Gore (Eds.), *Adolescent stress: Causes and consequences* (pp. 181–200). New York: Aldine de Gruyter.

Savin-Williams, R. C. (1990). *Gay and lesbian youth: Expressions of identity.* Washington, DC: Hemisphere.

Savin-Williams, R. C. (1994). Dating those you can't love and loving those you can't date. In R. Montemayor, G. R. Adamas, & T. P. Gullotta (Eds.), *Personal relationships during adolescence* (pp. 196–215). Thousand Oaks, CA: Sage.

Savin-Williams, R. C. & Berndt, T. J. (1990). Friendship and peer relationships. In S. S. Feldman and G. R. Elliott (Eds.), *At the threshold: The developing adolescent* (pp. 277–307). Cambridge, MA: Harvard University Press.

Schwendinger, H., & Schwendinger, J. S. (1985). *Adolescent subcultures and delinquency.* New York: Praeger.

Sebald, H. (1981). Adolescents' concept of popularity and unpopularity: Comparing 1960 with 1976. *Adolescence, 16,* 187–193.

Selnow, G. W., & Crano, W. D. (1986). Formal vs. informal group affiliations: Implications for alcohol and drug use among adolescents. *Journal of Studies on Alcohol, 47,* 48–52.

Sharabany, R., Gershoni, R., & Hofman, J. E. (1981). Girlfriend, boyfriend: Age and sex differences in intimate friendship. *Developmental Psychology, 17,* 800–808.

Simmons, R. G., & Blyth, D. A. (1987). *Moving into adolescence: The impact of pubertal change and school context.* New York: Aldine.

Skorepa, C. A., Horrocks, J. E., & Thompson, G. G. (1963). A study of friendship fluctuations of college students. *Journal of Genetic Psychology, 102,* 151–157.

Smetana, J. G., & Asquith, P. (1994). Adolescents' and parents' conceptions of parental authority and personal autonomy. *Child Development, 65*, 1147–1162.

Smith, T. E., Koob, J., & Wirtz, T. (1985). Ecology of adolescents' marijuana abuse. *International Journal of the Addictions, 20*, 1421–1428.

Stattin, H., & Magnussen, D. (1990). *Pubertal maturation in female development.* Hillsdale, NJ: Erlbaum.

Steinberg, L., Mounts, N. S., Lamborn, S. D., & Dornbusch, S. M. (1991). Authoritative parenting and adolescent adjustment across varied ecological niches. *Journal of Research on Adolescence, 1*, 19–36.

Stonehill, E., & Crisp, A. H. (1977). Psychoneurotic characteristics of patients with anorexia nervosa before and after treatment and at follow-up 4–7 years later. *Journal of Psychosomatic Research, 21*, 189–193.

Sussman, S., Dent, C. W., Stacy, A. W., & Burciaga, C. (1990). Peer group association and adolescent tobacco use. *Journal of Abnormal Psychology, 99*, 349–352.

Tanner, S. M., Miller, D. W., & Alongi, C. (1995). Anabolic steroid use by adolescents: Prevalence, motives, and knowledge of risks. *Journal of Sport Medicine, 5*, 108–115.

Tobler, N. S. (1986). Meta-analysis of 143 adolescent drug prevention programs: Quantitative outcome results of program participants compared to a control or comparison group. *Journal of Drug Issues, 16*, 537–567.

Urberg, K. A. (1992). Locus of peer influence: Social crowd and best friend. *Journal of Youth and Adolescence, 21*, 439–450.

Urberg, K. A., Shyu, S. J., & Liang, J. (1990). Peer influence in adolescent cigarette smoking. *Addictive Behaviors, 15*, 247–255.

Vilhjalmsson, R. (1994). Effects of social support on self-assessed health in adolescence. *Journal of Youth and Adolescence, 23*, 437–452.

Windle, M. (1992). Temperament and social support in adolescence: Interrelations with depressive symptoms and delinquent behaviors. *Journal of Youth and Adolescence, 21*, 1–21.

Zani, B. (1993). Dating and interpersonal relationships in adolescence. In S. Jackson & H. Rodriguez-Tome (Eds.), *Adolescence and its social worlds* (pp. 95–120). Hillsdale, NJ: Erlbaum.

8 Sexuality and Developmental Transitions During Adolescence

Jeanne Brooks-Gunn and Roberta Paikoff

Adolescent sexuality has been viewed through a panapoly of lenses and by a variety of disciplines – anthropology, demography, developmental psychology, sociobiology, adolescent medicine, sociology, and even economics. All societies have mechanisms for controlling youthful sexuality, some of which are more successful than others. Variations in the salience of parental control, peer groups, societal norms, and neighborhood composition exist both across and within societies. Historical changes also influence how much adherence to societal norms is seen (as well as the range of norms) across subgroups in a society. Indeed, the study of sexuality is a perfect example of why person, time, context, and period must be considered simultaneously (Bronfenbrenner 1977). In traditional societies marriage is often linked to sexual maturity, and first marriage occurs during the teenage years (Paige & Paige, 1985). However, in more industrialized societies, with their need for more formal educational skills, first marriages occur in young adulthood. The secular trend in menarche *and* the later age of marriage have resulted in an increase in the period between reproductive maturity and marriage. Figure 8.1 illustrates the interval between puberty (defined as menarche for girls and spermarche for males) and marriage for females in 1890 and 1988, as well as for males in 1988 (Alan Guttmacher Institute, 1994). For girls, the interval was a little over 7 years a century ago, compared to almost 12 years in 1988. First marriage occurs on average in the middle (to late) 20s. The 12 years may seem very long indeed to a teenager or a young adult experiencing sexual arousal.

At the same time (at least in the past 40 years, when data have become available on youth having intercourse by age 18), the percentages of sexually active teenagers have been rising for both boys and girls. Figure 8.2 illustrates these increases, from 1956 for girls and from 1968 for boys. By the end of the

The writing of this chapter was supported by funding from the National Institute of Child and Human Development (NICHD), the W. T. Grant Foundation, and the National Institute of Mental Health Office on AIDS. The NICHD Research Network on Child and Family Well-being also supported this work. We wish to thank our colleagues Doreen Rosenthal and Shirley Feldman for sharing their wonderful vignettes with us and Susan Millstein for her critical reading of our work. We finally wish to thank Andrea Bastiani for her assistance in the preparation of this chapter.

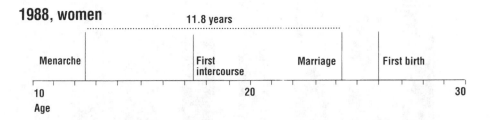

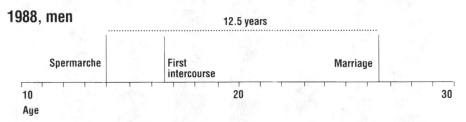

Figure 8.1. The interval for women and men between puberty and marriage. Reproduced with the permission of The Alan Guttmacher Institute from *Sex and America's Teenagers*, The Alan Guttmacher Institute, New York, 1994. *Sources: Menarche, 1890*: E. G. Wyshak & R. E. Frisch. (1982). Evidence for a secular trend in age of menarche. *New England Journal of Medicine, 306,* 1033–1035. *First marriage, 1890*: U. S. Bureau of the Census. (1991). Marital status and living arrangements: March, 1990. *Current Population Reports,* Series P-20, No. 450, Table A, p. 1. *First birth, 1890*: National Center for Health Statistics. (1976). *Fertility tables for birth cohorts by color,* United States, 1917–73 (Table 6A, p. 145). Rockville, MD, Public Health Service. *Menarche, first intercourse and first birth, and first marriage, 1988*: J. D. Forrest. (1993). Timing of reproductive life stages. *Obstetrics and Gynecology, 82,* 105–111, Table 3. *Spermache, 1988*: E. Atwater. (1992). *Adolescence* (3rd ed., p. 63). Englewood Cliffs, NJ: Prentice-Hall. *Notes: Menarche* is the beginning of menstruation in females. *Spermarche* is the beginning of sperm production in males. The data for the different time periods are not totally comparable. For 1890, age at first marriage is calculated in the usual manner as the age by which 50% of the ever-married population had married. (Median age at marriage in 1890 would be higher if it were calculated for the total population.) The 1890 first-birth figure is calculated from the 1917 birth cohort; the 1890 number is unavailable, but it is estimated to be lower. For 1988, the median ages at menarche, spermarche, first intercourse, marriage, and first birth are calculated as the age by which 50% of the total female (or male) population in 1988 had experienced the event. *Data points: 1890, women*: age at menarche, 14.8; marriage, 22.0; first birth, 23.8. *1988, women*: age at menarche, 12.5; first intercourse, 17.4; marriage, 24.3; first birth, 26.0. *1988, men*: age at spermarche, 14.0; first intercourse, 16.6; marriage, 26.5.

% of 12–19-year-olds, 1988

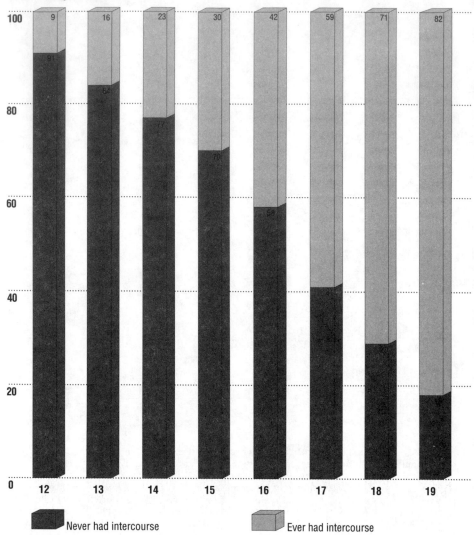

Figure 8.2. The percentage of women and men who have had intercourse by age. Reproduced with the permission of The Alan Guttmacher Institute from *Sex and America's Teenagers*, The Alan Guttmacher Institute, New York, 1994. *Sources: Women*: Adapted from AGI tabulations by S. L. Hofferth of data from the 1982 National Survey of Family Growth; AGI tabulations of data from the 1988 National Surveys of Family Growth. *Men*: F. L. Sonenstein, J. H. Pleck and L. C. Ku, "Sexual Activity, Condom Use and AIDS Awareness Among Adolescent Males," *Family Planning Perspectives*, *21*, 152–158, 1989, Table 1, p. 153. *Total Population*: F. W. Hollmann, "Estimates of the Population of the United States by Age, Sex, and Race," *Current Population Reports*, Series P-25, No. 1095, 1993, Table 1, p. 10. *Note:* The National Survey of Family Growth (NSFG) and NSAM (National Survey of Adolescent Males) do not survey youth under age 15. Estimates of age at first intercourse for 12–14-year-olds are based on data from the Youth Risk Behavior Survey (YRBS). Because the YRBS reports higher levels of sexual activity than the other two surveys, YRBS estimates were deflated on the basis of the ratio of YRBS to NSFG (or to NSAM for males) figures on proportions of 18-year-olds who have had intercourse.

1980s, three-quarters of boys and almost three-fifths of girls reported having had intercourse by age 18 (Alan Guttmacher Institute, 1994). Additionally, of those youth who are sexually active, intercourse is being experienced earlier. For example, 22% of 14-year-olds, 30% of 15-year-olds, 42% of 16-year-olds and 59% of 17-year-olds were sexually active (based on 1988 data; Alan Guttmacher Institute, 1994).

The impetus for strictures against youthful sexuality in earlier historical epochs was usually thought to be the control, timing, and context of childbearing (Paige & Paige, 1985). Today, the ensurance of physical health (absence of sexually transmitted diseases) is also a reason to be concerned about adolescent sexuality or at least the practice of safe sex. On a more emotional than physical level, concern is also raised about the ability of the young to engage in sexual intercourse in a way that respects both individuals, such that neither is being manipulated or coerced.[1] These concerns coexist with sexual desire that is part of becoming a man or woman. No matter how much adults might like to ignore it, sex has great meaning in the lives of youth, whether they have had any sexual experience or not. A sexual identity or identities have to be formed; sexual exploration (be it kissing, intercourse, or just dreaming) will occur during the adolescent years; and the negotiation of autonomy and intimacy will take place within sexual situations. On perhaps a more cautionary note, youth will also have to recognize situations in which sexual behavior is more difficult to control; in which others may use coercion or pressure to obtain sex; in which (one or both) partners may want intimacy but get sex instead; and in which their choices may not be accepted by their peer group (either to have or not to have sex). And sexuality is, in many ways, still gender specific, reflecting imbalances between dominance and status, much as we would like it to be otherwise.

This chapter is divided into five sections. The first one briefly considers the frameworks used to study adolescent sexual transitions. In the second section, we focus on aspects of the self that change during adolescence and that may have implications for sexual transitions. The third section highlights the ways in which relational change might affect the timing, nature, and meaning of sexual transitions. Then the meaning of sexuality is discussed by looking at what youth are actually saying. The final section returns to the definition of sexual well-being and the implications for studying sexual transitions.

Frameworks for the Study of Sexual Transitions

Antecedents of Sexual Intercourse

Typically, articles on adolescent sexuality (including those that we have written; e.g., Brooks-Gunn & Furstenberg, 1989; Brooks-Gunn & Paikoff, 1993; Miller, Card, Paikoff, & Peterson, 1992; Paikoff & Brooks-Gunn, 1991b) use frameworks that document all of the possible influences on sexual behavior. These include contexts such as family, peer, school, neighborhood, and work settings as well as individual biological, emotional, cognitive, and physical characteristics. The developmental challenges and potential pitfalls of adolescence are also charted. Factors that are associated with risk-taking behavior and conditions that connote resilience to risky situations are often used as organizing frames for examining sexual behavior.

Limitations of Current Frameworks

Although we believe that these approaches have provided insight into youthful sexuality, we also feel that they limit our understanding. Four topics are of concern: (1) sexual well-being and developmental transitions, (2) the gendered nature of sexuality, (3) decision making and sexuality, and (4) the meaning of sexuality to youth.

    1.   Sexuality is usually seen as a negative outcome for youth. Some effort has been made to discuss sexual well-being and to include feelings as well as behavior (Brooks-Gunn & Paikoff, 1993). However, these cases are rare and often seem forced. We have suggested, for example, that sexual well-being includes at least four components – feelings about pubertal changes, feelings about sexual arousal, sexual behavior, and safe sex. First, youth hopefully will develop positive feelings about their bodies during the transition to a reproductively mature body (Blyth, Simmons, & Zakin, 1985; Brooks-Gunn, Newman, Holderness, & Warren, 1994; Brooks-Gunn & Reiter, 1990; Brooks-Gunn & Warren, 1988; Petersen, Tobin-Richards, & Boxer, 1983). The second component of sexual well-being is defined as not experiencing distress over sexual arousal (Fine, 1988; Gaddis & Brooks-Gunn, 1985). Such transitions have not been studied in part because it is difficult to say exactly what constitutes positive feelings or no distress. The third component is labeled *sexual behavior* rather than *sexual intercourse*, even though behaviors such as masturbation (Chilman, 1983; Gaddis & Brooks-Gunn, 1985) and petting (Udry, 1988; Westney, Jenkins, & Benjamin, 1983) are not typically studied. Such behaviors often (but not always) precede intercourse and are an option in lieu of sexual intercourse. We know nothing about transitions associated with such behaviors. *Safe sex,* our fourth component, is usually defined as the use of contraception to reduce the likelihood of sexually transmitted diseases or pregnancy (Books-Gunn & Furstenberg, 1989). The beginning of contraceptive use and the more or less continuous use of contraceptives are the two transitions studied (Brooks-Gunn & Furstenberg, 1990; Hayes, 1987; Sonenstein, Pleck, & Leighton, 1989; Zabin & Hayward, 1993; Zelnik, 1983).

    The timing of these four dimensions are not well-studied. However, the one of sexual intercourse has been extensively documented, but we have little understanding of what it means to be off time with regard to one's peer group, let alone how accurate perceptions of peer group norms are (see the new Adolescent Health Survey being conducted at the University of North Carolina, which is providing much needed data on peer behaviors). We do know that today only about one-fifth of all youth do not have sex during their teenage years (Alan Guttmacher Institute, 1994). However, the timing of the onset of sexual behavior differs tremendously across subgroups, such that sexual intercourse at age 15 is normative in some groups, whereas intercourse at age 18 is the norm for other groups.

2.   Gendered aspects of sexuality are acknowledged but not studied in any depth. As an example, a *Psychological Bulletin* review identified 177 articles that considered sex differences in sexuality (Oliver & Hyde, 1993). Although gender differences in age of onset of intercourse and number of partners are smaller in recent cohorts than in earlier cohorts, they still exist. Additionally, the research reviewed (which is the bulk of the literature on sexuality) is really a catalogue of sexual behavior. The meaning of sexuality to boys and girls is not studied. Without an understanding of the process by which a sexual identity is forged and responses to situations are formed, we have no idea of how different or similar sexual experiences are for boys and girls (i.e., feelings, motivation, satisfaction).

3.   Almost nothing is known about how teenagers make choices to engage in or not to engage in sexual experiences, or how the choice to use contraceptives is made. Decision making is not studied to any great extent (for an exception, see Beyth-Marom & Fischhoff, chapter 5, this volume). Although about two-thirds of all youth report using contraceptives the first time they have intercourse (Alan Guttmacher Institute, 1994), and even more report using contraceptives later on, youth do not always use them consistently (Brooks-Gunn & Furstenberg, 1990).

4.   The voices of teenagers are not heard. What do youth say about the meaning of sexuality to them? What sexual scripts do they believe that they are carrying out? An example is our use of a rap song in the introduction to a chapter of ours (Brooks-Gunn & Paikoff, 1993). The song began as follows: "Sex is a gamble, kissing is a game." It goes on to take what might be seen by some to be a fairly cynical approach to sex and its meaning to boys and girls: "Nine months later and they say it's not mine." Several colleagues urged us to alter the title and make the rap song less prominent in our organization of the chapter. The most frequently cited reason was the belief that the song was not indicative of the ways in which youth understand and experience sexual encounters. Although we do not think that one rap song is representative of an entire generation's construction of sexual experiences, the response to our use of it illustrates how little we do know about the meaning of sex in youth's lives and how often youth's voices, when raised, are discounted.

Sexuality in the Context of the Self and of Relationships

In an attempt to "break set," we have started to think about the construction of sex as aspects of the self and of relationships more generally. Also, attention is being paid to the timing of sexual events for boys and girls and for different ethnic groups, since the link with self and other might be quite different for youth who engage in sex earlier than for those who do so later in adolescence. Of central importance are the voices of adolescents, vis-à-vis their hopes and desires, and the interpretation of their behavior. This chapter focuses on three general themes – the importance of self, of relationships, and of meaning in understanding sexual transitions. First, we consider aspects of the self – identity, feelings, and beliefs – as they develop during adolescence and influence choices made about sexual intercourse and perceived control over sexuality. The development of peer relationships as central to an understanding of sexuality is discussed in the next section. Much of the relevant work has taken social cognition as the frame. Then functions of sexuality, or its meaning in the life of youth and its impact on their health and well-being, is our focus. The research on the meaning of sexuality is quite different from that in the preceding two sections in that it is based on discourse – the construction of sexual experience through intensive interviews with youth rather than through structured survey methods.

Generally, we are most interested in understanding why some youth choose to have sexual experiences earlier than others. It is nearly impossible to put an age on the term *early*, given that the current literature is not consistent and that sexual onset varies by gender, ethnicity, family structure, family income, and academic engagement (Brooks-Gunn, 1993; Moore, Miller, Glei, & Morrison, 1995; Paikoff & Brooks-Gunn, 1990; Zabin & Hayward, 1993). We define *early* as the onset of sexual intercourse in the junior or middle high school years (sixth through ninth grades), when youth are less than age 16. An argument could be made to focus on three or four different groups – those who have intercourse before age 16, those who have intercourse at age 17 or 18, and those who have sex later (or who have sex at age 19 or 20 versus those who wait until age 21 or later; see Figure 8.3). Other sexual transitions are important, of course (i.e., sexual behaviors, the use of contraception, and comfort with one's body more generally). Most attention is paid to the onset of sexual intercourse, and the term *sexual transitions* usually refers to this event.

We have developed a model for understanding the impact of developmental processes on self-beliefs and health behaviors at adolescence (Paikoff & Brooks-Gunn, 1994). Self-beliefs (perceived control and self-concept) consider how pubertal change and the social challenges experienced by young adolescents contribute to the behavioral choices made by youth. What has been missing from this model is the role of relational change in moderating or mediating the pubertal, self, and social challenges confronting youth (Paikoff

% of women who have had intercourse by each age

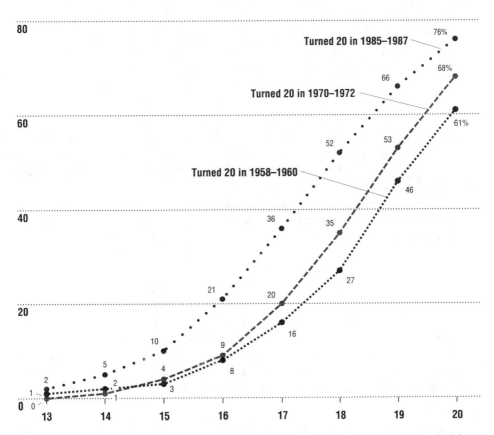

Figure 8.3. The percentage of women who have had intercourse by each age. Reproduced with the permission of The Alan Guttmacher Institute from *Sex and America's Teenagers*, The Alan Guttmacher Institute, New York, 1994. *Sources: Turned 20 in 1958–1960*: Adapted from tabulations by S. L. Hofferth of data from the 1982 National Survey of Family Growth. *Turned 20 in 1970–1972*: Adapted by AGI from tabulations by S. L. Hofferth of data from the 1982 National Survey of Family Growth, AGI tabulations of data from the 1988 National Survey of Family Growth. *Turned 20 in 1985–1987*: AGI tabulations of data from the 1988 National Survey of Family Growth. *Note*: Data are based on women aged 30–32 and 42–44 in 1982 and aged 21–23 and 36–38 in 1988.

& Brooks-Gunn, 1991a). The biological, psychological, and social changes of the young adolescent period demarcate childhood from adolescence (Brooks-Gunn, 1988; Brooks-Gunn & Petersen, 1984; Lerner & Foch, 1987). Changes are likely to impact on and alter the young person's significant relationships with others, such as parents and friends. The changes of puberty result in a reproductively mature individual, necessitating relational change (Paikoff & Brooks-Gunn, 1991a). Pubertal changes may open up a wide range of behavioral options to the young adolescent, via dating and unsupervised peer time (Stattin & Magnusson, 1990), resulting in a series of new social and sexual events to be mastered. Pubertal changes herald the intensification of sexual desire as well as changes in others' responses to the young adolescent. At the same time, cognitive and social-cognitive changes allow the individual to reflect on and organize thoughts about the self and relationships with others in more systematic and integrated ways (Keating, 1990). Enhanced social-cognitive abilities allow for the mastery of these relational and situational changes (Smetana, 1988, 1991); however, the specific mode by which these changes are mastered may vary dependent on self-beliefs, self-feelings, sexual desire, or a combination of these factors.

Pubertal maturity may trigger interest in sexual intimacy and increase sexual arousal (either directly via pubertal hormones or indirectly via secondary sex characteristics; see Udry, 1988). Relational changes that result in more unsupervised time and more time in dating situations may help create situations where sexual activity is possible (or conversely, increased parental restrictiveness may limit such opportunities). In either case, the propensity for social situations where early intercourse is possible is altered, as are motivation and desire. When social events arise that may potentiate early sexual activity, responses to these events are likely to vary as a function of biological, social-cognitive, and motivational characteristics. In addition, the occurrence of these events, as well as the relational changes of adolescence, may alter beliefs and feelings about the self, which themselves influence behavioral choices.

Self and Choice in Sexual Transitions

We wish to emphasize the importance of the self not only in the construction of a sexual identity, but also in the decisions made in the service of sexuality. Decision implies choice and control. Why are choice and control important in the study of adolescent sexuality? Youth are expected to take on increasing responsibility for their own behavior and decisions due to physical and cognitive maturity as well as social-relational changes (e.g., increase in the importance of and time spent with peers, decrease in direct monitoring by parents). Concern has been expressed over the choices made by adolescents with regard to health-compromising risk behaviors such as drinking and driving, substance use, and unprotected intercourse (Brooks-Gunn & Paikoff, 1993; Flynn-

Weitzman, Paikoff, & Brooks-Gunn, in press; Gardner, Scherer, & Tester, 1989; Melton, 1990), as well as the links concerning sex behavior (Donovan & Jessor, 1985; Jessor & Jessor, 1977).

The emphasis on negative behavioral outcome (or ultimate choice) has left unspecified the degree to which adolescents are in fact actively making choices as opposed to responding to contexts that enable or facilitate sexual activity. Perception of control over sexual situations is essential to an active choice-making strategy. Thus, the construct of control as we approach it overlaps that of perceived control, as discussed by Connell (1985), and of self-efficacy, as discussed by Bandura (1989). The presumption is that an individual can actively exert control over the situation and make a choice to engage in sexual behavior or not. The interesting research questions then become: (1) to what degree do adolescents perceive themselves as having control over these situations? (2) how much variation exists in perceptions of control over these situations? (3) how are these variations linked to behavioral choices? and (4) what are the situations in which youth perceive themselves as having control? Although our focus is on sexual situations, our arguments about choice and control may be extended to other health behaviors (see Beyth-Maron & Fischhoff, chapter 5, this volume).

Assuming that for the most part adolescents feel (and have) some control over sexual situations, how do they make choices? Choices are often made in social situations, where time is limited and the youth is sexually aroused. The situations possibly involve factors, or a relative weighing of factors, in ways that differ from what adults do. Ideally, an adolescent must anticipate, plan for, and recognize sexual situations in advance; indeed, these principles form the basis for many of the skill training programs aimed at preventing teenage pregnancy and sexually transmitted disease (Brooks-Gunn & Paikoff, 1993; Kirby, Barth, Leland, & Fetro, 1991). Yet, in order to benefit from such anticipatory planning or strategizing, the adolescent needs to have knowledge regarding the links between behavioral choices and sexual outcomes, as well as compelling motivation to avoid certain outcomes (intercourse or unsafe sex). Research has seldom investigated individual variation and behavioral correlates of motivational constructs with regard to sexuality, or even the age of the youth. Instead, sexual desire is assumed as the primary motivating factor; however, sex serves other functions as well (Moore & Rosenthal, 1993; Paikoff, 1995; Sprecher & McKinney, 1987).

In our own work with focus group data and interviews with fourth- , fifth- , and sixth-grade children, we find preliminary evidence that both adults and children are aware of the possible alternative functions of sex (Paikoff, 1995; Vera, Reese, Paikoff, & Jarrett, in press). Our data focus on African American preadolescents and young adolescents living in urban poverty; thus issues of both culture and context are important to consider in interpreting these results. First, parents display great concern regarding early sexual intercourse in their children, as well as sophisticated understanding of the possible motivations above and beyond the desire for sexual activity. Here a grandmother describes her concerns regarding early sexuality:

The thing that worries me, is that our kids are so sexually active, and I found out that there is more of African-Americans in contact with that disease AIDS, and I feel like they are too free. Maybe it's me, old as I am I know everything, and they know very little, and it concerns me because they are not aware of the different disease that are going on. Maybe they hear of places where they can go, but you know those places are not so easily accessible to us.

This grandmother expresses concern regarding the sexual activity of children in the neighborhood, particularly with regard to high rates of infectious disease also found in the community; she also discusses aspects of the context (urban poverty) that prohibit or limit treatment for sexually active children and adolescents. Other parents speculate more specifically about how the context in which they are raising their children may draw children towards early sexual activity (Vera et al., in press):

I'm going to say what I think maybe brought it on is, with all the gang activity going on, that a lot of girls was looking for protection too, that they don't get hurt, and so, hey, they [the boys] want their rewards so they say, "hey I ain't kept them off you for nothing"; so that's how they feel.

You know for yourself we can go on downstairs on the first floor of any of these buildings and we can see somebody's hands up somebody's daughter's skirt.

Both of these parents hypothesize that context is a powerful motivating factor for early sexual activity among their children: The first suggests that sex may be a trade-off for gang protection, and the second reveals that from a very young age, children are exposed to sexual activities through living in public housing. Children may model the behavior they are witnessing. In fact, quite a few poor urban fourth- and fifth-grade children are reporting high levels of being in situations where their peers (usually older peers) are having sex (12 of 44 participating in a pilot interview; Paikoff, 1995).

Although we know very little about the dialogue of negotiation between adolescents in a first-intercourse experience, we do know that such initial experiences are generally not planned (Paikoff & Brooks-Gunn, 1991b); hence, we can assume that choices are being made during the beginning of a sexual encounter, and that they involve elements of time pressure, intense affect, and sexual desire. In our model, we assume that there are meaningful differences between (1) those who end up in unplanned sexual situations and those who do not and (2) those who ultimately engage in unprotected intercourse and those who do not. We expected such differences on the basis of social-cognitive and self factors, as well as in association with particular relationships and circumstances. Thus, a girl might have relatively high self-beliefs regarding control and compelling motivations to avoid pregnancy, but might still engage in unprotected intercourse with a partner if she believes that she will not become pregnant, or believes that sex is necessary to continue the relationship, or believes that most of her friends are experimenting. Conversely, an adolescent with poor decision-making skills, low control beliefs, and no compelling motivations to avoid sexual situations may avoid such situations due to relatively late physical maturity or parental restrictiveness.

Development of the Self at Adolescence

Research on the development of the self has focused on reasoning about the self and the affective valence of beliefs regarding the self (Harter, 1983, 1990; Wylie, 1979). Multiple terms exist to describe each of these types of thinking: (1) *self-construction* refers to thinking about the self; (2) *self-beliefs* refers to cognitions about the self; and (3) *self-feelings* refers to the affective valence attributed to self-constructions and beliefs (Brooks-Gunn & Paikoff, 1992, p. 66).

1. Studies of the structure of thinking about the self (*self-constructions*) most often involve interviews probing individuals about hypothetical situations (Selman, 1980) or more open-ended speculations about the self (Broughton, 1981). Damon and Hart (1982) integrated the available research on self-understanding from infancy through adolescence, outlining the important changes in the structure of young adolescent thinking about the self. These include the following (Brooks-Gunn & Paikoff, 1992, p. 79): recognition of unconscious motivations regarding the self (Selman, 1980); recognition of self-subjectivity (Broughton, 1981; Selman, 1980); appreciation of the importance of individual and social characteristics in defining the self (Livesley & Bromley, 1973); perception of the self as malleable (Harter, 1990); and recognition of the importance of active processing and modifying of self-experiences (Damon & Hart, 1982). These developments enable young adolescents to create new organizations of their self-definitions, including dimensions of personality, social situation, unconscious volition, relativity, and reactivity. How these dimensions are associated with sexual behavior is not known.

2. Dimensions of *self-feelings* with regard to the self are clearly more emotional than cognitive in nature (though it is quite difficult to separate issues of affect and cognition with regard to self-conceptions; see Isen, 1985; Quintana & Lapsley, 1990). Self-esteem, self-worth, and negative affect are the major aspects of self-feelings that have been studied in adolescents to date. The premise of much of the research on self-feelings is that the transition to adolescence, given the concatenation of physical, social, and cognitive events co-occurring at this time, results in an increase in negative self-feelings (Brooks-Gunn, 1988, 1993; Hauser, Borman, Powers, Jacobson, & Noam, 1990; Holmbeck, 1996).

Research tends to support this premise, as negative self-feelings do appear to increase during the first half of adolescence, between the ages of 10 and 15 (Buchanan, Eccles, & Becker, 1992; Cantwell & Baker, 1991; Puigh-Antich & Gittelman, 1982; Rutter, Izard, & Read, 1968). A recent review of the literature on adolescent depression suggests that 7% of adolescents are identified with clinical depression, 15% with depressive syndrome, and about one-third with depressed mood (Compas, Petersen, & Brooks-Gunn, in press; Petersen et al., 1993). Increases in depression are more pronounced in girls than in boys (Kandel & Davies, 1986; Nolen-Hoeksma, 1987; Petersen, Sarigiani, & Kennedy, 1991; Radloff, 1991; Rutter, Graham, Chadwick, & Yule, 1976). Emotional lability (or mood swings) has received substantial theoretical interest, with excellent work on variability being done by Csikszentmihalyi, Larson and their colleagues (Csikszentmihalyi & Larson, 1984; Larson, Csikszentmihalyi, & Graef, 1980; Larson & Lampman-Petraitis, 1989). However, research is mixed vis-à-vis the size of the increase in lability during the early adolescent years.

Negative self-feelings may be associated with sexual choices. Depressive symptoms may involve pervasive feelings of lack of control, as well as confusion regarding life choices. Depression and other aspects of negative affect such as low self-esteem may result in lowered motivation to make health-promoting choices. It may also be the case, however, that some adolescents experiencing relatively high levels of negative affect and depression are less likely to wind up in sexual situations due to noninvolvement in peer activities. No research directly addresses these premises.

Sexual behavior also may be used to modulate affective states. In the interviews conducted by Feldman, Millstein, and colleagues of youth in Northern California, two statements from 19-year-old girls illustrate this point (Turner & Feldman, in preparation):

If you're like really down and you know you're with this person it's just when they say things to you that like make you feel good or you know "I like being with you" it just makes you feel like you're ten times bigger than everything else in life.

I was mad at my mom or my sister or my dad. So I wanted to release the anger in some way. . . . It's [sex] an escape from what you were thinking about.

Little is known about the ways in which negative self-feelings and sexual behavior are linked, let alone the causal nature of these associations. Many instances of the attribution of specific self-feelings to sexual intercourse may be cited as well. And it is likely that self-feelings as a motive for sexual engagement may change with development, as well as exhibit large individual differences.

3. During the transition to adolescence, the content of *self-beliefs* shifts from being more concrete to more comparative (Harter, 1983, 1990; Livesley & Bromley, 1973; Montemayor Eisen, 1977). The self is viewed as more complex, too (Harter, 1990). These changes in social comparison and evaluation may impact on perceived control and on choice behavior via comparison

of one's own ability to make choices. In a pilot study of decision making and choice behavior, the majority of young adolescents (90%) stated that they were better than (58%) or as good as (32%) peers in making decisions (Flynn-Weitzman et al., in press). Differences between these groups (especially with regard to the minority who believe they are worse decision makers than their peers) may be helpful in targeting those who perceive themselves as less in control than others with regard to choice behavior. The ability to consider the self and others systematically also may result in well-reasoned choices in sexual situations.

Sexual Identity

Developmentalists focusing on the transition to adolescent have conceptualized identity in Eriksonian terms (Erikson, 1968). Domains of identity have been expanded and refined (Grotevant, Thorbecke, & Meyer, 1982; Waterman, 1982). Some researchers are beginning to define *sexual identity* as one domain of identity rather than using the term to refer to sexual orientation or to a preference for same-sex or opposite-sex partners (Brooks-Gunn & Matthews, 1979; Gagnon & Simon, 1987; Money & Ehrhardt, 1972).

   The work of Rosenthal and her colleagues (Buzzwell & Rosenthal, in preparation; Moore & Rosenthal, 1993) is paradigmatic of this approach. In their forthcoming article, these authors suggest that at least three aspects of sexual identity can be identified – sexual self-esteem ("one's self-evaluation of worth as a sexual being"); sexual self-efficacy ("perceptions of mastery of one's sexual world"); and self-beliefs ("an individual's beliefs about . . . sexual image"). The last aspect includes "reactions to sexual contexts (anxiety), perceptions of physiology (arousal), externalization of desire (exploration), and interpersonal priorities (commitment)." The authors developed a questionnaire to tap these constructs and then tested 470 high school students in Melbourne, Australia.[2] Using cluster analyses, five sexual styles were found in this sample – sexually idealistic, sexually unassured, sexually competent, sexually adventurous, and sexually driven. (1) The sexually idealistic tended to be girls, virgins, and young. However, one-quarter had had intercourse. They rated themselves low in sexual self-efficacy, sexual self-esteem, sexual arousal, and sexual exploration and high on sexual anxiety. (2) The sexually unassured cluster tended to be male, young, and virgins (although one-quarter had had intercourse). They too had low sexual self-efficacy and sexual self-esteem, as well as very negative views about their bodies. They had higher scores than the first group vis-à-vis arousal and exploration even though they were very anxious about sex. (3) The third group – the sexually competent – were older, and 60% had had sexual experiences. Almost equal numbers of girls and boys were found in this cluster. Not surprisingly, members of this group had high self-efficacy and self-esteem vis-à-vis sexuality. They had intermediate attitudes toward exploration, arousal, and commitment. (4) The sexually adventurous were likely to be older males who had high self-efficacy and self-esteem and who reported high arousal levels and interest in exploration. Sixty percent had had intercourse. This group was also most likely to report having had a homosexual experience (14%). (5) The smallest group – the sexually driven – were also males. They differed from the sexually adventurous in reporting a great deal of difficulty in saying "no" to sexual activity. A little over one-quarter were virgins. They had the lowest sexual anxiety scores, the highest arousal and exploration scores, and the lowest sexual commitment scores.

Rosenthal and colleagues have gone on to describe the risk-taking behaviors (no contraceptive use) of these clusters with regular and casual partners. Of those within each cluster who were sexually active, cluster group differences were found. Other work has described sexual adventurers as those with multiple partners and often low contraceptive usage (Chilman, 1983). However, the Rosenthal approach is particularly valuable in that it describes different groups of youth, all of whom may react quite differently to sexual situations and may have somewhat different motivations for having sex, rather than focusing on two groups, the adventurers and the nonadventurers. It would be valuable to follow a cohort of youth over time to see how stable group membership is and to see what factors predict movement from one group to another.

The fact that the five clusters of students differ in their use of contraceptives also suggests that intervention strategies might be crafted as a function of sexual identity rather than the common use of a standard curriculum for all (Brooks-Gunn & Furstenberg, 1990). For example, we know that teenage boys were more likely to use condoms after the human immunodeficiency virus (HIV) epidemic was identified and publicized then before (based on national data; Sonenstein et al., 1989). Would differences in condom use increases be seen as a function of sexual style? We do know that the boys most at risk for HIV infection – those who had used drugs intravenously and who had had homosexual experiences – were least likely to use condoms consistently in the national U.S. sample studied by Sonenstein and colleagues (1989). However, nothing is known about links to sexual identity groups.

Relationships as a Context for Sexuality

Much of the work on peer relationships during adolescence has used a social-cognitive lens in which to frame the issues and research. Social-cognitive reasoning is thought to be central to the formation of reciprocal, flexible, and equal (peer) relationships (Hartup, 1989). The more emotional content of relationships may be less linked to social cognition, as exemplified by the early formation, intensity, and typically enduring nature of the mother–child relationship (Bowlby, 1969; Sroufe, 1985). Peer relationships have been studied vis-à-vis their content and structure, both of which are discussed in the following section.

Content of Peer Relationships

The most extensive documentation of the social-cognitive content related to understanding of friendship has been conducted by Berndt and his colleagues (Berndt, 1981, 1982; Berndt & Perry, 1990; see Berndt, 1996, for a review of this literature). Much of this work has involved extensive interviewing of children aged 6 through 14 regarding the important definitional features of friendships. In one such study (Berndt, 1981), when asked to comment on both ideal and actual friendships, sixth graders were more likely to mention intimacy or trust, loyalty, and nonaggressive behavior as definitions of friendship than were kindergartners or third graders. In contrast, kindergartners were more likely to define friendships tautologically (e.g., "he says I'm his best buddy") than were children in the later grades. At all ages, play or association was a primary defining feature of friendship. In studies of friendships over time (e.g., across a school year), few differences were found between fourth and eighth graders in terms of consistency or stability of friendships. However, there was a general decline in the strength of all children's friendships over the school year. Changes in the closeness of the children's friendships were accompanied by declines in positive comments regarding the friendship and increases in negative comments (Berndt, 1981).

The influence of friendship beliefs on choice behavior in sexual situations may be both developmentally and individually based. For example, expanding the definition of friendship as involving intimacy, loyalty, and trust may provide a powerful motivation to engage in or avoid sexual situations, depending on friendship norms. In addition, individual differences in friendship stability and change may be related to friendship group norms and hence to the probability of facing a sexual situation (see the classic work in Australia by Dunn, 1977).[3]

Structure of Relationships

The cognitive structural properties of relational knowledge have been examined by Selman (1980) and by Youniss (Youniss, 1980; Youniss & Smollar, 1985). Selman (1980) suggests that understanding of social relationships as mutual and reciprocal increases through early adolescence. Youniss (1980) also found support for changes in children's conceptions of the structure and function of friendships during the young adolescent years, suggesting the increasing importance of concepts such as equality, mutual understanding, and intimacy. Youniss suggests that social knowledge is altered in part through interactions with others (see also Lewis & Brooks-Gunn, 1979; Riegel, 1976;

Vygotsky, 1978). These perspectives have been applied directly to studying links between interpersonal negotiation strategies and peer therapy situations (Selman & Demorest, 1984; Selman & Schultz, 1990). Very little work has focused, however, on exploring more naturalistically occurring links between relationships and interactions (Laursen & Collins, 1988; Paikoff & Brooks-Gunn, 1991a).

Such changes may influence adolescent sexual choices. Do youth take the perspective of the other in sexual situations? Do youth anticipate social as well as health consequences in choosing to engage in sex or not? Depending on the nature of these views, adolescents may overestimate or underestimate their ability to control social sexual situations. Particular relationships and perceived consequences of behavior may provide the context for sexual behavior. Consequently, the meaning of relationships may be as important (or more so) than the social-cognitive level at which these relationships are understood.

The meaning of relationships may vary by gender as well as by age of child. For example, girls may be prone to construct the meaning of relationships through emotional closeness, intimacy, and sharing of feelings, whereas boys may be more familiar with the development of intimacy through time spent together in shared activities (Maccoby, 1988, 1990). With regard to age, pilot data on a high-risk sample of preadolescent African-American children living in urban poverty (considered at high risk due to their placement in classrooms for children with low reading levels for grade) suggest that initial viewing of others' sexual activity may be linked to playing running and chasing games with girls and boys together in unsupervised situations (Paikoff, 1995). Such a link would suggest a more playful than emotional or intimate initiation of sexual activity during the preadolescent years (see Westney et al., 1983).

The actual structure of peer relationships is thought to be more horizontal than vertical (e.g., interaction between relative equals; see Hartup, 1989). Peers presumably are able to discuss their feelings and experiences without concerns about punishment or lectures from adults (Savin-Williams & Berndt, 1990). However, little is known about the structure of peer interactions in adolescence or about the effects of these structures on sexual behavior. The one exception is work on dominance and leadership within the peer group. Perhaps the best example is the study of children in summer camps (Paikoff & Savin-Williams, 1983; Savin-Williams, 1987; Sherif & Sherif, 1964). Dominance hierarchies are formed early in summer camps and are quite stable over the life of the summer, especially for boys. Whether such structures would be found in peer groups where children are living at home, not together at camp, is not known (Brown, 1990).

However, dominance mechanisms may be particularly important in the study of sexual behavior. Fine (1988) has written eloquently on the discourse of sexual desire, making the important point that sexual relationships are often not equal, given differential dominance of boys and girls. Boys are more likely to be the pursuers and girls the pursued. And girls may find it difficult to refuse sexual overtures made by particular boys because of their status, their persistence, or their physical power (even in cases where sex is not forced). Fine has discussed potential gender power imbalances vis-à-vis the discourse of victimization. Contrary to what is often believed, sexual encounters as a match between boys as persuaders and girls as reluctant participants are not a vestige of the past. Some (but not all) adolescents still describe interchanges in these terms. Recent work by Rosenthal and her colleagues and by Feldman and her colleagues is most relevant here. Following are statements from a 19-year-old male in Feldman's Northern California study and a 16-year-old male in Rosenthal's Australian study (again, we regret that these examples are from older, not younger, adolescents).

As far as just sex for sex's sake ... guys, young guys are just walking hormones really ... one big walking wad of sexual tension. You know, that's a completely hormonal thing, they might not have anything to do with it, brainwise. ... Well, I need sex on a daily basis ... because I'm a teenage male, I do think about it a lot.

Interviewer: If you wanted to have sex and your partner did not, would you try to persuade them to have sex? How? 16-year old: Sure mate, shove it in. It is all part of the game. I would say "come on, come on, it's not that big." You have to say those things to virgins because they are scared.

Presumably, gender power divergences are much greater when males have high sexual arousal levels, high levels of sexual self-efficacy, low interest in commitment, and high interest in exploration. We suggest that the sexually adventurous and sexually driven males described by Rosenthal and colleagues (1994; Moore & Rosenthal, 1993) would be most likely to exhibit dominance behaviors in sexual interchanges. Of interest but unstudied is the reaction of different girls to boys with high arousal and low commitment. Also unknown is how many boys described as sexually competent use overt persuasion to initiate a sexual relationship, and whether the use of overt pursuit or dominance is tempered by the status of the girl, the relationship with the girl, or the age of the girl. This last point is very important given that young adolescent girls are likely to have intercourse with older boys (Zabin & Hayward, 1993).

The Meaning of Sexuality

Thus far, we have shied away from an examination of the meaning of sexuality in the adolescent's life. We are not alone; very little work has focused on meaning, other than a tepid listing of the functions of sex. The reluctance to address this quite obvious topic is akin to that seen with regard to puberty. Early work on the meaning of pubertal change to youth was difficult to conduct in terms of obtaining funding, school permission, and parental permission (Brooks-Gunn & Reiter, 1990; Brooks-Gunn & Ruble, 1982; Ruble &

Brooks-Gunn, 1987). It is still almost impossible to study some pubertal and sexual events (masturbation being an obvious example) vis-à-vis their meaning to youth (Gaddis & Brooks-Gunn, 1985).

Several authors are probing the meaning of sexuality within relationships as well as the meaning of sexuality to the individual (Moore & Rosenthal, 1991, 1993; Sprecher & McKinney, 1987; Turner & Feldman, in preparation). The two developmental processes considered previously – the development of the self and the development of relationships – are being linked to adolescent sexual transitions via a study of the meaning of sexuality. This approach does not take as its starting point a social-cognitive or a risk-taking framework, but rather begins with the functions that adolescent sex serves. Sexual interchanges serve intimacy, identity, and autonomy needs, as Turner and Feldman (in preparation) point out. Sprecher and McKinney (1987) have suggested that sex may have meaning as an act of exchange, interdependence, maintenance, intimacy, love, or self-disclosure. The salience of each of these functions of youth needs to be studied, as well as changes in their salience, in terms of age, sexual experience, arousal, or commitment. For example, Wyatt (1985; Wyatt & Riederle, 1994) asked 250 black and white women in Los Angeles County why they had sex the first time. Of those who had intercourse before age 18, just over half said that they were curious or were pressured by peer or partners. These women did not report that first intercourse was motivated by sexual desire (contrary to popular beliefs about "being carried away").

In the pilot study of high-risk children mentioned earlier (Paikoff, 1995), children were asked whether they had considered having sex but had not yet done so. Of the 20 children who responded in the affirmative, the reasons given for not having sex included not being ready (12/20), fear/desire to avoid disease (8/20), not wanting to have intercourse (7/20), feeling unprepared/not having contraceptives (6/20), or discussions with family members emphasizing the negative consequences of sex (5/20). These preliminary findings suggest that intervention programs targeted at delaying the onset of sexual intercourse for high-risk children may appeal to these youth by emphasizing some of these negative consequences, as well as by facilitating communication with family members regarding very early sexual intercourse.

Interviews with youth provide the most direct window into sexual experiences. Instead of more qualitative and rich descriptions, social scientists have focused on the surface characteristics, the easily quantifiable numbers – frequency, age of initiation, and use of birth control. The interviews provide the discourse to go with the digits.

One of the themes emerging from the interviews in Northern California is the way in which adolescents must learn to balance their own needs and those of others in the negotiations over sexual exchanges, as well as the definition of boundaries between self and other (Turner & Feldman, in preparation). The struggle between intimacy and autonomy, which recurs throughout development, is played out on the sexual stage as well as in relationships with parents, same-sex peers, and siblings. The theme of being manipulated or used by the other person was paradigmatic of this struggle. One 18-year-old male talked about the pain of having his former girlfriend dating his best friend while still visiting him for the sole purpose of sex (Turner & Feldman, in preparation). The physical pleasure was finally not worth the pain of feeling manipulated.

I guess . . . she manipulated me. . . . That's kinda all screwed up because she's still with him and the only thing I'm left with is this good physical feeling and I'm still hurting inside. And so . . . I'm getting used like a paper towel. I eventually told her . . . this is gonna stop here and now.

This young man yearned for intimacy with his former girlfriend; sex without intimacy was too painful, so it became necessary to reestablish sexual boundaries between them.

In another interview, a young woman in her 20s recounted one sexual relationship in which she felt used. She visited the man's room for several weeks.

Then, when he was through with me, he just like stopped calling, or I went over there once and he just didn't have anything to say to me and I felt, like, embarrassed and humiliated about having gone over there and I remember moaning that even though I was not into having a relationship any more than he was, I still felt like he had sort of called the shots, you know, he had used me, maybe because he finished with me first. . . . I remember that having something to do with my sort of starting to rethink this whole casual sex thing, that maybe I didn't want to be a part of that.

This young woman was speaking of the meaning of sex vis-à-vis experimenting with what it meant to be a sexual person. Indeed, she refers to the differences "between being myself having sex and just sort of playing a game and acting how I think somebody who is having sex should be acting" (Turner & Feldman, in preparation). Such a statement is reminiscent of the ways in which young adolescents try on different identities (Harter, 1990) – in this case, a specific sexual identity: that of explorer and game player. At the same time, this young woman acknowledged that she felt trashy, and she liked feeling that way for a while.

These vignettes are particularly interesting in light of the narratives supplied by Rosenthal's youth, who were all still in high school (in contrast, most of Feldman's respondents were out of high school and reflecting on adolescent experiences). No data exist on the developmental trajectories of the high school students in the five sexual style groups characterizing the Australian sample. That is, do many of the sexual adventurers find commitment more important as they age? And if so, what are the reasons for this change? A glimmer of such change is seen in this interview with a 22-year-old male talking about the decision to have sex with someone now, as opposed to when he was in high school.

When I have sex, I consider whether this is something she really wants, and I consider if it's something I really want because after sex often it will lead to more – at least when I have sex I want it to lead to more. I want to know if she wants it to lead to more. I want to know where I stand. I don't just want to have sex. I kind of got that over with in high school, that kind of thing. (Turner & Feldman, in preparation)

All three of the youths quoted imply that their behavior has changed, from experimentation with a sexual identity that manifested itself in terms of exploration of sex for sex's sake toward more intimacy and commitment. Such progression, if it occurs, needs to be documented, as well as the various paths that individuals take vis-à-vis their sexual selves.

Sexual Well-Being and Developmental Transitions

Even though the goal of this volume is to explicate how the construct of transitions underlies much of the adolescent literature, our chapter focuses less on transitions than we would like. The problem is that most of the research on sexual behavior has been done to understand sexual intercourse and the use of contraception rather than to take a more multifaceted and contextualized look at sexuality. We have attempted to broaden the definition of sexuality by including feelings about puberty and one's body more generally, sexual arousal and desire, sexual behavior as more than intercourse, and safe sex as more than the use of condoms (Brooks-Gunn & Paikoff, 1993). At least five development issues need to be brought to the forefront: (1) the timing of behaviors associated with sexuality more broadly defined, (2) the co-occurrence of sexual behaviors and other health-related behaviors, (3) the context in which various sexual transitions occur, (4) the age at which various sexual transitions occur, and (5) the gender of the youth experiencing sexual transitions.

1. The timing of various sexual transitions varies greatly within individuals (for the various indices of sexual well-being), as well as across individuals (for any specific index). Timing, of course, is a relative concept. Whether a particular transition occurs early or late depends on one's definition of early and late, the peer referent group, the historical time, and cultural mores (Brooks-Gunn, Petersen, & Eichorn, 1985). Considering the timing of various transitions adds to this complexity. For example, being an early-maturing girl is associated with having sexual intercourse, with smoking, and with drinking early. Indeed, maturing early sometimes results in a cascade of events (such as dating earlier, having older friends, being pursued by older males, demanding more autonomy from parents, spending more time in activities unsupervised by parents or other adults), which leads to early transitions in other behaviors (Costa, Jessor, Donovan, & Fortenberry, 1995; Gargiulo, Attie, Brooks-Gunn, & Warren, 1987; Stattin & Magnusson, 1990; Westney et al., 1983). These patterns may be seen more frequently in some contexts than others, although

data on this point are scanty (i.e., the co-occurrence of certain behaviors in early adolescence has been demonstrated in groups of American and Swedish youth and in middle-income and lower-income youth; however, few studies have included comparisons among groups of the strength of associations between the early timing of various transitions).

2. The importance of considering the co-occurrence of various health-related behaviors, our second developmental issue, is foreshadowed in the preceding paragraph. The confluence of a series of behaviors such as sexual intercourse, smoking, drinking, and illegal drug use, especially if occurring in the first half of the adolescent years, has been shown to place youth on a precarious developmental trajectory (Furstenberg, Brooks-Gunn, & Morgan, 1987; Jessor & Jessor, 1977).

It is still unclear whether or not certain behaviors are triggers for other behaviors; whether general patterns or trajectories exist; or whether the co-occurrence of several unhealthy behaviors among young adolescents is a reflection of underlying motivational characteristic (which are themselves influenced by biological, cognitive, social-cognitive, familial, peer, and other environmental factors). Jessor and his colleagues have suggested that the personality, environment, and behavior systems must be considered simultaneously when predicting which youth will exhibit a series of unhealthy behaviors (Jessor, 1991). One possible motivational characteristic underlying early transitions to sexual intercourse, drinking, and smoking involves the notion of unconventionality. *Unconventionality* has been defined as having "a higher value placed on independence relative to achievement [which occurs via] lowered expectations for academic achievement and higher tolerance for deviance" (Costa et al., 1995, p. 100). In a sample of 1,500 youth in the seventh, eighth, and ninth grades, Costa, Jessor, and their colleagues are examining the onset of various problem behaviors over a 3-year period. They find that unconventionality is associated with earlier sexual intercourse, as well as other so-called problem or unhealthy behaviors.

3. The underlying concomitants or precursors of early transitions to sexual behavior or to behaviors such as smoking and drinking need to be viewed in a more contextualized light. Research is becoming much more nuanced in this regard. As an example, we look at the work of Jessor and colleagues again. They find parallels in their samples of white youth seen in the 1970s and in the 1990s vis-à-vis the importance of unconventionality in predicting early onset of sexual intercourse, as well as smoking, drinking, and drug use (Costa et al., 1995; Jessor & Jessor, 1977). Thus, at least some of the antecedents of early sexual initiation may be similar even if historical conditions have resulted in a *change* in the number of youth having intercourse at an early age or the definition of an early transition.

At the same time, unconventionality did not predict early onset of intercourse in the black youth seen in the 1990s study (black youth were not included in the earlier study). It is critical to look at the mechanisms underlying these different findings for black and white youth, which can be done only by looking carefully at the contexts in which these youths reside. One possibility explored by the authors was that more black than white youth live in single-parent families. Such families are often unable to provide high levels of parental supervision, and sexual intercourse in part is predicated on unsupervised time (Sandefur, McLanahan, & Wojtkiewicz, 1992; Vera et al., in press). However, the number of single-parent families was not a determinant of these racial differences in the analyses reported by Costa et al. (1995). Other possibilities have to do with poverty, the persistence of poverty, neighborhood residence, school characteristics, and peer group norms (Brooks-Gunn, Duncan, Klebanov, & Sealand, 1993).

Another contextual factor may involve the timing of familial events, which may differ by income or racial group. For example, in the Baltimore Study of Teenage Parenthood, early sexual transitions in the first-borns of the original teenage mothers were associated with family structure in the early adolescent years but not in the childhood or preschool years. In contrast, family structure in the early adolescent years was not associated with grade failure, dropping out of high school, or literacy, whereas family structure earlier in life was (Baydar, Brooks-Gunn, & Furstenberg, 1993; Brooks-Gunn, Guo, & Furstenberg, 1993).

4. An underlying theme of our work is based on the belief that the concomitants of sexual intercourse, as well as the meaning of sexuality, differ as a function of the timing of such experiences. Regrettably, we could not organize the entire chapter around this premise, given the paucity of data comparing the experiences of adolescents who became sexually active in the earlier versus the later years of adolescence. Indeed, the quotations used throughout the chapter are from older adolescents who are reminiscing about their first or their early sexual experiences. Although valuable, it is unclear whether or not these recollections would be framed in the same way if the youth had been reporting when they were younger. We do know that reports of feelings about pubertal change vary, sometimes dramatically, based on whether girls are reporting about their experiences in the previous year or whether they are remembering events that took place years earlier (Brooks-Gunn & Ruble, 1982, 1983; Ruble & Brooks-Gunn, 1987).

Our conceptual model is based on the idea that changes in self-feelings, social cognition, puberty, and relationships render the decision making and the meaning of sexual intercourse quite different for adolescents in the first half of their second decade. Given the moral atmosphere surrounding teenage sexuality, especially early sexuality, studies of young adolescents are difficult. Overcoming parents' and teachers' reluctance to ask youth under 16 about sex is a major obstacle – even greater than their misgivings about studies of pubertal development (Brooks-Gunn, 1987). Even researchers may have some qualms; for example, the two of us disagreed as to the age at which the Chicago study of preadolescents and sexuality should begin (the debate centered on whether or not to ask fourth and fifth graders about their sexual experiences and behavior).

5. Our final transition issue involves gender. Indeed, all of the research on sexuality is gendered in that surveys always consider boys and girls separately. While Fine (1988) has written on the sexual discourse between boys and girls, we still do not understand how and when the meaning of sexuality diverges, as well as whether or not it even converges for males and females. We believe that the sexual experiences of young adolescent girls are frequently involuntary or at the very least occur in situations where dominance differentials play a role. How this state of affairs changes over time is not understood, although the vignettes presented in this chapter suggest that older adolescent girls are engaging in much more reciprocal sexual situations *and* that boys are experiencing feelings of intimacy and loss. Narrative research is the only window into such changes in sexual experiences.

In conclusion, the study of adolescent sexuality must be reframed in order to take into account behaviors *and* feelings, to promote a more multidimensional approach, and to explore sexual transitions other than age of first intercourse and of first contraceptive usage. Various pathways to healthy sexuality exist, as we have suggested. These include "practicing sexual abstinence but having positive feelings about one's body; not engaging in sexual intercourse with another but engaging in self-exploration; engagement in sexual behavior with another in the context of a committed relationship in middle or late adolescence and using safe sex practices; and engagement in preintercourse behaviors with another during the early and middle adolescent period, which may or may not result in intercourse in later years" (Brooks-Gunn & Paikoff, 1993, pp. 201–202). Unless such variations in sexual transitions and their concomitants are better understood, efforts to promote healthy sexual behaviors may not be particularly effective or at the very least will influence only a subset of youth.

Notes

1 This chapter is focused primarily on sexual activity that involves two individuals of the opposite sex and mutual consent. Information on involuntary sex during adolescence is sparse (but see Miller, Monson, & Norton, 1995; Moore, Nord, & Petersen, 1989). Of importance is the fact that for young girls, first intercourse is highly likely to be involuntary. Moore and colleagues (1989) report that three-fourths of 13-year-old girls who have had intercourse report the first experience to be involuntary, as do 50% of 15-year-old girls.

2 A major shortcoming of this work from our (limited) perspective is that sexual identity constructs were developed based on older adolescents. Given our interest in thinking of sexual transitions, we would welcome having comparable attention paid to younger adolescents.

Would the clusters found in the high school students in Australia be similar for junior high school students? And would the identity dimensions be relevant for different ethnic and cultural groups?

3 Older siblings' behavior also might play a role in a youth's definition of self as a sexual being and in a youth's subsequent behavior. One line of research has focused on the fact that girls whose older sisters were teenage mothers are more likely to have sex at an earlier age and to become teenage mothers. These findings hold across ethnic, economic, and geographic regions (i.e., rural versus urban; Cox, Emans, & Bithoney, 1990; East, Felice, & Morgan, 1993; Hogan & Kitagawa, 1985). Several mechanisms have been proposed for this association, including social learning theory by siblings as role models (Bandura, 1977), problem behavior theory, with siblings promoting lessened social controls on behavior (Jessor & Jessor, 1977), normative expectations theory (Hogan & Kitagawa, 1985), and maturational theory, as siblings are moderately similar in timing of menarche (Newcomer & Udry, 1985). In a direct test of some of these mechanisms, East (in press) found that younger sisters of a teenage childbearer were more likely to smoke, to be disengaged from school and to have low career expectations (girls were in sixth to eighth grades) than younger sisters of nonteenage childbearers; all of these characteristics are correlates of early sexuality. Additionally, sibling relationships described by the younger sister as warm, close, or rivalrous were associated with sexual intercourse (East, in press). Family demographic characteristics did not explain these findings. Thus, peer relationships within the family may play a role in determining how a young adolescent responds to sexual situations and expectations.

References

Alan Guttmacher Institute (AGI). (1994). *Sex and America's teenagers*. New York: Author.

Bandura, A. (1977). *Social learning theory*. Englewood Cliffs, NJ: Prentice-Hall.

Bandura, A. (1989). Human agency in social-cognitive theory. *American Psychologist, 44*, 1175–1184.

Baydar, N., Brooks-Gunn, J., & Furstenburg, F. F., Jr. (1993). Early warning signs of functional illiteracy: Predictors in childhood and adolescence. *Child Development, 64*, 815–829.

Berndt, T. J. (1981). Age changes and changes over time in prosocial intentions and behavior between friends. *Developmental Psychology, 17*, 408–416.

Berndt, T. J. (1982). The features and effects of friendship in early adolescence. *Child Development, 53*, 1447–1460.

Berndt, T. J. (1996). Transitions in friendship and friends' influence. In J. A. Graber, J. Brooks-Gunn, & A. C. Petersen (Eds.), *Transitions through adolescence: Interpersonal and contextual issues* (pp. 57–84). Hillsdale, NJ: Erlbaum.

Berndt, T. J., & Perry, T. B. (1990). Children's perceptions of friendships as supportive relationships. *Developmental Psychology, 5*, 640–648.

Blyth, D. A., Simmons, R. G., & Zakin, D. F. (1985). Satisfaction with body image for early adolescent females: The impact of pubertal timing within different school environments. *Journal of Youth and Adolescence, 14*, 207–225.

Bowlby, J. (1969). *Attachment and loss: Attachment I*. New York: Basic Books.

Bronfenbrenner, U. (1997). Lewinian space and ecological substance. *Journal of Social Issues, 33*, 199–212.

Brooks-Gunn, J. (1987). Pubertal processes and girls' psychological adaptation. In R. Lerner & T. T. Foch (Eds.), *Biological–psychosocial interactions in early adolescence: A life-span perspective* (pp. 123–153). Hillsdale, NJ: Erlbaum.

Brooks-Gunn, J. (1988). Transition to early adolescence. In M. Gunnar & W. A. Colling (Eds.), *Development during transition to adolescence: Minnesota symposia on child psychology* (Vol. 21, pp. 189–208). Hillsdale, NJ: Erlbaum.

Brooks-Gunn, J. (1993). Why do young adolescents have difficulty adhering to health regimes? In

N. Krasnegor, L. Epstein, S. B. Johnson, & S. J. Yaffee (Eds.), *Developmental aspects of health compliance behavior* (pp. 125–152). Hillsdale, NJ: Erlbaum.

Brooks-Gunn, J., Duncan, G., Klebanov P. K., & Sealand, N. (1993). Do neighborhoods influence child and adolescent development? *American Journal of Sociology, 99*, 353–395.

Brooks-Gunn, J., & Furstenburg, F. F., Jr. (1989). Adolescent sexual behavior. *American Psychologist, 44*, 249–257.

Brooks-Gunn, J., & Furstenburg, F. F., Jr. (1990). Coming of age in the era of AIDS: Sexual and contraceptive decisions. *Milbank Quarterly, 68*, 59–84.

Brooks-Gunn, J., Guo, G., & Furstenburg, F. F., Jr. (1993). Who drops out of and who continues beyond high school?: A 20-year follow-up of black urban youth. *Journal of Research on Adolescence, 3*, 271–294.

Brooks-Gunn, J., & Mathews, W. (1979). *He and she: How children develop their sex-role identity.* Englewood Cliffs, NJ: Prentice-Hall.

Brooks-Gunn, J., Newman, D., Holderness, C., & Warren, M. P. (1994). The experience of breast development and girls: Stories about the purchase of a bra. *Journal of Youth and Adolescence, 23*, 539–565.

Brooks-Gunn, J., & Paikoff, R. (1992). Changes in self feelings during the transition towards adolescence. In H. McGurk (Ed.), *Childhood social development: Contemporary perspective* (pp. 63–97). East Sussex, U.K.: Erlbaum.

Brooks-Gunn, J., & Paikoff, R. (1993). "Sex is a gamble, kissing is a game:" Adolescent sexuality, contraception and pregnancy. In S. P. Millstein, A. C. Petersen, & E. O. Nightingale (Eds.), *Promoting the health behavior of adolescents: New directions for the twenty-first century* (pp. 180–208). New York: Oxford University Press.

Brooks-Gunn, J., & Petersen, A. (1984). Problems in studying and defining pubertal events. *Journal of Youth and Adolescence, 13*, 181–196.

Brooks-Gunn, J., Petersen, A., & Eichorn, D. (1985). The study of maturational timing effects in adolescence. *Journal of Youth and Adolescence, 14*, 149–161.

Brooks-Gunn, J., & Reiter, E. O. (1990). The role of pubertal processes in the early adolescent transition. In S. Feldman & G. Elliott (Eds.), *At the threshold: The developing adolescent* (pp. 16–53). Cambridge, MA: Harvard University Press.

Brooks-Gunn, J., & Ruble, D. N. (1982). The experience of menarche. *Child Development, 53*, 1557–1566.

Brooks-Gunn, J., & Ruble, D. N. (1983). The experience of menarche from a developmental perspective. In J. Brooks-Gunn & A. Petersen (Eds.), *Girls at puberty: Biological and psychosocial perspective* (pp. 155–177). New York: Plenum.

Brooks-Gunn, J., & Warren, M. P. (1988). The psychological significance of secondary sexual characteristics in 9- to 11-year-old girls. *Child Development, 59*, 161–169.

Broughton, J. (1981). The divided self in adolescence. *Human Development, 24*, 13–32.

Brown, B. B. (1990). Peer groups and peer cultures. In S. Feldman & G. Elliott (Eds.), *At the threshold: The developing adolescent* (pp. 171–196). Cambridge, MA: Harvard University Press.

Buchanan, C. M., Eccles, J. S., & Becker, J. B. (1992). Are adolescents the victims of raging hormones? Evidence for activational effects of hormones on moods and behavior at adolescence. *Psychological Bulletin, 111*, 62–107.

Buzzwell, S., & Rosenthal, D. (in preparation). *Constructing a sexual self: Adolescents' sexual self perceptions and sexual risk-taking.*

Cantwell, D. P., & Baker, L. (1991). Manifestations of depressive affect in adolescence. Special issue: The emergence of depressive symptoms during adolescence. *Journal of Youth and Adolescence, 20*, 121–133.

Chilman, C. S. (1983). *Adolescent sexuality in a changing American society: Social and psychological perspectives for the human service professions* (2nd ed.). New York: Wiley.

Compas, B., Petersen, A., & Brooks-Gunn, J. (in press). *Depression in adolescence.* Newbury Park, CA: Sage.

Connell, J. P. (1985). A new multi-dimensional measure of children's perceptions of control. *Child Development, 56,* 1018–1041.

Costa, F. M., Jessor, R., Donovan, J. E., & Fortenberry, J. D. (1995). Early initiation of sexual intercourse: The influence of psychosocial unconventionality. *Journal of Research on Adolescence, 5,* 93–121.

Cox, J., Emans, S., & Bithoney, W. (1990). *Female siblings of adolescent mothers: A group at high risk for premature parenthood.* Paper presented at the Society for Adolescent Medicine Meetings, Atlanta, GA.

Csikszentmihalyi, M., & Larson, R. (1984). *Being adolescent: Conflict and growth in the teenage years.* New York: Basic Books.

Damon, W., & Hart, D. (1982). The development of self-understanding from infancy through adolescence. *Child Development, 53,* 841–864.

Donovan, J. E., & Jessor, R. (1985). Structure of problem behavior in adolescence and young adulthood. *Journal of Consulting and Clinical Psychology, 53,* 890–904.

Dunn, J. (1977). Patterns of early interactions: Continuities and consequences. In H. R. Schaffer (Ed.), *Studies in mother–infant interaction* (pp. 629–638). London: Academic Press.

East, P. (in press). The younger sisters of childbearing adolescents: Their attitudes, expectations, and behaviors. *Child Development.*

East, P., Felice, M., & Morgan, M. (1993). Sisters' and girlfriends' sexual and childbearing behavior: Effects on early adolescent girls' sexual outcomes. *Journal of Marriage and the Family, 55,* 953–963.

Erikson, E. H. (1968). *Identity: Youth and crisis.* New York: Norton.

Fine, M. (1988). Sexuality, schooling, and adolescent females: The missing discourse of desire. *Harvard Educational Review, 58,* 29–53.

Flynn-Weitzman, P., Paikoff, R., & Brooks-Gunn, J. (1995). *Mastering the possibilities: An exploratory look at how pre and young adolescents define and approach decisions.* Unpublished manuscript.

Furstenburg, F. F., Brooks-Gunn, J., & Morgan, S. P. (1987). Adolescent mothers and their children in later life. *Family Planning Perspectives, 19*(4), 142–151.

Gaddis, A., & Brooks-Gunn, J. (1985). The male experience of pubertal change. *Journal of Youth and Adolescence, 14*(1), 61–69.

Gagnon, J. H., & Simon, W. (1987). The sexual scripting of oral genital contacts. *Archives of Sexual Behavior, 16*(1), 1–25.

Gardner, W., Scherer, D., & Tester, M. (1989). Asserting scientific authority: Cognitive development and adolescent legal rights. *American Psychologist, 44,* 895–902.

Garigiulo, J., Attie, I., Brooks-Gunn, J., & Warren, M. P. (1987). Girls' dating behavior as a function of social context and maturation. *Developmental Psychology, 23,* 730–737.

Grotevant, H. D., Thorbecke, W. L., & Meyer, M. L. (1982). An extension of Marcia's identity status interview into the interpersonal domain. *Journal of Youth and Adolescence, 11,* 33–47.

Harter, S. (1983). Developmental perspectives on the self-system. In E. M. Heatherington (Vol. Ed.), *Socialization, personality and social development* (pp. 352–387). New York: Wiley.

Harter, S. (1990). Self and identity development. In S. Feldman & G. R. Elliott (Eds.), *At the threshold: The developing adolescent* (pp. 352–387). Cambridge, MA: Harvard University Press.

Hartup, W. (1989). Social relationships and their developmental significance. XXIV International Congress on Psychology (1988, Sydney, Australia). *American Psychologist, 44*(2), 120–126.

Hauser, S. T., Borman, E. H., Powers, S. I., Jacobson, A. M., & Noam, G. G. (1990). Paths of adolescent ego development: Links with family life and individual adjustment. *Psychiatric Clinics of North America, 13*(3), 489–510.

Hayes, C. (1987). *Risking the future: Adolescent sexuality, pregnancy, and childbearing* (Vol. I). Washington, DC: National Academy Press.

Hogan, D. P., & Kitagawa, E. (1985). The impact of social status, family structures, and the neighborhood on the fertility of black adolescents. *American Journal of Sociology, 90,* 825–855.

Holmbeck, G. N. (1996). A model of family relational transformation during the transition to adolescence: Parent–adolescent conflict and adaptation. In J. A. Graber, J. Brooks-Gunn, & A. C. Petersen (Eds.), *Transitions through adolescence: Interpersonal and contextual issues* (pp. 167–200). Hillsdale, NJ: Erlbaum.

Isen, A. M. (1985). Toward understanding the role of affect in cognition. In R. S. Wyer & T. K. Srull (Eds.), *Handbook of social cognition* (Vol. 3, pp. 179–227). Hillsdale, NJ: Erlbaum.

Jessor, R. (1991). Risk behavior in adolescence: A psychosocial framework for understanding and action. *Journal of Adolescent Health, 12,* 579–605.

Jessor, S. L., & Jessor, R. (1977). *Problem behavior and psychosocial development: A longitudinal study of youth.* New York: Academic Press.

Kandel, D. B., & Davies, M. (1986). Adult sequelae of adolescent depressive symptoms. *Archives of General Psychiatry, 43,* 225–262.

Keating, D. P. (1990). Adolescent thinking. In S. Feldman & G. R. Elliott (Eds.), *At the threshold: The developing adolescent* (pp. 54–89). Cambridge, MA: Harvard University Press.

Kirby, D., Barth, R. P., Leland, N., & Fetro, J. V. (1991). Reducing the risk: Input on a new curriculum on sexual risk-taking. *Family Planning Perspectives, 23*(6), 253–263.

Larson, R., Csikszentmihalyi, M., & Graef, R. (1980). Mood variability and the psychosocial adjustment of adolescents. *Journal of Youth and Adolescence, 9,* 469–490.

Larson, R., & Lampman-Petraitis, C. (1989). Daily emotional states as reported by children and adolescents. *Child Development, 60,* 1250–1260.

Laursen, B., & Collins, A. (1988). Conceptual changes during adolescence and effects upon parent–child relationships. *Journal of Adolescent Reseach, 3,* 119–139.

Lerner, R. M., & Foch, T. T. (Eds.). (1987). *Biological and psychosocial interactions in early adolescence.* Hillsdale, NJ: Erlbaum.

Lewis, M., & Brooks-Gunn, J. (1979). The search for the origins of self: Implications for social behavior and intervention. In L. Montada (Ed.), *Brennpunkte der entwicklungspsychologie [Developmental Psychology]* (pp. 157–172). Stuttgart: W. Kohlhammer.

Livesley, W. J., & Bromley, B. D. (1973). *Person perception in childhood and adolescence.* London: Wiley.

Maccoby, E. E. (1988). Gender as a social category. *Developmental Psychology, 24,* 755–765.

Maccoby, E. E. (1990). Gender and relationships: A developmental account. *American Psychologist, 45,* 513–520.

Melton, G. B. (1990). Knowing what we do know: APA and adolescent abortion. *American Psychologist, 45,* 1171–1173.

Miller, B., Card, J., Paikoff, R., & Peterson A. (1992). *Preventing adolescent pregnancy.* Newbury Park, CA: Sage.

Miller, B, Monson, B., & Norton, M. (1985). The effects of forced sexual intercourse on white female adolescents. *Child Abuse and Neglect, 19,* 1289–1301.

Money, J., & Ehrhardt, A. (1972). *Man and woman, boy and girl: The differentiation and dimorphism of gender identity from conception to maturity.* Baltimore: Johns Hopkins University Press.

Montemayor, R., & Eisen, M. (1977). The development of self-conceptions from childhood to adolescence. *Developmental Psychology, 13,* 314–319.

Moore, K., Miller, B., Glei, D., & Morrison, D. (1995). *Adolescent sex, contraception, and childbearing: A review of recent research.* Washington, DC: Child Trends, Inc.

Moore, K., Nord, C., & Peterson, J. (1989). Nonvoluntary sexual activity among adolescents. *Family Planning Perspectives, 21,* 110–114.

Moore, S., & Rosenthal, D. (1991). Adolescent invulnerability and perceptions of AIDS risk. *Journal of Adolescent Research, 6,* 164–180.

Moore, S., & Rosenthal, D. (1993). *Sexuality in adolescence.* Routledge, New York.

Newcomer, S. F., & Udry, J. R. (1985). Parent–child communication and adolescent sexual behavior. *Family Planning and Perspective, 17,* 169–174.

Nolen-Hoeksema, S. B. (1987). Reasons for studying: Motivational orientations and study strategies. *Cognition and Instruction, 5*(4), 269–287.

Oliver, M. B., & Hyde, J. S. (1993). Gender differences in sexuality: A meta-analysis. *Psychological Bulletin, 114*(1), 29–51.

Paige, K. E., & Paige, J. M. (1985). *Politics and reproductive rituals.* Berkeley: University of California Press.

Paikoff, R. L. (1995). Early heterosexual debut: Situation of sexual possibilities during the transition to adolescence. *American Journal of Orthopsychiatry, 65*, 389–401.

Paikoff, R. L., & Brooks-Gunn, J. (1990). Physiological processes: What role do they play during the transition to adolescence? In R. Montemayor, G. Adams, & T. Gullotta (Eds.), *Advances in adolescent development* (Vol. 2, pp. 63–81). Newbury Park, CA: Sage.

Paikoff, R. L., & Brooks-Gunn, J. (1991a). Do parent–child relationships change during puberty? *Psychological Bulletin, 110*, 47–66.

Paikoff, R. L., & Brooks-Gunn, J. (1991b). Interventions to prevent adolescent pregnancy. In R. M. Lerner, A. C. Petersen, & J. Brooks-Gunn (Eds.), *The encyclopedia of adolescence* (pp. 808–813). New York: Garland.

Paikoff, R. L., & Brooks-Gunn, J. (1994). Psychosexual development across the lifespan. In M. Rutter & D. Hay (Eds.), *Development through life: A handbook for clinicians* (pp. 558–582). Oxford: Blackwell Scientific.

Paikoff, R. L., & Savin-Williams, R. C. (1983). An exploratory study of dominancy interactions among adolescent females at summer camp. *Journal of Youth and Adolescence, 12*(5), 419–433.

Petersen, A. C., Compas, B., Brooks-Gunn, J., Stemmler, M., Ey, S., & Grant, K. (1993). Depression in adolescence. *American Psychologist, 48*(2), 155–168.

Petersen, A. C., Sarigiani, P. A., & Kennedy, R. E. (1991). Adolescent depression: Why more girls? *Journal of Youth and Adolescence, 20*, 247–271.

Petersen, A. C., Tobin-Richards, M., & Boxer, A. (1983). Puberty: Its measurement and its meaning. *Journal of Early Adolescence, 3*, 47–62.

Puigh-Antich, J., & Gittelman (1982). Depression in childhood and adolescence. In E. S. Piazket (Ed.), *Handbook of affective disorders* (pp. 379–392). New York: Guilford Press.

Quintana, S., & Lapsley, D. (1990). Rapprochment in late adolescent separation-individuation: A structural equations approach. *Journal of Adolescent Research, 4*, 371–385.

Radloff, L. S. (1991). The use of the center for epidemiologic studies depression scale in adolescents and young adults. Special issue: The emergence of depressive symptoms during adolescence. *Journal of Youth and Adolescence, 20*(2), 149–166.

Riegel, K. F. (1976). The dialectics of human development. *American Psychologist, 31*, 689–700.

Rosenthal, D., Moore, S., & Buzwell, S. (1994). Homeless youths: Sexual and drug-related behavior, sexual beliefs and HIV/AIDS risk. *AIDS Care, 6*(1), 83–94.

Ruble, D. N., & Brooks-Gunn, J. (1987). Perceptions of menstrual and premenstrual symptoms: Self-definitional processes at menarche. In B. E. Ginsberg & B. F. Carter (Eds.), *Premenstrual syndrome: Ethical and legal implications in a biomedical perspective* (pp. 237–251). New York: Plenum.

Rutter, M., Graham, P., Chadwick, O. F., & Yule, W. (1976). Adolescent turmoil: Fact or fiction? *Journal of Child Psychology and Psychiatry, 17*, 35–56.

Rutter, M., Izard, C. E., & Read, P. B. (Eds.). (1968). *Depression in young people: Clinical and developmental perspectives.* New York: Guilford Press.

Sandefur, G. D., McLanahan, S., & Wojtkiewicz, R. A. (1992). The effects of parental marital status during adolescence on high school graduation. *Social Forces, 71*, 103–121.

Savin-Williams, R. C. (1987). An ethological perspective on homosexuality during adolescence. *Journal of Adolescent Research, 2*(3), 283–302.

Savin-Williams, R. C., & Berndt, T. J. (1990). Friendship and peer relations. In S. Feldman & G. Elliott (Eds.), *At the threshold: The developing adolescent* (pp. 277–307). Cambridge, MA: Harvard University Press.

Selman, R. L. (1980). *The growth of interpersonal understanding: Developmental and clinical analyses.* New York: Academic Press.

Selman, R. L., & Demorest, A. P. (1984). Observing troubled children's interpersonal negotiation strategies: Implications of and for a developmental model. *Child Development, 55*(1), 288–314.

Selman, R. L., & Schultz, L. H. (1990). Bridging the gap between interpersonal thought and action in early adolescence: The role of psychodynamic processes. *Development and Psychopathology, 1*(2), 133–152.

Sherif, M., & Sherif, C. W. (1964). *Reference groups: Exploration in conformity and deviation of adolescents.* New York: Harper & Row.

Smetana, J. G. (1988). Concepts of self and social convention: Adolescents' and parents' reasoning about hypothetical and actual family conflicts. In M. Gunnar & W. A. Collings (Eds.), *Development during transition to adolescence: Minnesota symposia on child psychology* (Vol. 2, pp. 79–122). Hillsdale, NJ: Erlbaum.

Smetana, J. G. (1991). Adolescents' and mothers' evaluations of justifications for conflicts. In R. L. Paikoff (Ed.), *Shared views in the family during adolescence: New Directions for Child Development* (Vol. 5, pp. 71–86). San Francisco: Jossey-Bass.

Sonenstein, F. L., Pleck, J. H., & Leighton, C. K. (1989). *Sexual activity, condom use and AIDS awareness among adolescent males.* Paper presented at the annual meeting of the Population Association of America, Baltimore, MD.

Sprecher, S., & McKinney, K. (1987). Barriers in the initiation of intimate heterosexual relationships and strategies for intervention. Special issue: Intimate relationships: Some social work perspectives on love. *Journal of Social Work and Human Sexuality, 5,* 97–110.

Sroufe, A. (1985). Attachment classification from the perspective of infant–caregiver relationships and infant temperament. *Child Development, 56,* 1–12.

Stattin, H., & Magnusson, D. (1990). *Paths through life: Vol. 2. Pubertal maturation in female development.* Hillsdale, NJ: Erlbaum.

Turner, R., & Feldman, S. S. (in preparation). *The functions of sex in everyday life.*

Udry, J. R. (1988). Biological predispositions and social control in adolescent sexual behavior. *American Sociological Review, 53,* 709–722.

Vera, E. M., Reese, L., Paikoff, R. L., & Jarrett, R. (in press). Contextual factors of sexual risk taking in urban, African-American, preadolescent children. In B. Leadbeater & N. Way (Eds.), *Normative development of urban adolescent girls.* New York: New York University.

Vygotsky, L. (1978). *Mind in society: The development of higher psychological processes.* Cambridge, MA: Harvard University Press.

Waterman, A. S. (1982). Identity development from adolescence to adulthood: An extension of theory to a review of research, *Developmental Psychology, 18,* 341–358.

Wertsch, J. V. (1985). *Culture, communication, and cognition: Vygotskian perspectives.* Cambridge, MA: Cambridge University Press.

Westney, O. E., Jenkins, R. R., & Benjamin, C. M. (1983). Sociosexual development of preadolescents. In J. Brooks-Gunn & A. C. Petersen (Eds), *Girls at puberty: Biological and psychosocial perspectives* (pp. 273–300). New York: Plenum.

Wyatt, G. E. (1985). The sexual abuse of Afro-American and white women in childhood. *Child Abuse and Neglect: The International Journal, 9,* 507–519.

Wyatt, G. E., & Riederle, M. H. (1994). Reconceptualizing issues that affect women's sexual decision-making and sexual functioning. *Psychology of Woman Quarterly, 18,* 611–625.

Wylie, R. E. (1979). *The self-concept, Vol. 2: Theory and research on selected topics.* Lincoln: University of Nebraska Press.

Youniss, J. (1980). *Parents and peers in social development: A Sullivan–Piaget perspective.* Chicago: University of Chicago Press.

Youniss, J., & Smollar, J. (1985). *Adolescent relations with mother, father and friends.* Chicago: University of Chicago Press.

Zabin, L. S., & Hayward, S. C. (1993). *Adolescent sexual behavior and childbearing.* Newbury Park, CA: Sage.

Zelnik, M. (1983). Sexual activity among adolescents: Perspective of a decade. In E. R. McAnarey (Ed.), *Premature adolescent pregnancy and parenthood* (pp. 21–33). New York: Grune & Stratton.

9 Childbearing During Adolescence: Mental Health Risks and Opportunities

Cleopatra Howard Caldwell and Toni C. Antonucci

Adolescent childbearing represents a departure from what is thought to be the normative developmental course of adolescence in the United States. This early transition to parenthood coupled with the biological and psychosocial transformations of adolescence present enormous challenges to adolescent parents, their families, and society. Prior to the late 1960s, very little empirical data existed on the consequences of early childbearing. In fact, adolescent pregnancy and childbearing were not considered national concerns until the mid-1970s, when an Alan Guttmacher Institute report concluded that 1.1 million teenagers in the United States were becoming pregnant each year and that about half of these pregnancies resulted in live births (Furstenberg, Brooks-Gunn, & Morgan, 1987). Since that time, there has been a proliferation of research focusing on the impact of early childbearing on the life chances of adolescent mothers and their children (Chase-Lansdale, Brooks-Gunn, & Zamsky, 1994; Freeman & Rickels, 1993; Furstenberg, 1991; Hayes, 1987; Ladner & Gourdine, 1992; Miller & Moore, 1990; Musick, 1994; Nath, Borkowski, Whitman, & Schellenbach, 1991; Osofsky, Hann, & Pebbles, 1993; Plotnick, 1992; Thompson & Pebbles-Wilkins, 1992; Vinovskis, 1988; Voran & Phillips, 1993).

The results of most short-term studies on the consequences of early childbearing conclude that adolescent mothers do not do as well as those who delay childbearing until their 20s. Recently, however, several investigators have argued that the evidence supporting social, health, and economic differences between early and late childbearers may have been overstated (Brooks-Gunn & Furstenberg, 1989; Geronimus, 1991; Geronimus & Korenman, 1992; Horwitz, Klerman, Sung Kuo, & Jekel, 1991b; Luker, 1991). In their 17-year follow-up of over 300 African American women who had given birth as teenagers in the late 1960s, Furstenberg et al. (1987) found tremendous variation in the life circumstances of these mothers and their children. Their findings raised a critical question for future research: Why do some adolescent mothers make it, even under very difficult circumstances, whereas others fail to do so?

Changes in social norms regarding childbearing, health care, marital op-

220

tions, education, and employment, as well as availability and use of social support, have implications for the life chances of an adolescent mother. Individually, these factors represent different contexts in which early childbearing occurs; cumulatively, they begin to provide a more comprehensive framework for understanding different outcomes. Over the past two decades, the approach to studying adolescent childbearing has shifted from one of merely exploring sexual attitudes, knowledge, and contraceptive behavior to one examining more complex models that incorporate the influences of multiple environmental contexts on fertility, education, employment, and marital outcomes (Furstenberg et al., 1987; Hogan & Kitagawa, 1985).

Much of the literature characterizes early childbearing as a social and economic problem with dire consequences for the adolescent mother and her child (Brooks-Gunn & Furstenberg, 1986; Ladner & Gourdine, 1992; Zabin & Hayward, 1993). Research examining the consequences of early paternity for fathers is not as extensive. Studies focusing on adolescent fathers, however, have emerged over the past 15 years, suggesting that they too can suffer negative consequences from early paternity (Buchanan & Robbins, 1990; Christmon, 1990; Elster & Lamb, 1986; Ku, Sonenstein, & Pleck, 1993; Marsiglio, 1995, for review of literature; Miller, 1994; Pirog-Good, 1995; Robinson & Frank, 1994). Of particular interest for the present chapter is the impact of early parenting on the psychological well-being of the adolescent.

The mental health consequences of early parenthood have been examined from an individual difference perspective focusing on issues such as anxiety, stress, low self-esteem, low aspirations, suicidal ideation, alcohol or drug abuse, and conduct disorder (Stiffman, Earls, Robins, Jung, & Kulbok, 1987; Zabin & Hayward, 1993). Moreover, depression among adolescent mothers has been investigated, focusing on individual as well as intergenerational effects (Beardslee, Zuckerman, Amaro, & McAllister, 1988; Colletta, 1983; Horwitz et al., 1991b; Prodromidis, Abrams, Field, Scafidi, & Rahdert, 1994; Troutman & Cutrona, 1990; Turner, Grindstaff, & Phillips, 1990). Further, the mental health consequences of adolescent childbearing from a family perspective have recently gained attention in the social science literature. Characteristics of modern family life, especially regarding changing family structures, functions, and resources, can have powerful influences on the psychological well-being of adolescent parents and their children. A major step toward understanding the phenomenon and ramifications of early childbearing has been made with the recognition that adolescent parents are part of family systems. These family systems influence how well adolescents will care for their children and make the transition to adulthood. Research on these issues lags far behind that on the more sociostructural issues related to early childbearing.

The purpose of this chapter is to examine family factors that may account for outcome variations in the psychological well-being of African American and White adolescent parents. Intergenerational family relations as a social context for understanding early childbearing is the cornerstone of this chapter. The mother–daughter dyad will be the focus of most of the literature reviewed because early childbearing research typically focuses on this relationship. The contributions of and consequences for other family members, including the father of the baby, will be emphasized whenever possible as we try to broaden the family context for understanding outcome differences for individual adolescent parents and their children.

We begin with a historical overview of childbirth trends and social norms for adolescents, followed by an examination of racial differences in adolescent birth rates as background for understanding the meaning of early childbearing in contemporary Western society. The intergenerational family support relationships of adolescent mothers are then examined, and a conceptual model of how family relations may influence the psychological well-being of adolescent parents is proposed. The perspective of this chapter is that the birth of a baby to an adolescent is a family event that has economic, social, and psychological consequences for all family members. Thus, our central theme is the impact of family role transitions – due to an adolescent birth – on the emotional health of adolescent parents and their families. This conceptualization provides a broader approach to investigating early childbearing, and it allows for the inclusion of empirical work that uses individual and intergenerational analyses. Our ongoing study of family transitions to early childbearing is described, and findings are presented where appropriate to suggest directions for future research. Empirical studies focusing specifically on the psychological well-being of adolescent fathers are then presented. Finally, we provide a discussion of directions for future research and suggest ways in which adolescent parents' emotional health may be improved through family-centered interventions sensitive to their gender, unique developmental position, and cultural circumstances.

Early Childbearing in Historical Context

Early Childbearing as a Social Problem

Early childbearing as a critical social problem is a relatively contemporary concept explained in part by historical trends and interpretations of the rates of premarital pregnancies as far back as the 17th century (Smith & Hindus, 1975). The overall low rates (less than 10%) of premarital pregnancy during the 17th century were attributed to strict religious doctrine and the continuity between religious and sexual mores of society at that time. The dramatic rise (to about 30%) in premarital pregnancy in the latter half of the 18th century was a reflection of an increasingly sexually permissive society. However, during the mid-19th century, permissive sexual behavior declined in the United States as the strong social control of sexuality reemerged and the rate of premarital pregnancy returned to about 10%. The rate of premarital pregnancy again increased at the turn of the 20th century, reaching a high of 25% by 1950. Although the birth rate for adolescents has declined since the late 1950s, the current adolescent birth rate (62 per 1,000 in 1991) in the United States is substantially higher than that in other Western industrialized countries (Center on Budget and Policy Priorities, 1995).

Another important fertility-related issue has been the dramatic increase in the number of births to adolescents outside of marriage since the 1950s (Chase-Lansdale & Vinovskis, 1987). During the 1950s, almost 70% of first births to adolescent mothers were within marriage, whereas in 1991, 70% of adolescent mothers were unmarried and likely to be living with their parents or other relatives (Alan Guttmacher Institute, 1994). Additionally, the overwhelming majority (83%) of adolescents who decide to give birth today are from poor or low-income families, and 85% of this group is unmarried (Alan Guttmacher Institute, 1995).

Changing Social Norms

Societal concern about teenage births was minimal during the 1950s, when the rate of premarital pregnancy was relatively high (25%) for the nation (Furstenberg et al., 1987; Smith & Hindus, 1975). This was due, in part, to the expectation that if a woman became pregnant, a socially structured chain of events would occur wherein she would marry and form an independent, productive family unit. Concern about premarital pregnancy as a moral issue gave way to concern about early premarital childbearing as an economic issue when the number of births to adolescent mothers escalated after the post–World War II baby boomers reached their teen years (Furstenberg et al., 1987). From a policy perspective, adolescent motherhood today is considered to have more dramatic long-term implications for the welfare system, with government spending over $25 billion in 1990 for health and social services to adolescent mothers and their children (Alan Guttmacher Institute, 1993). Although policymakers have placed less emphasis on understanding the mental health costs of early childbearing, the long-term mental health consequences of early childbearing for both the adolescent parent and his or her child can result in limited or truncated labor force participation and greater health care expenditures. The full extent of these human capital costs have rarely been considered in policy debates about what should be done to provide more opportunities for adolescent parents.

Racial Differences in Adolescent Childbearing

Persistent racial differences in the number of reported births to adolescents have been evident throughout this century. In 1990, 21% of White adolescents and 40% of non-White adolescents became pregnant by age 18. Among

Whites, 2 in 10 first births were to adolescents in 1990, whereas among African Americans, 4 in 10 first births were to adolescents (Alan Guttmacher Institute, 1993). This 2:1 birth ratio of African American to White adolescents has been constant since 1920, regardless of changing fertility trends (Washington, 1982). It should be noted, however, that although the proportion of African American adolescents who become mothers is higher than that of White adolescents, in terms of absolute numbers, more babies are born to White than to African American adolescents.

Mental health outcomes (e.g., depression, efficacy) for African American and White adolescents, in general, in the United States can be highly influenced by race as an environmental factor (Lubin & McCollum, 1994; Peterson et al., 1993; Stiffman & Davis, 1990). For example, race plays an important role in options for specific types of social support available to adolescent mothers. One critical area of racial difference is in available support within the context of marriage. Literature from the 1950s and 1960s reflected anecdotal concerns about the negative effects of early marriage and childbirth (e.g., marital instability, large family size, economic hardship). However, more recent research suggests that continued involvement of the baby's father is an important predictor of the adolescent mother's psychological as well as economic well-being (Kissman & Shapiro, 1990; Thompson & Pebbles-Wilkins, 1992; Unger & Wandersman, 1988).

Although it is expected that 60% of all marriages will end in divorce (Luker, 1991), marriage and the ability to establish a separate household from the family of origin provide economic and psychosocial advantages for older adolescent mothers and their children (Brooks-Gunn & Furstenberg, 1989). African American adolescent mothers are at a greater disadvantage in this regard due to changes in social norms associated with age at first birth, options for marriage, and employment opportunities (Farber, 1990; Mare & Winship, 1991; Wilson, 1984).

White adolescent mothers historically have been more likely to marry than African American adolescent mothers. Specifically, 92% of births to African American adolescents and 57% of births to White adolescents were out of wedlock in 1990 (Alan Guttmacher Institute, 1993). Reasons why adolescent mothers are not making the decision to marry more often may be the result of a complex relationship between race and social class. For example, in a qualitative study of marital decisions among adolescent mothers, Farber (1990) found that more often than middle-class African American or White adolescents, lower-income African American adolescents did not expect to marry before the birth of their first child. Although they expressed a desire to marry, in reality their opportunities were limited by their social environment. Others have also found that poor African American females were more likely than any other group to experience early single parenting and to remain unmarried within the first 4 years of their baby's birth (Congressional Budget Office,

1990). When the adolescent mother remains single, her family assumes more responsibilities than when she is married (Chilman, 1980; Furstenberg, 1980). Numerous studies have found that without family support, adolescent mothers, regardless of race, are less likely to make a successful transition to adulthood and are often doomed to poverty (Furstenberg et al., 1987; Osofsky et al., 1993; Thompson & Pebbles-Wilkins, 1992).

Intergenerational Family Context

Family environments are central to the transmission of attitudes and values regarding issues of early childbearing. Families continue to have a tremendous influence on both positive and negative outcomes in the psychological as well as economic well-being of adolescent mothers (Richardson, Barbour, & Bubenzer, 1991; Unger & Wandersman, 1988). However, it is less clear what happens within the family to account for outcome variations and what role intergenerational relationships play in this process. Careful attention should be paid to strengths as well as vulnerabilities within family systems when intergenerational support relationships are explored. The advantage of an intergenerational focus is that it allows for a more complete understanding of reciprocal socialization influences across generations (Antonucci & Jackson, 1988). For example, repetition of early births across generations is one family mechanism expected to perpetuate the cycle of poverty from one generation to another (Kahn & Anderson, 1992). Intergenerational role modeling has been suggested as one possible explanation for why the cycle continues within a family (Hofferth, 1987). Additionally, within families with adolescent mothers, the new member (i.e., the infant) will impact everyone's life. Although family members may not have been involved in the decision to have the baby, they often are expected to provide essential support. Issues regarding support expectations are transmitted from one generation to another within the family and have psychological, social, and economic implications for the adolescent mother and her child.

A general model incorporating these major influences on the mental health of adolescent parents should consider both individual adolescent characteristics, family factors such as support provided to adolescent parents, and the impact of the interaction of these two elements on the psychological well-being of adolescent parents. Geronimus (1991) and her colleagues (Geronimus & Korenman, 1992) have suggested that family background characteristics, especially socioeconomic status, may account for many of the observed differences in the future life circumstances of adolescent mothers rather than the timing of first births. Components of the socioeconomic environment that have been investigated as predictors of negative outcomes for adolescent mothers include a history of childhood poverty, family economic instability, blocked employment opportunity structures, and living in risky

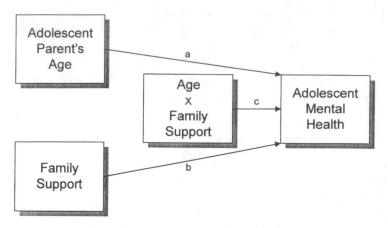

Figure 9.1. Family support as a moderator of mental health outcomes for adolescent parents.

neighborhoods (Hogan & Kitagawa, 1985; Kahn & Anderson, 1992; Kahn, Rindfuss, & Guilkey, 1990; Males, 1993; Zabin, Wong, Weinick, & Emerson, 1992). Building on these ideas, we propose that the relationship between individual characteristics of the adolescent parent and mental health outcomes are moderated by family characteristics.

Figure 9.1 presents a model of how these relationships may operate. The direct impact of the age of the adolescent parent on mental health outcomes (e.g., depressive symptoms, anxiety, stress, reduced self-esteem) is represented by path a, and the direct impact of family support (e.g., low versus high, satisfied versus not satisfied, good versus bad relationship) is depicted in path b. The interaction between the adolescent's age and the nature of family support (path c) represents the moderator hypothesis. In more descriptive terms, results showing that younger adolescent mothers experience less stress when family support is high, whereas highly supported older adolescent mothers experience more stress (Camp, Holman, & Ridgway, 1993; Kissman & Shapiro, 1990), is an example of the expected moderator relationship.

Differences in developmental needs and expectations for specific types of support for 14-year-old versus 19-year-old adolescent mothers could account for diverse mental health outcomes. If we consider age as a proxy for important developmental tasks (e.g., achieving emotional independence from parents and preparing for marriage and family life for older adolescents), we can better understand how family support may moderate the relationship between age and psychological well-being. Older adolescent mothers may perceive high levels of childrearing advice from their mothers as interference rather than support (Richardson et al., 1991) because they may be striving to become competent parents. Too much childrearing advice, then, could result in diminished psychological well-being. On the other hand, younger adolescent mothers may need to depend on their mothers for more emotional as well as instrumental support, especially in the area of childrearing, because they may not be capable of seeing themselves as competent parents. Future analyses from our Family Transitions to Early Childbearing Project will determine the merits of this model. Some preliminary data from this ongoing multigenerational study are presented in conjunction with previous research to emphasize the importance of examining early childbearing within an intergenerational family support context.

Family Transitions Study

In an effort to capture some of the dynamic changes that arise within families when early childbearing occurs, we initiated a longitudinal study of the mental health consequences of family transitions to early childbearing. This study uses a life span developmental perspective to examine intergenerational family relations as they influence the adjustment of individual family members and the family system as a whole (Antonucci, 1986; Brooks-Gunn & Furstenberg, 1989; Kahn & Antonucci, 1980). The adolescent mothers are 19 years old or younger at the time of the initial interview. In addition to face-to-face interviews with the adolescent mother, we conduct interviews with her mother and several other family members. Figure 9.2 depicts the relationships of potential study participants, with bold lines representing the link between required respondents and broken lines representing more tentative relationships (and thus greater difficulty in reaching and recruiting respondents). At minimum this is a three-generation family study of the adolescent mother, her 3-month-old infant, and her biological mother or "mother figure." In most cases, the adolescent mother's grandmother, biological father or "father figure," and the father of the baby are also interviewed.

Additional data are being collected through videotaped observations of unstructured and structured interactions between the adolescent mother and her infant when the infant is 3, 6, and 12 months of age. A second interview with multiple family members will be conducted about 1 year after the first interview. Issues of interest include the structure and function of social networks within these families, the influence of social relationships on psychological well-being, and the impact of supportive and conflictual familial relationships on individual and family adaptation.

Preliminary findings from 61 adolescent mother–grandmother dyads are presented throughout this section to suggest possible intergenerational family issues for consideration in future research and in developing interventions targeting adolescent mothers and their families. Several constructs are being explored from an intergenerational perspective. These include depressive symptomatology, anxiety, daily hassles, personal efficacy, self-esteem, coping, social support (including the structure, function, and quality of support rela-

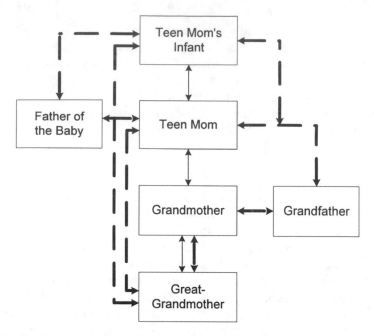

Figure 9.2. Familial relationship within the family transitions study.

tions), family adaptation, feelings about the birth, life changes since the birth, parental transitions and competencies, value transmissions, and future expectations. This study was piloted in Ypsilanti, Michigan, and New Orleans, Louisiana; however, because no site differences were found based on selected demographic factors (i.e., race, age, education, income, marital status), the results are reported for the sample as a whole. The adolescent mothers in this study are first-time mothers 14 to 19 years of age ($M = 17$, $SD = 1.47$). Their average educational level completed is 10th grade. The mean age of their mothers is 44 years ($SD = 7.06$), with an average of a high school education. Forty-three percent of the sample is African American and 57% is White. Annual family incomes ranged from \$2,500 to \$75,000. Median family income levels are significantly lower for African American (\$19,750) than for White (\$31,334) families, $F(1, 58) = 17.58$, $p < .001$.

Seventy-five percent of the adolescent mothers live with their family. However, several different household configurations exist. Forty-one percent live in single-mother households, 28% live in two-parent homes, and 11% live in either single-mother or two-parent homes with their partner present. Approximately 3% live in households with other relatives present, and 15% live alone with their partner. Only two adolescent mothers (3%) live alone with their infant. African American adolescent mothers are more likely than White adolescent mothers to live in single-mother households, X^2 (1) = 17.19, p < .001.

The remainder of this section provides a literature review of several issues that are important for understanding the structural and functional characteristics of multigenerational families that provide support to adolescent mothers and their children. We examine how flexible family structures and specific sources of social support can be beneficial in families with adolescent mothers. We also consider the consequences of multiple generations of early childbearers on mental health outcomes for adolescent mothers.

Flexible Family Structures and Sources of Social Support

Different patterns of family formation and dissolution have emerged since the 1950s. For example, the percentage of single-parent homes has risen to over 50%; overall births to unmarried women have increased dramatically; and there has been an increase in the number of extended family households due to an unstable economy (Beck & Beck, 1989; Center on Budget and Policy Priorities, 1995). When racial differences in family formation are considered, African Americans are less likely to marry, have higher divorce rates, and are more likely to become parents than Whites (Heaton & Jacobson, 1994). These characteristics of modern family life have strong implications for the family's ability to provide adequate support to an adolescent mother. The direction of current research findings suggests that adolescent mothers are a heterogeneous group with diverse concerns and needs. The type of family support that may be adequate for some may be a source of stress for others. Recent studies have identified several areas where the effect of family support on the psychological well-being of adolescent mothers has had mixed results. Findings on influential factors such as living arrangements and age of the adolescent mother, as well as sources of support and the grandmother's ability to provide support, are discussed.

Parenting and Living Arrangements. Changing family structures provide significant challenges for families trying to support an adolescent mother. The very concept of family includes providing for the emotional and physical care of children. However, the belief that the two-parent family – with the mother responsible for child care – is the only family structure within which effective parenting can occur has given way to an increasing recognition of the contributions of others in the childrearing process (Wilson, 1984; Wilson, Tolson, Hinton, & Kiernan, 1990). Within African American communities, Collins (1987) has described the boundaries distinguishing biological mothers of children from other women who care for children as being fluid and changing. Shared parenting responsibilities are common. Once considered a cultural elaboration of family, this point of view is now more prevalent in the early childbearing literature. The old African proverb "It takes a whole village to raise a child" is realized not only for African American families, but for families with adolescent mothers as well.

Childrearing in families with adolescent mothers is often the collective responsibility of the family and depends on female-centered networks. These "other mothers" are typically grandmothers, aunts, or female siblings who coparent the adolescent mother's child or who serve as surrogate parents. We found that grandmothers (the adolescents' mothers) are critical members of the adolescents' support networks, especially with regard to child care and parenting advice (Caldwell, Antonucci, Jackson, Osofsky, & Wolford, 1995). Grandmothers are a primary source of housing and financial assistance to adolescent mothers because most continue to live with their family for up to 5 years after the birth of their baby (Furstenberg, 1980). Previous studies also have found that the living arrangements of adolescent mothers have implications for a number of important outcomes other than child care. These include increased educational attainment, stable employment, less need for public assistance, better parenting ability, and more positive child developmental outcomes (Hayes, 1987; Stevens, 1988; Trent & Harlan, 1994; Wasserman, Brunelli, & Rauh, 1990). However, research on grandmothers' ability to promote psychological well-being among their daughters and grandchildren shows mixed results (Barth, Schinke, & Maxwell, 1983; Colletta & Lee, 1983; Davis & Rhodes, 1994; Kissman, 1989; Nath et al., 1991; Panzarine, 1986; Turner et al., 1990). Although it is expected that multigenerational households are more effective in promoting socioemotional health and more effective parenting than independent adolescent mother households (Furstenberg et al., 1987; Horwitz et al., 1991a), several studies present conflicting findings (Brooks-Gunn & Chase-Lansdale, 1991; Richardson et al., 1991; Unger & Cooley, 1992; Unger & Wandersman, 1988).

In a study of the quality of parenting in 99 African American multigenerational families with an adolescent mother, Chase-Lansdale et al. (1994) found that the quality of parenting provided by grandmothers varied with the age and living arrangements of the adolescent mother. Specifically, better parenting was provided by grandmothers to very young adolescent mothers than to older adolescent mothers living with them. Older, coresiding adolescent mothers reported a lower quality of parenting by grandmothers. In a similar vein, Voran and Phillips (1993) interviewed 20 African American adolescent mother–grandmother dyads and found that child-care support from grandmothers was negatively correlated with the adolescent mothers' self-esteem. That is, the more involved grandmothers were in providing child-care support, the lower the level of self-esteem adolescent mothers reported. The benefits of grandmother support may diminish as adolescent mothers age. For example, Unger and Wandersman (1988) found that having more support from the family was associated with less anxiety among adolescent mothers when their infant was 1 month old but not when the infant was 8 months old. These studies highlight the reality that there is a fine line between grandmothers' providing support and providing opportunities for adolescent mothers to feel competent as parents, especially with older adolescent mothers. Adolescence is the stage of life in which children begin to search for a sense of identity, independence, and self-sufficiency from family; yet, most adolescent mothers must remain dependent on their family for their very survival. By late adolescence, the need for support and the need to achieve independence may conflict, resulting in diminished benefits of support in conflictual mother–adolescent mother relationships. A renegotiation of family responsibilities is necessary as the adolescent mother ages (Unger & Cooley, 1992). Efforts to help grandmothers understand these distinctions based on the age of adolescent mothers are necessary if family psychological well-being is to be achieved.

Racial differences in the benefits of support also are apparent. Unger and Cooley (1992) showed that receiving child care and living with grandmothers resulted in more behavior problems among children of White adolescent mothers but not among children of African American adolescent mothers. In their study of primarily White adolescent mothers and their infants in various living arrangements, Spieker and Bensley (1994) found that high support from grandmothers was associated with more secure infant attachment when the adolescent mother lived away with her partner. On the other hand, low support from grandmothers for adolescent mothers living alone with their infants was related to more secure infants. Living away from the grandmother may facilitate accelerated role transitions for adolescent mothers. Yet, subtle racial differences may be operating through available options and choices for living arrangements.

African American adolescent mothers are less likely to maintain contact with the father of their baby and more likely to remain at home with their family than White adolescent mothers. For those who do remain at home, family values regarding the meaning of early childbearing should influence support relationships. We found a significant difference in the way African American and White grandmothers perceived their daughter's role within the family since the birth of the baby (Caldwell, Antonucci, Jackson, Osofsky, & Wolford, 1994). White grandmothers were more likely than African American grandmothers to say that they now treat their daughter more like an adult. Because most of our adolescent mothers lived with their mothers, and because we found no racial difference in level of conflict between mothers and daughters, it may be that the birth of the baby is more likely to be viewed as a rite of passage to adulthood (Spieker & Bensley, 1994) by White families than by African American families. This idea is supported by literature that suggests an expectation for independent family formation when an adolescent female gives birth more often among Whites than among African Americans (Farber,

1990; Hogan & Kitagawa, 1985). It also may be a reflection of flexible family boundaries and the ability to share mothering roles within historically extended, muitigenerational African American households (Billingsley, 1992; Burton, 1990; Collins, 1987; Wilson et al., 1990). Thus, the transition to adulthood for an adolescent mother is culturally determined and influenced by intergenerational expectations and obligations.

Adolescent Age and Social Support. An important direction of current research is the consequences of the timing of the first birth. Most of the work in this area has focused on the relationship between age and coresidence on quality of parenting among adolescent mothers and their mothers; differences in the type and amount of social support needed by adolescent mothers based on age; and age as a predictor of stress among adolescent mothers. In general, older adolescent mothers seem to need less parenting advice than younger mothers (Chase-Lansdale et al., 1994; Voran & Phillips, 1993). Additionally, younger adolescent mothers appear to experience less stress and rely more on their own mothers for both instrumental and emotional support, whereas older adolescent mothers experience more stress and need a wider variety of support resources (Camp et al., 1993; Kissman & Shapiro, 1990). These findings highlight the importance of a multigenerational development framework for understanding early childbearing. Given that the early, middle, and late stage of adolescence each has its own developmental tasks and transitions (Cobb, 1995), research approaches and interventions that consider adolescents as homogeneous miss the opportunity to achieve a more in-depth understanding of the impact of early childbearing on an adolescent's development. As previously stated, the developmental needs and capabilities of a 14-year-old mother are quite different from those of a 19-year-old mother. Developmental as well as individual and family differences must be recognized before adequate social support and effective interventions can be provided.

Father Support. The majority of empirical investigations of adolescent mothers and their families have focused on the adolescent's mother as her most common and preferred source of support. This may be partially due to earlier work on adolescent mother–father relationships, which indicated that the father was a passive and ineffectual figure in the adolescent mother's life (see the review by Landy, Schubert, Cleland, Clark, & Montgomery, 1983). Most of this research, however, was conceptualized within a psychoanalytic framework, and the samples were primarily clinical populations. More recently, community-based studies have found that the influence of the father of the adolescent mother has gained importance for encouraging more positive outcomes for adolescent mothers and their children. For example, Oyserman, Radin, and Benn (1993) found that the grandfather's involvement with his grandchild had a greater impact on the child's compliance with the adolescent mother's behavioral requests than the grandmother's involvement. This study demonstrated that there is added value in having family members other than the grandmother who support the adolescent mother–child dyad.

Partner Support. Support from the adolescent mother's partner also has been examined, with findings suggesting that grandmothers and partners affect the psychological well-being of the adolescent mother and child in different ways. Grandmothers provide significantly more types of support (e.g., social, emotional, financial, child care) than partners, though both provide emotional support (Spieker & Bensley, 1994). Adolescent mothers who have support from a partner exhibit more responsiveness to their infant (Unger & Wandersman, 1988), express more life satisfaction (Kissman, 1989), and report less distress (Thompson & Pebbles-Wilkins, 1992) than those who do not have partner support. These findings demonstrate the need to examine the influences of different family support sources. If we are to fully understand a supportive family environment, relationships with the adolescent mother, as well as the impact of relationships between other family members on the adolescent mother's psychological well-being, must be considered. An important footnote in this regard is that the fathers of adolescent mother's babies frequently are not teenagers themselves. In an analysis of partner age discrepancies, Males (1993) found that 7 out of 10 babies of adolescent mothers were fathered by men over the age of 20. Thus, the potential role of adolescent mother's partners should not be overlooked as sources of support as well as stress.

Grandmother Adaptation. Although grandmothers are expected to provide support to their adolescent daughters and grandchildren, the transition to grandmotherhood can be difficult, especially for younger grandmothers (Hagestad & Burton, 1986). Hagestad and Burton (1986) found that on-time grandmothers (i.e., those aged 39 or older) were better able to prepare for anticipated role transitions by becoming more flexible in other roles, whereas younger grandmothers had less time to prepare themselves because they typically found out about the pregnancy at a later stage. Additionally, younger grandmothers lacked avenues for expressing their feelings about their new responsibilities. Few studies have examined the impact of a birth to an adolescent mother on her mother (see Burton & Bengtson, 1985; Poole, Smith, & Hoffman, 1982; Sacco & MacLeod, 1990; and Voran & Phillips, 1993, for exceptions). We found that although almost all grandmothers indicated that they provided instrumental and emotional support to both the adolescent mother and her infant, for many this assistance was not without personal costs (Caldwell et al., 1994). Thus, the assumption that grandmothers are willing and able to assist their adolescent daughters who are mothers is not always realistic.

Other Support. Research is now emerging that explores the benefits of social support beyond family relationships. The role of "natural mentors" (i.e., non-parent, nonpeer supportive persons) in the psychological adjustment of adolescent mothers (Rhodes, Ebert, & Fischer, 1992) is an example of this work. It is intended to show the importance of other forms of social support (e.g., teachers, ministers, coaches) available to supplement family support or to act as an alternative source of support if conflictual family relationships make the cost of receiving support too high. An evaluation of informal support relationships beyond the mother–daughter dyad should be made before family support is considered unavailable.

Several family characteristics that appear to promote more positive psychological functioning among adolescent parents and their children emerged from this review. These include (1) flexible family structures that allow for the sharing of child care and child rearing; (2) coresidence and coparenting among younger adolescent mothers and their mothers; (3) grandmothers' understanding of the boundaries between promoting parental competence and undermining feelings of parental competence among older adolescent mothers; (4) the importance of sources of support beyond the grandmother for older adolescent mothers; and (5) the recognition that intergenerational family relations influence the psychological well-being of adolescent parents.

Multiple Generations of Early Childbearers

Family support, so critical for positive mental health outcomes, is often intergenerational in nature. The ability to provide adequate family support to adolescent mothers, however, may be influenced by a number of factors, including the actual structure of intergenerational linkages. For example, if a young girl gives birth at age 16, and her daughter gives birth at age 16, and her daughter's daughter also gives birth at age 16, the resultant intergenerational family configuration would be a young mother, an early grandmother, and a very young great-grandmother. This idea represents an age-condensed generational family structure (Burton, 1990) that highlights the mother–daughter relationship as critical to our understanding of how adolescent childbearing and the availability of social support may be passed from generation to generation (Musick, 1994). Just as compelling from a developmental perspective, however, is an age-condensed generational family structure based on the male lineage or on mixed-gender lineages. Unfortunately, research on father influences (i.e., the father of the baby and especially the father of the adolescent mother) in the early childbearing literature is limited; therefore, our conceptualizations of these relationships are female dominated. Burton's (1990) description of female age-condensed families as "having a greater number of people across and within generations who are closer in age than people in families with older mothers" would also be applicable to male contributions or lack of contributions to family support systems. Tendencies toward larger and younger families in family systems with multiple generations of early child-bearers have advantages and disadvantages in their ability to respond to the needs of adolescent parents and their children. The primary advantage is a wider array of people to serve as child-care providers, confidants, and com-forters; the major disadvantage is more demands on scarce financial (Burton, 1990, p. 127) as well as emotional resources. In general, there is less time for the accumulation of all types of resources.

Less common in the literature is the idea of early childbearing as an oppor-tunity for growth and development. However, Burton (1990) found that within some families, certain mechanisms promote adolescent childbearing as an alternative life course strategy. Although this work was based on a very small sample of 20 African American, low-income, rural families, the qualitative approach provided insight into the positive meaning of having children within these families. Family norms that include expectations for early childbearing should result in better family adjustments than those that do not because there may be less ambiguity in family role transitions. This is an area where future research can clarify the relationship between viewing early childbearing as normative and its impact on adolescent mental health. Although this area of research is not pervasive in the early childbearing literature, there are numer-ous studies of repetitions of early births across generations that suggest a family norm (Kahn & Anderson, 1992).

A few long-term investigations do not support these findings regarding repetitions of early births across generations. In a 20-year follow-up study of 121 African American, first-born children of women who were adolescent mothers in the late 1960s, Horwitz et al. (1991b) found that about 80% of the children had not become pregnant or fathered a child by age 19. Those who did tended to be the daughters of the adolescent mothers. Daughters who became pregnant as teens also reported significant depressive symptoms. Fur-ther, regardless of gender, children of adolescent mothers who had moved out of their parents' home about 2 years after their child's birth were more likely to become adolescent parents themselves. Finally, those who became young parents were more likely to have a mother suffering from lifetime depression. Similarly, Furstenberg and his colleagues (1987; Furstenberg, Levine, & Brooks-Gunn, 1990) did not find a persistent pattern of intergenerational transmission of early parenthood in their 17-year follow-up of 300 African American families in Baltimore. Although the percentage of repeated early childbearers was lower than expected (about 30%) in the Furstenberg study, Kahn and Anderson (1992) argued that it was still higher than that in samples of older mothers (20%), which suggests a greater risk.

The two most common characteristics of the children of adolescent parents who are at risk of becoming adolescent parents themselves are gender (i.e., daughters are at higher risk than sons) (Horwitz et al., 1991b; Kahn & Anderson, 1992) and being a child of a chronically depressed mother (Horwitz et al., 1991b). These same characteristics may place the adolescent mother at greater risk for negative mental health outcomes depending on the response of the family to the birth (Prodromidis et al., 1994).

Adolescent Fathers

Research on the psychological well-being of adolescent fathers is far less extensive than research on adolescent mothers. This may be due to the fact that most infants born to unmarried adolescent mothers remain with their mother and her family (Marsiglio, 1995; Wasserman et al., 1990). Nevertheless, an infant's birth can have adverse effects on an adolescent father's psychological well-being, regardless of whether or not he coresides or remains involved with the mother or baby. Several studies have found that adolescent fathers experience a variety of stressors associated with parenting (Cervera, 1991; Elster & Hendricks, 1986; Elster & Lamb, 1982; Miller, 1994; Rivara, Sweeney, & Henderson, 1986). The most frequently cited parent-related stressors included seeing the child, problems in the relationship with the child's mother and/or family, concerns about the health of the child, and the inability to provide economically for the child. The ability to cope with these stressors is compromised by the search for identity and other developmental issues during adolescence. The impact of these stressors also has implications for the child's emotional well-being because adolescent fathers often lack the cognitive, emotional, support, coping, and financial capabilities necessary for empathic, mature parenting (Applegate, 1988; Elster & Lamb, 1982). Thus, an early transition to parenthood for adolescent males presents developmental and parenting dilemmas similar to those experienced by adolescent females. Yet, the experience itself is very different because they are less likely to be involved in the day-to-day care of the child (Heath & McKenry, 1993; Marsiglio, 1986).

As with adolescent motherhood, most of the research on adolescent fatherhood focuses on the sociological aspects of early paternity (Applegate, 1988; Marsiglio, 1995), although a more extensive body of empirical work examining the mental health consequences of early paternity is beginning to emerge. Many studies of the psychological well-being of adolescent fathers highlight the importance of paternal responsibility for and involvement with their children as critical to their self-image, self-esteem, and diminished stress levels (Christmon, 1990; Elster & Lamb, 1982; Miller, 1994). However, comparative research on the short- and long-term mental health consequences for adolescent fathers shows conflicting results. For example, Robinson and Frank (1994) found that young fathers tended to have lower self-esteem than their nonfather peers. Similarly, Buchanan and Robbins (1990) found that adolescent fathers were more emotionally distressed as young adults than their peers who were not fathers as adolescents. Rivara et al. (1986), on the other hand, found that the mental health (i.e., depression/anxiety, mood states) of adolescent fathers was not significantly different from that of nonfathers. Contradictions in this literature may result from the use of cross-sectional designs using very small convenience samples to describe the experiences of adolescent fathers. This approach is further complicated by studies that interview the adolescent mother about the adolescent father (Cervera, 1991; Danziger & Radin, 1990) or lack of consistency in what constitutes the age range for an "adolescent father" (Marsiglio, 1995). Nevertheless, findings from these studies are beginning to focus attention on the fact that, like adolescent mothers, adolescent fathers need instrumental and emotional support from a variety of sources.

Differentials in the psychological well-being of adolescent fathers can be influenced by a number of factors, such as race, length of time since the birth of the first child, father's age, and family support. An interesting interaction between race and duration has been reported in the few studies that used a longitudinal design and a large sample. Buchanan and Robbins (1990) and Pirog-Good (1995) independently found that psychological distress among young adult men who were adolescent fathers compared to those who were not was more pronounced among White than among African American men. That is, the experience of having been an adolescent father resulted in low self-esteem (Buchanan & Robbins, 1990; Pirog-Good, 1995) and an external locus of control (Pirog-Good, 1995) among White males but not among African American males. Regarding parental satisfaction, Heath and McKenry (1993) demonstrated that as adults, men who fathered their first child during adolescence experienced more parental satisfaction than those who fathered later, especially for White fathers and older men. They also found that there was no significant difference in levels of marital instability or marital satisfaction among the men in the study, regardless of early paternity status.

The advantage of these large-scale longitudinal studies is that they raise several important issues that are not often considered in research on the emotional health of adolescent fathers: Does the initial level of psychological stress among adolescent fathers remain stable over time? How do family relationships moderate mental health outcomes for adolescent fathers as they age? Adolescent males, especially low-income ones, are often viewed as establishing their masculinity and improving their self-esteem through sexual activity and fathering children (Marsiglio, 1995; Robinson & Frank, 1994; Stiffman et al., 1987). Their initial feeling about the birth of their first child may be one of pride and a sense of accomplishment. Pirog-Good (1995) suggested that the self-esteem of White adolescent fathers in her study may have improved at the birth of their child, but it diminished over the 7 years of the study. High distress levels were apparent even among the young men who had married or lived with the mother of their child after birth in the Buchanan and Robbins

(1990) study. Because many White fathers have the opportunity to assume the father role more often than African American fathers, it could be that the distress White fathers experience as young adults reflects their success or lack of success at fathering based on their own desire and ability to be involved in parenting responsibilities for their first child.

The lower level of long-term distress among African American fathers could be a reflection of their decrease in direct involvement with their child over time (Rivara et al., 1986). However, Buchanan and Robbins (1990) found that men whose girlfriends had abortions and those whose child was primarily cared for by the adolescent mother were no less distressed than those who had married or lived with the mother. Thus, parenting responsibilities alone do not account for racial differences in long-term distress. An alternative explanation of the "absent father" phenomenon is more culturally based. That is, the families of African American adolescent fathers may assume more parenting responsibilities and provide continued support to the adolescent father through extended family efforts and living arrangements than the families of White adolescent fathers. Several studies of African American adolescent fathers have found that their family, especially their mother, usually had contact with their child and also was a great source of support for them (see Elster & Hendricks, 1986, for a review; see also Miller, 1994; Rivara et al., 1986). Additionally, longitudinal research has demonstrated that White adolescent fathers move into and out of their family household more often than African American adolescent fathers or those who delayed parenting, regardless of race (Pirog-Good, 1995). Getting married was one of the most frequently given responses as to the question of why White adolescent fathers left home. Independent living arrangements may have resulted in less support from the family of origin at a time when more support was needed to help these fathers negotiate the paradox of moving into adulthood while parenting.

The birth of a baby to an adolescent female fathered by an adolescent male can often result in stress for the adolescent father due to ambiguity in role definitions and uncertainty in role responsibilities, regardless of parenting status (i.e., involved versus not involved). Because the adolescent father typically lacks the ability to assume the major provider role expected of older fathers, his involvement with his baby often is curtailed by the adolescent mother and/or her family. There are no clear rules on how involved an adolescent father or his family should be when the adolescent parents do not marry (Cervera, 1991). The fact that an adolescent father does not live with and financially support his child does not mean that he cannot be involved and committed in other ways (Danziger & Radin, 1990). The contributions of the adolescent father's involvement to the mental health of the adolescent mother, the baby, and the father himself have been well documented throughout this chapter. Additionally, the influences of intergenerational family relations on the mental health of adolescent fathers has been suggested. Future research is necessary that addresses more complex questions regarding the factors that influence the psychological well-being of adolescent fathers before we can determine under what conditions their mental health will be compromised by the birth of a child during adolescence. Our family transitions study data will allow us to examine more fully some of these issues, such as the stability of adolescent father's psychological well-being over time, as well as the association between mental health outcomes and the influences of intra- and inter-generational relationships with the family of origin for both the adolescent mother and father.

Avenues for Future Research and Intervention

Our proposed model incorporating individual characteristics, family considerations, and the interaction of the two as important factors in predicting adolescent parents' mental health has been supported, to some extent, by our review of current empirical evidence – both from our own work and from the research of others. Directions for future research should include studies focusing on how the age of the adolescent parent and the type of support provided may interact to impact the psychological well-being of adolescent parents. Additionally, several empirical questions are raised by this review: (1) Will family support influence the relationship between parent gender and mental health for this population? (2) Will the influence of family support vary by the source of support once family members other than the mother of the adolescent mother are considered? (3) How are all of these relationships influenced by the race, ethnicity, and socioeconomic status of the family?

The next important step is to develop intervention strategies that utilize findings from this emerging research, noting the importance of intergenerational family influences on the mental health of early childbearers. Given that multiple transitions occur during adolescence, some researchers argue that this developmental period is an ideal time for interventions aimed at promoting healthy lifestyles (Brooks-Gunn & Warren, 1989). At the moment, there is clearly a public awareness concerning the potential problems that may occur as a result of adolescent parenting. Our review suggests that there are individual as well as family characteristics that render specific adolescents at risk for negative mental health outcomes. These include older adolescent mothers in need of support; adolescent mothers who are experiencing a conflict between the amount of family childrearing support needed and the amount provided by grandmothers; those whose mothers are chronically depressed; and adolescent fathers who want contact with their children. Academic and policy-oriented research indicates that the cost to society may be considerable if the needs of these adolescents are not met. From a simple human capital perspective, we should be highly motivated to intervene, considering the family factors described previously.

Some consideration should be given to models intervention designed to maximize the developmental accomplishments of each member of the family experiencing an early transition to childrearing and models that recognize individual needs based on gender. This should include sensitivity to the ages of both the adolescent parents and grandparents who are making these transitions. Belief systems regarding marital status and age at first birth within the context of families are also an important consideration. Finally, the availability and use of social supports beyond the adolescent mother–grandmother dyad should be assessed. Intervention programs are clearly very important and should include the family as early as possible after an adolescent has become a parent. Most programs tend to focus only on the adolescent mother's development and achievement. These programs typically encourage the adolescent mother to set goals in specific areas such as education and employment. Others are designed to enhance self-esteem and teach adolescent parenting skills (Chase-Lansdale, Brooks-Gunn, & Paikoff, 1991). Our work suggests, however, that we must not take a myopic view of an adolescent parent. We must acknowledge that adolescent mothers and fathers need assistance. This assistance should address their instrumental emotional as well as developmental needs. Further, we cannot assume that adolescent parents live in a neutral or isolated environment. Interventions, if they are to be successful, cannot ignore the context within which the adolescent parent must exist. We believe that it is critical to understand the family context if we are to design programs that will be effective for adolescent parents and their children in the long term. While emphasizing the broader family context, it is also important to recognize that although this context may be a significant source of support for many adolescent parents, it may also have a significantly negative impact on their potential for success. Nonetheless, we firmly believe that the broader family context will at least provide us with a more accurate assessment of the environment within which adolescent parents live and consequently improve the potential for the design of successful intervention programs based on more comprehensive family needs.

Conclusions

Studies of social support, especially from grandmothers, have been linked to positive as well as negative mental health among adolescent parents and their children. With numerous mental health risks associated with early childbearing, it is important to identify factors that may contribute to more positive long-term outcomes for adolescent parents and their family. Families as sources of support have been found to be important. However, transformations in family roles and obligations, as well as in resource allocations and the knowledge of adolescent developmental needs, must be considered as families adjust to the birth of a baby to an adolescent. It should also be noted that not all families are functional and thus capable of providing support. In some cases, an adolescent mother may have been seeking escape from a problematic family prior to her pregnancy. After the birth of her child, however, she must be even more dependent on her family. If that family is dysfunctional, poorly functioning, or otherwise unable to provide adequate and appropriate support, the negative mental health consequences of early childbearing will be exacerbated. Family structures are undergoing dramatic changes. Families are formed, disintegrated, reshaped, blended, and re-formed. As a consequence, a redefinition of family in general is necessary. Creative interventions should reach out not only to adolescent parents and their children, but also to the family members, whoever they may be, who will be responsible for assisting young parents in achieving a successful transition to adulthood.

References

Alan Guttmacher Institute. (1993, July). *Teenage sexual and reproductive behavior: Facts in brief.* Washington, DC: Author.

Alan Guttmacher Institute. (1994, August). *Teenage reproductive health in the United States: Facts in brief.* Washington, DC: Author.

Alan Guttmacher Institute. (1995, February). *Teenage pregnancy and the welfare reform debate: Facts in brief.* Washington, DC: Author.

Antonucci, T. C. (1986). Social support networks: A hierarchical mapping technique. *Generations, 10,* 10–12.

Antonucci, T. C., & Jackson, J. S. (1988). Successful aging and life course reciprocity. In A. M. Warnes (Ed.), *Human aging, and later life: Multidisciplinary perspectives* (pp. 83–95). London: Hodder & Stoughton.

Applegate, J S. (1988). Adolescent fatherhood: Developmental perils and potentials. *Child and Adolescent Social Work, 5,* 205–217.

Barth, R. P., Schinke, S. P., & Maxwell, J. S (1983). Psychological correlates of teenage motherhood. *Journal of Youth and Adolescence, 12,* 471–485.

Beardslee, W. R., Zuckerman, B. S., Amaro, H., & McAllister, M. (1988). Depression among adolescent mothers: A pilot study. *Developmental and Behavioral Pediatrics, 9,* 62–65.

Beck, R. W., & Beck, S. H. (1989). The incidence of extended households among middle-aged women: Estimates from a 15-year panel study. *Journal of Family Issues, 10,* 147–168.

Billingsley, A. (1992). *Climbing Jacob's ladder: The enduring legacy of African-American families.* New York: Simon & Schuster.

Brooks-Gunn, J., & Chase-Lansdale, P. L. (1991). Children having children: Effects on the family system. *Pediatric Annals, 20,* 467–481.

Brooks-Gunn, J., & Furstenberg, F. F. (1986). The children of adolescent mothers: Physical, academic and psychological outcomes. *Developmental Review, 6,* 224–251.

Brooks-Gunn, J., & Furstenberg, F. F. (1989). Long-term implications of fertility-related behavior and family formation on adolescent mothers and their children. In K. Kreppner & R. M. Lerner (Eds.), *Family systems and life-span development* (pp. 319–339). Hillsdale, NJ: Erlbaum.

Brooks-Gunn, J., & Warren, M. P. (1989). Biological and social contributions to negative affect in young adolescent girls. *Child Development, 60,* 40–55.

Buchanan, M., & Robbins, C. (1990). Early adult psychological consequences for males of adolescent pregnancy and its resolution. *Journal of Youth and Adolescence, 19,* 413–424.

Burton, L. M. (1990). Teenage childbearing as an alternative life-course strategy in multigeneration black families. *Human Nature, 1,* 123–143.

Burton, L. M., & Bengtson, V. L. (1985). Black grandmothers: Issues of timing and continuity of roles. In V. L. Bengtson & J. F. Robertson (Eds.), *Grandparenthood: Research and policy* (pp. 61–77). Beverly Hills, CA: Sage.

Caldwell, C. H., Antonucci, T. C., Jackson, J. S., Osofsky, J. D., & Wolford, M. L. (1994, July). *Families with adolescent mothers: The emergence of the interactive grandmother.* Paper presented at the Summer Institute on Successful Midlife Development sponsored by the MacArthur Foundation, International Society for the Study of Behavioral Development, and the Max Planck Institute for Human Development and Education, St. Moritz, Switzerland.

Caldwell, C. H., Antonucci, T. C., Jackson, J. S., Osofsky, J. D., & Wolford, M. L. (1995, March 31). *The availability of use of social support in families with adolescent mothers.* Paper presented at the Biennial Meeting of the Society for Research in Child Development, Indianapolis.

Camp, B. W., Holman, S., & Ridgway, E. (1993). The relationship between social support and stress in adolescent mothers. *Developmental and Behavioral Pediatrics, 14,* 369–374.

Center on Budget and Policy Priorities. (1995, March). *Welfare, out-of-wedlock childbearing, and poverty: What is the connection?* Working paper. Washington, DC.

Cervera, N. (1991, January). Unwed teenage pregnancy: Family relationships with the father of the baby. *Families in Society: The Journal of Contemporary Human Services,* 29–37.

Chase-Lansdale, P. L., Brooks-Gunn, J., & Paikoff, R. L. (1991). Research and programs for adolescent mothers: Missing links and future promises. *Family Relations, 40,* 369–403.

Chase-Lansdale, P. L., Brooks-Gunn, J., & Zamsky, E. S. (1994). Young African American multigenerational families in poverty: Quality of mothering and grandmothering. *Child Development, 65,* 373–393.

Chase-Lansdale, P. L., & Vinovskis, M. A. (1987). Should we discourage teenage marriage? *The Public Interest, 87,* 23–37.

Chilman, C. S. (1980). Social and psychological research concerning adolescent childbearing: 1970–1980. *Journal of Marriage and the Family, 42,* 793–805.

Christmon, K. (1990). Parental responsibility of African American unwed adolescent fathers. *Adolescence, 25,* 645–653.

Cobb, N. J. (1995). *Adolescence: Continuity, change, and diversity* (2nd ed.). Mountain View, CA: Mayfield.

Colletta, N. D. (1983). At risk for depression: A study of young mothers. *Journal of Genetic Psychology, 142,* 30–36.

Colletta, N. D., & Lee, D. (1983). The impact of support for black adolescent mothers. *Journal of Family Issues. 4,* 127–139.

Collins, P. H. (1987). The meaning of motherhood in black culture and black mother/daughter relationships. *SAGE: A Scholarly Journal on Black Women, 4,* 171–185.

Congressional Budget Office. (1990). *Sources of support for adolescent mothers.* Washington, DC: Congress of the United States.

Cooley, M. L., & Unger, D. G. (1991). The role of family support in determining developmental outcomes in children of teen mothers. *Child Psychiatry and Human Development, 21,* 217–234.

Danziger, S. K., & Radin, N. (1990). Absent does not equal uninvolved: Predictors of fathering in teen mother families. *Journal of Marriage and the Family, 52,* 636–642.

Davis, A. A., & Rhodes, J. E. (1994). African-American teenage mothers and their mothers: An analysis of supportive and problematic interactions. *Journal of Community Psychology, 22,* 12–20.

Elster, A. B., & Hendricks, L. (1986). Stresses and coping strategies of adolescent fathers. In A. B. Elster & M. E. Lamb (Eds.), *Adolescent fatherhood* (pp. 55–65). Hillsdale, NJ: Erlbaum.

Elster, A. B., & Lamb, M. E. (1982). Adolescent fathers: A group potentially at risk for parenting failure. *Infant Mental Health Journal, 3*, 148–155.

Elster, A. B., & Lamb, M. E. (Eds.). (1986). *Adolescent fatherhood.* Hillsdale, NJ: Erlbaum.

Farber, N. (1990). The significance of race and class in marital decisions among unmarried adolescent mothers. *Social Problems, 37*, 51–63.

Freeman, E. W., & Rickels, K. (1993). *Early childbearing: Perspectives of black adolescents on pregnancy, abortion, and contraception.* Newbury Park, CA: Sage.

Furstenberg, F. F. (1980). Burdens and benefits: The impact of early childbearing on the family. *Journal of Social Issues, 36*, 64–87.

Furstenberg, F. F. (1991). As the pendulum swings: Teenage childbearing and social concern. *Family Relations, 40*, 127–138.

Furstenberg, F. F., Brooks-Gunn, J., & Morgan, P. (1987). *Adolescent mothers in later life.* Cambridge, MA: Cambridge University Press.

Furstenberg, F. F., Levine, J. A., & Brooks-Gunn, J. (1990). The children of teenage mothers: Patterns of early childbearing in two generations. *Family Planning Perspectives, 22*, 54–61.

Geronimus, A. T. (1991). Teenage childbearing and social and reproductive disadvantage: The evolution of complex questions and the demise of simple answers. *Family Relations, 40*, 463–471.

Geronimus, A. T., & Korenman, S. (1992). The socioeconomic consequences of teen childbearing reconsidered. *Quarterly Journal of Economics, 107*, 1187–1214.

Hagestad, G. O., & Burton, L. (1986). Grandparenthood, life context, and family development. *American Behavioral Scientist, 29*, 471–484.

Hayes, C. D. (Ed.), (1987). *Risking the future: Adolescent sexuality, pregnancy, and childbearing.* Washington, DC: National Academy Press.

Heath, D. T., & McKenry, P. C. (1993). Adult family life of men who fathered as adolescents. *Families in Society: The Journal of Contemporary Human Services, 74*, 36–45.

Heaton, T. B., & Jacobson, C. K. (1994). Race differences in changing family demographics in the 1980s. *Journal of Family Issues, 15*, 290–308.

Hofferth, S. L. (1987). Factors affecting initiation of sexual intercourse. In S. L. Hofferth & C. D. Hayes (Eds.), *Risking the future: Adolescent sexuality, pregnancy and childbearing* (Vol. 2, pp. 7–35). Washington, DC: National Academy Press.

Hogan, D. P., & Kitagawa, E. M. (1985). The impact of social status, family structure, and neighborhood on the fertility of black adolescents. *American Journal of Sociology, 90*, 825–855.

Horwitz, S. M., Klerman, L. V., Sung Kuo, H., & Jekel, J. F. (1991a). Intergenerational transmission of school-age parenthood. *Family Planning Perspectives, 23*, 168–172.

Horwitz, S. M., Klerman, L. V., Sung Kuo, H., & Jekel, J. F. (1991b). School-age mothers: Predictors of long-term educational and economic outcomes. *Pediatrics, 87*, 862–868.

Kahn, J. R., & Anderson, K. E. (1992). Intergenerational patterns of teenage fertility. *Demography, 29*, 39–57.

Kahn, R. L., & Antonucci, T. C. (1980). Convoys over the life course: Attachment, roles, and social support. In P. B. Baltes & O. Brim (Eds.), *Life-span development and behavior* (pp. 253–286). New York: Academic Press.

Kahn, J. R., Rindfuss, R. R., & Guilkey, D. K. (1990). Adolescent contraceptive method choices. *Demography, 27*, 323–335.

Kissman, K. (1989). Social support, parental belief systems, and well being. *Youth and Society, 21*, 120–130.

Kissman, K., & Shapiro, J. (1990). The composites of social support and well-being among adolescent mothers. *International Journal of Adolescence and Youth, 2*, 165–173.

Ku, L., Sonenstein, F. L., & Pleck, J. H. (1993). Neighborhood, family, and work: Influences on the premarital behaviors of adolescent males. *Social Forces, 72*, 479–503.

Ladner, J., & Gourdine, R. L. (1992). Adolescent pregnancy in the African-American community.

In R. L. Braithwaite & S. E. Taylor (Eds.), *Health issues in the black community* (pp. 206–221). San Francisco: Jossey-Bass.

Landy, S., Schubert, J., Cleland, J. F., Clark, C., & Montgomery, J. S. (1983). Teenage pregnancy: Family syndrome? *Adolescence, 71*, 679–694.

Lubin, B., & McCollum, K. L. (1994). Depressive mood in black and white female adolescents. *Adolescence, 29*, 241–245.

Luker, K. (1991, Spring). Dubious conceptions: The controversy over teen pregnancy. *The American Prospect*, 73–83.

Males, M. (1993). School-age pregnancy: Why hasn't prevention worked? *Journal of School Health, 63*, 429–432.

Mare, R. D., & Winship, C. (1991). Socioeconomic change and the decline of marriage for blacks and whites. In C. Jencks & P. E. Peterson (Eds.), *The urban underclass* (pp. 175–202). Washington, DC: The Brookings Institution.

Marsiglio, W. (1986). Teenage fatherhood: High school completion and educational attainment. In A. B. Elster & M. E. Lamb (Eds.), *Adolescent fatherhood* (pp. 67–87). Hillsdale, NJ: Erlbaum.

Marsiglio, W. (1995). Young nonresident biological fathers. *Marriage and Family Review, 20*, 325–348.

Miller, B. C., & Moore, K. A. (1990). Adolescent sexual behavior, pregnancy, and parenting: Research through the 1980s. *Journal of Marriage and the Family, 52*, 1025–1044.

Miller, D. B. (1994). Influences on parental involvement of African American adolescent fathers. *Child and Adolescent Social Work Journal, 11*, 363–378.

Musick, J. S. (1994). Grandmothers and grandmothers-to-be: Effects on adolescent mothers and adolescent mothering. *Infants and Young Children, 6*, 1–9.

Nath, P. S., Borkowski, J. G., Whitman, T. L., & Schellenbach, C. J. (1991). Understanding adolescent parenting: The dimensions and functions of social support. *Family Relations, 40*, 411–420.

Osofsky, J. D., Hann, D. M., & Pebbles, C. (1993). Adolescent parenthood: Risks and opportunities for mothers and infants. In C. H. Zeanah (Ed.), *Handbook of infant mental health* (pp. 106–119). New York: Guilford Press.

Oyserman, D., Radin, N., & Benn, R. (1993). Dynamics in a three-generational family: Teens, grandparents, and babies. *Developmental Psychology, 29*, 564–572.

Panzarine, S. (1986). Stressors, coping and social supports of adolescent mothers. *Journal of Adolescent Health Care, 7*, 153–161.

Peterson, A. C., Compas, B. E., Brooks-Gunn, J., Stemmler, M., Ey, S., & Grant, K. E. (1993). Depression in adolescence. *American Psychologist, 48*, 155–168.

Pirog-Good, M. A. (1995). The family background and attitudes of teen fathers. *Youth and Society, 26*, 351–376.

Plotnick, R. D. (1992). The effects of attitudes on teenage premarital pregnancy and its resolution. *American Sociological Review, 57*, 800–811.

Poole, C. J., Smith, M. S., & Hoffman, M. A. (1982). Mothers of adolescent mothers. *Journal of Adolescent Health Care, 3*, 41–43.

Prodromidis, M., Abrams, S., Field, T., Scafidi, F., & Rahdert, E. (1994). Psychosocial stressors among depressed adolescent mothers. *Adolescence, 29*, 331–343.

Rhodes, J. E., Ebert, L., & Fischer, K. (1992). Natural mentors: An overlooked resource in the social networks of young, African American mothers. *American Journal of Community Psychology, 20*, 445–461.

Richardson, R., Barbour, N. B., & Bubenzer, D. L. (1991). Bittersweet connections: Informal social networks as sources of support and interference for adolescent mothers. *Family Relations, 40*, 430–434.

Rivara, F. P., Sweeney, P. J., & Henderson, B. F. (1986). Black teenage fathers: What happens when the child is born? *Pediatrics, 78*, 151–158.

Robinson, R. B., & Frank, D. I. (1994). The relation between self-esteem, sexual activity, and pregnancy. *Adolescence, 29*, 27–35.

Sacco, W. P., & Macleod, V. A. (1990). Interpersonal responses of primary caregivers to pregnant adolescents differing on depression level. *Journal of Clinical Child Psychology, 19*, 256–270.

Smith, D. S., & Hindus, M. S. (1975). Premarital pregnancy in America 1640–1971: An overview and interpretation. *Journal of Interdisciplinary History, 4*, 537–570.

Spieker, S. J., & Bensley, L. (1994). Roles of living arrangements and grandmother social support in adolescent mothering and infant attachment. *Developmental Psychology, 30*, 102–111.

Stevens, J. H., Jr. (1988). Social support, locus of control, and parenting in three low-income groups of mothers: Black teenagers, black adults, and white adults. *Child Development. 59*, 635–642.

Stiffman, A. R., & Davis, L. E. (Eds.). (1990). *Ethnic issues in adolescent mental health.* Newbury Park, CA: Sage.

Stiffman, A. R., Earls, F., Robins, L. N., Jung, K. G., & Kulbok, P. (1987). Adolescent sexual activity and pregnancy: Socioenvironmental problems, physical health, and mental health. *Journal of Youth and Adolescence, 16*, 497–509.

Thompson, M. S., & Pebbles-Wilkins, W. (1992). The impact of formal, informal, and societal support networks on the psychological well-being of black adolescent mothers. *Social Work, 37*, 322–328.

Trent, K., & Harlan, S. L. (1994). Teenage mothers in nuclear and extended households: Differences by marital status and race/ethnicity. *Journal of Family Issues, 15*, 309–337.

Troutman, B. R., & Cutrona, C. T. (1990). Nonpsychotic postpartum depression among adolescent mothers. *Journal of Abnormal Psychology, 99*, 69–78.

Turner, R. J., Grindstaff, C. F., & Phillips, N. (1990). Social support and outcome in teenage pregnancy. *Journal of Health and Social Behavior, 31*, 43–57.

Unger, D., & Cooley, M. (1992). Partner and grandmother contact in black and white teen parent families. *Journal of Adolescent Health, 13*, 546–552.

Unger, D. G., & Wandersman, L. P. (1988). The relations of family and partner support to the adjustment of adolescent mothers. *Child Development, 59*, 1056–1060.

Vinovskis, M. A. (1988). Teenage pregnancy and the underclass. *The Public Interest, 93*, 87–96.

Voran, M., & Phillips, D. (1993). Correlates of grandmother child care support to adolescent mothers: Implications for development in two generations of women. *Children and Youth Services Review, 15*, 321–334.

Washington, A. C. (1982). A cultural and historical perspective on pregnancy-related activity among U.S. teenagers. *Journal of Black Psychology, 9*, 1–28.

Wasserman, G. A., Brunelli, S. A., & Rauh, V. A. (1990). Social supports and living arrangements of adolescent and adult mothers. *Journal of Adolescent Research, 5*, 54–66.

Wilson, M. N. (1984). Mother's and grandmothers' perceptions of parental behavior in three-generational black families. *Child Development, 55*, 1333–1339.

Wilson, M. N., & Tolson, T. F. J. (1990). Familial support in the black community. *Journal of Clinical Child Psychology, 19*, 347–355.

Wilson, M. N., Tolson, T. F. J., Hinton, I. D., & Kiernan, M. (1990). Flexibility and sharing of child care duties in black families. *Sex Roles, 22*, 409–425.

Wilson, W. J. (1984). *The truly disadvantaged: The Inner city, the underclass and public policy.* Chicago: University of Chicago Press.

Zabin, L. S., & Hayward, S. C. (1993). *Adolescent sexual behavior and childbearing.* Newbury Park, CA: Sage.

Zabin, L. S., Wong, R., Weinick, R. M., & Emerson, M. R. (1992). Dependency in urban black families following the birth of an adolescent's child. *Journal of Marriage and the Family, 54*, 496–507.

10 Marriage, Divorce, and Parenthood During the Transition to Young Adulthood: Impacts on Drug Use and Abuse

Jerald G. Bachman, Katherine N. Wadsworth,
Patrick M. O'Malley, John Schulenberg,
and Lloyd D. Johnston

Introduction

Becoming married and becoming a parent are two of the most important events that can define the transition from late adolescence to young adulthood. These events are richly complex in their impacts, for they involve commitments to new roles and responsibilities that usually extend over many years, changing both the physical and psychological environments of the individual. New roles and responsibilities may involve many changes in social contexts, often including new living arrangements, new neighborhoods and neighbors, and new sets of friends and acquaintances, and can be accompanied by important changes in personality and attitude (Antonucci & Mikus, 1988). Throughout adulthood, changing situations and roles elicit new behaviors by providing new rewards and sanctions (Baltes, Reese, & Lipsett, 1980), and increasing identification with adult roles may also increase investment in conforming to normative expectations (Jessor, Donovan, & Costa, 1991; Kandel, 1984; Yamaguchi & Kandel, 1985a). Clearly there is great potential for change in behavior during the transition to young adulthood.

Our focus in this chapter is on the ways in which transitions into (and out of) marriage, and into parenthood, are related to the use of cigarettes, alcohol, and illicit drugs. Although these are by no means the only health-related behaviors that may be affected by marriage and parenthood, they are among the most important. The use of cigarettes can have serious long-term health consequences (U.S. Department of Health and Human Services, 1989). The excessive use of alcohol can involve immediate as well as long-term risks (Baer, 1993; Hilton, 1991; Zucker, 1987). Similarly, the use of illicit drugs such as marijuana and cocaine can involve immediate risks of accident and injury due to impairment, risks of arrest and other negative outcomes due to involvement in illegal activities, and longer-term risks of physiological and psychosocial problems (Baumrind & Moselle, 1985; Kandel, 1980). The detrimental effects of smoking tobacco and using alcohol, marijuana, and cocaine during

Data are drawn from the Monitoring the Future project, a study supported by a grant from the National Institute on Drug Abuse (RO1-DA-01411).

pregnancy also have been documented consistently (Chasnoff, 1991; Hatch & Bracken, 1986; McDonald, Armstrong, & Sloan, 1992; Serdula, Williamson, Kendrick, Anda, & Byers, 1991). Although smoking during pregnancy seems to have declined as public awareness of the risks increases (Kleinman & Kopstein, 1987; Streissguth, Darby, Barr, Smith, & Martin, 1983), findings regarding declines in alcohol and other drug use during pregnancy have not been as consistent (Little, Snell, Gilstrap, Gant, & Rosenfeld, 1989; Serdula et al., 1991; Streissguth et al., 1983). One recent study found that nearly 15% of pregnant women enrolled in public or private prenatal care tested positive for alcohol, marijuana, cocaine, or opiates (Chasnoff, Landress, & Barrett, 1990).

Change, Stability, and Age-Related Shifts in Drug Use

There have been many changes in drug use during recent decades, including large secular trends as particular substances have increased and/or decreased in popularity, differences from one cohort to another, and changes in the drug-using behaviors of individuals. And, of course, all of these changes are to some degree interrelated (see O'Malley, Bachman, & Johnston, 1984, 1988, for discussion of such distinctions and analyses based on Monitoring the Future data).

Among the changes of particular interest to us in this chapter are age-related shifts in drug use that occur during late adolescence and young adult-hood. It has long been recognized that heavy alcohol use and use of some illicit drugs decline on average among individuals during their 20s (e.g., Bachman, O'Malley, & Johnston, 1981, 1984; Donovan, Jessor, & Jessor, 1983; Jessor et al., 1991; Kandel, 1984; O'Malley et al., 1984, 1988; Zucker, 1979). Figure 10.1 illustrates such changes for heavy drinking and for use of marijuana.

Corresponding to the declines in use shown in Figure 10.1 are increases in the proportions of young people who become married and who become parents. Thus, one of the key questions to be addressed in this chapter is whether marriage and parenthood can explain most or all of the overall age-related changes in drug use among young adults.

We have thus far noted a variety of mean-level changes in drug use, but we must also stress the considerable rank-order stability in drug and alcohol use over time (Bachman, O'Malley, & Johnston, 1984; O'Malley, Bachman, & Johnston, 1983). In particular, most young adults who use cigarettes on a daily basis are chemically dependent, which contributes greatly to the stability of use. Stability in drug use may also reflect stability in other potentially causal factors. For example, a good deal of stability in some basic dimensions of personality during the transition to young adulthood has been demonstrated (e.g., McGue, Bacon, & Lykken, 1993; Troll, 1985). In the face of these and other stabilizing influences, why should marriage and parenthood produce significant change in drug use behaviors? We have already suggested a likely

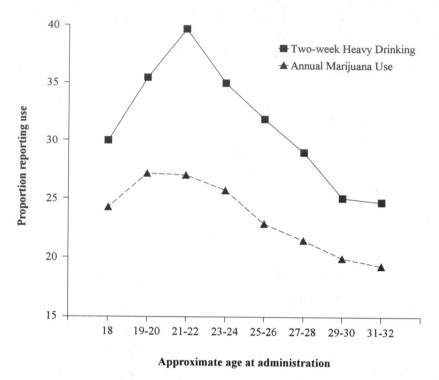

Figure 10.1. Age-related changes in drug use: heavy alcohol use and annual marijuana use.

answer: Marriage and parenthood are two of the most powerful role transitions that typically define the assumption of adulthood.

Marriage and Parenthood: Changes in Social Contexts and Commitments

Transitions into new roles can be stressful and destabilizing, but in spite of its stresses and demands, marriage appears to protect people from many physical and psychological problems, including depression, suicide, victimization, injuries, alcohol abuse, and overall mortality (as summarized by Miller-Tutzauer, Leonard, & Windle, 1991). Parenthood clearly is an emotionally and physically stressful undertaking, but it is also a highly valued social role (Fawcett, 1978; Hoffman, 1978), which becomes a central aspect of the self-concept and a key component of life satisfaction for many people (Chilman, 1980; Cowan & Cowan, 1988; Hoffman & Manis, 1978). If such transitions increase the likelihood of being looked on, treated, and expected to act as an adult, the effect may be to prompt more adultlike behavior. If excessive use of alcohol and the use of illicit drugs are seen more as "sowing wild oats" than as fully adult behavior, then the assumption of other adult roles may involve the expectation of reducing or eliminating some drug-using behavior.

In addition to such broad changes in role expectations, a number of specific changes in social contexts also are involved in marriage and parenthood. Marriage usually involves a change in residence for at least one of the spouses; if there is also a substantial shift in geographic location, that in turn can prompt changes in friendship patterns and other social contacts. Even when no change in neighborhood is involved, newly married partners generally commit more time to each other and to establishing their homes (Wallerstein, 1994), thereby leaving less time for hanging out with friends in settings conducive to drinking and other drug use. Parenthood also transforms social interactions and social networks as parents are forced to reassess their needs for social support and advice versus leisure time and fun, increasing the importance and intensity of some relationships (notably extended family members and other parents) and decreasing that of others (single friends) (Gottlieb & Pancer, 1988). Further role changes and reduced opportunities for socializing result from the sheer burdens of parenthood (Antonucci & Mikus, 1988). Parents who are busy caring for their young children simply have less time available for hanging out or partying with friends, thereby reducing their opportunities for drug use.

In addition to changes in social patterns, the personal commitment made to a spouse may inhibit excessive drinking, illicit drug use, and other potentially damaging behaviors. Frequent close contact with a caring partner may be enough to tip the scales against such behaviors. Becoming a parent can also drastically alter one's psychological landscape and interpersonal commitments, introducing a whole new set of priorities and values (Galinsky, 1981; Heath, 1978; Mikus, 1981), and drug use may become less compatible with those new priorities and values.

Marriage is often undertaken with the expectation that parenthood will soon follow; accordingly, some of the personal and social transformations observed to coincide with marriage actually may be better understood as anticipatory to parenthood. Indeed, many couples who already live together or are sexually intimate choose to marry precisely because they feel ready to have children and prefer to do so as a married couple. Some anticipatory reductions in drug use may occur well before pregnancy as young adults planning for parenthood become more sensitized to health practices in general, particularly those practices (such as smoking, alcohol use, and use of illicit drugs) that could adversely affect their ability to conceive and/or affect the health of their child both before and after birth (Serdula et al., 1991). Further reductions in drug use occur during pregnancy, and although these are most pronounced among women, reductions in some behaviors (such as heavy drinking) also occur among husbands with pregnant spouses (Bachman, O'Malley, Johnston, Rodgers, & Schulenberg, 1992). Some portions of such pregnancy effects seem to be transitory; however, to the extent that there are any lasting effects of drug reduction during pregnancy, lower levels of use would be expected among parents. Finally, young children soon become astute observers of parents' behaviors, and the need to set a good example could further contribute to lowered levels of drug use by parents.

Single parenthood may operate very differently from the processes we have just described. Single fathers rarely reside with their children, and thus would not experience many of the practical restraints of parenthood or perhaps many of the psychological ramifications. And although single mothers usually do reside with their children, they may be less likely than married mothers to receive social approval or clear norms for their behavior.

Nonmarital cohabitation might also be viewed as anticipatory to marriage and might be expected to have some of the same effects on drug use as marriage. However, nonmarital cohabitation has been linked to *higher* drug use (Bachman et al., 1984), especially among men (Newcomb, 1987), which may be due in part to lower traditionalism and higher deviance among people who choose to cohabit outside of marriage (Newcomb, 1987; Thornton, Axinn, & Hill, 1992; Yamaguchi & Kandel, 1985b). However, much of the research in this area has concentrated on cohabitation very early in adulthood and has not addressed other factors, such as the timing, duration, or commitment in the relationship. In addition, substantial cohort differences in the prevalence of premarital cohabitation complicate interpretation of the meaning of this living arrangement. This complex issue deserves further consideration and is one we plan to address in future work (Wadsworth, Bachman, Schulenberg, O'Malley, & Johnston, in preparation).

Several studies have shown what may be "marriage effects" on the drug use of women but not men. Horwitz and White (1991) found declines in alcohol use among newly married women but not men; Yamaguchi and Kandel (1985a) reported declines in marijuana use after marriage among women; and Newcomb and Bentler (1987) reported that marriage was significantly linked to decreases in women's use of alcohol, marijuana, and cocaine. Brunswick, Messeri, and Titus (1992) also reported changes in women's "heavy drug use" (including both marijuana and cocaine) as a function of marriage. However, Donovan et al. (1983) found declines in problem drinking after marriage for both men and women; and Miller-Tutzauer et al. (1991) found that both married men and women moderated their alcohol use after marriage, and that this effect stabilized within a year after marriage. Yamaguchi and Kandel (1985a) also found declines in marijuana use among both men and women in the year preceding marriage.

Thus, (1) there is evidence for an influence of marital status on drug and alcohol use for both men and women, but perhaps stronger in the case of women, and (2) there is also some evidence of anticipatory effects, that is, changes that may take place after commitment to marriage but before the wedding actually occurs. Stronger, more consistent results found for women in these studies may in part reflect effects of pregnancy and the assumption of a primary caregiving role.

Changes Involved in Divorce

If being married contributes to lower than average drug use, for reasons outlined previously, then we might expect that getting divorced would contribute to increased use, at least in terms of a rebound to the earlier levels of drug use typical of single persons. Becoming divorced can lead one back to old friendships as well as to the singles scene, both of which could contribute to a rebound in alcohol and other drug use. Divorce also may reverse effects associated with parenthood, at least for a parent who ceases to reside with children after separation or divorce. Another reason for expecting an increase in drug use following divorce is that divorce is almost always somewhat stressful, often quite traumatic, and sometimes leads to depression (Aseltine & Kessler, 1993); one response to such stresses may be heavy drinking and other drug use.

Some studies have linked divorce with increases in substance use. Cross-sectional data have long suggested a greater risk of substance abuse among divorced men and women, but longitudinal evidence has produced a mixed picture. Hanna, Faden, and Harford (1993) found that women who separated or divorced increased their drinking, and Hallberg (1992) found sustained increases in both alcohol use and tobacco smoking among men for up to 5 years after divorce. However, other research has suggested that although divorce and heavy drinking are closely linked, this is primarily due to the greater likelihood of divorce among heavy drinkers (Power & Estaugh, 1990).

Linking Marriage, Divorce, and Parenthood to Drug Use

In sum, when young adults make transitions into marriage and/or into parenthood, several other changes occur in their lives. Many of these changes may contribute to reducing or stopping the use of cigarettes, alcohol, and illicit drugs. Conversely, the changes in lifestyle associated with divorce or separation may contribute to increased drug use. In this chapter, we examine data indicating whether such changes in drug use are in fact associated with marriage, divorce/separation, and parenthood. We present data showing changes in drug use during the interval in which a marital transition occurs. This allows us to differentiate changes that are anticipatory to the transition, occur during the transition, or continue beyond the transition interval. We also disentangle marriage and parenthood effects and assess whether the various transition groups have distinctly different starting points in terms of drug use.

Data Source: The Monitoring the Future Project

All findings presented here are drawn from the Monitoring the Future project, which has been studying American high school seniors and young adults since 1975. A detailed discussion of the research design is available elsewhere (Bachman, Johnston, & O'Malley, 1991; Johnston, O'Malley, & Bachman, 1994). Briefly, the project surveys nationally representative samples of high school seniors each year and then follows smaller subsamples from each cohort throughout their late teens and 20s. Data are collected via self-completed questionnaires, with the first wave group-administered in schools during the senior year. Follow-ups are conducted by mail. The initial mailing to respondents selected for follow-up occurs 1 year after high school for a random half of the target cases and 2 years after high school for the other half; subsequent follow-ups are on a biennial schedule.

Prior Analyses Examining Marriage and Parenthood

An early analysis of Monitoring the Future panel data focused on some of the linkages between marriage and drug use during the first 3 years after high school, and found that those who married reduced the use of alcohol and illicit drugs (Bachman et al., 1984). Later analyses, extended to 10 years after high school, confirmed this pattern of findings for marriage occurring at any point within the 10-year interval, and showed also that becoming a parent is linked with some further decreases in drug use for married men and women (Bachman et al., 1992). We did not find much evidence that people with different levels of drug use during high school were differentially predisposed toward marriage or parenthood, except in the case of single parents, who were distinctly more likely to have smoked tobacco and used other drugs during high school and to continue their use in young adulthood.

These earlier analyses, like those reported in the present chapter, focused on before-and-after changes in drug use; however, the earlier analyses differed from the present ones in two important respects. First, in the earlier analyses the senior year of high school was treated as the "before" point, and each follow-up survey (examined one at a time) was treated as the "after" point. Second, measures of *change* in drug use (raw gain scores) were treated as dependent variables, and this made it a straightforward matter to carry out multivariate analyses that simultaneously controlled a variety of background factors as well as a number of post–high school roles, environments, and experiences.

The earlier analyses supported our conclusion that both marriage and parenthood contribute to reduced drug use; moreover, the multivariate approach demonstrated that substantial portions of these relationships do not overlap with other relationships with drug use (Bachman et al., 1992). However, such multivariate analyses of change scores are undertaken at some cost; they involve a good deal of complexity and abstraction and some corresponding loss of descriptive clarity.

Present Analysis Approach

This chapter relies heavily on the earlier multivariate findings and reports some of them in summary fashion. But the new analyses reported in this chapter differ from our earlier work in several important respects. First, the present analyses take a more descriptive approach to how the transitions to marriage and to parenthood seem to influence drug use. Second, these analyses focus on change in substance use across the specific intervals in which transitions occurred. Third, these analyses include our first examination of transitions *out of* marriage – that is, separation and divorce.

Two sets of analyses are reported. The first defines subgroups according to marital transition patterns – that is, patterns of change (or nonchange) in marital status over the 3- to 4-year periods defined by three consecutive survey measurements (as described later). Then for each of these subgroups we examine levels of drug use (percentages reporting use at a given level) at each of the three points in time. This descriptive approach (1) shows the changes in drug use during the interval in which a marital transition occurred, (2) gives us some indications of the extent to which such changes are anticipatory and/or continue after the transition interval, and (3) provides important data on whether the various subgroups have distinctly different starting points in terms of drug use.

The second set of analyses takes a somewhat similar approach, this time defining subgroups according to parental transition patterns. Specifically, these analyses examine changes (or nonchanges) in parental status, as well as marital status, over the 2-year (or 1-year) intervals between consecutive surveys.[1] The inclusion of marital status in these analyses was necessary so that we could see the extent to which the transition to parenthood seems to have impacts above and beyond any associated with marriage transitions.

Samples Included

The Monitoring the Future project includes extensive follow-up data on each high school graduating class cohort from 1976 on. Consistent with the earlier multivariate analyses (Bachman et al., 1992), the present analyses include the senior classes of 1976 through 1988, plus follow-up data for up to 10 years (five follow-up surveys) but no later than 1993 (which was the latest year for which data were available at the time of these analyses). The age range covered is from approximately 18 (end of 12th grade) to 28 (for those completing the fifth follow-up survey).

All intervals between follow-up surveys are (approximately) 2 years. A random half of the intervals between the senior year survey and the first follow-up survey are also 2 years, and the other half are 1 year. Thus the large majority of all intervals between surveys are 2 years, and we will generally speak of 2-year periods (keeping in mind that in a few cases the interval is shorter).[2]

This selection of samples was designed to exploit all of our panel data available at the time of analysis. Because there was less time for the more recent senior classes to be followed longitudinally, the data from these classes are limited to transitions that occurred relatively soon after high school. Accordingly, (1) our data on transitions that occurred when respondents were in their middle or late 20s are based only on respondents who finished high school in the late 1970s or early 1980s, and (b) later-occurring transitions are in general somewhat underrepresented in these analyses. If our purpose was to provide descriptions of those transitions that are highly accurate demographically for specific cohorts, such distortions would represent a problem. But because our purpose is to describe changes in drug use associated with these transitions, and because our earlier research (Bachman et al., 1992) showed that these changes in drug use are generally similar across a variety of ages and cohorts, we are comfortable with the present sample selection. On the whole, the samples used remain large and broadly representative of the transitions in drug use that occur during young adulthood.

Analysis Strategy

Many respondents completed follow-up surveys on five (or more) occasions at 2-year intervals. Such individuals contributed four separate and overlapping transition intervals to the analyses of possible transitions in and out of marriage (senior year plus Follow-ups 1 and 2, Follow-ups 1, 2, and 3, Follow-ups 2, 3, and 4, and Follow-ups 3, 4, and 5) and five different intervals to the analyses of transitions to parenthood (senior year plus Follow-up 1, Follow-ups 1–2, 2–3, 3–4, and 4–5). Respondents from the most recent cohorts had not completed five follow-ups as of 1993 and thus contributed fewer intervals to these analyses.

The strategy of using respondents' full panel data records to contribute up to five different intervals is somewhat unusual, although we have used it in prior analyses of Monitoring the Future panel data (Bachman et al., 1984, 1992). Our rationale is that we want to make use of all available respondents when focusing on key transitions such as becoming married or becoming a parent. Accordingly, our unit of analysis is the transition rather than the individual. On the one hand, this practice of including all possible sets of intervals substantially increases the number of cases available for analysis of transitions into (or out of) marriage as well as into parenthood. On the other hand, respondents who remain consistently married or consistently single throughout most or all of the follow-up period contribute multiple times to those steady-state transition patterns.

The use of several sets of data from the same respondents in the steady-state patterns, as just described, provides an increase in precision in contrast to using only one set of data from each respondent; however, in estimating confidence intervals around percentages, it would not be appropriate to treat all such cases as completely independent. A conservative approach would be to make such estimates based on the number of independent cases for any transition set (these numbers are provided in Table 10.1).

In general, the number of respondents is sufficiently large, and the findings to be presented are sufficiently clear, that we did not need to perform significance testing – particularly since much of what is displayed descriptively here is fully consistent with our earlier multivariate analyses.[3] One important exception involves transitions from married to divorced or separated; the number of cases is smaller, and earlier analyses did not include this transition. For these reasons, we undertook additional analyses to test specifically whether women and men who reported a transition from married to divorced/separated tended to increase or decrease their use of cigarettes, alcohol, and illicit drugs. In these analyses we calculated change scores (raw gain scores) for each drug, focusing specifically on the 2-year interval in which the divorce or separation occurred.[4] For all four drug use dimensions and for both women and men (tested separately), the mean changes in drug use following divorce/separation were positive and significantly greater than zero.

Results: Marriage, Engagement, and Divorce

We turn our attention first to patterns of transition into and out of marriage. At each data collection point, respondents were asked, "What is your present marital status?" and they were given four alternatives in the following order: "Married, Engaged, Separated/divorced, Single." Strictly speaking, these alternatives are not mutually exclusive because those who are engaged or divorced would also be considered single; however, the ordering of the alternatives was designed to encourage such respondents to choose the earlier and more specific options. Our findings suggest that our measure of marital status is reasonably accurate.

An important limitation in our data on marital status is that it was assessed only at each data collection point, and the follow-up surveys were spaced at 2-year intervals. Consequently, if an individual went from married to divorced, then to engaged, then to a second marriage, and made all three transitions within the 2-year span between follow-up surveys, the data record would simply indicate "Married-Married." Fortunately, such rapid transitions are sufficiently rare that we are confident that even though our follow-up measures assess marital status only at 2-year intervals, they do capture the large majority of important changes (e.g., single to married or married to divorced) and thus provide a good basis for examining the impacts of marital status on drug use.

If we consider the four categories of marital status (M = married, E = engaged, D = separated/divorced, S = single), assessed at three points in time, there are 64 logically possible combinations ($4 \times 4 \times 4 = 64$); however, some combinations did not actually occur in our sample and others involved too few cases to analyze. We focused our analyses on nine of the most frequently occurring patterns; two involve no change (S-S-S = single at each time, M-M-M = married at each time), three involve transitions into marriage (S-S-M, S-E-M, S-M-M), and four involve divorce at some point (S-M-D, M-M-D, M-D-D, M-D-M). As we shall see, examining these nine transition patterns provides a fairly clear picture of the ways in which both marriage and divorce are related to drug use.

Age and Background Differences Linked to Transition Patterns

The upper portion of Table 10.1 displays the nine major marriage transition patterns. For each of these patterns, the table also reports means of approximate age (at the end of the transition sequence), high school grades, and parents' educations, as well as the percentage who were attending college or another post–high school educational institution (more than half of the time) at the time of the first follow-up (1 or 2 years after high school). The age data indicate, of course, that those who are married tend to be older than those who are single. More important, the data on high school grades, parents' education, and college attendance remind us that educational success and college attendance often cause marriage to be deferred (Marini, 1987), which means that those who attended college are underrepresented in the transition sequences involving (early) marriage. We note also that high school performance levels, as reflected in grades, were lowest among those who would later experience divorce. In short, Table 10.1 reminds us that some important dimensions are not fully controlled in the present descriptive analyses. We should add, however, that in other analyses (notably Bachman et al., 1992) we statistically controlled such factors; the findings reported here remained strong after such controls were imposed.

Cigarette Use

Cigarette use tends to start well before the end of high school. Prior longitudinal analyses of Monitoring the Future data showed cigarette use to be more stable than other drug use behaviors and less affected by differences in post–high school experiences (Bachman et al., 1984; O'Malley et al., 1983; Schulen-

Table 10.1. *Transition patterns, number of cases, mean ages, and background characteristics*

	Women						Men					
	No. of cases[a]	Indep. no.[b]	Age[c]	H.S. grades[d]	Parent ed.[e]	% college students[f]	No. of cases	Indep. no.	Age	H.S. grades	Parent ed.	% college students
Marriage transition groups												
Single–single–single	13,120	6,391	23.3	6.38	3.69	72.3	13,433	6,371	23.4	5.91	3.74	68.5
Single–single–married	2,007	2,006	23.6	6.28	3.44	62.1	1,587	1,586	24.0	5.68	3.49	54.1
Single–engaged–married	1,528	1,528	23.9	6.39	3.51	61.0	957	957	24.5	5.82	3.51	57.3
Single–married–married	1,929	1,929	24.3	6.14	3.28	47.9	1,167	1,167	24.9	5.57	3.34	45.7
Married–married–married	3,939	2,358	26.1	6.12	3.08	33.5	1,778	1,195	26.4	5.40	3.16	33.1
Single–married–divorced	187	187	23.7	5.98	3.39	36.2	112	112	24.6	5.31	3.28	42.3
Married–married–divorced	311	310	25.8	5.86	3.11	28.5	130	130	26.3	5.24	3.09	28.9
Married–divorced–divorced	221	221	25.9	5.85	3.19	31.4	86	86	26.4	5.20	3.19	34.5
Married–divorced–married	115	113	25.4	6.10	3.08	26.9	54	54	26.2	5.09	2.91	25.9
Parenthood transition groups												
Single nonparent–single nonparent	26,992	11,619	21.7	6.34	3.68	69.8	25,826	10,798	21.9	5.82	3.72	65.1
Single nonparent–single parent	823	821	21.7	5.36	3.06	37.2	522	513	22.1	5.06	3.28	38.8
Single nonparent–married nonparent	3,929	3,909	22.9	6.35	3.41	54.5	2,393	2,384	23.8	5.77	3.50	55.8
Single nonparent–married parent	1,212	1,211	22.3	5.76	3.26	37.4	875	868	23.0	5.18	3.31	32.4
Married nonparent–married nonparent	2,499	1,734	25.0	6.50	3.33	53.4	1,297	970	25.6	5.78	3.45	55.0
Married nonparent–married parent	1,697	1,696	24.7	6.21	3.22	42.3	897	896	25.3	5.60	3.24	42.1

[a] Total number of transitions analyzed.

[b] Total number of individuals who contributed at least one transition case in each category.

[c] Average age at the end of the transition period, assuming an average age of 18 at the base year data collection (end of 12th grade). For marriage transition groups this is the age at Time 3; for parenthood transition groups this is the age at Time 2.

[d] High school grades are based on a 9-point scale from D or below (1) through A (9).

[e] Parent education is measured using the average of mother's and father's education on a 6-point scale, from grade school or less (1) through graduate or professional school after college (6).

[f] The percentage of each transition group who indicate more than half-time enrollment in college or other post-high school education at follow-up Time 1.

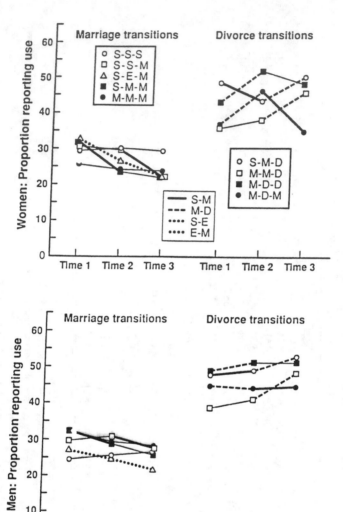

Figure 10.2. Drug use related to transitions in marital status: 30-day prevalence of cigarette use.

berg, Bachman, O'Malley, & Johnston, 1994). These findings of relatively high stability in smoking behavior are certainly consistent with the conclusion that this is the most widespread addiction among young people. Nevertheless, our more recent analyses have shown some modest relationships with marital status (Bachman et al., 1992), and these are confirmed and expanded in the present analyses.

Figure 10.2 shows, separately for women and men in each of the nine transition patterns, proportions who reported any use of cigarettes during the 30-day period preceding each follow-up survey. The findings are a bit stronger and clearer for women, but the results for men are in the same direction.

The left side of Figure 10.2 shows that the transition from single to married status involved a decline in the proportion of cigarette users. The drop was 7% or more among women and somewhat less among men (3.2% to 3.4%). Those in the S-E-M (single-engaged-married) pattern showed declines across both 2-year intervals, thus suggesting that some of the "marriage effect" is actually anticipatory.

The right side of Figure 10.2 reveals several interesting findings. First, it shows that among women the transition from married to divorced was associated with a 7% or more increase in the proportion of smokers, whereas among men the increase associated with divorce was smaller and less consistent (2.4% to 7.2%). Second, the figure shows that higher rates of smoking were actually predictive of divorce. Each of the four subgroups involving divorce showed smoking proportions of 35% or higher *prior to divorce* (range, 38.2% to 48.4%), whereas none of the other groups showed rates that high at any point.

We conclude (1) that marriage, as well as the anticipation of marriage, contributes to modest reductions in the likelihood of smoking and (2) that divorce contributes to modest increases, especially among women. Is it also true that smoking increases the likelihood of divorce? We are not prepared to assert such a conclusion (although it is not implausible). Rather, we are convinced that smoking is part of a relatively long-standing syndrome of nonconforming behavior, including low grades in high school and a low likelihood of attending college (Schulenberg et al., 1994), and it seems likely that individuals high in such tendencies are also more prone to divorce. In other words, we think that smoking is primarily an indicator of a broader range of behavior problems that may also contribute to divorce, but we can easily imagine that smoking itself makes some additional contribution to the likelihood of divorce – particularly if the spouse is a nonsmoker.

Alcohol Use and Abuse

Very large majorities of young men and women report some use of alcohol, making it (in statistical terms, at least) a normative behavior among young adults. Most young adult drinkers report only occasional use – typically once or twice a week (Johnston et al., 1994). If this occasional use consisted of only one or two drinks, there would be little cause for concern, but often consumption reaches five or more drinks, which involves both short-term risks (automobile and other accidents, risky sexual behavior, etc.) and long-term risks (eventual addiction and other health problems).

Alcohol use shows considerable stability during the years after high school, although not as much as cigarette use (O'Malley et al., 1983; Schulenberg et al., 1994; but see Schulenberg, O'Malley, Bachman, Wadsworth, & Johnston, 1996). Most high school students and young adults who consume alcohol are not addicted (in contrast to cigarette users); thus alcohol use may be more susceptible to the impacts of new responsibilities and social environments associated with marriage.

Figure 10.3 compares subgroups in terms of proportions who reported that on one or more occasions during the preceding 2 weeks they consumed five or more drinks in a row, which we term an *instance of heavy drinking*. This level of consumption involves considerable impairment for most individuals, particularly women (given male–female differences in body weight and metabolism of alcohol); nevertheless, it is a behavior reported by about one-half of the unmarried men and about one-third of the unmarried women.

Focusing first on the left side of the figure, we see again that becoming married was associated with a drop in alcohol use. Among both women and men, the transition to marriage was linked to about a 15% drop in the proportion reporting any instances of heavy drinking in the past 2 weeks. Stated differently, this level of drinking was reported by only about two-thirds as many married men and only about one-half as many married women compared with their unmarried counterparts. Here also we see that the transition from single to engaged was associated with considerable reductions in use, suggesting some anticipatory socialization. In addition, we see that those who were single at all three points in time were among the most likely to report instances of heavy drinking, whereas those married at all three points were least likely. Finally, we can see that (except for the subgroup showing the transition through engagement), the overall shifts occurred only during the interval in which the transition into marriage actually occurred.

The right side of Figure 10.3 shows that for those who had been or soon would be divorced, a transition *into* marriage was linked to a drop in instances of heavy drinking; more important, it shows a corresponding rise in such instances when there was a transition *out of* marriage. Each of the four patterns indicates that becoming divorced increased the likelihood of some heavy drinking, and these increases were generally comparable in size to the decreases associated with becoming married.

Our earlier multivariate analyses showed that the marriage effect on alcohol use was not limited to instances of heavy drinking; being married was associated with less frequent use of alcohol in general. Moreover, these analyses showed that such effects were not explainable in terms of background (e.g., race, region, high school grades, college plans) or other post–high school experiences (e.g., college attendance, employment); indeed, the marriage effect was largely independent of such factors (Bachman et al., 1992; Schulenberg et al., 1996).

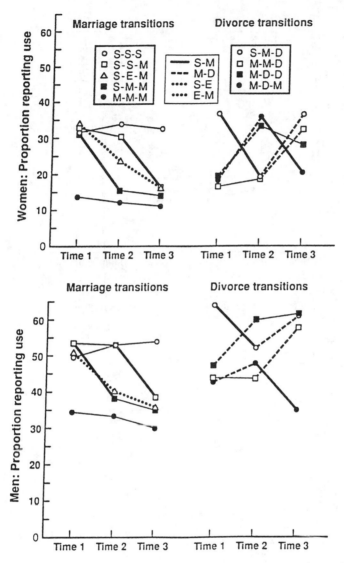

Figure 10.3. Drug use related to transitions in marital status: 2-week prevalence of heavy alcohol use.

The present analyses, in addition to confirming the earlier results, show for the first time that the impacts of divorce were roughly the mirror image of the marriage effect. All of these findings suggest that it is primarily the present condition of being either married or unmarried, rather than the longer-term history of marital status, that is associated with the differences in levels of alcohol use.

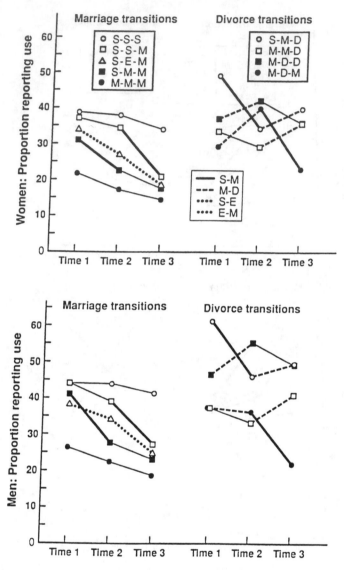

Figure 10.4. Drug use related to transitions in marital status: annual prevalence of marijuana use.

Marijuana Use

Marijuana was the most widely used drug in recent decades, but its use declined somewhat during most of the historical period covered by our present analyses. Still, it is clear from Figure 10.4 that changes associated with marriage and divorce were substantially larger than the slight declines among those who were consistently single or consistently married. Here again we see that marriage was associated with decreased proportions of substance users, whereas divorce was associated with increased proportions. For women at least, there is also some indication that engagement was associated with some anticipatory decline in marijuana use.

Cocaine Use

Cocaine use involved fewer than half as many young men and women than marijuana use. Nevertheless, the patterns of change in the use of the two drugs, as related to marriage and divorce, appear quite similar. Figure 10.5 shows that each transition pattern involving a shift from single to married also involved a drop in the proportion of cocaine users. Additionally, each shift from married to divorced involved a rise in the proportion of cocaine users. Finally, those moving from single to engaged to married showed declines fairly similar to those moving from single to married (any distinctions linked specifically to engagement are too small for us to consider them statistically trustworthy).

Results: Becoming a Parent

We turn now to the question of whether becoming a parent influences substance use above and beyond that associated with marriage. At each data collection point respondents were asked whether they had children, so it is a straightforward matter to determine whether respondents went from nonparents to parents during any 2-year (or 1-year) interval between data collections. Based on earlier analyses, we also considered it important to distinguish between married and unmarried parenthood because the implications for role responsibilities and social environment are often very different – especially among males. Moreover, many respondents made the transition into parenthood during the same interval in which they made the transition from being single to married.

Because marriage appears to have important impacts on substance use, as demonstrated in the preceding section, it was necessary to examine several different transition patterns so that we could maintain distinctions between those who were single and those who were (or became) married. We limited these analyses to those who were married at two adjacent time points (M-M), those who were single at both (S-S), and those who went from single to married (S-M); we then divided each of the three groups into those who remained nonparents at both times (NP-NP) and those who made the transition into parenthood (NP-P). Thus these analyses focus on the transition into parenthood while controlling the marriage transition (or nontransition). This approach generated six different transition patterns when dealing with just two points in time; extending the analyses to three

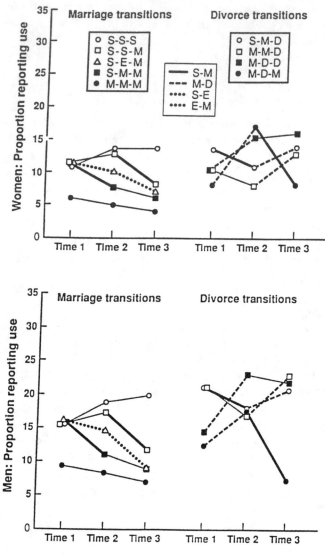

Figure 10.5. Drug use related to transitions in marital status: annual prevalence of cocaine use.

time points was judged to be impractical (and, as we shall see, largely unnecessary).

The lower portion of Table 10.1 shows that with marital status controlled, there were no substantial age differences between those who made the transition into parenthood and those who did not; however, the differences in the percentage who were students during the first year or two after high school remind us that young adults who went to college were more likely to defer parenthood.

Cigarette Use

Figure 10.6 shows changes in cigarette use for men and women who did and did not make the transition from nonparent to parent. In addition to showing men and women separately, the figure shows three contrasting pairs of transitions – in each case distinguishing between those who became parents and those who did not.

Turning first to the left side of the figure, we see that among those who remained single, there was little change in smoking rates whether they became parents or not. Much more interesting, however, is the fact that those who became single parents were substantially more likely to have been smokers beforehand (as well as afterward). In other words, smokers were more likely than nonsmokers to become single parents. Here, as before, we are not inclined to attribute much of a causal role directly to smoking; smoking is associated with many problem behaviors, and we view this overall pattern as contributing to the likelihood of becoming a single parent. In particular, we note that those who became single parents had the lowest high school grades of any of the transition groups, and low rates of college attendance as well (see Table 10.1).

Interestingly, the middle portion of Figure 10.6 indicates that among those who made the transition from single to married, those who also became parents during the same interval were more likely to have been smokers at the outset. The differences here are not as large as those on the left side of Figure 10.6, but they are in the same direction and consistent across males and females. Of course, it is likely that some in this category married only after pregnancy occurred, making them in some respects similar to those who became single parents; further similarities between the two groups include low high school grades and low rates of college attendance (see Table 10.1). In any case, the figure suggests that smokers are somewhat more likely than nonsmokers to make the transition into pregnancy and parenthood soon after becoming married (and in some cases shortly in advance of marriage).

The middle portion of Figure 10.6 also shows the declines in the proportion of smokers after marriage that we first observed in Figure 10.2. Here again, the declines are more substantial among females. Most important, we see here that among those females who became mothers during the same interval in which they married, the proportions of smokers dropped appreciably (about 10%). Our earlier analyses showed that being pregnant was linked to substantial drops in cigarette use (Bachman et al., 1992), and it seems likely that those who became both wives and parents in a 2-year interval (or less) were especially likely to have only recently ceased to be pregnant. In other words, some of

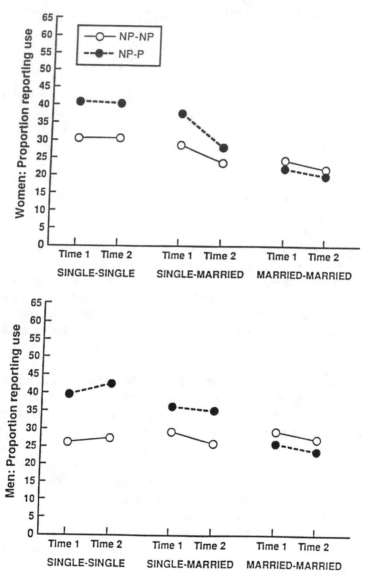

Figure 10.6. Drug use related to marriage and parenthood: 30-day prevalence of cigarette use.

the decline in the proportion of smokers among these particular women may have been residual effects of very recent pregnancies (i.e., some individuals may have stopped smoking while pregnant and had not yet resumed smoking).

The right side of Figure 10.6 shows that among those married at both times, there were only small differences in the proportion of smokers between those

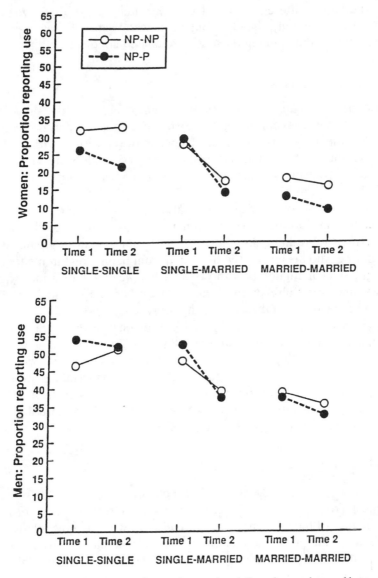

Figure 10.7. Drug use related to marriage and parenthood: 2-week prevalence of heavy alcohol use.

who became parents and those who did not, nor were there any differential changes during the interval.

In sum, we see relatively little evidence that parenthood per se has a strong or consistent impact on smoking rates, although there is some indication that pregnancy and parenthood among newly married women is linked to a decline. The larger differences revealed in this analysis are that *prior* rates of smoking were generally higher among those who become parents – especially single parents – than among those who remained childless.

Alcohol Use and Abuse

The left side of Figure 10.7 shows only slight declines in the proportion of occasional heavy drinkers among those who become single parents. A comparison across the three parts of the figure does show (consistent with the findings in the previous section) that those who remained single were most likely to have reported one or more instances of consuming five or more drinks in a row during the past 2 weeks.

The middle portion of Figure 10.7 also repeats an earlier finding – that making the transition from single to married was associated with a drop in heavy drinking. Additionally, there is a slight suggestion of greater declines among those who also made the transition from being nonparents to parents. The right side of Figure 10.7 shows an even weaker indication of greater declines among the already married who then became parents, but it is too small to be treated as statistically trustworthy.

In sum, the data presented in Figure 10.7 provide little evidence that becoming a parent for the first time has substantial effects on instances of heavy alcohol use. This finding is generally consistent with our earlier work; bivariate analyses showed greater than average declines in heavy drinking among those who were married parents, but multivariate analyses showed such differences to be mostly explainable in terms of other factors such as marital status and living arrangements (Bachman et al., 1992).

Marijuana Use

The left side of Figure 10.8 shows that those who became single nonparents were most likely to have used marijuana beforehand (about 50% of the men and over 40% of the women). The figure also shows there was relatively little decline in use among single men after they became parents, whereas among single mothers there was a somewhat larger drop (in contrast to single women who did not become mothers).

The middle portion of Figure 10.8 shows the now familiar drop in drug use during the transition from single to married, and shows also that among women – but not men – the transition to parenthood involved a small additional drop in the proportion of marijuana users.

The right side of Figure 10.8 shows that among married women who made the transition into parenthood there was a further drop in the already low proportion of marijuana users, whereas among married men there was a smaller shift in the same direction, regardless of whether they became parents.

In sum, the data in Figure 10.8 provide some indication that becoming a

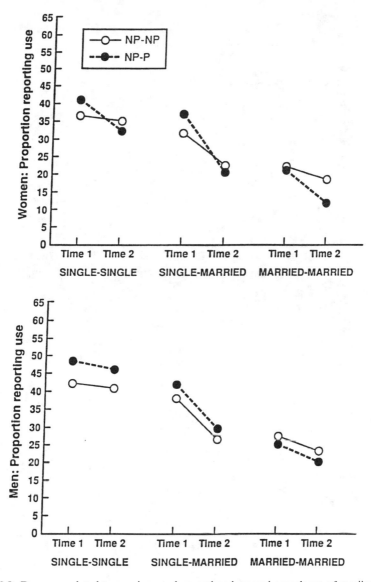

Figure 10.8. Drug use related to marriage and parenthood: annual prevalence of marijuana use.

parent may reduce the likelihood of being a marijuana user, at least among women. Our earlier analyses, which focused on *amounts* of marijuana use in the past year (not just users versus nonusers), showed declines linked to being a married parent among both men and women, and roughly half of the initial bivariate relationships remained after multivariate controls for other factors – findings that were clearly statistically significant (Bachman et al., 1992).

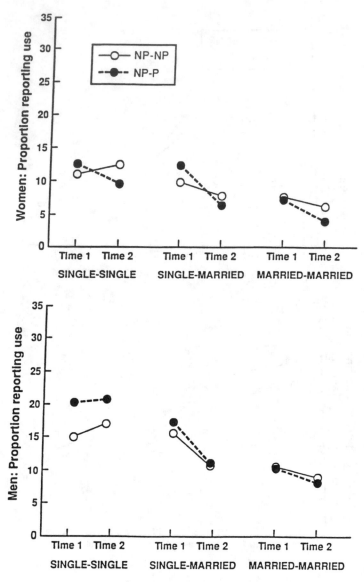

Figure 10.9. Drug use related to marriage and parenthood: annual prevalence of cocaine use.

Cocaine Use

The findings for cocaine use, shown in Figure 10.9, are in most respects quite similar to those in Figure 10.8 – except, of course, for the fact that fewer than half as many respondents used cocaine as used marijuana. Here again we see the fairly substantial differences in use associated with marriage. We also see that parenthood was associated with some decline in the proportions of cocaine users. Figure 10.9 indicates that the declines associated with parenthood were rather small, especially among men; however, our earlier work showed that even after multivariate controls for other factors, the lower levels of cocaine use among married parents were statistically significant (Bachman et al., 1992).

Discussion and Conclusions

In this chapter we have used panel data from the Monitoring the Future project to examine ways in which transitions into marriage, parenthood, and divorce may influence the drug use of young adults. We have taken a largely descriptive approach, examining these transitions over intervals spanning up to 4 years. The findings are consistent with several earlier analyses examining many of the same respondents but using different approaches. The findings also extend our understanding in several important ways, as noted in this section.

Impacts of Marriage

Being married, and apparently also the anticipation of becoming married, contribute to reduced drug use. Even among cigarette smokers, a small proportion give up the habit after, or sometimes soon before, they get married. Our earlier analyses provided little evidence that those with different levels of drug use were differentially disposed to marriage, and our multivariate analyses suggested that *being* married was linked to lower use compared with being single (Bachman et al., 1992). The present analyses, focusing on more complex transition patterns, clearly demonstrate that declines in drug use occur during the interval in which the transition from single to married occurs. But that does not mean that all the change takes place subsequent to the actual exchange of vows. To the contrary, our look at the S-E-M pattern reveals that some of the decline in drug use is anticipatory. Nevertheless, the central finding is that the changes in drug use occur relatively promptly, with relatively little change thereafter, except for that attributable to additional changes in roles and responsibilities.

Impacts of Parenthood

It must be kept in mind that other factors closely related to marriage, particularly pregnancy and parenthood, also appear to contribute to reduced drug use; however, earlier multivariate analyses clearly established that a considerable proportion of the marriage effect on drug use remains after such other factors are controlled statistically (Bachman et al., 1992). Our earlier multivariate work showed that married parents were significantly less likely than married nonparents to use alcohol, marijuana, or cocaine (Bachman et al., 1992). The present analyses show some parenthood effects, more so among women than among men, but the effects seem modest at best, certainly much smaller than the effects of marriage.

Impacts of Divorce

Separation and divorce involve, in many respects, a set of role changes opposite to those of marriage and parenthood. Thus, at the beginning of this chapter, we speculated that drug use might rebound after divorce to the levels associated with being single. A further speculation is that the stresses and disappointments associated with divorce might actually lead to even higher levels of drug use, a sort of "extra trauma effect." Our results show, fairly clearly and consistently, that drug use rises during the interval in which individuals make the transition from married to divorced or separated. More specifically, the *increases* in proportions of drug users following divorce seem roughly as large as the *decreases* associated with marriage. That may not fit particularly well with the "extra trauma" notion, but it is consistent with the view that the current set of role requirements and expectations, rather than the longer-term history, contributes to the drug use differences associated with marital status.

A longer-term history of substance use does show a relationship to the likelihood of becoming divorced. In general, individuals who would later experience divorce had histories that included relatively low educational success and a relatively high likelihood of cigarette use. The most plausible interpretation of these findings is that those with less successful adjustments early in life (reflected in poor high school grades, cigarette addiction, not going to college) are also less likely to be successful, perhaps for some of the same reasons, in sustaining a marriage.

Can Marriage and Other Transitions Explain Age-Related Changes in the Drug Use of Young Adults?

So far, we have discussed the effects of role transitions in the context of psychological and sociological influences. However, it is possible that both marriage and lower drug use are outcomes of a more global, and simple, maturation effect – that the simple influence of age results in both more marriages and less drug use. Marriage and reduced drug use could be seen as parallel side effects of a general "settling down" or "maturing out" of adolescent behavior patterns, with no causal link between the two.

Rather than believing that maturational effects explain marriage effects, we feel it is much more likely that marriage and other major role changes in adulthood explain the bulk of the maturation effect. First, if the effects shown here were fully explained by maturation, we would expect change to occur in one direction. Thus, we might not expect an increase in substance use to be associated with the end of a marital relationship. However, this alternative hypothesis is contradicted by the results presented here because divorce is accompanied by an increase in substance use. It might still be argued that whereas maturation caused the decline, the stress associated with the divorce produced the increase. Thus, although change does go in both directions, the causes may not be linked. However, because the increase in substance use associated with divorce so closely matches the size of the decrease occurring with marriage, it seems parsimonious to link these changes of similar magnitude rather than posit two separate causes.

Although there is some change toward lower use of some drugs with age, with or without marriage, marriage has the greater impact regardless of when it occurs. Previous analyses, illustrated in Figure 10.10 (from Bachman, 1987), as well as the analyses reported here, have shown that the magnitudes of change associated with marriage and parenthood are similar whether they occur relatively early or relatively late; thus they appear to be independent of age (see also Bachman, Johnston, O'Malley, & Schulenberg, 1996). However, other explanations for the effects shown here may be related to maturation. Personality and value changes, as well as identification with adult roles, may be dimensions of psychological maturation, but these factors vary considerably on an individual level and are not directly linked to the simple passage of time. A major question that runs throughout this chapter concerns the exact mechanisms by which marriage and parenthood influence change in drug use, and even if we have set aside the maturational argument, several different psychological, social, and pragmatic explanations remain.

If we postulate a direct causal link between marriage and lower drug use, we might posit that the relation between marriage and drug use reflects the direct practical restrictions on leisure time that impinge on drug use and other immature impulses, rather than influencing the individual through a psychological mechanism. There is some interesting evidence to suggest that people generally marry others similar to themselves in many ways, including age, race, education, religious commitment, and expectations for the marital relationship and parenting (Buss, 1984; Coombs, & Fernandez, 1978; Mare, 1991), as well as in the frequency and type of substance use (Yamaguchi & Kandel, 1993). This homophily in drug use between marital partners suggests that the marital relationship itself need not *necessarily* impose constraints on drug use behavior and might in fact be expected to promote stability.

Yamaguchi and Kandel (1993) also report little evidence that the drug use behavior or attitudes of one spouse influence a marital partner's drug use behavior over time, arguing that perhaps it is not primarily the people in a

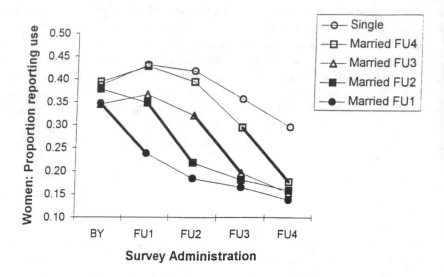

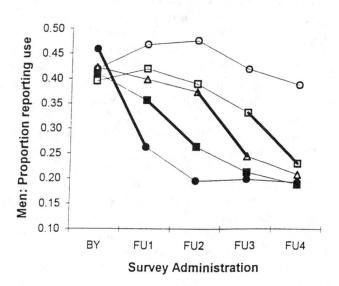

Figure 10.10. Drug use related to marital status across five points in time: annual marijuana use.

marriage who change one another's behavior, but rather some larger or shared influence that shapes them in tandem. A plausible explanation, given these results, is that regardless of substance use and similarity of substance use, both partners are exposed to societal expectations and pressures or may share a mutual psychological openness to these influences, a readiness for change, or a commitment to move toward a more mature adult status.

If changes were due solely to practical aspects of marriage impinging on the free time of individuals who would otherwise choose to continue previous levels of substance use, then we would not expect to see any effects prior to marriage. Similarly, if married people change their behaviors in direct response to the societal expectations that accompany that role, change would not be expected before the role was assumed. The existence of anticipatory effects – that is changes occurring before the marriage itself – points to a mechanism involving purposeful individual change, such as the conscious adoption of adult identity or the gradual assumption of married social roles. The process of becoming a couple may include gradually increasing contact with one another and with each other's family and friends, and social expectations about appropriate couple behavior may also change gradually, such as how much time the couple spend together versus with friends. Becoming a couple also may involve increases in commitment and intimacy, and a feeling of responsibility to the new loved one may inhibit risky behaviors such as drug and alcohol use. The wedding day itself may be only the final consolidation of this gradual merging of two life plans.

Understanding the Overlapping Influences of
Marriage and Parenthood

These and previous results have shown overlap between marriage, pregnancy, and parenthood effects. The overlap can be interpreted in at least two ways. First, parenthood may not have a strong influence above and beyond marriage because individuals who are likely to change their substance use behavior in response to parenthood have already done so in response to marriage, whereas those resistant to the moderating influence of the marital role will also be resistant to change when they make the transition to parenthood. Second, it is possible that some of the observed marriage effect reflects the anticipation of parenthood. This explanation may be supported by our findings of a stronger marriage effect for women. If changes related to marriage reflect preparation for parenthood (i.e., preconception and pregnancy), then these preparations would differentially influence women as the bearers and primary caregivers of infants and young children.

In conclusion, marriage certainly involves new sets of responsibilities, mutual caring, commitments, intimacy, and increased adult contacts. These new roles are likely to inhibit the recreational use of illicit drugs, as well as heavy use of alcohol. In particular, being married may mean spending less time in bars and at parties frequented by singles – the singles scene, where a lot of smoking, drinking, and illicit drug use can take place. Furthermore, to the extent that the marriage effect is due to the progressive mutual commitment and responsibility that begins prior to the exchange of marriage vows and continues thereafter, then it is probable that our findings regarding substance use can be generalized to other lifestyle threats to health, including, for example, other problem behaviors or nutritional deficiencies. Examination of the far-reaching influences of marriage and parenthood on the psychology and the daily lives of men and women is beyond the scope of this chapter, but our current results outline some of the key influences.

Notes

1 We considered extending these analyses to a 3- or 4-year period involving three points in time, as in the first set of analyses; however, we judged that impractical due to the complexities and the reduced sizes of subgroups that would have resulted.
2 We could, of course, have limited our analysis to intervals between follow-up periods, but that would have reduced the number of cases and would have eliminated early transitions into marriage and parenthood – those occurring within the first 2 years after high school.
3 In the descriptive analyses reported in this chapter, we applied three criteria before treating any change, or difference between groups, as meaningful: (a) the change or difference had to be large enough to be of *substantive* importance; (b) it had to meet conventional criteria for *statistical* significance ($p < .05$, two-tailed) of differences between percentages; and (c) it had to be reasonably consistent with our earlier (Bachman et al., 1992) multivariate analyses.
4 See Bachman et al. (1992, especially pp. 15–16) for a summary of our reasons and evidence in support of the use of such change scores in this type of analysis.

References

Antonucci, T. C., & Mikus, K. (1988). The power of parenthood: Personality and attitudinal changes during the transition to parenthood. In G. Y. Michaels & W. A. Goldberg (Eds.), *The transition to parenthood: Current theory and research* (pp. 62–84). New York: Cambridge University Press.

Aseltine, R. H., & Kessler, R. C. (1993). Marital disruption and depression in a community sample. *Journal of Health and Social Behavior, 34*(3), 237–251.

Bachman, J. G. (1987). *Changes in deviant behavior during late adolescence and early adulthood.* Paper presented at the Ninth Biennial Meetings of the International Society for the Study of Behavioral Development, Tokyo. (ERIC Document ED No. 309 365).

Bachman, J. G., Johnston, L. D., & O'Malley, P. M. (1991). *Monitoring the future project after seventeen years: Design and procedures.* (Monitoring the Future Occasional Paper No. 33.) Ann Arbor, MI: Institute for Social Research.

Bachman, J. G., Johnston, L. D., O'Malley, P. M., & Schulenberg, J. (1996). Transitions in alcohol and other drug use and abuse during late adolescence and young adulthood. In J. A. Graber, J. Brooks-Gunn, & A. C. Petersen (Eds.), *Transitions through adolescence: Interpersonal domains and contexts* (pp. 111–140). Hillsdale, NJ: Erlbaum.

Bachman, J. G., O'Malley, P. M., & Johnston, L. D. (1981). *Changes in drug use after high school as a function of role status and social environment.* (Monitoring the Future Occasional Paper No. 11.) Ann Arbor, MI: Institute for Social Research.

Bachman, J. G., O'Malley, P. M., & Johnston, L. D. (1984). Drug use among young adults: The impacts of role status and social environments. *Journal of Personality and Social Psychology, 47,* 629–645.

Bachman, J. G., O'Malley, P. M., Johnston, L. D., Rodgers, W. L., & Schulenberg, J. (1992). *Changes in drug use during the post-high school years.* (Monitoring the Future Occasional Paper No. 35.) Ann Arbor, MI: Institute for Social Research.

Baer, J. S. (1993). Etiology and secondary prevention of alcohol problems with young adults. In

J. S. Baer, G. M. Marlatt, & R. J. McMahon (Eds.), *Addictive behaviors across the life span: Prevention, treatment, and policy issues* (pp. 111–137). Newbury Park, CA: Sage.

Baltes, P. B., Reese, H. W., & Lipsitt, L. P. (1980). Life-span developmental psychology. *Annual Review of Psychology, 31,* 65–110.

Baumrind, D., & Moselle, K. (1985). A developmental perspective on adolescent drug abuse. *Advances in Alcohol and Substance Abuse, 4*(3–4), 41–67.

Brunswick, A. F., Messeri, P. A., & Titus, S. P. (1992). Predictive factors in adult substance abuse: A prospective study of African American adolescents. In M. Glantz & R. Pickens (Eds.), *Vulnerability to drug abuse* (pp. 419–472). Washington, DC: American Psychological Association.

Buss, D. M. (1984). Marital assortment for personality dispositions: Assessment with three different data sources. *Behavior Genetics, 4*(2), 111–123.

Chasnoff, I. J. (1991). Cocaine and pregnancy: Clinical and methodologic issues. *Clinical Perinatology, 18,* 113–123.

Chasnoff, I. J., Landress, H. J., & Barrett, M. E. (1990). The prevalence of illicit-drug or alcohol use during pregnancy and discrepancies in mandatory reporting in Pinellas County, Florida. *New England Journal of Medicine, 322*(17), 1202–1206.

Chilman, C. S. (1980). Social and psychological research concerning adolescent childbearing: 1970–1980. *Journal of Marriage and the Family, 42*(4), 793–805.

Coombs, L. C., & Fernandez, D. (1978). Husband–wife agreement about reproductive goals. *Demography, 15,* 57–73.

Cowan, P. A., & Cowan, C. P. (1988). Changes in marriage during the transition to parenthood: Must we blame the baby? In G. Y. Michaels & W. A. Goldberg (Eds.), *The transition to parenthood: Current theory and research* (pp. 114–156). New York: Cambridge University Press.

Donovan, J. E., Jessor, R., & Jessor, L. (1983). Problem drinking in adolescence and young adulthood: A follow-up study. *Journal of Studies on Alcohol, 44,* 109–137.

Fawcett, J. T. (1978). The value and the cost of the first child. In W. B. Miller & L. F. Newman (Eds.), *The first child and family formation* (pp. 244–265). Chapel Hill: University of North Carolina, Carolina Population Center.

Galinsky, E. (1981). *Between generations: The stages of parenthood.* New York: Berkeley Books.

Gottlieb, B. H., & Pancer, S. M. (1988). Social networks and the transition to parenthood. In G. Y. Michaels, & W. A. Goldberg (Eds.), *The transition to parenthood: Current theory and research* (pp. 235–269). New York: Cambridge University Press.

Hallberg, H. (1992). Life after divorce: A five-year follow-up study of divorced middle-aged men in Sweden. *Family Practice, 9*(1), 49–56.

Hanna, E., Faden, V., & Harford, T. (1993). Marriage: Does it protect young women from alcoholism? *Journal of Substance Abuse, 5*(1), 1–14.

Hatch, E. E., & Bracken, M. B. (1986). Effect of marijuana use in pregnancy on fetal growth. *American Journal of Epidemiology, 124,* 986–993.

Heath, D. H. (1978). What meaning and effects does fatherhood have for the maturing of professional men? *Merrill-Palmer Quarterly, 24*(4), 265–278.

Hoffman, L. W. (1978). Effects of the first child on the woman's role. In W. B. Miller & L. F. Newman (Eds.), *The first child and family formation* (pp. 340–367). Chapel Hill: University of North Carolina, Carolina Population Center.

Hoffman, L. W., & Manis, J. (1978). Influences of children on marital interaction and parental satisfactions and dissatisfactions. In R. M. Lerner & G. W. Spanier (Eds.), *Child influences on marital and family interaction: A life-span perspective* (pp. 165–213). New York: Academic Press.

Howitz, A. V., & White, H. R. (1991). Becoming married, depression, and alcohol problems among young adults. *Journal of Health and Social Behavior, 32,* 221–237.

Jessor, R., Donovan, J. E., & Costa, F. M. (1991). *Beyond adolescence: Problem behavior and young adult development.* New York: Cambridge University Press.

Johnston, L. D., O'Malley, P. M., & Bachman, J. G. (1994). *National survey results on drug use from the Monitoring the Future Study, 1975–1993, Volume I: High school seniors* (DHHS Pub. No. (ADM) 94-3809) and *Volume II: College students and young adults* (DHHS Pub. No. (ADM) 94-3810). Rockville, MD: National Institute on Drug Abuse.

Kandel, D. B. (1980). Drug and drinking behavior among youth. *Annual Review of Sociology, 6,* 235–285.

Kandel, D. B. (1984). Marijuana users in young adulthood. *Archives of General Psychiatry, 41,* 200–209.

Kleinman, J. C., & Kopstein, A. (1987). Smoking during pregnancy, 1967–80. *American Journal of Public Health, 77*(7), 823–825.

Little, B. B., Snell, L. M., Gilstrap, L. C., Gant, N. F., & Rosenfeld, C. R. (1989). Alcohol abuse during pregnancy: Changes in frequency in a large urban hospital. *Obstetrics and Gynecology, 74*(4), 547–550.

Mare, R. D. (1991). Five decades of educational assortative mating. *American Sociological Review, 56,* 15–32.

Marini, M. M. (1987). Measuring the process of role change during the transition to adulthood. *Social Science Research, 16*(1), 1–38.

McDonald, A. D., Armstrong, B. G., & Sloan, M. (1992). Cigarette, alcohol, and coffee consumption and prematurity. *American Journal of Public Health, 82,* 87–90.

McGue, M., Bacon, S., & Lykken, D. (1993). Personality stability and change in early adulthood: A behavioral genetic analysis. *Developmental Psychology, 29*(1), 96–109.

Mikus, K. (1981). *Paradoxes of early parenthood.* Ann Arbor, MI: University Microfilms.

Miller-Tutzauer, C., Leonard, K. E., & Windle, M. (1991). Marriage and alcohol use: A longitudinal study of "maturing out." *Journal of Studies on Alcohol, 52,* 434–440.

Newcomb, M. D. (1987). Cohabitation and marriage: A quest for independence and relatedness. *Applied Social Psychology Annual, 7,* 128–156.

Newcomb, M. D., & Bentler, P. M. (1987). Changes in drug use from high school to young adulthood: Effects of living arrangement and current life pursuit. *Journal of Applied Developmental Psychology, 8,* 221–246.

O'Malley, P. M., Bachman, J. G., & Johnston, L. D. (1983). Reliability and consistency of self-reports of drug use. *International Journal of the Addictions, 18,* 805–824.

O'Malley, P. M., Bachman, J. G., & Johnston, L. D. (1984). Period, age, and cohort effects on substance use among American youth. *American Journal of Public Health, 74,* 682–688.

O'Malley, P. M., Bachman, J. G., & Johnston, L. D. (1988). Period, age, and cohort effects on substance use among young Americans: A decade of change, 1976–1986. *American Journal of Public Health, 78,* 1315–1321.

Power, C., & Estaugh, V. (1990). The role of family formation and dissolution in shaping drinking behavior in early adulthood. *British Journal of Addiction, 85*(4), 521–530.

Schulenberg, J., Bachman, J. G., O'Malley, P. M., & Johnston, L. D. (1994). High school educational success and subsequent substance use: A panel analysis following adolescents into young adulthood. *Journal of Health and Social Behavior, 35*(1), 45–62.

Schulenberg, J., O'Malley, P. M., Bachman, J. G., Wadsworth, K, N., & Johnston, L. D. (1996). Getting drunk and growing up: Trajectories of frequent binge drinking during the transition to young adulthood. *Journal of Studies in Alcohol, 57,* 289–304.

Serdula, M., Williamson, D., Kendrick, J., Anda, R., & Byers, T. (1991). Trends in alcohol consumption by pregnant women: 1985 through 1988. *Journal of the American Medical Association, 265*(7), 876–879.

Streissguth, A. P., Darby, B. L., Barr, H. M., Smith, J. R., & Martin, D. C. (1983). Comparison of drinking and smoking patterns during pregnancy over a six-year interval. *American Journal of Obstetrics and Gynecology, 145*(6), 716–724.

Thornton, A., Axinn, W. G., & Hill, D. H. (1992). Reciprocal effects of religiosity, cohabitation, and marriage. *American Journal of Sociology, 98*(3), 628–651.

Troll, L. E. (1985). *Early and middle adulthood* (2nd ed.). Monterey, CA: Brooks/Cole.

U.S. Department of Health and Human Services. (1989). *Reducing the health consequences of smoking: 25 years of progress. A report of the Surgeon General* (DHHS Pub. No. (CDC) 89-8411). Rockville, MD: Office on Smoking and Health.

Wadsworth, K. N., Bachman, J. G., Schulenberg, J. E., O'Malley, P. M., & Johnston, L. D. (In preparation). Patterns of pre-marital cohabitation and influences on drug and alcohol use: A longitudinal perspective.

Wallerstein, J. S. (1994). The early psychological tasks of marriage. *American Journal of Orthopsychiatry, 64*(4), 640–650.

Yamaguchi, K., & Kandel, D. (1985a). On the resolution of role incompatibility: Life event history analysis of family roles and marijuana use. *American Journal of Sociology, 90*, 1284–1325.

Yamaguchi, K., & Kandel, D. (1985b). Dynamic relationships between premarital cohabitation and illicit drug use: An event-history analyses of role selection and role socialization. *American Sociological Review, 50*(4), 530–546.

Yamaguchi, K., & Kandel, D. (1993). Marital homophily on illicit drug use among young adults: Assortative mating or marital influence? *Social Forces, 72*(2), 505–528.

Zucker, R. A. (1979). Developmental aspects of drinking through the young adult years. In H. T. Blane & M. E. Chafetz (Eds.), *Youth, alcohol, and social policy* (pp. 91–146). New York: Plenum Press.

Zucker, R. A. (1987). The four alcoholisms: A developmental account of the etiologic process. In P. C. Rivers (Ed.), *Nebraska Symposium on Motivation, 1987: Alcohol and addictive behavior* (pp. 27–83). Lincoln: University of Nebraska Press.

Part III

Achievement Transitions and Health

11 The Association of School Transitions in Early Adolescence with Developmental Trajectories Through High School

Jacquelynne S. Eccles, Sarah E. Lord, Robert W. Roeser, Bonnie L. Barber, and Debra M. Hernandez Jozefowicz

By whatever criteria one uses, many of America's adolescents are not succeeding. Between 15% and 30% drop out before completing high school (Office of Educational Research and Improvement, 1988); a substantial number consume alcohol and other drugs on a regular basis (Johnston, O'Malley, & Bachman, 1994); increasing numbers of youth experience serious social, emotional, and behavioral problems (Kazdin, 1993; Rutter, 1995); and many others are disenchanted with school and education (Dryfoos, 1990). Many of these problems begin to appear during the early adolescent years (Carnegie Council on Adolescent Development, 1989). Why? Several investigators have suggested that the transition to junior high school may contribute to the emergence of these problems (Eccles et al., 1993; Simmons & Blyth, 1987). This transition occurs at a time when most young adolescents are also experiencing the physical, psychological, and social changes associated with puberty, including the new role demands presented by parents, peers, and teachers. Moreover, the school environments of traditional junior high schools are usually quite different from those of elementary schools. Several investigators have argued that these differences undermine healthy development for many youth (e.g., Eccles et al., 1993; Simmons & Blyth, 1987). The first part of this chapter focuses on this hypothesis.

Difficulties with this transition, however, are not universal. Hirsch and Rapkin (1987), for example, found no change in self-esteem in students making the transition from sixth grade into a junior high school (see also Fenzel & Blyth, 1986; Hawkins & Berndt, 1985; Nottelmann, 1987). Although some of the discrepancies in findings undoubtedly reflect variations across studies in populations, school environments, and methodology, it is also likely that indi-

Funding for this project was provided by grants from the National Institute of Child Health and Human Development, the National Science Foundation, Spencer Foundation, the William T. Grant Foundation, and the MacArthur Foundation Research Network on Successful Adolescent Development among Youth in High Risk Settings to the first author. We wish to thank the following people for their help throughout data collection and analysis: Janis Jacobs, Harriet Feldlaufer, Dave Klingel, Douglas Mac Iver, Karen McCarthy, Carol Midgley, David Reuman, Allan Wigfield, and Doris Yee. We would also like to thank all of the school districts, teachers, and students who participated in these studies.

vidual differences in young adolescents' responses to the transition to junior high school are important. For example, Simmons and Blyth (1987) found that girls already involved in dating and showing the most advanced pubertal development were most at risk for negative changes in their self-esteem in conjunction with the transition to junior high school (see also Hirsch & Rapkin, 1987). Similarly, Midgley, Feldlaufer, and Eccles (1988a, 1989) found more extreme negative effects of the junior high school transition on low-achieving rather than on high-achieving students. Thus, although some adolescents adapt well to the transition, others find it more difficult. In the second section of this chapter, we discuss factors that might account for individual differences in early adolescents' response to the junior high school transition. In the final section, we present data on the long-term sequelae of individual differences in adolescents' response to the junior high school transition. We argue that individual differences in adjustment to the transition to junior high school can launch adolescents on developmental trajectories that can influence their later adjustment.

General Developmental Changes in Adolescents' School Motivation and Self-Confidence: A Case of Stage–Environment Mismatch

Several investigators have reported mean level declines in such motivational constructs as interest in school (Epstein & McPartland, 1976), intrinsic motivation (Harter, 1981), and self-concepts and self-esteem (Eccles et al., 1989; Eccles, Midgley, & Adler, 1984; Simmons & Blyth, 1987; Wigfield, Eccles, Mac Iver, & Reuman, 1991) in conjunction with the junior high school transition. There is also evidence of similarly timed increases in such negative motivational and behavioral characteristics as focus on self-evaluation rather than task mastery (Maehr & Anderman, 1993; Midgley, Anderman, & Hicks, 1995; Nicholls, 1980; Roeser, Midgley, & Maehr, 1994), test anxiety, and both truancy and dropping out of school (Rosenbaum, 1976; see Eccles et al., 1984, for a full review). Finally, several investigators have found a marked decline in some young adolescents' school grades as they move into junior high school – the magnitude of which predicts subsequent school failure and dropping out (e.g., Roderick, 1991; Simmons & Blyth, 1987). Although these changes are not extreme for most adolescents, there is sufficient evidence of a gradual decline in various indicators to make one wonder what is happening (see Eccles & Midgley, 1989, for review).

A variety of explanations have been offered. Some scholars attribute these declines to the intrapsychic upheaval assumed to be associated with early pubertal development (e.g., Freud, 1969; Hamburg, 1974). Others have suggested that they result from the coincidence of multiple life changes. For example, drawing on cumulative stress theory, Simmons and her colleagues suggest that declines in motivation result from the fact that adolescents making the transition to junior high school at the end of Grade 6 (average age, 12) must cope with two major transitions: pubertal change and school change (e.g., Blyth, Simmons, & Carlton-Ford, 1983; Simmons & Blyth, 1987; see also Crockett, Petersen, Graber, Schulenberg, & Ebata, 1989).[1] Simmons and her colleagues tested the hypothesis that early adolescents making a school transition are at greater risk for negative outcomes than early adolescents who only have to cope with pubertal change during this developmental period. Specifically, they compared the pattern of changes on several indicators of adjustment for two groups of adolescents: a group who moved from sixth (age 12) to seventh grade (age 13) in the same building complex (i.e., a K–8 school building), and a group who went from a K–6 school building to a different junior high school building that included Grades 7 through 9. This design unconfounds age, grade, and the time of transition into a new school environment.

Simmons and her colleagues found clear evidence, especially among girls, of greater negative change between sixth and seventh grades for those adolescents making the junior high school transition (i.e., those in a K–6 to 7–9 system) than for those remaining in the same school setting (i.e., those in a K–8 system). The fact that the junior high school transition effects were especially marked for girls was interpreted as additional support for the cumulative stress theory because girls are more likely to be experiencing both a school transition and pubertal change at this age.

We obtained a similar pattern of results using the data from the National Educational Longitudinal Study. We compared eighth graders in K–8 school systems with eighth graders in either junior high school systems (systems with K–6, 7–9, and 10–12 grade buildings) or middle school systems (systems with a K–5, 6–8, and 9–12 grade clustering configuration). The eighth-grade students in the K–8 systems looked better on several motivational indicators, such as self-esteem, coming to class prepared, and attending school on a regular basis, than the students in the other two school systems (Eccles, Lord, & Midgley, 1991). In addition, the eighth-grade teachers in the K–8 system reported fewer student problems, less truancy, and more student engagement than teachers in the other school systems. Clearly, both young adolescents and their teachers fare better in K–8 school systems than in either junior high school or middle school systems. Why?

Several investigators have suggested that the changing nature of the educational environments experienced by many young adolescents help explain both these school system differences and the mean level declines in motivation associated with the junior high school transition (e.g., Eccles, 1993; Eccles et al., 1984; Eccles & Midgley, 1989; Lee, Statuto, & Kedar-Voivodas, 1983; Lipsitz, 1981; Midgley, 1993; Simmons & Blyth, 1987). Drawing on person–environment fit theory (see Hunt, 1975), Eccles and Midgley (1989) proposed that these motivational and behavioral declines could result from the fact that junior high schools are not providing appropriate educational environments for many young adolescents. According to person–environment theory, behavior, motivation and mental health are influenced by the fit between the characteristics individuals bring to their social environments and the characteristics of these social environments. Individuals are not likely to do very well, or be very motivated, if they are in social environments that do not fit their psychological needs. If the social environments in the typical American junior high school do not fit well the psychological needs of adolescents, then person–environment fit theory predicts a decline in adolescents' motivation, interest, performance, and behavior as they move into this environment. Furthermore, Eccles and Midgley (1989) argued that this effect should be even more marked if the young adolescents experience a fundamental change in their school environment when they move into a junior high school or middle school, that is, if the environment of the junior high school or middle school fits their psychological needs less well than the environment of the elementary school.

Is there any evidence that such a negative change in the school environment occurs with the transition to junior high school? Yes. For example, Simmons and Blyth (1987) enumerated the following types of macro-level changes: increased school size, increased bureaucratic organization, increased departmentalization, and decreased teacher–student individual contact and opportunity for close relationships with teachers. Simmons and Blyth suggested that such changes put young adolescents at risk in several ways. Because early adolescence is a period of exploration, youth are likely to try out various behaviors and identities. Although such experimentation is both healthy and normal, it can also be quite risky. Successful passage through this period of experimentation requires a tight safety net carefully monitored by caring adults – adults who provide opportunities for experimentation without letting the youth seriously mortgage their futures in the process (see Carnegie Council on Adolescent Development, 1989). Clearly, the large, bureaucratic structure of the typical junior high and middle school is ill suited to such a task. In addition, Higgins and Parsons (1983) suggested that the increased size results in the disruption of one's peer network at a time when peer relations are especially important. Each of these characteristics of the junior high school transition could have detrimental effects on young adolescents, especially those already somewhat at risk due to psychological, social, or academic problems.

There is also evidence of negative changes at the classroom level. First, junior high school classrooms, compared to elementary school classrooms, tend to be characterized by a greater emphasis on teacher control and discipline, and by fewer opportunities for student decision making, choice, and self-management (e.g., Brophy & Everston, 1976; Midgley & Feldlaufer, 1987;

Midgley, Feldlaufer, & Eccles, 1988a; Moos, 1979). Such differences in the opportunity for participation in decision making and self-control are likely to be especially problematic for young adolescents. This is a time in development when youth begin to think of themselves as young adults. It is also a time when they increase their exploration of possible identities. Adolescents believe they are becoming more responsible and, consequently, deserving of greater adult respect. Presumably, the adults responsible for their socialization would also like to encourage them to become more responsible for themselves as they move toward adulthood. And in fact, this is what typically happens across the elementary school grades (see Eccles & Midgley, 1989). Unfortunately, the evidence suggests that this developmentally appropriate progression is disrupted by the transition to junior high school. According to stage–environment fit theory, such a developmentally regressive disruption is likely to undermine the motivation and engagement of the young adolescents experiencing the change.

Second, junior high school classrooms, compared to elementary school classrooms, are characterized by less personal and positive teacher–student relationships (see Eccles & Midgley, 1989; Feldlaufer, Midgley, & Eccles, 1988; Midgley, Feldlaufer, & Eccles, 1988b). Such a shift in the quality of student–teacher relationships is also likely to be especially detrimental at early adolescence. As adolescents begin to explore their own identity, they are prone to question the values and expectations of their parents. In more stable social groups, young adolescents often have the opportunity to do this questioning with supportive nonparental adults such as religious counselors, neighbors, and relatives. In our highly mobile, culturally diverse society, such opportunities are not as readily available. Teachers are the one stable source of nonparental adults left for many American youth. Unfortunately, the sheer size and bureaucratic nature of most junior high schools, coupled with the stereotypes we hold regarding the negative characteristics of adolescents, lead teachers to distrust their students and to withdraw from them emotionally (see Eccles et al., 1993; Miller et al., 1990). Consequently, these youth have little choice but to turn to peers as nonparental guides in their exploration of alternative identities. Evidence from a variety of sources suggests that this can be a very risky venture (e.g., Elliott, Huizinga, & Menard, 1989; Jessor & Jessor, 1977). The reduced opportunity for close relationships between students and junior high school teachers has another unfortunate consequence for young adolescents: It decreases the likelihood that teachers will be able to identify students on the verge of getting into serious trouble and get these students the help they need. This way, the holes in the safety net may become too big to prevent unnecessary failures.

Third, junior high school teachers, again compared to elementary school teachers, tend to feel less effective as teachers, especially for low-ability students. For example, the seventh-grade junior high teachers discussed by Midgley et al. (1988b) expressed much less confidence in their teaching efficacy than sixth-grade elementary school teachers in the same school districts. This decline in teachers' sense of efficacy in teaching less competent students could help explain why it is precisely these students who give up on themselves following the junior high school transition (Lord, Eccles, & McCarthy, 1994; Midgley et al., 1989).

Finally, junior high school teachers appear to use a more competitive standard in judging students' competence and in grading their performance than do elementary school teachers (see Eccles & Midgley, 1989). There is no stronger predictor of students' self-confidence and sense of personal efficacy for school work than the grades they receive (Eccles, 1983). If grades change, then we would expect to see a concomitant shift in the adolescents' self-perceptions and academic motivation. And in fact, this is what happens. For example, Simmons and Blyth (1987) found a greater drop in grades between sixth and seventh grades for adolescents making the junior high school transition at this point than for adolescents enrolled in K–8 schools. Furthermore, this decline in grades was not matched by a decline in the adolescents' scores on standardized achievement tests, supporting the conclusion that the decline reflects a change in grading practices rather than a change in the rate of the students' learning (Kavrell & Petersen, 1984). Imagine what this decline in grades could do to young adolescents' self-confidence, especially in light of the fact that the material they are being tested on is not likely to be more intellectually challenging.

Changes such as those just reviewed are likely to have a negative effect on many indices of students' school-related motivation at any grade level. But Eccles and Midgley (1989) have argued that these types of changes are particularly harmful at early adolescence given what is known about psychological development during this stage of life, namely, that early adolescent development is characterized by increases in the desire for autonomy, peer orientation, self-focus and self-consciousness, salience of identity issues, concern over intimate relationships, and capacity for abstract cognitive activity (see Simmons & Blyth, 1987). Simmons and Blyth (1987) have argued that adolescents need a reasonably safe as well as an intellectually challenging environment to adapt to these shifts – an environment that provides a "zone of comfort" as well as challenging new opportunities for growth. In light of these needs, the environmental changes often associated with the transition to junior high school seem especially harmful in that they disrupt the possibility of close personal relationships between youth and nonfamilial adults at a time when youth have an increased need for precisely this type of social support. These environmental changes emphasize competition, social comparison, and ability self-assessment at a time of heightened self-focus; they decrease decision making and choice at a time when the desire for self-control and respect from adults is growing; and they disrupt peer social networks at a time when adolescents are especially concerned with peer relationships and social acceptance. Thus, at a time when identity-relevant questions such as "Who am I?" "Where do I belong?" and "How do I fit in?" are most salient for young teens, the social environment of junior high school may become a venue for anonymity or alienation, rather than a place of support and guidance that serves to assist youth in their unfolding development.

In sum, we believe that the nature of these environmental changes, coupled with the normal course of development, is likely to result in a developmental mismatch. That is, the fit between early adolescents' needs and the opportunities provided to them in their school environment deteriorates as early adolescents move into junior high school, and this lack of fit increases the risk of negative motivational outcomes, especially for those adolescents who are already having academic difficulties.

To test these predictions, we conducted a large-scale longitudinal study of the impact of changes in the school and classroom environments on adolescents' achievement-related beliefs, motives, values, self-evaluations, affective reactions, and behaviors (the Michigan Study of Adolescent Life Transitions – MSALT). The first 2 years of this study focused intensively on the junior high school transition. Although all of the adolescents made this transition between Grades 6 and 7 and all districts had a K–6, 7–9, 10–12 grade structure at the time of this study, we purposely selected 12 school districts in southeastern Michigan that differed in the nature of the junior high school environment along the dimensions reviewed earlier. The data summarized in this part of the chapter come from the first 2 years of this study, during which time questionnaires were administered at school during the fall and spring terms of 2 consecutive school years: the students' sixth- and seventh-grade years.

Approximately 1,500 young adolescents participated at all four waves of the first 2 years of this study. The median family income for these students was approximately $30,000 per year in 1983. Most families would be classified as working or middle class based on their occupation, education, and family income; most lived in working- and middle-class communities surrounding Detroit. Seventy-five percent of the mothers reported being married, 8% reported being remarried, and 13% reported being separated or divorced. Eighty-five percent of the sample were White, 8% were African American, and the remaining 7% were a mix of other ethnic groups.

By and large, our findings support the prediction that changes in school experiences like those described previously are linked to declines in motivation and self-esteem (see Eccles et al., 1993; Eccles, Lord, & Roeser, in press; Midgley et al., 1988a, 1989, for full descriptions). For example, as predicted, the adolescents who moved from a high-efficacy sixth-grade teacher to a low-efficacy seventh-grade teacher ended their first year in junior high school with lower expectancies for themselves in math, lower perceptions of their performance in math, and higher perceptions of the difficulty of math than adolescents who experienced no change in teacher efficacy or who had moved from low- to high-efficacy teachers as they made the junior high school transition. Also, as we had predicted, teacher efficacy beliefs had a much stronger impact on the low-achieving adolescents' beliefs than on the high-achieving adolescents' beliefs. By the end of the junior high school year, the confidence of those low-achieving adolescents who had moved from high- to low-efficacy teachers had declined dramatically. It is also important to note that the decline in self-confidence and efficacy for learning math was not characteristic of either the low- or high-achieving adolescents who moved into a high-teacher-efficacy classroom in seventh grade, suggesting that the decline is not a general feature of early adolescent development. Rather, it seems to be a consequence of the fact that so many young adolescents experience a debilitating shift in their classroom environments as they make the junior high school transition (Midgley et al., 1989).

Similarly, we found that changes in the affective relationship between students and teachers also predicted changes in the adolescents' motivation. As we had expected, it was the young adolescents who moved from elementary teachers they perceived to be high in support to teachers they perceived to be low in support who showed the decline in the value they attached to math. In contrast, the young adolescents who moved from teachers they perceived to be low in support to junior high school teachers they perceived to be high in support showed an increase in the value they attached to math. Again, it was the low-achieving students who were at particularly high risk when they moved to less facilitative classroom environments after the transition (Midgley et al., 1988a).

It is important to note that in both of these studies many more students experienced the developmentally regressive pattern of change over the junior high school transition than experienced the developmentally appropriate pattern of change. More specifically, based on median splits that characterized sixth- and seventh-grade teachers as either high or low in teaching efficacy, 42% of the students went from a sixth-grade teacher with a high sense of efficacy to a seventh-grade teacher with a low sense of efficacy. This compared to 9% of the students who went from a low-efficacy sixth-grade teacher to a high-efficacy teacher and 13% who had a high-efficacy teacher in both years. Futhermore, 21% of the students went from a supportive sixth-grade teacher to an unsupportive seventh-grade teacher, compared to the 15% who moved from an unsupportive sixth-grade teacher to a supportive seventh-grade teacher.

Individual Differences in the Adjustment to School Transitions During Early Adolescence

More central to the concerns of this chapter, the MSALT study also provides strong support for the existence of individual differences in adolescents' response to the junior high school transition. In both the study on the impact of changes in teacher efficacy and the study on the impact of changes in student–teacher relationships, low-achieving students were more negatively affected by the change than high-achieving students. In this section, we explore the issue of individual differences in response to the junior high school transition more thoroughly.

Both Simmons and Blyth (1987) and Fenzel (1991) have analyzed the transition to junior high school in terms of stress and coping. From this perspective, transitions are considered stressful events in that they tap the individual's resources for adaptation. Within the stress and coping literature (e.g., Garmezy, 1983; Rutter, 1981), differences in individuals' responses to stressful life events are assumed to result from the balance between the protective and risk factors that individuals have at their disposal. Protective factors buffer against the potentially anxiety-producing or adverse effects of life or environmental transitions, whereas risk factors tend to exacerbate these effects.

We have now completed a set of analyses of the MSALT data based on an application of the risk–protective factors paradigm to the junior high school transition (Lord et al., 1994). We investigated both psychological and general family environment factors as potential moderators of adolescents' responses to the junior high school transition. The psychological factors we examined included adolescents' ability self-concepts, worries, and self-consciousness; the family environmental factors included decision-making opportunities and developmental attunement to the needs of adolescents. The rationale for each of these sets of moderators is summarized in the following subsection, along with a summary of our findings.

Psychological Protective and Risk Factors

In thinking about the psychological protective and risk factors most likely to affect adjustment to the junior high school transition, we decided to focus on a set of constructs directly related to the school setting. In terms of protective factors, several investigators have suggested that personal coping resources are key influences on individuals' adjustment to stressful situations such as school transitions. Personal coping resources typically include a set of relatively stable personality, attitudinal, and cognitive dispositions that promote effective adaptation (Fenzel, 1991). The personal coping resources that seem most likely to buffer against the detrimental effects of a stressful school transition include a sense of autonomy, a sense of personal efficacy, and confidence in one's competence (Bandura, 1986; Compas, 1987; Garmezy, 1983; Harter, 1990).

Several studies point to the relevance of perceptions of one's competencies for understanding the changes in self-esteem associated with major life changes such as the junior high school transition. For example, in Bohrnstedt and

Felson (1983), adolescents' perceived academic and athletic competence were predictive of high self-esteem. Similarly, Harter (1990) has shown that perceived competence in academic, social, athletic, and physical appearance domains is related to high self-esteem, with confidence in one's physical appearance and social competence having the strongest relations. Other studies have focused on the protective role that actual abilities play. This work demonstrates that sixth-grade success in academic and social domains predicts increases in self-esteem following the junior high school transition (e.g., Hirsch & Rapkin, 1987; Simmons & Blyth, 1987; Simmons, Burgeson, Carlton-Ford, & Blyth, 1987).

Achievement-related worries and self-consciousness seem the most likely candidates as psychological risk factors for the junior high school transition adjustment process. Elkind and Bower (1979) have shown that self-consciousness is negatively related to self-esteem. Similarly, several studies indicate that anxiety about one's performance in the academic and social domains is negatively related to adolescents' school performance (e.g., Payne, Smith, & Payne, 1983; Willig, Harnisch, Hill, & Maehr, 1983). Eccles and her colleagues have suggested that both anxiety and self-consciousness may be particularly detrimental as the early adolescent is forced to adjust to a new school environment characterized by increased rigor in grading, less variety in evaluation techniques, and an increase in social comparison among students (Eccles & Midgley, 1989; Feldlaufer et al., 1988). Furthermore, these detrimental effects are likely to be especially salient during early adolescence because this developmental period is characterized by increased self-focus and self-consciousness (e.g., Eccles et al., 1984; Elkind & Bower, 1979; Eccles & Midgley, 1989).

Support for these hypotheses concerning risk and protective factors associated with the junior high school transition is provided in a recent study we conducted (Lord et al., 1994). In this study, we tested the relation of sixth-grade indicators of these psychological protective and risk factors (e.g., competence beliefs, anxieties, self-consciousness) to several indicators of adjustment to the junior high school transition. By and large, the results supported our hypotheses. These results are reviewed more fully later.

Family Protective and Risk Factors

In thinking about the possible impact of the family environment on adolescents' adaptation to the junior high school transition, it is useful to consider the salient developmental tasks confronting adolescents during this time. A central task of adolescence is developing a sense of oneself as an autonomous individual while at the same time retaining a good relationship with one's parents (Blos, 1979; Eccles et al., 1993; Steinberg, 1990). In keeping with our stage–environment fit perspective, we have focused on the fit between early adolescents' family environment and adolescents' developmental needs in terms of support for increasingly autonomous decision making and self-direction (e.g., Eccles et al., 1993; see also Hunt, 1975). Similar to our earlier discussion regarding the importance of fit in the school environment, person–environment fit theory suggests that the fit between adolescents' need for autonomy and the amount of control their parents exert over their decision making should affect their motivation and sense of satisfaction with their environment. Adopting a developmental framework, we assume that the fit between desire for self-control and opportunities for self-control is likely to change as the individual develops, unless the environment changes at the same rate and in the appropriate direction. As adolescents mature, they are likely to desire more self-control and more opportunities for decision making. When they enter early adolescence, the rate of increase in this desire for control over one's own life likely accelerates, increasing the need for the family to rene-gotiate the power balance between parent and child (Collins, 1990; Eccles, Miller-Buchanan, et al., 1991; Hill, 1988; Montemayor, 1986; Steinberg, 1990). It seems plausible that those parents who are able to adjust to the adolescent's changing needs with relatively little conflict will provide a better match be-tween the early adolescent and the family environment. This better match should then serve as a protective factor in the adolescent's developmental trajectory.

In support of this hypothesis, researchers have shown that family environ-ments that provide adolescents with opportunities for personal autonomy and involvement in family decision making are associated with positive out-comes such as increased self-esteem and self-reliance, greater satisfaction with school and student–teacher relations, positive school adjustment, ad-vanced moral reasoning, and a mastery orientation toward problem solving in the classroom (e.g., Epstein & McPartland, 1977; Flanagan, 1985, 1986, 1989; Yee, 1986, 1987; Yee & Flanagan, 1985). Conversely, a parenting style that is coercive, authoritarian, and not attuned to the adolescent's need for more decision-making opportunities is associated with greater self-consciousness and lower self-confidence (Leahy, 1981; Ryan & Lynch, 1989; Yee & Flanagan, 1985).

Consistent with this perspective, the period of early adolescence has been acknowledged by developmentalists (e.g., Collins, 1990; Eccles et al., 1993; Hill, 1988; Paikoff & Brooks-Gunn, 1991; Steinberg, 1990), family sociologists (e.g., Aldous, 1977), and clinicians (e.g., Blos, 1979) as a time of transition that requires a renegotiation of family rules and roles for successful adapta-tion. Research and clinical evidence suggest that the family's ability to adapt to the changing needs of the early adolescent has implications for the process of identity formation (Grotevant, 1983), for the development of psychopathol-ogy such as eating disorders (Minuchin, Rosman, & Baker, 1978), and possibly for how the early adolescent negotiates the transition to junior high school

(Eccles, Miller-Buchanan, et al., 1991; Eccles et al., 1993). It is reasonable to postulate that family environments that are responsive and developmentally sensitive to the needs of early adolescents serve as protective factors for the transition to junior high school. To test these hypotheses, we examined adolescents' perceptions of the family environment with regard to two general dimensions: parent–adolescent mismatch related to issues of autonomy and control and the provision of decision-making opportunities (Lord et al., 1994). The results of the analyses using these measures are summarized below.

Risk and Protective Factors During the Junior High School Transition: Findings of the Lord, Eccles, and McCarthy Study

Lord et al. (1994) tested the hypotheses outlined previously using the following indicators of protective and risk factors as predictors of adjustment outcomes at both the beginning (Wave 3) and end (Wave 4) of the seventh-grade school year: sixth-grade school achievement level, perceptions of one's own abilities, worries about one's abilities and self-consciousness, and the two ratings of their family environment. Here we focus only on the results for changes in self-esteem because self-esteem is widely acknowledged as central to adolescents' general psychological adjustment (see Harter, 1985, 1990). We believe changes in self-esteem provide a global indicator of the reactivity of the self-system to the junior high school transition. Wave 2 self-esteem (measured with Harter's Self-Worth Scale, 1982), collected during the spring of the students' sixth grade prior to the transition, was entered into the regression equation first in order to test the impact of the other predictors on *change* in self-esteem from Wave 2 to Waves 3 and 4. Because of the importance of achievement level as a general protective factor (e.g., Rae-Grant, Thomas, Offord, & Boyle, 1989), teacher-rated academic ability was also included as a control. By controlling for both Wave 2 self-esteem and academic ability, these regression models tested the extent to which our other predictors were associated with a gain or loss in self-esteem between the end of sixth grade and the beginning (or end) of the seventh-grade year, controlling for prior achievement level.

The other predictors, all collected in the spring of the sixth grade, were then entered in two sets: the psychological protections and risks (e.g., ability self-concepts, worries) and then the family protections and risks (e.g., involvement in decision making, lack of developmental attunement between parent and child). Finally, given the evidence of greater vulnerability for females during this transition (Simmons & Blyth, 1987), gender was entered at the last step.

Psychological Protective and Risk Factors. As expected, both sixth-grade self-esteem and sixth-grade academic performance measures were related to seventh-grade self-esteem (also measured with Harter's Self-Worth Scale) in the fall and spring, suggesting considerable stability in self-esteem across these time periods. However, sixth-grade academic performance was not a significant predictor of self-esteem change between Wave 2 and Wave 3 or 4. As predicted, the psychological protective factors were associated with positive change in self-esteem. This was particularly true for the adolescents' ratings of their physical attractiveness, their math ability, and their peer social ability. Also, as hypothesized, the psychological risk factors were associated with declines in self-esteem over the junior high school transition. This was particularly true for social and academic self-consciousness.

That confidence in one's peer-related social skills and one's physical attractiveness, coupled with low social self-consciousness, emerged as salient contributors to adolescents' adjustment to junior high school probably reflects the impact of the changing roles adolescents take on at this particular period of life. Several investigators have suggested that there is an increased emphasis at this time, by both peers and families, on physical appearance, social presentation, and popularity with the opposite sex (Higgins & Parsons, 1983; Hill & Lynch, 1983). Coupled with the new and much larger social environment of the junior high setting, confidence in one's competence in peer social relationships and in one's physical attractiveness may be particularly important protective factors.

The salience of physical appearance for self-esteem across the transition to junior high can also be problematic, particularly for females. Given that the standards for female physical attractiveness in the United States are outside the normal range of variation, excessive focus on physical attractiveness may propel some adolescent females toward the extreme efforts linked with eating disorders in order to make their bodies fit these unrealistic societal standards.

Family Protective and Risk Factors. As predicted, the perception that one's parents are too controlling and intrusive was associated with a decline in self-esteem. In contrast, the perception that one's family provides sufficient opportunities for engagement in family decision making was associated with an increase in self-esteem across the junior high school transition.

Female Gender as a Risk Factor. Gender added little to the predictive power of the regression equation at Wave 3. In contrast, at Wave 4, gender had a negative relation to self-esteem change, indicating that males' self-esteem increased more than that of females even after controlling for all of the other measures. Given that this effect did not occur between Waves 2 and 3, these results suggest that the decline has more to do with the conjoint effect of early adolescent development and the school transition than with the junior high school transition per se. This conclusion is consistent with the reports of several other studies on female development during the early adolescent period (e.g., AAUW, 1992; Brown & Gilligan, 1992; Simmons & Blyth, 1987).

Summary. The results of the Lord et al. (1994) study are consistent with our predictions based on stage–environment fit theory. Adolescents who experience good support for decision making at home and who think their parents provide them with sufficient autonomy respond to the junior high school transition with gains in their self-esteem. Similarly, consistent with other discussions of the role of risk and protective factors during adolescence (e.g., Compas, 1987, 1994; Masten et al., 1988; Maughan, 1988), those adolescents who had relatively high levels of self-esteem prior to the junior high school transition, and who were confident of their academic competencies and physical attractiveness, experienced gains in self-esteem following the junior high school transition. In the next section, we build on this work by looking at individual differences in the short- and long-term consequences of self-esteem change in response to the junior high school transition.

Profiles of Adjustment to the Junior High School Transition

The junior high transition is a developmentally normative contextual change that can serve as a turning point for early adolescents. It is a transition that can launch early adolescents on alternative developmental pathways. Adolescents differ in how they respond to this transition, and not all individuals experience difficulty as they move from the elementary to the junior high school environment. For some, the transition provides opportunities for growth and positive development, whereas for others, the challenges of this school transition, amid a variety of concurrent biopsychosocial changes, appear to undermine their sense of self-worth. As a result, some adolescents may shift to developmental pathways that can have quite negative long-term consequences, mediated by disengagement from school, increased psychological distress, and/or engagement in risky and potentially dangerous activities. We address this issue in the remainder of this chapter.

First, in an effort to understand how different students adjust to the demands of the junior high school transition, we examine a profile of indices of psychological and behavioral functioning both before and after the transition. Next, we examine the long-term sequelae of individual differences in adolescents' response to this school transition. Is the junior high school transition a turning point in the developmental trajectories of adolescents? Does a decline in self-esteem at this point predispose an adolescent to a more negative high school trajectory?

In order to understand how students who manifest different patterns of response to the junior high school transition look on a variety of contemporaneous and long-term indices of psychosocial adjustment and well-being, we created three groups of students based on change in their self-esteem. These groups were created by regressing Wave 3 self-esteem on Wave 2 self-esteem and saving the residuals – which represent a change in adolescents' self-esteem over the junior high school transition. The residual scores ranged from −1.82 to 1.84, with negative values reflecting a decline in self esteem across the transition and positive values reflecting an increase in self-esteem from Wave 2 to Wave 3. The adolescents were grouped into one of three categories based on cut points on the residual score at ±.5 standard deviation – yielding 553 decreasers, 888 no changers, and 595 increasers.

We selected change in self-esteem as our central indicator of these early adolescents' reactivity to the junior high school transition for two reasons. First, self-esteem is related conceptually and empirically to one's feelings of personal competence and valuing of various activity domains (see Bohrnstedt & Felson, 1983; Eccles, 1983; Harter, 1990; Simmons & Blyth, 1987), to social-emotional functioning (Covington, 1992; Petersen et al., 1993), and to behavioral outcomes (e.g., Owens, 1994; Rosenberg, Schooler, & Schoenbach, 1989). Because we wanted to examine academic, social-emotional, and behavioral outcomes in this report, we thought that self-esteem provided the best single construct from which to predict changes in these other domains of functioning. Second, changes in self-beliefs, values, and emotions related to academics that are linked to self-esteem (e.g., competence beliefs, self-consciousness) are known to change, often in negative directions, as a function of the transition to junior high school (see Eccles & Midgley, 1989; Eccles et al., 1984; Harter, Whitesell, & Kowalski, 1992). Thus, we expect self-esteem to be a good proximal indictor of these other self-system changes that reflect, at least in part, students' reactivity to the junior high school transition.

Profiles of Self-Esteem Change. In order to test whether or not grouping students by self-esteem served our purpose of describing a general pattern of response to the school transition, we compared our three groups (decreasers, no changers, and increasers) on a variety of other personal and psychological characteristics. To differentiate these groups further for our assessments of short- and long-term adjustment, we divided each of the three self-esteem change groups into high and low achievers based on a median split of the sixth-grade math teacher's rating of the student's academic ability relative to other students in the class. The number of students, girls and boys, and high and low achievers present in each of the self-esteem change groups during Waves 1–6 are presented in Table 11.1. Focusing on the Wave 1–4 column only, one can see that females are overrepresented in both of the two decreaser groups, and in the high-achieving no-change group (significantly so based on a chi-square analysis, $p < .01$).

Table 11.1. *Self-esteem change group cell numbers and participation rate by achievement group and gender*

Self-esteem change group	Waves 1–4 6th–7th grade	Wave 5 10th grade	Wave 6 12th grade
Decliners	553	206 (36%)	241 (44%)
High achievement			
Females	149	68 (46%)	74 (50%)
Males	86	39 (45%)	45 (52%)
Low achievement			
Females	172	64 (37%)	77 (45%)
Males	146	35 (24%)	45 (31%)
Same	888	364 (41%)	415 (47%)
High achievement			
Females	236	113 (48%)	122 (52%)
Males	196	85 (43%)	98 (50%)
Low achievement			
Females	231	94 (41%)	104 (45%)
Males	225	72 (32%)	91 (40%)
Incliners	595	243 (41%)	275 (46%)
High achievement			
Females	156	77 (49%)	81 (52%)
Males	149	64 (43%)	71 (48%)
Low achievement			
Females	141	51 (36%)	57 (40%)
Males	149	51 (35%)	66 (44%)

Note: Numbers in parentheses represent the percentage of adolescents remaining from the original sample at Waves 1–4.

Our next step was to describe the profiles of adjustment of the different groups of students across the span of their sixth and seventh grades on other indicators. Using multivariate analysis of variance techniques (MANOVA), we examined how the three groups differed in terms of psychological characteristics that were assessed around the transition event. These characteristics included the criterion measure of self-esteem, self-reports of anxiety, self-consciousness, school engagement, and teacher ratings of adolescents' general resourcefulness. Gender, academic achievement (high versus low), and self-esteem change group (decliners, no change, increasers) were included as between-subject factors; times of measurement (Waves 1–4) was the within-subjects factor. The measures are summarized in Appendix A.

For purpose of this chapter, we focus primarily on the effects involving both wave and self-esteem change group (SE Change). Figure 11.1 illustrates the results for self-esteem across Waves 1–4 (SE Change by Time $F[6, 1,880] = 266, p < .001$; eta-squared $= .23$). What is most interesting in this figure is the fact that the three change groups have quite similar self-esteem ratings prior to

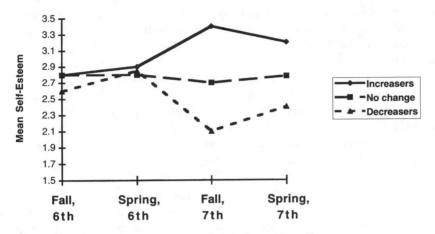

Figure 11.1. Self-esteem changes across sixth and seventh grades.

the junior high school transition (in the fall and spring of their sixth-grade year). The marked divergence immediately following the transition reflects the way the groups were created. However, this divergence persists across the seventh-grade school year to Wave 4, when the three groups are still significantly different from one another ($p < .001$). The other results from this MANOVA are consistent with findings reported elsewhere on this sample. As reported in Eccles et al. (1989), there is a curvilinear main effect ($F[3, 1,884] = 38.8, p < .001$; eta-squared = .02) for time, with self-esteem increasing from fall to spring during the sixth grade, then falling sharply across the transition to junior high school (Waves 2 to 3) and recovering somewhat by the end of the seventh grade. The magnitude of this pattern, however, differed for females and males (Time by Gender $F[3, 1,885] = 23.3, p < .001$; eta-squared = .01), with females showing a more marked decline following the transition than males. The pattern also differed across the two achievement groups, with the low achievers showing less within-year increase in self-esteem in both grades than the high achievers (Time by Achievement Group $F[3, 1,885] = 5.5, p < .01$; eta-squared = .003). As we discuss later, the significant group differences we found here for changes in self-esteem are significant not only at the end of seventh grade but also later, during the high school years. Whatever it is about the response to the junior high school transition that separates these groups from one another at grade 7 appears to have long-term consequences for development during the adolescent period.

Profiles of Anxiety Change. Next, we compared these groups on measures of psychological adjustment. Given our previous work on risk and protective factors associated with the junior high school transition (Lord et al., 1994), we examined how adolescents in each of the three self-esteem change groups looked in terms of their academic anxiety in math and their feeling of social self-consciousness. Math anxiety (measured at all four waves; see Appendix A) assessed the extent to which students felt nervous or worried either before or during tests in mathematics (alphas $\geq$ .85). Social self-consciousness (measured at Waves 2 and 4) assessed students' concerns about how others perceived them or how well they thought they were liked on meeting significant others (alphas $\geq$ .80). Again, although we included gender, achievement group, and self-esteem change group as the between-subject factors and wave as the within-subject factors in these analyses, we focus only on the results involving self-esteem change group and time.

The analyses of math anxiety yielded significant main effects for change group, gender, achievement group, and time. The SE change by time effect was not significant, however. As one would expect, females reported more math anxiety than males ($F[1, 1,846] = 75.4, p < .001$; eta-squared = .04), and low-achieving students reported more math anxiety than high-achieving students ($F[1, 1,846] = 68.1, p < .001$; eta-squared = .04). More relevant to this chapter, although all students reported declining levels of math anxiety across the four waves ($F[3, 1,845] = 76.9, p < .001$; eta-squared = .04), students whose self-esteem declined over the transition to junior high school reported more anxiety about math at all waves than did those students whose self-esteem either increased or did not change across the transition ($F[3, 1,846] = 40.2, p < .001$; eta-squared; = .04). This difference did not increase over time, suggesting that school-related anxiety is more of a precursor of SE change than a concomitant response to the transition. Consistent with this interpretation, recall that math anxiety was one of the significant predictors of self-esteem change in the Lord et al. (1994) study.

Similar results were obtained for the social self-consciousness measures. Significant effects for both self-esteem change group and gender for adolescents's social self-consciousness were found. Both females ($F[1, 1,885] = 61.6, p < .001$) and students whose self-esteem declined ($F[2, 1,885) = 15.1, p < .001$) across the transition were more self-conscious in social situations than their peers at both time points. Additionally, there was also a small, significant time by change group effect (eta-squared = .004), which is illustrated in Figure 11.2. Although there was a general decline in social self-consciousness across the sixth to seventh grade time span, the magnitude of this decline varied slightly across the three self-esteem change groups: Those students who experienced an increase in self-esteem across the transition to junior high school also experienced a significantly greater decline in social self-consciousness from Wave 2 to Wave 4. So, unlike the effects for math anxiety, social self-consciousness appears to serve as both a protective factor for self-esteem change (Lord et al., 1994) and an indicator of the response to the junior high school transition. The results suggest that adolescents whose self-esteem goes up with the transition to junior high school experience gains in other positive

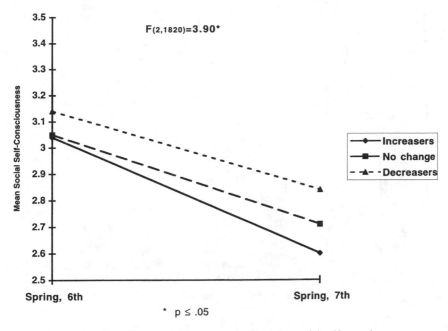

Figure 11.2. Time by self-esteem change group effect for social self-consciousness across the transition to junior high school.

psychological characteristics, such as self-assurance and comfort with themselves in social situations. This protective relation may be particularly important during the adolescent years, when multiple changes and pressures from peers can result in social awkwardness and insecurity.

Social-Emotional Adjustment at the End of Seventh Grade. To assess social-emotional functioning at the end of seventh grade, we examined both psychological and behavioral indicators of adjustment. First, as a primary indicator of psychological adjustment, we selected depressive affect. It is well established that the prevalence of depressive symptomatology increases during the adolescent years, particularly for females (e.g., Petersen et al., 1993). It is also believed that this change may be related to early adolescents' adjustment to school changes amid a variety of other life changes (Simmons & Blyth, 1987). To assess adolescents' social-emotional functioning in terms of depressed symptomatology, we used a three-item scale that assessed the frequency of adolescents' feelings of unhappiness, sadness, depression, or loneliness. Items were derived from the SCL-90 and had good internal reliability (alpha ≥ 70).

We also examined indicators of two other types of change adolescents often experience. The early adolescent years are a time when peer cliques and the desire for acceptability and belonging become more salient. This shift

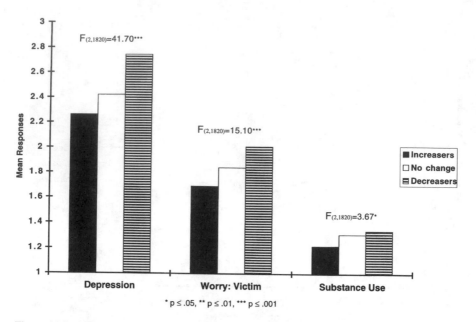

Figure 11.3. Adjustment at the end of seventh grade.

can have both positive and negative consequences (e.g., Brown, 1990; Fuligni & Eccles, 1993). We have focused on two possible negative consequences of an increased orientation toward peers: increased pressure for involvement in risky behaviors, such as drug or alcohol use (Elliott et al., 1989), and increased peer–peer violence and victimization (Simmons & Blyth, 1987).

In order to assess our hypothesis that individual differences in changes in self-esteem across the transition to junior high school are associated with corresponding differences in adjustment posttransition, a series of MANOVAs was conducted, with the adjustment indicators as dependent measures and self-esteem change group, achievement group, and gender as between-subject factors. Since these variables were not measured at Waves 1–3, we could not test for longitudinal change during early adolescence in these outcomes. The results of these MANOVAs are summarized here, and the means for the three significant self-esteem change group effects are illustrated in Figure 11.3. Consistent with previous literature (e.g., Elliott et al., 1989; Kazdin, 1993; Petersen et al., 1993), females reported more frequent depressive symptoms than males ($F[1, 1,820] = 75.6$, $p < .001$; eta-squared = .04). There were also main effects for achievement group for each of the three adjustment indicators: High achievers reported significantly fewer depressive symptoms ($F[1, 1,820] = 6.44$, $p < .01$; eta-squared = .003), less alcohol and drug use ($F[1, 1,820] = 26.4$, $p < .001$; eta-squared = .01), and less victimization ($F[1, 1,820] = 22.8, p < .001$; eta-squared $= .01$) than their low-achieving counterparts.

More central to the premise of this chapter, however, are the findings for the three self-esteem change groups. Individual differences in self-esteem change across the transition to junior high school were systematically related to group differences in depressive symptoms ($F[2, 1,820] = 41.7, p < .001$; eta-squared $= .05$), feelings of peer victimization ($F[2, 1,820] = 15.1, p < .001$; eta-squared $= .02$), and alcohol/drug/cigarette use ($F[2, 1,820] = 3.67, p < .03$; eta-squared $= .005$) at the end of seventh grade. Univariate one-way analyses were conducted to determine the precise nature of these group differences. Early adolescents who experienced a decrease in self-esteem across the junior high transition reported significantly more depressive symptomatology at the end of seventh grade than did those who experienced an increase in self-esteem across the transition. Adolescents whose self-esteem did not change across the transition reported fewer depressive symptoms than the decreasers and more symptoms than those whose self-esteem increased across the transition.

The picture was similar for the adolescents' reports of feeling victimized. Early adolescents who experienced an increase in self-esteem across the transition were significantly better off at the end of seventh grade than those whose self-esteem did not change across the transition. This latter group, in turn, reported less peer victimization than adolescents whose self-esteem declined across the transition from sixth to seventh grade.

The results for substance use were less marked but still statistically significant. Early adolescents who experienced an increase in self-esteem across the transition into seventh grade reported significantly less involvement in substance use relative to the other change groups. These results suggest that a positive change in self-esteem at the onset of junior high school may have a buffering or protective effect on the adolescent's substance use later during that year.

As one final indicator of social-emotional adjustment, we assessed whether adolescents across our SE Change groups differed in terms of their seventh-grade math teachers' rating of their psychological resourcefulness (tolerance for frustration, getting along with others, helping others with school work, etc.; see Appendix A for details) at both Waves 3 and 4. There was a significant SE Change group effect ($F[2, 1,820] = 12.5, p < .001$; eta-squared $= .01$). Students who experienced a drop in self-esteem across the transition to seventh grade were rated as significantly less resourceful in both the fall and spring of seventh grade than were those whose self-esteem increased or stayed the same across the transition.

Academic Adjustment at the End of Seventh Grade. Another aspect of adjustment we examined was students' level of engagement with school. Although the relations among academic motivation, achievement, and mental health during adolescence are not highly developed in the literature, given that school is a focal life arena for early adolescents, it is likely that academic engagement and achievement are critical to continued patterns of personal adjustment during this period of development (e.g., Maughan, 1988). School commitment and achievement can serve as protective factors against the emergence of negative outcomes that appear later in adolescence, such as problem behaviors, affiliation with negative peers, and mental health problems (Achenbach, Howell, Quay, & Conners, 1991; Compas, 1994; Cowen, 1991; Dryfoos, 1990; Rae-Grant et al., 1989). Conversely, academic underachievement and alienation in early adolescence are likely to be risk factors for later adjustment (e.g., Dryfoos, 1990; Cairns, Cairns, & Neckerman, 1989; Finn, 1989; Offord & Fleming, 1995; Owens, 1994).

For example, in a recent study of 1,500 adolescents and their families (Roeser, Lord, & Eccles, 1994), we found a strong association between school alienation, academic competence, motivation, and mental health during early adolescence. In this study, groups of adolescents were differentiated by their self-reports of alienation from academics (e.g., not liking school; devaluing the importance of a good education), school disengagement (e.g., belief that classes are boring, school is a waste of time), and behavioral alienation (skipping classes, failing a class). Relative to those seventh graders who were not alienated, the profile of measures that differentiated adolescents who were highly alienated from school included both adolescent self-reports and parent reports of lower academic values and ability self-concepts, lower self-esteem and less personal resourcefulness, and higher anger and depressive symptomatology. Highly alienated students also reported less social support, poor overall evaluations of the quality of their schools, and more negative teacher expectancies for them in school.

Another worrisome set of differences also distinguished the three groups: Relative to low-alienated students, high-alienated adolescents reported being involved in peer groups with more antisocial characteristics (e.g., involvement in drugs, vandalism, gangs, unprotected sex) and fewer prosocial characteristics (e.g., value school, good education). These findings are particularly troubling given evidence that adolescents who are alienated from conventional groups (e.g., school and family) often establish strong social bonds with antisocial peer groups in order to obtain a sense of belonging (see Elliott et al., 1989; Fuligni & Eccles, 1993).

Given the importance of school engagement for adolescents' future choices and options, as well as its relation to other domains of functioning, we wanted to assess how adolescents in each of the three self-esteem change groups differed in terms of their engagement with school. As an indicator of school disengagement, we used the adolescents' self-ratings of how frequently they had engaged in various disruptive or unethical behaviors at school during the previous 3 weeks (e.g., be verbally or physically harsh to another student,

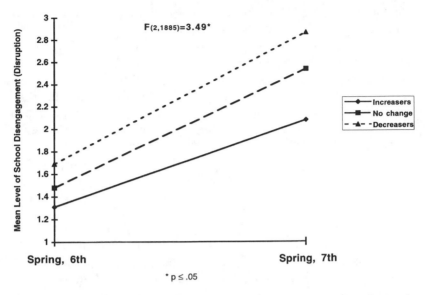

Figure 11.4. Time by self-esteem change group effect for school disengagement across the transition to junior high school.

vandalizing school property, disrupting class, and cheating – measured at the end of sixth and seventh grades). A repeated-measures MANOVA was conducted to determine whether there were differences between the change groups in terms of these indicators of the adolescents' engagement with school. Between-subject results indicated that there were change group, gender, and achievement main effects. In general, early adolescents whose self-esteem declined across the transition to junior high school exhibited greater school disengagement than did those whose self-esteem increased over the transition at both waves ($F[2, 1,820] = 10.7, p < .001$; eta-squared = .01). In addition, males and low achievers reported more school disengagement than females and high achievers at both waves ($p < .01$ in each case at each wave; eta-squared = .03 and .003, respectively).

More pertinent to our predictions, however, are the within-subject results. There was a significant time effect for school disengagement, as assessed at the end of sixth and seventh grades: In general, students became more disengaged from school over this time span. Pertinent to our predictions was the finding that the nature of this change depended on the pattern of change in adolescents' self-esteem. Students whose self-esteem increased across the transition to junior high school showed markedly smaller increases in their level of school disruption than did those whose self-esteem declined across the same transition. This pattern is presented in Figure 11.4. Positive adjustment to the junior high school transition may serve a protective role in the development of school problem behaviors, some of which seem to be fairly common during early adolescence (e.g., Offord & Fleming, 1995).

We found additional support for the risk/protective role of the self-esteem change across the transition and school behavior. SE Change group status was reliably associated with levels of truancy from school and end-of-year academic grades. Students who experienced a decrease in self-esteem across the transition also reported more truancy (i.e., skipped classes, skipped school) than those whose self-esteem either did not change or increased across the transition ($F[2, 1,820] = 6.50, p < .001$; eta-squared $= .01$). This change group effect was more pronounced for males than for females ($F[2, 1,820] = 2.98$, $p < .05$). Students whose self-esteem decreased across the transition also had lower mathematics grades than the SE Increasers ($F[2, 1,138] = 3.03, p < .05$; eta-squared $= .01$).

Summary. In summary, these results, which included multiple indices of functioning, lend support to our assertion that change in self-esteem across the transition to junior high school is a valid indicator of early adolescents' more general adjustment to this normative transition. Our change groups differed in predictable ways on several related indicators of adjustment, such that students who experienced a decline in self-esteem during this time also evidenced more negative patterns of adjustment in terms of their own reports of anxiety and mental health, their teachers' reports of their personal resourcefulness and ego resilience, their engagement with academics and behavior at school, and their academic marks.

Using these profiles of adjustment to the junior high school transition as a point of departure, we now turn to the question of the longer-term consequences of this adjustment to the transition. Does the direction of change in self-esteem across the transition to junior high school predict later adjustment? What are the short- and long-term sequelae of the transition to junior high school? Does the positive or negative transition to junior high school set the adolescent on a developmental trajectory, that is, does this transition serve as a protective purpose, or does it put the adolescent at risk for a trajectory toward maladaptive adjustment?

Long-term Sequelae of Individual Differences in Adolescents' Response to the Junior High School Transition

In this section, we address the issue of whether or not adolescents' adjustment to the junior high transition has long-term implications for their psychological and behavioral adjustment later in adolescence. To do this, we examine the association of our junior high self-esteem change groups with various indicators of social-emotional and behavioral adjustment in 10th and 12th grades. Approximately 900 of the students from the initial four waves of the study also provided us with data during their 10th- and 12th-grade years.[2] A series

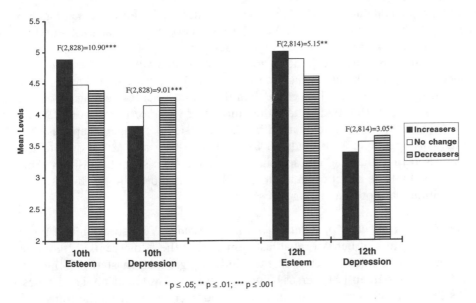

Figure 11.5. Adjustment during high school.

of MANOVAs were conducted using 10th- and 12th-grade self-esteem and depressive symptoms, and 12th-grade academic achievement and drug/alcohol use as dependent measures.

Implications of the Transition for Later Adjustment During High School

Social-Emotional Indices of Adjustment in 10th Grade. Consistent with our earlier findings and with existing literature, males reported significantly higher self-esteem ($F[1,828] = 11.5, p < .001$; eta-squared $= .01$) and fewer depressive symptoms ($F[1,828] = 102.7, p < .001$; eta-squared $= .11$) than females. But more pertinent to the central premise of this chapter, and consistent with our hypotheses, adolescents' social-emotional functioning depended on their junior high school self-esteem change group. As shown in Figure 11.5, adolescents whose self-esteem increased during the transition into junior high school reported significantly higher self-esteem in 10th grade than did those who had experienced a decline in self-esteem going into junior high (eta-squared $= .03$). Adolescents whose self-esteem had increased also reported significantly fewer depressive symptoms than those whose self-esteem had decreased (eta-squared $= .02$).

Social-Emotional Indices of Adjustment in 12th Grade. As was true in 10th grade, adolescents whose self-esteem had increased during the transition into junior high school reported significantly higher self-esteem (see Figure 11.5) in

12th grade than those who had experienced a decline in self-esteem going into junior high (eta-squared = .01). Females also reported lower self-esteem than males ($F[1,814] = 9.24$, $p < .001$; eta-squared = .01).

Similarly, as was true in 10th grade, adolescents whose self-esteem had increased during the junior high school transition reported significantly fewer depressive symptoms in 12th grade than those whose self-esteem had dropped (eta-squared = .01). In addition, the amount of variance in reported depressive symptoms that was explained by the self-esteem change group was substantially higher in 12th grade (8%) than in 10th grade (2%), despite the increased time that had elapsed since the junior high school transition. This suggests that the effect of an adolescent's response to the junior high school transition was not attenuating across time.

Behavioral Indicators of Adjustment in 12th grade. We also examined three main indicators of behavioral adjustment during the adolescents' 12th-grade school year: academic achievement, students' graduation status (being on track to graduate in 1990 versus being delayed), and use of alcohol and drugs. As expected, students whose self-esteem had decreased across the transition to 7th grade had significantly lower grade point averages (GPAs) in 12th grade than those whose self-esteem had increased ($F[2, 1,138] = 3.21$, $p < .05$; eta-squared = .01). In addition, there was a significant change group by gender interaction for 12th grade GPA ($F[2, 1,138] = 4.51$, $p < .01$; eta-squared = .01): Boys in the decreasing or no-change self-esteem groups had significantly poorer overall GPAs than girls in these groups.

Next, we examined whether or not students were on time in meeting their graduation requirements for their expected 1990 graduation date. Table 11.2 presents the numbers and percentages of students who did not graduate on time at the end of the 1990 school year. Some of these students eventually dropped out, entered alternative education programs, or graduated at some point after 1990. Chi-square analyses yielded a trend at the .10 level of significance for self-esteem change group membership by 12th-grade graduation status. Students in the declining self-esteem group, particularly those in the low-achiever group, were slightly overrepresented in the nongraduation group.

Next, we examined the substance use measures. Unlike the results for the psychological and academic variables, the patterns of associations involving drug and alcohol use were quite complex. We focus here on the one effect that is particularly intriguing given the issues outlined in this chapter: the result for drug use (see Appendix A for details on the measure). Several researchers now suggest that alcohol and drug use is a very complex behavior in adolescents. For some youth, it is linked with other indicators of problematic development; for others, it appears to be linked more with healthy exploratory behaviors (Maggs, chapter 13, this volume; Maggs, Almeida, & Galambos, 1995; Schulenberg et al., 1996). Our results suggest a similar complexity. As

Table 11.2. *Self-esteem change group cell numbers and nongraduation status during 12th grade by achievement group and gender*

Self-esteem change group	Number of students set to graduate at the end of the 1990 school year	Number of students not set to graduate at the end of the 1990 school year
Decreasers	304	32 (11%)
High achievement		
Females	97	4 (4%)
Males	57	3 (5%)
Low achievement		
Females	87	12 (14%)
Males	63	13 (21%)
Same	535	48 (9%)
High achievement		
Females	153	6 (4%)
Males	127	7 (6%)
Low achievement		
Females	135	13 (10%)
Males	120	22 (18%)
Increasers	358	21 (6%)
High achievement		
Females	102	3 (3%)
Males	99	3 (3%)
Low achievement		
Females	69	7 (10%)
Males	88	8 (9%)
Missing Data	1,787	

Note: Nongraduation status during the 1990 school year contains several categories, including students who dropped out, enrolled in an alternative program, or fell behind in meeting graduation requirements.

Note: Numbers in parentheses represent the percentage of students in each group who had valid data but who did not graduate from 12th grade on time.

pictured in Figure 11.6, we found a significant interaction between self-esteem change group and achievement level in predicting this substance use construct in 12th grade (eta-squared = .02). Among the low achievers, those whose self-esteem increased across the transition reported the most drug use. In contrast, among the high achievers, the decreasers reported the most frequent drug use. And in fact, this latter group stood out among all groups in terms of the frequency with which it reported drug use. Similar results were found for alcohol use, including a significant self-esteem change group by achievement level interaction ($F[2,756] = 4.07$, $p < .05$; eta-squared = .01). The high achievers who experienced a decline in self-esteem across the transition reported more frequent alcohol use than low achievers whose self-esteem had also declined during the transition. Within the low-achieving group, those

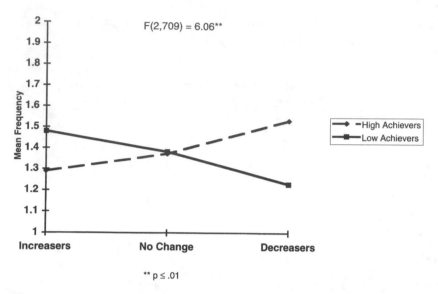

Figure 11.6. Achievement by self-esteem change group effect for 12th-grade drug use.

students whose self-esteem had decreased across the transition reported the least frequent use of alcohol during 12th grade.

Overall, among the low-achieving adolescents, those whose self-esteem increased during the transition to junior high school reported the most frequent use of alcohol and drugs in 12th grade. One possible explanation for this pattern of results is that these adolescents became increasingly disengaged from school and moved toward a pattern of peer affiliations characterized by the use of alcohol and drugs. This group of students may represent those who place more value on the increased social network of the junior high experience, gain feelings of self-worth more from these affiliations than from school, and become the "partiers" of the school. We are in the process of conducting further analyses to characterize more clearly the nature of this group of adolescents and their peer network.

The results for both high- and low-achieving students whose self-esteem decreased across the transition are a bit more complex. Post hoc analyses were conducted to explore the nature of the drug and alcohol use findings in more detail. We suspected that one explanation for differences in the substance use of the high- and low-achieving decreasers might lie in the sample distribution of students in these groups by the time they got to the end of high school. Indeed, chi-square analyses revealed an overrepresentation of high achievers in the decreasers group by 12th grade, based on the fact that a sizable proportion of the low-achieving decliners were not available for assessment at this time for a variety of reasons (enrolled in alternative programs, dropped out of school, fallen behind grade level, etc.).

Although such variation in attrition could account in part for this difference, it is also likely that the results for the high-achieving SE decreasers have substantive meaning as well. To explore this possibility, we ran several additional analyses to describe this group more fully. First, in order to see how different the high-achieving students whose self-esteem declined were from the other two groups of high achievers, we compared these three groups with each other on measures of mental health and grades in 12th grade. High-achieving adolescents in the SE decreaser group were significantly more depressed ($F[2, 507] = 5.6, p < .004$) than those in the SE increaser group and continued to have significantly lower self-esteem ($F[2, 507] = 8.2, p < .001$) than adolescents in both of the other two high-achieving groups. In contrast, these youth continued to have just as high grades as those in the other two groups (and higher than those of the low-achieving groups: $F[1, 182] = 48.3$, $p < .001$, eta-squared $= .21$). Next, we compared the high and low achievers within the SE decreasers group. These two groups differed only on their GPA (see the previous statistic), not on their self-reports of depression and self-esteem. Finally, we checked back to see if this group of high achievers had stood out in their drug and alcohol use at earlier waves, and found that they did not in the same manner as they did during 12th grade. This suggests that the higher rates of reported substance use among these adolescents may be unique to their situation in Grade 12.

In many ways, this high-achieving group of adolescents appears to have experienced quite negative consequences of their junior high school transition. Despite their high achievement in Grade 6 and their continued relatively high academic achievement throughout junior and senior high school, their self-esteem was undermined by the junior high school transition and remained low throughout their high school years. These students are now facing another major school transition: out of high school and potentially into college. Perhaps these prospects are particularly difficult for them psychologically, and they are turning to drugs and alcohol to cope with the associated stress. We are currently conducting further analyses to characterize the nature of these students' experiences more clearly and to discern patterns of continuity/discontinuity vis-à-vis a proclivity toward substance use. Furthermore, we are interested in understanding the developmental trajectories of the low-achieving, decreasing self-esteem adolescents who did not appear to use substances as much in the face of their difficulties. Further elucidation of the mechanisms involved in these processes could help guide the development of prevention and intervention strategies for this important area of concern in adolescence.

Conclusion

We began this chapter with a review of the evidence of a decline in school motivation and attachment during early adolescence. We outlined a theoretical perspective, the stage–environment fit perspective, for understanding how changes in school context might contribute to this decline. Stage–environment fit theory suggests that the fit between an individual's psychological needs and the opportunities afforded by the school environment (as well as other contexts) that serve to meet these needs influences an adolescent's motivation and attachment to the school. We focused on two specific psychological needs: (1) the increasing need for autonomy and participation in decisions regarding one's experiences and (2) the continuing need for strong social supports and close, trusting relationships with adults. For example, we argued that the perceived match between adolescents' desires for autonomy and democratic participation in decision making at home and in school is likely to decrease to the extent that these environments do not respond to these needs in a developmentally appropriate manner. Furthermore, we argued that adolescents who are not afforded opportunities for autonomy and decision making at home and in school at a level appropriate to their developmental stage are more likely to develop a negative view both of the particular social context and of themselves. Similarly, to the extent that the quality of social relationships with teachers deteriorate as young adolescents move into junior high school, the mismatch between their social needs and the opportunity for positive, healthy relationships with adults at school may increase, causing young adolescents to turn away from the adults in the school as a source of emotional support.

In the first section, we summarized the support we found for these hypotheses. In particular, we provided evidence of developmentally regressive changes in the school environments that many adolescents experience as they make the transition to junior high school, as well as the predicted negative impacts of these changes on aspects of adolescent development. Finally, we summarized findings suggesting that family and school environments that are responsive and developmentally sensitive to these changes in young adolescents' needs and desires can serve a protective function during the transition to junior high school.

In the second section, we focused on individual differences in adolescents' coping with the junior high school transition. Although this transition can be stressful for many adolescents, particularly those who experience developmentally regressive changes in the social context both at school and at home, many adolescents survive the transition quite well. Consistent with predictions based on both stage–environment fit theory, as well as with other research on risk and resilience (e.g., Jessor, 1993; Masten et al., 1988; Maughan, 1988), those adolescents who experienced good support for decision making at home, who felt that their parents respected them, and who had confidence in their academic and social skills adjusted best to the junior high school transition.

In the final section, we reported results related to the short- and long-term sequelae of the junior high school transition. The results provide consistent evidence that the self-esteem change experienced during the transition to junior high school is related to different subsequent developmental pathways. Although we have yet to investigate fully the processes that likely underlie these associations, the evidence is clear that the three SE Change groups we created are different from each other in consistent ways both at the end of 7th grade and later, in 10th and 12th grades. Adolescents who experience an increase in self-esteem as they make the junior high school transition report better psychological adjustment at the end of seventh grade and later, during their high school years, than those who experience a decrease in self-esteem in conjunction with the junior high school transition. These results are particularly interesting given the fact that these two groups of adolescents did not differ in self-esteem during the sixth-grade school year just prior to the junior high school transition. Our results provide compelling evidence that the junior high transition is a pivotal period for many young adolescents. In the future, we will explore what it is about these youth that make them differentially responsive to the junior high school transition, as well as the social-environmental experiences at home, with peers, and at school that may have contributed to the differing patterns of change in self-evaluation and personal adjustment during this critical life period. Finally, we plan to explore the processes that underlie the continuity across time in the differences we observed between these three groups of adolescents in order to develop recommendations for appropriate prevention and intervention programs.

Appendix A

*Scale Summaries and Sample Items**

Waves 1–4
Teacher-Rated Resourcefulness   *5 items, Alpha = .76*
(1 − rarely, 3 = often)
This student gives up when faced with a difficult academic problem or situation (R).
This student handles stress and frustration well.

Social Self-consciousness   *2 items, Alpha = .80*
(1 = not at all true of me, 4 = very true of me)
When I meet new people my age, I wonder what they'll think of me.

Math Anxiety   *5 items, Alpha = .85*
(1 = not at all nervous, 7 = very nervous)
Before you take a test in math, how nervous do you get?

Depressive Symptoms   *5 items, Alpha = .70*
(1 = never, 5 = very often)
How often do you feel unhappy, sad, or depressed?

Victimization   *2 items, Alpha = .55*
(1 = never, 5 = very often)
How often do you worry about getting picked on or beaten by other kids at school?

School Disruption   *5 items, Alpha = .79*
(0–12 or more times)
In the last 3 weeks at school, about how many times did you wise off and disrupt a class?

School Truancy   *3 items, Alpha = .71*
(0–12 or more times)
In the last 3 weeks at school, about how many times did you skip a class?
Since this past January, how many times have you not come to school when
you were supposed to?

Substance Use   *3 items, Alpha = .67*
(1 = never, 5= very often; 0–12 or more times)
How often do you drink alcohol or use illicit drugs outside of school?
In the last 3 weeks at school, about how many times did you bring alcohol or drugs to school?
(0–12 or more times)

Waves 5–6
Depressive Symptoms   *3 items, Alpha = .70*
(1 = never, 7 = daily)
How often do you feel unhappy, sad, depressed?

Drug Use   *4 items, Alpha = .75*
(1 = never, 7 = 21 or more times)
Think about the last 6 months. About how often in those 6 months did you do the things listed
below?
Bring alcohol or drugs to school
Sell drugs

Alcohol Use   *2 items, Alpha = .94*
(1 = never, 7 = 21 or more times)
Think about the last 6 months. About how often in those 6 months did you do the things listed
below?
Get drunk
Drink alcohol

---

*Alphas presented here are representative of the scale's reliability at each wave in which it was
measured. The alphas presented are taken from the first time of measurement that a particular
scale was assessed.

Notes

1 In the public school system in the United States, an intermediate school structure called *junior
   high school or middle school* exists between elementary schools that serve children and high
   schools that serve older adolescents. This school structure requires most early adolescents to
   make a transition into an intermediate school environment during their early adolescent years
   while they are also experiencing pubertal change.
2 The sample size is reduced in 10th grade because half of the school districts were eliminated
   from the study. This was due to a lack of sufficient funds to follow the entire sample into and

through high school. Districts that were eliminated during Wave 5 included a school district that had the greatest minority representation (primarily African Americans). Thus, minority students were underrepresented during Wave 5. However, in 12th grade, this demographically diverse district was again included in the sample. By reintroducing this district during Wave 6, there was no differential attribution or distortion of the sample due to community/demographic characteristics at this time.

References

Achenbach, T. M., Howell, C. T., Quay, H. C., & Conners, C. K. (1991). National survey of problems and competencies among four to sixteen year olds. *Monographs for the Society of Research in Child Development, 56*(3).

Aldous, J. (1977). Family interaction patterns. *Annual Review of Sociology, 3*, 105–135.

American Association of University Women (AAUW), (1992). *How schools shortchange girls. The AAUW report: A study of major findings on girls in education.* Washington, DC: American Association of University Women, Educational Foundation, National Education Association.

Bandura, A. (1986). The explanatory and predictive scope of self-efficacy theory. Special issue: Self-efficacy theory in contemporary psychology. *Journal of Social and Clinical Psychology, 4*(3), 359–373.

Blos, P. (1979). Modifications in the classical psychoanalytic model of adolescence. *Adolescent Psychiatry, 7*, 6–25.

Blyth, D. A., Simmons, R. G., & Carlton-Ford, S. (1983). The adjustment of early adolescents to school transitions. *Journal of Early Adolescence, 3*, 105–120.

Bohrnstedt, G., & Felson, R. (1983). Explaining the relations among adolescents' actual and perceived performances and self-esteem: A comparison of several causal models. *Journal of Personality and Social Psychology, 45*(1), 43–56.

Brophy, J. E., & Evertson, C. M. (1976). *Learning from teaching: A developmental perspective.* Boston: Allyn & Bacon.

Brown, B. B. (1990). Peer groups and peer culture. In S. S. Feldman & G. R. Elliott (Eds.), *At the threshold: The developing adolescent* (pp. 171–196). Cambridge, MA: Harvard University Press.

Brown, L. M., & Gilligan, C. (1992). *Meeting at the crossroads: Women's psychology and girls' development.* Cambridge, MA: Harvard University Press.

Cairns, R. B., Cairns, B. D., & Neckerman, H. J. (1989). Early school dropout: Configurations and determinants. *Child Development, 60*, 1437–1452.

Carnegie Council on Adolescent Development. (1989). *Turning points: Preparing American youth for the 21st century.* New York: Carnegie Corporation.

Collins, W. A. (1990). Parent–child relationships in the transition to adolescence: Continuity and change in interaction, affect, and cognition. In R. Montemayor, G. Adams, & T. Gullotta (Eds.), *Advances in adolescent development* (Vol. 2, pp. 85–106). Newbury Park, CA: Sage.

Compas, B. E. (1987). Coping with stress in childhood and adolescence. *Psychological Bulletin, 101*, 393–403.

Compas, B. (1994). Promoting positive mental health during adolescence. In S. G. Millstein, A. C. Petersen, & E. O. Nightingale (Eds.), *Promoting the health of adolescents: New directions for the twenty-first century* (pp. 159–179). New York: Oxford University Press.

Covington, M. (1992). *Making the grade: A self-worth perspective on motivation and school reform.* New York: Cambridge University Press.

Cowen, E. L. (1991). In pursuit of wellness. *American Psychologist, 46*, 404–408.

Crockett, L. J., Petersen, A. C., Graber, J. A., Schulenberg, J. E., & Ebata, A. (1989). School transitions and adjustment during early adolescence. *Journal of Early Adolescence, 9*, 181–210.

Dryfoos, J. G. (1990). *Adolescents at risk: Prevalence and prevention.* Oxford: Oxford University Press.

Eccles, J. S. (1983). Expectancies, values and academic behaviors. In J. T. Spence (Ed.), *The development of achievement motivation* (pp. 283–331). Greenwich, CT: JAI Press.

Eccles, J. S. (1993). School and family effects on the ontogeny of adolescents' interests, self-perceptions, and activity choice. In J. Jacobs (Ed.), *Nebraska symposium on motivation, 1992: Developmental perspectives on motivation* (pp. 145–208). Lincoln: University of Nebraska Press.

Eccles, J. S., Lord, S., & Midgley, C. M. (1991). What are we doing to adolescents? The impact of educational contexts on early adolescents. *American Journal of Education, 99,* 521–542.

Eccles, J. S., Lord, S. E, & Roeser, R. W. (in press). Round holes, square pegs, rocky roads, and sore feet: A discussion of stage–environment fit theory applied to families and school. In D. Cicchetti & S. L. Toth (Eds.), *Rochester symposium on developmental psychopathology, Vol. VII: Adolescence: Opportunities and challenges.* Rochester: University of Rochester Press.

Eccles, J. S., & Midgley, C. (1989). Stage/environment fit: Developmentally appropriate classrooms for early adolescents. In R. E. Ames & C. Ames (Eds.), *Research on motivation in education* (Vol. 3). New York: Academic Press.

Eccles, J., Midgley, C., & Adler, T. (1984). Grade-related changes in the school environment: Effects on achievement motivation. In J. G. Nicholls (Ed.), *The development of achievement motivation* (pp. 283–331). Greenwich, CT: JAI Press.

Eccles, J. S., Midgley, C., Buchanan, C. M., Wigfield, A., Reuman, D., & Mac Iver, D. (1993). Developmental during adolescence: The impact of stage/environment fit. *American Psychologist, 48,* 90–101.

Eccles, J. S., Miller-Buchanan, C., Flanagan, C., Fuligni, A., Midgley, C., & Yee, D. (1991). Control versus autonomy during adolescence. *Journal of Social Issues, 47*(4), 53–68.

Eccles J. S., Wigfield, A., Flanagan, C. A., Miller, C., Reuman, D. A., & Yee, D. (1989). Self-concepts, domain values, and self-esteem: Relations and changes at early adolescence. *Journal of Personality, 57*(2), 283–309.

Elkind, D., & Bower, R. (1979). Imaginary audience behavior in children and adolescents. *Developmental Psychology, 15,* 38–44.

Elliott, D. S., Huizinga, D., & Menard, S. (1989). *Multiple problem youth: Delinquency, substance use, and mental health problems.* New York: Springer-Verlag.

Epstein, J. L., & McPartland, J. M. (1976). The concept and measurement of the quality of school life. *American Educational Research Journal, 13,* 15–30.

Epstein, J. L., & McPartland, J. M. (1977). *Family and school interactions and main effects on affective outcomes* (Rep. No. 235). Baltimore: Johns Hopkins University, Center for Social Organization of Schools.

Feldlaufer, H., Midgley, C., & Eccles, J. S. (1988). Student, teacher, and observer perceptions of the classroom environment before and after the transition to junior high school. *Journal of Early Adolescence, 8,* 133–156.

Fenzel, L. M. (1991, April). *A prospective study of the relationships among role strain, self-esteem, competence, and social support in early adolescence.* Paper presented at the Biennial Meeting of the Society for Research in Child Development, Seattle.

Fenzel, L. M., & Blyth, D. A. (1986). Individual adjustment to school transitions: An exploration of the role of supportive peer relations. *Journal of Early Adolescence, 6,* 315–329.

Finn, J. (1989). Withdrawing from school. *Review of Educational Research, 59,* 117–142.

Flanagan, C, (1985, April). *The relationship of family environments in early adolescence and intrinsic motivation in the classroom.* Paper presented at the meeting of the American Educational Research Association, Chicago.

Flanagan, C. (1986, April). *Early adolescent needs and family decision-making environments: A study of person–environment fit.* Paper presented at the meeting of the American Educational Research Association, San Francisco.

Flanagan, C. (1989, April). *Adolescents' autonomy at home: Effects on self-consciousness and intrinsic motivation at school.* Paper presented at the meeting of the American Educational Research Association, Montreal.

Freud, A. (1969). Adolescence as a developmental disturbance. In G. Kaplan & S. Lebovici (Eds.), *Adolescence: Psychosocial perspectives* (pp. 5–10). New York: Basic Books.

Fuligni, A., & Eccles, J. S. (1993). Perceived parent–child relationships and early adolescents' orientation toward peers. *Developmental Psychology, 29,* 622–632.

Garmezy, N. (1983). Stressors of childhood. In N. Garmezy & M. Rutter (Eds.), *Stress, coping and development in adolescents* (pp. 43–84). New York: McGraw-Hill.

Grotevant, H. D. (1983). The contribution of the family to the facilitation of identity formation in early adolescence. *Journal of Early Adolescence, 3*(3), 225–237.

Hamburg, B. A. (1974). Early adolescence: A specific and stressful stage of the life cycle, In G. V. Coelho, B. A. Hamburg, & J. E. Adams (Eds.), *Coping and adaptation.* New York: Basic Books.

Harter, S. (1981). A new self-report scale of intrinsic versus extrinsic orientation in the classroom: Motivational and informational components. *Developmental Psychology, 17,* 300–312.

Harter, S. (1982). The perceived competence scale for children. *Child Development, 53,* 87–97.

Harter, S. (1985). Competence as a dimension of self-evaluation: Toward a comprehensive model of self-worth. In R. L. Leahy (Ed.), *The development of the self* (pp. 55–122). New York: Academic Press.

Harter, S. (1990). Developmental differences in the nature of self-representations: Implications for the understanding, assessment, and treatment of maladaptive behavior. *Cognitive Therapy and Research, 14,* 113–142.

Harter, S., Whitesell, N. R., & Kowalski, P. (1992). Individual differences in the effects of educational transitions on young adolescents' perceptions of competence and motivational orientations. *American Educational Research Journal, 29,* 777–808.

Hawkins, J. A., & Berndt, T. J. (1985). *Adjustment following the transition to junior high school.* Symposium paper presented at the Biennial Meeting of the Society for Research in Child Development, Toronto.

Higgins, E. T., & Parsons, J. E. (1983). Social cognition and the social life of the child: Stages as subcultures. In E. T. Higgins, D. W. Ruble, & W. W. Hartup (Eds.), *Social cognition and social development* (pp. 15–62). New York: Cambridge University Press.

Hill J. P. (1988). Adapting to menarche: Familial control and conflict. In M. Gunnar & W. A. Collins (Eds.), *Minnesota symposia on child development* (Vol. 21, pp. 43–77). Hillsdale, NJ: Erlbaum.

Hill, J. P., & Lynch, M.E. (1983). The intensification of gender-related role expectations during early adolescence. In J. Brooks-Gunn & A. C. Petersen (Eds.), *Girls at puberty: Biological and psychosocial perspectives.* (pp. 201–228). New York: Plenum.

Hirsch, B., & Rapkin, B. (1987). The transition to junior high school: A longitudinal study of self-esteem, psychological symptomatology, school life, and social support. *Child Development, 58,* 1235–1243.

Hunt, D. E. (1975). Person–environment interaction: A challenge found wanting before it was tried. *Review of Educational Research, 45,* 209–230.

Jessor, R. (1993). Successful adolescent development among youth in high-risk settings. *American Psychologist, 48,* 117–126.

Jessor, R., & Jessor, S. L. (1977). *Problem behavior and psychosocial development: A longitudinal study of youth.* San Diego, CA: Academic Press.

Johnston, L. D., O'Malley, P. M., & Bachman, J. G. (1994). *National survey results on drug use from the Monitoring the Future Study, 1975–1993.* Rockville, MD: National Institute on Drug Abuse.

Kavrell, S. M., & Petersen, A. C. (1984). Patterns of achievement in early adolescence. In M. L. Maehr (Ed.), *Advances in motivation and achievement* (pp. 1–35). Greenwich, CT: JAI Press.

Kazdin, A. E. (1993). Adolescent mental health: Prevention and treatment programs. *American Psychologist, 48*, 127–141.

Leahy, R. L. (1981). Parental practices and the development of moral judgment and self-image disparity during adolescence. *Developmental Psychology, 17*(5), 580–594.

Lee, P. C., Statuto, C. M., & Kedar-Voivodas, G. (1983). Elementary school childrens' perceptions of their actual and ideal school experience: A developmental study. *Journal of Educational Psychology, 75*, 838–847.

Lipsitz, J. (1981). Educating the early adolescent: Why four model schools are effective in reaching a difficult age group. *American Education, 17*, 13–17.

Lord, S., Eccles, J. S., & McCarthy, K. (1994). Risk and protective factors in the transition to junior high school. *Journal of Early Adolescence, 14*, 162–199.

Maehr, M. L., & Anderman, E. M. (1993). Reinventing schools for early adolescents: Emphasizing task goals. *Elementary School Journal, 93*, 593–610.

Maggs, J., Almeida, D. M., & Galambos, N. L. (1995). Risky business: The paradoxical meaning of problem behavior for young adolescents. *Journal of Early Adolescence, 15*, 339–357.

Masten, A. S., Garmezy, N., Tellegren, A., Pellegrini, D. S., Larkin, K., & Larsen, A. (1988). Competence and stress in school children: The moderating effects of individual and family qualities. *Journal of Child Psychology and Psychiatry, 29*, 745–764.

Maughan, B. (1988). School experiences as risk/protective factors. In M. Rutter (Ed.), *Studies of psychosocial risk: The power of longitudinal data* (pp. 200–220). New York: Cambridge University Press.

Midgley, C. (1993). Motivation and middle level schools. In P. R. Pintrich & M. L. Maehr (Eds.) *Advances in motivation and achievement: Motivation in the adolescent years* (Vol. 8, pp. 217–294). Greenwich, CT: JAI.

Midgley, C., Anderman, E., & Hicks, L. (1995). Differences between elementary and middle school teachers and students: A goal theory approach. *Journal of Early Adolescence, 15*, 90–113.

Midgley, C., & Feldlaufer, H. (1987). Students' and teachers' decision-making fit before and after the transition to junior high school. *Journal of Early Adolescence, 7*, 225–241.

Midgley, C., Feldlaufer, H., & Eccles, J. S. (1988a). Student/teacher relations and attitudes toward mathematics before and after the transition to junior high school. *Child Development, 60*, 375–395.

Midgley, C., Feldlaufer, H., & Eccles, J. S. (1988b). The transition to junior high school: Beliefs of pre- and post-transition teachers. *Journal of Youth and Adolescence, 17*, 543–562.

Midgley, C., Feldlaufer, H., & Eccles J. S. (1989). Change in teacher efficacy and student self- and task-related beliefs during the transition to junior high school. *Journal of Educational Psychology, 81*, 247–258.

Miller, C. L., Eccles, J. S., Flanagan, C., Midgley, C., Feldlaufer, H., & Harold, R. D. (1990). Parents' and teachers' beliefs about adolescents: Effects of sex and experience. *Journal of Youth and Adolescence, 19*, 363–394.

Minuchin, S., Rosman, B. L., & Baker, L. (1978). *Psychosomatic families: Anorexia nervosa in context.* Cambridge, MA: Harvard University Press.

Montemayor, R. (1986). Family variation in parent-adolescent storm and stress. *Journal of Adolescent Research, 1*, 15–31.

Moos, R. H. (1979). *Evaluating educational environments.* San Francisco: Jossey-Bass.

Nicholls, J. G. (1980, June). *Striving to develop and demonstrate ability: An intentional theory of achievement motivation.* Paper presented at a Conference on Attributional Approaches to Human Motivation, Center for Interdisciplinary Studies, University of Bielefeld, West Germany.

Nottelmann, E. D. (1987). Competence and self-esteem during the transition from childhood to adolescence. *Developmental Psychology, 23*, 441–450.

Office of Educational Research and Improvement. (1988). *Youth indicators 1988*. Washington, DC: U.S. Government Printing Office.

Offord, D. R., & Fleming, J. E. (in press). Child and adolescent psychiatry and public health. In M. Lewis (Ed.), *Child and adolescent psychiatry: A comprehensive textbook* (2nd ed.). Baltimore: Williams & Wilkins.

Owens, T. J. (1994). Two dimensions of self-esteem: Reciprocal effects of positive self-worth and self-deprecation on adolescent problems. *American Sociological Review, 59*, 391–407.

Paikoff, R. L., & Brooks-Gunn, J. (1991). Do parent–child relationships change during puberty? *Psychological Bulletin, 110*, 47–66.

Payne, B. D., Smith, J. E., & Payne, D. A. (1983). Grade, sex, and race differences in test anxiety. *Psychological Reports, 53*(1), 291–294.

Petersen, A. C., Compas, B. E., Brooks-Gunn, J., Stemmler, M., Ey, S., & Grant, K. E. (1993). Depression in adolescence. *American Psychologist, 48*, 155–168.

Rae-Grant, N., Thomas, H., Offord, D. R., & Boyle, M. H. (1989). Risk, protective factors, and the prevalence of behavioral and emotional disorders in children and adolescents. *Journal of American Academy of Child and Adolescent Psychiatry, 28*, 262–268.

Roderick, M. R. (1991). The path to dropping out among public school youth: Middle school and early high school experiences. *Dissertation Abstracts International, 52*, 1644–1645.

Roeser, R. W., Lord, S. E., & Eccles, J. S. (1994, February). *A portrait of academic alienation in early adolescence: Motivation, mental health and family indices*. Paper presented at the meeting of the Society for Reserach on Adolescence, San Diego.

Roeser, R. W., Midgley, C. M., & Maehr, M. L. (1994, February). *Unfolding and enfolding youth: A developmental study of school culture and student well-being*. Paper presented at the meeting of the Society for Research on Adolescence, San Diego, CA.

Rosenbaum, J. E. (1976). *Making inequality: The hidden curriculum of high school tracking*. New York: Wiley.

Rosenberg, M., Schooler, C., & Schoenbach, C. (1989). Self-esteem and adolescent problems: Modeling reciprocal effects. *American Sociological Review, 54*, 1004–1018.

Rutter, M. (1981). Stress, coping, and development: Some issues and some questions. *Journal of Child Psychology and Psychiatry, 22*, 323–356.

Rutter, M. (1995). *Psychosocial disturbances in young people: Challenges for prevention*. New York: Cambridge University Press.

Ryan, R. M., & Lynch, J. H. (1989). Emotional autonomy versus detachment: Revisiting the vicissitudes of adolescence and young adulthood. *Child Development, 60*, 340–356.

Schulenberg, J., O'Malley, P. M., Bachman, J. G., Wadsworth, K. N., & Johnston, L. D. (1996). Getting drunk and growing up: Trajectories of frequent binge drinking during the transition to young adulthood. *Journal of Studies on Alcohol, 57*, 289–304.

Simmons, R. G., & Blyth, D. A. (1987). *Moving into adolescence: The impact of pubertal change and school context*. Hawthorn, NY: Aldine de Gruyter.

Simmons, R. G., Burgeson, R., Carlton-Ford, S., & Blyth, D. A. (1987). The impact of cumulative change in early adolescence. Special issue: Schools and development. *Child Development, 58*, 1220–1234.

Steinberg, L. (1990). Autonomy, conflict, and harmony in the family relationship. In S. S. Feldman & G. R. Elliott (Eds.), *At the threshold: The developing adolescent* (pp. 255–276). Cambridge, MA: Harvard University Press.

Wigfield, A., Eccles, J. S., Mac Iver, D., & Reuman, D. A. (1991). Transitions during early adolescence: Changes in adolescents' domain-specific self-perceptions and general self-esteem across the transition to junior high school. *Developmental Psychology, 27*(4), 552–565.

Willig, A. C., Harnish, D. L., Hill, K. T., & Maehr, M. L. (1983). Sociocultural and educational correlates of success-failure attributions and evaluation anxiety in the school setting for Black, Hispanic, and Anglo Adolescents. *American Educational Research Journal, 20*(3), 385–410.

Yee, D. K. (1986, April). *Family decision-making, classroom decision-making, and student self-*

320   ECCLES, LORD, ROESER, BARBER, AND JOZEFOWICZ

and achievement-related attitudes. Paper presented at the meeting of the American Educational Research Association, San Francisco.

Yee, D. K. (1987, April). *Participation in family decision-making: Parent and child perspectives.* Paper presented at the meeting of the Society for Research in Child Development, Baltimore.

Yee, D. K., & Flanagan, C. (1985). Family environments and self-consciousness in early adolescence. *Journal of Early Adolescence, 5,* 59–68.

12 Transition Into Part-Time Work: Health Risks and Opportunities

Michael D. Finch, Jeylan T. Mortimer, and Seongryeol Ryu

Introduction

In prior generations, American youth typically had limited work experience prior to leaving school; when they did have paid jobs, their work was usually sporadic and informal, in the homes of neighbors, relatives, and friends. Youth sometimes held more formal jobs (in nonhousehold settings) during the summer months, but most did not do this kind of work when school was in session. In contrast, in the contemporary United States, almost all adolescents work at some time during high school. A recent national study (Manning, 1990) showed that 70% of 16- to 18-year-olds were employed during the preceding month; the median number of hours worked was 17.5. Bachman and Schulenberg's (1993) study of 71,863 high school seniors in the annual Monitoring the Future surveys showed that 75% of boys and 73% of girls did paid work; 47% of the employed boys and 38% of the employed girls worked more than 20 hours per week.

Though very little systematic research has focused on informal work or on summer jobs (Greenberger & Steinberg, 1981), there is an apparent consensus that these kinds of employment are not detrimental for youth; instead, they are viewed as rather salutary. Indeed, babysitting may be one of the most desirable teenage jobs (Greenberger & Steinberg, 1981; Mortimer, Finch, Shanahan, & Ryu, 1992a). Youth who do informal work in private households generally have considerable discretion over the number and scheduling of work hours; friendly and supportive relationships with employers, who are neighbors and sometimes family friends and relatives; and sometimes even permission to attend to other tasks, such as homework, while working. In contrast, formal work usually imposes firmer temporal constraints with respect to the total hours worked, as well as the scheduling of that time, and more formal employer–employee relations. In summer jobs, youth can benefit from all the work world has to offer – opportunities to learn about how to get and

The research described in this chapter was supported by a grant from the National Institute of Mental Health, "Work Experience and Mental Health: A Panel Study of Youth" (MH 42843).

keep a job; to earn and manage money; to build work-relevant interpersonal skills; and to gain knowledge about the kinds of jobs one likes and doesn't like – without interference with schoolwork.

Because this contemporary pattern of employment – formal jobs held during the school year – has elicited the most concern, we focus on the transition to this kind of part-time work in this chapter. What benefits or risks to adolescent health, or more generally, to healthy youth development, might derive from this transition? This question is complicated given the many potential implications of adolescent employment for a wide range of health-relevant outcomes.

In fact, the health benefits and costs of adolescent employment have been subject to considerable scrutiny, yielding divergent findings and much ensuing controversy. With some risk of oversimplification, this body of work can be divided into two general camps. In the first camp are those who conclude that working is good for youth. According to this view, employment in adolescence creates special opportunities for growth and development, which can potentially enhance health (particularly mental health). In the second camp are those who argue that teenage employment, particularly during the school year, is detrimental, especially when it occurs in large doses; therefore, hours of work should be strictly monitored.

In this chapter, we briefly review these two positions, evaluate the evidence, and then pose what we believe to be a third, more plausible, opinion on this issue: that the consequences of the transition to part-time work depend preeminently on its quality, its meaning, and the context in which it occurs. We argue that although some kinds of work indeed pose risks to health, for most employed adolescents work is a salutary experience. We summarize empirical evidence from the ongoing Youth Development Study (as well as other evidence) that supports this third point of view.

The Transition to Part-Time Work Is Beneficial

Consideration of adolescent health in a broad sense – including the developing self-concept and other dimensions of psychological well-being – raises sensitivity to many potentially health-enhancing consequences of the transition to part-time work. Working part-time during adolescence constitutes a transitional or in-between role location (Allen & van de Vliert, 1984, p. 13); the young person is no longer entirely out of the labor force but is still not yet a full-time worker whose economic support depends on the job. Part-time jobs provide experience with employment, but there are neither expectations of a long-term commitment nor extensive costs associated with inadequate performance or withdrawal from the work role.

The acquisition and successful maintenance of the work role is, of course, one of the most important markers of the transition to adulthood. It is the path to economic independence, as well as a major aspect of the identity of most adults. Almost all adolescent girls, as well as boys, expect to work during a substantial part of their adult lives. Thus, it might be argued that the role of future worker is a key component of the adolescent future "possible self" (Markus, Cross, & Wurf, 1990). Heightened self-awareness generally occurs in unfamiliar environments (Hormuth, 1984), and youth often find themselves in new work contexts, given the frequency of job changes in this initial phase of the work career. Such exposure to diverse work environments encourages thinking about self with respect to future occupational goals and reflection on issues of great significance for vocational development: "What kind of job would I like to have in the future?" and "What am I good at?" The adolescent may develop firm opinions about the kinds of jobs she or he likes and does not like, rendering the educational credentials necessary to move beyond the secondary labor market increasingly salient.

If this transition to part-time work signifies progress in moving toward the adult work role, clarifying both work values and preferences, one would expect it to have positive implications for mental health. The adolescent may also acquire skills on the job that, although seemingly mundane from the standpoint of the adult worker, may be highly salient for a young person: for example, the knowledge that one is able to find a job, meet supervisors' expectations, and accept responsibility. From this perspective, what is learned at work, even in a so-called menial job, is not inconsequential: how to relate to supervisors, cooperate with coworkers, deal with customers and clients, manage money, be on time, and even gain task-related skills that are transferable to other jobs (e.g., learning to use a cash register, keyboard, or computer).

Employed adolescents may learn to manage their time better so as to juggle effectively the multiple roles and responsibilities of worker, student, friend, and family member. They may realize that such conflicting responsibilities and time demands are pervasive in adult life. Their growing capacity to handle these circumstances in adolescence could promote a general sense of efficacy, a self-image of one who is able to meet the challenges of multiple adult roles (Elder & Caspi, 1990; Rutter, 1990). A positive self-concept and a sense of self-efficacy are important resources for coping with problems and risks in adolescence; thus, any enhancement of the adolescent self-image would constitute a significant ingredient in health maintenance (Hurrelmann & Losel, 1990).

Consistent with these considerations, public attitudes toward youth work are highly favorable. Several national task forces (Carnegie Council on Policy Studies in Higher Education, 1980; National Commission on Youth, 1980; Panel on Youth, 1974; Wirtz, 1975) have called for increasing adolescent involvement in the workplace. They point out that schools are detached from the real work of adulthood, restrict pupils to a limited range of occupational role models, and do not provide exposure to practical tasks necessary for the acquisition and successful performance of adult occupational roles. Most parents approve of the increasing autonomy and independence that derive from their adolescent children's employment (Phillips & Sandstrom, 1990). Parents see their children's jobs as providing opportunities to take responsibility and to manage their time more effectively.

There is, in fact, empirical evidence that employment can have positive consequences for youth. Although Greenberger and Steinberg's (1986) study of students in four California high schools generally emphasized negative consequences (as described later), they found that teenage employment was associated with self-reported punctuality, dependability, and personal responsibility (see also Greenberger, 1984; Steinberg, Greenberger, Garduque, Ruggiero, & McAuliffe, 1982) and with girls' self-reliance (Greenberger, 1984). Moreover, there is evidence that employment can have positive consequences for academic achievement. D'Amico's (1984) analysis of the National Longitudinal Study (NLS) youth data showed that employment at low intensity (fewer than 20 hours per week) lessened high school dropout rates. He argues that both employers and schools reward personality traits that promote achievement. Self-discipline, mobilization of effort, and application to a task are necessary even for marginal jobs (Snedeker, 1982). Moreover, adolescent part-time work has been found to have positive consequences for employment and income in the years following high school (see Steel, 1991; Stern & Nakata, 1989).

The Transition to Part-Time Work Is Detrimental

In the 1980s, as the findings of Greenberger and Steinberg's (1986) research became increasingly visible, the notion that adolescent work is good was replaced by the opposite stance: that work is bad, placing adolescents at risk with respect to their present health and development, as well as diminishing the likelihood of salutary future outcomes. In accord with this perspective, the predominant tone of much recent scientific commentary on youth employment is negative.

Why might working pose risks to health or to healthy development more generally? With respect to physical health risks, teenagers may be subject to particular hazards of work, such as dangerous machinery, noxious fumes, or excessive heat and cold (Parker, Carl, French, & Martin, 1994). Approximately 64,000 teenagers (aged 14–17) are injured on the job each year severely enough to require emergency room treatment (Associated Press, 1994). The American Public Health Association has recently voiced its concern to the U.S. Department of Labor that adolescents are exposed to potential occupational injuries when they work with deep fryers or grills, enter walk-in coolers and freezers, and lift heavy loads (Fernandez, 1994). Furthermore, adolescent job demands could increase susceptibility to disease. Adolescents who work long hours or at night may be vulnerable to exhaustion, chronic fatigue, and consequently lowered resistance to infections and other illnesses. Bachman and Schulenberg (1993), in their study of more than 70,000 Monitoring the Future respondents nationwide, found evidence that work intensity contributes to unhealthy lifestyles, including diminished sleep and a lack of exercise.

Greenberger and Steinberg (1986) stressed that young workers take on adult responsibilities prematurely, without adequate coping skills (Greenberger, 1983, 1988; see also Cole, 1980). Stressors on the job could pose risks to mental health, increasing strain and depressive affect, and could weaken the immune system. Greenberger (1988) notes that adolescent work sites are highly age segregated. Although youth workers have ample contact with their age-mates, relations with peer coworkers are often rather superficial, and the conditions of youth work may hamper the development of close, meaningful friendships. If working disrupts ongoing social relationships, such as ties to peers or bonds with parents, the consequent reduction in social support could likewise interfere with mental health and increase the risk of maladaptive behaviors (Gottlieb, 1991; House, Umberson, & Landis, 1988; Kessler, Price, & Wortman, 1985; Rutter, 1990; Turner, 1983).

Employment might also foster unhealthy behaviors outside the workplace. For example, relationships with older coworkers could introduce adolescents prematurely to substance use – more adultlike ways of handling stress or spending leisure time. Such use could pose immediate risks to health (e.g., automobile accidents linked to alcohol consumption) or lead to longer-term negative outcomes (e.g., alcohol addiction, cancer and other smoking-related diseases). Employment also provides the financial wherewithal to support these often costly, unhealthy habits.

Sometimes the risks of paid work are framed in terms of its opportunity costs. Greenberger and Steinberg (1986) warn that because work typically consumes so much time, adolescents risk losing a valuable "moratorium" period that should be available to explore alternative identities and interests and to develop close interpersonal bonds. Unlike many other role transitions, on the transition to part-time work, adolescents' former roles are not relinquished. Despite widespread approval of adolescent employment, school is still considered the most important "business" of the adolescent's life. In fact, much of the concern about youth work derives from a fear that working draws students away from school, promotes behaviors that interfere with learning, and reduces the investment in homework and academic achievement. A part-time job, coupled with a full school schedule and extracurricular activities, can produce role overload and consequent distress. High school students who work at night may more frequently be late for school in the morning and experience fatigue, which may interfere with their concentration throughout the school day. From the standpoint of health, given the importance of educa-tion (and social stratification position more generally) for multiple health outcomes (House et al., 1994), any detrimental implication that part-time work may have for educational attainment is a serious matter.

Those in the "work is bad" camp sometimes compare students who are working with those who are not employed; more typically, they examine differences between those who work more and fewer hours. Investigators (Bachman, Bare, & Frankie, 1986; Bachman & Schulenberg, 1993; Green-berger, 1984; Greenberger & Steinberg, 1986; Steinberg & Dornbusch, 1991; Steinberg, Greenberger, Garduque, Ruggiero, & Vaux, 1982) have linked decrements in adjustment to hours of work, finding that adolescents who work long hours are particularly prone to the use of cigarettes, alcohol, illicit drugs, and delinquency. Indeed, work may provide a new arena for delinquent (even criminal) acts, such as stealing from the cash register.

Employed adolescents have higher rates of school tardiness (Greenberger & Steinberg, 1986) and misconduct (Steinberg & Dornbusch, 1991) than those who are not employed; as hours of work increase, less time is spent doing homework (Greenberger & Steinberg, 1986). Several investigators observe negative associations between employment, or hours spent working, and grades (Finch & Mortimer, 1985; Lewin-Epstein, 1981; Marsh, 1991; McNeil, 1984; Mortimer & Finch, 1986; Steinberg & Dornbusch, 1991; Steinberg, Greenberger, Garduque, Ruggiero, & McAuliffe, 1982; Steinberg, Greenberger, Garduque, Ruggiero, & Vaux, 1982). However, the causal relationship between grade point average and employment is by no means clear.[1]

Whereas prior studies are for the most part cross-sectional, longitudinal data are considerably more useful in ascertaining whether diminished achievement and involvement in school are the antecedents or the conse-quences of employment. Using longitudinal data from a panel of California and Wisconsin high school students, Steinberg, Fegley, and Dornbusch (1993) compared students who entered the workforce with those who remained unemployed over a 1-year period. They found that nonworkers in Year 1 who entered the workforce in Year 2 earned lower grades and also spent less time on homework, had lower educational expectations, and expressed more disengagement from school at time 1 than those who remained nonemployed at both times. This pattern would support a selection argument. That is, students who are less interested, involved, or successful in school choose to enter the labor force, perhaps seeking a new domain in which to demonstrate competence.

Consistent with such selectivity, Bachman and Schulenberg (1993) suggest that a lack of success in school fosters youth employment, which may be one component of a syndrome of "pseudomaturity" or "precocious development" that precipitates a hastened transition to adulthood – early involvement in adultlike behaviors like drinking and smoking, as well as withdrawal from the more dependent, preadultlike student role.

Alternatively, poorer grades on the part of working students could be due to the influence of employment. However, Steinberg and his colleagues' (1993) assessment of change in grade point average, considered as a consequence of employment, yielded mixed findings. Among students employed 1–20 hours per week in Year 1, those who increased their hours (to 21 or more) had significantly lower grade point averages at Time 2 than those who became nonworkers the following year. (In these analyses, prior grade point average was controlled.) However, these students (employed 1–20 hours at Time 1) constituted just 28% of the panel. Among the remainder (those initially out of the labor force or working more than 20 hours per week), the pattern of employment (change or stability in the intensity of work) had no significant effects on grades.

The Consequences of the Transition to Part-Time Work Depend on the Quality of the Work Experience, Its Meaning, and the Context in Which It Occurs

We believe that both the "work is good" and the "work is bad" perspectives are simplistic. The literature that has just been briefly summarized pays scant attention to the quality of the adolescent work experience. Investigators compare working and nonworking adolescents or, more frequently, measure work experience solely in terms of its quantity: the number of hours worked per week. Adolescents select themselves into employment or are selected by employers; they work a given number of hours per week; and benefits or costs are observed. Investigators sometimes speculate about possible causal mechanisms. However, because little is known about what is actually occurring at work, employment is essentially a black box.

The findings of research on adults, if considered at all applicable to adolescents, dictate a very different approach. That is, the quality of adult work, particularly its complexity and self-directed character, has important implications for psychological functioning, the self-concept, and other indicators of mental health (Baker & Green, 1991; Johansson & Aronsson, 1991; Kohn & Schooler, 1983; Mortimer, Lorence, & Kumka, 1986). Similarly, stressors in the workplace are key determinants of physical health (Baker & Green, 1991). Given this pervasive pattern, we should examine the quality of adolescent work experience and consider its relationship to health-related outcomes.

It must be recognized, however, that what constitutes a quality work experience may be different for an adolescent and an adult. For example, unlike adults, adolescent novices to the workplace may need more direction and clarity of instruction. To new workers, autonomy may be somewhat frightening, given their lack of experience and skill. Shanahan, Finch, Mortimer, and

Ryu (1991), in fact, report that decision-making autonomy in youth jobs is significantly associated with youth distress.

In a notable exception to the dearth of research on the quality of adolescent work, Schulenberg and Bachman (1993), using data collected over a decade from Monitoring the Future cohorts, report a series of interactions between work intensity and work quality in affecting health outcomes. That is, students suffered when they worked in poor-quality jobs for long periods of time. Poor-quality jobs included those that did not make use of their talents, were unconnected to anticipated future jobs, and were being done only for the money. In addition, Schulenberg and Bachman report many direct benefits of high-quality work experience in terms of reduced substance use and other health outcomes.

Furthermore, the broader meaning and social context of working must be taken into account. How do the adolescent's significant others view the work role? Is employment seen as something that will benefit the family collectively or is it only a source of individual reward? Are parents critical of the adolescent for wasting earnings on designer jeans, admiring of their offspring's diligence in saving for college, or grateful for the youth's contributions to the family coffer? Marsh (1991) reports positive effects of employment on grades, but only when the worker is using earnings to save for college. Marsh's finding suggests that much depends on the social meaning of adolescent work. When there is high academic involvement and a clear linkage between earnings and future educational attainment, work may even be educationally beneficial.

There is evidence from the Depression era that adolescents in economically deprived families, who contributed to the family economy by paid work, gained a sense of self-confidence and efficacy from helping their families at a time of crisis (Elder & Rockwell, 1979). The positive mental health and subsequent socioeconomic attainment of these young people were attributed to these early helping experiences; caring for others is often thought to be developmentally beneficial (Garmezy, 1988; Hetherington, 1989; Werner, 1984; Werner & Smith, 1982). Similarly, Shanahan and Elder (1993) found that in economically hard-pressed farm settings of rural Iowa, relationships with parents actually improved when sons had higher earnings.

Bachman (1983) raises the specter of "premature affluence" that derives from large amounts of disposable income at a time when most basic expenses are being taken care of by parents. He questions whether adolescents can learn realistically about the uses and value of money when much of their income is being spent rather frivolously. However, he presents data indicating that the majority (62%) of students who plan to complete 4 years of college save at least some of their earnings for this purpose, and almost half give at least some money to help pay family living expenses. These uses of earnings suggest salutary contextual meanings of work.

An extensive literature documents the mental health benefits of multiple roles in adulthood (Thoits, 1983). Multiple roles provide access to social contacts, diverse activities, and opportunities to cope with challenging problems and tasks. The social support and confidence gained from these experiences can constitute important resources in dealing with future stressors. Moreover, given the stressors that exist in any role or social context, social support and positive experiences derived from other contexts can enable more effective coping. If distress is prevented or alleviated, the likelihood of disease diminishes. In the same way, adolescent work could also function as an "arena of comfort" (Simmons, in press) when there are family disruptions or problems in school.

Evidence from the Youth Development Study

The findings to be reported were obtained from a 4-year study (1988–1991) of the effects of work experience on adolescent mental health and development. The panel was chosen randomly from a list of ninth graders enrolled in the St. Paul (Minnesota) School District. Consent to participate was obtained from 1,139 parents and 1,139 adolescents who constituted 64% of eligible cases. (Eligibility to participate in the study was defined by enrollment in the school district at the time of the initial data collection and by the absence of disabilities that would prevent the completion of a questionnaire.)[2]

The 64% response to the letter of invitation is problematic because those who decided to participate in the study could be systematically different from those who refused. For example, more highly educated parents could be more positively disposed to research of this kind. To investigate this possibility, a probit analysis (using LIMDEP; Greene, 1992) of the decision to participate was conducted, with neighborhood socioeconomic context indicators obtained from census tract tapes and other variables obtained from school records assigned to each case as predictors (Finch, Shanahan, Mortimer, & Ryu, 1991). Girls were more likely to participate than boys (there are 476 boys and 524 girls in the general sample), and older students (i.e., older than their ninth-grade peers) were less likely to be in the study. Most important, no socioeconomic contextual variables predicted participation. We conclude that the initial sample well represents the student body in the St. Paul public schools. (For further information about the sample, see Mortimer et al., 1992a.)

Self-administered questionnaires were distributed in school classrooms each year (Grades 9–12); those students who were not present for either of two scheduled administrations (and those who were not attending school, e.g., 10% in Wave 4) had questionnaires mailed to their homes, using procedures recommended by Dillman (1983). Of the initial 1,000 participants, 93% were retained over the 4-year period (that is, 93% of those who participated in

Table 12.1. *Work status, type of work, and hours of work by grade and gender*

	Grade 9	Grade 10	Grade 11	Grade 12
	Boys/Girls	Boys/Girls	Boys/Girls	Boys/Girls
Employed	40% 63%	42% 52%	53% 63%	58% 70%
Workers in formal employment	65% 28%	91% 66%	97% 87%	97% 94%
Hours worked				
Median	7.5 9.5	20.0 15.0	20.0 18.0	20.0 20.0
Mean	11.3 11.5	19.6 15.8	21.9 18.6	21.8 19.8
SD	9.7 8.8	10.8 8.3	9.9 8.5	10.6 9.2

Wave 1 also completed surveys in Wave 4). Questionnaire data were also obtained during the first wave from parents of 96% of the adolescent participants. Information concerning family socioeconomic background was obtained directly from the parents.

The Transition to Formal Work

Table 12.1 shows the percentage of employed students, the percentage holding formal jobs, and the hours worked by gender and high school year. Because all four surveys took place during the school year, these numbers reflect the contemporary pattern of working while school is in session. In each year, the majority of girls report employment, defined here as work that takes place outside the adolescent's own home at least once a week for pay. The majority of boys are working by the 11th grade. Only 35% of boys held informal employment in the ninth grade compared to 72% of the employed girls, most of whom worked in private households as babysitters. The figures thus indicate the timing of the transition from informal to formal work rather clearly for girls, whereas boys' employment was heavily formal even in the first wave of the study. By Grade 10, almost two-thirds of the employed girls held formal jobs. In fact, the decline in girls' total employment rate between Waves 1 and 2, from 63% to 52%, could be due to the difficulties that some girls experience in moving from informal to formal work. By the 12th grade, practically all employed boys and girls are working in formal settings.[3]

It is interesting to speculate on the reasons that precipitate the move to formal employment, particularly for girls. An obvious consideration is the earnings advantage; for example, 10th-grade girls who continued to do babysitting (or other informal work) earned, on the average, $2.79 per hour; those who moved into the formal workplace had mean earnings of $4.28 per hour. Of course, formal work is also more adultlike and may therefore be more attractive, aside from its greater profitability. Moreover, it is likely that widely

Boys

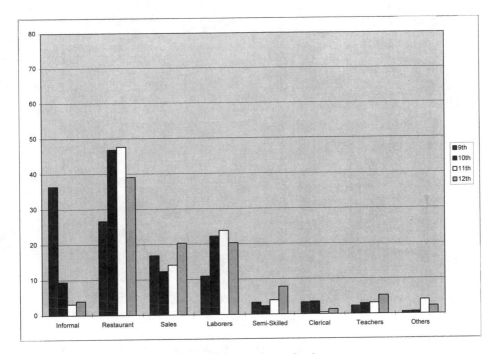

Figure 12.1a. Percentage distributions of job types by gender: boys.

held norms govern the shift. Given that job change often necessitates some period of search, girls' dip in employment between Waves 1 and 2 could be attributed to the plight of girls who are considered too old for babysitting but cannot readily find formal work.

However, it is also possible that parents monitor adolescent girls' activities more closely than those of boys, and that some are reluctant to give permission to their 10th-grade daughters to do more adultlike work that may entail threats to their well-being (like working at night, locking up stores, etc.). Given the limitations of the data, we cannot determine the microdynamics of these intriguing employment changes.

As they go through school, students report substantial, and increasing, hours of work; 9th-grade boys worked 11.3 hours per week on the average and 21.8 hours per week in the fourth wave; boys exhibited a large increase in work hours between the 9th and 10th grades. The corresponding mean hours for girls are 11.5 and 19.8 in Waves 1 and 4, with girls showing more gradual increments in work hours over time. By the fourth wave, about one-fourth of the panel worked more than 20 hours per week.

As shown in Figure 12.1a and b, the character of adolescent work also changes over time, with informal work prominent in Year 1, concentration in

Girls

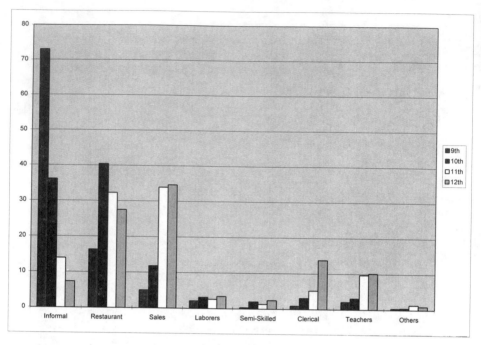

Figure 12.1b. Percentage distributions of job types by gender: girls.

restaurant work in Years 2 and 3, and then greater dispersion across various types of jobs in Year 4.

The changing pattern of involvement in restaurant work, the archetypal teenage job in the United States, is especially noteworthy. Almost half of the employed 10th-grade boys and 40% of the girls perform this kind of work. However, by the 11th grade, only a little more than a quarter of girls continue to be employed in restaurants; boys show a similar but somewhat delayed trend. Although Figure 12.1 presents aggregate data, not the progression of individual careers, this pattern suggests trends in adolescent employment. High school youth are not stuck in fast-food jobs, but rather move into and then out of them. Other analyses show that youth work also becomes more complex, involving more training and greater supervisory responsibility as young people move through high school (Mortimer, Finch, Dennehy, Lee, & Beebe, 1994).

Because detailed analyses relevant to the question of whether work is good or bad for adolescent health have been published (Finch et al., 1991; Mortimer et al., 1994; Mortimer, Finch, Shanahan, & Ryu, 1992a, 1992b; Mortimer & Shanahan, 1994; Mortimer, Shanahan, & Ryu, 1993; Shanahan et al., 1991) or are under review (e.g., Mortimer, Finch, Ryu, Shanahan, & Call, 1996), we only summarize the findings here. We have utilized various measures of work experience, comparing students on the basis of their work status (employed or not), the hours they worked at each wave, their cumulative work involvement (in formal jobs over the entire 4-year period of high school), and, finally, the quality of their work experience at each time of measurement. We have examined a range of health-related outcomes, including indicators of self-concept and mental health (self-esteem, self-efficacy, and depressive affect), involvement in school (grade point average, time spent doing homework), behavioral adjustment (frequency of alcohol use and smoking), educational and occupational aspirations, and measures of the quality of the adolescent's relationships with parents and peers.

We have taken a variety of analytic approaches, estimating ordinary least squares regressions (controlling important background variables as well as the lagged outcomes), more complex structural equation models, and fixed effects models (Mortimer & Finch, 1994). Although we have not examined all work features and health outcomes, we can bring a considerable amount of evidence to bear on the question at issue. That is, what have we learned from these analyses about the impact of the transition to part-time work on adolescents' health and well-being?

Comparisons of Workers and Nonworkers

We find virtually no differences, considering a wide range of outcomes, between students who work and those who do not at any wave. The consistent pattern of null findings with respect to work status supports the conclusion that working per se is neither beneficial nor harmful with respect to the healthy development of youth (Mortimer, Finch, et al., 1996).

Assessment of the Effects of Work Intensity, Measured Each Year

We obtained yearly measures of the intensity or amount of work at the time of each survey administration: operationalized as dummy variables indicating high-intensity (more than 20 hours per week) and low-intensity (20 or fewer hours) employment. The reference category in these analyses consisted of nonworking youth. Intensity of work bore no consistently significant relationship to measures of adolescent mental health, homework time, academic achievement, or relationships with parents and peers (Mortimer, Finch, et al., 1996; Mortimer & Shanahan, 1991, 1994; Mortimer et al., 1993). Apparently, contrary to the notion that work time functions as an opportunity cost with respect to more educationally beneficial activities, adolescents in the Youth Development Study who worked fewer hours did not choose to invest their extra time in homework activity.

However, in a highly stringent analysis incorporating relevant controls (e.g., socioeconomic background, race, family composition) as well as the lagged outcome, we found that 10th- and 11th-grade students who worked at higher intensity did engage in more alcohol use (Mortimer, Finch, et al., 1996). But by the senior year, because alcohol use had become quite stable, controlling the lagged variable (measured 1 year previously) rendered the effect of work hours on the frequency of drinking statistically nonsignificant. Consistent with the selection argument that characteristics of the person determine the level of involvement in employment, prior alcohol use in each year (Waves 9, 10, 11) significantly predicted the number of hours worked in the following year. But selection did not explain the effect of more intensive work; the effects of work hours on alcohol use were manifest even when the lagged dependent variable (alcohol use measured 1 year previously) was controlled. Considering the congruence of the findings of the Youth Development Study, Steinberg's research (Steinberg & Dornbusch, 1991; Steinberg et al., 1993), and Bachman and Schulenberg's (1993) large-scale study, the linkage between working long hours and alcohol use appears to be one of the most robust findings on this subject. However, the contention that work intensity influences mental health, academic achievement, and cigarette smoking did not withstand the extensive controls applied in these analyses.

Assessment of Cumulative Work Intensity Over a 4-Year Period

Measures of work intensity used in prior studies generally assess investment in work at a single time only (D'Amico, 1984; Schill, McCartin, & Meyer, 1985; Steinberg & Dornbusch, 1991) or on two or more occasions, considered serially (Mortimer, Finch, et al., 1996; Steinberg et al., 1993). Such studies do not capture the variability in work investment over a period of time. But usually youth move into and out of the labor force over the course of a year. Even among those whose labor force participation remains stable, job hours are likely to change. As a result, work intensity at any given time may be a quite fallible indicator of involvement over a longer duration. Therefore, we examined cumulative work intensity, measured over the entire high school period.

In annual surveys commencing in February of the 9th, 10th, 11th, and 12th grades, we asked students for a detailed list of their work obligations throughout the previous year. We compiled these data into monthly summaries of the cumulative hours worked in both informal and formal jobs. In analyzing the effects of cumulative work on health outcomes, we used the number of hours spent in formal work during each of 3 school years (omitting ninth-grade data given the concentration of the younger students in informal work) and the number of hours spent in formal work during the summers. That is, from continuous monthly data files, we computed the number of hours worked each school year and summer prior to our measures of mental health, which were obtained toward the end of the school year (February to June).

When examined in the context of ordinary least squares models, neither during the school year nor during the summer did cumulative formal work hours manifest significant effects on three dimensions of mental health: self-esteem, self-efficacy, and depressive affect (Mortimer & Finch, 1994). But consistent with the "work is bad" school of thought, cumulative formal work during the school year had a significantly negative effect on grade point average; work during the summer had a significantly positive effect on grades (Finch, Mortimer, & Ryu, 1994). Cumulative work during the school year also had a significantly positive effect on the frequency of alcohol use and smoking.

In summary, our investigation of the effects of work intensity, or the amount of time students spend working, on mental health outcomes has yielded many null findings. With respect to behavioral adjustment, we find consistent evidence that more intensive work promotes alcohol use. Our studies of achievement (grade point average) are inconsistent; they yield null findings (when hours of work are measured each year) and negative findings (when hours of work are measured cumulatively). Let us now turn to the quality of adolescent work, that is, to the character of the tasks adolescents work on, the nature of their interpersonal relationships on the job, and their own accounts of their experiences.

Effects of the Quality of the Work Experience on Adolescents' Health Outcomes

We find that employed adolescents who have opportunities for advancement, who perceive little conflict between school and work, and who feel that they are paid well (thus, appreciated by their employers) increase in self-efficacy over a 1-year period (Finch et al., 1991). However, when they experience problems on the job – for example, time pressure, overload, or conflicts between school and work – they express more depressive affect over time (Shanahan et al., 1991). Given that analyses demonstrating these effects incorporated numerous controls as well as lagged variables, we have considerable confidence that the quality of work does matter for adolescent mental health. Moreover, we have found evidence that when boys have work that involves mastery of new skills, the quality of their relationships with their parents and their peers improves over time (Mortimer & Shanahan, 1991, 1994). Moreover, the opportunity to learn skills on the job has positive implications for occupational value formation. Employed adolescents with this opportunity became more aware of the variety of rewards that work has to offer, affecting both intrinsic and extrinsic value dimensions (Mortimer, Pimentel, Ryu, Nash, & Lee, 1996). Employed girls with opportunities to help others on the job manifested a stronger sense of self-efficacy over time (Call, Mortimer, & Shanahan, 1995).

A recently completed doctoral dissertation (Call, 1994) demonstrates that "comfort" in the work environment (as indicated by good relationships with supervisors, absence of stress, etc.) moderates (alleviates) the detrimental effects of discomfort with parents (strain in parent–adolescent relationships) on mental health. Interestingly, a substantial minority of the employed students (more than one-third each year) reported that they were "Quite Close" or "Very Close" to their supervisors and that the supervisor was "Often" or "Always" willing to listen to problems and help find solutions. When the adolescent lacked supervisory support at work, discomfort in the parent–child relationship diminished self-esteem, mastery, and the sense of well-being. However, when support from the supervisor was present, such discomfort had no significant effects on these mental health outcomes. Similarly, under conditions of high work stress (e.g., time pressure, overload, excessive heat, cold, or noise), change in the father's employment status diminished adolescent self-esteem; this change in the family context had no significant effect when there was little work stress.

If the quality of work is so important, it becomes crucial to know to what extent adolescents actually have high- or low-quality jobs. Contrary to the report of Greenberger and Steinberg (1986), we find much evidence that the character of adolescent work is, for the most part, not a cause for concern. Most of our job quality indicators are positively skewed. For example, only a minority of employed students feel that their jobs do not provide them with "a chance to learn new things" (16%) or challenges (19%), place them under time pressure (31%), or subject them to role conflict (22%). By contrast, 70% report that it is "somewhat" or "very true" that the job "gives me a chance to be helpful to others"; 65% say they are "never" or "rarely" held responsible for things that are outside their control. Only 9% say that their pay is not good, and 71% believe that they can keep their jobs as long as they want. Moreover, as mentioned earlier, adolescents' jobs become increasingly complex, as indicated by U.S. Department of Labor (1977, 1986) *Dictionary of Occupational Titles* ratings, involve increasingly lengthy training, and involve more supervisory responsibility as adolescents move through school (Mortimer et al., 1994). Overall, the perceptions of the students themselves do not indicate wholesale dissatisfaction with work or widespread exposure to detrimental work environments. In fact, they are quite satisfied with their jobs.

Discussion

On the basis of our data, we do not dispute the fact that working, in some circumstances and with respect to certain outcomes, may be bad for adolescents. When considering whether work is good or bad, we believe it is important to specify what outcomes are at issue. In some respects, there is congruence between our findings and the findings of those who are most squarely in the "work is bad" camp – Steinberg, Dornbusch, Greenberger, and their collaborators: We both find that long hours of work foster alcohol use, and this is certainly cause for concern.

We would also like to draw attention to another kind of congruence: the numerous null findings both in our research and in the research of investigators in the "work is bad" camp. For example, Steinberg et al. (1993) report that once initial distress levels were taken into account, there were no differences in adolescent distress related to the work history, that is, to increases or decreases in working hours (or movement into and out of employment) over the 1-year period of study. Similarly, we find no effect of work hours on depressive affect in any year and no effect of cumulative work hours, measured over the entire period.

In Steinberg et al.'s (1993) longitudinal analyses (over a 1-year period), significant differences in mental health indicators were associated with the work career pattern only in particular subgroups; they did not occur across the board. For example, they found that among students who were *not employed* at Time 1, those who were working more than 20 hours per week at Time 2 scored significantly lower on self-esteem at Time 2 than previously non-employed peers who were working 20 or fewer hours per week at Time 2. Self-reliance exhibited a nearly significant tendency in the same direction. Still, for those students who were employed in the first wave of their study, neither increase nor decrease in work intensity bore a significant relationship to self-esteem or self-reliance. Steinberg and his colleagues' (1993) analyses of academic achievement yielded a similar mixed pattern.[4]

In fact, only 15 of 54 contrasts (27.8%) that Steinberg et al. (1993) make between their employment history groups yield statistically significant differences, a rate that is better than chance but not a basis for a wholly convincing argument that work is bad. Steinberg et al. choose to emphasize the detrimental effects of work. However, if high levels of work are really so harmful, shouldn't increases in working hours have a more pervasive detrimental influence?

Furthermore, there is room for difference in interpretation even when findings across studies are essentially the same. For example, both the Youth Development Study (Mortimer & Shanahan, 1994) and Steinberg et al.'s (1993) research indicate that youth become more independent of parents when they work more hours. Steinberg and his colleagues view this as an ominous trend – raising the specter of employed students lacking parental supervision and out of control. We find that both parents and adolescents agree that working makes students more independent of their families. But the parents in our study view this as a very good thing (Phillips & Sandstrom, 1990). Surely, acquiring independence from parents is a normal developmental task in adolescence, one that may be hastened by part-time work.

It should be noted that our study is mute with respect to many presumed outcomes that have been linked to adolescent work. Restrictions imposed by school officials prevented us from investigating the effects of working on deviant and illegal behaviors. Thus, we do not know whether paid work fosters serious risks to health and well-being among the Youth Development Study participants: use of illegal drugs, juvenile delinquency, and problems with the law.

As we see it, the strongest evidence in support of the "work is bad" argument lies in the area of substance use, particularly alcohol, which is now the drug of choice for adolescents and an important "gateway" drug, preceding more socially unacceptable drug involvement (Kandel, 1989; Wagenaar & Perry, 1994). Correlational evidence also strongly links intensive paid work to illegal drug use (Bachman & Schulenberg, 1993); longitudinal data would provide an even more powerful basis for this linkage. What needs to be addressed now is whether these correlates of employment are transitory or persistent. Although adolescents who work more intensively are found to engage in more alcohol use, does this signify only earlier onset, a premature acquisition of adultlike leisure time behavior, or do those who worked (and drank) more in adolescence continue to be heavier drinkers as adults? Is more frequent alcohol use a short-lived reaction to stress entailed by initial acquisition of the work role and the new responsibilities (and, perhaps, overloads) it involves, a response that lessens over time as youth acquire more confidence and experience in the new role? Or does early youthful drinking among the more intensive workers signify the onset of a lifelong pattern of greater substance use? We will be able to address these questions in future waves of the Youth Development Study.

Because most studies to date have drawn information about youth jobs from self-reports, it is difficult to separate the objective work situation from individual reactions to it. Information about work from supervisors and employers would be very useful in this regard. Comparative studies of selected workplaces would also be instructive. Whereas prior research has investigated aggregate effects of work on adolescent health outcomes, it would be useful in the future to examine whether youth have different responses to their jobs depending on prior expectations, achievement orientations, family background, or other factors that are external to the work situation.

It would also be worthwhile to extend the array of health outcomes under consideration. In our research, mental health benefits and detriments are emphasized; the Monitoring the Future research program has given considerable attention to healthy lifestyle factors (such as exercise, sleep, and nutrition). Further studies might assess whether adolescent workers are more prone to infectious illnesses or other minor health complaints, such as headaches or intestinal disorders, which might decrease the regularity of their school attendance.

An additional task for future research is to assess the long-term implications of adolescent work for adult socioeconomic outcomes that are likely to affect future health. It is generally accepted that prior anticipatory socialization, providing an opportunity to learn and practice future roles, is a good predictor of successful role adaptation at a later time (Mortimer & Simmons, 1978). But in fact, we do not yet know whether the transition to part-time work in adolescence constitutes a valuable or even necessary anticipatory socialization experience with respect to the future adult work role. The answer to this question may again depend on the quality of work, as indicated by Stern and Nakata's (1993) finding that skill utilization in adolescent work predicts success in the job market during the first 3 years after graduating from high school. When further information becomes available from the Youth Development Study, we will be able to examine the extent to which working in adolescence or differences in the quality of youth work predict subsequent differences in the acquisition of, and effective coping with, full-time work.

Although we focus here on the consequences of the transition to part-time work, it might be worthwhile to consider the consequences of not working at all or having only minimal involvement in work (e.g., only occasional babysitting) during the high school years. Research on unemployed adults emphasizes that they lack a valuable arena for the development of skills, an important outlet for the exercise of physical and mental energy, a source of social contacts, the temporal structuring of the day that work provides, and a major locus of personal identity (Warr, 1984). Although they would not likely suffer all of these losses, students who do not work may violate widely held expectations on the part of parents and peers, be more financially dependent on their parents (and perhaps emotionally dependent as well; see Shanahan et al., 1991), and miss out on valuable anticipatory socialization experiences with respect to the adult work role. They would miss the opportunity to test a role that is an integral part of the adult "possible self."

Given these considerations, the fact that minority teenagers are less likely to be employed than White youth may create additional disadvantage in an already discriminatory labor market (Bachman & Schulenberg, 1993; Mortimer et al., 1994). Among Youth Development Study seniors, 70% of White students but only 47% of non-Whites were employed. Moreover, although others have expressed concern about the opportunity costs of employment with respect to developmentally salutary activities, paid jobs may, to the contrary, lessen the likelihood of getting into trouble and of participating in deviant, even criminal, behaviors (Sullivan, 1989). It is noteworthy that a historical study of troubled youth in early modern England found that work was considered a highly effective antidote for youthful vagrancy and delinquency (Moran & Vinovskis, 1994).

In conclusion, investigators have examined different facets of adolescent work (employment status, intensity, quality); they have examined different health-relevant outcomes; they have utilized varying methodological techniques and analytic procedures; and they have attributed differential importance to null findings. The findings obtained thus far in the Youth Development Study, taken in tandem, as well as our review of other studies of the consequences of adolescent work, lead us to believe that it is the quality, social meaning, and context of adolescent work that is most important, not whether a student is employed or not, nor even whether a small or large number of hours are committed to work each day. That is, consistent with the extensive literature on work experience in adulthood (Mortimer & Lorence, 1995), what happens on the job, coupled with the meaning and significance of that work experience for both the self and significant others, are the things that matter for adolescent health and positive developmental outcomes. Consistent with this pattern, policymakers, employers, and educators who wish to improve adolescent health might profitably give greater attention to the quality of adolescent jobs instead of focusing exclusively, as has been typical up to the present, on work hour restrictions.

Notes

1 However, some studies fail to find statistically significant associations between student employment and grades (Gottfredson, 1985; Hotchkiss, 1982; Meyer & Wise, 1982). Others report curvilinear relationships, with those working moderate numbers of hours (e.g., 20 hours or less) reporting higher grades than non-working students and those who work more intensively (Mortimer, Finch, et al., 1993; Schill et al., 1995).

2 This school district contained a large concentration of Hmong families, who constituted 9% of both the student body and the initially selected sample. Because the Hmong are very recent immigrants with a distinctive cultural tradition, they required special data collection procedures. The analyses of the Hmong data are focused on issues of acculturation; they are reported elsewhere (Call & McNall, 1992; Dunnigan, McNall, & Mortimer, 1993). This chapter presents findings based on the general (non-Hmong) panel ($N = 1,000$).

3 Despite the fact that informal employment is rare for both genders by the fourth wave, the employment differential in favor of girls continues. Recent national studies indicate no gender difference in youth labor force participation and employment (see Bachman, O'Malley, & Johnston, 1987; U.S. Department of Labor, 1985, 1987).

4 The very low 1-year retention rate in the Steinberg et al. (1993) research – only 30% of adolescents studied in the first year were included in the second-year data analyses – raises the possibility of sample selection biases and diminishes confidence in the results. They show that those who left and stayed in the panel do not differ on a number of first-wave characteristics. However, the extent to which those who stayed and left were similar subsequently, that is, whether they had different patterns of change in health-relevant outcomes in response to work over time, is unknown.

References

Allen, V. L., & van de Vliert, E. (1984). A role theoretical perspective on transitional processes. In V. L. Allen & E. van de Vliert (Eds.), *Role transitions: Explorations and explanations* (pp. 3–18). New York: Plenum.

Bachman, J. G. (1983). Premature affluence: Do high school students earn too much? *Economic Outlook USA*, Vol. 10, No. 3. Ann Arbor, MI: Survey Research Center, Institute for Social Research.

Bachman, J. G., Bare, D. E., & Frankie, E. I. (1986). *Correlates of employment among high school seniors*. Ann Arbor, MI: Institute for Social Research.

Bachman, J. G., O'Malley, P. M., & Johnston, J. (1987). *Youth in transition: Vol VI. Adolescence to adulthood – change and stability in the lives of young men*. Ann Arbor, MI: Survey Research Center, Institute for Social Research.

Bachman, J. G., & Schulenberg, J. (1993). How part-time work intensity relates to drug use, problem behavior, time use, and satisfaction among high school seniors: Are these consequences or merely correlates? *Developmental Psychology, 29*, 220–235.

Baker, F., & Green, G. M. (1991). Work, health, and productivity: Overview. In G. M Green & F. Baker (Eds.), *Work, health, and productivity* (pp. 3–29). New York: Oxford University Press.

Call, K. T. (1994). *Arenas of comfort and adolescent stress: Evidence from a prospective longitudinal study*. Unpublished doctoral dissertation, University of Minnesota.

Call, K. T., & McNall, M. (1992). Poverty, ethnicity, youth adjustment: A comparison of poor Hmong and non-Hmong adolescents. In W. Meeus, M. de Goede, W. Kox, & K. Hurrelmann (Eds.), *Adolescence, careers, and cultures* (pp. 373–392). Berlin and New York: De Gruyter.

Call, K. T., Mortimer, J. T., & Shanahan, M. (1995). Helpfulness and the development of competence in adolescence. *Child Development, 66*, 129–138.

Carnegie Council on Policy Studies in Higher Education. (1980). *Giving youth a better chance*. San Francisco: Jossey-Bass.

Cole, S. (1980). *Working kids on working*. New York: Morrow.

D'Amico, R. J. (1984). Does employment during high school impair academic progress? *Sociology of Education, 57*, 152–164.

Dillman, D. A. (1983). Mail and other self-administered questionnaires. In P. H. Rossi, J. D. Wright, & A. B. Anderson (Eds.), *Handbook of survey research* (pp. 359–377). New York: Academic Press.

Dunnigan, T., McNall, M., & Mortimer, J. T. (1993). The problem of metaphorical nonequivalence in cross-cultural survey research: Comparing the mental health statuses of Hmong refugee and general population adolescents. *Journal of Cross-Cultural Psychology, 24*, 344–365.

Elder, G. H., & Caspi, A. (1990). Studying lives in a changing society: Sociological and personological explorations. In A. I. Rabin, R. A. Zucker, R. Emmons, & S. Frank (Eds.), *Studying persons and lives* (pp. 201–247). New York: Springer.

Elder, G. H., Jr., & Rockwell, R. C. (1979). Economic depression and postwar opportunity in men's lives: A study of life patterns and health. In R. G. Simmons (Ed.), *Research in community and mental health* (Vol. 1, pp. 249–303). Greenwich, CT: JAI Press.

Fernandez, P. V. (1994, September). Reemerging child labor issue prompts health concerns. *The Nation's Health*, pp. 2–4.

Finch, M. D., & Mortimer, J. T. (1985). Adolescent work hours and the process of achievement. In A. C. Kerckhoff (Ed.), *Research in sociology of education and socialization* (Vol. 5, pp. 171–196). Greenwich, CT: JAI Press.

Finch, M. D., Mortimer, J. T., & Ryu, S. (1994, February). *Work intensity and the academic achievement of high school students: A test of three behavioral models*. Paper presented at the Biennial Meeting of the Society for Research on Adolescence, San Diego, CA.

Finch, M. D., Shanahan, M. J., Mortimer, J. T., & Ryu, S. (1991). Work experience and control orientation in adolescence. *American Sociological Review, 56*, 597–611.

Garmezy, N. (1988). Longitudinal strategies, causal reasoning and risk research: A commentary. In M. Rutter (Ed.), *Studies of psychosocial risk: The power of longitudinal data* (pp. 29–44). Cambridge: Cambridge University Press.

Gottfredson, D. C. (1985). Youth employment, crime, and schooling: A longitudinal study of a national sample. *Developmental Psychology, 21*, 419–432.

Gottlieb, B. H. (1991). Social support in adolescence. In M. E. Colten & S. Gore (Eds.), *Adolescent stress: Causes and consequences* (pp. 281–306). New York: Aldine de Gruyter.

Greenberger, E. (1983). A researcher in the policy arena: The case of child labor. *American Psychologist, 38,* 104–111.

Greenberger, E. (1984). Children, families, and work. In N. D. Reppucci, L. A. Weithorn, E. P. Mulvey, & J. Monahan (Eds.), *Children, mental health, and the law* (pp. 103–122). Beverly Hills, CA: Sage.

Greenberger, E. (1988). Working in teenage America. In J. T. Mortimer & K. M. Borman (Eds.), *Work experience and psychological development through the life span* (pp. 21–50). Boulder, CO: Westview.

Greenberger, E., & Steinberg, L. D. (1981). The workplace as a context for the socialization of youth. *Journal of Youth and Adolescence, 10,* 185–210.

Greenberger, E., & Steinberg, L. D. (1986). *When teenagers work.* New York: Basic Books.

Greene, W. H. (1992). *LIMDEP Version 6.0 user's manual and reference guide.* Belport, NY: Econometric Software, Inc.

Hetherington, E. M. (1989). Coping with family transitions: Winners, losers, and survivors. *Child Development, 60,* 1–14.

Hormuth, S. E. (1984). Transitions in commitments to roles and self-concept change: Relocation as a paradigm. In V. L. Allen & E. van de Vliert (Eds.), *Role transitions: Explorations and explanations* (pp. 109–124). New York: Plenum.

Hotchkiss, L. (1982). *Effects of work time on school activities and career expectations* (working paper). Columbus, National Center for Research in Vocational Education.

House, J. S., Lepkowski, J. M., Kinney, A. M., Mero, R. P., Kessler, R. C., & Herzog, A. R. (1994). The social stratification of aging and health. *Journal of Health and Social Behavior, 35,* 213–234.

House, J. S., Umberson, D., & Landis K. (1988). Structures and processes of social support. *Annual Review of Sociology, 14,* 293–318.

Hurrelmann, K., & Lösel, F. (1990). Basic issues and problems of health in adolescence. In K. Hurrelmann & F. Lösel (Eds.), *Health hazards in adolescence* (pp. 1–21). Berlin and New York: Walter de Gruyter.

Johansson, G., & Aronsson, G. (1991). Psychosocial factors in the workplace. In G. M. Green & F. Baker (Eds.), *Work, health, and productivity* (pp. 179–197). New York: Oxford University Press.

Kandel, D. B. (1989). Issues of sequencing of adolescent drug use and other problem behaviors. *Drugs and Society, 3,* 55–76.

Kessler, R. C., Price, R. H., & Wortman, C. B. (1985). Social factors in psychopathology. *Annual Review of Psychology, 36,* 531–72.

Kohn, M. L., & Schooler, C. (1983). *Work and personality: An inquiry into the impact of social stratification.* Norwood, NJ: Ablex.

Lewin-Epstein, N. (1981). *Youth employment during high school.* Washington, DC: National Center for Educational Statistics.

Manning, W. D. (1990). Parenting employed teenagers. *Youth and Society, 22,* 184–200.

Markus, H., Cross, S., & Wurf, E. (1990). The role of the self-system in competence. In R. J. Sternberg & J. Kolligan, Jr. (Eds.), *Competence considered* (pp. 205–226). New Haven, CT: Yale University Press.

Marsh, H. W. (1991). Employment during high school: Character building or a subversion of academic goals? *Sociology of Education, 64,* 172–189.

McNeil, L. (1984). *Lowering expectations: The impact of student employment on classroom knowledge.* Madison: Wisconsin Center for Educational Research.

Meyer, R. M., & Wise, D. A. (1982). High school preparation and early labor force experience. In R. B. Freeman & D. A. Wise (Eds.), *The youth labor problem: Its nature, causes and consequences* (pp. 277–347). Chicago: University of Chicago Press.

Moran, G. F., & Vinovskis, M. A. (1994). Troubled youth: Children at risk in early modern

England, colonial America, and 19th century America. In R. D. Ketterlinus & M. E. Lamb (Eds.), *Adolescent problem behaviors: Issues and research* (pp. 1–16). Hillsdale, NJ: Erlbaum.

Mortimer, J. T., & Finch, M. D. (1986). The effects of part-time work on self-concept and achievement. In K. Borman & J. Reisman (Eds.), *Becoming a worker* (pp. 66–89). Norwood, NJ: Ablex.

Mortimer, J. T., & Finch, M. D. (1994, July). *Work intensity and the mental health of high school students: A test of three behavioral models.* Paper presented at the World Congress of Sociology, Bielefeld, Germany.

Mortimer, J. T., Finch, M. D., Dennehy, K., Lee, C., & Beebe, T. (1994). Work experience in adolescence. *Journal of Vocational Education Research, 19,* 39–70.

Mortimer, J. T., Finch, M. D., Ryu, S., Shanahan, M. J., & Call, K. T. (1996). The effects of work intensity on adolescent mental health, achievement and behavioral adjustment: New evidence from a prospective study. *Child Development, 67,* 1243–1261.

Mortimer, J. T., Finch, M. D., Shanahan, M., & Ryu, S. (1992a). Work experience, mental health, and behavioral adjustment in adolescence. *Journal of Research on Adolescence, 2,* 25–57.

Mortimer, J. T., Finch, M. D., Shanahan, M., & Ryu, S. (1992b). Adolescent work history and behavioral adjustment. *Journal of Research on Adolescence, 2,* 59–80.

Mortimer, J. T., & Lorence, J. (1995). The social psychology of work. In K. Cook, G. Fine, & J. House (Eds.), *Sociological perspectives on social psychology* (pp. 497–523). Boston: Allyn & Bacon.

Mortimer, J. T., Lorence, J., & Kumka, D. (1986). *Work, family and personality: Transition to adulthood.* Norwood, NJ: Ablex.

Mortimer, J. T., Pimentel, E., Ryu, S., Nash, K., & Lee, C. (1996). Part-time work and occupational value formation in adolescence. *Social Forces, 74,* 1405–1418.

Mortimer, J. T., & Shanahan, M. J. (1991). *Adolescent work experience and relations with peers.* Paper presented at the annual meeting of the American Sociological Association, Cincinnati, OH.

Mortimer, J. T., & Shanahan, M. J. (1994). Adolescent work experience and family relationships. *Work and Occupations, 21,* 369–384.

Mortimer, J. T., Shanahan, M., & Ryu, S. (1993). The effects of adolescent employment on school-related orientation and behavior. In R. K. Silbereisen & E. Todt (Eds.), *Adolescence in context: The interplay of family, school, peers and work in adjustment* (pp. 304–326). New York: Springer-Verlag.

Mortimer, J. T., & Simmons, R. G. (1978). Adult socialization. *Annual Review of Sociology, 4,* 421–454.

National Commission on Youth. (1980). *The transition to adulthood: A bridge too long.* Boulder, CO: Westview Press.

New York Times (1994, April 22). U.S. says 64,000 teen-agers a year are injured on the job, p. A8.

Panel on Youth of the President's Science Advisory Committee (Chair: James S. Coleman). (1974). *Youth: Transition to adulthood.* Chicago: University of Chicago Press.

Parker, D., Carl, W., French, L., & Martin. F. (1994). Characteristics of adolescent work injuries reported to the Minnesota Department of Labor and Industry. *American Journal of Public Health, 84,* 606–611.

Phillips, S., & Sandstrom, K. L. (1990). Parental attitudes towards youth work. *Youth and Society, 22,* 160–183.

Rutter, M. (1990). Psychosocial resilience and protective mechanisms. In J. Rolf, A. S. Masten, D. Chicchetti, K. H. Nuechterlein, & S. Weintraub (Eds.), *Risk and protective factors in the development of psychopathology* (pp. 181–214). Cambridge: Cambridge University Press.

Schill, W. J., McCartin, R., & Meyer, K. (1985). Youth employment: Its relationship to academic and family variables. *Journal of Vocational Behavior, 26,* 155–163.

Schulenberg, J., & Bachman, J. G. (1993, March). *Long hours on the job? Not so bad for some adolescents in some types of jobs: The quality of work and substance use, affect, and stress.*

Paper presented at the meeting of the Society for Research on Child Development, New Orleans.

Shanahan, M. J., & Elder, G. H., Jr. (1993, March). *Rural contexts of adolescent work experiences: Cause and consequence.* Paper presented at the meeting of the Society for Research in Child Development, New Orleans.

Shanahan, M. J., Finch, M. D., Mortimer, J. T., & Ryu, S. (1991). Adolescent work experience and depressive affect. *Social Psychology Quarterly, 54,* 299–317.

Simmons, R. G. (in press). Comfort with the self. In S. Stryker (Ed.), *Self, affect and society.*

Snedeker, G. (1982). *Hard knocks. Preparing youth for work.* Baltimore: Johns Hopkins University Press.

Steel, L. (1991). Early work experience among white and non-white youth. *Youth and Society, 22,* 419–447.

Steinberg, L., & Dornbusch, S. M. (1991). Negative correlates of part-time employment during adolescence: Replication and elaboration. *Developmental Psychology, 27,* 304–313.

Steinberg, L. D., Fegley, S., & Dornbusch, S. M. (1993). Negative impact of part-time work on adolescent adjustment: Evidence from a longitudinal study. *Developmental Psychology, 29,* 171–180.

Steinberg, L. D., Greenberger, E., Garduque, L., Ruggiero, M., & McAuliffe, S. (1982). High school students in the labor force: Some costs and benefits to schooling and learning. *Education Evaluation and Policy Analysis, 4,* 363–372.

Steinberg, L. D., Greenberger, E., Garduque, L, Ruggiero, M., & Vaux, A. (1982). Effects of work in adolescent development. *Developmental Psychology, 18,* 385–395.

Stern, D., & Nakata, Y. (1993). Characteristics of high school students' paid jobs, and employment experience after graduation. In D. Stern & D. Eichorn (Eds.), *Adolescence and work: Influences of social structure, labor markets, and cultures* (pp. 189–233). Hillsdale, NJ: Erlbaum.

Sullivan, M. L. (1989). *Getting paid: Youth crime and work in the inner city.* Ithaca, NY: Cornell University Press.

Thoits, P. A. (1983). Dimensions of life events that influence psychological distress: An evaluation and synthesis of the literature. In H. B. Kaplan (Ed.), *Psychological stress: Trends in theory and research* (pp. 33–103). New York: Academic Press.

Turner, R. J. (1983). Direct, indirect, and moderating effects of social support upon psychological distress and associated conditions. In H. Kaplan (Ed.), *Psychosocial stress: Trends in theory and research* (pp. 105–155). New York: Academic Press.

U.S. Department of Labor. (1977). *Dictionary of occupational titles* (4th ed.). Washington, DC: U.S. Government Printing Office.

U.S. Department of Labor. (1985). *Handbook of labor statistics* (Bureau of Labor Statistics, Bull. No. 2217). Washington, DC: U.S. Government Printing Office.

U.S. Department of Labor. (1986). *Dictionary of occupational titles* (4th ed., Suppl.). Washington, DC: U.S. Government Printing Office.

U.S. Department of Labor. (1987). *Employment and earnings* (Vol. 34, 10). Washington, DC: U.S. Government Printing Office.

Wagenaar, A. C., & Perry, C. L. (1994). Community strategies for the reduction of youth drinking: Theory and application. *Journal of Research on Adolescence, 4,* 319–345.

Warr, P. (1984). Reported behavior changes after job loss. *British Journal of Social Psychology, 23,* 271–275.

Werner, E. E. (1984). *Child care: Kith, kin and hired hands.* Baltimore: University Park Press.

Werner, E. E., & Smith, R. S. (1982). *Vulnerable, but not invisible: A longitudinal study of resilient children and youth.* New York: McGraw-Hill.

Wirtz, W. (1975). *The boundless resource: A prospectus for an education/work policy.* Washington, DC: New Republic Book Co.

13 Alcohol Use and Binge Drinking as Goal-Directed Action During the Transition to Postsecondary Education

Jennifer L. Maggs

When adults reminisce about their college days, a common activity is swapping tales about wild parties, experiments with bizarre and often unknown concoctions, outrageous and funny things done while drinking, and other hilariously presented, legendary exploits. Sometimes the tone of the conversation momentarily grows sober as people wonder aloud how they made it through this phase safely or remember an old friend who was not so lucky. But even in the context of such self-reflection, there is also a feeling of regret that this exciting time of life is over, a time when you shared everything with your friends, partied every weekend, and had only yourself to worry about. Of course, this mythical depiction of the carefree life of the college student does not represent the diversity of actual experiences, but as a legend it is a powerful image that evokes nostalgia in some adults, a feeling of having missed out in others, and excitement in adolescents who still have college to look forward to.

Approximately half of North American adolescents go on to some form of postsecondary education after completing high school (W. T. Grant, 1988). In addition to greatly enhancing occupational prospects, going to college tends to slow the passage to adulthood (Sherrod, Haggerty, & Featherman, 1993). Because individuals typically leave school before commencing full-time employment or starting a family, the timing of the assumption of adult roles (e.g., worker, spouse, parent) is greatly influenced by the amount of time spent in formal education (Marini, 1984, 1985). That is, adolescents who go to college tend to start their first full-time job, marry, and have children later than those who complete their education by the end of high school. Even when adult roles are initiated prior to final departure from schooling, involvement in any postsecondary education tends to delay adult transitions. A more gradual passage toward adulthood can have many noneducational benefits (W. T. Grant, 1988). For many individuals, the college years represent an opportunity to postpone the assumption of full adult responsibilities while continuing to learn, explore ideas, and pursue personal and academic interests (Pascarella &

The preparation of this chapter was supported by a Social Sciences and Humanities Research Council of Canada research grant to the author.

Terenzini, 1991). Likewise, individuals can experiment with various adult behaviors, values, and lifestyles. In other words, the college experience can provide a safe haven for exploration, a developmental moratorium (Sherrod et al., 1993).

This chapter focuses on the use of alcohol as a representative risk behavior during the transition to university life. (The terms *university* and *college* will be used interchangeably to denote postsecondary educational institutions.) The chapter argues that late adolescent and young adult alcohol use and binge drinking can be usefully conceived of as purposive action directed toward the pursuit of developmentally normative goals. The introduction discusses the characteristics of this major developmental transition, the prevalence and functions of risk-taking during adolescence and young adulthood, and the theoretical assumptions and hypotheses that guided the research. Subsequent sections describe the study, in which late adolescent university students completed questionnaires about their adjustment, goals, beliefs about alcohol, and drinking behavior on two occasions as they began their first year and were adjusting to life in a college residence.

Transition to University Life: Opportunities and Challenges

The passage from adolescence into young adulthood is a major developmental transition during which discontinuity in life trajectories increases (Schulenberg, O'Malley, Bachman, Wadsworth, & Johnston, 1996; Sherrod et al., 1993). For many adolescents, this period begins when they move away from their parents' home to begin university, and many initially live in a student residence (Cantor, Norem, Niederthal, Langston, & Brower, 1987; Flanagan, Schulenberg, & Fuligni, 1993; Takahashi & Majima, 1994). This major developmental transition represents the co-occurrence of at least two major role changes: the transformation from being a high school student to a university student and from being a child living at home to an independent person living in a college dormitory. In Western societies, moving away from home and pursuing vocational goals are important markers on the path toward adulthood (Compas, Wagner, Slavin, & Vannatta, 1986). Living on one's own greatly increases opportunities for self-governance in that it allows or forces the adolescent to make daily decisions about time use, lifestyle choices, and many other aspects of life without direct input from parents (Flanagan et al., 1993). Like other developmental advances and role transformations, the transition to university life involves both gains and losses (Baltes, 1987; Cantor & Langston, 1989), such as the initiation of new roles (e.g., roommate) but the end of others (e.g., high school student); new friendship networks but separation from family and old friends; more academic choices and opportunities (e.g., different courses, areas of specialization) but corresponding new academic demands (e.g., much larger classes, less direction from instructors, increased competition); and increased independence and self-direction but decreased parental guidance and support.

Clearly, beginning university demands substantial adaptation and reorganization (Aseltine & Gore, 1993; Hays & Oxley, 1986; Hogan & Astone, 1986; Simmons & Blyth, 1987). Thus, it may be a time of growth but also of vulnerability (Compas et al., 1986; Sherrod et al., 1993; Takahashi & Majima, 1994; Zirkel, 1992). Finishing high school and moving away from home involve the disruption of and the potential for changes in patterns of life, habits, and lifestyle behaviors. In many ways, this period represents a new beginning for adolescents. There is the opportunity to make new friends, enjoy new-found freedom, direct one's own daily life, explore educational and future career alternatives, and experiment with different behaviors and lifestyles. For some, the transition may reduce exposure to stressful situations such as conflicted family relations or high school unpopularity, providing the opportunity to make a break with a troubled past (cf. Aseltine & Gore, 1993). Moving away from home to live in an unfamiliar university environment can also be a stressful experience, particularly for more vulnerable individuals (Compas et al., 1986; Shaver, Furman, & Buhrmester, 1985; Zirkel, 1992). The new environment presents individuals with various normative demands, such as being independent, succeeding academically, and establishing new friends and social networks (Cantor et al., 1987; Hays & Oxley, 1986; Takahashi & Majima, 1994). New university students also confront the opportunity for and often the expectation of high levels of some risk behaviors, particularly alcohol use and binge drinking (Prentice & Miller, 1993).

Developmental Transitions and Risk Behaviors

Why is the transition to postsecondary education a particularly interesting time to study risk behaviors such as alcohol use? First, moving away from home to begin postsecondary education leads to dramatic changes in the physical context and in normative expectations for social and academic behavior (Aseltine & Gore, 1993; Compas et al., 1986; Hays & Oxley, 1985; Prentice & Miller, 1993; Shaver et al., 1985). As students begin life in this new environment, they are likely to set personal goals for the upcoming year (Cantor et al., 1987). Focusing on students' personal characteristics, goals, and beliefs as factors shaping their drinking behavior will advance our understanding of the functions served by risky behaviors such as binge drinking (Nurmi, 1993). Second, moving away from home leads to significant changes in situational affordances and opportunities in many domains (Cantor, 1994), not the least of which is risky behavior. University administrators and resident assistants do not and cannot care for individual adolescents and protect them from harm to the same extent as loving parents do. Thus opportunities for potentially risky activities such as eating unhealthy foods, drinking, using drugs, and having risky sex are likely to increase. Desires to experiment that were previously suppressed or limited to rare occasions may be more easily fulfilled in the new, more independent living situation. Therefore, this period of transition, during which opportunities to experiment expand greatly, provides a window into how adolescents shape their own behavior, given the opportunity.

Prevalence of Substance Use on Campus

Cigarette Use. Individuals who become habitual smokers typically start to smoke prior to the end of high school (Johnston, O'Malley, & Bachman, 1994). Youth in college smoke less than noncollege youth: for example, 9% of full-time college students smoked half a pack or more daily in 1993 compared to 20% of similar-aged youth not in college (Johnston et al., 1994). These differences precede the end of high school and thus are not a consequence of college attendance.

Illicit Drug Use. In contrast, there is little difference in illicit drug use between college and noncollege youth (Johnston et al., 1994). For example, the annual prevalence of any illicit drug use in 1993 was 31% for college students and 30% for their same-age noncollege peers. Between 1980 and 1993, there were marked declines in illicit drug use among adolescents and young adults in the United States. For example, among college students the annual prevalence of using any illicit drug dropped from 56% to 31% (Johnston et al., 1994).

Alcohol Use. Secondary and postsecondary students report using alcohol more than any other substance (Johnston et al., 1994; Siggner, 1988). For example, 72% of 20- to 24-year-old Canadians reported drinking alcohol regularly, and 20% of males and 4% of females reported consuming eight or more drinks on one occasion in the previous week (Siggner, 1988). The frequency and quantity of drinking increase throughout adolescence, peak in late adolescence or early adulthood, and then tend to decline as adult roles are initiated (Bachman, O'Malley, Wadsworth, Johnston, & Schulenberg, chapter 10, this volume; Jessor, Donovan, & Costa, 1991; Kandel & Yamaguchi, 1985; Sharpe & Lowe, 1989). In addition to these age trends, alcohol use is particularly high among postsecondary students, especially those living in dormitories and fraternities/sororities (Crowley, 1991; O'Hare, 1990). The annual U.S. Monitoring the Future surveys, for example, show that among 19- to 22-year-old Americans, college students have a slightly higher annual prevalence of alcohol use than noncollege youth (87% versus 84%, respectively), a higher monthly prevalence of use (72% versus 63%), and a higher 2-week prevalence of binge drinking (40% versus 34%) (Johnston et al., 1994).

Functions of Alcohol Use and Binge Drinking

Alcohol consumption was selected as the focus risk behavior for this study because of the very high prevalence of alcohol use and binge drinking among late adolescent and young adult students and because of the potential for serious negative consequences due to alcohol misuse (Siggner, 1988). The role played by drinking alcohol in adolescents' lives is paradoxical, just as it is for other so-called problem behaviors (Maggs, Almeida, & Galambos, 1995; Maggs & Hurrelmann, 1996). Despite the possibility of serious harm from binge drinking and alcohol misuse, drinking also may serve important constructive functions for adolescents, such as helping them to make friends, let off steam, indicate a transition to a more mature status, or explore personal identities (Chassin, Presson, & Sherman, 1989; Jessor, 1987; Silbereisen & Eyferth, 1986). Prevalence studies show that it is more normative to drink during adolescence than it is not to drink (Johnston et al., 1994; Moffitt, 1993). In fact, some scientists have argued that experimenting with risk behaviors such as drinking alcohol has become one of the developmental tasks or rites of passage of adolescence in Western societies (e.g., Baumrind, 1985; Jessor, 1987; Schulenberg, O'Malley, Bachman, Wadsworth, & Johnston, 1996; Shedler & Block, 1990). Understanding how and why adolescents use alcohol as they negotiate the transition into adulthood is essential for planning health promotion efforts aimed at minimizing the negative consequences of alcohol misuse (Leventhal & Keeshan, 1993).

Behavior as Goal-Directed Action:
Theoretical Perspective and Hypotheses

The developmental action perspective provides a useful framework for understanding adolescent alcohol use. The action perspective assumes that human development is initiated and directed by the intentions and goals of developing individuals (Brandtstädter, 1984; Chapman & Skinner, 1985; Hurrelmann, 1989; Silbereisen, 1985). That is, humans shape their own development through goal-directed action. The term *action* is used to denote purposive, self-directed behavior (Silbereisen & Eyferth, 1986). Applying a developmental action perspective to adolescent alcohol use, individuals are assumed to have attributes that direct their decisions about engaging in this potentially risky behavior (cf. Hurrelmann, 1990; Silbereisen & Eyferth, 1986). These attributes can be said to motivate drinking behavior (Jessor, 1987). Thus, drinking can be viewed as rational, goal-directed action. In the present study, individual differences in psychosocial adjustment, personal goals, and beliefs about drinking alcohol were hypothesized to predict levels of alcohol use and binge drinking. In the following three subsections, each of these sets of predictors is discussed in turn.

Psychosocial Adjustment and Risk-Taking: Alternative Views. There are conflicting views concerning the nature and direction of the relationship between
psychosocial adjustment and risk-taking behaviors. One hypothesis is that low
self-esteem, psychological maladjustment, and inadequate social skills lead
young people to engage in behaviors such as substance use, precocious sexual
activity, and delinquency. Some studies have observed negative relationships
between psychosocial adjustment and some risk behaviors (Newcomb,
Bentler, & Collins, 1986); others have failed to observe any relationship
(Jessor et al., 1991; Windle & Barnes, 1988). A second hypothesis is that
psychosocial competence rather than pathology leads to developmentally
appropriate risk-taking, such as experimental substance use (Baumrind, 1985,
1987; Shedler & Block, 1990). A third hypothesis is that risk behaviors have
both positive and negative correlates (Chassin et al., 1989; Maggs et al., 1995;
Moffitt, 1993; Silbereisen & Noack, 1988). For example, Silbereisen and colleagues proposed that drinking and smoking are aimed at integrating the
adolescent into the peer group and thus may lead to changes in self-esteem
(Silbereisen & Noack, 1988; Silbereisen, Schönpflug, & Albrecht, 1990; see
also Semmer et al., 1987). Similarly, Maggs and colleagues have shown that
risk-taking among young adolescents was associated with higher family conflict and a negative self-image but also with higher levels of peer involvement
and perceived peer acceptance and leadership (Maggs & Galambos, 1993;
Maggs & Hurrelmann, 1996; Maggs et al., 1995).

Thus, risk-taking behaviors may be indicative of psychosocial adjustment
and competence, but they may also arise out of maladjustment and low self-
esteem. An interesting question is whether it is the *level* of risk-taking (e.g.,
frequency, severity of potential consequences) that distinguishes between
competent and poorly adjusted risk takers. For example, Shedler and Block
(1990) found that childhood psychological adjustment was associated with
experimental substance use during adolescence, but childhood maladjustment
predicted adolescent abuse of substances. An alternative possibility is that
risk-taking has both positive and negative antecedents and consequences *for
the same individuals.* This has been called the *paradox of risk-taking* (Maggs &
Hurrelmann, 1996; Maggs et al., 1995). The present study examines the extent
to which self-image and peer acceptance predict levels of drinking behavior
among older adolescents beginning university. It was hypothesized that a
negative self-image and high peer acceptance would predict higher levels of
drinking behavior during the transition to college life. In order to examine
whether the psychosocial predictors of drinking differed by level, dependent
variables included a quantity-frequency measure of drinking, as well as the
frequency of binge drinking.

Personal Goals: How Individuals Shape Their Own Development. People
shape and influence their own behavior and development by setting personal

goals, making plans for their accomplishment, and taking corresponding action (Brandtstädter, 1984; Cantor, 1990; Chapman & Skinner, 1985; Nurmi, 1991, 1993). Personal goals have been variously referred to as *life tasks* (Cantor, 1990), *personal projects* (Little, 1983), *personal strivings* (Emmons, 1986), and *possible selves* (Markus & Nurius, 1986). Common to these concepts is the view that self-articulated personal goals, based on individual values and beliefs about future options and culturally defined tasks, motivate and shape individual behavior (Nurmi, 1993; Nurmi, chapter 15, this volume). By actively selecting environments and activities, individuals expose themselves to various developmental opportunities, and thus mold their experience and development (Brandtstädter, 1984; Zirkel, 1992). Goal orientation and planfulness are related to psychosocial competence and subjective well-being. That is, people who are psychosocially competent tend to set and work toward realistic goals (Clausen, 1991), and commitment to goals, attainability of goals, and progress in goal achievement predict positive changes in subjective well-being (Brunstein, 1993). The extent to which individuals are able to accomplish their plans is also dependent on situational affordances, that is, opportunities to meet personal needs and goals (Cantor, 1994).

As discussed previously, the transition to postsecondary education presents students with many challenges and opportunities. Common goals or life tasks of college students include succeeding academically and establishing or maintaining interpersonal relationships (Cantor, 1990; Cantor et al., 1987; Shaver et al., 1985). Although the exact content of individuals' personal goals is idiosyncratic, developmentally normative goals can be assessed on nomothetic variables, such as their importance or salience (Brunstein, 1993). The present study assessed students' self-rated importance of achieving social, academic, and health goals during the upcoming academic year (e.g., making friends, doing well in courses, and staying healthy, respectively). Social and academic goals were assessed because of their direct relevance to the normative demands of the undergraduate environment (Cantor et al., 1987; Pascarella & Terenzini, 1991). Health goals were measured because of their potential relevance for decisions about alcohol use. It was assumed that drinking would be viewed by students as having a facilitative social effect, but also as potentially interfering with academic success and physical health. Thus, it was hypothesized that individual differences in students' self-articulated importance of accomplishing social goals would be positive predictors of alcohol use, and individual differences in the importance of academic goals and health goals would be negative predictors of alcohol use.

Beliefs About Alcohol Use. When individuals make decisions about whether to engage in any behavior, they may consider the potential costs and benefits of both doing the act and of not doing it (Beyth-Marom & Fischhoff, chapter 5, this volume; Furby & Beyth-Marom, 1992; Gardner, 1993). In other words, any potential activity involves the possibility for gain and for loss. For example, going to a lot of parties and drinking every weekend might provide gains such as having fun and making new friends, but also might lead to potential losses such as falling behind in schoolwork. Thus adolescent behavior such as alcohol use, despite being seen as problematic by adults, may also be interpreted as a reasonable act from the perspective of the adolescent. Knowledge about adolescents' perceptions of the risks and benefits of alcohol use and binge drinking provides a window into their subjective meaning and functions, information that is essential for the design of effective prevention programs (Hurrelmann, 1989; Leventhal & Keeshan, 1993). Research indicates that adolescents who believe that using alcohol, cigarettes, or other drugs is rewarding are more likely to initiate and continue using these substances (e.g., Bauman, Fisher, Bryan, & Chenoweth, 1985; Johnston & O'Malley, 1986). The present study assessed participants' perceptions of two global benefits and costs of drinking alcohol, namely, fun and risk. The extent to which beliefs about fun and risk predicted levels of alcohol use and binge drinking was examined. Following Maggs et al. (1995), the belief that drinking is fun was hypothesized to be positively related to drinking, and the belief that drinking is risky was hypothesized to be negatively related to drinking.

Motivations to Drink versus Motivations to Limit Drinking. Considerations of costs and benefits, or gains and losses, can be distinguished in terms of whether they refer to the possibility of experiencing positive consequences (e.g., having a good time with friends) or of avoiding negative consequences (e.g., not getting a hangover). Many programs and campaigns aimed at preventing risk behaviors such as cigarette use, binge drinking, or unsafe sex aim to inform people about negative consequences and to convince them that they can and should avoid these dangers by not engaging in the activities (Hurrelmann, 1990; Leventhal & Keeshan, 1993). Thus it is assumed that fear of negative consequences should lead to an avoidance of the risky activity. Often much less attention is given to the positive consequences one may experience by engaging in risk behavior, that is, the positive functions served by actions like alcohol use or sexual relationships (Jessor, 1987; Turner & Feldman, 1994). Health education programs have often assumed that the fear of negative consequences should motivate people to avoid risky behaviors. However, if the desire to experience certain positive consequences is a more powerful predictor of behavior, health promotion programs that target alternative means of achieving these same consequences might be more successful (Leventhal & Keeshan, 1993). In the present study, the unique contributions of motivations *to* drink (social goals, beliefs that drinking is fun) and of motivations to *not* drink or to *limit* drinking (academic goals, health goals, beliefs that drinking is risky) to the prediction of drinking behavior were contrasted. It was hypothesized that prodrinking motivations would be more predictive of alcohol use and binge drinking than antidrinking motivations.

Summary and Hypotheses

The present study viewed students' alcohol use as a purposive behavior directed toward the attainment of instrumental, developmentally relevant goals. Participants were older adolescents moving into student residences at the start of their first year of university. The extent to which psychosocial adjustment, personal goals, and beliefs about alcohol predicted alcohol use and binge drinking was examined. The hypotheses were as follows: (1) students with more positive self-images will drink less and students who feel more accepted by their peers will drink more; (2) students with high social goals will drink more, and students with high academic goals and high health goals will drink less; and (3) beliefs about the fun and risk of alcohol will predict drinking. Finally, it was hypothesized that (4) goals and beliefs that *promote* or *encourage* drinking (social goals, the belief that drinking is fun) will be much more strongly related to drinking than goals and beliefs that *hinder* or *discourage* drinking (academic goals, health goals, the belief that drinking is risky). The criterion variables in the analyses were plans to drink alcohol and to binge drink; actual alcohol use and binge drinking; and differences between planned and actual drinking.

Method

Participants and Procedure

The participants were 344 students living in on-campus residences at a medium-sized Canadian university. The estimated response rate was 79%. The mean age was 18.7 years (SD = 1.0); 74% were younger than the provincial drinking age of 19 years. However, participants reported experiencing relatively few obstacles to drinking. For example, when they wanted to drink, 76% reported having people to drink with, 78% were able to acquire alcohol, and 88% had a place to drink most or all of the time. Questionnaires were completed by the participants during their first week of the fall semester as they began living in a university residence. Three weeks later, a second set of questionnaires was completed (matched n = 169). The collection of data concerning plans to drink and actual drinking permitted the evaluation of the extent to which psychosocial adjustment, personal goals, and beliefs about alcohol predicted planned drinking, actual drinking, and differences between planned and actual drinking. Participants were assured that all responses would be anonymous, and informed consent was obtained in writing. Although there was considerable attrition between Time 1 and Time 2, analyses revealed no significant differences between those who remained and those who dropped out with respect to demographic or situational variables, alcohol use, consequences of drinking, or any other measured variable (Maggs, 1993). Thus, attrition did not appear to be selective.[1]

Measures

Psychosocial Adjustment. Three subscales from the Adolescent Self-Image Questionnaire (Offer, Ostrov, & Howard, 1982) assessed adolescents' feelings about themselves: Impulse Control measured adolescents' resistance to impulsive, violent, or angry behavior (9 items, e.g., "Even under pressure, I manage to remain calm"); Mastery and Coping assessed confidence in coping (10 items, e.g., "When I decide to do something, I do it"); and Emotional Tone measured positive affect (9 items, e.g., "Most of the time, I am happy"). Subjects rated items on a 6-point scale ranging from 1 = Does not describe me at all to 6 = Describes me very well, with higher scores indicating a more positive self-image. Offer et al. (1982) demonstrated the psychometric adequacy of these measures. In the present sample, alphas were .64, .67, and .80, for the three subscales, respectively. The three self-image subscales were closely interrelated. To reduce the number of predictors and the potential for multicollinearity, the three self-image subscales were entered into a principal components analysis. A strong one-component solution accounted for 69% of the variance in self-image, with factor loadings of .80, .81, and .87. Thus, factor scores were computed using the regression method and were used in all subsequent correlational analyses.

Peer Acceptance was measured using the Offer et al. (1982) nine-item peer acceptance scale. Participants indicated how confident and positive they felt about their relationships with their peers. A sample item was "I do not have a particularly difficult time in making friends," rated on the same scale as for self-image. Mean scores were computed, with higher scores indicating that adolescents felt more accepted by their peers. Cronbach's alpha was .80.

Personal Goals. Students were asked to rate the importance of achieving certain goals during the upcoming academic year. Three categories of goals were assessed: Social Goals (six items, e.g., "make new friends"), Academic Goals (three items, e.g., "do well in all your courses"), and Health Goals (three items, e.g., "work out/participate in sports regularly"). Possible responses ranged from 1 = Not at all important to me to 5 = Very important to me. Alphas for the three scales were .80, .82, and .71, respectively. As evidence of the content validity of this measure, Cantor and colleagues' (Cantor et al., 1987; Cantor & Langston, 1989) interview and beeper studies of first-year university students found that 81% of students' spontaneously articulated goals and 50% of their activities (sampled via beepers) fell into interpersonal or achievement domains.

Beliefs About Drinking Alcohol. Participants indicated how Fun and how Risky they thought it was to drink alcohol (cf. Maggs et al., 1995). Possible responses on these two single-item measures ranged from 1 = Not at all Fun to 4 = Very Fun and from 1 = Not at all Risky to 4 = Very Risky.

Drinking Behavior. Questions adapted from previous research were used to measure alcohol use and binge drinking (Donovan, Costa, & Jessor, 1985; Health & Welfare Canada, 1988). To measure Planned Alcohol Use, participants were asked (1) how often they planned to drink alcohol in the upcoming three weeks (possible responses ranged from 1 = Never to 6 = Every day) (frequency) and (2) how many drinks they planned to drink per average drinking occasion (possible responses ranged from 1 = none to 7 = 12 or more) (quantity). These two items were multiplied to yield a quantity-frequency estimate of alcohol use. To measure Planned Binge Drinking, participants indicated (3) how many times they planned to consume five or more drinks on one occasion in the next 3 weeks and (4) how many times they planned to get drunk in the next 3 weeks. Response formats were the same as for item (1). The mean of these two items was taken. At Time 2, these four questions were repeated with respect to the quantity and frequency of Actual Alcohol Use and Actual Binge Drinking in the 3 weeks between Time 1 and Time 2. Coefficient alphas for the binge drinking scales were .93 for planned drinking and .92 for actual drinking.

Results

Descriptive Analyses

Table 13.1 presents the means, standard deviations, and intercorrelations for the seven predictor variables. These descriptive statistics are presented separately for females and males. A one-way MANOVA was performed with gender as a between-subjects factor and these seven variables as the dependent variables. This analysis showed that males and females differed in their levels of these variables, multivariate $F(7, 325) = 5.13, p < .001$. On average, students felt positively about themselves (self-image) and felt accepted by their peers. Males' self-image was more positive, on average, than females', $F(1, 331) = 5.79, p < .05$; however, there was no gender difference in peer acceptance. All three personal goals were seen as somewhat to very important. Males rated the importance of social goals higher than females, $F(1, 331) = 5.57, p < .05$, and females rated the importance of health goals higher than males, $F(1, 331) = 7.07, p < .01$. Academic goals were equally important to

Table 13.1. *Descriptive statistics: Psychosocial adjustment, personal goals, and beliefs about alcohol*

	Females	Males	Total sample	Intercorrelations					
	M (SD)	M (SD)	M (SD)	1.	2.	3.	4.	5.	6.
Psychosocial adjustment[a]									
Self-image[b]	4.56 (.57)	4.72 (.52)	4.62 (.56)						
Peer acceptance	4.45 (.78)	4.55 (.77)	4.48 (.78)	.64**					
Personal goals[c]									
Social	3.52 (.67)	3.70 (.73)	3.58 (.70)	.07	.29**				
Academic	4.80 (.38)	4.82 (.36)	4.77 (.42)	.13*	.10	.05			
Health	4.82 (.36)	4.77 (.42)	4.17 (.65)	.24**	.22**	.25**	.21**		
Beliefs about alcohol[d]									
Fun	2.60 (.91)	2.80 (.97)	2.67 (.94)	.05	.28**	.41**	−.06	.04	
Risk	2.86 (.84)	2.50 (.97)	2.73 (.89)	−.14*	−.15*	−.22**	.11*	.11*	−.36**

Note: n = 334–340.

[a] Higher scores represent higher adjustment.

[b] Mean of three self-image subscales. Mean (*SD*) of self-image composite = .02 (.98).

[c] Response format: 1 = Not at all important to me to 5 = Very important to me.

[d] Response format: 1 = Not at all Fun/Risky to 4 = Very Fun/Risky.

* *p* < .05. ** *p* < .001.

males and females. Academic goals were rated as most important to achieve during the upcoming year, followed by health goals, and social goals were rated as the least important, all $p < .001$. With respect to fun and risk ratings, females viewed drinking as more risky than did males, $F(1, 331) = 13.17, p < .001$, and there was a nonsignificant tendency for males to rate drinking as more fun than did females, $F(1, 331) = 3.33, p < .07$.

Levels of planned and actual drinking were similar to those found in other Canadian and American surveys (e.g., Johnston et al., 1994; Siggner, 1988). For example, 74% and 45% of students planned to use alcohol and get drunk at least once, respectively, in the upcoming 3 weeks; 72% and 49% actually did so. Plans to drink were quite closely related to actual drinking behavior, as indicated by large correlations between planned and actual alcohol use and between planned and actual binge drinking, $r = .69$ and $.67$, both $p < .001$. The quantities of alcohol respondents reported actually consuming per average drinking occasion were 1 drink (9%), 2 to 3 drinks (33%), 4 to 6 drinks (34%), 7 to 9 drinks (18%), and 10 or more drinks (7%). Two one-way MANOVAs examined gender differences in alcohol use and binge drinking. Planned and actual drinking were analyzed in separate analyses because of the different n. Both multivariate F values were significant at $p < .001$. Univariate tests showed that, relative to females, males had higher planned alcohol use, $F(1, 343) = 12.3, p < .001$, planned binge drinking, $F(1, 343) = 17.0, p < .001$, actual alcohol use, $F(1, 167) = 4.27, p < .05$, and actual binge drinking, $F(1, 166) = 12.2, p < .01$.

Table 13.1 also presents the intercorrelations among the predictors. These were computed for the sample as a whole because subsequent analyses did not find evidence that the pattern of relationships differed by gender, despite mean-level differences. The two indicators of psychosocial adjustment, self-image and peer acceptance, were strongly and positively related. With respect to personal goals, the importance of health goals was positively related to the importance of academic and social goals. Four of the six correlations between psychosocial adjustment and personal goals were significant, with positive self-image and higher peer acceptance being positively related to viewing the goals as more important. Adolescents who believed alcohol use was more fun felt more accepted by their peers and viewed social goals as more important, and those who believed alcohol use was more risky had a less positive self-image, felt less accepted by their peers, and viewed academic and health goals as more important. Fun and risk were moderately negatively related.

Prediction of Intended and Actual Drinking Behavior

The first three hypotheses stated that drinking behavior would be predicted by psychosocial adjustment, personal goals, and beliefs about alcohol. These hypotheses were evaluated using a series of multiple regression analyses.

Table 13.2. *Multiple regressions predicting planned and actual alcohol use and binge drinking by psychosocial adjustment, personal goals, and beliefs about drinking*

Step and predictors	Plans to drink			Actual drinking			Plans to binge drink			Actual binge drinking		
	r	β	ΔR^2	r	β	ΔR^2	r	β	ΔR^2	r	β	ΔR^2
Step 1: Gender	.23***	.23***	.05***	.19*	.19*	.04*	.23***	.23***	.05***	.27***	.27***	.07***
Step 2: Psychosocial adjustment												
Self-image	.06	−.26**		.02	−.29**		.01	−.31***		.01	−.29**	
Peer acceptance	.30***	.46***	.12***	.30***	.46***	.14***	.25***	.44***	.12***	.29***	.46***	.14***
Step 3: Personal goals												
Social	.43***	.36***		.29***	.23**		.40***	.33***		.33***	.23**	
Academic	−.08	−.08		−.12	−.06		−.11*	−.10*		−.15	−.06	
Health	−.05	−.13**	.11***	−.13	−.15	.06**	−.06	−.12*	.10***	−.11	−.15	.06**
Step 4: Beliefs about alcohol												
Fun	.71***	.58***		.60***	.44***		.63***	.48***		.55***	.44***	
Risk	−.35***	−.05	.28***	−.41***	−.14*	.21***	−.38***	−.12*	.22***	−.40***	−.14*	.21***
Total R^2 (adjusted R^2)			.57 (.56)***			.44 (.42)***			.49 (.47)***			.44 (.42)***

Note: $n = 340$ for Plans, $n = 164$ for Actual. r = Pearson correlation. β = standardized beta. ΔR^2 = change in R^2 for each step.
* $p < .05$. ** $p < .01$. *** $p < .001$.

Gender was entered on a first step as a control variable because males' physical size and metabolism allow them to drink more alcohol than females. Three subsequent steps added the psychosocial adjustment variables (self-image, perceived peer acceptance), personal goals (social, academic, and health goals), and beliefs about alcohol (fun, risk), respectively.[2] Table 13.2 presents the results of these analyses, including bivariate correlations between the predictors and criterion variables, standardized regression coefficients for each predictor at the step it was added to the equation, change in R^2 for each step, and total R^2, for each of the four criterion variables.

On the first step, gender predicted 4–7% of the variance in drinking, with males drinking and binge drinking more than females, as expected. The second step examined the relationship of psychosocial adjustment with alcohol use and binge drinking. From 12% to 14% of the variance in drinking was explained by the two predictors. Inspection of the correlations shows that students who felt more accepted by their peers planned to and actually did engage in more alcohol use and binge drinking, as hypothesized. Contrary to the hypothesis, self-image was not related bivariately to alcohol use or binge drinking. Nonetheless, self-image was a consistent predictor of drinking when levels of peer acceptance were controlled. That is, peer acceptance appeared to suppress the relationship of self-image and drinking (Pedhazur, 1982). In other words, students who had a more negative self-image than their level of peer acceptance would predict tended to drink more than students whose self-image was more positive than their level of peer acceptance would predict. Follow-up analyses designed to explore the nature of this relationship are discussed later in this chapter.

The third step added the students' social, academic, and health goals to the equation, explaining an additional 6–11% of the variance in the drinking measures. The importance of social goals consistently predicted alcohol use and binge drinking, both bivariately and when entered with the other predictors. That is, students who felt it was more important that they make friends and be popular tended to drink more alcohol. The importance of academic goals and health goals was much less consistently related to drinking, and the magnitude of the bivariate correlations and regression coefficients was much smaller than those for social goals. Believing academic goals were important predicted less planned binge drinking during the first 3 weeks of the semester but was not related to planned or actual alcohol use or to actual binge drinking. Believing health goals were important predicted less planned alcohol use and binge drinking but was not related to actual drinking. Only one of the eight bivariate correlations was significant.

A final step added students' beliefs about how fun and how risky they thought it was to drink alcohol. These two single-item predictors explained an additional 21–28% of the variance in planned and actual alcohol use and binge drinking. The bivariate correlations showed that the belief that drinking was fun was consistently strongly related to higher alcohol use and binge drinking (r = .55 to .71), and the belief that drinking was risky was consistently related to drinking less (r = −.35 to .41), both as hypothesized. When entered together with the other predictor variables, Fun maintained a strong positive independent prediction (β = .44 to .58) and Risk retained a minimal independent prediction (β = −.05 to −.14). A total of 44–57% of the variance in drinking was explained by the full set of predictors.

The Relative Salience of Motivations to Drink and Motivations to Not Drink

In order to address the hypothesis that motivations to drink would be more predictive of levels of alcohol and binge drinking than motivations to not drink or to limit drinking, a separate set of regressions was performed. The first two steps were identical to the previous analyses. On the third step, two blocks of predictors were entered simultaneously. One block contained the prodrinking characteristics and motivations to drink: social goals and the belief that drinking is fun (Block A). The other block contained the antidrinking motivations: academic goals, health goals, and the belief that drinking is risky (Block B). Because Blocks A and B were entered into the equation simultaneously, the R^2 associated with each block represents the unique contribution of the prodrinking and antidrinking motivations, respectively, to the prediction of alcohol use and binge drinking (Block R^2 is analogous to squared beta coefficients for sets of predictors). The results of this analysis showed that, as hypothesized, prodrinking motivations made a substantially larger unique contribution to the prediction of alcohol use and binge drinking (R^2 = .13 to .31) than did antidrinking motivations (R^2 = .01 to .03). Examination of the bivariate correlations and regression coefficients of the prodrinking variables (social goals, fun) versus the antidrinking variables (academic goals, health goals, risk) also supported the greater relative salience of prodrinking factors.

Predictors of Drinking More or Less Than Intended

The previous analyses showed that the predictors of planned and actual alcohol use were very similar, and these did not vary systematically by level of drinking (i.e., alcohol use versus binge drinking). The strong relationship between planned and actual alcohol use and binge drinking indicated that plans to drink were often realized. However, these correlations between intended and actual drinking also showed that over half of the variance in actual alcohol use was *not* accounted for by plans to drink ($1 - .69^2 = 52\%$). A final series of analyses examined the extent to which psychosocial adjustment, personal goals, and beliefs about alcohol accounted for *differences* between

Table 13.3. *Multiple regressions predicting discrepancy between planned and actual alcohol use by self-image, personal goals, and beliefs about drinking*

Step and predictors	Actual drinking			Actual binge drinking		
	spr	β	ΔR^2	spr	β	ΔR^2
Step 1: Control variables						
Planned alcohol use[a]	.69***[b]	.68***		.67**[b]	.65***	
Gender	.05	.03	.47***	.21**	.16**	.48***
Step 2: Psychosocial adjustment						
Self-image	.01	−.15*		.09	−.09	
Peer acceptance	.21**	.25***	.04***	.21**	.21**	.03*
Step 3: Personal goals						
Social	−.05	−.05		.05	.02	
Academic	−.03	−.04		−.01	−.00	
Health	−.09	−.07	.01	−.04	−.03	.00
Step 4: Beliefs about alcohol						
Fun	.22**	.17*		.20**	.18*	
Risk	−.19*	−.09	.02**	−.17*	−.07	.03**
Total R^2 (adjusted R^2)			.54 (.51)***			.53 (.51)***

Note: n = 164. spr = semipartial correlation, controlling for Time 1 drinking measure. β = standardized beta. ΔR^2 = change in R^2 for each step.
[a] Planned alcohol use and planned binge drinking.
[b] Correlation of Time 1 with Time 2 score.
*$p < .05$. ** $p < .01$. *** $p < .001$.

intended and actual drinking. Thus these analyses examined factors that predicted drinking more or less than intended.

Table 13.3 presents the results of the two multiple regressions, which followed the same strategy as those reported in Table 13.2 with the addition on Step 1 of plans to drink and binge drink, respectively. The criterion variables were actual drinking and binge drinking at Time 2. By thus controlling for plans to drink alcohol on the first step, the remaining steps in the regression analyses examined the extent to which the set of predictors accounted for discrepancies between intentions to drink and actual drinking behavior. As before, the first step also included gender.

The results for Step 1 showed that in addition to the large and significant relationship of planned to actual drinking, gender was a significant predictor of binge drinking. Examination of the means for males and females showed that males binge drank more than planned and females binge drank less than planned. Step 2 added self-image and peer acceptance. The pattern of results for drinking was similar to that in the previous regressions, with low self-image emerging as a predictor of drinking more than intended only when peer acceptance was included in the equation. Having high peer acceptance was related to drinking more and binge drinking more than intended. Step 3 added the three personal goals variables to the equation, with no additional significant relationships. Finally, Step 4 added beliefs about the fun and risk associated with drinking alcohol, with an additional 2% of the variance explained for drinking and 3% for binge drinking. Believing that drinking alcohol was fun predicted drinking and binge drinking more than intended during the first 3 weeks of school, and believing that drinking alcohol was risky predicted drinking less than intended.

Peer Acceptance and the Suppression of Negative Self-Image

Suppression occurs when a relationship between two variables is hidden (or suppressed) by the presence of a third variable (Pedhazur, 1982). Only when the effects of a third variable are controlled is the true relationship between the first two made visible. The negative relationship between self-image and drinking behavior appeared to be suppressed by peer acceptance, as the bivariate correlations between self-image and drinking were not significantly different from zero, yet self-image was negatively related to drinking when levels of peer acceptance were taken into account. Before accepting a conclusion of suppression, however, several analyses were performed to rule out competing possibilities. First, because self-image and peer acceptance were positively related to each other ($r = .64$) and, to a lesser extent, to the other predictors, multicollinearity was a potential concern. However, none of the tolerances was lower than .55, indicating that the correlations among the predictors were unlikely to be causing spuriously significant betas for self-image. Second, to investigate whether self-image might moderate (or statistically interact with) the relationships of peer acceptance and drinking, two series of regressions were computed, adding the interaction of self-image and peer acceptance both before and after the addition of the main effects. In all cases, the interaction explained no variance. The analyses reported in Tables 13.2 and 13.3 were also rerun separately for participants with negative and positive self-image (based on a median split). Across all criterion variables, the results for self-image and peer acceptance were replicated. That is, self-image was a negative predictor of drinking when levels of peer acceptance were controlled. Thus it appeared that peer acceptance suppressed the relationship of self-image with alcohol use and binge drinking.

Discussion

Psychosocial Adjustment

The relationship between the psychosocial adjustment variables and drinking behavior supported the paradox hypothesis about normative risk-taking behaviors. That is, although people who felt accepted by their peers also reported feeling good with respect to themselves in general, peer acceptance and general self-image were differentially related to alcohol use and binge drinking. Those who felt more accepted by their peers planned to and actually did drink more, and those who felt positively about their own impulse control, mastery, and emotional tone planned to drink less, consistent with previous research on younger adolescents (Maggs et al., 1995). Higher peer acceptance and more negative self-image together also predicted drinking more than planned. Subsequent analyses in the present sample supported the interpretation that the positive effect of drinking on feelings of peer acceptance suppressed the negative bivariate relationship of self-image and drinking. That is, self-image emerged as a significant predictor of drinking only when levels of peer acceptance were controlled. Thus, the portion of self-image that was unrelated to feelings of peer acceptance was negatively related to drinking.

The suppression by peer acceptance of the relationship between self-image and drinking behavior may help to explain past inconsistent results with respect to self-esteem and alcohol use (e.g., Jessor et al., 1991; Newcomb et al., 1986; Windle & Barnes, 1988). If some risk behaviors have both positive and negative antecedents and consequences for individuals, understanding the precise nature of these relationships may be very difficult. This finding is not surprising considering the strong contradictory messages about alcohol in North American culture (Peele, 1993). Films, television programs, beer advertisements, and popular legends about late adolescent binge drinking present a positive and alluring image of the fun and good times associated with alcohol use. In contrast, many negative images about alcohol use and abuse also abound: public service announcements against drinking and driving, rigorously enforced minimum purchase ages (21 in the United States, 18 or 19 in Canada), stiff penalties for drinking and driving, alcohol-related fatality statistics, and so on. The current results are consistent with the opposing influences on adolescents (and adults) with respect to drinking alcohol. That is, drinking was associated with greater interpersonal competence and confidence in interpersonal domains but also was related to less positive psychological adjustment. Thus the paradoxical regard in which alcohol is held in North American culture was reflected at the individual level: drinking appeared to be both good and bad.

Personal Goals

Developmental role transitions such as starting university or moving away from home have important consequences for personal goal setting because they provide a basis for anticipating what is possible, acceptable, and desirable at different ages and in different contexts (Nurmi, 1993). The results for the importance of social goals supported the proposition that drinking alcohol can be a rational behavior directed toward the attainment of developmentally and situationally relevant personal goals (Cantor, 1994; Silbereisen & Eyferth, 1986). The lack of consistent inhibitory effects of academic and health goals on alcohol use or binge drinking suggests that (1) students do not view drinking during the first weeks of the semester as having a negative effect on their academic performance and health; (2) drinking is so subjectively rewarding that any negative consequences are viewed as acceptable side effects; (3) drinking behavior is guided by forces other than rational decision making; or (4) some combination of these three factors. The fact that social, academic, and health goals did not predict differences between intentions to drink and actual drinking behavior suggests that the effect of personal goals on drinking was already accounted for by intentions or plans to drink. An important caveat to these results is that all data were collected during the first month of the first year of university, before academic demands and deadlines were in full swing. It is probable that the importance of academic goals would be significantly related to variables such as the cumulative number of nights spent socializing per semester or to alcohol use data collected during midterms or final exams.

Beliefs About Fun and Risk

The magnitude of the relationship between fun and risk ratings with planned and actual drinking behavior is remarkable in light of the simplicity of the measurement of fun and risk. By themselves, the single-item measures of fun and risk accounted for 30–50% and 12–17% of the variance in drinking, respectively. These two variables also added substantially to the prediction of planned drinking, actual drinking, and differences between planned and actual drinking above and beyond the effects of psychosocial adjustment and personal goals. This result underscores the importance of taking seriously the perspective of adolescents and the factors they consider as they make decisions about potentially risky yet immediately rewarding behaviors such as alcohol use and binge drinking (cf. Beyth-Marom & Fischhoff, chapter 5, this volume; Furby & Beyth-Marom, 1992). In particular, programs aiming to prevent or reduce undue risk-taking by adolescents need to acknowledge the positive functions served by these behaviors.

Relative Salience of Positive versus Negative Consequences

Prodrinking motivations (social goals, believing that drinking is fun) were much more strongly predictive of alcohol use and binge drinking than were antidrinking motivations (academic goals, health goals, believing that drinking is risky). This suggests that despite the potential dangers and disadvantages of drinking too much, the desire to partake in social activities involving alcohol is a strong force for students beginning university. Why would motivations to drink be so much more salient than motivations to not drink or to limit drinking? Positive functions of drinking, such as making friends and having fun, may be more salient because they are experienced more immediately than negative functions such as damaging one's health or failing an exam. A related possibility is that positive outcomes may seem more likely than negative ones. For example, the likelihood of meeting new people at any given party is relatively high, whereas the likelihood of getting fat or having an accident on any given night is relatively low.

Limitations

The results should be interpreted in light of several limitations of the design and the sample. First, a brief and specific period of transition (the start of university) was targeted in order to examine proximal predictors of and short-term change in self-directed behavior. The results might have been different during other periods of the school year; for instance, academic goals would be much more likely to predict the frequency of socializing and drinking during exam periods. Second, an intriguing finding was the apparent suppression of the relationship between self-image and alcohol use by peer acceptance. This result needs to be replicated, preferably with measures of peer acceptance and psychological adjustment selected to be more independent of each other than those in the present study. Third, the present study assessed the importance of personal goals. Goals have many other attributes than can be assessed, such as their salience, desirability, likelihood, and so on (Bauman et al., 1985; Emmons, 1986). Finally, although a period of transition was targeted, measures were not obtained concerning individual variations in the timing, characteristics, or experience of this transition. All research participants were beginning their first year in a university residence. Thus certain hypotheses could not be addressed, for example, contrasting the drinking behavior of adolescents who attend college versus those who do not, or between students who live in residence, with their parents, or in a fraternity/sorority house.

Health Promotion and Policy Implications

The present study has interesting implications for policies governing campus alcohol policies and health promotion efforts for adolescents and young adults. Students have strong personal needs that they will seek to meet through available means. Whether alcohol use is a means to an end or an end in itself, it is clear that students will not forgo opportunities to drink without the availability of equally attractive alternatives that serve the same instrumental functions. One harm-reduction strategy is to encourage responsible drinking in a protected environment. At the university studied in the present research, alcohol use was prohibited in public areas of the residences but permitted in private rooms, with the rationale that drinking close to home would be safer than drinking in downtown bars and transportation home would not be required. As in most Canadian and European universities, there are no fraternities or sororities at this institution; thus all on-campus housing is governed directly by the university.

Many students arrive at university with clear plans to drink alcohol, and they are typically successful in acting on these plans relatively quickly. University administrations and residence coordinators are faced with the challenges of trying to maintain a safe, orderly, and pleasant living environment, help students to adapt to college life, and prevent accidents. One possible strategy is rigid enforcement of campus antialcohol policies and other codes of student conduct. However, more democratic tactics may achieve better results, particularly if the longer-term goal is to help students learn to make responsible decisions about drinking as adults. For example, Triplet, Cohn, and White's (1988) study of residence hall judicial policies suggested that direct student input and participation in dormitories' rule enforcement fosters students' sense of personal control and responsibility, as well as promoting less tolerant attitudes toward serious rule breaking.

Campuses and communities can help make it possible for adolescents to drink responsibly. For example, bars could be required to actively encourage designated drivers and to provide free nonalcoholic drinks to volunteers. Campus policing can focus on penalizing excessive use rather than underage purchase of alcohol. Nonjudgmental counseling and support should be available to all. Individuals also need a certain level of knowledge and interpersonal skills to drink responsibly. For example, all students should know the best ways to help a friend who has drunk too much. Based on an innovative series of experiments where the alcoholic content of beer and mixed drinks at fraternity parties was secretly manipulated, Geller, Kalsher, and Clarke (1991) argued for the utility of nontraditional methods of reducing alcohol-related traffic accidents. The authors point to numerous strategies of promoting socially responsible drinking at parties, pubs, and other informal gatherings of friends, such as serving lower-alcohol beer, using smaller measuring instruments for drinks, administering free sobriety tests, and making blood alcohol meters available to patrons and guests.

Finally, students tend to overestimate the frequency and quantity of alcohol use and the prevalence of alcohol-related consequences among their friends, living group (e.g., residence, sorority house), and students in general (Baer & Carney, 1993; Baer, Stacy, & Larimer, 1991; Prentice & Miller, 1993). Because these systematic biases may serve as a means of prodrinking influence, campus alcohol abuse prevention programs can challenge these overestimates by providing students with accurate data on the very wide range of drinking norms and behaviors on campus, the prevalence of abstinence, and the relatively large number of students who do not get drunk.

Directions for Future Research

The current results support the argument that risk behaviors play a constructive role in adolescent development (Jessor, 1987; Maggs et al., 1995; Maggs & Hurrelmann, 1996; Silbereisen & Noack, 1988). The strong relationship between prodrinking motivations and alcohol use/binge drinking underscores the importance of taking very seriously the subjective functions served by risk behaviors such as drinking for adolescents and young adults. Future research would benefit by explicitly considering adolescents and young adults as active shapers and directors of their own behavior and development within the opportunities furnished by their environments (Hurrelmann, 1989; Silbereisen, 1985). Prevention and health promotion programs that target individual behavior typically assume that individuals have the power or ability to change their own behavior: We need theoretical models that test and support the conditions under which this assumption is true.

As mentioned previously, the suppression of the relationship between self-image and drinking by peer acceptance needs to be replicated, ideally with more independent measures of adjustment. Sociometric data on students' popularity would be an interesting addition to data on perceived peer acceptance. In other words, do people just *feel* more accepted by their peers when they drink more, due to overestimating positive social norms toward drinking (Baer & Carney, 1993; Baer et al., 1991; Prentice & Miller, 1993), or are people who drink and binge drink more often *actually* more popular?

An important direction for future research on this topic would be to systematically incorporate normative variations in the transition to university life as an aspect of the research design, as has been done, for example, concerning the transition to junior and senior high schools (see Eccles, Lord, Roeser, Barber, & Jozefowicz, chapter 11, this volume; Simmons & Blyth, 1987). Inter- and intracampus variations in college housing options (e.g., dormitory versus living with parents versus off-campus housing versus fraternity/sorority house), housing policies (e.g., no alcohol versus limited use permitted), and recreational opportunities (e.g., active campus culture versus commuter community) could be examined to determine their impact on students' drinking habits, social integration, and general adjustment to campus life. Longer-term longitudinal studies are needed to assess the continuing impact of personal characteristics on social and academic behavior, as well as potential consequences of behaviors such as drinking on multiple domains of life. Nancy Cantor's multiple-method (e.g., questionnaire, diary, beeper) studies of college students are excellent models that could be applied to the study of risk behavior (e.g., Cantor & Langston, 1989; Cantor et al., 1987). A very interesting issue that could be addressed using this approach would be the alternative strategies that students use to fulfill their strong social needs and goals.

Notes

1 Although it is impossible to verify empirically, a large portion of the attrition appeared to be due to differences in the commitment of the (unpaid) resident advisers who distributed and collected the questionnaires, rather than to differential dropout of the participants themselves.
2 To test for the possibility that the pattern of relationships was different between males and females, exploratory analyses added the two-way interactions of Gender and the seven predictors on three additional steps. Only 1 of 18 steps (three blocks × six criterion variables) yielded significant Step R^2/β values (thus not exceeding chance levels). Therefore, interactions are not presented.

References

Aseltine, R. H., Jr., & Gore, S. (1993). Mental health and social adaptation following the transition from high school. *Journal of Research on Adolescence, 3*, 247–270.

Baer, J. S., & Carney, M. M. (1993). Biases in the perceptions of the consequences of alcohol use among college students. *Journal of Studies on Alcohol, 54*, 54–60.

Baer, J. S., Stacy, A., & Larimer, M. (1991). Biases in the perception of drinking norms among college students. *Journal of Studies on Alcohol, 52*, 580–586.

Baltes, P. B. (1987). Theoretical propositions of life-span developmental psychology: On the dynamics between growth and decline. *Developmental Psychology, 23*, 611–626.

Bauman, K. E., Fisher, L. A., Bryan, E. S., & Chenoweth, R. L. (1985). Relationship between subjective expected utility and behavior: A longitudinal study of adolescent drinking behavior. *Journal of Studies on Alcohol, 46*, 32–38.

Baumrind, D. (1985). Familial antecedents of adolescent drug use: A developmental perspective. In C. LaRue Jones & R. J. Battjes (Eds.), *Etiology of drug use: Implications for prevention. NIDA Research Monograph 56: A RAUS Report* (pp. 13–44). Rockville, MD: National Institute on Drug Abuse.

Baumrind, D. (1987). A developmental perspective on risk taking in contemporary America. In C. E. Irwin (Ed.), *Adolescent social behavior and health: New Directions for Child Development, 37*, 93–125. San Francisco: Jossey-Bass.

Brandtstädter, J. (1984). Personal and social control over development: Some implications of an action perspective in life-span psychology. In P. B. Baltes & O. G. Brim (Eds.), *Life-span development and behavior* (Vol. 6, pp. 2–28). New York: Academic Press.

Brunstein, J. C. (1993). Personal goals and subjective well-being: A longitudinal study. *Journal of Personality and Social Psychology, 65*, 1061–1070.

Cantor, N. (1990). From thought to behavior: "Having" and "doing" in the study of personality and cognition. *American Psychologist, 45*, 735–750.

Cantor, N. (1994). Life task problem solving: Situational affordances and personal needs. *Personality and Social Psychology Bulletin, 20*, 235–243.

Cantor, N., & Langston, C. A. (1989). Ups and downs of life tasks in a life transition. In L. A. Pervin (Ed.), *Goal concepts in personality and social psychology* (pp. 127–167). Hillsdale, NJ: Erlbaum.

Cantor, N., Norem, J. K., Niedenthal, P. M., Langston, C. A., & Brower, A. M. (1987). Life tasks, self-concept ideals, and cognitive strategies in a life transition. *Journal of Personality and Social Psychology, 53*, 1178–1191.

Chapman, M., & Skinner, E. A. (1985). Action in development: Development in action. In M. Frese & J. Sabini (Eds.), *Goal-directed behavior: The concept of action in psychology* (pp. 200–213). Hillsdale, NJ: Erlbaum.

Chassin, L., Presson, C. C., & Sherman, S. J. (1989). "Constructive" vs. "destructive" deviance in adolescent health-related behaviors. *Journal of Youth and Adolescence, 18*, 245–262.

Clausen, J. S. (1991). Adolescent competence and the shaping of the life course. *American Journal of Sociology, 96*, 805–842.

Compas, B. E., Wagner, B. M., Slavin, L. A., & Vannatta, K. (1986). A prospective study of life events, social support, and psychological symptomatology during the transition from high school to college. *American Journal of Community Psychology, 14,* 241–257.

Crowley, J. E. (1991). Educational status and drinking patterns: How representative are college students? *Journal of Studies on Alcohol, 52,* 10–16.

Donovan, J. E., Costa, F. M., & Jessor, R. (1985). *Health questionnaire.* Boulder, CO: University of Colorado, Institute of Behavioral Science.

Emmons, R. A. (1986). Personal strivings: An approach to personality and subjective well-being. *Journal of Personality and Social Psychology, 51,* 1058–1068.

Flanagan, C., Schulenberg, J., & Fuligni, A. (1993). Residential setting and parent–adolescent relationships during the college years. *Journal of Youth and Adolescence, 22,* 171–189.

Furby, L., & Beyth-Marom, R. (1992). Risk taking in adolescence: A decision-making perspective. *Developmental Review, 12,* 1–44.

Gardner, W. (1993). A life-span rational-choice theory of risk taking. In N. J. Bell & R. W. Bell (Eds.), *Adolescent risk taking* (pp. 66–83). Newbury Park, CA: Sage.

Geller, E. S., Kalsher, M. J., & Clarke, S. W. (1991). Beer versus mixed-drink consumption at fraternity parties: A time and place for low-alcohol alternatives. *Journal of Studies on Alcohol, 52,* 197–204.

Hays, R. B., & Oxley, D. (1986). Social network development and functioning during a life transition. *Journal of Personality and Social Psychology, 50,* 305–313.

Health and Welfare Canada (1988). *Canada's health promotion survey: Technical report.* Ottawa, Ontario: Minister of Supply and Services Canada.

Hogan, D. P., & Astone, N. M. (1986). The transition to adulthood. *Annual Review of Sociology, 12,* 109–130.

Hurrelmann, K. (1989). Adolescents as productive processors of reality: Methodological perspectives. In K. Hurrelmann & U. Engel (Eds.), *The social world of adolescents: International perspectives* (pp. 107–118). Berlin: Walter de Gruyter.

Hurrelmann, K. (1990). Health promotion for adolescents: Preventive and corrective strategies against problem behavior. *Journal of Adolescence, 13,* 231–250.

Jessor, R. (1987). Problem-behavior theory, psychosocial development, and adolescent problem behavior. *British Journal of Addiction, 82,* 331–342.

Jessor, R., Donovan, J. E., & Costa, F. M. (1991). *Beyond adolescence: Problem behavior and young adult development.* New York: Cambridge University Press.

Johnston, L. D., & O'Malley, P. M. (1986). Why do the nation's students use drugs and alcohol? Self reported reasons from nine national surveys. *Journal of Drug Issues, 16,* 29–66.

Johnston, L. D., O'Malley, P. M., & Bachman, J. G. (1994). *National survey results on drug use from the Monitoring the Future Study, 1975–1993.* Rockville, MD: National Institute on Drug Abuse.

Kandel, D. B., & Yamaguchi, K. (1985). Developmental patterns of the use of legal, illegal, and medically prescribed psychotropic drugs from adolescence to adulthood. In C. LaRue Jones (Eds.), *Etiology of drug use: Implications for prevention. NIDA research monograph 56: A RAUS report* (pp. 13–44). Rockville, MD: National Institute on Drug Abuse.

Leventhal, H., & Keeshan, P. (1993). Promoting healthy alternatives to substance abuse. In S. G. Millstein, A. C. Petersen, & E. O. Nightingale (Eds.), *Promoting the health of adolescents: New directions for the twenty-first century* (pp. 260–284). New York: Oxford University Press.

Little, B. R. (1983). Personal projects: A rationale and method for investigation. *Environment and Behavior, 15,* 273–309.

Maggs, J. L. (1993). *Adolescent alcohol use as a goal-directed behaviour.* Unpublished doctoral dissertation, University of Victoria, Victoria, B.C., Canada.

Maggs, J. L., Almeida, D. M., & Galambos, N. L. (1995). Risky business: The paradoxical meaning of problem behavior for young adolescents. *Journal of Early Adolescence, 15,* 339–357.

Maggs, J. L., & Galambos, N. L. (1993). Alternative structural models for understanding adolescent problem behavior in two-earner families. *Journal of Early Adolescence, 13,* 79–101.

Maggs, J. L., & Hurrelmann, K. (1996). *Do substance use and delinquency have different implications for adolescents' peer relations?* Manuscript in review.

Marini, M. M. (1984). The order of events in the transition to adulthood. *Sociology of Education, 57,* 63–84.

Marini, M. M. (1985). Determinants of the timing of adult role entry. *Social Science Research, 14,* 309–350.

Markus, H., & Nurius, P. (1986). Possible selves. *American Psychologist, 41,* 954–969.

Moffitt, T. E. (1993). Adolescence-limited and life-course-persistent antisocial behavior: A developmental taxonomy. *Psychological Review, 100,* 674–701.

Newcomb, M. D., Bentler, P. M., & Collins, C. (1986). Alcohol use and dissatisfaction with self and life: A longitudinal analysis. *Journal of Drug Issues, 16,* 479–494.

Nurmi, J.-E. (1991). How do adolescents see their future? A review of the development of future orientation and planning. *Developmental Review, 11,* 1–59.

Nurmi, J.-E. (1993). Adolescent development in an age-graded context: The role of personal beliefs, goals, and strategies in the tackling of developmental tasks and standards. *International Journal of Behavioral Development, 16,* 169–189.

Offer, D., Ostrov, E., & Howard, K. I. (1982). *The Offer self-image questionnaire for adolescents: A manual* (3rd ed.). Chicago: Michael Reese Hospital.

O'Hare, T. M. (1990). Drinking in college: Consumption patterns, problems, sex differences, and legal drinking age. *Journal of Studies on Alcohol, 52,* 500–502.

Pascarella, E. T., & Terenzini, P. T. (1991). *How college affects students.* San Francisco: Jossey-Bass.

Pedhazur, E. J. (1982). *Multiple regression in behavioral research: Explanation and prediction* (2nd ed.). New York: Holt, Reinhart, & Winston.

Peele, S. (1993). The conflict between public health goals and the temperance mentality. *American Journal of Public Health, 83,* 805–810.

Prentice, D. A., & Miller, D. T. (1993). Pluralistic ignorance and alcohol use on campus: Some consequences of misperceiving the social norm. *Journal of Personality and Social Psychology, 64,* 243–256.

Schulenberg, J. E., O'Malley, P. M., Bachman, J. G., Wadsworth, K. N., & Johnston, L. D. (1996). Getting drunk and growing up: Trajectories of frequent binge drinking during the transition to young adulthood. *Journal of Studies on Alcohol, 57,* 289–304.

Schulenberg, J. E., Wadsworth, K. N., O'Malley, P. M., Bachman, J. G., & Johnston, L. D. (1996). Adolescent risk factors for binge drinking during the transition to young adulthood: Variable- and pattern-centered approaches to change. *Developmental Psychology, 32,* 659–674.

Semmer, N. K., Dwyer, J. H., Lippert, P., Fuchs, R., Cleary, P. D., & Schindler, A. (1987). Adolescent smoking from a functional perspective: The Berlin-Bremen study. *European Journal of Psychology of Education, 2,* 387–402.

Sharpe, D. J., & Lowe, G. (1989). Adolescents and alcohol: A review of the recent British research. *Journal of Adolescence, 12,* 295–307.

Shaver, P., Furman, W., & Buhrmester, D. (1985). Transition to college: Network changes, social skills, and loneliness. In S. Duck (Ed.), *Understanding personal relationships: An interdisciplinary approach* (pp. 193–219). London: Sage.

Shedler, J., & Block, J. (1990). Adolescent drug use and psychological health: A longitudinal inquiry. *American Psychologist, 45,* 612–630.

Sherrod, L. R., Haggerty, R. J., & Featherman, D. L. (1993). Introduction: Late adolescence and the transition to adulthood. *Journal of Research on Adolescence, 3,* 217–226.

Siggner, A. J. (1988). *Canada's health promotion survey: Technical report series: Special study on youth.* Ottawa: Minister of Supply and Services Canada.

Silbereisen, R. K. (1985). Action theory perspectives in research on social cognition. In M. Frese & J. Sabini (Eds.), *Goal-directed behavior: Psychological theory and research on action.* Hillsdale, NJ: Erlbaum.

Silbereisen, R. K., & Eyferth, K. (1986). Development as action in context. In R. K. Silbereisen,

K. Eyferth, & G. Rudinger (Eds.), *Development as action in context: Problem behavior and normal youth development* (pp. 3–16). Berlin: Springer-Verlag.

Silbereisen, R. K., & Noack, P. (1988). On the constructive role of problem behavior in adolescence. In N. Bolger, A. Caspi, G. Downey, & M. Moorehouse (Eds.), *Persons in context: Developmental processes* (pp. 152–180). Cambridge: Cambridge University Press.

Silbereisen, R. K., Schönpflug, U., & Albrecht, H. T. (1990). Smoking and drinking: Prospective analyses in German and Polish adolescents. In K. Hurrelmann & F. Lösel (Eds.), *Health hazards in adolescence* (pp. 167–190). Berlin: Walter de Gruyter.

Simmons, R. G., & Blyth, D. A. (1987). *Moving into adolescence: The impact of pubertal change and school context.* New York: Aldine de Gruyter.

Takahashi, K., & Majima, N. (1994). Transition from home to college dormitory: The role of preestablished affective relationships in adjustment to a new life. *Journal of Research on Adolescence, 4,* 367–384.

Triplet, R. G., Cohn, E. S., & White, S. O. (1988). The effect of residence hall judicial policies on attitudes toward rule-violating behaviors. *Journal of Applied Social Psychology, 18,* 1288–1294.

Turner, R., & Feldman, S. S. (1994, February). *The functions of sex in everyday life.* Paper presented at the Biennial Meetings of the Society for Research on Adolescence, San Diego, CA.

W. T. Grant, (1988). *The forgotten half: Pathways to success for America's youth and young families.* Washington, DC: Youth and America's Future: The William T. Grant Commission on Work, Family, and Citizenship.

Windle, M., & Barnes, G. M. (1988). Similarities and differences in correlates of alcohol consumption and problem behaviors among male and female adolescents. *International Journal of the Addictions, 23,* 707–728.

Zirkel, S. (1992). Developing independence in a life transition: Investing the self in the concerns of the day. *Journal of Personality and Social Psychology, 62,* 506–521.

14   Health Risks and Deviance in the Transition from School to Work

Eduard Matt, Lydia Seus, and Karl F. Schumann

Introduction

In recent decades, youth as a biographical phase has become increasingly characterized by numerous structural and individual risks. In particular, the reduction of occupational training and work options for adolescents with limited levels of education forces them into longer periods of qualification; this, in turn, leads to a delayed entry into the labor force. This development not only implies postponement but also differentiation and individualization of transitions into qualified work and adult life. The achievement of a favorable position within economic and employment structures can still be considered as the main criterion for the successful transition to adulthood (Buchmann, 1989; Heinz, 1993; National Research Council, 1993; Pätzold, 1988). The degree of success or failure in the process of finding a promising trajectory from school to work via occupational training is mainly dependent on social and other resources available to adolescents. In this chapter, we present some results from our study on the transition from school to work of German youths with low-level education, with a special focus on health and delinquency.

The German educational system is quite different from the American one (Petersen, Leffert, & Hurrelmann, 1993; Schumann, 1995). At the age of about 11 or 12 years, German pupils attend Grades 5 and 6 in a so-called phase of orientation. This phase enables the pupils, their parents, and the teachers to select from three school types the one that best fits the youth's capabilities. The three types of school are *Hauptschule* (Grades 7 to 10; students can also leave after Grade 9 or after having completed the prescribed years of schooling, in this case mostly without any certificate), *Realschule* (Grades 7 to 10), and *Gymnasium* (Grades 7 to 13). The three school types are stratified. Only

This research project is funded by a generous grant of the Deutsche Forschungsgemeinschaft (DFG). Under the title "Selection Processes in the Transition from School to Work and Deviant Behavior," the project is part of the Special Research Centre "Status Passages and Risks in the Life Course" (Sfb 186), which is jointly funded by the University of Bremen and the Deutsche Forschungsgemeinschaft (DFG). We are grateful for criticism and assistance from the other members of the research team: Gerhard-Uhland Dietz, Beate Ehret, Volker Mariak, and Fred Othold.

those pupils considered capable of entering university will go to the *Gymnasium*. The second type, *Realschule*, is attended by the largest number of adolescents. The pupils graduate at the age of 16 years with a certificate that enables them to continue training at school for technical and commercial occupations. The pupils judged to be the least skilled go to the *Hauptschule*, which is considered low-level education. There is still another type of school, *Sonderschule*, a school for the handicapped, attended by pupils with learning disabilities and behavioral, mental, or other problems.

For youth who have graduated from the *Hauptschule*, apprenticeship is the core of vocational training and education. Apprenticeships are available in about 420 occupations covering most blue- and white-collar jobs that do not require college or university training. An apprenticeship, which lasts for 3 or $3\frac{1}{2}$ years, combines firm-based training with 1 day of schooling per week in state-led vocational schools. Together these components form the so-called dual system. It is completed with a final examination in practice and theory and afterward confers job titles of office employee, skilled blue-collar worker, or white-collar worker (see Schumann, 1995).

In Germany, entry into the labor market is strongly dependent on the acquisition of formal certificates. Certain certificates are considered to be prerequisites for entering specific occupational careers. Graduates from both the *Hauptschule* and the *Realschule* compete for places in vocational training. Youths who leave school after having attended for only the minimum number of years prescribed by compulsory education experience particularly strong competition. They are victimized by a widespread process of displacement in which students with higher levels of education increasingly occupy the slots in the dual system of occupational training originally designed for students with regular (minimal) education provided mainly in the *Hauptschule*. However, the competition takes place not only between graduates of the *Hauptschule* and those with higher levels of education (*Realschule, Gymnasium*). In addition, immigrant adolescents compete with Germans for proper places in the system of occupational training. Furthermore, the system is highly segregated along gender lines; girls from the *Hauptschule* have access to only a small range of occupations with low incomes and poor employment prospects. For example, Seidenspinner (1988) has argued, "It has to be stressed that the equation poor qualification equals poor chances in the labor market has never been true for female youth. . . . In the actual situation of competition the qualified female graduate of the *Realschule* has at best the same chances as the male graduate of the *Hauptschule*" (pp. 63–64).

Competition is especially intense for youths who graduate from the lower-status schools, that is, *Hauptschule* and *Sonderschule*. More and more, the *Realschule* has become the standard type of education for the majority of youth. Seven out of 10 students today graduate from *Realschule* or attain an even higher level of education (Bertram & Gille, 1990). As a result, the

Hauptschule is now considered as the school for those who fail to comply with normal educational expectations. That is, "The more it becomes normal to receive higher education the more those who graduate from the *Hauptschule* understand that they will live a life in the lower stratum of society" (Schumann, 1994, p. 136).

Problems Related to the Status Passage

The differentiation within occupational structures, as well as the addition of substitutes for regular occupational training, has produced a variability that demands that youth make decisions under conditions of continuous change. It is not at all clear if one's chosen occupational training will guarantee permanent employment in the future. In addition to this complicated decision, the youth of today face transitions in other dimensions of their lives; various forms of interpersonal partnership, as well as of living accommodations, provide options among which adolescents must choose. The timing of these transitions is heterogeneous and not necessarily linked to the transition to work. An increased asyncrony between the various transitions within the status passage makes adolescents more dependent on psychosocial, familial, and economic resources; this creates a number of risks (Hogan & Astone, 1986; Hurrelmann, Holler, & Nordlohne, 1988; Strauss & Glaser, 1971).

The lack of synchrony, in which adolescents may experience success in some dimensions of their lives and failure in others, may lead to complications. These asynchronies are solved on the basis of the biographical perspective of youth. That is, the meaning an event has for a given person differs greatly according to his or her earlier experiences. Rather than the given status as such (e.g., being married, being a worker), it is the relevance this status has for the individual and his or her commitment to it that will lead to the adoption of adult changes in behavior (e.g., reduction of delinquency), as Sampson and Laub (1992) have convincingly argued. The same event, then, can have quite different consequences for the future of a particular youth. Sociological theory stresses that risks in the life course may have quite different meanings and relevance for different people. The ways in which individuals cope with these challenges can also be very different – for example, withdrawal from social situations, delinquency, psychosomatic symptoms, or health risk behavior. Therefore, events and changes in the life course can be understood only in the context of the individual biography. It is also important to consider gender differences. Any status passage will depend both on the structural conditions provided by the labor market and the resources available to the individual (e.g., education, social capital, relationships, parental support, health, motivation, aspiration, orientation toward work) (Keupp, 1990; Leisering, Geissler, Mergner, & Rabe-Kleberg, 1993; SFB186, 1993).

Individual Risk Behavior

Let us first discuss patterns of behavior that may threaten individual health. *Youth* and *health risks* seem to be concepts that do not go together well because *youth* seems to symbolize health, energy, success, and so on, not health risks or disease. However, some researchers, such as Hurrelmann and colleagues in Germany (e.g., Engel & Hurrelmann, 1989, 1993; Hurrelmann & Lösel, 1990), suggest that youths are showing increasing signs of illness. Behaviors that may jeopardize health seem to be an integral part of the everyday life of adolescents. Sociologists and other scholars in the humanities and social sciences are concerned about the increasing number of adolescents who act in risky ways: "In terms of socialization theory, risk behavior includes all types of behavior which in the long run may lead to a high probability of difficulties in social integration or of problems in the development of a stable and healthy personality" (Engel & Hurrelmann, 1993, p. 9, our translation). Behaviors that may generally reduce the chances of living a successful life as an adult include the use of legal and illegal drugs, dropping out of school, dropping out of occupational training (the dual system), and delinquent and aggressive behavior.

The health of adolescents has been studied with increasing intensity during the last decade (see, e.g., Hurrelmann and colleagues, cited earlier; National Research Council, 1993). In addition, the definition and conceptualization of health and illness have been broadened by the World Health Organization to include physical, psychological, and social well-being, providing a new perspective for understanding the situation of adolescents. "This broader view of health – emphasizing mental and social, as well as physical, aspects and a sense of well-being as well as the absence of problems – can be said to fit the period of adolescence much better than does a narrow focus on the absence of physical health problems" (U.S. Office of Technology Assessment, 1991, p. 4).

Although recent studies of substance use (Deutsche Hauptstelle gegen die Suchtgefahren, 1989; Scheerer & Vogt, 1989) do not distinguish between the use of legal (e.g., alcohol, nicotine) and illegal (e.g., hashish, heroin) drugs, only the latter would be considered delinquent from a legal perspective. Both drug use and other forms of delinquency may constitute severe health risks and are potentially detrimental to future life chances. When we focus on nonaccepted behavior in general, we use the term *deviance*. Looking at such behavior in a legal and criminological context, we use the term *delinquency*.

Although the use of legal drugs by adults in Western societies is rarely questioned, in the case of adolescents it is considered as deviant and problematic (Zielke, 1993). There has been a reduction in the primary drug of choice, alcohol, since the mid-1970s (Bundesministerium für Gesundheit, 1991). This development, however, should not be misunderstood because although it is true that today fewer adolescents consume alcohol, the amount they consume is about the same as that drunk by youths in the early 1980s. If one includes the social status of the adolescents in the analysis, one finds differences between the youths of today and those of the 1980s in patterns of alcohol use only with regard to the modalities or context of first consumption and with respect to predispositions for misuse. In Germany, unemployed youths, young workers, and youths from the lower social strata seem to be at a much higher risk of alcohol misuse (Franzkowiak & Stoessel, 1990). This is also true when referring to the definition by Engel and Hurrelmann (1993) of conditions that create stress: "As has been shown in our research, enduring demands on youth for achievement under conditions of growing competition and reduced guarantees to obtain a desirable occupational training and/or position may be said to trigger psychosocial and psychosomatic symptoms of stress" (pp. 2–3).

The youths studied in our own research (e.g., Schumann, 1995) may be considered to be at high risk with respect to social background, occupational prospects, and risky behavior. Another risk factor that is relevant to our sample is involvement in delinquent behaviors such as theft, bodily harm, and property damage. In Germany, self-reported delinquency reaches its peak after the majority of adolescents have left school, not before (Feest, 1993). In two large cities, the peak for males has been found to be 17 years, which may be a good estimate for male youths living in urban areas in general (Albrecht, Howe, & Wolferhoff-Neetix, 1988). According to criminological studies, another risk for students with the lowest level of education (such as those studied in our own research) is involvement in illegal behavior (e.g., Farrington, Gallagher, Morley, Ledger & West, 1986; Hagan, 1993; Sack, 1987). Failure in the school system seems to be correlated with deviant and criminal behavior: prisoners, for example, often lack education and occupational training. Thus graduates from *Hauptschule* and *Sonderschule* can be seen as youths who face a particularly difficult and risky period during the status passage from school to work.

In the following section, we describe the sample and methods of our study. Next, we present some results. First, we focus on the description of health-risk behavior and delinquency in order to determine the level of these behaviors, as well as some consequences for the transition into the occupational system. Then we discuss the causal link of risk factors and further development. We contrast two alternative concepts to analyze these relationships: the *causation hypothesis*, namely, that failure in occupational training leads to an increase in risk behavior, and the *selection hypothesis*, namely, that health damage and risk behavior lead to failure in the integration into occupational training. We will discuss which one is more relevant in this portion of the life span. We attempt to show some relationships between health-risk behavior, delinquency, and failure and success in the occupational system.

The Bremen Study: Methods and Sampling Procedure

The Bremen study is a longitudinal study of a cohort of German adolescents who left school after having completed the compulsory 9 years of schooling. Our main research purpose is to determine the effect of different transitions from school to work on delinquency. The transition into work life may be negotiated via apprenticeships, training schemes, phases of unemployment, part-time work, and so on; these different trajectories may have an impact on substance use as well as delinquency. We study a cohort of former pupils who have the lowest level of schooling because we expect these individuals to face the highest risk of unemployment and involvement in deviant behavior. The cohort (macro panel) consists of 424 former pupils representing all those who left *Hauptschulen* and *Sonderschulen* in 1989 in the city of Bremen who were willing to participate in our research. They were questioned shortly before leaving school in 1989 (Time 1) and again in 1992–1993 (Time 2). At Time 1, we asked questions about their occupational wishes and plans, their first contacts with the police, and their attitude toward work. The questionnaires were distributed and filled out in classrooms under the supervision of a member of the research team. At Time 2, we asked questions concerning occupational career, social network, relationships with family and peers, level of alcohol and drug use, problems related to drinking alcohol, health-related behavior, work attitudes, finances, attitudes toward delinquency, job satisfaction, and other issues. The questions were asked by an interviewer, primarily in the youth's home. A second questionnaire concerning major delinquent activities was filled out separately and anonymously. Delinquency was measured by a self-report questionnaire similar to that used by other criminologists and researchers (e.g., Thornberry, Lizotte, Krohn, Farnworth, & Jang, 1991). Adolescents indicated how many times they had engaged in each of 32 delinquent activities (e.g., vandalism, burglary, fraud). Scores were available for three time periods: (1) prior to leaving school, (2) from the time of leaving school to the end of 1991, and (3) the year of 1992. Participants also indicated whether their delinquent acts had led to contact with the police or the court system. The absolute number of delinquent acts was transformed into a logarithmic scale. All these items were transformed into a delinquency index by time periods.

From this cohort, a micro panel of 60 adolescents was selected and so far has been interviewed four times (in 1989, 1990, 1992, and 1994) using an unstructured open interview technique. We were able to link information collected at Time 1 of the macro panel to Time 1 of the micro panel and have used insights from the micro panel at Times 2 and 3 for data collection and analysis of Time 2 of the macro panel, and so forth.

For the cohort of 424 youths, the mean age at Time 1 was 15.9 years. Forty-five percent of the cohort were female, and 17% had a minority status (immigrants and persons with other than German nationality). The majority of the adolescents started an apprenticeship directly after school (69% of the males, 57% of the females). Many participated in training schemes before they started their apprenticeships (17.8% of the males, 17.4% of the females). Others went into another type of schooling or into unskilled work. Not all have managed to enter the dual system; a substantial group were forced to settle for less attractive substitutes.

Risky Behavior and Delinquency in the Transition from School to Work

We now present some results concerning success and failure in occupational training, delinquent and health-related behavior, and the impact of these behaviors on the trajectory from school to work. We start with some descriptive data on occupation and health-risk behavior. In the second subsection, we explore the direction of the causal link between health risks and occupational success.

Occupational Training and Delinquency

We distinguish six groups that describe the variety of courses used to obtain an appropriate level of occupational training along the lines of success and failure, first entry, and changes in the course of training. The first group consists of youths who after 3 years had graduated from the dual system and were eligible for advanced positions in their respective crafts (e.g., for males: car mechanic, locksmith, joiner; for females: hairdresser, salesperson). The second group consists of those who entered into an apprenticeship directly after school and still occupied this status in 1992. The youths in the third group also started an apprenticeship but later switched to another one, which was still in progress in 1992. The fourth group did not make it into an apprenticeship after school and needed an interim period of additional training (on the level of substitutes) until they managed to obtain an apprenticeship contract. The fifth group consists of those who, after dropping out of the dual system, started unskilled work. The sixth and last group comprises adolescents who did not manage to enter the dual system and started with unskilled work immediately after leaving school. At Time 2, a considerable proportion of the youths in Groups 5 and 6 was unemployed. Figure 14.1 shows the distribution of the six groups according to gender.

Only half of the adolescents managed to remain in the dual system contin-

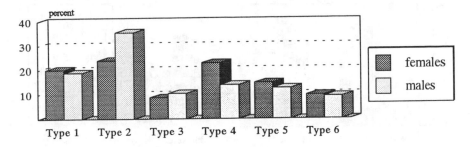

Chi-square: 10.2; df = 5; p = .063; n = 424

Type 1: Graduated from the dual system, n = 82
Type 2: In apprenticeship, n = 129
Type 3: Switch to another apprenticeship, n = 41
Type 4: Apprentice after some additional training, n = 75
Type 5: Drop out from the dual system, n = 57
Type 6: No qualification attempts; unskilled work, n = 40

Figure 14.1. Gender distribution of occupational training status 3 years after leaving school.

uously. The other half began a more complicated, and therefore more risky, process of occupational training. Ten percent dropped out of the dual system for some time but managed to reenter it (Type 3). Seventeen percent started in a substitute type of occupational training and were later accepted for an apprenticeship (Type 4). Some of the dropouts from apprenticeships did not manage to obtain a new contract (13.4%); some did not even manage to enter the dual system at any time and are now working as unskilled laborers (9.4%). These data are quite representative of Germany in general (Bundesminister für Bildung und Wissenschaft, 1992). Moreover, the report of the U.S. National-al Research Council (1993) suggested that one-fourth of all youth in the United States are at risk because of their dim occupational prospects. With regard to gender, the distribution among the six groups is less favorable for women, although the significance level of $p < .05$ was not reached. We now turn to a discussion of delinquency and health-risk behavior and their possible impacts on success or failure in occupational training.

In order to test the hypothesis that delinquency may play a role with regard to success or failure in the transition from school to work, we divided the time period between graduation from school and Time 2 into two phases (B, C). We did so because the structure of the data from Wave 2 allowed us to determine the level of delinquency among the youths in our sample for each of these phases and thus to say something about changes in delinquency from school-time (Phase A) to the period after leaving school in 1989. Phase B covers the first $2\frac{1}{2}$ years after graduation (1989–1991), and Phase C includes the entire 1992 year (mean age: 19.6 years). Figure 14.2, combining changes in delin-

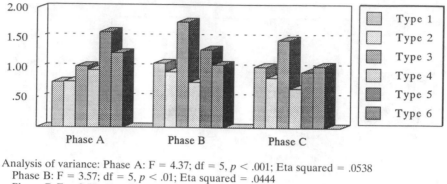

Analysis of variance: Phase A: F = 4.37; df = 5, p < .001; Eta squared = .0538
    Phase B: F = 3.57; df = 5, p < .01; Eta squared = .0444
    Phase C: F = 2.57; df = 5, p < .05; Eta squared = .0323
    Differences between Phase A and C: F = 1.09; df = 5; n.s.; Eta squared = .025
    Differences between Phase B and C: F = 1.94; df = 5; n.s.; Eta squared = .025
(n = 391)
Type 1: Graduated from the dual system, n = 76
Type 2: In apprenticeship, n = 122
Type 3: Switch to another apprenticeship, n = 34
Type 4: Apprentice after some additional training, n = 73
Type 5: Drop out from the dual system, n = 49
Type 6: No qualification attempts, n = 37

Figure 14.2. Delinquency (means) according to success in occupational training for three phases: school (A), 1989–1991 (B), 1992 (C).

quency and types of trajectories in occupational training (or work), does not show a conclusive picture.

Although there is a significant correlation between the occupational course and delinquency, the relationship is not very strong. According to these data, success and failure in occupational training are not clearly related to the levels of delinquency in phases B and C. Contrary to our expectations, the trend shows that successful youths (Types 1–3) seem to increase their delinquency, whereas those who fail tend to reduce it. The least delinquent are those who, after spending some time in training substitute positions, managed to enter the dual system at last (Type 4). Those with a high delinquency rate while attending school experienced the greatest problems entering the occupational system. They failed more than others in getting an apprenticeship. However, many of those with high levels of delinquency also succeeded in entering the dual system. Thus, our first major finding is that success and failure are not clearly related to risk behavior in terms of delinquency, and changes in the level of delinquency are not significantly related to types of occupational course.

Taking Personal Risks

The transition from school to work may also be influenced by the extent to which the individuals take personal risks. Let us describe the frequency of risk behaviors in our sample at Time 2 (1992). With respect to alcohol use, only 2.5% of males and 8.3% of females reported never drinking alcohol; 40.1% of males and 70.2% of females drank one or two times a month; 31.8% and 16%, respectively, drank once weekly; 22.7% and 5.0%, respectively, drank several times a week; and 2.9% and 0.6%, respectively, drank daily. This represented a significant gender difference in the frequency of drinking (chi-square = 59.6, $df = 4$, $p < .001$). This result corresponds to findings from other research demonstrating different drinking patterns between males and females (Engel & Hurrelmann, 1993; Franzkowiak & Stoessel, 1990). Females tend to prefer wine, whereas males tend to select beer and hard liquor. With respect to the quantity of beer consumed per drinking occasion, 52.7% of males drank six or more glasses (compared to 14.4% of females), 32.1% drank three to five glasses (28.8% of females), and 13.2% of males drank one to two glasses (37.2% of females) (chi-square = 67.3, $df = 3$, $p < .001$). With respect to the quantity of wine consumed, 23.4% of females drank three to five glasses per occasion (compared to 3.3% of males), and 35.1% drank one to two glasses (15.6% of males) (chi-square = 30.1, $df = 2$, $p < .001$). With respect to drunkenness, 39.3% of males and 67.2% of females had never been drunk in the month preceding Time 2; 39.7% and 29.9%, respectively, had been drunk once or twice; 11.7% and 1.5%, respectively, had been drunk three or four times; and 9.3% and 1.5%, respectively, had been drunk even more often (chi-square = 34.8, $df = 3$, $p < .001$). It should be noted that German youth consume alcohol less frequently than American youth (see, e.g., Hamilton, 1987).

A study from Baden-Württemberg (a state in southwest Germany) conducted in 1989 among 12- to 25-year-old youths showed that 19% consumed alcohol regularly and 33% did so occasionally (MAGS, 1989). The respective percentages we found in our study are considerably higher (42.1% regularly, 53% occasionally).

The frequencies for the use of cannabis, the most widespread illegal drug, are rather high. In Engel and Hurrelmann's (1993) sample, 15–30% of 20-year-olds had had experiences with hashish or marijuana. In our sample, self-reports of drug use indicated that 21.6% had consumed such drugs at least once in their lives. Hurrelmann and Engel (1993) reported that 5% of their sample regularly used soft drugs. In our sample, only 3.2% of the youths could be considered regular users: Only 2.5% of the males and 1.1% of the females used soft drugs several times a week; 2.1% and 0.5%, respectively, did so once a week; 7.5% and 3.3%, respectively, did so once or twice per month; and 88% and 95.1%, respectively, never used them. There were no statistical differences in illegal drug use between females and males, in contrast to the consumption of alcohol.

The use of hard drugs was very infrequent in our sample. Only four adolescents (1%) reported that they used hard drugs, 0.5% of them daily and 0.5% occasionally. These figures are similar to those reported by the Bundeszentrale

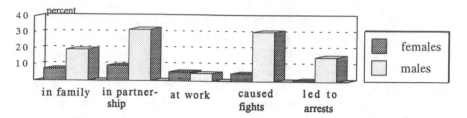

Figure 14.3. Youth reporting that drunkenness causes (once or more often) problems in social relationships.

für gesundheitliche Aufklärung (Federal Drug Prevention Office, 1990), which found that 0.3% of 12- to 25-year-old youths consumed cocaine and 0.2% consumed heroin.

To conclude, it can be said that the majority of our sample (which may be considered representative of German graduates from *Hauptschule* and *Sonderschule*) do not use alcohol or drugs excessively. We now turn to the consequences of the consumption patterns described with respect to social reactions to such risky behavior (see Figure 14.3).

Drunkenness causes many problems, especially in relationships and with agents of social control. Not surprisingly males reported more problems with family and romantic partners; they also reported more fights and arrests due to drinking. Alcohol may not cause many health problems at this age, but it does contribute to troubles in other realms: fighting and delinquency. Impacts on work and occupational training seem to be negligible; not surprising, if one considers that drunkenness occurs mostly on weekends.

The Impact of Health Status on Integration Into the Job Market

The transition from school to work is also influenced by aspects of physical health. For example, 11.3% of both male and female respondents stated that they were not able to choose their favorite occupational career because of health problems. In addition, in the course of occupational training, 41.1% ($n = 163$) dropped out and/or switched to another form of education. The main reasons for dropping out and changing are presented in Table 14.1.

Of the reasons measured by our checklist, the main reasons for dropping out and changing in both sexes were conflicts with teachers or instructors and disappointment with the type of occupational training chosen. Women cited health reasons more often, whereas men suffered more from dissatisfying working conditions. Unfortunately, the questionnaire did not ask respondents to explain what they meant by "health reasons." Therefore, the actual conditions, subjective experiences, and types of behavior that they may have asso-

Table 14.1. *Main reasons given for changes of and dropping out from apprenticeships or other qualification attempts (n = 163)*

	Females	Males	Total (%)	*n*
Conflicts with teachers	14.3%	12.7%	13.5%	22
Disappointments	13.1%	13.9%	13.5%	22
Health*	16.7%	6.3%	11.7%	19
Do not like school	9.5%	6.3%	7.5%	13
Bad working conditions	2.4%	11.4%	6.3%	11
Other reasons	44.0%	49.4%	46.6%	76

*$p < .01$ for gender difference.

ciated with the answer "health reasons" can only be illustrated by drawing on the qualitative material collected from our micro panel.

In these interviews, the adolescents reported problems with allergies, psychosomatic disturbances due to conflicts at the work site, and various other handicaps, such as poor eyesight, back pain, and general physical weakness. One has to consider, though, that to some extent "illness" is treated as an objective quality or status beyond personal control. Because illness, in this sense, may not be regarded as a matter of personal responsibility, the adolescent may have been using it as an excuse to drop out or change. Nonetheless, we agree with many researchers (e.g., Petermann, Bode, & Schlack, 1990) that health problems, especially allergies and chronic respiratory diseases, seem to increase rather than decrease during adolescence. Those who experienced health impairments were less successful than others (see later). However, not only are objective indicators of health important for successful completion of occupational training, but even more essential is the capacity to cope with problems. If the adolescent succeeds in finding an alternative (e.g., another apprenticeship contract), then the consequences for his or her future will not be at all negative. But without such an alternative, health becomes a very restrictive factor. These relationships can be demonstrated with reference to some case studies of adolescents who belong to the small sample for which we have qualitative data.

Due to illnesses in school, for example, *Adele* had to leave the *Realschule* and go back to the lower-status *Hauptschule*. As a graduate from this type of school she later had no chance to become a merchant, her favored profession. She also failed to enter occupational training as a hairdresser, her second preferred choice, due to an allergy. Eventually, however, she found a type of training (shop assistant in a bakery) that, at least in part, seemed to fit her interest in sales. She liked it and was successful.

Due to illness, *Afra* did not attend school regularly; however, this did not reduce her success in school. A physical handicap prevented her from obtaining a contract for her preferred apprenticeship as a nurse. Her grandmother and mother had been nurses, and *Afra* urgently wanted to continue this family tradition. She could not think of any alternative and ended up with no occupational training at all.

These examples illustrate how illness or health risks may have quite different consequences for entry into and progress in occupational training. Health problems may limit a person's life course options, in some cases leading to a complete breakdown of a self-determined life and career trajectory.

In apprenticeship, health problems do not seem to bother the youth too much. Seventeen percent of the youths (19.1% of males, 15.8% of females; chi-square $= 9.4$, $df = 2$, $p < .01$) report having accepted health risks during work to avoid being fired. Following are three examples from case studies based on our qualitative data.

Francis mentions health problems with his hip and spine that may force him to give up his occupation; but he wants at least to complete his apprenticeship. Thereafter he hopes to begin his training in the field of computers.

Fleming's case is similar. He suffers from back pain, so he does not expect to be able to work in his occupation as a mechanic. He intends, however, to complete his training and is attempting to add to his education a diploma completed at night school.

Jack is a waiter who has serious back problems. He does not want to lose his job, so he ignores the illness and does not ask for medical advice because he is afraid the physician might suggest that he quit his job. Despite his pain, he even works overtime when required. He identifies strongly with his occupation as well as his colleagues, and does all he can to keep his job.

The strong interest in completing the apprenticeship is understandable if one considers the particular value of graduation from the dual system for success in the German labor market. A certificate is necessary for further career plans and is important for providing good chances in the labor market, even for jobs in other trades or for unskilled work. Graduation broadens a person's future occupational options, even if he or she cannot stay in the field where the training was obtained.

Health Risks and Prevention During Occupational Training

As indicated before, the health status of adolescents plays an important role in the process of occupational training. In some crafts, applicants for training are required to undergo health checks. Sometimes training cannot be continued as a result of health problems. It is also important to consider health damage due to work conditions. This relationship between work and health may be illustrated by some figures: 18% of the youths confirmed that they already had accepted health risks at the workplace to keep their jobs, 11% reported that they had to change to another apprenticeship due to health problems, and 38% agreed with the statement "I do not care what work does to my health." Despite all these health problems, the question remains: Does health impairment lead to failure in occupational training?

In the scientific discussion of youth health problems, the relationships between occupational training and health risks have thus far received little attention. Is health damage a consequence of compliance with the instructors' expectations? Are vocational training instructors concerned with the health of the trainees at all? Is there any relationship between success in occupational training and health status? In a related field, Elkeles and Seifert (1993) studied whether and how unemployment and health problems are related. Based on data from the German socioeconomic panel, they tried to determine whether the causation hypothesis or the selection hypothesis is more powerful. The causation hypothesis implies that failure in the labor market causes health problems. The selection hypothesis implies that persons with poor health may be discriminated against in the labor market. According to the results of Elkeles and Seifert, the selection hypothesis seems to be more consistent with the data. Similar questions can be addressed based on our data. The causation hypothesis could be expressed as follows:

A: Failure in occupational training causes behavior that may damage health (e.g., less successful youths drink alcohol more often).

The selection hypothesis may be stated this way:

B1:   Those who accept health risks will be less successful than others. For example, individuals who use drugs will be less likely to graduate from the dual system.

The selection hypothesis may also be expressed in the reverse direction as far as job-related health risks are concerned:

B2:   The acceptance of health risks at the workplace may increase the chances of being successful.

Because we have panel data, we are able to evaluate the support for the causation hypothesis by relating success or failure in occupational training after about 2 years (i.e., at the end of 1991) to risk behavior in 1992. For a test of the selection hypothesis, we can use our knowledge of health-related behavior prior to the end of 1991 to predict the status in occupational training achieved by the end of 1992. However, one must keep in mind that the true direction of the relationship between health-damaging behavior and work conditions and success or failure in occupational training cannot be determined specifically. This is due to autocorrelative effects that may exist with regard to each of the variables (health, success/failure) but that have not been measured. That is, if youths drop out from their first apprenticeship, their chances of obtaining a new apprenticeship contract are reduced, so that early failure may cause consecutive failures. Also, the readiness to take health risks such as drinking alcohol may increase over time. This process can be perpetuated if an adolescent belongs to a peer group that has been continuously involved in assaults or heavy consumption of alcohol since secondary school.

Table 14.2. *Relationship between health-related behavior and vocational training failure*

Health-related behavior in 1992	Failure in vocational training before the end of 1991
Consumption of alcohol	.15*
Consumption of soft drugs	.12
Consumption of hard drugs	.12*
Frequency of assaults	.04
Frequency of drug offenses	.10

*$p < .05$.

Such autocorrelations of the variables over time may obscure the existing relationships. However, it is possible to examine which of the two directions of the relationship between health and success/failure has stronger supporting evidence.

Causation Hypothesis

If one considers success or failure in occupational training as an independent variable and looks at its effect on later health-related behavior, the results presented in Table 14.2 are obtained. No relationships were observed between failure in occupational training and participation in violent acts, the consumption of soft drugs, or drug offenses in 1992. However, adolescents who had experienced failure in their vocational training before the end of 1991 were at increased risk for consumption of alcohol and hard drugs in 1992. In other words, those who ran into problems during their apprenticeships consumed alcohol more often than others and were more likely to consume hard drugs. Thus, vocational difficulties did not seem to lead to an increase in violent behavior, but they did result in increased drug use. Because hard drug use is not widespread, we do not wish to state that failure in the vocational system leads to drug addiction. But it is important to note that the time span measured is not very long, so the potentially more detrimental long-term effects of failure could not be assessed.

Selection Hypothesis

Unfortunately, we cannot use the same set of variables to test the selection hypothesis because we did not collect health-related data for earlier phases of the adolescents' lives. This was impossible because the youths were still in school at Time 1 and had not reached the legal age, which forced us to restrict

Table 14.3. *Health-related behavior as a precondition for failure*

Failure in sustaining occupational training occurred more often:	
in case of drug use in school	$p < .05$
in case of drug offenses after leaving school until 1991	$p < .05$
if assaults were committed during school time	$p < .05$
if assaults were committed after leaving school	n.s.
if respondents suffered from diseases after leaving school	$p < .05$

our data collection in order to obtain parental consent. Table 14.3 gives a first overview.

From this perspective, we find more evidence for detrimental effects of risk behavior on vocational training. A high level of drug use and assaults during school time are negatively related to later success in entering the dual system. For those who succeed in entering the dual system, drug use but not assaults seems to have a further negative effect on success. In addition, health problems experienced after leaving school are associated with more negative occupational outcomes. We conclude that assaults have a negative effect at the beginning of the transition but not in the course of the apprenticeship. Drug use (especially hard drugs) and drug-related delinquency seem to have a negative effect both in school and during the apprenticeship. Thus, the selection hypothesis must be modified. Not every type of delinquency has detrimental effects. Depending on an individual's personal situation, some health-related behaviors may cause negative effects under some circumstances, whereas others may lead to negative consequences only under certain conditions during their transition from school to work. Furthermore, as expected, Table 14.3 shows that the effect of health problems during occupational training is more important than delinquency.

For an explanation of the limited impact of health variables on success and failure in occupational training, one should know more about how the selection process works. We can answer this question only in a very preliminary way if we examine the tolerance of youths toward health risks associated with working conditions (a measure of attitude), as well as the actual acceptance of suffering from health damage due to work (a measure of behavior). Such attitudes and behaviors are potential strategies employees may use as a safeguard against possible dismissal. We found that failure occurs more often when apprenticeship contracts are canceled due to health-related reasons (chi-square $= 41.6$, $df = 3$, $p < .001$) than when adolescents demand that the work must not endanger their health (n.s.) or when they refuse to tolerate health risks at work (n.s.). The results do not suggest that instructors in any way select according to health-related behavior. Rather, it seems that self-selection may take place among those who switch from one apprenticeship to another. This at least is true of health risks that occur in the workplace.

If, however, the youths commit delinquent acts that entail health risks, this may have negative consequences in terms of the reactions of their instructors or others. Finally, the expectations youths have concerning guarantees of their health provided by arrangements at the workplace are not correlated with the use of drugs or alcohol, nor are they related to selection due to health handicaps. However, there is a statistical relationship between such expectations and a lack of participation in violence ($F = 3.1$, eta-square $= .0235$, $df = 3, p < .05$). And, of course, this preventive orientation is strongly related to the degree of toleration of health risks at work (chi-square $= 15.1, df = 6$, $p < .05$).

Youths accept health risks at the workplace only to a certain degree. However, the range of this tolerance seems to be very unstable, as noted by the unimpressive correlation between two measurements of this tolerance taken in 1989 and 1992 ($r = .206, p < .001$). The low relationship between this protective attitude and the fact that health risks have already been taken at the work place is another case in point (chi-square $= 16.071, df = 6, p < .05$). The experience of such damage is also not significantly correlated with success or failure in training. If at all, selection seems to be taking place in relation to health-risk behavior outside of the job. The use of alcohol produces substantial problems in other realms, and the use of drugs undermines attempts to obtain vocational training.

These relationships have been confirmed, in part, in an additional study (Mariak, in preparation) in which qualitative data were collected from instructors in the dual system. The instructors seemed to judge such risk behavior outside the job in terms of moral evaluations inasmuch as such behavior is believed to have negative consequences for trainees' attitudes toward their work. Such moral evaluations may be the basis for selection (dismissal) of these "deviants" (see Mariak & Matt, 1993).

Conclusion

The status passage from school to work is important for the placement of individuals in the social structure. Due to the variability and lack of regulation of this transition, risks of many kinds influence the course of the passage. One should expect that deviance, the general status of health, and health-risk behaviors may have negative effects. In particular, we would expect that an accumulation of such risks may contribute to a less than optimal development.

The results of our study, however, show a different picture. Drinking large amounts of alcohol does lead to problems within the family, as well as with one's girlfriend or boyfriend, but it does not seem to cause difficulties at the workplace, the sector we focus on mainly in our study. The relationship between risky behavior and delinquency, on the one hand, and success or failure in obtaining occupational training, on the other, seems to be rather weak, with the exception of illegal (hard) drug use. Deviance seems to be widely unrelated: The successful apprentices score as high on deviance as the unsuccessful. It is important to examine not only health-risk behaviors per se, but also the consequences and problems these behaviors may cause in other realms of life.

We believe that one explanation for the joint occurrence of success in obtaining occupational training and deviance may lie in the separation of work and leisure. Youths who commit deviant acts seem to do so more frequently on weekends and seem to take care that their performance in the dual system is not affected by their behavior during their leisure time. This separation of work and leisure seems also to play a role in relation to health. Here, however, a general tendency of youths to disregard health, possibly based on the assumption that health is an everlasting resource, may lead to behavior that objectively causes health risks while subjectively the youths are not too concerned. Risky behavior means "normal" behavior for youths in today's world, which demands more and more independence and self-regulation from individuals. Only when health risks lead to symptoms that demand attention do individuals seem to take corrective action (e.g., change to another area of vocational training, cease violent activities).

Only the general status of health (chronic illnesses and other health impairments) seems to have an impact on vocational success. Because the general status of adolescent and adult health is unlikely to improve dramatically in industrial nations in the near future, for many adolescents the transition from school to work will continue to be a difficult and precarious one.

References

Albrecht, G., Howe, C. N., & Wolterhoff-Neetix, J. (1988). Neue Ergebnisse zum Dunkelfeld der Jugenddelinquenz. In G. Kaiser, H. Kury, & H. J. Albrecht (Eds.), *Kriminologische Forschung in den 80er Jahren* (pp. 661–696). Freiburg: Max Planck Institut.

Bertram, H., & Gille, M. (1990). *Datenhandbuch – Zur Situation von Familien, Kindern und Jugendlichen in der Bundesrepublik Deutschland*. Weinheim: Juventa.

Buchmann, M. (1989). *The script of life in modern society*. Chicago and London: University of Chicago Press.

Bundesminister für Bildung und Wissenschaft (Ed.). (1992). *Berufsbildungsbericht 1992*. Bad Honnef: Bock.

Bundesministerium für Gesundheit (Ed.). (1991). *Gesundheitsverhalten im Kindes- und Jugendalter*. Baden-Baden: Nomos.

Bundeszentrale für gesundheitliche Aufklärung. (1990). *Die Entwicklung der Drogenaffinität Jugendlicher. Zusammenfassende Ergebnisse einer Trendanalyse*. Cologne: Selbstverlag.

Deutsche Hauptstelle gegen die Suchtgefahren (Ed.). (1989). *Jahrbuch 1990 zur Frage der Suchtgefahren*. Hamburg: Neuland.

Elkeles, T., & Seifert, W. (1993). Unemployment and health impairments. Longitudinal analyses for the Federal Republic of Germany. *European Journal of Public Health, 3,* 28–37.

Engel, U., & Hurrelmann, K. (1989). *Psychosoziale Belastung im Jugendalter.* Berlin: de Gruyter.

Engel, U., & Hurrelmann, K. (1993). *Was Jugendliche wagen. Eine Längsschnittstudie über Drogenkonsum, Stressreaktionen und Delinquenz im Jugendalter.* Weinheim and Munich: Juventa.

Farrington, D. P., Gallagher, B., Morley, L., Ledger, R. J., & West, D. J. (1986). Unemployment, school leaving, and crime. *British Journal of Criminology, 26,* 335–356.

Feest, J. (1993). Alterskriminalität. In G. Kaiser, H. J. Kerner, F. Sack, & H. Schellhoss (Eds.), *Kleines Kriminologisches Wörterbuch* (pp. 14–17). Heidelberg: Müller.

Franzkowiak, P., & Stoessel, U. (1990). Jugend und Gesundheit. In Sachverständigenkommission 8. Jugendbericht (Ed.), *Risiken des Heranwachsens. Probleme der Lebensbewältigung im Jugendalter. Materialien zum 8. Jugendbericht* (Vol. 3, pp. 53–101). Munich: Verlag Deutsches Jugendinstitut.

Hagan, J. (1993). The social embeddedness of crime and unemployment. *Criminology, 31,* 465–491.

Hamilton, S. F. (1987). Work and maturity: Occupational socialization of non-college youth in the United States and West Germany. *Research in the Sociology of Education and Socialization, 7,* 283–312.

Heinz, W. (1993). Einleitung. Widersprüche in der Modernisierung von Lebensläufen: Individuelle Optionen und institutionelle Rahmungen. In L. Leisering, B. Geissler, U. Mergner, & U. Rabe-Kleberg (Eds.), *Moderne Lebensläufe im Wandel* (pp. 10–19). Weinheim: Deutscher Studien Verlag.

Hogan, D. P., & Astone, N. M. (1986). The transition to adulthood. *Annual Review of Sociology, 12,* 109–130.

Hurrelmann, K., Holler, B., & Nordlohne, E. (1988). Die psychosozialen "Kosten" verunsicherter Statuserwartungen im Jugendalter. *Zeitschrift für Pädagogik, 34,* 25–44.

Hurrelmann, K., & Lösel, F. (1990). Basic issues and problems of health in adolescence. In K. Hurrelmann & F. Lösel (Eds.), *Health hazards in adolescence* (pp. 1–21). Berlin: de Gruyter.

Keupp, H. (1990). Lebensbewältigung im Jugendalter aus der Perspektive der Gemeindepsychologie. Förderung präventiver Netzwerkressourcen und Empowermentstrategien. In Sachverständigenkommission 8. Jugendbericht (Ed.), *Risiken des Heranwachsens. Probleme der Lebensbewältigung im Jugendalter. Materialien zum 8. Jugendbericht* (Vol. 3, pp. 1–52). Munich: Verlag Deutsches Jugendinstitut.

Leisering, L., Geissler, B., Mergner, U., & Rabe-Kleberg, U. (Eds.). (1993). *Moderne Lebensläufe im Wandel.* Weinheim: Deutscher Studien Verlag.

MAGS (Ministerium für Arbeit, Gesundheit und Sozialordnung Baden-Württenberg) (Eds.). (1989). *Junge Menschen und Sucht.* Stuttgart: Selbstverlag.

Mariak, V. (in preparation). *Arbeitsmoral und Normalität im Alltag beruflicher Ausbildung.*

Mariak, V., & Matt, E. (1993). *Sozialisation und Selbstsozialisation in der beruflichen Ausbildung. über Selektionskriterien und -entscheidungen von AusbilderInnen und Jugendlichen.* Sfb 186, Arbeitspapier Nr. 15, Bremen.

National Research Council. (1993). *Losing generations. Adolescents in high-risk settings.* Washington DC: National Academy Press.

Pätzold, G. (1988). Jugend, Ausbildung und Beruf. In H. H. Krüger (Ed.), *Handbuch der Jugendforschung* (pp. 273–291). Opladen: Leske + Budrich.

Petermann, F., Bode, U., & Schlack, H. G. (1990). *Chronisch kranke Kinder und Jugendliche.* Cologne: Deutscher Ärzte Verlag.

Petersen, A. C., Leffert, N., & Hurrelmann, K. (1993). Adolescence and schooling in Germany and the United States: A comparison of peer socialization to adulthood. *Teachers College Record, 94,* 611–628.

Sack, F. (1987). Jugendarbeitslosigkeit im Lichte der Kriminalitätstheorien. In J. Münder, F. Sack, H. J. Albrecht, & H. J. Plewig (Eds.), *Jugendarbeitslosigkeit und Jugendkriminalität* (pp. 15–40). Neuwied: Luchterhand.

Sampson, R. J., & Laub, J. H. (1992). Crime and deviance in the life course. *Annual Review of Sociology, 18*, 63–84.

Scheerer, S., & Vogt, I. (Eds.). (1989). *Drogen und Drogenpolitik*. Frankfurt am Main: Campus.

Schumann, K. F. (1994). Lebensperspektiven nach Ende der Schulpflicht. In H. Peisert & W. Zapf (Eds.), *Gesellschaft, Demokratie und Lebenschancen* (pp. 135–153). Stuttgart: Deutsche Verlags-Anstalt.

Schumann, K. F. (1995). The deviant apprentice. The impact of the German dual system of vocational training on juvenile delinquency. In J. Hagan (Ed.), *Delinquency and disrepute in the Life Course (Current Perspectives on Aging and the Life Cycle*, Vol. 4, pp. 91–103). Greenwich, CT: JAI Press.

Seidenspinner, G. (1988). Verschärfung durch Konkurrenz: Von der Schwierigkeit Jugendlicher, über Arbeit ihr Leben zu verwirklichen. In F. Benseler, W. Heitmeyer, D. Hoffmann, D. Pfeiffer, & D. Sengling (Eds.), *Risiko Jugend* (pp. 63–66). Münster: Votum.

SFB (Sonderforschungsbereich) 186. (1993). *Statuspassagen und Risikolagen im Lebensverlauf. Arbeits- und Ergebnisbericht*. Bremen: Selbstverlag.

Strauss, A., & Glaser, B. (1971). *Status passage*. London: Routledge & Kegan Paul.

Thornberry, T. P., Lizotte, A. J., Krohn, M. D., Farnworth, M., & Jang, S. J. (1991). Testing interactional theory. An examination of reciprocal causal relationships among family, school, and delinquency. *Journal of Criminal Law and Criminology, 82*, 3–35.

U.S. Office of Technology Assessment. (1991). *Adolescent health: Vol. I. Summary and police options. OTA-H-468*. Washington, DC: U.S. Government Printing Office.

Zielke, B. (1993). *Deviante Jugendliche. Individualisierung, Geschlecht und soziale Kontrolle*. Opladen: Leske & Budrich.

Part IV

Identity Transitions and Health

15 Self-Definition and Mental Health During Adolescence and Young Adulthood

Jari-Erik Nurmi

Introduction

During adolescence and young adulthood, people are frequently faced with developmental transitions in several different domains of their lives. These transitions provide a basis for two major psychosocial processes during adolescence. First, in order to manage these new challenges successfully, it is necessary for young people to become interested in age-graded role transitions, to solve related developmental tasks, and finally, to commit themselves to behaviors leading to major adult roles (Erikson, 1959; Havighurst, 1948). This process of directing and controlling one's own life (Brandtstädter, 1984; Lerner, 1983) by setting personal goals, constructing plans for their realization, and evaluating goal achievements is defined here as a self-definition process (see Karoly, 1993). Second, in the course of this process, adolescents and young adults form conceptualizations about and attitudes toward themselves. These outcomes of the self-definition process have been described in terms of identity formation (Bosma, 1992; Marcia, 1980) and self-concept (Harter, 1990).

Although the self-definition process that accompanies life transitions typically promotes positive developmental outcomes and leads to successful socialization, it may lead to negative outcomes in some cases. It has been suggested, for example, that about 10–20% of adolescents exhibit some form of severe mental health problems (Petersen et al., 1993). Negative pathways include underachievement and dropping out of school (Nurmi, Onatsu, & Haavisto, 1995a), unemployment during early adulthood (Nurmi, Salmela-Aro, & Ruotsalainen, 1994b), problems in interpersonal relationships (Laursen, 1993), delinquency and criminal behavior (Patterson, DeBaryshe, & Ramsey, 1989), frequent binge drinking (Schulenberg, O'Malley, Bachman, Wadsworth, & Johnston, 1996), and even suicide (Garland & Zigler, 1993). At

The preparation of this chapter was supported by a grant from the Social Science Research Council of Finland. I am grateful to Katariina Salmela-Aro and the editors for their helpful comments on earlier drafts and to Joan Nordlund for correcting the English.

395

the psychological level, these reactions are reflected in mental health problems, such as low self-esteem, depression, loneliness, and anxiety (Petersen et al., 1993; Powers, Hauser, & Kilner, 1989). In this chapter, *mental health* is defined as a psychological state characterized by an accumulation of positive moods, personal well-being, and adjustment to the current life situation. By contrast, *mental health problems* are characterized by an accumulation of low subjective well-being, negative moods, and maladjustment to the present life context. Mental health also typically promotes rather than prevents subsequent positive developmental outcomes and well-being.

In this chapter, I first review the literature on how people direct and control their future in terms of setting personal goals, planning for the realization of these goals, evaluating success in goal achievements, and constructing self-definitions. Research on related mental health consequences is also reviewed. To illustrate some of these mechanisms, the results of two preliminary studies are presented. In Study 1, the role of one dysfunctional cognitive and attributional strategy, a failure-trap strategy, as a pathway to dropping out of society and to related problem behavior is examined. In Study 2, the impact of another dysfunctional strategy, self-handicapping, and negative life events on depression is investigated. Finally, prospectives for future research on and interventions in young people's dysfunctional self-definitions and mental health problems are discussed.

The Self-Definition Process

There has been an increasing amount of theoretical and empirical work on the psychology of the self during the last 15 years. This literature has concerned a wide range of concepts, such as *self-esteem* (Rosenberg, 1979), *self-concept* (Harter, 1990), *self-identity* (Marcia, 1980), *possible selves* (Markus & Nurius, 1986), and *self-regulation* (Karoly, 1993). One problem with this literature is that these concepts refer to quite different types of psychological phenomena. Some, such as *self-concept*, refer to the cognitive schemata people have about themselves, whereas others, such as *possible selves*, refer to individual motivation. In turn, identity formation (Marcia, 1980) describes a general socialization process. The aim of this chapter is to review some of these concepts and relate them to the wider self-definition process.

It is important to recognize that adolescent development, and the related self-definition process, occur in a cultural and societal context that consists of such characteristics as age-graded role transitions (Elder, 1985) and developmental tasks (Havighurst, 1948), life events (Baltes, Reese, & Lipsitt, 1980), institutional careers (Mayer, 1986), opportunity structures (Grotevant, 1987), and developmental standards (Caspi, 1987). In other words, adolescents construct their own future out of the various alternative options provided by their developmental context (Nurmi, 1993). Although these environmental factors

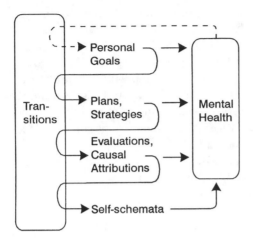

Figure 15.1. The self-definition process in the context of developmental transitions.

play an important role in adolescents' mental health and well-being (for a review, see Nurmi, 1993), this chapter concentrates on the self-definition process as a way of dealing with these transitional patterns and how it influences later development and well-being.

The self-definition process is described in Figure 15.1 in terms of developmental transitions, four substages of the self-definition process, and their mental health consequences. According to the model (see also Nurmi, 1993), young people direct their own lives first by constructing personal goals. This process includes a comparison between their individual motives and the challenges and options provided by the developmental transitions they are currently facing. The second stage includes an effort to find the means for goal actualization in the context of developmental transitions. The process has been described in terms of planning, problem solving, and strategy construction. After attempting to realize their goals and plans, adolescents reach a certain point at which they evaluate their goal achievements. The normative standards for the appropriate ways of managing the developmental transitions provide a basis for these evaluations. In the course of these three substages, adolescents gain various self-definitions that are reflected in their self-schemata and self-attitudes. The model suggests further that each of these self-definition substages has consequences for adolescents' mental health.

The self-definition model is applied here as a heuristic tool for understanding the ways in which young people try to negotiate different age-graded developmental transitions. Although the pattern of these transitions may vary across different cultures and societies, it is expected that the model will still have heuristic value in quite different environments. This is because self-definition is not conceptualized as representing a developmental transition as such, but rather as a process by which young people try to manage it.

Because people are faced with frequent developmental transitions during adolescence and young adulthood (Schulenberg et al., 1996), the self-definition process is likely to be particularly important during these stages of life. However, contrary to identity theories (Erikson, 1959; Marcia, 1980), self-definition is not considered a typical developmental task of these age periods. On the contrary, it is assumed to occur whenever people are facing major developmental transitions during their lives.

I now take a closer look at the four stages of self-definition and review related research on their mental health consequences.

Constructing Personal Goals

It has been suggested that constructing personal goals plays an important role in directing one's own development (Nurmi, 1991, 1993). This goal setting (see Figure 15.1) is based on a comparison of individual needs and motives that developed earlier in life, and of different challenges and options provided by the developmental transitions people are currently facing (Nurmi, 1993; Nuttin, 1984). It is influenced by various processes providing information about future options such as age-graded normative expectations, available adult role models, and negotiations with significant others, such as parents, peers, and teachers.

Personal Goals. An increasing amount of research has been done recently on human motivation (Cantor & Zirkel, 1990; Emmons, 1986; Klinger, 1977; Little, 1983; Markus & Nurius, 1986; Nurmi, 1989a). This research has been aimed at describing the ways in which individual motives and needs are translated into personal goals, how they regulate behavior in specific life contexts, and the consequences they have for people's well-being (Cantor & Zirkel, 1990; Karoly, 1993). A wide range of concepts has been used in this research field, such as *future-oriented goals* (Nurmi, 1989a, 1989b), *personal projects* (Little, 1983) and *strivings* (Emmons, 1986), *current concerns* (Klinger, 1977) and *possible selves* (Markus & Nurius, 1986). Despite the differences in terminology, all these concepts refer to self-articulated goals that (1) are based on a comparison between abstract individual motives and knowledge of future options, (2) refer to some culturally defined tasks or challenges, (3) are organized in terms of a complex hierarchy, the levels of which differ according to the generality and abstractness of the motives and goals involved (Emmons, 1989; Leontjev, 1977), (4) provide a basis for motivated behavior in specific situations, and finally (5) are realized by means of different cognitive strategies (Nurmi, 1993).

A number of conceptualizations have also been suggested for measuring personal goals. The first two reflect the relational nature of goal construction (Nuttin, 1984): *personal goals* always refer to some of the individual's basic needs, as well as to certain objectives in the environment. Consequently, the content of personal goals has been analyzed according to either the basic needs they refer to, such as achievement, power, and affiliation (Emmons, 1991), or the domains of life they concern, such as education, occupation, and leisure time (Nurmi, 1991). For example, when adolescents and young adults are asked about their future goals, they typically mention topics related to future education, occupation, family, and leisure activities (Nurmi, 1991, 1992a).

On the other hand, personal goals are formulated and realized through a complex process in which people construct different schemata, beliefs, and emotions concerning their goals. To describe the outcomes of this process, a number of concepts, such as *goal importance, specificity* (Emmons, 1992), *challenge, self-efficacy, control beliefs* (Bandura, 1986), *difficulty, valence* (Wright & Brehm, 1989), *complexity, stress, personal control* (Lecci, Karoly, Briggs, & Kuhn, 1994), and *temporal distance* (Gjesme, 1974), have been introduced (for a review, see Lee, Locke, & Latham, 1989).

Mental Health Consequences. Adolescents' and young adults' personal goals, and how they are worked out, have been shown to have consequences for their well-being and mental health. There is an increasing amount of evidence suggesting that goal contents are associated with personal well-being. For example, it has been found that a high level of interest in affiliative goals among young adults is associated with positive affect, power-related goals with a low level of well-being (Emmons, 1991), self-related goals with mental health problems (Salmela-Aro, 1992), and projects concerned with promoting one's own health with somatic complaints (Karoly & Lecci, 1993). Moreover, a lack of commitment to school and family has been found to be associated with adolescent suicide attempts (Kandel, Raveis, & Davies, 1991). Furthermore, the personal well-being of young people with achievement-oriented goals has been found to be influenced by life events in this domain, whereas affiliative-oriented people are more influenced by interpersonal events (Emmons, 1991).

The ways in which young people appraise their personal goals have also been found to be related to their personal well-being and mental health. For example, young adults who rated their goals as more important, more enjoyable, and less difficult were more satisfied with their life than those who rated them as less important, less enjoyable, and more difficult (Palys & Little, 1983). Moreover, young people who rated their goals as difficult, stressful, beyond their personal control, and unlikely to be achieved were found to be more depressed and anxious than those who showed the reverse pattern (Lecci et al., 1994). Furthermore, those who reported high-level, reflective, abstract goals were shown to be more psychologically distressed and depressed than those who had more concrete, specific, low-level goals. This was perhaps because these goals were also seen to be more difficult and to require more effort than low-level goals (Emmons, 1992). Salmela-Aro and Nurmi (1994b) found that young adults who rated their affiliative goals as difficult, stressful, and anxiety-provoking had lower self-esteem and higher depression and loneliness than those who rated them as easy to accomplish and not stress or anxiety provoking.

The person–environment fit theory suggests that mental health is influenced by the fit between adolescents' individual needs and the social environments in which they live. For example, according to Eccles et al. (1993), a decrease in well-being (e.g., self-concept, intrinsic motivation, and confidence in personal skills) during the transition into junior high school occurs because this context fits poorly with the increasing needs of autonomy and social support among preadolescents. Similarly, Hurrelmann and Engel (1992) suggested that an increased risk of delinquency arises when the fulfillment of formal cultural values is threatened by a lack of favorable opportunities.

Planning and Strategy Construction

Once young people have constructed personal goals, they have to find the means for their realization in the context of age-graded transitions (Figure 15.1). This has often been described in terms of planning and strategy construction (for a review, see Nurmi, 1991). In the course of this process, people also make certain decisions and gradually become committed to pertinent behaviors, such as a choice of school track, occupation, and way of life (Marcia, 1980).

Planning. How individuals use self-knowledge and knowledge about the social world to translate their goals into behavior has been described in terms of planning (Norem, 1989). When people are faced with a challenge or demand about which they have some experience, they typically apply some of the personal skills or strategies they have previously developed (Markus & Wurf, 1987). However, faced with new demands and challenges, people need to devise new strategies, which they do by means of planning and strategic problem solving (Cantor, 1990; Markus & Wurf, 1987; Nurmi, 1989a). This is typical in the context of frequent developmental transitions, which are common during adolescence and young adulthood. Problem-solving skills and decision strategies might also be expected to play an important role when young people try to devise a strategy for managing a challenging life transition.

Although planning has typically been described in terms of cognitive processes, emotional and evaluative aspects may also play an important role. For example, negative affect, failure expectations (Jones & Berglas, 1978), and a lack of belief in personal control (Seligman, 1975) have been found to be typical of inefficient, dysfunctional, and nonrational strategies.

Strategies. Several researchers have recently discussed the different types of strategies people use to respond to the situational demands they face during their lives. For example, Cantor (1990) described a typical successful strategy in achievement contexts in terms of an *illusory glow optimism*. This strategy was characterized by straightforward striving for success based on high outcome expectations, high levels of effort and task-oriented behavior, and a desire to enhance an already strong image of competence.

Other strategies have been found to lead to problem behavior. For example, Jones and Berglas (1978) introduced *self-handicapping* in the context of poor academic performance. Because self-handicappers expect failure, they concentrate on task-irrelevant behavior in order to create behavioral excuses. Later on, if they fail, they use this behavior as an attributional excuse. Another typical maladaptive strategy is *learned helplessness* (Abramson, Seligman, & Teasdale, 1978; Seligman, 1975). Helpless individuals have been shown to lack belief in personal control and therefore to be passive in achievement-related situations (Diener & Dweck, 1978).

A few studies have also examined the strategies people use in social situations. For example, Nurmi, Toivonen, Salmela-Aro, and Eronen (in press) described an optimistic, planning-oriented strategy that seems to lead to success in peer relationships. On the other hand, a pessimistic-avoidance strategy, characterized by failure expectations, social withdrawal, and self-handicapping, seems to lead to dissatisfaction and loneliness in social life.

Mental Health Consequences. There is growing evidence that the features of strategy construction may influence adolescents' and young adults' well-being and mental health. For example, a self-handicapping strategy has been found to be associated with different types of problem behavior, such as underachievement at school (Nurmi et al., 1995a), and alcohol use (Jones & Berglas, 1978). Similarly, learned helplessness has been shown to be related to depression (Rosenhan & Seligman, 1984) and problems in school (Diener & Dweck, 1978).

It has also been shown that problem-solving and planning skills are associated with mental health. For example, a lack of problem-solving skills among young adults has been found to be related to hopelessness and suicide ideation (Dixon, Heppner, & Anderson, 1991), later psychological stress (D'Zurilla & Sheedy, 1991), and depression (Blankstein, Flett, & Johnston, 1992; Elliott, Herrick, & Witty, 1992; Heppner, Baumgardner, & Jackson, 1985). Jorgensen and Dusek (1990) found that well-adjusted adolescents made more effort to develop a plan of action, to utilize social resources, and to become involved in task-related activities than did maladjusted adolescents.

It has also been found that dysfunctional strategies in affiliative situations, such as a pessimistic-avoidance strategy (Nurmi et al., in press) and a similar social constraint strategy (Langston & Cantor, 1989), have negative effects on well-being, including subjective dissatisfaction, stress, negative adjustment, and loneliness. In turn, the use of an optimistic, planning-oriented strategy has been found to decrease loneliness, particularly among young men (Nurmi et al., in press). A lack of social skills has also been found to be associated with feelings of loneliness and problems in peer relationships (Inderbitzen-Pisaruk, Clark, & Solano, 1992; Savin-Williams & Berndt, 1990). Moreover, poor inter-personal problem-solving skills, involving difficulties in generating alternatives, decision making, and implementing solutions, for example, have been found to be associated with young people's depression (Sacco & Graves, 1984), suicide attempts, and psychiatric symptoms (Cole, 1989; Rotheram-Borus, Troutman, Dopkins, & Shrout, 1990; Sadowski & Kelley, 1993).

Evaluation of Goal Attainments

After constructing personal goals and trying to find the means for their realization, young people end up with certain outcomes and, consequently, need to evaluate the extent to which these outcomes are in line with their original goals (Figure 15.1). This evaluation, and the way it is processed psychologically, provides a basis for the way people think and feel about themselves, that is, their self-schemata (Nurmi, 1993).

Affects, Causal Attribution, and Illusions. The evaluation of goal attainments has been suggested to consist of various subsequent substages. According to Weiner (1985), a comparison of the fit between achievements and original personal goals is first followed by an unspecific positive or negative emotion, depending on whether the outcome is interpreted as a success or a failure. The second stage consists of an exploration of the causes of the outcome. Third, as a consequence of these causal attributions, a number of attribution-specific emotions follow. Moreover, how people feel about their achievements and to what they attribute the causes may be important in determining the extent to which goal attainments influence their self-concept and moods (Abramson et al., 1978). For example, if failure is ascribed to self-related factors, self-esteem is lower than if it is attributed to other people and circumstances (Weiner, 1986).

It has also been shown that people apply different evaluative strategies for self-protecting purposes. According to Taylor and Brown (1988), mentally healthy individuals seem to have the enviable capacity to distort reality in the direction that enchances self-esteem, maintains the belief in personal control, and promotes an optimistic view of the future. For example, normal or relatively well-adjusted people have been shown to take credit for success but to blame other people and situational factors for failure, indicating the use of self-serving attributional bias (Zuckerman, 1979). Other self-protecting and self-enhancing strategies include excuse making (Snyder & Higgins, 1988), downward social comparisons (Wills, 1981), and impression management (Leary & Kowalski, 1990).

The evaluation of goal attainments during adolescence and early adulthood typically occurs in interpersonal contexts. Young people not only estimate the fit of their personal goals and achievements, but also negotiate them with their significant others, such as peers and parents (Higgins & Snyder, 1991). Moreover, many evaluations during adolescence are public and have multiple audiences, such as school class or sports teams. Interestingly, feedback about behavioral outcomes has been shown to have a stronger impact on self-esteem in public than in private situations (e.g., Tice, 1992).

Mental Health Outcomes. It has been found that the evaluation of goal attainments in the context of developmental transitions influences young people's self-schemata and problem behavior. For example, goal attainment related to major developmental tasks, such as finding a girlfriend or boyfriend (Silbereisen & Noack, 1990), and scholastic competence and social acceptance (Harter, 1990), have been shown to influence adolescents' self-concept (for a review, see Nurmi, 1993). Moreover, strong success orientation, and simultaneous failures at school, have been reported to increase the risk of delinquency (Hurrelman & Engel, 1992). Similarly, Baumeister (1990) suggested that high standards, as well as failures in related domains of life, create a risk of suicidal behavior.

There is also an extensive amount of evidence suggesting that the causal attributions and self-serving biases people apply in the evelation of behavioral outcomes have important mental health consequences (for a review, see Taylor & Brown, 1988). It has been shown, for example, that a lack of self-serving causal attributions – that is, the attribution of negative life events to internal, stable, and global causes and attribution of positive life events to external and unstable causes – is associated with depression among adolescents (Craighead, 1991; Kaslow, Rehm, & Siegel, 1984) and young adults (Cohen, van der Bout, Kramer, & van Vliet, 1986; Feather, 1987; Seligman, Abramson, Semmel, & von Baeyer, 1979). This attributional pattern has also been found to be associated with other mental health–related problems among young adults, such as low self-esteem (Feather, 1987; Tennen & Herzberger, 1987), shyness (Johnson, Petzel, & Johnson, 1991) and loneliness (Anderson, Horowitz, & deSales French, 1983). In addition, other self-protecting strategies have been found to be associated with mental health. For example, downward social comparison has been shown to bolster self-evaluation and increase expectations of success (Wills, 1981).

Self-Schemata as Self-Definitions

In the process of directing their future lives, adolescents and young adults construct different self-definitions in terms of self-concept, self-esteem, and self-identity (Figure 15.1). Together with the evaluation of goal achievements, goal setting and strategy construction provide a basis for the way young people see themselves. Self-schemata are also influenced by broader social and societal sources. For example, young people receive behavioral outcome feedback from their significant others, such as peers, parents, and teachers (Nurmi, 1993). They are also involved in various institutions, such as schools, universities, and sports teams, which all rate individual achievements on a regular basis (Eccles et al., 1993).

The schemata about and attitudes toward the self, being based on the self-definition process, are important because they might be expected to influence subsequent mental health and subjective well-being in various ways (Figure 15.1). For example, low self-esteem has been found to be associated with mental health problems, such as depression (Harter, 1990; Petersen et al., 1993), hopelessness, suicidal ideation (Harter, 1990), and a lack of self-serving attributional bias (Taylor & Brown, 1988). It has also been found to be related to several types of problem behavior, for example, underachievement (Nurmi et al., 1995a) and unsuccessful socialization (Nurmi et al., 1994b).

Finally, adolescents' and young adults' mental health might also be expected to influence the ways in which they try to direct their own future lives. For example, depression may influence the ways people see their developmental transitions and the types of personal goals they construct in order to handle them.

Developmental Pathways

In the course of the self-definition process, adolescents and young adults orient and commit themselves to, and end up following, certain developmental pathways and cycles that consist of both psychological and environmental factors. Although in most cases these developmental cycles are positive, consisting of an accumulation of feelings of competence, high self-esteem, interest in developmental tasks, and successful socialization, they are sometimes negative cycles or downward spirals (Eccles et al., 1993). For example, Petersen et al. (1993) suggested that adolescent depression may increase the likelihood of problems in peer relations, which, in turn, may increase depression later on. Similarly, Brightman (1990) found, in achievement contexts, that depressed adolescents who were exposed to unsolvable tasks showed significant performance deficits in terms of effort, problem solving, and persistence. This can then be expected to increase the likelihood of failure and related external attributions, and consequently to lead to increased depression (Abramson et al., 1978). Moreover, Patterson et al. (1989) described a negative cycle leading to antisocial behavior. First, inefficient parenting leads to childhood conduct disorders. This then increases the likelihood of academic failure and peer rejection. Because this pattern leads to increased depression and involvement with deviant peer groups, it increases the risk of chronic delinquent behavior. Typical of these negative pathways is the accumulation of both psychological and contextual determinants that strengthen the negative developmental spirals at each stage. The same type of sequential cumulation is, of course, typical of positive pathways.

Two Example Studies

To illustrate some of the processes described in the theoretical framework (Figure 15.1), two preliminary studies will be briefly described. The aim of both studies was to examine the extent to which (1) the ways young people handle different challenges in the context of developmental transitions and (2) the ways they define themselves, influence their subsequent success, risk-taking behavior, and mental health.

Study 1: A Failure-Trap Strategy and Unsuccessful Socialization

The self-definition model suggests that one pathway to problem behavior and related mental health problems may be that young people use dysfunctional strategies in managing major developmental transitions. To investigate this, we carried out a series of studies among different problem behavior groups, such as underachievers (Nurmi et al., 1995a), society dropouts (Nurmi et al., 1994b) and young prisoners. In one preliminary study in this research program, we were interested in investigating the extent to which young people who showed evidence of problems in handling the transition to an adult career used a higher level of dysfunctional cognitive and attributional strategies than well-adapted youths. Moreover, we were interested in examining the extent to which the use of a dysfunctional strategy was associated with different types of problem behavior, such as the use of alcohol and criminal actions.

Method. Three groups of young Finnish people were examined: (1) a *problem behavior group* consisting of twenty 16- to 24-year-old young adults (fifteen males, five females) who showed serious problems in getting involved with working life due to a low level of education, long periods of unemployment, and short periods of employment; (2) a *health problem group* consisting of fourteen 16- to 26-year-old young adults (nine males, five females) who had a variety of health problems (e.g., an allergy or asthma); and (3) a *control group* consisting of twenty-three 18- to 33-year-old young people (twenty-two males, one female) who attended a vocational school (Nurmi et al., 1994b). The participants were asked to fill in the following measures.

Cognitive and behavioral strategies were assessed using the Strategy and Attribution Questionnaire (SAQ, Form-B; Nurmi et al., 1994b). The Failure Expectations, Task-irrelevant Behavior, and Externality summary scores were calculated from this scale (for sample items and reliability information, see Nurmi et al., 1994b). *Self-esteem* was assessed using the Finnish version of Rosenberg's (1979) Self-esteem scale.

Attributional strategies were analyzed using a Cartoon-Attribution-Strategy Test (CAST; Nurmi et al., 1994b). The CAST is a test in which the participants are shown six situations in the form of two-picture cartoons in an interview. The first picture shows a challenging situation, and the second describes the situation ending in either success or failure. After the showing of the second picture, the subjects were asked how they would explain the outcome. Based on these causal attributions, a score for *self-serving attributional bias* was calculated for each subject as follows: The self-related causal attribution concerning success, and other related attributions related to failure, were summed. Then the self-related causal attribution in the failure situation, and the other related attributions concerning success, were subtracted from the first score (for the scoring details and reliability information, see Nurmi et al., 1994b).

Information about the *use of alcohol* and *criminal behavior* was requested in a clinical interview. The participants were asked "How many times per week do you use alcohol?" and "How many times have you been convicted of any crimes in court?" These data are available only for the problem behavior and health problem groups.

Results. The three groups were compared using a one-way analysis of variance. Moreover, pairwise comparisons between the groups were carried out using Tukey's HSD procedure. The results (Figure 15.2) showed that the problem behavior group reported lower levels of self-esteem and self-serving attributional bias than the control group. Moreover, they reported a higher level of failure expectations than the control group and a higher level of task-irrelevant behavior than the health problem and control groups. Thus, young adults who displayed evidence of problems in handling one major developmental transition seem to apply a dysfunctional cognitive and attributional pattern that can be characterized as a failure-trap strategy: Due to low self-esteem, they expect failure. Because they believe this expected outcome to be beyond their control, they turn to task-irrelevant and blunting behavior, perhaps to reduce their anxiety. However, it seems that they do not refer to their

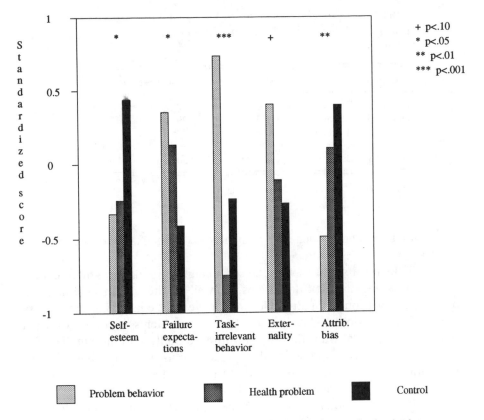

Figure 15.2. Self-esteem and the use of cognitive and attributional strategies for the three groups.

task-irrelevant behavior as an excuse for the failure, but rather blame themselves and do not take credit for success. Because this strategy not only increases the likelihood of failure but also maximizes the negative feedback for self-definitions, it might be expected to provide a basis for repeated failures in tackling developmental transitions.

I was also interested in examining the extent to which young people's self-esteem, and the cognitive and attributional strategies they use, are associated with their problem behavior, such as alcohol use and criminal actions. The correlations between these variables were calculated for the problem behavior and health problems groups (these data were available only for these two groups). The results (Table 15.1) showed that the higher the levels of task-irrelevant behavior and failure expectations the young people reported, the more frequently they used alcohol and the higher the level of criminal behavior they showed. These results suggest that the application of a dysfunctional strategy in achievement situations seems to be associated with different types

Table 15.1. *Correlations between self-esteem and strategy variables, and alcohol use and criminal behavior*

Variable	Alcohol use	Criminal behavior
Self-esteem	.00	−.22
Failure expectations	.35*	.29
Task-irrelevant behavior	.66***	.48**
Externality	.20	.16
Self-serving bias	−.63***	−.30

***$p < .001$,**$p < .01$, *$p < .05$; $n = 34$.

of risk-taking behavior, which may even increase the negative consequences of this strategy in the long run.

Overall, the results fit well with the self-definition model presented earlier. As expected, negative self-definitions, as well as the use of dysfunctional cognitive and attributional strategies in achievement contexts, seemed to be typical of young people who show evidence of problems in coping with one major developmental transition: socialization to adult working life. The fact that the application of dysfunctional strategies was associated with alcohol use and criminal behavior suggests that these maladjusted young people are already on a negative developmental pathway: Due to negative self-definitions, they apply a dysfunctional strategy to cope with their failure expectations and related anxiety, which then increases the likelihood of failure. Moreover, their efforts to cope with repeated failures (and the related negative feedback) by using more alcohol might be expected to contribute to subsequent maladjustment.

Study 2: Self-Handicapping, Life Events, and Depression

The self-definition model also suggests that the use of dysfunctional cognitive strategies in developmental transitions and related life events should decrease personal well-being and even lead to mental health problems. To examine this hypothesis, we used data from the Helsinki Longitudinal Student Study (HELS Study). In these analyses, we were interested in examining the extent to which the impact of negative and positive life events is different for people who use a self-handicapping versus a functional strategy.

Method and Procedure. A total of 272 (70 men, 202 women) 18- to 32-year-old undergraduates at the University of Helsinki were examined at two measurement points.

1. A total of 303 university undergraduates participated in a study at the beginning of their first autumn term. They were asked to complete (a) the SAQ (Nurmi, Salmela-Aro, & Haavisto, 1995b) and (b) the revised Beck Depression inventory (Beck, Rush, Shaw & Emery, 1979).
2. One year later, the same subjects were asked to complete the revised Beck Depression inventory again and also a Life Event Questionnaire. The retention rate at this stage of the study was 90%.

Cognitive and attributional strategies were assessed using the SAQ (Form A; Nurmi et al., 1995b). For the purpose of this chapter, only two of the subscales were used (Cronbach alphas in brackets): *failure expectation* (.78) and *task-irrelevant behavior* (.70). Because both of these scales have been suggested to be typical of self-handicappers (Jones & Berglas, 1978), a new self-handicapping score was calculated by summing them. In turn, *depression* (.87) was assessed using a revised version of the Beck Depression inventory (Beck et al., 1979).

Positive and negative life events were assessed at the second measurement occasion using a Life-Event Checklist for Students (Nurmi & Salmela-Aro, 1993). In this measure, the participants were asked to rate whether 20 different types of life events had happened to them during the last year. To examine the meaning of these life events, an independent sample of 30 students was asked to evaluate them as positive or negative (ranging from 2 = very positive to −2 = very negative). These independent evaluations were used as a basis for calculating the summary scores for positive and negative life events for the original sample.

Results. The results showed, first, that the use of self-handicapping slightly increased the likelihood of negative life events ($r = .14, p < .01$) but had no impact on positive life events ($r = .06, p =$ n.s.). After partialling out depression at Time 1, negative life events were positively associated with depression at Time 2 (*partial* $r = .20, p < .001$) and positive events were negatively associated (*partial* $r = −.12, p < .05$). However, self-handicapping was not associated with an increase in depression (*partial* $r = .08, p =$ n.s.).

Our major aim was to investigate the extent to which positive and negative life events had different impacts on depression, depending on the type of strategy young people used. We divided the students into two groups using a median split: self-handicappers and normals. Correlations were calculated between positive and negative life events and depression at Time 2, after depression at Time 1 was partialled out, separately for these two groups. Then the group differences in the relative magnitude of these correlations were compared by transforming the correlations into z-scores (Fisher's transformation; see Table 15.2).

The results (Table 15.2) showed that negative life events increased depression among self-handicappers but not among the normal group. On the other hand, positive life events did not influence depression among self-

Table 15.2. *Partial correlations between negative and positive life events and depression at Time 2 after partialling out depression at Time 1 separately for self-handicappers and non-self-handicappers*

	Depression			
Variables	Self-handicappers[a]	Normal group[b]	z	p
Negative life events	.32***	.08	1.96	.05
Positive life events	.00	−.22***	1.72	.09

***$p < .001$, **$p < .01$, *$p < .05$.
[a]$n = 123$.
[b]$n = 129$.

handicappers, whereas they decreased depression among the non-self-handicappers.

The self-definition model suggests that the strategies young people use when facing negative life events during a developmental transition should influence their subsequent subjective well-being and mental health. The results of Study 2 showed that negative life events increased depression only among young people who used a self-handicapping strategy. In contrast, those who did not show signs of using a dysfunctional strategy were able to cope with negative life events in such a way that there was no decrease in their subjective well-being. The results further showed that self-handicappers were not able to use positive life events to increase their subjective well-being, as those using a functional type of strategy were able to do.

Conclusions

This chapter described adolescent development in the context of life transitions as a self-definition process that consists of setting personal goals, planning for their realization, and evaluating goal achievements. It also described how young people construct schemata about and attitudes toward themselves during this process of self-definition. Research on how this process is related to young people's mental health was summarized.

Summary

The review of the literature showed that adolescent self-definition in the context of frequent developmental transitions plays an important role in the development of personal well-being and mental health. First, a lack of personal goals concerning major developmental tasks of adolescence and young adulthood, and the lack of fit between these goals and environmental options, seem to lead to problems in personal well-being and mental health. Thus, adolescents and young adults who are unable to adapt their personal goals to age-graded transitions and related options are in danger of developing mental health problems. Second, the evaluation of personal goals as difficult to accomplish, stressful, anxiety provoking, and abstract was found to be associated with mental health problems. This suggests that not only the goals, but also how they are concretely worked out in the context of life transitions, play an important role for later personal well-being. Third, dysfunctional strategies and poor problem-solving skills in achievement contexts were found to lead to problem behavior, such as underachievement, dropping out of school, and alcohol use, as well as psychological stress and depression. Moreover, dysfunctional strategies in affiliative situations seemed to increase the likelihood of problems in peer relationships, loneliness, and depression. Finally, the research suggests that the use of different self-serving causal attributions and biases to cope with failure and negative events has positive mental health consequences. For example, linking positive life events to the self and negative ones to external factors was found to be related to a low level of depression. Because age-graded transitions may be either health-promoting or risk factors in adolescent development, the key issue seemed to be the extent to which young people are able to construct personal goals and strategies to work out these normative demands, and the extent to which they are able to cope with negative feedback.

It was also suggested that in the course of the self-definition process, adolescents and young adults commit themselves to and end up on certain developmental pathways, which in most cases are positive, opening new developmental prospects and strengthening positive self-definitions. In some cases, however, these developmental pathways seem to lead to negative cycles and downward spirals characterized by the accumulation of negative developmental markers, such as low self-esteem, depression, dysfunctional strategies, lack of self-protecting attributional bias, problem behavior, and subsequent mental health problems. Earlier negative self-definitions, in particular, seem to provide a basis for further negative developmental cycles.

The results of the two studies presented in this chapter provide some support for the self-definition model and illustrate a few examples of negative developmental pathways. The findings from Study 1 suggested that young people who showed evidence of having problems in managing the developmental transition to adult work roles seemed already to have embarked on a severely negative developmental pathway: Their negative self-definitions provide a basis for the use of a failure-trap strategy in achievement contexts, which leads to repeated failures and related negative feedback. Because this dysfunctional strategy seemed to be associated with frequent use of alcohol and criminality, all this can be expected to lead to the strengthening of a negative developmental cycle. Study 2 indicated that the use of a self-handicapping strategy in the face of negative life events in the context of a developmental transition leads to increased depression. By contrast, negative life events do not decrease subjective well-being among those who apply a more functional strategy.

Limitations of Earlier Studies and Directions for Future Research

However, there are at least three limitations that should be considered in any attempt to generalize these findings. These limitations also provide direction for future research. First, the majority of research thus far has been carried out on young adults. Therefore, it is possible that some of the processes described here proceed differently during early and middle adolescence. For example, adolescence is characterized by rapid cognitive development (Blasi & Hoeffel, 1974) that may influence young people's goal setting, life planning, and the applications of different biases (Nurmi, 1991). Moreover, it has been suggested that in the process of cognitive development, adolescents move from describing themselves in concrete, situation-specific terms to the application of more abstract, stable self-descriptions (Harter, 1990). This change may well increase their use of different attributional biases because their self-concept becomes less dependent on concrete feedback regarding their behavior. This, then, may influence their self-definitions.

Consequently, there is a need for future research to investigate the impact of cognitive development on managing developmental transitions in terms of setting personal goals, constructing plans for their realization, dealing with negative feedback about goal nonachievement, and forming related self-definitions during early and middle adolescence in particular.

Second, most of the research concerning the self-definition process has been done in Western Europe and the United States. However, there is evidence suggesting that some of these processes may vary across cultures. For example, Americans have been shown to apply higher levels of self-serving attributional bias than Finnish people (Nurmi, 1992b). Moreover, it can be expected that, in some non-Western traditional societies, the self-definition process is influenced less by individual factors and more by family decisions than in some Western societies (Nurmi, 1991). In addition to the fact that some age-graded transitions vary across cultures and societies, the features of an efficient self-definition process may well be different in various sociocultural environments.

To examine these issues, there is a need for cross-cultural studies in which the self-definition process is examined in sociocultural environments that vary according to educational systems, to the timing of institutional transitions, and to the traditions, values, and norms associated with family decision making, parental practices, and social support. Although a few studies have focused these issues (Nurmi, 1991; Nurmi, Seginer, & Poole, 1995c), more research is needed on how young people direct their lives and define themselves in the context of developmental transitions in different sociocultural environments.

Third, all the research reviewed on the relationships between the four substages of the self-definition process and mental health was correlational. Although success in constructing personal goals and strategies to deal with developmental transitions, and ways of coping with related negative feedback, were found to be associated with subjective well-being and mental health, it is possible that, at least in some cases, mental health influences the self-definition process rather than vice versa (see Figure 15.1). As an example, Salmela-Aro and Nurmi (in press) found, in a longitudinal cross-lagged study, that depression had a stronger impact on the ways people appraised their personal goals than goal appraisals had on depression.

Thus, there is a need for careful cross-lagged longitudinal studies, covering a specific transitional period several times, concerning the ways in which adolescents direct their own lives and define themselves, as well as their subjective well-being and mental health. Only this type of design provides the opportunity to examine causal relationships between self-definition and mental health over time. Moreover, it would afford the use of a person-oriented approach (Magnusson & Bergman, 1988; see also Schulenberg et al., 1996) to examine the development and precursors of different negative developmental pathways and related mental health problems.

Interventions for Negative Developments

Because the self-definition process during adolescence and young adulthood was found to be associated with mental health, another important consideration involves interventions that could change some of these negative developments. Because mental health problems have been assumed to consist of negative cycles and downward spirals, the first requirement for intervention would be to define the early markers of different negative developments for the early detection of the problem groups.

The next step would be to develop clinical interventions. One way to do this would be to look at interventions separately according to different self-definition processes. For example, one group of adolescents in need of help are those who have problems adapting their personal goals to age-graded transitions. One intervention might be to encourage these youths to become interested in age-graded developmental tasks and related institutional careers. This may consist of vocational and educational counseling, which might help them to construct realistic future perspectives in these domains. Moreover, providing them with appropriate role models for positive development in their own environments, and knowledge about future options, may encourage them to orient themselves toward successful socialization patterns. It has also been suggested that discussions aimed at changing false beliefs about acceptable levels of performance into more realistic evaluations may help these adolescents to use more functional ways of handling developmental challenges (Higgins & Berglas, 1990).

A second intervention may be aimed at those who have problems constructing appropriate strategies for handling major developmental demands and transitions. This group may be best helped by providing them with information for future decision making and life planning, as well as different types of skill training. The skill training may vary from planning future education to having successful interpersonal relationships. It may even consist of programs aimed at the improvement of some family management practices (Patterson et al., 1989). Abramson et al. (1978) suggested that one intervention for people using dysfunctional strategies might be to redirect some beliefs of uncontrollability related to life planning toward personal control, again by providing some skill training.

Third, if cognitive and behavioral strategies also include dysfunctional attributional and evaluative patterns, as is the case with learned helplessness and the failure-trap strategy, there may be a need to develop more clinical types of intervention. For example, Abramson et al. (1978) suggested that a certain kind of reattribution therapy may be valuable for these types of problem groups. This therapy could consist of making unrealistic attributions of failure more external and specific and those of success more internal and global.

Finally, negative self-schemata seem to play an important role in the development of mental health problems. Consequently, one intervention may consist of efforts to change some of these negative schemata toward more positive ones. The most efficient way to do this may be to try to change adolescents' environments so as to decrease the likelihood of continuous negative feedback by making sure that all individuals have a chance to succeed and to receive positive feedback, at least in some domains of their lives. One important issue in this context is how to transform school institutions into settings that provide positive and rewarding developmental contexts for a whole cohort.

Using some of these ideas, we (Nurmi, Anttonen, & Jarvikoski, 1994a) have recently made an effort to plan an intervention program for young "society dropouts" who have severe problems in becoming socialized into adulthood. These problems include a low level of education, long unemployment periods, and various types of problem behavior ranging from heavy alcohol use to criminality. In this program, a group of maladjusted youths participated in an intensive 5-month course that included vocational guidance, help in life management, individual counseling, and working in different types of work clinics and private companies. The major principles of this intervention program are similar to those described earlier: to encourage these youths to plan their lives by helping them to construct realistic educational and occupational goals, providing them with some skill training, helping them to become more conscious about their dysfunctional cognitive and attributional strategies, and finally, trying to provide them with an environment in which they have the opportunity to succeed in concrete tasks and therefore receive positive feedback for their future self-definitions. The program is currently at the stage of testing some of our ideas in preliminary intervention studies.

References

Abramson, L. Y., Seligman, M. E. P., & Teasdale, J. D. (1978). Learned helplessness in humans: Critique and reformulation. *Journal of Abnormal Psychology, 87*, 49–74.

Anderson, G. A., Horowitz, L. M., & deSales French, R. (1983). Attributional style of lonely and depressed people. *Journal of Personality and Social Psychology, 87*, 127–136.

Baltes, P. B., Reese, H. W., & Lipsitt, L. P. (1980). Life-span developmental psychology. *Annual Review of Psychology, 31*, 65–100.

Bandura, A. (1986). *Social foundation of thought and action*. Englewood Cliffs, NJ: Prentice-Hall.

Baumeister, R. F. (1990). Suicide as escape from self. *Psychological Review, 97*, 90–113.

Beck, A. T., Rush, A. J., Shaw, B. F., & Emery, G. (1979). *Cognitive therapy of depression*. Chichester, U.K.: Wiley.

Blankstein, K. R., Flett, G. L., & Johnston, M. E. (1992). Depression, problem-solving ability, and problem-solving appraisals. *Journal of Clinical Psychology, 48*, 749–759.

Blasi, A., & Hoeffel, E. C. (1974). Adolescence and formal operations. *Human Development, 17*, 344–363.

Bosma, H. A. (1992). Identity in adolescence: Managing commitments. In G. R. Adams, T. P. Gullotta, & R. Montemayor (Eds.), *Adolescent identity formation* (pp. 91–121). Newbury Park, CA: Sage.

Brandtstädter, J. (1984). Personal and social control over development: Some implications of an action perspective in life-span psychology. In P. B. Baltes & O. G. Brim (Eds.), *Life span development and behaviour* (Vol. 6, pp. 2–28). New York: Academic Press.

Brightman, B. G. (1990). Adolescent depression and the susceptibility to helplessness. *Journal of Youth and Adolescence, 19*, 441.

Cantor, N. (1990). From thought to behavior: "Having" and "doing" in the study of personality and cognition. *American Psychologist, 45*, 735–750.

Cantor, N., & Zirkel, S. (1990). Personality, cognition, and purposive behavior. In L. A. Pervin (Ed.), *Handbook of personality: Theory and research* (pp. 135–164). New York: Guilford Press.

Caspi, A. (1987). Personality in the life-course. *Journal of Personality and Social Psychology, 53*, 1203–1213.

Cohen, L., van den Bout, J., Kramer, W., & van Vliet, T. (1986). A Dutch attributional style questionnaire: Psychometric properties and findings of some Dutch–American differences. *Cognitive Therapy and Research, 10*, 665–669.

Cole, D. A. (1989). Psychopathology of adolescent suicide: Hopelessness, coping behavior, and depression. *Journal of Abnormal Psychology, 98*, 248–255.

Craighead, W. E. (1991). Cognitive factors and classification issues in adolescent depression. *Journal of Youth and Adolescence, 20*, 311–326.

Diener, C. I., & Dweck, C. S. (1978). An analysis of learned helplessness: Continuous changes in performance, strategy, and achievement cognitions following failure. *Journal of Personality and Social Psychology, 36*, 451–462.

Dixon, W. A., Heppner, P. P., & Anderson, W. P. (1991). Problem solving appraisal, stress, hopelessness, and suicide ideation in a college population. *Journal of Counseling Psychology, 38*, 51–56.

D'Zurilla, T. J., & Sheedy, C. F. (1991). Relation between social problem-solving ability and subsequent level of psychological stress in college students. *Journal of Personality and Social Psychology, 61*, 841–846.

Eccles, J. S., Midgley, C., Wigfield, A., Miller-Buchanan, C., Reuman, D., Flanagan, C., & MacIver, D. (1993). Development during adolescence. *American Psychologist, 48*, 90–101.

Elder, G. H., Jr. (1985). Perspectives on the life course. In G. H. Elder, Jr. (Ed.), *Life course dynamics* (pp. 23–49). Ithaca, NY: Cornell University Press.

Elliott, T. R., Herrick, S. M., & Witty, T. E. (1992). Problem-solving appraisal and the effects of social support among college students and persons with physical disabilities. *Journal of Counseling Psychology, 39*, 219–226.

Emmons, R. A. (1986). Personal strivings: An approach to personality and subjective well-being. *Journal of Personality and Social Psychology, 51*, 1058–1068.

Emmons, R. A. (1989). The personal striving approach to personality. In L. A. Pervin (Ed.), *Goal concepts in personality and social psychology* (pp. 87–126). Hillsdale, NJ: Erlbaum.

Emmons, R. A. (1991). Personal strivings, daily life events and psychological and physical well-being. *Journal of Personality, 59*, 455–472.

Emmons, R. A. (1992). Abstract versus concrete goals: Personal striving level, physical illness, and psychological well-being. *Journal of Personality and Social Psychology, 62*, 292–300.

Erikson, E. H. (1959). *Identity and the life cycle.* New York: International Universities Press.

Feather, N. T. (1987). The rosy glow of self-esteem: Depression, masculinity, and causal attributions. *Australian Journal of Psychology, 39*, 25–41.

Garland, A. F., & Zigler, E. (1993). Adolescent suicide prevention. Current research and social policy implications. *American Psychologist, 48*, 169–182.

Gjesme, T. (1974). Goal distance in time and its effects on the relations between achievement motives and performance. *Journal of Research in Personality, 8*, 161–171.

Grotevant, H. D. (1987). Toward a process model of identity formation. *Journal of Adolescent Research, 2*, 203–222.

Harter, S. (1990). Process underlying adolescent self-concept formation. In R. Montemayor, G. R. Adams, & T. P. Gullotta (Eds.), *From childhood to adolescence: A transitional period* (pp. 205–239). Newbury Park, CA: Sage.

Havighurst, R. J. (1948). *Developmental tasks and education.* New York: McKay.

Heppner, P., Baumgardner, A., & Jackson, J. (1985). Problem-solving self-appraisal, depression, and attributional style: Are they related? *Cognitive Therapy and Research, 9*, 105–113.

Higgins, R. L., & Berglas, S. (1990). The maintenance and treatment of self-handicapping. From risk-taking to face-saving – and back. In R. L. Higgins, C. R. Snyder, & S. Berglas (Eds.), *Self-handicapping. The paradox that isn't* (pp. 187–238). New York: Plenum.

Higgins, R. L., & Snyder, C. R. (1991). Reality negotiation and excuse-making. In C. R. Snyder & D. R. Forsyth (Eds.), *Handbook of social and clinical psychology* (pp. 79–95). New York: Pergamon Press.

Hurrelmann, K., & Engel, U. (1992). Delinquency as a symptom of adolescents' orientation toward status and success. *Journal of Youth and Adolescence, 21*, 119–137.

Inderbitzen-Pisaruk, H., Clark, H., & Solano, C. H. (1992). Correlates of loneliness in midadolescence. *Journal of Youth and Adolescence, 21*, 151–167.

Johnson, J. M., Petzel, T. P., & Johnson, J. E. (1991). Attributions of shy persons in affiliation and achievement situations. *Journal of Psychology, 125*, 51–58.

Jones, E. E., & Berglas, S. (1978). Control of attributions about the self through self-handicapping: The appeal of alcohol and the rate of underachievement. *Personality and Social Psychology Bulletin, 4*, 200–206.

Jorgensen, R. S., & Dusek, J. B. (1990). Adolescent adjustment and coping strategies. *Journal of Personality, 58*, 503–513.

Kandel, D. B., Raveis, V. H., & Davies, M. (1991). Suicidal ideation in adolescence: Depression, substance use, and other risk factors. *Journal of Youth and Adolescence, 20,* 289–307.

Karoly, P. (1993). Mechanisms of self-regulation: A systems view. *Annual Review of Psychology, 44,* 23–52.

Karoly, P., & Lecci, L. (1993). Hypochondriasis and somatization in college women: A personal project analysis. *Health Psychology, 12,* 103–109.

Kaslow, N. J., Rehm, L. P., & Siegel, A. W. (1984). Social-cognitive and cognitive correlates of depression in children. *Journal of Abnormal Psychology, 12,* 605–620.

Klinger, E. (1977). *Meaning and void. Inner experience and the incentives in people's lives.* Minneapolis: University of Minnesota Press.

Langston, C. A., & Cantor, N. (1989). Social anxiety and social constraint: When making friends is hard. *Journal of Personality and Social Psychology, 56,* 649–661.

Laursen, B. (Ed.). (1993). *Close friendships in adolescence.* San Francisco: Jossey-Bass.

Leary, M. R., & Kowalski, R. M. (1990). Impression management: A literature review and two-component model. *Psychological Bulletin, 107,* 34–47.

Lecci, L., Karoly, P., Briggs, C., & Kuhn, K. (1994). Specificity and generality of motivational components in depression: A personal project analysis. *Journal of Abnormal Psychology, 103,* 404–408.

Lee, T. W., Locke, E. A., & Latham, G. P. (1989). Goal setting theory and job performance. In L. A. Pervin (Ed.), *Goal concepts in personality and social psychology* (pp. 291–321). Hillsdale, NJ: Erlbaum.

Leontjev, A. N. (1977). *Toiminta, tietoisuus, persoonallisuus [Action, cognition, and personality].* Helsinki: Kansankulttuuri.

Lerner, R. M. (1983). A "goodness of fit" model of person–context interaction. In D. Magnusson & V. L. Allen (Eds.), *Human development: An interactional perspective* (pp. 279–294). New York: Academic Press.

Little, B. R. (1983). Personal projects: A rationale and method for investigation. *Environment and Behavior, 15,* 273–309.

Magnusson, D., & Bergman, L. R. (1988). *A pattern approach to the study of pathways from childhood to adulthood* (Re. No. 679). University of Stockholm, Department of Psychology.

Marcia, J. E. (1980). Identity in adolescence. In J. Adelson (Ed.), *Handbook of adolescent psychology* (pp. 159–187). New York: Wiley.

Markus, H., & Nurius, P. (1986). Possible selves. *American Psychologist, 41,* 954–969.

Markus, H., & Wurf, E. (1987). The dynamic self-concept: A social psychological perspective. *Annual Review of Psychology, 38,* 299–337.

Mayer, K. U. (1986). Structural constraints on the life course. *Human Development, 29,* 163–170.

Norem, J. K. (1989). Cognitive strategies as personality: Effectiveness, specificity, flexibility, and change. In D. M. Buss & N. Cantor (Eds.), *Personality psychology: Recent trends and emerging directions* (pp. 45–60). New York: Springer-Verlag.

Nurmi, J.-E. (1989a). Adolescents' orientation to the future: Development of interests and plans, and related attributions and affects, in the life-span context. *Commentationes Scientiarum Socialium* (Vol. 39). Helsinki: Finnish Society for Sciences and Letters.

Nurmi, J.-E. (1989b). Planning, motivation, and evaluation in orientation to the future: A latent structure analysis. *Scandinavian Journal of Psychology, 30,* 64–71.

Nurmi, J.-E. (1991). How do adolescents see their future? A review of the development of future orientation and planning. *Developmental Review, 11,* 1–59.

Nurmi, J.-E. (1992a). Age differences in adult life-goals, concerns, and their temporal extension: A life course approach to future-oriented motivation. *International Journal of Behavioral Development, 15,* 487–508.

Nurmi, J.-E. (1992b). Cross-cultural differences in self-serving bias: Responses to the attributional style questionnaire by American and Finnish students. *Journal of Social Psychology, 132,* 69–76.

Nurmi, J.-E. (1993). Adolescent development in an age-graded context: The role of personal beliefs, goals, and strategies in the tackling of developmental tasks and standards. *International Journal of Behavioral Development, 16*, 169–189.

Nurmi, J.-E., Anttonen, M., & Jarvikoski, A. (1994a). *Notes for life.* A research program in progress. Helsinki: Malminkartano Rehabilitation Center, Merikoski Rehabilitation Center, and University of Helsinki.

Nurmi, J.-E., Onatsu, T., & Haavisto, T. (1995a). Underachievers' cognitive and behavioral strategies – self-handicapping at school. *Contemporary Educational Psychology, 20*, 188–200.

Nurmi, J.-E., & Salmela-Aro, K. (1993). *Life-event checklist for students.* Unpublished data. University of Helsinki.

Nurmi, J.-E., Salmela-Aro, K., & Haavisto, T. (1995b). The strategy and attribution questionnaire: Psychometric properties. *European Journal of Psychological Assessment, 11*, 108–121.

Nurmi, J.-E., Salmela-Aro, K., & Ruotsalainen, H. (1994b). Cognitive and attributional strategies among unemployed young adults: A case of the failure-trap strategy. *European Journal of Personality, 8*, 135–148.

Nurmi, J.-E., Seginer, R., & Poole, M. E. (1995a). Searching for the future in different environments: A comparison of Australian, Finnish and Israeli adolescents' future orientations, explorations and commitments. In P. Noack, M. Hofer, & J. Youniss (Eds.), *Psychological responses to social change: Human development in changing environments* (pp. 219–238). Berlin: de Gruyter.

Nurmi, J.-E., Toivonen, S., Salmelo-Aro, K., & Eronen (in press). Social strategies and loneliness. *The Journal of Social Psychology.* University of Helsinki.

Nuttin, J. R. (1984). *Motivation, planning, and action. A relational theory of behavior dynamics.* Hillsdale, NJ: Erlbaum.

Palys, T. S., & Little, B. R. (1983). Perceived life satisfaction and the organization of personal project systems. *Journal of Personality and Social Psychology, 44*, 1221–1230.

Patterson, G. R., DeBaryshe, B. D., & Ramsey, E. (1989). A developmental perspective on antisocial behavior. *American Psychologist, 44*, 329–335.

Petersen, A. C., Compas, B. E., Brooks-Gunn, A., Stemmler, M., Ey, S., & Grant, K. E. (1993). Depression in adolescence. *American Psychologist, 48*, 155–168.

Powers, S. I., Hauser, S. T., & Kilner, L. A. (1989). Adolescent mental health. *American Psychologist, 44*, 200–208.

Rosenberg, M. (1979). *Conceiving the self.* Malabar, FL: Krieger.

Rosenhan, D. L., & Seligman, M. E. P. (1984). *Abnormal psychology.* New York: Norton.

Rotheram-Borus, M. J., Troutman, P. D., Dopkins, S. C., & Shrout, P. E. (1990). Cognitive style and pleasant activities among female adolescent suicide attempters. *Journal of Consulting and Clinical Psychology, 58*, 554–561.

Sacco, W. P., & Graves, D. J. (1984). Childhood depression, interpersonal problem-solving, and self-ratings of performance. *Journal of Clinical Child Psychology, 13*, 10–15.

Sadowski, C., & Kelley, M. L. (1993). Social problem solving in suicidal adolescents. *Journal of Consulting and Clinical Psychology, 61*, 121–127.

Salmela-Aro, K. (1992). Struggling with self: The personal projects of students seeking psychological counselling. *Scandinavian Journal of Psychology, 33*, 330–338.

Salmela-Aro, K., & Nurmi, J.-E. (in press). Depressive symptoms and personal project appraisals: A cross-lagged longitudinal study. *Personality and Individual Differences.*

Salmela-Aro, K., & Nurmi, J.-E. (1996). Uncertainty and confidence in interpersonal projects: Consequences for social relationships and well-being. *Journal of Social and Personal Relationships, 13*, 109–122.

Savin-Williams, R. C., & Berndt, T. J. (1990). Friendship and peer relations. In S. S. Feldman & G. R. Elliott (Eds.), *At the threshold: The developing adolescent* (pp. 277–302). Cambridge, MA: Harvard University Press.

Schulenberg, J., O'Malley, P., Bachman, G., Wadsworth, K., & Johnston, L. (1996). Getting drunk and growing up: Trajectories of frequent binge drinking during the transition to young adulthood. *Journal of Studies on Alcohol, 57*, 289–304.

Seligman, M. E. P. (1975). *Helplessness: On depression, development and death.* San Francisco: Freeman.

Seligman, M. E. P., Abramson, L. Y., Semmel, A., & von Baeyer, C. (1979). Depressive attributional style. *Journal of Abnormal Psychology, 88*, 242–247.

Silbereisen, R., & Noack, P. (1990). Adolescents' orientation for development. In H. Bosma & S. Jackson (Eds.), *Coping and self-concept in adolescence* (pp. 112–124). Berlin: Springer-Verlag.

Snyder, C. R., & Higgins, R. L. (1988). Excuses: Their effective role in the negotiation of reality. *Psychological Bulletin, 104*, 23–35.

Taylor, S. E., & Brown, J. (1988). Illusion and well-being: A social psychological perspective on mental health. *Psychological Bulletin, 103*, 193–210.

Tennen, H., & Herzberger, S. (1987). Depression, self-esteem, and the absence of self-protective attributional biases. *Journal of Personality and Social Psychology, 52*, 72–80.

Tice, D. M. (1992). Self-concept change and self-presentation: The looking glass self is also a magnifying glass. *Journal of Personality and Social Psychology, 3*, 435–451.

Weiner, B. (1985). An attributional theory of achievement motivation and emotions. *Psychological Review, 92*, 548–573.

Weiner, B. (1986). *An attributional theory of motivation and emotion.* New York: Springer-Verlag.

Wills, T. A. (1981). Downward comparison principles in social psychology. *Psychological Bulletin, 90*, 245–271.

Wright, R. A., & Brehm, J. W. (1989). Energization and goal attractiveness. In L. A. Pervin (Ed.), *Goal concepts in personality and social psychology* (pp. 169–210). Hillsdale, NJ: Erlbaum.

Zuckerman, M. (1979). Attribution of success and failure revised, or: The motivational bias is alive and well in attribution theory. *Journal of Personality, 47*, 245–287.

16   Ethnic and Racial Identity Development and Mental Health

Jean S. Phinney and Eric L. Kohatsu

It is well recognized that identity formation is a key developmental task of adolescence (Blos, 1979; Erikson, 1968; Kroger, 1989). For Erikson, ego identity formation takes place as adolescents, through a process of exploration and commitment, achieve a sense of self based on an understanding and integration of their abilities, interests, and opportunities. The successful resolution of the identity crisis, ideally by late adolescence, leads to an achieved identity, that is, a secure sense of self that serves as a guide to one's adulthood. Research within this framework provides strong evidence that an achieved identity is associated with positive psychological outcomes, including self-assurance, self-certainty, and a sense of mastery (Adams, Gullotta, & Montemayor, 1992; Marcia, Waterman, Matteson, Archer, & Orlofsky, 1994).

Ego identity research has focused on the adolescent's ways of dealing with the challenges presented by the need to choose one's occupation, ideology, and life style. The role of the context in identity formation has been less explored, although increasing attention is being paid to historical and sociocultural factors in development (Elder, Model, & Parke, 1993; Silbereisen & Todt, 1994). The importance of the context in identity formation is accentuated for adolescents who are distinct from the dominant majority group by reason of culture, ethnicity, or race. Ward (1990) states, with reference to African Americans, that "During adolescence, the need to identify strongly with a sense of peoplehood or a shared social identity is heightened by a consciousness of belonging to a specific group that is characteristically different from other groups" (p. 118). For adolescents of color, the successful transition to healthy functioning in adulthood requires the achievement of a secure sense of their ethnic and/or racial identity, in the face of stereotypical images of their group, cultural differences and conflicts, and restricted opportunities. This process, which is typically neither salient nor important for White adolescents, is of central importance to American adolescents from non-European backgrounds (Aries & Moorehead, 1989; Helms, 1990; Phinney & Alipuria, 1990).

420

This chapter has two goals. The first is to examine the process of ethnic and racial identity formation. This process is assumed to involve progression through a number of phases. Adolescents of color begin with an unexamined (diffuse or foreclosed) ethnic or racial identity based on received views of their ethnicity, such as positive attitudes derived from parents or stereotypes and negative attitudes toward their group originating from the dominant society. They proceed through an intermediate exploration phase to an achieved, internalized identity based on a conscious awareness and understanding of the implications of their race or ethnicity and a secure, grounded sense of themselves as members of an ethnic or racial group (Helms, 1990; Phinney, 1993).

The second goal of the chapter is to consider how this process is related to mental health, especially psychological adjustment. Each phase presents different challenges to adolescents. In the initial phase, adolescents may be unaware of or ignore problems associated with race or ethnicity, particularly if they are in a supportive, homogeneous environment. On the other hand, they may be vulnerable to stress and a poor self-image because of cultural conflicts, discrimination, and internalized stereotypes. The intermediate exploration phase may be a period of psychological instability due to changing world views and conflicts with parents, peers, and school personnel. However, this phase may also elicit positive feelings of empowerment. The achievement of an ethnic or racial identity is assumed to be accompanied by the development of both psychological resilience and more appropriate ways of dealing with threats to identity. However, it does not eliminate the conflicts and contradictions that exist in society regarding race and ethnicity.

Our focus is on adolescents in the United States from non-European and non-Middle Eastern backgrounds, specifically African Americans, Latinos,[1] Native Americans, and Asian/Pacific Islander Americans. We use the term *ethnocultural* to refer to these youth. We have generally avoided using the term *minority* because of its often pejorative connotations and its misleading implications, given that in many cities and in some regions of the country traditional minority groups are in fact in the majority. We focus on a process that is common across these ethnocultural groups, but we recognize that there are important differences both among and within these groups in terms of group and individual history, experience, and position in society. Both the intergroup and intragroup differences influence the process of group identity formation, creating tremendous complexity in adequately understanding this phenomenon.

We begin with some definitions and an overview of the three central issues that must be negotiated in the formation of ethnic and racial identity. The central sections of the chapter trace the process of group identity formation for ethnocultural adolescents and consider the mental health implications of each phase.

Definitions: Ethnic Identity and Racial Identity

There is little consensus on the paradigms or approaches to use in the study of ethnic and racial identity. Sociologists and anthropologists (e.g., Alba, 1990; DeVos & Romanucci-Ross, 1982; Waters, 1990) have examined ethnic identity primarily among European immigrants who are racially indistinguishable from the White majority. The systematic study of group identity among non-European ethnocultural groups is relatively recent. For these individuals, identity as a member of a distinct group is likely to include elements of both ethnic and racial identity, although the emphasis on these components will vary across individuals and groups. Both ethnicity and race can be considered as part of the broad construct of social identity, defined by Tajfel (1981) as "that part of an individual's self-concept which derives from his [sic] knowledge of his [sic] membership of a social group (or groups) together with the value and emotional significance attached to that membership" (p. 255). Because the term *social identity* can have varied meanings, we use the term *group identity* to refer to this broad sense of group membership, whether it is based on race, ethnicity, or both.

Although both ethnicity and race can form the basis of group identity, ethnic identity and racial identity have been studied within different research traditions encompassing different theoretical and methodological approaches. The study of ethnic identity among non-European American ethnocultural groups has focused on Hispanics (e.g., Bernal & Knight, 1993; Garcia, 1982; Keefe & Padilla, 1987), Asians (e.g., Matute-Bianchi, 1986; Ting-Toomey, 1981; Wooden, Leon, & Toshima, 1988), and, more recently, African Americans (e.g., Aries & Moorehead, 1989; Phinney, 1992; Phinney, DuPont, Espinosa, Revill, & Sanders, 1994). Many different methods have been used to assess ethnic identity; there is little agreement on exactly what it is, what its components are, or how it should be measured (Phinney, 1990). It is clearly a complex, multidimensional concept including, at a minimum, self-identification, a sense of belonging and commitment to one's ethnic group, and the cognitive and affective meanings of one's group membership (Bernal, Knight, Ocampo, Garza, & Cota, 1993; Keefe, 1992; Phinney, 1990). Ethnic identity in adolescence has been examined developmentally within the framework of Erikson's (1968) theory of ego identity, as operationalized by Marcia (1980; Marcia et al., 1994), in studies with both high school and college students (Phinney, 1989; Phinney & Alipuria, 1990).

In contrast to ethnic identity, racial identity was studied initially with reference to African Americans (Cross, 1978, 1991; Helms, 1990; Jackson, 1976), although it has been extended to other ethnocultural groups (e.g., Atkinson, Morten, & Sue, 1993; Kohatsu, 1992; Lee, 1988; Sue & Sue, 1990). Racial identity is based on the perception of a shared racial history and reflects the quality or manner of identification with one's racial group (Helms, 1990). Racial identity theorists have focused on the effects of racism and oppression imposed by White Americans on an ethnocultural person's psychological functioning. Although racial identity theory has a precise meaning in the literature, the concept of *race* remains vague and undefined (Betancourt & Lopez, 1993; Helms, 1994; Yee, Fairchild, Weizmann, & Wyatt, 1993). However, as a socially constructed concept based on phenotypic differences, it has a clear psychological impact on development (Spencer & Markstrom-Adams, 1990). The racial identity literature examines the psychological changes that take place as ethnocultural individuals struggle with the personal, social, and political implications of their membership in a racial group. Most racial identity models are based on Nigrescence theory (Cross, 1991), that is, the process of becoming (psychologically) Black. The bulk of this research has been with late adolescents, mainly college students (e.g., Carter, 1991; Helms, 1990: Kohatsu, 1992; Mitchell & Dell, 1992; Parham & Helms, 1985a, 1985b), although recent work has examined racial identity across the life span (e.g., Parham & Williams, 1993). It should be noted that ethnic or racial self-labels (e.g., *Black* versus *African American*; *Hispanic* versus *Latino*) are not synonymous with one's group identity (Kohatsu, 1992; Kohatsu & Richardson, 1996). Self-labels simply identify one's group affiliation and may be transitory indicators of the current social environment rather than an accurate reflection of one's underlying identity structure (Parham & Helms, 1981).

A distinction should be made between group identity and acculturation. Generally, *acculturation* refers to both individual and group-level changes in behaviors, attitudes, and values that take place over time as two or more cultural groups come into contact (Berry, 1990). The nature of the relationship between acculturation and group identity is complex and has not been widely studied (Birman, 1994), although Kohatsu (1992) demonstrated that acculturation and racial identity are two different constructs. As immigrants become more acculturated to American society and adopt American values, attitudes, and behaviors, they may increasingly identify themselves as American. However, their sense of belonging to a distinct ethnic or racial group can remain strong. In discussing ethnic identity, we focus on this subjective sense of group belonging and commitment, which can be maintained even though specific attitudes, behaviors, and values from the ethnic culture are no longer present (Keefe & Padilla, 1987).

In this chapter, our focus is on a common element of ethnic and racial identity, specifically, the transition process by which adolescents and young adults come to understand and internalize a positive sense of their ethnic and racial background. This process requires the resolution of three conceptually distinct challenges, which will be explored.

Three Facets of Ethnic and Racial Identity Formation

A clear statement of the three issues involved in establishing a secure group identity is provided by Boykin and Toms (1985). With reference to African Americans, they describe the "triple quandary," that is, the need to negotiate three distinct realms: Black or African culture, minority status, and mainstream American society. Cross (1991), discussing ways in which a secure identity guides everyday life for African Americans, identifies three functions of Black identity that correspond to Boykin and Toms' quandaries. According to Cross, an internalized Black identity functions (1) to provide a sense of group affiliation, (2) to defend the individual from the psychological stress of prejudice and discrimination, and (3) to provide a basis for links to the wider society. These three aspects have received different emphasis, depending on the ethnic or racial group in question; for example, the minority experience has been a particularly salient focus in discussion of Black identity (Helms, 1990), and the relationship to one's ethnic culture has been especially important for Mexican Americans (Bernal et al., 1993).

The first issue focuses on adolescents' sense of belonging and commitment to their ethnic or racial group. In a discussion of Chicano culture and identity, Arce (1981) points out that "For minority group members, identification with others who share their origins and traditions is critical to developing both a positive personal identity and feelings of self-esteem and efficacy, rather than self-blame and powerlessness" (p. 182). The idea that a social or group identity is important for psychological functioning generally, not just for people of color, is a central tenet of social identity theory, as elaborated by Tajfel and his colleagues (Tajfel & Turner, 1986). In addition, Tajfel (1981, chap. 15) has emphasized the particular need for ethnocultural group members to establish a satisfactory sense of group belonging, The importance and centrality of ethnic or racial identity is supported in empirical studies. For example, ethnic identity has been found to be most predictive of overall identity status for African Americans (Aries & Moorehead, 1989). Ethnicity was rated as a quite or very important identity issue by nearly three-quarters of Asian American, African American, and Mexican American college students compared to less than one-quarter of White students (Phinney & Alipuria, 1990).

The second aspect of ethnic and racial identity for ethnocultural adolescents is their minority status within the larger society, particularly the problematic effects of racism, prejudice, and discrimination (Spencer & Markstrom-Adams, 1990). Tajfel (1981) states that "minorities . . . share one difficult psychological problem which can be described . . . as a conflict between satisfactory self-realization and the restrictions imposed upon it by the realities of membership of a minority group" (p. 322). Historically, internalized racism was assumed by some psychologists to be the basis for low self-regard among African Americans (Cross, 1991). The tendency of young Black children to

choose White dolls as most like themselves (Clark & Clark, 1947) was attributed to the negative images of African Americans in society and was assumed
to indicate both the lack of a positive racial identity and poor self-esteem. In
contrast to that view, current writing emphasizes that internalized racism is not
related in any simple way to group identity and self-esteem (Cross, 1991). The
critical issue is the way in which the individual interprets and responds to the
awareness and experience of these phenomena (Helms, 1990). A number of
writers have noted that awareness of racism plays a role in the identity formation process (e.g., Keefe, 1992; Ward, 1990). Some sociologists (e.g., Porter &
Washington, 1993; Portes & Rumbaut, 1990) suggest, in fact, that discrimination experienced by ethnocultural groups accounts in part for their retention
of an ethnic identity despite residence for several generations in the United
States. The extent and timing of experiences with racism and discrimination
may be key factors in the development of an ethnic or racial identity.

The third theme for ethnocultural adolescents is their relationship to the
dominant Euro-American culture, to other ethnocultural groups, and to the
larger society. According to Cross (1991), an internalized group identity serves
a "bridging function," promoting connections with other groups and individuals "who constitute the larger non-Black world within which the Black world
is nestled" (p. 218). The issue for ethnocultural adolescents centers on the
meaning and implications of being bicultural or multicultural (LaFromboise,
Coleman, & Gerton, 1993). Much of the early literature on this topic assumed
that being bicultural was psychologically damaging (Stonequist, 1935), that is,
that the person who was part of two cultures really belonged to neither and
was therefore marginalized. However, this view has been clearly rejected by
theoretical and empirical work showing that identity with reference to both
one's ethnic culture and the dominant culture are independent dimensions
(Phinney et al., 1994; Ramirez, 1984), that is, that one can strongly identify
with one, with both, or with neither culture.

The relationship to the larger society has not been emphasized in the study
of group identity. However, a recent study (Phinney & Devich-Navarro, in
press) illustrates its importance in the psychological functioning of ethnocultural adolescents. African American and Mexican American adolescents were
interviewed regarding their sense of being ethnic, American, and bicultural,
and were given questionnaire measures of ethnic and American identity. All
of the adolescents expressed a positive sense of their ethnicity, and there was
little variation in their ethnic identity scores. However, there were substantial
differences in American identity scores and wide variation in their perceptions
of American society. Some adolescents felt that they were American; for
them, America signified diversity. For example, one student stated that America is "a very diverse culture . . . I do not think there is any true blood American; people have come from all different places." Other adolescents did not
think of themselves as American: "White is American to me, and no one in my

family is White." Adolescents' resolution of these conflicting views of the larger society plays an important role in their group identity.

The Phases of Ethnic and Racial Identity Development

Several models of ethnic and racial identity development have been proposed, based on different theoretical perspectives, focusing on different issues and ethnic or racial groups, and using different terminology. Table 16.1 provides an overview of the terms that have been used in various models, including the related concept of *ego identity*. Although there are similarities and parallels across models, the meanings of specific components are by no means the same, as each model has a different focus. Furthermore, although there is some evidence that this process is sequential, we do not imply that these are necessarily stages in the strict sense. We use the term *phase* as a general term for aspects of the identity formation process. However, in our discussion of particular research traditions, we use the terms used by the researchers themselves.

The Initial Phase

Before they reach adolescence, children have learned their appropriate ethnic or racial group label and the particular behaviors and traditions, as well as societal images, associated with their group (Aboud, 1987; Bernal, Knight, Garza, Ocampo, & Cota, 1990). This early understanding of one's ethnicity or race could be considered the foundation on which a mature ethnic or racial identity is formed. Adolescents' conceptions of their ethnicity or race are initially embedded in the family and ethnic community (Keefe, 1992). Most ethnocultural parents educate their children about their culture, race (including race relations), or ethnicity, and this socialization has an impact on group identity (Phinney & Chavira, 1995; Thornton, Chatters, Taylor, & Allen, 1990). A number of other factors interact in various ways to influence the developing sense of self as a member of an ethnic or racial group. These factors include the immediate community and school contexts, as well as exposure to messages from the media and the wider society about the individual's worth (Helms, 1990; Phinney & Rosenthal, 1992). Thus, as a result of these influences, ethnocultural children enter adolescence with group identities of varying salience and differing valence.

The predominant characteristic of the initial phase is that the meaning and implications of one's group have not been examined and evaluated by the adolescent. This can be related to low salience or lack of concern (diffusion) or to fixed ideas derived from external sources (foreclosure). Adolescents with a diffuse group identity have little interest in exploring their ethnic culture or have not examined the possible meanings of being a minority person in the United States (Phinney, 1993). This low salience is exemplified by the state-

Table 16.1. *Terminology used in models of ego identity and ethnic and racial identity development*

	Initial phase	(Transition)	Intermediate phase	Final phase
Ego identity (Marcia et al., 1994)	Diffusion/foreclosure	(Identity crisis)	Moratorium	Identity achievement
Ethnic identity (Phinney, 1989, 1993)	Unexamined	(Exposure, experience)	Exploration	Achievement
Racial identity theory (Cross, 1991; Helms, 1990)	Preencounter	(Encounter)	Immersion/emmersion	Internalization/ commitment
Minority identity model (Atkinson, Morten, & Sue, 1993; Sue & Sue, 1990)	Conformity	(Dissonance)	Resistance and immersion	Introspection/integrative awareness

ment of an African American high school student: being Black "is just a skin color; I don't think it is any more special than any other group" (Phinney & Devich-Navarro, in press).

Cross (1991) suggests that some African Americans in this initial phase simply do not place much significance on race in the context of their daily lives. Other factors may be more salient, such as their religion. Similarly, the socio-political implications of racial group membership are not a part of their conscious awareness. According to Cross (1991), this lack of interest may be due to a Eurocentric educational system that leaves adolescents oblivious to the contributions of people of their own race and culture. "The most damning aspect of miseducation is not necessarily poor mental health but the development of a world view and cultural-historical perspective that can inhibit knowledge about, and thus the capacity to be an advocate for, the . . . interests of Black people" (p. 193).

Many ethnocultural adolescents in the initial phase have a foreclosed group identity based on views derived from others. Their attitudes will vary widely, depending on the socialization messages the child has received in the family, community, and society. Minority identity models (Atkinson et al., 1993), and racial identity models in particular (Cross, 1991; Helms, 1990), have emphasized the strong adherence to and belief in the dominant White culture that often occurs in this phase. A person in this phase, termed *preencounter* or *conformity*, is oriented to White Americans as a reference group; for example, some ethnocultural adolescents express a wish to be White (Phinney, 1989). Cross (1991) refers to the "idealization of the dominant traditional White world view" (p. 20) that is characteristic of this phase.

Concomitantly, preencounter or conformity adolescents may denigrate their ethnic culture and group members (Atkinson et al., 1993; Sue & Sue, 1990). This denigration is also often accompanied by a denial of their racial/ethnic group membership and of its sociopolitical implications (Cross, 1991; Sue & Sue, 1990). Mitchell and Dell (1992) found that Black students with high levels of preencounter attitudes tended not to participate in Black cultural organizations. The extreme version of this perspective is adolescents' internalization of negative stereotypes of their own racial/ethnic group; for example, they "loathe other Blacks; they feel alienated from them and do not see Blacks or the Black community as potential or actual sources of personal support" (Cross, 1991, p. 191). In short, some adolescents in this phase function psychologically from racist stereotypes of their own racial group. One African American college student stated:

I was never taught to be proud of my African heritage. . . . I went through a very long stage of identifying with my oppressors. Wanting to be like, live like, and be accepted by them. Even to the point of hating my own race and myself for being a part of it. Now I am ashamed that I ever was ashamed. I lost so much of myself in my denial of and refusal to accept my people. (Tatum, 1992, p. 10)

As a result of their White cultural orientation, ethnocultural individuals in this phase typically do not appreciate or understand other minority groups, and the degree of psychological contact with them may be minimal. These adolescents may even harbor negative or racist attitudes toward other ethnocultural groups and individuals (Atkinson et al., 1993).

However, it is not clear how common negative attitudes toward one's ethnic or racial groups are. Although over half the high school students in an interview study of ethnic identity (Phinney, 1989) were in the initial unexamined phase, relatively few of them expressed the strong negative feelings toward their own group suggestive of preencounter attitudes. When the family and community provide a supportive environment, some adolescents may avoid internalizing negative views of their group. For example, an African American woman reflecting on her early life stated:

I have really strong Black females in my life ... I've never looked at it as a negative ... I can't even really remember ever wishing I was a different color or anything like that. By the way I was brought up, it was always positive. (Shorter-Gooden & Washington, 1996)

Several studies with college students have found relatively low endorsement of preencounter attitudes (Helms, 1990; Pyant & Yanico, 1991). The expression of negative views of one's racial/ethnic group may have become less acceptable, and individuals therefore disguise them in more socially desirable attitudes.

The implications of the initial phase for psychological functioning have not been widely studied, but most ethnic or racial identity development models assume that this phase is likely to be negatively associated with psychological well-being. High self-esteem, defined as a generally positive self-concept or self-evaluation, is assumed to underlie healthy psychological functioning, and measures of self-esteem have often been used as indicators of overall adjustment. In an interview study with African American, Asian American, and Latino adolescents (Phinney, 1989), students assigned to the initial or unexamined phases of ethnic identity were found to have significantly more negative self-concept scores than students in other phases. In a study with second-generation Cuban American youths (Szapocznik, Kurtines, & Fernandez, 1980), those adolescents who rejected their roots and became highly Americanized showed poorer psychological adjustment than those who were more bicultural. These adolescents may reject their parents along with their culture of origin and, by extension, rebel against all authority figures, in a pattern often resulting in maladjustment and highly disruptive discipline problems.

Among college students, preencounter or conformity attitudes, that is, negative feelings about one's own racial group and preference for Whites (Helms, 1990), have been found to be significantly related to feelings of inferiority, inadequacy, and hypersensitivity (Parham, 1982, cited in Carter, 1991). Moreover, African American college students with high levels of preencounter attitudes were more likely to exhibit low self-actualizing tendencies, low self-regard, and high anxiety (Parham & Helms, 1985a, 1985b). Pyant and Yanico (1991) found that preencounter attitudes in African American female college students were significant negative predictors of general well-being and self-esteem. Finally, preencounter attitudes have been shown to be predictive of anxiety, memory impairment, paranoid thoughts, hallucinations, and concern with alcohol among college students (Carter, 1991), as well as low levels of autonomy and mature interpersonal relationships among Black college women (Taub & McEwen, 1992).

Most of the studies cited were done with college students, and thus the findings may not be applicable to younger adolescents or to those who do not go to college. Nevertheless, these studies provide considerable empirical support for the position that trying to fit into the White world while shunning one's own group and culture is related to feelings of anxiety and insecurity. More generally, the denial and/or denigration of one's race or ethnicity seems to be negatively associated with the development of a healthy sense of self and of psychological functioning overall.

However, the evidence for poor psychological outcomes in this phase is generally weak, and it seems clear that not all adolescents in the initial phase are prone to psychological problems. As Cross (1991) wrote:

It would be a mistake to assume that Preencounter is a form of mental illness. . . . The great majority of Preencounter Blacks are probably as mentally healthy as Blacks in the more advanced stages of [racial identity development]. (p. 198)

Mental health in this phase may be a factor of both the prior socialization of the adolescent, as discussed earlier, and the particular context in which the adolescent is living. With a supportive family and minimal exposure to negative experiences, the adolescent with an unexamined (diffuse or foreclosed) group identity may have no problems. Nevertheless, young people who have not examined and resolved for themselves the meaning of their ethnic and racial group membership may be vulnerable to new experiences that disrupt their existing world view. Commenting on the foreclosure status of ego identity, Marcia (1993) pointed out that these individuals "have a problem, because they depend on a particular external structure. . . . When you do not have the flexibility . . . to look at what a new situation can mean when your context changes, you are in trouble" (p. 70). At some point in development, ethnocultural adolescents will be faced with situations that challenge their unexamined ethnic or racial attitudes and sense of group membership. Such an experience, or series of experiences, could precipitate an identity crisis (Erkison, 1968), termed an *encounter* in racial identity theory, that will stimulate a transition to the next phase.

Transition

All models of racial and ethnic identity postulate a critical period in which adolescents begin to question their existing world views and cultural frame of reference. This period may be triggered either by personal encounters with prejudice, stereotypes, or racism, or by exposure to positive role models, such as Malcolm X, or to information about the history and culture of one's group. Experiences with racism may draw adolescents' attention to their minority status and force them to question whether a person of color can ever be fully accepted in the White world. According to racial identity theory, these incidents are not amenable to interpretation via conformity or preencounter attitudes, so a certain amount of confusion (i.e., cognitive dissonance) and emotional turmoil takes place (Helms, 1990). A Korean American college student stated:

Before when racial comments were said around me I would somehow ignore it and pretend that nothing was said. By ignoring comments such as these, I was protecting myself. . . . In realizing that there is racism out in the world and that there are comments concerning race that are directed towards me, I feel as if I have reached the first step. (Tatum, 1992, p. 11)

As ethnocultural adolescents begin to think about these often painful experiences directed at them personally because of their race, they are likely to seriously question their values, attitudes, and beliefs about the world and about themselves as persons of color (Cross, 1991). Psychologically, the ethnocultural individual will react with "confusion, alarm, anomie, or even depression" (Cross, 1991, p. 201). Concomitantly, they might feel anger and resentment towards Whites and shame for past denigration of their racial or ethnic group. "Inner-directed guilt, rage at White people, and an anxiety about becoming the right kind of Black person combine to form a psychic energy that flings the person into a frantic, determined . . . search for Black identity" (Cross, 1991, p. 201). In short, ethnocultural adolescents are ready to embark on a journey of transforming their existing group identity.

Within racial identity theory, these attitudes and experiences define an intermediate phase called *encounter* or *dissonance* (e.g., Atkinson et al., 1993; Cross, 1991; Helms, 1990; Sue & Sue, 1990). Some research has shown that college students who endorse encounter or dissonance attitudes tend to be highly aware of institutional racism and anxious and unassertive in interracial situations (Kohastsu, 1992). However, the existence of encounter as a distinct phase is controversial. Although some studies provide evidence for the reliability and validity of the encounter phase (e.g., Kohatsu, 1992), others show low or inconsistent reliability (Ponterotto & Wise, 1987) or a high correlation of encounter attitudes with the next phase (Pyant & Yanico, 1991). Furthermore, research with the encounter subscale has yielded inconsistent results as to its positive or negative psychological correlates. In any case, this appears to be a dynamic, transitory, and changeable period, making it difficult to assess adequately and to evaluate in terms of mental health implications. It may not be an identifiable or discrete phase but rather a transition to the next phase.

Intermediate Phase

Once adolescents have begun to question their world view, they embark on a period of exploring, examining, and perhaps rejecting their existing views and beliefs as they strive to make sense of their experience as members of a minority group. This phase, variously termed *moratorium, exploration, resistance*, or *immersion/emersion*, is seen as essential if minority adolescents are to become well-functioning adults in society. Adolescents begin to lay the foundations for resolving each of the three interrelated issues discussed earlier. Specifically, this phase is characterized by (1) increased awareness of racism, prejudice, and discrimination, (2) a distancing from or rejection of White society, and (3) an often intense involvement in one's ethnic culture.

The salience of these issues differs widely, and the literature dealing with different groups reflects these differences. Research on Black racial identity has emphasized the growing awareness and understanding of discrimination and racism and the related rejection of Whites and White society (Cross, 1978; Helms, 1990). The focus in studies of Hispanics and Asian Americans has more frequently been on the conflicting demands of two different cultures (Ramirez, 1984; Sung, 1985). Furthermore, the importance of each of these issues is likely to vary for individual adolescents, depending on contextual factors. We examine each of these themes separately.

The most salient aspect of the exploration or resistance phase, discussed in virtually all the writings on racial and ethnic identity, is the heightened awareness of racism and ethnic and racial stereotypes. Keefe (1992) discusses the perception of prejudice and discrimination against one's ethnic group as a key component of ethnic identity among Chicanos. According to Cross (1978), writing about African Americans, the process of becoming increasingly aware of racism can be accompanied by "rage . . . perturbation, effrontery, high risk taking, a destructive mood in constant tension with dreams of revitalization" (p. 17); these feelings of anger contribute to "the tendency to denigrate White people and White culture" (p. 17).

The second aspect of this phase is therefore a distancing from the dominant society. Jackson's (1976) model of racial identity development describes this period as including "a total rejection of all that is White . . . White relationships, White values, and activities that support White people or White institutions" (p. 160). Much of the anger that occurs in this phase seems to stem from a realization of the inconsistency between the ideals of America as a country of justice and equality and the reality of racism as experienced by minority youth (Tatum, 1992). Among African American 10th and 11th graders who were interviewed regarding their views of being American (Phinney & Devich-Navarro, in press), some adolescents exhibited the characteristics of this phase, that is, strong ethnic allegiance and rejection of the mainstream. They made comments such as "I wish it wasn't a thing called America . . . because it does not work. I think we should have stayed apart." These adolescents, responding both to the experience of discrimination and to their increased knowledge about the history of oppression, made statements such as these: "Some people see us as just Black; they do not include us in America"; "Most of the time we can't get along; we should just be separate, not talk to one another." Anger may also arise when students realize how much of their group's history and culture is ignored in the school curriculum and in the society at large.

As a result of these feelings, adolescents may react by rejecting other so-called White values, such as schooling and education. Fordham and Ogbu (1986) suggest that awareness of discrimination contributes to the development of an oppositional identity, that is, an identity that opposes everything that the mainstream encourages. Other writers as well have described the alienation of ethnocultural youth who feel that they have no stake in the society (Matute-Bianchi, 1986; Steele, 1992). Several writers have suggested that the awareness of racism and discrimination, which is characteristic of this phase, promotes a sense of solidarity among members of ethnocultural groups as they come together to oppose racism (Keefe, 1992; Porter & Washington, 1993).

The third, concomitant aspect of this phase is the strong, often intense, interest and involvement in one's ethnic culture. As Ward (1990) states about African Americans, "The adolescent must . . . construct an identity that includes one's Blackness as positively valued and desired. . . . If this process of positive identification with the Black reference group . . . is not completed and internalized, identity formation will be at risk" (p. 219). Cross (1978) refers to an "intense sense of intimacy toward Black life" (p. 17) that is characteristic of this phase. The process often includes active searching for information about one's heritage. Many ethnocultural junior and senior high school students are actively involved in learning more about their culture; they talk with family or friends about ethnic issues, read books (beyond those required for school courses), and go to ethnic museums (Phinney, 1989; Phinney & Tarver, 1988). These activities are typically accompanied by a growing understanding and appreciation of the accomplishments of the group and of outstanding figures who can be positive role models.

For some adolescents, this phase of identity development may be a period of high risk. If the exploration process leads to a feeling that they have no place in a society the discriminates against them and provides few positive roles for them, they may become alienated from society (Steele, 1992). The outcome of the exploration is likely to be largely dependent on the social supports an adolescent receives. Parents and other adult role models can be an important influence, and community organizations can provide opportunities for positive involvement. During this time, high school and college ethnic organizations can serve a valuable function in providing a forum for exploration and discussion around the topics of race and ethnicity. Ward (1990) found that in a predominantly White school, Black students experienced a discovery of self through participation in Black student organizations that provided a forum for mutual recognition and connection. "Such organization can provide needed social support as the adolescents struggle with complicated issues of identity, inclusion and exclusion" (Ward, 1990, p. 226).

There is relatively little research that specifically addresses the mental health implications of this phase of ethnic or racial identity development. Theoretically, it is thought to be a period of uncertainty and possibly psychological distress, although empirical evidence is weak. With reference to the moratorium status within the ego identity paradigm, Marcia (1994) states that during this period the individual may be anxious and confused; the psychological uncertainty may be reflected in less than optimal functioning. In research with high school students, Phinney (1989) found that adolescents in the exploration phase of ethnic identity scored lower on self-concept than those with an achieved ethnic identity. Because involvement in one's cultural or racial background is a pivotal aspect of this phase, a positive sense of one's group may be central to one's self-perceptions. In a recent study of ethnocultural high school students (Phinney & Devich-Navarro, in press) stages were not explicitly assessed, but some African American students expressed attitudes that are characteristic of the exploration or immersion phase, that is, a positive ethnic identity, together with very negative views of the mainstream or American culture. For these adolescents, ethnic identity scores were highly correlated with scores on the Tennessee self-concept scale ($r = .80$). Thus, for individuals with attitudes associated with this phase, a positive affirmation of group membership may be an important correlate of a positive sense of self.

In research that assesses stages of racial identity in college students, using the Racial Identity Attitudes Scale, Parham and Helms (1985a, 1985b) found that strong immersion/emersion attitudes were predictive of low self-regard, low self-actualizing tendencies, high anxiety, and hostility. Carter (1991) reported a heightened concern with drug use associated with this phase and suggested that immersion/emersion attitudes may lead to experimentation with drugs as a way to identify with stereotypical images of African Americans. Also during this phase, college students were more aware of interpersonal and institutional racism (Kohatsu, 1992).

In summary, this phase appears to be characterized by psychological instability and often strong emotions. However, the exploration process, "although painful, is necessary and ultimately productive" (Marcia, 1994, p. 41). Most adolescents or young adults move beyond the resistance or moratorium phase to an achieved internalized identity.

Final Phase

Within the ego identity literature, identity achievement is characterized by a commitment to a particular direction (occupation, lifestyle) that follows an examination of alternatives and consideration of one's abilities, interests, and opportunities. This commitment and sense of direction serve as a guide for future decisions. Waterman's (1984) extensive review of the literature on identity development strongly indicates that an achieved ego identity is linked to effective psychological functioning. Similarly, a secure, committed sense of one's racial or ethnic group membership is assumed to provide the foundation for healthy adjustment among members of ethnocultural groups (Cross, 1991; Phinney, 1993). This secure sense of self is based on the successful resolution of the three interrelated issues discussed earlier: ethnicity, minority status, and relationship to the larger society.

The central component of an achieved, internalized identity is a strong, positive feeling about oneself as a member of one's ethnic or racial group. Writing about Mexican Americans, Arce (1981) stated that "Following [a] period of cultural and political consciousness . . . individuals develop a deeper sense of belonging to the group. . . . When a person finally comes to feel at one with the group, the internalization process has been completed, and ethnic identity established" (p. 186). In describing this phase among African Americans, Cross (1978) states, "Tension, emotionality, and defensiveness are replaced by a calm, secure demeanor. Ideological flexibility, psychological openness, and self-confidence about one's Blackness are evident" (p. 18). Adolescents may reflect on the changes that have occurred from an earlier period when they rejected their race or ethnicity:

I used to want to be White, because I wanted long flowing hair; and I wanted to be real light. I used to think being light was prettier, but now I think there are pretty dark-skinned girls and pretty light-skinned girls. I don't want to be White now. I'm happy being Black. (Phinney, 1989, p. 44)

The second aspect of the achieved, internalized group identity involves the manner of handling racism, prejudice, and discrimination. Various writers have suggested that the awareness of these problems remains, but the anger that accompanied it in earlier phases is tempered, and individuals have developed more adaptive means of handling these obstacles (Cross 1991). Many youths express the need to work harder to overcome these obstacles (Ward, 1990). Others express a commitment to disproving negative stereotypes by excelling in their own field and by trying to educate those who hold such views (Phinney & Chavira, 1995). This active approach to coping with such problems may contribute to positive self-esteem. An interview study with African

American, Asian American, and Mexican American adolescents identified several ways in which these youths dealt with problems such as prejudice and discrimination (Phinney & Chavira, 1995). Although this study did not assess stages of ethnic identity, adolescents who used a proactive style, including self-affirmation, discussion, and attempts to disprove stereotypes, showed higher scores on both self-esteem and ethnic identity than did adolescents who responded to such incidents with anger and verbal retorts, a strategy more likely to occur among adolescents at the earlier phase of resistance and exploration.

The final aspect of an achieved or internalized ethnic or racial identity is a resolution of the adolescent's relationship with the dominant culture. Theoretical models assume that at this stage, individuals have positive attitudes toward and relationships with the dominant culture (Atkinson et al., 1993; Cross, 1991). For many ethnocultural youths it is a virtual necessity to be bicultural, to participate both in their ethnic culture and in the mainstream. However, there are many different models describing ways of being bicultural (LaFromboise et al., 1993). Before considering the implications of biculturalism, we examine the evidence that an achieved ethnic or racial identity is associated with positive psychological adjustment.

Existing models strongly suggest that an achieved, internalized group identity, compared to earlier phases, is associated with better psychological adjustment, including a positive self-concept and the absence of psychological distress (Helms, 1990; Phinney, 1993). Research that used an interview technique to assign Asian American, African American, and Hispanic high school students to one of three ethnic identity stages (Phinney, 1989) found that those with an achieved ethnic identity scored significantly higher on self-concept than those in the other stages. Research using a continuous scale of ethnic identity (Phinney, 1992) has shown consistent but low positive correlations between ethnic identity and self-esteem among a number of different ethnocultural groups. This relationship has been demonstrated among Asian American, African American, and Hispanic high school students ($r = .31$) and college students ($r = .25$) (Phinney, 1992) and, in a separate study of high school and college students, among Asian Americans ($r = .25$), African Americans, ($r = .24$), and Latinos ($r = .27$) (Phinney et al., 1994). These relatively low correlations suggest that although ethnic identity is implicated in self-esteem, the two constructs are independent and other variables need to be considered.

One problem in interpreting these data is that they are correlational, and thus direction of effect cannot be inferred. In a longitudinal study that assessed self-concept and ethnic identity among a group of ethnocultural adolescents at ages 16 and 19 (Phinney & Chavira, 1992), ethnic identity and self-esteem were both correlated at each time period and predicted each other over time, suggesting an interactive effect. Specifically, a clear, positive sense of one's background may contribute to positive self-attitudes; at the same time, high self-esteem may provide the confidence needed for the exploration of difficult issues, such as the questioning of stereotypes, that leads to an achieved ethnic identity. Rosenberg and his colleagues (Rosenberg, Schooler, & Schoenbach, 1989) have noted that self-esteem can be seen as either the cause or the outcome of developmental variables. Factors that enhance self-esteem, such as family support and personal accomplishments, are likely to contribute as well to a secure sense of self as a member of an ethnic or racial group. Further longitudinal research is needed to clarify these interrelationships.

Research using the Racial Identity Attitudes Scale (Helms, 1990) has shown mixed results regarding the psychological implications of the final phase of identity development. Some research has found no relationship of internalization with measures of psychological well-being (Parham & Helms, 1985a; Pyant & Yanico, 1991), whereas other research has shown internalization attitudes to be significant predictors of assertiveness and awareness of racism (Kohatsu, 1992). Carter (1991) reported that internalization was associated with paranoia among college students; he suggested that paranoia at this phase of development may be indicative of the psychological price that ethnocultural adolescents pay for their efforts to become bicultural. Paranoia may in fact serve as a psychologically adaptive response to a racist and hostile environment (Ridley, 1984).

As we have discussed, an important part of the identity formation process concerns the way adolescents perceive and relate to the mainstream society. There is substantial support for the view that being bicultural, that is, incorporating elements from both the ethnic culture and the mainstream culture into one's identity, provides the basis for better psychological functioning than an emphasis on either culture alone (LaFromboise et al., 1993; Oetting & Beauvais, 1991; Ramirez, 1984). Evidence from cross-cultural research suggests that for members of ethnocultural groups, "selective involvement in two cultural systems may provide the most supportive sociocultural base for the mental health of the individual" (Berry & Kim, 1988, pp. 213–214). In research with Cuban American adolescents, Szapocznik and his colleagues (1980) found that the best-adjusted youths were fully involved with both Cuban and American culture. However, as noted earlier, the effects may be interactive, with the more adjusted youths having better interpersonal skills that make such involvement easier.

In addition to relating well to the larger society, individuals with an internalized ethnic or racial identity are assumed to have positive relations with members of other ethnic groups (Atkinson et al., 1993). The importance of attitudes toward other groups was illustrated in a study of African American and Mexican American adolescents (Phinney & Devich-Navarro, in press). For those students who indicated that they considered themselves to be bicultural, that is, both ethnic and American, self-concept and attitudes toward other ethnic groups were significantly positively correlated.

The studies just discussed focus on bicultural adaptation, that is, the ability to function effectively in two or more cultural settings. Thus, they do not involve group identity or identification as such. Several studies have assessed identification with the Euro-American culture as a factor in adjustment. In a study of Native American adolescents, Oetting and Beauvais (1991) independently assessed identification with Indian culture and White American culture by asking youths separate questions assessing the extent to which they "live by or follow the White American [or American Indian] way of life." They found that self-esteem and school adjustment were related to both Indian and White identification; the highest self-esteem and best school adjustment were among those who had high identification with both groups. They conclude that "It is not mixed cultural identification but weak cultural identification that creates problems" (p. 679). A study by Sanchez and Fernandez (1993) used direct questions to assess identification, for example, "I consider myself a person from Hispanic background [an American]." Those high on American identification showed significantly less acculturative stress.

In summary, the research on the psychological implications of an achieved or internalized group identity is very diverse. Results from various studies cannot be directly compared because of the different ethnic and racial groups involved and the use of different procedures and measures. However, overall, the research reviewed suggests that psychological adjustment among ethnocultural adolescents is associated with positive attitudes and interactions with members of their own group, of other groups, and of the larger society. Furthermore, this combination of attitudes is most likely to be found among adolescents who have actively engaged in a process of ethnic or racial identity development and have reached a secure, integrated understanding of themselves as members of an ethnic and/or racial group.

Concluding Comments

We have discussed ethnic and racial identity development among ethnocultural youths as a process that cuts across groups and is comparable in some respects to ego identity development. At the broadest level, it can be thought of as an aspect of the general developmental process of increasing differentiation and integration. A successful transition to adulthood requires ethnocultural adolescents to differentiate stereotypes of their group from the reality of the group as they know and experience it. To function effectively as adults in a diverse society, they must also distinguish between those aspects of American society that are destructive to their group, such as individual and institutional racism, and those forces working for change, for example toward a more equitable society. An internalized group identity for these adolescents involves an integrated sense of self as a member of an ethnic or racial group and as a member of the larger society, able to participate competently in various contexts in a multicultural society.

However, there is little solid evidence in the literature to suggest how the transition to a secure sense of self is accomplished. Even within the more widely studied area of ego identity, the processes of identity transition and resolution are little understood (LaVoie, 1994). Most of the emphasis has been on individual, internal processes, notably exploration and commitment. Yet contextual factors are clearly important in that they often provide the impetus for exploration and the opportunity for expressing commitment (Phinney & Goosens, 1996). Changing sociocultural factors present adolescents with varying challenges and opportunities for understanding the self. For ethnocultural adolescents, these challenges depend in part on the structure and composition of the ethnic community and on the nature and extent of contacts with the larger society, as well as on historical events that affect these relationships. For example, the civil rights movement provided the chance for dramatic changes in the expression of racial identity (Cross, 1991).

Because historical and cultural factors are important influences on group identity, it is essential to keep in mind the differences among ethnic and racial groups. Each group has distinct cultural traditions and resources and faces unique problems and challenges. A key factor in determining the value and significance of research on group identity will be how accurately it reflects the perspectives of different ethnocultural individuals and groups. For this reason, research can be enriched by the use of ethnographic and qualitative methods that allow participants to express their own points of view. Researchers who are themselves from these groups can, through their own knowledge and background, play an essential role in generating research and calling attention to the limitations of mainstream research that fails to consider ethnocultural diversity. They provide what Greenfield (1994) terms an *insider perspective*. However, Greenfield notes the importance of having an outsider perspective as well in order to get a complete picture of psychological reality. It is important to bring both perspectives to bear. Therefore, collaboration among researchers from diverse backgrounds holds promise for research that can further our understanding of this topic.

Clearly, there are many interacting factors that affect the development of racial and ethnic identity in ethnocultural adolescents. Most research has focused on a limited number of factors and has studied individuals at one point in time. The relationships between ethnic and racial identity and between group identity and cultural adaptation have not been systematically studied. There is a need for longitudinal research that includes a range of interacting factors that influence group identity, including the immediate context and the larger sociopolitical environment. By considering the interactions among these variables and by developing more complex and dynamic models, we can begin to understand the ways in which ethnocultural adolescents develop a psychologically healthy sense of themselves both as individuals and as members of a particular ethnic and racial group.

Note

1 Labels for American ethnic groups have changed over time (e.g., *Negro, Black, African American*). The terms *Latino* and *Hispanic* are roughly synonymous ways of referring to people of Latin American origin, but the former is currently preferred by many members of that group and we use it as the general term. However, in citing previous research, we use the term used by the researchers.

References

Aboud, F. (1987). The development of ethnic self-identification and attitudes. In J. Phinney & M. Rotheram (Eds.), *Children's ethnic socialization: Pluralism and development* (pp. 32–55). Newbury Park, CA: Sage.

Adams, G., Gullotta, T., & Montemayor, R. (1992). *Adolescent identity formation.* Newbury Park, CA: Sage.

Alba, R. (1990). *Ethnic identity: The transformation of white America.* New Haven, CT: Yale University Press.

Arce, C. (1981). A reconsideration of Chicano culture and identity. *Daedalus, 110*(2), 177–192.

Aries, E., & Moorehead, K. (1989). The importance of ethnicity in the development of identity of black adolescents. *Psychological Reports, 65*, 75–82.

Atkinson, D., Morten, G., & Sue, D. (1993). *Counseling American minorities* (4th ed.). Dubuque, IA: W. C. Brown.

Bernal, M., & Knight, G. (Eds.). (1993). *Ethnic identity: Formation and transmission among Hispanics and other minorities.* Albany, NY: State University of New York Press.

Bernal, M., Knight, G., Garza, C., Ocampo, K., & Cota, M. (1990). The development of ethnic identity in Mexican-American children. *Hispanic Journal of Behavioral Sciences, 12*, 3–24.

Bernal, M., Knight, G., Ocampo, K., Garza, C., & Cota, M. (1993). Development of Mexican American identity. In M. Bernal & G. Knight (Eds.), *Ethnic identity: Formation and transmission among Hispanics and other minorities* (pp. 31–46). Albany, NY: State University of New York Press.

Berry, J. (1990). Psychology of acculturation. In J. Berman (Ed.), *Cross-cultural perspectives: Nebraska symposium on motivation* (pp. 201–234). Lincoln: University of Nebraska Press.

Berry, J., & Kim, U. (1988). Acculturation and mental health. In P. Dasen, J. Berry, & N. Sartorius (Eds.), *Health and cross-cultural psychology: Toward applications* (pp. 207–236). Newbury Park, CA: Sage.

Betancourt, H., & Lopez, S. (1993). The study of culture, ethnicity, and race in American psychology. *American Psychologist, 48*(6), 629–637.

Birman, D. (1994). Acculturation and human diversity in a multicultural society. In E. Trickett, R. Watts, & D. Birman (Eds.), *Human diversity: Perspective on people in context* (pp. 261–284). San Francisco: Jossey-Bass.

Blos, P. (1979). *The adolescent passage.* New York: International Universities Press.

Boykin, A. W., & Toms, F. (1985). Black child socialization: A conceptual framework. In H. McAdoo & J. McAdoo (Eds.), *Black children: Social, educational, and parental environments* (pp. 33–51). Thousand Oaks, CA: Sage.

Carter, R. (1991). Racial attitudes and psychological functioning. *Journal of Multicultural Counseling and Development, 19*, 105–114.

Clark, K., & Clark, M. (1947). Racial identification and preference in Negro preschool children. In

T. Newcomb & E. Hartley (Eds.), *Readings in social psychology* (pp. 169–178). New York: Holt.

Cross, W. (1978). The Thomas and Cross models of psychological nigrescence. *Journal of Black Psychology, 4*, 13–31.

Cross, W. (1991). *Shades of black: Diversity in African-American identity.* Philadelphia: Temple University Press.

DeVos, G., & Romanucci-Ross, L. (Eds.). (1982). *Ethnic identity: Cultural continuities and change.* Chicago: University of Chicago Press.

Elder, G., Modell, J., & Parke, R. (1993). *Children in time and place: Developmental and historical insights.* New York: Cambridge University Press.

Erikson, E. (1968). *Identity: Youth and crisis.* New York: Norton.

Fordham, S., & Ogbu, J. (1986). Black students' school success: Coping with the burden of "acting white." *The Urban Review, 18*(3), 31–58.

Garcia, J. (1982). Ethnicity and Chicanos: Measurement of ethnic identification, identity, and consciousness. *Hispanic Journal of Behavioral Sciences, 4*, 295–314.

Greenfield, P. (1994). Independence and interdependence as developmental scripts: Implications for theory, research, and practice. In P. Greenfield & R. Cocking (Eds.), *Cross-cultural roots of minority child development* (pp. 1–25). Hillsdale, NJ: Erlbaum.

Helms, J. (1990). *Black and white racial identity: Theory, research, and practice.* New York: Greenwood.

Helms, J. (1994). How multiculturalism obscures racial factors in the therapy process. *Journal of Counseling Psychology, 41*, 162–165.

Jackson, B. (1976). Black identity development. In L. Golubschick (Ed.), *Urban social and educational issues* (pp. 158–164). Dubuque: Kendall/Hunt.

Keefe, S. (1992). Ethnic identity: The domain of perceptions of and attachment to ethnic groups and cultures. *Human Organizations, 51*(1), 35–43.

Keefe, S., & Padilla, A. (1987), *Chicano ethnicity.* Albuquerque: University of New Mexico Press.

Kohatsu, E. L. (1992). *The effects of racial identity and acculturation on anxiety, assertiveness, and ascribed identity among Asian American college students.* Doctoral dissertation, University of Maryland, College Park. *Dissertation Abstracts International* B 54/2. (University Microfilms No. AAC 9315670).

Kohatsu, E., & Richardson, T. (1996). Racial and ethnic identity assessment. In L. A. Suzuki, P. J. Meller, & J. G. Ponterotto (Eds.), *Multicultural assessment: Clinical, psychological, and educational applications* (pp. 611–650). San Francisco: Jossey-Bass.

Kroger, J. (1989). *Identity in adolescence: The balance between self and other.* New York: Routledge.

LaFromboise, T., Coleman, H., & Gerton, J. (1993). Psychological impact of biculturalism: Evidence and theory. *Psychological Bulletin, 114*, 395–412.

LaVoie, J. (1994). Identity in adolescence: Issues of theory, structure, and transition. *Journal of Adolescence, 17*, 17–28.

Lee, E. (1988). Cultural factors in working with Southeast Asian refugee adolescents. *Journal of Adolescence, 11*, 167–179.

Marcia, J. (1980). Identity in adolescence. In J. Adelson (Ed.), *Handbook of adolescent psychology* (pp. 159–187). New York: Wiley.

Marcia, J. (1993). Discussion comment. In J. Kroger (Ed.), *Discussions on ego identity* (p. 70). Hillsdale, NJ: Erlbaum.

Marcia, J. (1994). Identity and psychotherapy. In S. Archer (Ed.), *Interventions for adolescent identity development* (pp. 29–46). Thousand Oaks, CA: Sage.

Marcia, J., Waterman, A., Matteson, D., Archer, S., & Orlofsky, J. (1994). *Ego identity: A handbook of psychosocial research.* New York: Springer-Verlag.

Matute-Bianchi, M. (1986). Ethnic identities and pattern of school success and failure among Mexican-descent and Japanese-American students in a California High School. *American Journal of Education, 95*, 233–255.

Mitchell, S. L., & Dell, D. M. (1992). The relationship between black students' racial identity attitude and participation in campus organizations. *Journal of College Student Development, 33,* 39–43.

Oetting, E., & Beauvais, F. (1991). Orthogonal cultural identification theory: The cultural identification of minority adolescents. *International Journal of the Addictions, 25,* 655–685.

Parham, T., & Helms, J. (1981). The influence of black students' racial identity attitudes on preferences for counselor's race. *Journal of Counseling Psychology, 28,* 250–257.

Parham, T. A., & Helms, J. E. (1985a). Relation of racial identity attitudes to self-actualization and affective states of black students. *Journal of Counseling Psychology, 32,* 431–440.

Parham, T. A., & Helms, J. E. (1985b). Attitudes of racial identity and self-esteem: An exploratory investigation. *Journal of College Student Personnel, 26,* 143–146.

Parham, T. A., & Williams, P. T. (1993). The relationship of demographic and background factors to racial identity attitudes. *Journal of Black Psychology, 19,* 7–24.

Phinney, J. (1989). Stages of ethnic identity development in minority group adolescents. *Journal of Early Adolescence, 9,* 34–49.

Phinney, J. (1990). Ethnic identity in adolescents and adults: A review of research. *Psychological Bulletin, 108,* 499–514.

Phinney, J. (1992). The Multigroup Ethnic Identity Measure: A new scale for use with diverse groups. *Journal of Adolescent Research, 7,* 156–176.

Phinney, J. (1993). A three-stage model of ethnic identity development. In M. E. Bernal & G. P. Knight (Eds.), *Ethnic identity: Formation and transmission among Hispanics and other minorities* (pp. 61–79). Albany, NY: State University of New York Press.

Phinney, J., & Alipuria, L. (1990). Ethnic identity in college students from four ethnic groups. *Journal of Adolescence, 13,* 171–184.

Phinney, J., & Chavira, V. (1992). Ethnic identity and self-esteem: An exploratory longitudinal study. *Journal of Adolescence, 15,* 271–281.

Phinney, J., & Chavira, V. (1995). Parental ethnic socialization and adolescent outcomes in ethnic minority families. *Journal of Research on Adolescence, 5,* 31–53.

Phinney, J., & Devich-Navarro, M. (in press). Variations in bicultural identification among African American and Mexican American adolescents. *Journal of Research on Adolescence.*

Phinney, J., DuPont, S., Espinosa, C., Revill, J., & Sanders, K. (1994). Ethnic identity and American identification among ethnic minority adolescents. In A. Bouvy, F. van de Vijver, P. Boski, & P. Schmitz (Eds.), *Journeys into cross-cultural psychology* (pp. 167–183). Amsterdam: Swets & Zeitilinger.

Phinney, J., & Goosens, L. (Eds.). (1996). Identity development in context. Special issue of the *Journal of Adolescence, 19*(5).

Phinney, J., & Rosenthal, D. (1992). Ethnic identity formation in adolescence: Process, context, and outcome. In G. Adams, T. Gulotta, & R. Montemayor (Eds.), *Identity formation during adolescence* (pp. 145–172). Newbury Park, CA: Sage.

Phinney, J., & Tarver, S. (1988). Ethnic identity search and commitment in black and white eighth graders. *Journal of Early Adolescence, 8,* 265–277.

Ponterotto, J., & Wise, S. (1987). Construct validity study of the Racial Identity Attitude Scale. *Journal of Consulting Psychology, 34,* 218–223.

Porter, J., & Washington, R. (1993). Minority identity and self-esteem. *Annual Review of Sociology, 19,* 139–161.

Portes, A., & Rumbaut, R. (1990). *Immigrant America: A portrait.* Berkeley: University of California Press.

Pyant, C., & Yanico, B. (1991). Relationship of racial identity and gender-role attitudes to black women's psychological well-being. *Journal of Counseling Psychology, 38,* 315–322.

Ramirez, M. (1984). Assessing and understanding biculturalism-multiculturalism in Mexican-American adults. In J. Martinex & R. Mendoza (Eds.), *Chicano psychology* (pp. 77–94). Orlando, FL: Academic Press.

Ridley, C. (1984). Clinical treatment of the nondisclosing black client. *American Psychologist, 39,* 1234–1244.

Rosenberg, M., Schooler, C., & Schoenbach, C. (1989). Self-esteem and adolescent problems: Modeling reciprocal effects. *American Sociological Review, 54,* 1004–1018.

Sanchez, J., & Fernandez, D. (1993). Acculturative stress among Hispanics: A bidimensional model of ethnic identification. *Journal of Applied Social Psychology, 23,* 654–668.

Shorter-Gooden, K., & Washington, C. (1996). Young, black, female: The challenge of weaving an identity. *Journal of Adolescence, 19* (5).

Silbereisen, R., & Todt, E. (Eds.). (1994). *Adolescence in context: The interplay of family, school, peers, and work in adjustment.* New York: Springer-Verlag.

Spencer, M., & Markstrom-Adams, C. (1990). Identity processes among racial and ethnic minority children in America. *Child Development, 61,* 290–310.

Steele, C. (1992, April). Race and the schooling of black Americans. *The Atlantic Monthly,* 68–78.

Stonequist, E. (1935). The problem of a marginal man. *American Journal of Sociology, 41,* 1–12.

Sue, D. W. & Sue, D. (1990). *Counseling the culturally different: Theory and practice* (2nd ed.). New York: Wiley.

Sung, B. (1985). Bicultural conflicts in Chinese American immigrant children. *Journal of Comparative Family Studies, 16,* 255–269.

Szapocznik, J., Kurtines, W., & Fernandez, T. (1980). Bicultural involvement and adjustment in Hispanic-American youths. *International Journal of Intercultural Relations, 4,* 353–365.

Tajfel, H. (1981). *Human groups and social categories.* Cambridge: Cambridge University Press.

Tajfel, H., & Turner, J. (1986). The social identity theory of intergroup behavior. In S. Worchel & W. G. Austin (Eds.), *Psychology of intergroup relations* (pp. 7–24). Chicago: Nelson-Hall.

Tatum, B. (1992). Talking about race, learning about racism: The application of racial identity development theory in the classroom. *Harvard Educational Review, 62,* 1–24.

Taub, D., & McEwen, M. (1992). The relationship of racial identity attitudes to autonomy and mature interpersonal relationships in black and white undergraduate women. *Journal of College Student Development, 33,* 439–446.

Thornton, M., Chatters, L., Taylor, R., & Allen, W. (1990). Sociodemographic and environmental correlates of racial socialization by black parents. *Child Development 61,* 401–409

Ting-Toomey. (1981). Ethnic identity and close friendship in Chinese-American college students. *International Journal of Intercultural Relations, 5,* 383–406.

Ward, J. (1990). Racial identity formation and transformation. In C. Gilligan, N. Lyons, & T. Hanmer (Eds.), *Marking connections: The relational worlds of adolescent girls at Emma Willard School* (pp. 215–232). Cambridge, MA: Harvard University Press.

Waterman, A. (1984). *The psychology of individualism.* New York: Praeger.

Waters, M. (1990). *Ethnic options: Choosing identities in America.* Berkeley: University of California Press.

Wooden, W., Leon, J., & Toshima, M. (1988). Ethnic identity among Sansei and Yonsei church-affiliated youth in Los Angeles and Honolulu. *Psychological Reports, 62,* 268–270.

Yee, A., Fairchild, H., Weizmann, F., & Wyatt, G. (1993). Addressing psychology's problems with race. *American Psychologist, 48,* 1132–1140.

17 Religion and Adolescent Health-Compromising Behavior

John M. Wallace, Jr., and David R. Williams

As a result of both real and perceived increases in the prevalence of teenage pregnancy, sexually transmitted diseases, drug use, violence, delinquency, school dropout, and mental health problems, there has been a substantial increase in research concerning adolescent health and well-being (OTA, 1991). Despite the continued and growing interest in behaviors that compromise adolescents' health, and the search for protective factors relevant to the prevention of these behaviors, social scientists typically ignore one potentially important protective factor to which nearly 50% of American youth are regularly "exposed." This factor is broadly termed *religion*. Although some researchers (Dryfoos, 1990; Hawkins, Catalano, & Miller, 1992) have identified lack of religiosity or low religiousness as a risk factor for a number of problem behaviors, religion measures are not routinely included in research, nor is religion widely acknowledged as an important correlate (if not predictor) of adolescent health-related attitudes, beliefs, and behaviors.

The purpose of this chapter is to begin to bridge the gap between research on religion (i.e., attitudes, beliefs, values, and behaviors concerning things spiritual) and research on adolescent health outcomes. In the first section we describe the "epidemiology" of religion among American youth. In the second section we discuss the relative neglect of religion by researchers interested in adolescent health. In the third section we review, selectively, empirical research on the relationship between religion and the two potentially health-compromising behaviors in which American youth are most likely to engage – precocious sexual involvement and the use of licit and illicit drugs. In the fourth section we discuss problems and limitations in the extant research on religion and adolescent health outcomes. The chapter concludes with the discussion of a conceptual framework designed to guide future research on the relationship between religion and adolescent health.

Religion and American Youth

American youth exhibit high levels of pro-religious beliefs, attitudes, and behaviors (Gallup & Bezilla, 1992). For example, 95% of American teens aged

444

13 to 17 believe in God (or a universal spirit), 76% believe that God observes their actions and rewards or punishes them, 93% believe that God loves them, 91% believe in heaven, 76% believe in hell, and 86% believe that Jesus Christ is God or the Son of God. Eighty percent of American teenagers say that religion is at least fairly important to them, and 40% report that they seriously try to follow the teaching of their religion. Ninety-three percent report being affiliated with a religious group or denomination (59% Protestant, 30% Catholic, 1% some other Christian denomination, 2% Jewish, 1% report some other affiliation) (Gallup & Bezilla, 1992).

With regard to their religious practices, 42% of teenagers report that they frequently pray alone, 48% report that they have attended church or syna-gogue within the last 7 days, and 36% report that they read the Bible weekly or more. Forty-one percent of American teens report that they are currently involved in Sunday school, 36% report being involved with a church youth group, 23% are involved in church-sponsored activities to help the less fortu-nate, and 18% are involved in a church choir or music group.

Figure 17.1 presents trend data on religious involvement among American teenagers from 1976 to 1993.[1] These data reveal that there has been a gradual decline in religious attendance over the past two decades and, concomitantly, a gradual increase in the percentage of youth who claim no religious affiliation. For example, in 1976, 41% of high school seniors reported that they attended services weekly; by 1993 this figure had decreased to 32%. Only 11% of 12th-grade students reported that they had no religious affiliation in 1976; by 1993 this figure had increased to 16%. Despite the decline in church attendance and the increase in the number of unaffiliated youth, a substantial proportion of the American youth population remains religiously involved and the impor-tance that young people ascribe to religion has remained unchanged. For example, the same percentage of American high school seniors who reported that religion was very important to them in 1976 (29%) reported that religion was very important to them in 1993.

Data on the sociodemographic correlates of religious attendance, impor-tance, and affiliation indicate the following: (1) In general, age does not appear to be strongly related to the importance that adolescents ascribe to religion or to the likelihood that they are not affiliated with a religious denomination. Age does, however, relate to attendance at religious services, with older adoles-cents attending less frequently than younger adolescents. (2) On average, females are slightly more religious than males, as measured by the importance, attendance, and affiliation variables. (3) Relative to White and Hispanic youth, Black youth are more religious across all three religion indicators. (4) Although adolescents from single- and two-parent families are equally likely to report that religion is very important to them, those in two-parent families attend religious services more often and are less likely to report that they are not religiously affiliated. (5) Parental education is not strongly related to the

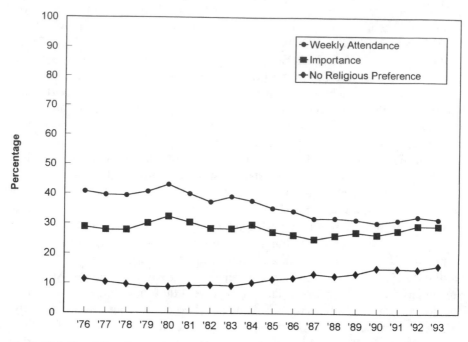

Figure 17.1. Trends in religion variables, 1976–1993.

importance that adolescents place on religion, but students with highly educated parents attend church more often and are less likely to say that they have
no religious affiliation. (6) Adolescents who live in nonurban areas report
greater importance of religion and more frequent attendance at religious
services than do adolescents from medium-sized and large cities. (7) Relative
to adolescents in the other regions of the country, southern youth attend
church more often, are more likely to say that religion is very important to
them, and are least likely to say that they do not belong to a religious group.

   In sum, although there is considerable variation in the extent to which
American young people attend religious services, feel that religion is a very
important part of their life, engage in various religious practices, and hold
specific beliefs about God, Satan, Jesus Christ, and other spiritual beings, one-
third to one-half of them might be considered highly religious, with perhaps
another 40% being considered at least mildly religious. Given the high prevalence of religious attitudes, beliefs, and practices among American youth, one
would expect a substantial body of research examining religion and its causes
and consequences in the lives of American adolescents; such is not the case.
Having examined the epidemiology of religion among American youth, we
now turn our attention to the relative neglect of this important topic as it
relates to research on adolescence broadly and to research on adolescent
health in particular.

Adolescence, Health, and the Neglect of Religion

There is little communication between scholars who do research on religion, those who do research on adolescence, and those who do research on health. As a result of this lack of conversation, relatively little is known concerning religion and its relationship to adolescent health. The lack of intellectual exchange between scholars of religion, adolescence, and health is evidenced in at least four ways. First, research on adolescence typically ignores religion. For example, an examination of 60 textbooks published in the last three decades in the areas of child and adolescent development revealed that 44 had no mention of religion, 9 only briefly mentioned religion, 5 had what might be considered an extensive discussion of religion, and only 2 had chapters that included the topic of religion in a chapter title (Thomas & Carver, 1990).

Second, research on adolescent religion typically omits any discussion of adolescent health. For example, neither a recent review of the research on adolescence and religion (Benson, Donahue, & Erickson, 1989) nor a recent book (Hyde, 1990) that comprehensively reviewed published research on religion in childhood and adolescence had a subsection or even references to adolescent health issues other than sex, drug use, or suicide.

Third, the adolescent health literature has largely ignored the relationship between religion and health. For example, perhaps the most important summary of research on adolescent health to date, the U.S. Congress's 726-page document entitled Adolescent Health (OTA, 1991), summarizes hundreds of studies relevant to adolescent health, and yet the index includes only two references to religion. The first reference simply mentions the importance of churches and synagogues as places to offer activities to adolescents. The second notes that there is a negative relationship between religiousness and initiation into sexual activity.

Fourth, when religion is included in research relevant to adolescent health, it is typically a nonfocal variable that is not taken seriously. For example, a recent review of research on the relationship between religion and drug abuse found it to be the most consistently replicated correlate of nonabuse and often the most significant predictor in the study. Despite this fact, however, researchers often failed to discuss the inverse relationship between religion and drug use in the abstract or the text of their research articles (Gorsuch, 1988).

Religion and Adolescent Health-Compromising Behavior: Empirical Research

Among adults, religion has been found to relate positively to health status, longevity, specific health outcomes, and a variety of health behaviors (for reviews, see King, 1990; Levin, 1994; Levin & Schiller, 1987). Despite a long history of research on the relationship between religion and health among adults, relatively little research has focused on religion as it relates to adoles-

cent health. In fact, research on religion and adolescent health issues is virtually nonexistent with the exception of that on the extent to which religion acts
as a "social control" against what has broadly been referred to as *delinquency*
or *deviance*.

We now review a number of the more rigorous studies that examine empirically the relationship between religion and the two most widespread adolescent health-compromising behaviors – precocious, typically unprotected sex
and drug use. Where possible, the samples for the studies discussed are drawn
from the general adolescent population (approximately 13 to 19 years old)
rather than from more restricted populations (e.g., first-year psychology
undergraduates).

Sexual Behaviors

Relatively high proportions of American adolescents are sexually active. For
example, among high school students, 44% of 9th graders, 53% of 10th
graders, 65% of 11th graders, and 71% of 12th graders reported ever having
sexual intercourse (Kann et al., 1991). Of those who are sexually active, more
than 40% reported that they had had four or more sexual partners. Trend data
on the prevalence of sexual intercourse among young people suggest that the
age of initiation into sexual intercourse continues to decline. For example, in
1970 less than 30% of 15- to 19-year-old girls reported having had premarital
intercourse; by 1988 this figure had increased to nearly 52%. The relatively
high rates of sexual intercourse among adolescents and the relatively high
number of sexual partners among those who are sexually active place them at
increased risk for a broad range of health problems including pregnancy,
childbearing, abortion, cervical cancer, and a variety of sexually transmitted
diseases (e.g., syphilis, gonorrhea, human immunodeficiency virus [HIV]).

Each year an estimated 1 million girls between the ages of 10 and 19 become
pregnant in the United States. It is also estimated that more than 40% of
America's 17 million adolescent females will become pregnant before their
20th birthday (OTA, 1991). Of the 1 million adolescent girls who get pregnant
each year, slightly more than half give birth, about 40% have abortions, and
approximately less than 15% miscarry.

Annually, 3 million teenagers (one out of eight) are infected with a sexually
transmitted disease (National Commission on AIDS, 1994). In 1989 there
were 11,820 new cases of gonorrhea among adolescents aged 10 to 14 years
(69.7 cases per 100,000) and 204,023 new cases among adolescents aged 15 to
19 years (1,145.4 cases per 100,000). Recent data suggest that there have been
increases not only in gonorrhea but also in syphilis and a variety of other
sexually transmitted diseases, including HIV/AIDS. By the end of March 1993
there were 1,167 cases of AIDS among teenagers aged 13 to 19. The estimated
10-year lag between HIV infection and the onset of AIDS suggests that many

of the 10,949 20- to 24-year-olds with AIDS and the 44,171 25- to 29-year-olds with AIDS in the United States (as of March 1993) were actually infected as teenagers.

Clearly, early and typically unprotected sexual intercourse poses serious threats to the health and long-term well-being of young people. A variety of factors have been identified as key risk factors for pregnancy, HIV, and other sexually transmitted diseases. These risk factors include, but are not limited to, age at first intercourse, frequency of intercourse, number of sexual partners, and the absence and inappropriate use of contraceptives. The question that is relevant in the current context is: To what extent does religion relate to adolescent sexual activity and risk factors for sex-related health problems?

Religion can affect adolescent sexuality in a variety of ways, including influencing attitudes and beliefs about contraception; influencing attitudes and beliefs about the appropriateness and type of sexual activity permissible outside of marriage; and/or influencing the situations, environments, and relationships in which adolescents place themselves. A number of studies have examined the relationship between religion and adolescent sexual behaviors. In general, past reviews of the literature and recent findings from both national and local studies indicate a strong negative relationship between religion and sexual attitudes and behaviors (Hayes, 1987; Miller & Moore, 1990; Murry, 1994). Specific findings from selected studies will now be outlined.

One of the most comprehensive studies on the relationship between religion and adolescent females' sexual behavior was that conducted by Zelnick, Kantner, and Ford (1981). The study, based on two national U.S. surveys of adolescent females aged 15 to 19 years, examined the extent to which religious affiliation and religiosity (an index combining the importance of religion to the young woman, her perception of the importance of religion in her family, and her frequency of attendance at religious services) related to a number of sex-related outcomes, including the prevalence of premarital sex, age at initiation into sex, number of sexual partners, and patterns of contraceptive use. Both religion measures had strong bivariate relationships with the prevalence of premarital intercourse. On average, young women who were more religious and who belonged to more fundamentalist versus liberal or no religious groups were less likely to report engaging in premarital sex. Fundamentalist religious denominations are those that are theologically (and often politically) conservative and that hold doctrines such as the inerrancy of Scripture, the virgin birth, and the resurrection of Jesus Christ. In 1976 the prevalence of premarital sex among fundamentalist females was 44% compared to 58% among those with no religious affiliation. Similarly, only 24% of the young women in the high category of the religiosity index reported having premarital sex compared to 54% of those in the low-religiosity category. Compared to sexually active young women from fundamentalist religious backgrounds and those with high levels of religiosity, religiously less involved, sexually active young women initiated sex earlier, had more sexual partners, and had more frequent premarital sexual experiences. Controlling for a number of variables (e.g., race, age, parental education, family stability, age at menarche), one or both of the religion measures continued to relate significantly to the prevalence of intercourse, mean age at first intercourse, number of sexual partners, and frequency of intercourse. Generally, neither denominational affiliation nor religiosity strongly or consistently related to whether or not sexually active females had used contraception during their first or last intercourse experience.

Thornton and Camburn (1989) examined the relationship between several measures of religiosity (i.e., denominational affiliation, frequency of church attendance, and self-rated importance of religion) and attitudes toward premarital sex, the likelihood of ever having had intercourse, the number of sexual partners, and recency of intercourse. They tested the hypothesis that religiosity would influence sexual behaviors and attitudes, and alternatively, that sexual behaviors and attitudes would influence religiosity. Overall, denominational affiliation (i.e., Protestant, Catholic, none) did not differentiate sexual attitudes or behaviors very well. Having said this, however, we should note that, on average, adolescents with no religious affiliation were more likely to have had sex, had a greater number of sexual partners, and had sex more often than adolescents who were affiliated with some religious group. Attendance at religious services and importance of religion were both strongly negatively related to sexual involvement. For example, 78% of adolescents who never attended religious services reported having had sex compared to only 39% of those who attended church once or several times a week. Similarly, 70% of those who said religion was not important to them had had sex compared to 50% of those for whom religion was very important. The average number of sexual partners and recency of sexual intercourse were also strongly related to religiosity. Adolescents who never attended religious services reported an average of nearly three sexual partners compared to less than one partner for those who attended services several times a week. The hypothesis that sexual attitudes and behaviors would impact religiosity also received some support; having positive attitudes toward premarital sex was significantly related to reduced attendance at religious services. Having had sex was also related to reduced attendance, but the relationship was not statistically significant.

In a study examining the relationship between religiosity (attendance, importance, and affiliation) and contraceptive use, Strader and Thornton (1989) found that although highly religious, sexually experienced female adolescents were no less likely than less religious, sexually experienced females to use some form of contraception, they were less likely to use medical methods of contraception (i.e., the pill or intrauterine device).

Using a nationally representative sample of African American females,

Murry (1994) investigated factors that differentiated late versus early coital initiators. Early initiators (57.3%) were much less likely than late initiators (85.2%) to be frequent (once a week or more) church attendees. Discriminant function analyses revealed that church attendance remained a significant predictor of late initiation, even after controls for parental teaching about sexuality, contraceptive knowledge, number of hours worked, family structure, age at puberty, family income, parental control, mothers' employment, family income, and urbanicity. In fact, church attendance was one of the strongest predictors of late coital initiation, second only to parental teaching.

In a recent study of 16- to 18-year-olds, Sheeran, Abrams, Abraham, and Spears (1993) examined the relationship between religiosity and personal sexual attitudes, attitudes toward sexually active others, virginal status, anticipation of sexual intercourse, and frequency of both coitus and noncoital sexual experiences over the previous year. The religiosity indicators included measures of religious upbringing (were you brought up according to a religion?), denominational affiliation, ritual/behavior (church attendance), self-attitude/self-schema (would you say that you are religious?), and salience of religious identity (religious beliefs would influence my decisions about sex).

All of the religion measures related significantly to adolescents' personal sexual standards and their judgments of others. Specifically, having been brought up according to a religion, being brought up Catholic or Protestant (versus another affiliation), frequent church attendance, feeling that they were religious, and indicating that religious beliefs would influence their decisions about sex were all related to negative attitudes toward engaging in premarital sex and to negative evaluations of persons who change partners a number of times during a year. Only religious self-attitude and frequency of church attendance were related significantly to being a virgin. Having a religious upbringing and the three measures of current religiosity (self-attitude, attendance, and identity salience) were associated with the respondent's not anticipating having sex in the next year or having had sex in the past year. Interestingly, only religious identity salience was significantly related to frequency of sexual experience with and without intercourse (the question did not ask about the specific nature of the experience). When all of the variables were simultaneously controlled, frequent church attendance, high religious self-attitude, and high salience of religious identity related significantly to more conservative sexual attitudes and less anticipation of having sex in the next year. Only religious self-attitude (feeling that they were religious) related significantly to having negative attitudes toward others being involved in many different relationships. Religious self-attitude was also significantly and positively related to being a virgin, whereas being raised Catholic (versus Protestant or another affiliation) was significantly and negatively related to being a virgin and significantly and positively related to frequency of intercourse and nonintercourse sexual experience. Religious identity salience continued to relate to frequency of nonintercourse sexual experiences, net of the other factors.

In sum, although the research that explicitly examines the relationship between religion and adolescent sexual behaviors in a sophisticated fashion is not large, sufficient work has been done to allow us to reach some tentative conclusions. Attendance at religious services, self-rated importance of religion, and denominational affiliation have all been found to relate significantly to lower levels of sexual involvement. The research suggests that on average, highly religious adolescents initiate sex later, have fewer sexual partners, and have sex less often than their less religious peers (Hayes, 1987; Miller & Moore, 1990; Murry, 1994; Thornton & Camburn, 1989; Zelnick et al., 1981). Accordingly, they are at less risk of experiencing the negative physical and social health problems associated with early sexual involvement. On the other hand, sexually active religious females appear less likely to use medical (i.e., the most reliable) methods of contraception and thus may be at increased risk of pregnancy (Strader & Thornton, 1989; Zelnick et al., 1981). Having said this, however, we should note that empirical examination of the data on this issue indicates no significant differences in the prevalence of contraception (Zelnick et al., 1981).

Alcohol, Tobacco, and Other Drug Use

The use of alcohol, tobacco, and other drugs is widespread among American youth. For example, in 1994, the lifetime prevalence of illicit drug use was nearly 26% among 8th graders, 37% for 10th graders, and 46% for 12th graders (Johnston, Bachman, & O'Malley, 1995). The illicit drugs used most widely by adolescents are inhalants and marijuana. The lifetime prevalence of inhalant use was 20% for 8th graders, 18% for 10th graders, and 18% for 12th graders. Lifetime prevalence rates for marijuana use were 17% for 8th graders, 30% for 10th graders, and 38% for 12th graders. Use of those drugs that are legal for adults – alcohol and cigarettes – is even more widespread among American adolescents. For example, the annual prevalence of alcohol use in 1994 was 47% among 8th graders, 64% among 10th graders, and 73% among 12th graders. The prevalence of heavy drinking (five or more drinks in a row on a single occasion within the last 2 weeks) was 15% among 8th graders, 24% among 10th graders, and 28% among 12th graders. The 1994 30-day prevalence of cigarette use was 19% among 8th graders, 25% among 10th graders, and 31% among 12th graders. Further, 9% of 8th graders, 15% of 10th graders, and 19% of 12th graders were daily smokers. Despite the substantial declines in drug use among American youth during the 1980s, recent trend data suggest that drug use among American adolescents is on the increase (Johnston et al., 1995).

Given the link between drug use, motor vehicle accidents, school problems, delinquency, violence, and other problem behaviors (Dryfoos, 1990), researchers have invested considerable effort in the identification of risk and protective factors for the abuse of alcohol, tobacco, and other drugs. A recent publication from the Office of Substance Abuse Prevention (OSAP) listed over 100 specific risk and protective factors for drug use (Gopelrud, 1992). A recent review of empirical research on risk and protective factors for drug use identified 17 categories of variables (Hawkins et al., 1992). Interestingly, the OSAP list did not include religion at all, and the review by Hawkins et al. included it under the subheading of alienation and rebellion. Specifically, Hawkins et al. noted that "alienation from the dominant values of society, low religiosity, and rebelliousness have been shown to relate positively to drug use and delinquent behavior" (p. 85). The limited attention given to religion as it relates to drug use is particularly curious in light of Gorsuch's earlier finding that religion was "the most consistently replicated correlate of nonabuse" (1988, p. 209). Despite the fact that recent risk and protective factor research has paid relatively little attention to the importance of religion as it relates to drug use, a number of researchers have explicitly examined this relationship. Several of these studies will now be reviewed.

Using data from over 3,000 Canadian adolescents, Adlaf and Smart (1985) examined the relationship between drug use (measured by the frequency of use of alcohol, cannabis, and hallucinogens; medical and nonmedical use of stimulants, barbiturates, or tranquilizers; and a polydrug use index) and religious affiliation (Protestant, Catholic, none), religiosity (very religious, moderately religious, do not care one way or the other), and frequency of church attendance (never to very frequently). They found that Catholic students were less likely than Protestant or unaffiliated students to report cannabis, nonmedical, or hallucinogenic drug use in the previous year. They also found that religiously unaffiliated youth were less likely than Catholic and Protestant youth to have used alcohol in the last year (68% versus 76% and 75% respectively). (This seemingly contradictory finding might be the result of Catholic and Protestant youth's ritual use of alcohol for communion.) The religiosity and church attendance measures both had strong negative relationships with drug use. For example, students who reported that they were very religious were much less likely to use drugs than those who indicated that they did not care about religion one way or the other: alcohol (61% versus 80%), cannabis (8% versus 39%), nonmedical (6% versus 31%), hallucinogenic (2% versus 22%), and medical drug use (10% versus 20%). Similarly, students who reported that they attended religious services very frequently were much less likely to use drugs than students who never attended or who attended less frequently. The drug use prevalences for the very frequent attendees versus those who never attended religious services were as follows: 62% versus 77% for alcohol, 11% versus 36% for cannabis, 10% versus 28% for nonmedical use, 3% versus 21% for hallucinogens, and 12% versus 21% for medical use. Based on multivariate analyses run separately for males and females and controlling for age, Adlaf and Smart concluded that (1) religious affiliation had relatively little impact on drug use; (2) church attendance was more strongly related to drug use than was the attitudinal religiosity measure; and (3) generally, the strength of the relationship between religion and drug use increased as the drug in question approached the illicit end of the licit–illicit drug continuum.[2]

Analyzing data from a nationally representative sample of U.S. high school seniors. Bachman and Wallace (in press) also found a strong negative relationship between religious commitment (an index that combines self-rated importance and attendance) and drug use (see also Wallace & Bachman, 1991). For example, relative to seniors with low religious commitment, highly religious seniors were much less likely to report daily cigarette use (3% versus 18%), heavy drinking (12% versus 37%), 30-day marijuana use (4% versus 21%), and annual cocaine use (1% versus 6%). Examination of the relationship between religion and trends in drug use suggests that religion "protected" religiously highly committed youth from the drug epidemic experienced by much of the nation.

Hadaway, Elifson, and Petersen (1984) explored the relationship between religion and drug use, paying particular attention to the potential impact of family and the extent to which the impact varied, depending on societal constraints surrounding a particular behavior. The study dealt with multiple measures of religion, including frequency of attendance at religious services, parental attendance at religious services, salience of religion (self-rated importance of religion), respondents' belief that God answers prayer, an index of religious orthodoxy (items like "God really exists"), and a denominational variable trichotomized into fundamentalist Protestant, liberal Protestant, and Catholic. Additionally, they included an attitudinal "morality" variable that asked respondents' level of agreement with the statement "Children should obey all the rules their parents make for them." The dependent measures focused on attitudes toward persons of their own age using alcohol, as well as marijuana and other illicit drugs, and on the respondents' annual use of alcohol, as well as marijuana and other illicit drugs. All the religion measures and the morality measures had a moderate to strong negative relationship with attitudes toward drug use and with actual self-reported use (gammas = $-.27$ to $-.57$). Further, with the exception of the relationship between parents' church attendance and adolescents' drinking, all of the relationships were statistically significant.

A more detailed examination of the relationship between the importance of religion and drug use and church attendance and drug use suggested that the relationships are quite strong (Hadaway et al., 1984). For example, among those who said that religion was extremely important to them, in the previous year 52% did not use alcohol, 83% did not use marijuana, and 97% did not use other illicit drugs. Among adolescents who indicated that religion was not too important, the corresponding figures were 21%, 47%, and 75%, respectively. Denominational affiliation was also an important correlate of substance use: Adolescents belonging to fundamentalist Protestant denominations reported more negative attitudes toward drugs and less substance use than did their Catholic and liberal Protestant counterparts. Similarly, the strength of the negative relationships between alcohol use and attitudes toward drug use tended to be stronger among fundamentalist Protestants than among the other two groups. Multiple discriminant analyses controlling for peer marijuana use, parents' views about peers, fighting with parents, grade in school, academic performance, sex, and closeness to mother revealed that religious salience and peer use were the two best predictors of negative attitudes toward drug and alcohol use. Religious salience was the third strongest predictor of marijuana use (after peer use and grades) and only fifth best in discriminating students who did and did not use an illicit drug other than marijuana. Based on the findings of this study, the authors conclude that (1) higher levels of religious activity, belief, salience, and orthodoxy are associated with lower levels of drug use and (2) the role of religion as an agent of social control appears to be most salient when few other constraining social forces are at work.

In a panel study of the link between religion and marijuana use among 264 American high school youths, Burkett and Warren (1987) found that the negative impact of religion on adolescent marijuana use was primarily indirect, through its impact on the selection of non-marijuana-using peers. Following this study, Burkett (1993) investigated the extent to which parents' religiosity, as perceived by their children, influenced adolescents' alcohol use. He concluded that parental influence was largely indirect, through its impact on both adolescents' peer selection and religious commitment.

In a novel follow-up to an earlier study, Lorch and Hughes (1988) collected data from pastors regarding their church's or denomination's stance on the use of alcohol and other drugs, as well as their efforts to educate youth in their congregations about these substances. The study revealed that religious groups with the most liberal attitudes toward alcohol and drug use (e.g., Jews and Catholics) were least likely to have alcohol and drug education programs, were least likely to forbid alcohol and drug use as part of their teaching about alcohol and drugs, were most likely to view alcohol and drug addiction as an illness, and were least likely to view alcohol and drug addiction as a sin. When they compared their results with the data from their earlier study of alcohol and drug use patterns among over 13,000 youths from various religious denominations (Lorch & Hughes, 1985), the authors found that the liberal groups had the highest prevalence of alcohol and drug use among young members. Alternatively, those denominations with the most proscriptive beliefs about alcohol and drug use had the greatest number of education programs and the lowest prevalences of alcohol and drug use among their youths. The results of this study suggest that denominational affiliation influenced adolescent drug use through explicit teachings and group expectations, as well as through norms contrary to alcohol and drug use.

In sum, research on adolescent drug use suggests that there is a moderate yet significant inverse relationship between religiosity (attitudes, beliefs, affiliations, and behaviors) and drug use. Young people who frequently attend religious services, who report that religion is important to them, and who belong to religious denominations that explicitly prohibit drug use on average are less likely to be involved with drugs than are their less religiously engaged counterparts. The research suggests that one of the important ways in which religion is related to drug use is through the type of young people adolescents select as peers. Specifically, it appears that religious adolescents are less likely than nonreligious ones to choose young people as friends who use drugs.

Religion and Adolescent Health-Compromising Behaviors: Problems and Limitations

A number of limitations plague the small body of research that has attempted to examine the relationship between religion and adolescent health-compromising behaviors. These limitations include problems in design, problems in the measurement of religion and health-compromising behaviors, and problems in the match between the theoretical frameworks used to guide the research and the actual operationalization of the theoretical constructs.

The design problems most common to research in the area of religion and adolescent health-compromising behaviors are the use of samples that are often small, nonrepresentative, and typically homogeneous with regard to economic and racial/ethnic representation (i.e., middle-class white youth). Another major design limitation is that much of the research has been done on college students instead of on adolescents of various ages in the general population. Given the selection bias with regard to college attendance, as well as the potential effects of the college experience and environment itself on young people's health behaviors and religious attitudes and behaviors, findings from these studies lack generalizibility.

In addition to design problems, serious measurement problems are typical of research on religion and adolescent health. Perhaps the most basic measurement problem in this body of research is the way in which religion is measured. Religion scholars have long theorized about and empirically verified the multidimensional nature of religion (see Spilka, Hood, & Gorsuch,

1985). These dimensions include but may not be limited to a belief or an ideological component, a ritual or behavioral component (e.g., church attendance), an experiential component, and a consequential component (i.e., how religion influences the way in which one lives one's daily life) (Stark & Glock, 1968).

Despite a voluminous body of research on the multidimensionality of religion, the vast majority of research on religion and adolescent health behaviors treats religion as a unidimensional construct, typically assessed by the measures attendance, importance, and affiliation. Williams (1994) has recently provided a comprehensive overview of the weaknesses of these unidimensional measures of religious involvement. The operationalization of religious affiliation as Catholic versus Protestant versus Jewish is problematic because it fails to capture the variation among religious groups. It has long been noted, for example, that there is more variation within the Protestant category than between Protestants and Catholics. The distinction between church and sect is perhaps a more useful way in which to classify denominations (see Iannaccone, 1988). The church–sect distinction may be particularly important as it pertains to health-related behaviors because emphasis on morality and living a distinctive lifestyle are the defining characteristics of religious sects, whereas more traditional religious organizations (i.e., churches) are less likely to emphasize these issues.

Although the frequency of attendance at religious services is a robust correlate of adult and adolescent health outcomes, it is not always an indicator of anything intrinsically religious, it is an inadequate measure of public religious participation, and it captures only a small part of religious commitment and activity (Williams, 1994). Unidimensional measures like attendance and denominational affiliation are particularly problematic as indicators of adolescent religiosity given that the frequency with which most adolescents attend church and the denomination to which they belong are not solely under their personal control; these are choices determined largely by their parents. Measures of subjective religiosity (i.e., how important adolescents feel religion is in their lives) fail to capture the extent to which religiosity is a critical force in helping to define adolescents' identity or the extent to which it is a central part of who they perceive themselves to be. Broad multidimensional measures of religious involvement exist (e.g., Hilty, Morgan, & Burns, 1984) that can facilitate identification of the specific aspects of religious commitment that relate to adolescent health attitudes, beliefs, and behaviors, but they have seldom been used in research on the relationship between religion and adolescents' involvement in health-compromising behavior.

Beyond problems with the measurement of religion, the operationalization of the dependent health outcome variables is also often problematic. Many of the health-related variables with which researchers are concerned are highly skewed, particularly for younger adolescents (e.g., number of sexual partners, frequency of cocaine use in the last month). Given the limited variability in these dependent measures, it is difficult for any single factor to significantly (in a statistical sense) predict the level of involvement in the behavior in question. This is particularly the case when the distributions of the dependent and independent variables violate the assumptions of the statistical procedures being used.

Related to the measurement problems typical of research on religion and adolescent health outcomes is the mismatch that often occurs between the theoretical issue under investigation and the operationalization of the theoretical constructs. For example, a paper may have as its stated research question "Are religious youth less likely to be sexually active than nonreligious youth?" Although this appears to be a relatively straightforward research question, readily amenable to empirical investigation, differences in sample composition, the way in which the independent variable (religion) and the dependent variable (sexual behavior) are operationalized, and the statistical technique used to examine the relationship may cause researchers to arrive at drastically different conclusions. For example, if the study is conducted on a sample of middle school students, the dependent variable is frequency of sex in the last month (measured zero to one time, two or three times, four or more times), the religion variable is frequency of church attendance ("often," "sometimes," "never"), and the data analytic technique is ordinary least squares regression, it is quite likely that the study will conclude that "religion has relatively little influence on adolescent sexual involvement." The reasons for this conclusion will include the following: (1) there is little variability to explain in the dependent variable because very few middle school students will have had sex in the last month; (2) the religion measure is poor because the response categories are vague and because the frequency with which the average middle school age student attends church is probably not under his or her control; and (3) the use of ordinary least squares regression does not directly address whether religious youth are less likely to be sexually active than nonreligious youth; rather, it addresses the extent to which adolescents' (subjective) church attendance predicts how often they will have had sex in the last month. As a result of the theory–operationalization mismatch, the skewed distribution of the sex variable, the relatively poor measurement of religion, and the mismatch between the chosen data analytic technique and the research question, it is highly unlikely that a substantively significant relationship will be found between religion and adolescents' sexual involvement. On the other hand, a study that closely matches theory and operationalization, utilizes data analytic techniques appropriate for the distribution and form of the dependent variable, and measures religion concretely and multidimensionally will, in all likelihood, conclude that "religion is strongly related to adolescent sexual involvement."

Religion and Adolescent Health-Compromising Behavior: Problems and Prospects

Research on adolescent drug use and research on adolescent sexual activity suggest that religion plays an important, if not central, role in understanding why some young people are less likely to engage in these health-compromising behaviors than others. Nevertheless, religion remains outside the set of widely accepted variables (e.g., peer influence) that researchers recognize must be included in investigations concerning adolescent health. In fact, religion is typically treated as simply a sociodemographic marker that must be "controlled" for, rather than as a variable of primary theoretical and empirical importance. This lack of conceptual and theoretical clarity and sophistication with regard to how, why, when, and under what circumstances religion is expected to relate to health outcomes is perhaps the central problem of research linking religion and adolescent health-compromising behaviors.

As a preliminary effort to address this problem and to take advantage of the opportunity that this problem presents, we have developed a conceptual framework within which to begin to investigate the relationship between religion and adolescent health outcomes (Figure 17.2). The model consists of five basic components: (1) the primary socialization influence of the family; (2) three secondary socialization influences; (3) the mechanisms by which the secondary socialization influences are thought to relate to adolescent health outcomes; (4) the health outcomes themselves; and (5) the macrosociocultural context in which adolescents' lives are nested. Before describing the various components of the model, it is important to reiterate the importance of the measurement of religion.

Measurement of Religion. The model explicitly recognizes religion as a key socialization influence and calls for researchers to recognize the ways in which religious influence operate cooperatively, interactively, or antagonistically with the other socialization influences. A full understanding of the role of religion as it relates to adolescent health outcomes is contingent on the assessment of religion in all of its complexity. Current methods of measuring religion (e.g., denominational affiliation) used in research that examines religion's relationship to adolescent health outcomes are simplistic and, as a result, yield inconsistent results. Future research that measures religion multidimensionally and uses the framework provided by the socialization influence model should yield findings that demonstrate consistently the importance of religion as a key socialization influence on adolescent health outcomes through its effects on the other socialization influences and mechanisms.

Religion and the Primary Socialization Influence. The socialization influence model postulates that adolescent health outcomes, and health-compromising

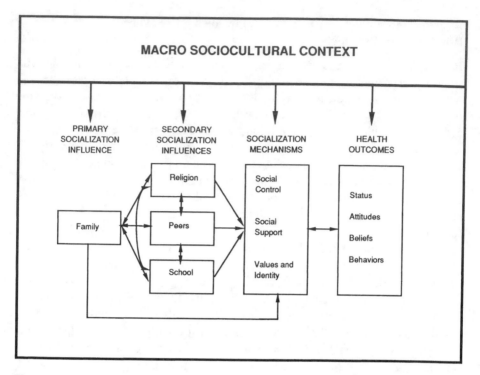

Figure 17.2. Socialization influence framework.

behavior in particular, are the result of a dynamic socialization process that begins in childhood and extends over the life course. As the first source of socialization into the norms and values of the larger society, the family is viewed as the primary socialization influence. Although adolescents experience increasingly greater influence from secondary socialization sources as they age, the influence of parents does not cease; rather, adolescents experience parental influence along with the influence of other domains. Because parents, peer networks, schools, and religion are all presumed to influence adolescents' health outcomes, it is necessary to understand the influence of each of these domains, but the impact of the family is viewed as primary.

The family is typically the child's primary socialization influence during the first few years of life. As children age, however, they are exposed to other socialization influences for increasingly longer periods of time. Eventually, as the children move into adolescence, they begin to attend school full time, to participate in extracurricular activities, to date, and so on, and only a small amount of their day may be under the direct influence, supervision, and observation of parents. Nevertheless, the family remains an important influence in the lives of young people, particularly with regard to their religious socialization and development.

Greater attention needs to be given to the ways in which the primary socialization of children and adolescents within the family context is shaped by religion. Fowler's (1991) work on religious development provides some insights that can be used to examine this relationship. Building on and integrating Piaget's theory of cognitive development, Kohlberg's theory of moral development, and Erikson's theory of psychosocial development, Fowler has proposed a stage model of faith development that begins with the family as the first and primary religious socializer of children. The first stage, primal faith, begins during infancy and lays the foundation for the later stages (Fowler, 1991). During this stage, infants learn to develop trust and to overcome the anxiety that results from separation from significant others. Thus, the foundation for religious faith begins with basic faith in parents, the primary caregivers. The second stage, intuitive-projective faith, emerges during early childhood. During this stage, "imagination, stimulated by stories, gestures, and symbols but not yet controlled by logical thinking, combines with perception and feelings to create long-lasting faith images" (p. 35). Children's perceptions of and thinking about God are drawn from their experiences and interactions with parents and the other adults with whom they have significant emotional attachments. The third stage, the mythic-literal faith stage, begins in and extends through the elementary school years. During this stage, "concrete-operational thinking, the developing ability to think logically, emerges to help [children] order the world with categories of causality, space, time and number" (p. 35). Religious beliefs and concepts are transmitted primarily through stories from parents, religious classes, sermons, and so on, and are taken and interpreted literally.

The fourth stage, the synthetic-conventional faith stage, is hypothesized to begin during early adolescence. Cognitively, this stage is characterized by the emergence of formal operational thinking, the ability to reflect on and integrate past experiences, and concern about identity, the future, and personal relationships (Fowler, 1991). According to Fowler, concerns about personal relationships (e.g., with family members and peers) during this stage "correlate with a hunger for a personal relationship to God in which we feel ourselves to be known and loved in a deep and comprehensive way"(p. 38). During this stage, adolescents integrate the various messages, influences, and pieces of information they receive in their primary roles and relationships into their value system and worldview. The fifth stage of faith, the individuative-reflective stage, emerges during middle to late adolescence and may last through middle adulthood (Fowler, 1991). This is the stage during which adolescents question, examine, and reconstitute the values and beliefs they received from their families and from others responsible for their religious training. It is also during the individuative-reflective stage that adolescents

begin to establish their autonomy with regard to decisions concerning commitments, relationships, and self-identity, including those pertaining to religious
commitments and beliefs. Although not yet tested fully and verified empirically, Fowler's theory of the stages of faith development effectively integrates
past theoretical work on identity development, moral development, and cognitive development into a useful framework within which to begin to investigate the family's role in religious development across the lifespan.

Religion and the Secondary Socialization Influences. Within the socialization
influence model, it is imperative to understand how the influence of religion on
the family, and on parents in particular, impacts the other secondary socialization influences. Parents for whom religion is particularly important may seek
to shape the other domains of socialization to fit with their religious convic-
tions. More specifically, highly religious parents may send their children to
religious schools, may choose the community in which they live based on its
religious composition, and may even seek to constrain, either directly or
indirectly, their children's choice of friends based on their religious background. The socialization influence model posits that religion is an important
socialization influence that operates independently, interdependently, and
perhaps even in competition with the other secondary socialization influences
to help create and shape the socialization mechanisms that, in turn, impact
adolescent health outcomes.

Religion, the Socialization Mechanisms, and Health Outcomes. Theoretical and
empirical research has largely ignored the importance of religion as a key
factor in understanding adolescent health outcomes. The socialization influence model suggests that religion relates to health outcomes but only indirectly, through its influence on various socialization mechanisms, including social
control, social support, and value and identity formation. Given religion's
consistently negative relationship to health-compromising behavior, it seems
imperative for future research to understand better the social control, social
support, and values and identity mechanisms through which religion protects
young people from acting in ways potentially detrimental to their long-term
health and well-being.

In recent years, considerable debate has arisen concerning the nature of
religion's social control effect on adolescent behavior. The impetus for this
debate was the publication of Hirschi and Stark's 1969 article "Hellfire and
Delinquency." According to Stark (1984), the original purpose of this study
was merely to document what everyone knew to be true: that religious commitment is negatively related to delinquent behavior. What Hirschi and Stark
found, however, was that young people who attended church and believed in
hell and the afterlife were no less likely to engage in deviant acts than were
their nonattending, nonbelieving counterparts. As a result of this finding,

Hirschi and Stark concluded that "the church is irrelevant to delinquency because it fails to instill in its members love for their neighbors and because belief in the possibility of pleasure and pain in another world cannot now, and perhaps never could, compete with the pleasures and pains of everyday life" (1969, pp. 213–214).

"Hellfire and Delinquency" and the subsequent efforts to confirm or refute its findings all tested an implicitly psychological model. The psychological model tested by Hirschi and Stark posited that religion operates primarily at the individual level as an internalized psychological control against deviant behavior. In time, however, a number of researchers attempted to replicate Hirschi and Stark's findings. Using a sample of youth from a southern U.S. city, Rhodes and Reiss (1970) found that church attendance had a strong negative relationship to delinquent behaviors. The authors suggested that the discrepancy between their findings and those of Hirschi and Stark might have resulted from the higher level of religiosity in the South relative to the West. According to Stark and colleagues, this suggestion provided the key to understanding the relationship between deviance and religion (Stark, 1984). This key was to understand religion not as an individual-level psychological restraint against deviant behavior, but rather as a group or contextual phenomenon, consistent with a more sociological theoretical framework. Stark (1987) concluded, "We cannot assess the impact of religion on conformity unless we examine variations among groups. Put another way, to rediscover religious effects we must rediscover the moral community" (p. 114).

Stark (1984) and Stark et al. (1982) characterize moral communities as those in which people express traditional religious beliefs and engage in traditional religious practices such as attending worship services, praying, and belonging to local churches. In order to test their moral community hypothesis, Stark et al. used data collected in 1966 from a study of white males located in 87 schools. Schools were used as representative of communities. A school was classified as a *secular community* if 60% or more of the sample from that school scored below the mean on a religious values index and if no more than 20% scored at the highest level of the index. *Moral communities* were those not classified as secular. A religious values index was developed that included four questions that asked if it was a good thing (1) to be devout about one's religious faith; (2) to attend religious services regularly; (3) to live one's religion in daily life; and (4) to encourage others to attend services and live religious lives.

Stark et al. empirically demonstrated that there were higher levels of delinquency in the secular communities relative to the moral communities and that the correlation between religiosity (measured by self-rated importance) and delinquency was significantly lower in the secular communities (gamma = .15) than in the moral communities (gamma = .31). Based on these findings, Stark and colleagues concluded that religiosity has a strong negative impact on deviance within the moral community.

Following the lead of "Hellfire and Delinquency," the theoretical models used to guide the empirical investigation of the relationship between religion and health have placed disproportionate emphasis on the constraining, conformist, or other negative social control functions of religion while ignoring the positive control functions that come about by providing a system of social integration and social support. Some recent research has highlighted the social support function of religion (see Brownfield & Sorenson, 1991; Burkett & Warren, 1987). Specifically, this research suggests that one of the most important ways in which religion relates to drug use (and presumably other problem behaviors) is that it influences adolescents' peer selection to include other young people who are not engaged in problem behaviors, and it provides encouragement and social rewards for engaging in conventional behaviors (e.g., doing well in school) versus problem behaviors. In an example from the adult literature, Williams, Larson, Buckler, Heckman, and Pyle (1991) found that religious attendance was not related to psychological well-being once initial health status was controlled; however, further examination revealed that in the face of stress, the social support provided by religious attendance reduced the negative consequences of stress on psychological well-being.

A third key mechanism through which religion is expected to influence adolescents' health outcomes is by its impact on their values and identity. As noted by Williams (1994), "religious socialization, including identification with religious characters or groups, can play a critical role in the establishment of religious identity in particular, and identity formation in general" (p. 140). For many American young people, religion may be much more than just going to church, claiming a denominational affiliation, or believing in the existence of God. For many, their religion – that is, what they believe to be their personal relationship with God and the fellowship they experience with like-minded others – may be central to their identity. If the religion with which these young people identify prohibits the use of drugs, extramarital sex, or other potentially health-compromising behaviors, it is likely that these young people will refrain from them.

Religion and the Macrosociocultural Context. Future research should seek to understand the manner and extent to which the larger macrosociocultural context affects religion, the other socialization influences, and adolescent health outcomes. The socialization influence model suggests that adolescents, their families, their religious beliefs and affiliations, their peer networks, their schools, the socialization mechanisms that influence their health outcomes, and the health outcomes themselves are all nested within and influenced by the larger sociocultural context. Thus, in addition to the condition of the economy, the images presented in the mass media, and other factors, religion at a macro (e.g., national) level might also influence adolescent health outcomes. For example, the relatively high rate of religious commitment and belief among American youth may be a key factor in understanding why America has a higher rate of teenage pregnancy than other nations, even though American teens report levels of sexual involvement similar to those in other nations (OTA, 1991).

If American youths' religious beliefs cause them to feel that sexual involvement before marriage is morally wrong, the consistent use of birth control devices would bring them face to face with the discrepancy between their stated beliefs and their behavior. Youths who are unable to resolve the cognitive dissonance that results from this situation may be less likely to use contraception and thus more likely to conceive a child, even though they are not less likely to be sexually active. A positive relationship between religion and pregnancy among sexually active teenagers and a reciprocal relationship between religion and sex (i.e., resolving the dissonance between being sexually active and religious by becoming less religious) are both possibilities (see Thorton & Camburn, 1989). In other words, although the vast majority of research has viewed religion as a control against health-compromising behavior, such may not be the case. In fact, religion, depending on how it is defined and what it means in a particular sociocultural context, can relate to adolescent health outcomes at multiple levels and in multiple ways. Simplistic theoretical models that hypothesize about adolescents' fear of future "hellfire" and its supposed constraining effects on adolescent health-compromising behaviors are misguided in that they ignore the complex inter-relationships that exist between adolescents, their families, their peers, and the social contexts, both micro and macro, in which they live. In order to assess accurately the relationship between religion and adolescent health outcomes, future research must begin to recognize the potential complexity of the relationship. It is hoped that the socialization influence model will assist future research toward this end.

Conclusion

Substantial proportions of American youth report that they believe in God, that they are affiliated with a religious denomination, that they regularly attend church, that religion is important to them, and that they try to live their lives in accord with their religious beliefs. Although past research suffers from a number of design, measurement, and theoretical problems, there appears to be a negative relationship between religion and at least two of the most pressing adolescent health-compromising behaviors in the United States: sexual involvement and drug use. Accordingly, a better understanding of religion may have important implications for research and interventions aimed at preventing health-compromising behaviors among adolescents. In light of this information, scientists, particularly those concerned with prevention, should not ignore the potential opportunities that lie in understanding the mechanisms through which religion influences adolescent's health-compromising behavior.

Further, given that religious leaders and institutions are ubiquitous to American communities, that clergy are often sought out before or instead of other mental health professionals, and given that religious organizations are the only American institutions that have frequent, often weekly, access to entire families, political, religious and ideological biases must be put aside in a collaborative effort to promote the health and well-being of America's young people.

Notes

1 The data are unpublished data from the University of Michigan's Monitoring the Future study. The principal investigators are Lloyd Johnston, Jerald Bachman, and Patrick O'Malley.
2 Adlaf and Smart's conclusion that religious affiliation has relatively little impact on drug use is probably a result of the weak measurement of affiliation rather than the lack of a relationship. This assertion is supported by studies reviewed later and by the section of the present chapter on problems and limitations of research on religion and adolescent health-compromising behaviors.

References

Adlaf, E. M., & Smart, R. G. (1985). Drug use, religious affiliation, feelings, and behaviour. *British Journal of the Addictions, 80*, 163–171.

Bachman, J. G., & Wallace, J. M., Jr. (in press). Religion and drug use. In R. Clayton (Ed.), *Encyclopedia of Drugs and Alcohol*. New York: Macmillan.

Benson, P. L., Donahue, M. J., & Erickson, J. A. (1989). Adolescence and religion: A review of the literature from 1970 to 1986. *Research in the Social Scientific Study of Religion, 1*, 153–181.

Brownfield, D., & Sorenson, A. M. (1991). Religion and drug use among adolescents: A social support conceptualization and interpretation. *Deviant Behavior, 12*, 259–276.

Burkett, S. R. (1994). Perceived parent's religiosity, friends' drinking, and hellfire: A panel study of adolescent drinking. *Review of Religious Research, 35*, 134–154.

Burkett, S. R., & Warren, B. O. (1987). Religiosity, peer associations, and adolescent marijuana use: A panel study of underlying causal structures. *Criminology, 25*, 109–131.

Dryfoos, J. G. (1990). *Adolescents at risk: Prevalence and prevention*. New York: Oxford University Press.

Fowler, J. W. (1991). Stages in faith consciousness. In F. K. Oser & W. G. Scarlett (Eds.), *New directions for child development, Special issue on religious development in childhood and adolescence* (Vol. 52, pp. 27–45). San Francisco: Jossey-Bass.

Gallup, G. H., Jr., & Bezilla, R. (1992). *The religious life of young Americans*. Princeton, NJ: George H. Gallup International Institute.

Gopelrud, E. N. (Ed.). (1992). *Breaking new ground for youth at risk: Program summaries*. OSAP Technical Rep. 1. DHHS Pub. No. (ADM) 92-1658. Washington, DC: U.S. Department of Health and Human Services.

Gorsuch, R. L. (1988). Psychology of religion. *Annual Review of Psychology, 39*, 201–221.

Hadaway, C. K., Elifson, K. W., & Petersen, D. M. (1984). Religious involvement and drug use among urban adolescents. *Journal for the Social Scientific Study of Religion, 23*, 109–128.

Hawkins, J. D., Catalano, R. F., & Miller, J. Y. (1992). Risk and protective factors for alcohol and other drug problems in adolescence and early adulthood: Implications for prevention. *Psychological Bulletin, 112*, 64–105.

Hayes, C. (Ed.). (1987). *Risking the future: Adolescent sexuality, pregnancy, and childbearing* (Vol. 1). Washington, DC: National Academy Press.

Hilty, D. M., Morgan, R. L., & Burns, J. E. (1984). King and Hunt revisited: Dimensions of religious involvement. *Journal for the Scientific Study of Religion, 23*, 252–266.

Hirschi, T. (1969). *Causes of delinquency.* Berkeley: University of California Press.

Hirschi, T., & Stark, R. (1969). Hellfire and delinquency. *Social Problems, 17*, 202–213.

Hyde, K. E. (1990). *Religion in childhood and adolescence: A comprehensive review of the research.* Birmingham, AL: Religious Education Press.

Iannaccone, L. R. (1988). A formal model of church and sect. *American Journal of Sociology, 94*, 241–268.

Johnston, L. D., Bachman, J. G., & O'Malley, P. M. (1993). *Monitoring the future: Questionnaire responses from the nation's high school seniors.* Ann Arbor, MI: Institute for Social Research.

Johnston, L. D., O'Malley, P. M., & Bachman, J. G. (1995). *National survey results on drug use from the Monitoring the Future Study, 1975–1994* (Vol. 1). Washington, DC: U.S. Government Printing Office.

Kann L., Anderson, J. E., Holtzman, D., Ross, J., Truman, B. I., Collins, J., Lloyd, J., & Kolbe, L. J. (1991). HIV-related knowledge, beliefs, and behaviors among high school students in the United States: Results from a national survey. *Journal of School Health, 61*, 397–401.

King, D. G. (1990). Religion and health relationships: A review. *Journal of Religion and Health, 29*, 101–112.

Levin, J. S. (1994). Religion and health: Is there an association, is it valid, and is it causal? *Social Science and Medicine, 38*, 1475–1482.

Levin, J. S., & Schiller, P. S. (1987). Is there a religious factor in health? *Journal of Religion and Health, 26*, 9–36.

Lorch, B. R., & Hughes, R. H. (1985). Religion and youth substance use. *Journal of Religion and Health, 24*, 197–208.

Lorch, B. R., & Hughes, R. H. (1988). Church, youth, and drug education programs and youth substance use. *Journal of Alcohol and Drug Education, 33*, 14–26.

Miller, B. C., & Moore, K. A. (1990). Adolescent sexual behavior, pregnancy, and parenting: Research through the 1980s. *Journal of Marriage and the Family, 52*, 1025–1044.

Murry, V. (1994). Black adolescent females: A comparison of early versus late coital initiators. *Family Relations, 43*, 342–348.

National Commission on AIDS (1994). Preventing HIV/AIDS in adolescents. *Journal of School Health, 64*, 39–51.

Office of Technology Assessment (OTA). (1991). *Adolescent health: Vol. 2. Background and the effectiveness of selected prevention and treatment services.* OTA-H-466. Washington, DC: U.S. Government Printing Office.

Rhodes, A., & Reiss, A. L., Jr. (1970). The religious factor and delinquent behavior. *Journal of Research in Crime and Delinquency, 7*, 83–89.

Sheeran, P., Abrams, D., Abraham C., & Spears, R. (1993). Religiosity and adolescent's premarital sexual attitudes and behaviour: An empirical study of conceptual issues. *European Journal of Social Psychology, 23*, 39–52.

Spilka, B., Hood, R. W., & Gorsuch R. L. (1985). *The psychology of religion.* Englewood Cliffs, NJ: Prentice-Hall.

Stark R. (1984). Religion and conformity: Reaffirming a sociology of religion. *Sociological Analysis, 45*, 273–282.

Stark, R., & Glock, C. Y. (1968). *American piety: The nature of religious commitment.* Berkeley: University of California Press.

Stark, R., Kent, L., & Doyle, D. P. (1982). Religion and delinquency: The ecology of a lost relationship. *Journal of Research in Crime and Delinquency, 19*, 4–24.

Strader, M., & Thornton, A. (1989). Adolescent religiosity and contraceptive usage. *Journal of Marriage and the Family, 49*, 117–128.

Thomas, D. L., & Carver, C. (1990). Religion and adolescent social competence. In T. P. Gullota, G. R. Adams, & R. Montemayor (Eds.), *Developing social competency in adolescence* (Vol. 3, pp. 195–219). Newbury Park, CA: Sage.

Thornton, A., & Camburn, D. (1989). Religious participation and adolescent sexual behavior and attitudes. *Journal of Marriage and the Family, 51*, 641–653.

Wallace, J. M., Jr., & Bachman, J. G. (1991). Explaining racial/ethnic differences in adolescent drug use: The impact of background and lifestyle. *Social Problems, 38*, 333–357.

Williams, D. R. (1994). The measurement of religion in epidemiologic studies. In J. S. Levin (Ed.), *Religion in aging and health: Theoretical foundations and methodological frontiers* (pp. 125–148). Thousand Oaks, CA: Sage.

Williams, D. R., Larson, D. B., Buckler, R. E., Heckman, R. E., & Pyle, C. M. (1991). Religion and psychological distress in a community sample. *Social Science and Medicine, 32*, 1257–1262.

Zelnick, M., Kantner, J., & Ford, K. (1981). *Sex and pregnancy in adolescence.* Beverly Hills, CA: Sage.

Part V

Intervention: Altering Transition–Health Risk Connections

18   Promoting Mental Health During the Transition Into Adolescence

Anne C. Petersen, Nancy Leffert, Barbara Graham,
Jan Alwin, and Shuai Ding

Introduction

The transition from childhood into adolescence is one of the major developmental transitions occurring over the life course. It involves significant biological and social changes in every aspect of individual development and every important social context (Petersen, 1988). The challenges experienced by the young person may involve significant stress that produces a negative developmental trajectory through adolescence into adulthood (e.g., Petersen, Kennedy, & Sullivan, 1991; Petersen & Leffert, 1995). Because of all the changes at this time of life, there is a significant opportunity to intervene in the lives of young people to prevent difficulties and increase the likelihood of positive developmental trajectories (e.g., Ebata, Petersen, & Conger, 1990; Petersen & Ebata, 1987). This chapter describes adolescence as a time of transition, aspects of mental health and psychopathology during adolescence, current models of adolescent mental health promotion, and approaches to intervention. In addition, it describes one program to promote mental health in early adolescence by teaching information about the age period and by providing skills to cope more positively with the challenge of early adolescence. Finally, the chapter describes implications for future work in the area of prevention and intervention during adolescence.

Adolescent Development: A Time of Transition

Adolescence is considered a time of transition because major changes take place in all domains of development (e.g., physical, cognitive) and in all social contexts (Petersen, 1988). The transition into adolescence is usually defined as

Some of the results described here were presented by A. Petersen in three symposia: (1) "Adolescent Development and Its Problems" at the biennial meeting of the International Society for Behavioral Development, Recife, Brazil, July 1993, (2) "Facilitating Transitions for Elementary, Middle, and Junior High School Children" at the annual meeting of the American Psychological Association, Toronto, Ontario, Canada, August 1993, and (3) "Developmental Transitions during Adolescence: Health Risks, Health Benefits" at the biennial meeting of the Society for Research in Child Development, Indianapolis, IN, March 30–April 2, 1995.

471

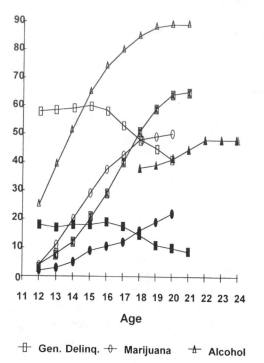

Figure 18.1. Age-specific prevalence rate for selected lifestyle behaviors: 3-year running averages. (Reproduced with permission from Elliott, D. S. (1993). Health enhancing and health compromising lifestyle. In S. G. Millstein, A. C. Petersen, & E. O. Nightingal (Eds.), *Promoting the health of adolescents: New directions for the twenty-first century.* New York: Oxford University Press.

beginning with puberty, the biological changes that involve the development of adult shapes and sizes as well as mature reproductive potential (e.g., Petersen & Taylor, 1980). These changes are the most dramatic biological changes since infancy, but they also involve significant social and psychological responses as these changes are noticed by both the adolescent and others interacting with him or her. Similarly significant in the United States is the change from elementary school to middle or junior high school, which involves moving to a larger, more anonymous environment that is generally more distant from home (Eccles, Lord, Roeser, Barber, & Jozefowicz, chapter 11, this volume; Simmons & Blyth, 1987). The primary changes of puberty and the contextual change of school also affect changes with family, peers, and self in a variety of domains (Petersen, 1988).

A period that is characterized by all of these changes can provide challenges and new opportunities or it can become overwhelming and stressful. The individual trajectory following a developmental transition depends on the timing of the transition, whether changes are normative or nonnormative, the social context in which the transition occurs, and the individual's reponse to these changes. Nonnormative changes such as the death of a family member

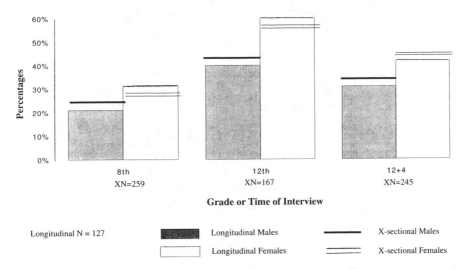

Figure 18.2. Increases in depressive episodes over the course of adolescence. Reproduced with permission of the Jacobs Institute of Women's Health from Depression and body image disorders, by A. C. Petersen, N. Leffert, B. Graham, S. Ding, & T. Overbey, WOMEN's HEALTH ISSUES, Vol. 4, No. 2, pp. 98–108. Copyright 1994.

or divorce add a source of stress at any age (e.g., Kessler, Price, & Wortman, 1985) and may have amplified effects when they occur simultaneously with a developmental transition such as adolescence.

There is increasing research evidence that the sheer number of changes experienced simultaneously is related to worse outcomes for the adolescent (e.g., Simmons & Blyth, 1987). This supports Coleman's (1978) focal theory, which stated that developmental tasks are manageable if they are experienced sequentially or without too many changes at once.

Although developmental changes tend to be primarily positive over the adolescent years, the nature of health problems is particularly affected in adolescence. Both externalizing and internalizing problems tend to increase over adolescence. As can be seen in Figure 18.1, Elliott (1993) has documented changes in externalizing problems such as substance use and delinquency.

Internalizing problems also increase. Figure 18.2 shows an example from our research in which depressive episodes increase over the course of adolescence (Petersen, Leffert, Graham, Ding, & Overbey, 1994). It is important to note, however, that most adolescents develop increasing competence and self-esteem over the adolescent decade (McCarthy & Hoge, 1982; O'Malley & Bachman, 1983), although some may have difficulties at some point (Petersen & Leffert, 1995). The question, then, is not what causes adolescents to have difficulty, but why some develop significant problems and others do not.

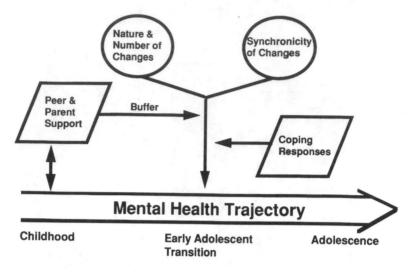

Figure 18.3. A model of developmental transitions. (Adapted with permission of Walter de Gruyter & Co. from Petersen & Ebata, 1987).

Our research has focused particularly on internalizing problems. Consistent with other research (e.g., Simmons & Blyth, 1987), prior research by our group has demonstrated that girls have more internalizing problems than boys because they are more likely to have especially challenging timing of transitions, such as becoming pubertal before or at the same time as changing schools (e.g., Petersen, Kennedy, & Sullivan, 1991). Several studies have found that girls are more likely to experience parental divorce in early adolescence (Block, Block, & Gjerde, 1988; Morgan, Lye, & Condran, 1988; Petersen, Sarigiani, Camarena, & Leffert, in press), a factor that amplifies any other stress at this time. We have found that good relationships with parents can minimize any negative effects of other changes (Petersen, Kennedy, & Sarigiani, 1991). We have not found that peers buffer negative effects in early adolescence, but they do play such a role later in adolescence (Petersen et al., in press).

The model for development of mental health in adolescence that is depicted in Figure 18.3 describes how the number and timing of changes in early adolescence affect mental health. Moderators of these effects include parental and peer support, as well as coping skills of the adolescent. We developed a school-based intervention program that attempted to teach effective coping skills to young adolescents so that they might be better able to deal with the challenges of the period (Petersen, 1989; Rice, Herman, & Petersen, 1993).

Influences on Adolescent Mental Health

Observers and scholars of adolescent development continue to view the adolescent decade only as involving significant risk. It has been demonstrated (e.g., Grinker & Werble, 1974; Offer, 1969; Offer & Offer, 1975; Rutter, Graham, Chadwick, & Yule, 1976) that not all adolescents experience significant psychological turmoil and that the majority of adolescents traverse the period in a much calmer fashion than had been previously assumed. Not until recently, however, have researchers begun to examine resilience in the face of stress and challenge (e.g., Garmezy, 1984; Garmezy & Rutter, 1983; Rutter, 1983, 1987). The following section reviews some of the risk and protective factors that may influence adolescent mental health.

Risk Factors

Risk factors that influence mental health during adolescence include family stress, social or school stress, or factors that may pertain to individual vulnerabilities that adolescents have brought with them to the period.

Family Stress. The family has long been assumed to have a major influence on the development of children and adolescents (e.g., Maccoby & Martin, 1983). However, the family has changed significantly in recent decades; divorce rates have increased, increasing the likelihood that adolescents will grow up either with a single parent or with a "reconstituted" family including a stepparent and perhaps stepsiblings. In addition, women have entered the labor force in large numbers, especially when children become adolescents (Hess, 1995).

Family changes are often considered to be stressful events at any point in the life course. As mentioned earlier, we found that girls are three times as likely as boys to experience a parental divorce during early adolescence (Petersen et al., in press). This increased rate has been seen in other longitudinal studies (e.g., Block et al., 1988) as well as national probability samples (Cherlin et al., 1991; Morgan et al., 1988).

Social/School Stress. A great deal of evidence suggests that the transition from elementary school to middle school or junior high can have negative effects on certain groups of young people (e.g., Eccles et al., chapter 11, this volume; Eccles & Midgley, 1989; Simmons & Blyth, 1987). This transition generally involves a change to a much larger and more anonymous school that is farther from home than the neighborhood elementary school. Research by Eccles and colleagues (Eccles & Midgley, 1989; Eccles et al., 1993) has further demonstrated that these teachers are less supportive of autonomy and more demanding of compliant behavior than elementary school teachers despite the increased capacities of adolescents relative to children.

Research has demonstrated that academic performance drops with every school transition (Blyth, Simmons & Carlton-Ford, 1983) compared to the achievement of same-age peers who are not making a school transition. The effects are stronger with more transitions or with other changes that occur at or near the same time (Crockett, Petersen, Graber, Schulenberg, & Ebata, 1989). There also may be negative effects on self-esteem, although only for girls (Simmons & Blyth, 1987) and not in all populations (Crockett et al., 1989; Fenzel & Blyth, 1986).

Research has shown that synchronous changes (e.g., experiencing a school change during puberty) during adolescence can affect the adolescent's ability to cope. Very few boys go through puberty before a school transition, whereas girls usually experience puberty before or during this transition (Petersen, Kennedy, et al., 1991; Simmons & Blyth, 1987); this may put girls at particular risk for coping difficulties during this period. We examined the effects of the synchrony of pubertal timing and school transitions on psychosocial variables (Leffert, Graham, & Petersen, 1994; Petersen, Kennedy, & Sullivan, 1991), including Emotional Tone, a measure of negative as well as positive feelings of well-being (Petersen, Schulenberg, Abramowitz, Offer, & Jarcho, 1984). We found that boys and girls were very similar when the data were analyzed this way. Both boys and girls who experienced puberty after the school transition had more positive Emotional Tone. Taken together with family changes, the synchronicity of puberty and school change explain the emergence of depression in adolescence in both boys and girls, and they entirely explain the gender difference in depression that emerges during adolescence (Petersen et al., 1994; Petersen, Sarigiani, & Kennedy, 1991). We also found that parent support during early adolescence, but not peer support, eliminates this effect on 12th-grade depression measures (Petersen, Sarigiani, & Kennedy, 1991).

Individual Vulnerability. Individual vulnerabilities may particularly influence mental health during the course of adolescence. Adolescents may enter the period already vulnerable as a result of chronic illness, disability, prior psychopathology, or family dysfunction. As discussed previously (Ebata et al., 1990; Petersen & Ebata, 1987; Petersen & Leffert, 1995), there are many examples in the literature of these particular vulnerabilities that may put adolescents at further risk for negative mental health outcomes. For example, adolescents who have difficulty coping with stress or adversity may turn to health-compromising behaviors (e.g., smoking or the use of other substances) as a means of dealing with or muting the anxiety they feel as a result of weaknesses in coping skills (Compas, 1993).

Protective Factors

The challenges and potential stress of development during adolescence may be buffered by factors exogenous to the individual, such as family and peer support. In addition, individuals may have coping skills that serve to protect them from stressors.

Family Support. Traditionally, psychoanalytic models characterized parent–child relationships during the course of adolescence as stormy (Blos, 1970; Freud, 1958). This storminess was thought to be a necessary part of the development of autonomy and the process of individuation. In most cases, however, research has shown that individuation does not lead to detachment from parents (Crockett & Petersen, 1993; Galambos & Ehrenberg, chapter 6, this volume). In fact, closeness to parents continues into adulthood (Youniss & Smollar, 1985). As discussed earlier, we found that parent support actually eliminates the negative effects of the synchronicity of puberty and school change on 12th-grade depression measures.

Adolescents do report decreased closeness to parents over the adolescent decade (Petersen, White, & Stemmler, 1991). In addition, parent–child relationships during adolescence are not conflict free. Research has shown that conflict increases during early adolescence (e.g., White, Petersen, Stemmler, & Mikesell, in preparation), an increase that has been shown to be related to pubertal development (Hill, Holmbeck, Marlow, Green, & Lynch, 1985; Steinberg, 1981). Conflict reaches a plateau during midadolescence and then declines (Montemayor, 1983). Conflicts that occur between most parents and their adolescent children seem to center on rather mundane issues such as clothing, chores, and hairstyles (Laursen & Collins, 1994); only 15% of families report conflicts that are thought to be severe and related to psychopathology (Montemayor, 1983; Rutter et al., 1976).

Peer Support. The structure of the peer group changes over the course of adolescence (Crockett et al., 1989). During early adolescence, young people move from small groups of friends that are most often formed in the neighborhood to larger groups that are based more often in the school (e.g., Brown, 1990). Recent research documents the role of peer groups in influencing developmental trajectories (e.g., Brown, 1989; Brown, Dolcini, & Leventhal, chapter 7, this volume). For example, groups of athletes in some schools are given higher status by other students and given preferential treatment by teachers and other adults (e.g., Eckert, 1989).

Although the peer group has been found to influence the appearance and preferences of adolescents, there is no evidence that peers divert young people from the values of their family on issues such as religion and politics (Kandel & Lesser, 1972; Lerner, Karson, Meidels, & Knapp, 1975). The peer pressure that adolescents perceive for involvement in problem behavior does appear to increase over the adolescent decade (Brown, Clasen, & Eicher, 1986). Some young people may be more at risk for this negative influence to participate in risky behaviors, such as young people with weak or dysfunctional family ties or early maturing girls (Magnusson, 1987).

Peers can also provide supportive and positive influences during the course of adolescence (e.g., Brown et al., 1986; Brown et al., chapter 7, this volume;

Hill & Holmbeck, 1986). By later adolescence, peers especially provide social support. There is also evidence that good peer relationships can buffer negative parental or other influences (e.g., Klepp, Halper, & Perry, 1986; Sarigiani, 1990).

Coping. Individuals vary in their responses to the same changes. Some adolescents cope more effectively than others with the changes they experience during adolescence. Over the past decade, a body of research on the coping responses of adolescents has emerged (e.g., Compas, 1987a, 1987b, 1993; Nurmi, chapter 15, this volume). We have found that girls respond differently to interpersonal challenge than boys (Petersen, Kennedy, & Sullivan, 1991). These differences may contribute to the gender differences in depressed affect. For example, Mikesell (1988) identified four family types based on several measures of parent–adolescent relationships. Girls in the most dysfunctional families (as defined by low cohesion, communication, and organization) reported depressed affect and poor functioning. In contrast, boys from such families reported even better mood than boys from the other family contexts. Mikesell (1988) found that these boys were inflating or exaggerating their social skills and popularity based on data from other sources. This is entirely consistent with Nolen-Hoeksema's (1987) hypothesis that girls amplify negative mood and boys are more likely to distract themselves from a depressed mood (Petersen, Kennedy, & Sullivan, 1991).

Compas and colleagues (Compas, Orosan, & Grant, 1993) have suggested a model of the role of stress and coping in the development of depression and other psychopathology during adolescence. The biological changes of puberty combined with interpersonal stressful events may result in depressed affect. The way an individual copes with this experience of depressed mood may explain the development of depression. Specifically, Compas et al. (1993) posit that emotion-focused coping increases during adolescence. The emotion-focused coping style is used particularly by females; by contrast, males tend to use distraction. The emotion-focused style of coping may result in depression when it is combined with the stressful changes of puberty and life events.

In an earlier report from our research, Herman-Stahl, Stemmler, and Petersen (1995) reported on the use of approach-oriented coping and avoidant-coping based on the Seiffe-Krenke and Shulman (1990) coping questionnaire. Approach-oriented coping represents both internal and active ways of coping, whereas avoidant-oriented coping suggests passive avoidant methods of coping. Females in all grades used higher levels of approach-oriented coping than did males. Only the approach method showed a significant main effect for grade, with no clear pattern of those grade differences. Herman-Stahl et al. (1995) also examined the relation between coping style and depressive symptoms. Young people who usually or primarily use an approach-oriented style of coping report fewer depressive symptoms, whereas adolescents who use an avoidant-oriented style are more depressed. Thus the use of active methods of coping with problems may contribute to positive adaptation.

In another report from our research group, Herman-Stahl and Petersen (in press) show that youths with positive adjustment and those who are considered resilient use more approach-oriented coping and less avoidant-oriented coping than young people with negative adjustment scores and those considered vulnerable (see Herman-Stahl & Petersen, 1995a, for a complete description of the adjustment groups). In regression analyses, Herman-Stahl and Petersen (submitted) report that adolescents with symptoms of depression are more likely to report lower levels of perceived competence and an active coping style, as well as unsupportive family relationships. These results are consistent with those of others (e.g., Ebata & Moos, 1991), suggesting that young people with depressive symptoms use less effective coping strategies, have fewer or lower expectations of controlling events, and come from more dysfunctional or less supportive family environments.

These data suggest that young adolescents need help coping with the challenges of early adolescence and ways of using parents and peers as supporters rather than stressors. All of these results were used in designing the intervention presented in this chapter.

Adolescent Mental Health Promotion

Adolescent mental health promotion is an essential part of any comprehensive health program for young people. Promotion programs, in fact, complement any treatment effort (Compas, 1993). However, mental health promotion requires a model based on health rather than the traditional medical model derived from illness (Compas, 1993).

Models

Several different models underlie adolescent mental health promotion or prevention efforts. Some models focus on contexts for adolescents such as schools, whereas others focus on the adolescents themselves. Current approaches to adolescent mental health promotion focus on either primary or secondary prevention efforts. Primary prevention programs are designed to reduce the incidence of dysfunctional mental health by stopping problems before they begin. Secondary prevention is aimed at reducing the severity of expression in adolescents who already show signs of problems (Kazdin, 1993). In addition to focusing on reducing either incidence or severity, these models can be either specific to a particular problem (e.g., smoking cessation) or aimed at general aspects of mental or physical health (e.g., promoting coping behaviors or social competence). These different characteristics lead to many different interventions that provide various options, all with the ultimate goal of improving adolescent functioning (Kazdin, 1993).

Prevention of adolescent depression can be either primary or secondary. First, as primary prevention, services can be delivered to the entire population of adolescents. This method is based on the assumption that all adolescents are at some risk for some level of depressed mood, and that all adolescents are exposed to at least the sources of risk for depression, such as stressful life experiences (Petersen, Compas, & Brooks-Gunn, 1992). This method focuses on reducing the incidence of depression in the adolescent population and hence reducing the overall risk of depressive disorders. Second, adolescents who have been shown to be at risk for depression can be specifically targeted for preventive efforts. For example, an adolescent with a parent who is depressed is considered particularly at risk and can be specifically targeted in a prevention program (Petersen et al., 1992).

The study presented here represents one of the few evaluations of a controlled study of an intervention focused on adolescent depression with an appropriate comparison sample. Programs to enhance social competence and problem-solving skills do exist, however, and are relevant to the prevention of depression (Weissberg, Caplan, & Silvo, 1989). Teaching social competence and problem solving to young people will foster positive social, emotional, and academic development. However, previous studies have not included measures of depression as outcomes of these programs.

Few prevention programs are designed specifically to reduce depression. However, interventions have been developed to address some of the stressors and problems that may be linked to depression, such as programs to assist adolescents in coping with the stress of their parents' divorce (see Grych & Fincham, 1992, for a review; Petersen et al., 1992). Like the studies addressing social competence and problem solving, the prevention programs have not assessed depressed affect or depressive symptoms directly, although they have reported results on similar constructs, such as anxiety symptoms and other internalizing problems (Petersen et al., 1992) as well as adolescent behavior problems. For example, Goldstein's general skill-streaming training was developed to help acting-out young people learn prosocial skills (Goldstein, Sprafkin, Gershaw, & Klein, 1980).

Primary prevention programs such as those described previously may not be sufficient for young people who are considered to be at high risk for depression. Secondary preventive programs may be directed to those who have been identified on the basis of this risk (Petersen et al., 1992). The most powerful source of risk for adolescent depression is the presence of a depressive disorder in the parent (Downey & Coyne, 1990; Fendrich, Warner, & Weissman, 1990; Phares & Compas, 1992). Therefore the diagnosis of depression in parents is a distinct marker of the need for either a preventive or a treatment-oriented intervention for the children of these individuals (Petersen et al.,

1992). Beardslee and colleagues (Beardslee, 1990; Beardslee et al., 1992; Beardslee & Podorefsky, 1988) have developed interventions targeted to depressed parents and their children, using research evidence of the characteristics of adolescents who have shown resilience in spite of the depressive disorders of their parents (Petersen et al., 1992). Clarke and Lewinsohn (1986) developed a group treatment program for clinical depression.

An Example of Coping Intervention: The Penn State Adolescent Study

The study presented here is an example of a primary prevention effort targeted to a population-based group of young people. The Penn State Adolescent Study (PSAS) is a cohort sequential longitudinal study of early adolescence ($N = 335$). The subjects were recruited from two successive cohorts of sixth graders from two communities, which included two middle schools (Grades 6–8) in one community and one junior high school (Grades 7–9) in the other.[1] Students in the two communities represented varied demographic backgrounds. One community had a major university and students from the middle and upper middle classes but also included some students from the working class, with an average of 52.62 (representing approximately a major occupational grouping of "Technicians and Related Support") on an occupational prestige index developed by the National Opinion Research Center (NORC; Stevens & Hoisington, 1987). The second community was represented by two schools that tapped working-class to middle-class populations; the NORC index averaged 42.47 (representing approximately a major occupational grouping of "Sales") for this community.[2]

Design

Approximately half of the students in the study sample in both school districts in 2 successive years were randomly assigned to the intervention or control groups. To ensure that there were enough participants with a high risk of depressive symptoms, we oversampled on risk status, which was established in two successive assessments in sixth and seventh grades. Adolescents were thought to be at high risk if they reported depressive mood (i.e., in the lower third of the distribution in the fall of both sixth and seventh grades, based on prior research evidence in another longitudinal study) (Ebata, 1987). This produced five factors in the analytic design: intervention status, risk group, gender, community, and cohort. The subjects were assessed six times – three times before, once immediately after, and 6 and 12 months after a school-based psychoeducational intervention (see the design in Figure 18.4).

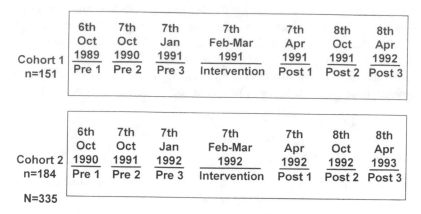

Cohort 1	6th Oct 1989 Pre 1	7th Oct 1990 Pre 2	7th Jan 1991 Pre 3	7th Feb-Mar 1991 Intervention	7th Apr 1991 Post 1	8th Oct 1991 Post 2	8th Apr 1992 Post 3
n=151							

Cohort 2	6th Oct 1990 Pre 1	7th Oct 1991 Pre 2	7th Jan 1992 Pre 3	7th Feb-Mar 1992 Intervention	7th Apr 1992 Post 1	8th Oct 1992 Post 2	8th Apr 1993 Post 3
n=184							

N=335

Figure 18.4. The design of the PSAS.

A Psychoeducational Intervention Program

The intervention program developed for the PSAS (Meyer et al., 1992; Petersen, 1989) was designed as a psychoeducational approach to teach young adolescents adaptive emotional, cognitive, and behavioral responses to stressors or challenges and to decrease the development of depressive symptoms and affect. Emphasis was placed on ways of coping with the normal levels of distressed affect that are common reactions to chronic strains, stressful life events, developmental transitions, and daily hassles in early adolescence (Petersen, 1989; Rice & Meyer, 1994). The idea behind this program was to develop or support intrapersonal and interpersonal ways of coping with challenges (Rice & Meyer, 1994).

The specific content of the program, as well as suggestions for the didactic material and role-playing exercises, were taken from skill-streaming (Goldstein et al., 1980) and a group treatment of clinical depression in adolescence (Clarke & Lewinsohn, 1986). In addition, the work of Compas and colleagues (Compas et al., 1991; Compas, Phares, & Ledoux, 1989) on the enhancement of coping and stress management skills in children and adolescents was added during the pilot phases of intervention program design.

The program consisted of 16 sessions conducted in school.[3] Sessions were led by clinically trained graduate students or psychologists. Each session focused on a particular social skill or coping method (Table 18.1). Each session began with a group activity to serve as a "warm-up", followed by a didactic presentation that emphasized the topic for that session. Additional activities following the presentation were intended to help adolescents practice the content discussed; these activities involved role-playing, assertiveness exercises, discussion of videos, or games designed specifically for the intervention (Petersen, 1989; Rice & Meyer; 1994). The session closed with a summary of the important points and activities during the session. Closing comments also

Table 18.1. *Psychoeducational intervention program*

Session	Topic	Description
1	Introduction to challenges of adolescence	Provide orientation to the program and an overview of some of its challenges, opportunities, and risks.
2	Wheel of Life	Increase awareness of different areas of life (e.g., friends, family, school) and importance of using strengths when challenges in other areas are causing stress.
3	Problem-solving method	Outline five-step approach to coping with challenges • Stop and think. • Set a positive goal. • Brainstorm solutions. • Evaluate consequences. • Choose the best plan.
4	Generating alternative solutions	Learn how to brainstorm solutions to relevant problems.
5	Assertiveness	Differentiate between passive, aggressive, and assertive communication.
6	Emotion-focused coping	Learn how to cope with uncontrollable situations and how to manage feelings.
7	Relaxation training	Learn relation techniques and appropriate uses of relaxation strategies.
8	Anticipating consequences	Consider possible consequences of solutions, and assess positive and negative attributes of consequence.
9	Review and practice	Use strategies discussed and practiced thus far in role-played situations.
10	Wheel of Life game	Play large, human-sized, board game integrating Wheel of Life concepts (Harder, 1990) with coping methods.
11	Self-esteem	Decrease irrational thinking and enhance positive self-affirming thoughts and actions.
12	Shyness	Explore shyness in different social contexts and ways to increase social skills.
13	Friendship	Resolve problems and deal with challenges in peer relationships.
14	Peer pressure	Apply assertive strategies to cope with problematic pressure from peers.
15	Problem solving in the family	Coping with problems with parents and siblings.
16	Summary/wrap-up	Review program and encourage maintenance of program goals.

attempted to bridge the gap between the current and following sessions as a means of maintaining continuity throughout the program.

Each of the 16 sessions lasted approximately 40 minutes. The early sessions focused on the nature of challenges, which were discussed as opportunities or potential risks (Rice & Meyer, 1994). Later sessions offered the practice of specific problem-solving methods and ways of applying those strategies to specific challenges that young adolescents may confront. For example, the second session focused on a framework for understanding challenges: The Wheel of Life (Harder, 1990). The Wheel of Life describes areas of life that may be more or less important to individuals, depending on their unique values and priorities. The areas include school, family, social, physical, mental, spiritual, community, and financial. Students were encouraged to consider their own priorities in these areas and how those priorities may result in conflicts between areas. The areas of the wheel also represent sources of potential challenge, as well as resources that may help in meeting those challenges.

After the first two sessions, students were given opportunities to practice specific problem-solving methods and to apply them to challenges that may be experienced during early adolescence (e.g., peer pressure, friendships, conflicts or problems in the family). The last session included a role-played review of the previous 15 sessions, completion of a personal contract in which the adolescent agreed to use certain skills learned during the program, feedback, and a closing party.

The hypotheses were as follows: (1) a psychoeducational program delivered at school will decrease the development of depressive affect and symptoms and (2) the proximal mechanism for the effect on depression will be more effective coping skills. We hypothesized that both effects would be stronger for girls than for boys because a psychoeducational curriculum arguably could be more salient to girls and because previous studies have found stronger effects on girls' coping.

Measures

The measurement design for students included both paper-and-pencil questionnaires and assessments gained through individual interviews. Additional assessments (e.g., responses to pagers) are not discussed here. This discussion focuses on measures of coping and depression-related phenomena.

Coping was assessed with several measures, all demonstrated to have good reliability and validity. These measures include the Mastery and Coping scale of the Self-Image Questionnaire for Young Adolescents (SIQYA; Petersen et al., 1984), and two scales formed from the Seiffe-Krenke Coping Questionnaire to measure problem- and affect-focused coping, each in the interpersonal and school domains (Seiffe-Krenke & Shulman, 1990). The Mastery and

Coping scale of the SIQYA ranges from 1 ("describes me very well") to 6 ("does not describe me at all") and the scale score is the average across all items. Reliabilities, as measured by alpha coefficients of interitem consistency, are .75 for boys and .67 for girls. The scale is scored so that higher scores reflect better mastery and coping.

Depression was assessed with several measures. Clinical depression was assessed with the Diagnostic Interview Schedule for Children (DISC; NIMH, 1991). The DISC is a structured psychiatric interview designed to elicit a diagnosis of childhood psychopathology. It is used primarily for research purposes and is generally scored to yield a diagnosis of childhood and adolescent psychiatric disorder. Five essential features are necessary for making a clinical diagnosis of depression: (1) the presence of either depressed affect (or irritability in children and adolescents) or anhedonia, (2) the presence of five out of nine symptoms of depression, (3) a duration of at least 2 weeks, (4) symptoms that reflect a change in functioning, and (5) symptoms that are not attributable solely to loss (e.g., death, divorce, moving away). For these analyses, we used data from all subjects on a scale counting the number of criteria for diagnosis, with 0 representing no criteria and 5 representing the number required to be diagnosed with depression.

Depressive symptoms were assessed with two measures: the Children's Depression Inventory (CDI; Kovacs & Beck, 1977) and the Achenbach Youth Self Report (YSR; Achenbach & Edelbrock, 1987). The CDI is a self-report measure derived from the Beck Depression Inventory and is designed to assess depressive symptoms in both children and adolescents. Items include a range of depressive symptoms such as sadness, suicidal ideation, and sleep/appetite disturbances. The item format is multiple choice; respondents choose which of the three multiple-choice descriptors are most true of themselves. The YSR is a standardized, empirically derived rating scale that yields scores for externalizing (e.g., conduct problems and attentional problems) and internalizing behaviors (e.g., depression). The present study used both the internalizing and externalizing scales, as well as the anxious/depressed syndrome.

Depressive affect was measured by the Emotional Tone scale of the SIQYA (Petersen et al., 1984). The Emotional Tone scale is made up of 11 items providing an index of well-being from negative to positive feelings and tapping dimensions such as depression and anxiety. The scale is scored in the same fashion as the Mastery and Coping scale described earlier, with higher scores reflecting better emotional tone. Reliabilities, as measured by alpha coefficients of interitem consistency, are .81 for boys and .85 for girls.

Analyses

Time 1 data were analyzed to check that random assignment to treatment and control groups was achieved; this was verified. At Time 5, there were no main

Table 18.2. *Frequencies and percentage missing by cohort across time*

Cohort	Time 1 (sixth grade, Oct.)	Time 2 (seventh grade, Oct.)	Time 3 (seventh grade, Jan.)	Time 4 (seventh grade, Apr.)	Time 5 (eighth grade, Oct.)	Time 6 (eighth grade, Apr.)
1	151	147	146	140	128	116
2	184	184	174	164	140	157
Total	335	331	320	304	268	273
% missing	0%	1.2%	4.5%	8.7%	20.6%	18.5%

Note: Some subjects were inadvertently dropped from the mailing list following the intervention. This problem was not discovered until after the Time 5 data collection for Cohort 2.

effects or interactions for community or cohort, suggesting that neither demographic differences in the two communities nor historical effects (e.g., the Gulf War)[4] had an impact directly or on modifying the intervention effects.

The data were then analyzed for effects of the intervention in two ways. MANOVAs were conducted on the gain scores from Time 3 to Time 4 (January 1991 to April 1991 for Cohort 1 and January 1992 to April 1992 for Cohort 2), just before and just after the intervention. These analyses compare the direction and magnitude of change in the intervention group with that of the control group, thus controlling for effects of maturation and other artifacts. (We also conducted MANCOVAs because there were instances in which the two groups had become different on the dependent variable by Time 3; the results were not generally different from those with gain scores, suggesting that differences by Time 3 did not affect the results.) Finally, to check for long-term effects, we compared the groups at Time 5 (October 1991 and October 1992) (see Figure 18.4 for the design). Only significant ($p \leq .05$) effects are discussed here. In all cases, effects were tested a priori, as determined by the design.

Because we did not attempt to ensure that we involved all participants in the study at each time of assessment, or especially for each measure, attrition is not a useful concept in this study. For example, a student might have missed a day of school due to illness and thereby missed a day of study assessments, but still might have participated in all other study assessments. Instead of examining attrition, we investigated bias in missing data. We found no significant bias in missing data for any independent variable or on any of the dependent variables studied thus far. (See Table 18.2 for percent missing by cohort across time points.)

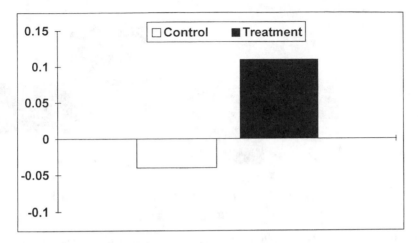

Figure 18.5. An example of the effects of the intervention on coping.

Results

The results revealed that the intervention was effective in producing better coping in the short term. There was a significant multivariate main effect of group on the coping measures, with results in the same direction for all measures. The short-term effects of the intervention on the Mastery and Coping scale of the SIQYA are shown in Figure 18.5 as an example. There was no stronger effect on the coping of girls, contrary to our hypothesis.

The short-term effects on measures of depression were more mixed. With Achenbach's internalizing and externalizing scales, the control group reported increasing externalizing problems, whereas the intervention group reported decreasing problems in this area. On internalizing problems, both groups reported decreases, with the intervention group reporting significantly fewer problems than the control group (Figure 18.6).

In the MANOVA with the CDI and Emotional Tone, group interacted with gender, F (2, 233) = 4.07, p < .01. For example, on the CDI the gender differences in the control group were consistent with expectations, but in the intervention group we found the hypothesized improvement among girls but increased depressive symptoms among boys (Figure 18.7).

As would be expected, there was a significant multivariate effect of risk on the MANOVA on Emotional Tone and CDI, F (2, 234) = 13.24, p < .001, such that high-risk youths reported more depressed affect and depressive symptoms. There were no significant univariate results on the CDI. Group interacted with gender and risk on Emotional Tone, F (2, 241) = 4.71, p < .031. Both of the high-risk groups showed improvement on Emotional Tone; high-risk

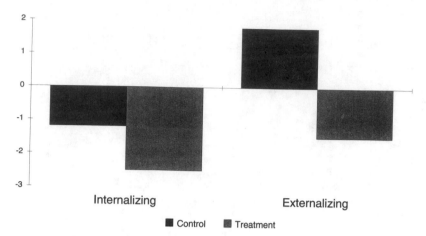

Figure 18.6. The effects of the intervention on internalizing and externalizing problems.

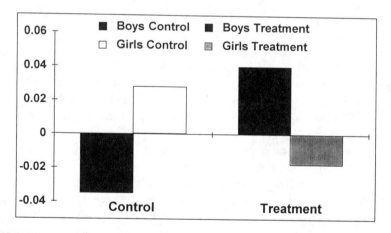

Figure 18.7. The effects of the intervention by gender on depressive affect (CDI).

girls in the intervention group showed the largest gains in Emotional Tone.
The high-risk girls in the intervention group showed an increase more than
three times that of the high-risk girls in the control group. (The mean gain
score for the high-risk intervention group girls was .85, and the score for the
high-risk control group girls was .28. Standard deviations were approximately
equal at .83 and .76, respectively) (Figure 18.8).

The MANOVA on internalizing and externalizing symptoms revealed a
significant multivariate interaction of group and risk status, $F(2, 228) = 4.47$,
$p < .01$, showing that, overall, the high-risk control group increased on both
internalizing and externalizing symptoms, whereas both low-risk groups decreased on both target symptoms. Univariate results showed a main effect of

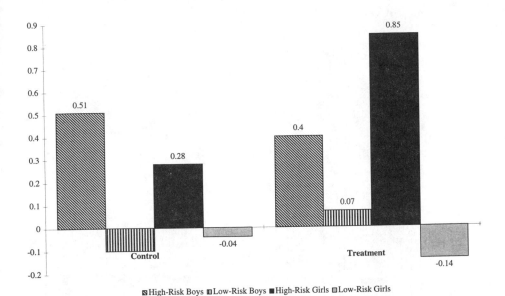

Figure 18.8. Intervention Group × Sex × Risk: interaction on Emotional Tone gain score.

risk on internalizing symptoms, $F(1, 235) = 6.90$, $p < .009$, with the high-risk group increasing on internalizing symptoms, as would be expected. Group interacted with risk on externalizing symptoms, $F(1, 235) = 8.38$, $p < .004$, with the high-risk group showing the greatest reduction of externalizing symptoms (Figure 18.9). As with internalizing symptoms, there was a significant main effect of risk on the DISC, $F(1, 268) = 5.11$, $p < .025$, with the high-risk group showing increased depressive symptoms compared to the low-risk group. There were no interactions of group and risk on this measure of clinical depression.

Over the longer term (by Time 5) there were no main effects of group, although this variable interacted with others. These interactions are not easily interpretable, and they do not fit our original hypotheses or any hypotheses generated post hoc. Thus we infer that the intervention did not persist in influencing coping and depression nearly a year later.

Discussion

The results of this study are both promising and disappointing. It is promising to know that coping skills can be taught and that these skills decrease the likelihood of depressive symptoms at least in girls. The results with boys on the CDI are interesting. Because there was no Group × Sex interaction on

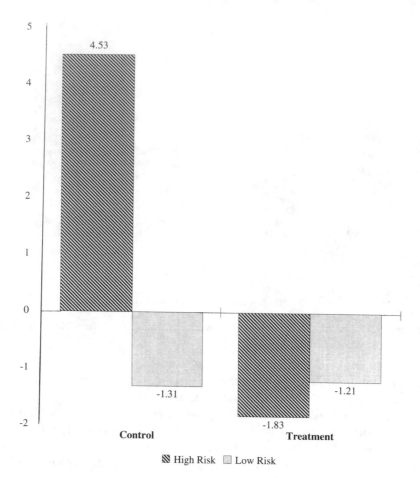

Figure 18.9. Intervention Group × Risk: interaction on externalizing gain score.

the coping measures, the result cannot be due to different effects of the intervention on the coping behaviors of boys compared to girls.

That the effects of the intervention did not persist is disappointing but not surprising. Given all the changes occurring during early adolescence, it would be surprising for a brief intervention to have strong long-term effects. With interventions into smoking behavior, the most effective interventions with adolescent behavior, researchers have achieved significant effects over longer periods of time by using booster sessions at periodic follow-up intervals and by creating "no smoking" environments at school and within peer groups (e.g., Leventhal & Keeshan, 1993; Perry & Kelder, 1992). None of these approaches was used in the present case. Further, effective coping is not always prevalent among adults, providing modeling of negative behaviors. And finally, effective coping may decrease the extent to which young people experience depressive symptoms, but it cannot entirely counteract the effects of the many changes that occur in these young lives. These young people experienced a higher level of serious loss than we have seen in prior research involving the death of loved ones, marital breakup of parents, and so forth. "Sleeper" or delayed effects could, of course, be found subsequently (e.g., Dielman, 1994). This would require further follow-up of this sample in order to test such effects.

The results do suggest that interventions can help during developmental transitions. We hope that others will improve on our efforts so that more young people can be guided through the difficulties of this decade of life.

Implications for Further Research

As the first study examining the promotion of effective coping and the reduction of depressed affect and symptoms among adolescents, the study described here makes a significant contribution. Placed within the framework of health promotion and disease prevention studies more generally, however, it clearly demonstrates that much work is yet to be done.

Future work should examine ways to extend benefits over a longer period of time. As noted earlier, research on other problems (e.g., smoking) demonstrates that repetition of support for effective behavior is required, especially throughout a challenging developmental period such as adolescence. It is also possible that longer-term effects were not found because the approaches taken in the intervention began to be more broadly diffused throughout the school population. We recognize, of course, that establishing such a diffusion process would require specific follow-up research.

Specificity of the intervention is another question requiring attention. This study provides some information on this issue because externalizing behaviors were also reduced over the short term, suggesting that the intervention extends beyond effects on the target outcome. There is other evidence of the efficacy of behavioral procedures for the treatment of externalizing problems such as aggression, hyperactivity, and attentional difficulties (e.g., Barkley, 1987; Hinshaw, 1994). The intervention described here has components of problem solving, an area of difficulty for children with externalizing problems. On the other hand, research examining the covariation of depression with other problems demonstrates that depression has especially high rates of comorbidity with other disorders and related behaviors and symptoms (Compas & Hammen, 1994; Petersen et al., 1993). Strong covariation of problems is even more prevalent in childhood and adolescence than in adulthood (e.g., Compas & Hammen, 1994), making it difficult to conclude that externalizing problems are distinct from internalizing problems, especially depression. Additional data from the present project could be examined to further clarify this issue.

Whether this primary population-targeted intervention is effective in adolescents with more severe problems is another important consideration. The fact that youths at high risk for depression benefited even more than those at low risk suggests that the intervention is effective even for those with more serious problems. On the other hand, the fact that we did not find intervention effects on clinical depression suggests that this intervention is not effective with those already manifesting serious depression. This latter result is not surprising and is rather reassuring because we would expect that a more specific treatment would be needed for clinically depressed youth.

Another question is whether this intervention is effective with young people experiencing acute challenges such as a significant family change (e.g., parental divorce or death) likely to result in at least temporary depression. Other data from this project would permit an examination of this question. Furthermore, depressive episodes among adolescents are frequently related to the loss of a relationship with a boyfriend or girlfriend (e.g., Camarena, 1990). Whether the intervention is effective with young people experiencing such depressive episodes will be pursued in future analyses.

Policy Implications

If further analyses support the finding that this intervention is effective at least over the short term, should it be recommended for implementation in schools? We attempted to conduct the intervention in such a way as to make it usable for school implementation. Indeed, one of the school districts participating in the research asked to work with us so that teachers would be able to integrate the intervention into their regular curriculum. We conducted special workshops in this community for teachers interested in the intervention. Thus, we believe that the program could be implemented with relatively little assistance to school personnel.

Given the fact that a program such as the one described here could be implemented in a typical school district at low cost, we believe it should be recommended to schools. Even short-term benefits could give adolescents another year or two on a more positive trajectory, improving the likelihood of longer-term effects for at least some youths. We would be more enthusiastic, of course, with evidence of longer-term effects.

There is substantial evidence that depression is a significant problem for adolescents. The related morbidity in the form of problems such as drug and alcohol use, as well as mortality resulting from suicide and risky behavior, suggests strongly that reducing depression among adolescents should be a high priority. Today's youths are our future, and we must invest wisely in them to ensure their well-being as well as our own.

Notes

1 Junior high schools have a course-based curriculum like that of high schools but house younger students. Middle schools, more recent in origin, focus more in design and curriculum on the developmental status of young adolescents. Studies of schools for young adolescents, however, find that there are few differences in practice.
2 The NORC index (Stevens & Hoisington, 1987) classifies parental occupational prestige on a scale ranging from 14.7 to 81.1 ($SD = 16.0$) based on 1980 prestige ratings.
3 In one school, sessions were offered during free periods; in the other, they were scheduled during a period designed to focus on material like this. Because there were no systematic differences, we conclude that this difference did not contribute systematic variation to the outcome variables.
4 The Gulf War of 1991 began just prior to the intervention for Cohort 2.

References

Achenbach, T. M., & Edelbrock, C. (1987). *Manual for youth self-report and profile*. Burlington: Department of Psychiatry, University of Vermont.

Barkley, R. A. (1987). *Hyperactive children: A handbook for diagnosis and treatment*. New York: Guilford Press.

Beardslee, W. R. (1990). Development of a clinician-based preventive intervention for families with affective disorders. *Journal of Preventive Psychiatry and Allied Disciplines, 4*, 39–61.

Beardslee, W. R., Hoke, L., Wheelock, I., Rothberg, P., van de Velde, P., & Swatling, S. (1992). Initial findings on preventive interventions for families with parental affective disorders. *American Journal of Psychiatry, 149*, 1335–1340.

Beardslee, W. R., & Podorefsky, D. (1988). Resilient adolescents whose parents have serious affective and other psychiatric disorder: The importance of self-understanding and relationships. *American Journal of Psychiatry, 145*, 67–69.

Block, J., Block, J. H., & Gjerde, P. F. (1988). Parental functioning and the home environment in families of divorce: Prospective and concurrent analyses. *Journal of the American Academy of Child and Adolescent Psychiatry, 27*(2), 207–213.

Blos, P. (1970). *The adolescent passage*. New York: International Universities Press.

Blyth, D. A., Simmons, R. G., & Carlton-Ford, S. (1983). The adjustment of early adolescents to school transitions. *Journal of Early Adolescence, 3*, 104–120.

Brown, B. (1989). The role of peer groups in adolescents' adjustment to secondary school. In T. J. Berndt & G. W. Ladd (Eds.), *Peer relationships in child development* (pp. 188–216). New York: Wiley.

Brown, B. (1990). Peer groups and peer cultures. In S. S. Feldman & G. R. Elliott (Eds.), *At the threshold: The developing adolescent* (pp. 171–196). Cambridge, MA: Harvard University Press.

Brown, B., Clasen, D., & Eicher, S. (1986). Perceptions of peer pressure, peer conformity dispositions, and self-reported behavior among adolescents. *Developmental Psychology, 22*, 521–530.

Camarena, P. (1990). *Science and personal stories of psychological well-being across the adolescent years: An exploration of gender and mental health*. Unpublished doctoral dissertation, Pennsylvania State University.

Cherlin, A. J., Furstenberg, F. F., Jr., Chase-Lansdale, P. L., Kiernan, K. E., Robins, P. K., Morrison, D. R., & Teitler, J. O. (1991). Longitudinal studies of effects of divorce on children in Great Britain and the United States. *Science, 252*, 1386–1389.

Clarke, G. N., & Lewinsohn, P. M. (1986). *The coping with depression course: Parent version*. Eugene: Oregon Research Institute.

Coleman, J. (1978). Current contradictions in adolescent theory. *Journal of Youth and Adolescence*, 7, 1–11.

Compas, B. E. (1987a). Coping with stress during childhood and adolescence. *Psychological Bulletin, 101*, 393–403.

Compas, B. E. (1987b). Stress and life events during childhood and adolescence. *Clinical Psychology Review*, 7, 275–302.

Compas, B. E. (1993). Promoting positive mental health during adolescence. In S. G. Millstein, A. C. Petersen, & E. O. Nightingale (Eds.), *Promoting the health of adolescents: New directions for the twenty-first century* (pp. 159–179). New York: Oxford University Press.

Compas, B. E., & Hammen, C. L. (1994). Child and adolescent depression: Covariation and comorbidity in development. In R. J. Haggerty, L. R. Sherrod, N. Garmezy, & M. Rutter (Eds.), *Stress, risk, and resilience in children and adolescents: Processes, mechanisms, and interventions* (pp. 225–267). New York: Cambridge University Press.

Compas, B. E., Ledoux, N., Howell, D. C., Phares, V., Williams, R. A., Giunta, C. T., & Banez, G. A. (1991). *Enhancing coping and stress management skills in children and adolescents: Evaluation of a school-based preventive intervention*. Unpublished manuscript, University of Vermont.

Compas, B. E., Orosan, P. G., & Grant, K. E. (1993). Adolescent stress and coping: Implications for psychopathology during adolescence. *Journal of Adolescence, 16*, 331–349.

Compas, B. E., Phares, V., & Ledoux, N. (1989). Stress and coping preventive interventions for children and adolescents. In L. A. Bond & B. E. Compas (Eds.), *Primary prevention and promotion in the schools* (pp. 319–340). Newbury Park, CA: Sage.

Crockett, L. J., & Petersen, A. C. (1993). Adolescent development: Health risks and opportunities for health promotion. In S. G. Millstein, A. C. Petersen, & E. O. Nightingale (Eds.), *Promoting the health of adolescents: New directions for the twenty-first century* (pp. 13–37). New York: Oxford University Press.

Crockett, L. J., Petersen, A. C., Graber, J. A., Schulenberg, J. E., & Ebata, A. (1989). School transitions and adjustment during early adolescence. *Journal of Early Adolescence, 8*, 405–419.

Dielman, T. E. (1994). School-based research on the prevention of adolescent alcohol use and misuse: Methodological issues and advances. *Journal of Research on Adolescence, 4*, 271–293.

Downey, G., & Coyne, J. C. (1990). Children of depressed parents: An integrative review. *Psychological Bulletin, 108*, 50–76.

Ebata, A. T. (1987). *A longitudinal study of psychological distress during early adolescence*. Unpublished doctoral dissertation, Pennsylvania State University.

Ebata, A. T., & Moos, R. H. (1991). Coping and adjustment in distressed and healthy adolescents. *Journal of Applied Developmental Psychology, 17*, 33–54.

Ebata, A. T., Petersen, A. C., & Conger, J. J. (1990). The development of psychopathology in adolescence. In J. E. Rolf, A. S. Masten, D. Cicchetti, K. Nuechterlein, & S. Weintraub (Eds.), *Risk and protective factors in the development of psychopathology* (pp. 308–333). New York: Cambridge University Press.

Eccles, J. S., & Midgley, C. (1989). Stage/environment fit: Developmentally appropriate classrooms for early adolescents. In R. E. Ames & C. Ames (Eds.), *Research on motivation in education* (Vol. 3, pp. 139–186). New York: Academic Press.

Eckert, P. (1989). *Jocks and burnouts: Social categories and identity in the high school*. New York: Teachers College Press.

Elliott, D. S. (1993). Health enhancing and health compromising lifestyles. In S. G. Millstein, A. C. Petersen, & E. O. Nightingale (Eds.), *Promoting the health of adolescents: New directions for the twenty-first century* (pp. 119–145). New York: Oxford University Press.

Fendrich, M., Warner, V., & Weissman, M. M. (1990). Family risk factors, parental depression, and psychopathology in offspring. *Developmental Psychology, 26*, 40–50.

Fenzel, L. M., & Blyth, D. A. (1986). Individual adjustment to school transitions: An exploration of the role of supportive peer relations. *Journal of Early Adolescence, 6*, 315–329.

Freud, A. (1958). Adolescence. *Psychoanalytic study of the child, 13*, 255–278.

Garmezy, N. (1984). Stress-resistant children: The search for protective factors. In J. E. Stevenson (Ed.), *Recent research in developmental psychology* (pp. 213–233). Oxford: Pergamon Press.

Garmezy, N., & Rutter, M. (Eds.). (1983). *Stress, coping, and development in children.* New York: McGraw-Hill.

Goldstein, A. P., Sprafkin, R. P., Gershaw, N. J., & Klein, P. (1980). *Skill-streaming the adolescent.* Champaign, IL: Research Press.

Grinker, R. R., & Werble, B. (1974). Mentally healthy young men (homoclites): Fourteen years later. *Archives of General Psychiatry, 30*, 701–704.

Grych, J. H., & Fincham, F. D. (1992). Interventions for children of divorce: Towards greater integration of research and action. *Psychological Bulletin, 111*, 434–454.

Harder, C. (1990). *The winner's seminar: A leadership experience for youth.* Cedar Rapids, IA: Carole Harder.

Herman-Stahl, M. A., & Petersen, A. C. (in press). Stressed and depressed: The protective role of coping and social resources for depressive symptoms among young adolescents. *Journal of Youth and Adolescence.*

Herman-Stahl, M. A., & Petersen, A. C. (submitted). *Depressive symptoms during adolescence: Direct and stress-buffering effects of coping, control beliefs, and family relationships.*

Herman-Stahl, M. A., Stemmler, M., & Petersen, A. C. (1995). Approach and avoidant coping: Implications for adolescent mental health. *Journal of Youth and Adolescence, 24*, 649–665.

Hess, L. E. (1995). Changing family patterns in Western Europe: Opportunity and risk factors for adolescent development. In M. Rutter & D. J. Smith (Eds.), *Psychosocial disorders in young people: Time trends and their causes* (pp. 104–193). New York: Wiley.

Hill, J., & Holmbeck, G. (1986). Attachment and autonomy during adolescence. In G. Whitehurst (Ed.), *Annals of child development* (pp. 145–189). Greenwich, CT: JAI Press.

Hill, J., Holmbeck, G., Marlow, M., Green, T., & Lynch, M. (1985). Menarcheal status and parent–child relations in families of seventh-grade girls. *Journal of Youth and Adolescence, 14*, 301–316.

Hinshaw, S. P. (1994). Attention deficits and hyperactivity in children. *Developmental clinical psychology and psychiatry* (Vol. 29). Thousand Oaks, CA: Sage.

Kandel, D., & Lesser, G. (1972). *Youth in two worlds.* San Francisco: Jossey-Bass.

Kazdin, A. E. (1993). Adolescent mental health. *American Psychologist, 48*, 127–141.

Kessler, R. C., Price, R. H., & Wortman, C. B. (1985). Social factors in psychopathology: Stress, social support and coping processes. *Annual Review of Psychology, 36*, 351–372.

Klepp, K. I., Halper, A., & Perry, C. L. (1986). The efficacy of peer leaders in drug abuse prevention. *Journal of School Health, 56*, 407–411.

Kovacs, M., & Beck, A. T. (1977). An empirical-clinical approach toward a definition of childhood depression. In J. G. Schulterbrandt & A. Raskin (Eds.), *Depression and childhood: Diagnosis, treatment and conceptual models* (pp. 1–26). Rockville, MD: National Institute of Mental Health.

Laursen, B., & Collins, W. A. (1994). Interpersonal conflict during adolescence. *Psychological Bulletin, 155*, 197–209.

Leffert, N., Graham, B. L., & Petersen, A. C. (1994, May). Gender-based development of behavioral and emotional problems during early adolescence. In J. A. Graber (Chair), *Methods for studying stress during reproductive transitions.* Symposium conducted at the conference on "Psychosocial and Behavioral Factors in Women's Health: Creating an Agenda for the 21st Century," Washington, DC.

Lerner, R. M., Karson, M., Meidels, M., & Knapp, J. R. (1975). Actual and perceived attitude of late adolescents and their parents: The phenomenon of the generation gaps. *Journal of Genetic Psychology, 126*, 195–207.

Leventhal, H., & Keeshan, P. (1993). Promoting healthy alternatives to substance abuse. In S. G. Millstein, A. C. Petersen, & E. O. Nightingale (Eds.), *Promoting the health of adolescents: New directions for the twenty-first century* (pp. 260–284). New York: Oxford University Press.

Maccoby, E., & Martin, J. (1983). Socialization in the context of the family: Parent–child interaction. In E. M. Hetherington (Ed.), *Handbook of child psychology* (Vol. 4, pp. 103–196). New York: Wiley.

Magnusson, D. (1987). *Individual development in an interactional perspective: Vol. 1. Paths through life.* Hillsdale, NJ: Erlbaum.

McCarthy, J. D., & Hoge, D. R. (1982). Analysis of age effects in longitudinal studies of adolescent self-esteem. *Developmental Psychology, 18,* 372–379.

Meyer, A., Miller, S., Grund, E., Herman, M., Rice, K., Sullivan, P., & Kennedy, R. (1992). *Penn State adolescent study (PSAS): Intervention program manual.* Unpublished manual, Pennsylvania State University, University Park, PA.

Mikesell, J. (1988). *The relationship between patterns of family functioning and adolescent self-image: A multivariate, multi-process approach.* Unpublished doctoral dissertation, Pennsylvania State University.

Montemayor, R. (1983). Parents and adolescents in conflict: All families some of the time and some families most of the time. *Journal of Early Adolescence, 3,* 83–103.

Morgan, S. P., Lye, D. N., & Condran, G. A. (1988). Sons, daughters, and the risk of marital disruption. *American Journal of Sociology, 94,* 110–129.

National Institute of Mental Health (NIMH). (1991). *NIMH diagnostic interview schedule for children.* Rockville, MD: Author.

Nolen-Hoeksema, S. (1987). Sex differences in unipolar depression: Evidence and theory. *Psychological Bulletin, 101,* 259–282.

Offer, D. (1969). *The psychological world of the teenager: A study of normal adolescent boys.* New York: Basic Books.

Offer, D., & Offer, J. (1975). *From teenage to young manhood.* New York: Basic Books.

O'Malley, P. M., & Bachman, J. G. (1983). Self-esteem: Change and stability between ages 13 and 23. *Developmental Psychology, 19,* 257–268.

Perry, C. L., & Kelder, S. H. (1992). Models for effective prevention. *Journal of Adolescent Health, 13,* 355–363.

Petersen, A. C. (1988). Adolescent development. *Annual Review of Psychology, 39,* 583–607.

Petersen, A. C. (1989). *Coping with adolescent challenge: Gender-related mental health outcomes.* Study supported by the William T. Grant Foundation, Grant 89127289.

Petersen, A. C., Compas, B. E., & Brooks-Gunn, J. (1992). *Depression in adolescence: Current knowledge, research directions, and implications for programs and policy.* Washington, DC: Carnegie Council on Adolescent Development, Carnegie Corporation of New York.

Petersen, A. C., & Ebata, A. T. (1987). Developmental transitions and adolescent problem behavior: Implications for prevention and intervention. In K. Hurrelmann, F. X. Kaufmann, & F. Lösel (Eds.), *Social intervention: Potential and constraints* (pp. 167–184). New York: Walter de Gruyter.

Petersen, A. C., Kennedy, R. E., & Sullivan, P. (1991). Coping with adolescence. In M. E. Colten & S. Gore (Eds.), *Adolescent stress: Causes and consequences* (pp. 93–110). New York: Aldine de Gruyter.

Petersen, A. C., & Leffert, N. (1995). What is special about adolescence? In M. Rutter (Ed.), *Psychosocial disturbances in young people: Challenges for prevention* (pp. 3–36). New York: Cambridge University Press.

Petersen, A. C., Leffert, N., Graham, B., Ding, S., & Overbey, T. (1994). Depression and body image disorders in adolescence. *Women's Health Issues, 4,* 98–108.

Petersen, A. C., Sarigiani, P., Camarena, P., & Leffert, N. (in press). Resilience in adolescence. *International Annals of Adolescent Psychiatry.*

Petersen, A. C., Sarigiani, P. A., & Kennedy, R. E. (1991). Adolescent depression: Why more girls? *Journal of Youth and Adolescence, 20,* 247–271.

Petersen, A. C., Schulenberg, J. E., Abramowitz, R. H., Offer, D., & Jarcho, H. D. (1984). A self-image questionnaire for young adolescents (SIQYA): Reliability and validity studies. *Journal of Youth and Adolescence, 13,* 93–111.

Petersen, A. C., & Taylor, B. (1980). The biological approach to adolescence: Biological change and psychological adaptation. In J. Adelson (Ed.), *Handbook of adolescent psychology* (pp. 117–155). New York: Wiley.

Petersen, A. C., White, N., & Stemmler, M. (1991, April). *Familial risk and protective factors influencing adolescent mental health.* Symposium presentation at the biennial meetings of the Society for Research in Child Development, Seattle.

Phares, V., & Compas, B. E. (1992). The role of fathers in child and adolescent psychopathology: Make room for daddy. *Psychological Bulletin, 111,* 387–412.

Rice, K. G., Herman, M. A., & Petersen, A. C. (1993). Challenge in adolescence: A conceptual model and psycho-educational intervention. *Journal of Adolescence, 16,* 235–251.

Rice, K. G., & Meyer, A. L. (1994). Preventing depression among young adolescents: Preliminary process results of a psycho-educational intervention program. *Journal of Counseling and Development, 73,* 145–152.

Rutter, M. (1983). Stress, coping, and development: Some issues and some questions. In N. Garmezy & M. Rutter (Eds.), *Stress, coping, and development in children* (pp. 1–41). New York: McGraw-Hill.

Rutter, M. (1987). The role of cognition in child development and disorder. *British Journal of Medical Psychology, 60,* 1–16.

Rutter, M., Graham, P., Chadwick, O., & Yule, W. (1976). Adolescent turmoil: Fact or fiction. *Journal of Child Psychology and Psychiatry, 17,* 35–56.

Sarigiani, P. (1990). *A longitudinal study of relationship adjustment of young adults from divorced and nondivorced families.* Unpublished doctoral dissertation, Pennsylvania State University.

Seiffe-Krenke, I., & Shulman, S. (1990). Coping style in adolescence. A cross-cultural study. *Journal of Cross-Cultural Psychology, 21*(3), 351–377.

Simmons, R. G., & Blyth, D. A. (1987). *Moving into adolescence: The impact of pubertal change and school context.* Hawthorne, NY: Aldine de Gruyter.

Steinberg, L. (1981). Transformation in family relations at puberty. *Developmental Psychology, 17,* 833–838.

Stevens, G., & Hoisington, E. (1987). Occupational prestige and the 1980 labor force. *Social Science Research, 16,* 74–105.

Weissberg, R. P., Caplan, M. Z., & Silvo, P. J. (1989). A new conceptual framework for establishing school-based competence promotion programs. In L. A. Bond & B. E. Compas (Eds.), *Primary prevention and promotion in the schools* (pp. 255–296). Newbury Park, CA: Sage.

White, N. R., Petersen, A. C., Stemmler, M., & Mikesell, J. (in preparation). *Affective family environment and adjustment in early adolescence.*

Youniss, J., & Smollar, J. (1985). *Adolescents' relations with mothers, fathers, and friends.* Chicago: University of Chicago Press.

19 Preventing Health-Compromising Behaviors Among Youth and Promoting Their Positive Development: A Developmental Contextual Perspective

Richard M. Lerner, Charles W. Ostrom, and Melissa A. Freel

In every nation of the world, children and adolescents are dying – from violence, from drug and alcohol use and abuse, from unsafe sex, from poor nutrition, and from the sequelae of persistent and pervasive poverty (Dryfoos, 1990; Hamburg, 1992; Huston, 1991; Lerner, 1993a, 1993b, 1995; Little, 1993; McKinney, Abrams, Terry, & Lerner, 1994; Schorr, 1988; Wilson, 1987; World Health Organization, 1986, 1993). If our youth are not dying, their life chances are being squandered – by school failure, underachievement, and dropping out; by crime; by teenage pregnancy and parenting; by lack of job preparedness; by challenges to their health (e.g., lack of immunizations, inadequate screening for disabilities, insufficient prenatal care, and lack of sufficient infant and childhood medical services); and by the feelings of despair and hopelessness that pervade the lives of children whose parents have lived in poverty and who see themselves as having little opportunity to do better, that is, to have a life marked by societal respect, achievement, and opportunity (Dryfoos, 1990; Huston, 1991; Huston, McLoyd, & Garcia Coll, 1994).

There are numerous manifestations of the severity and breadth of the problems besetting the youth, families, and communities of our world. To illustrate, consider four major categories of risk behaviors in late childhood and adolescence: (1) drug and alcohol use and abuse; (2) unsafe sex, teenage pregnancy, and teenage parenting; (3) school underachievement, school failure, and dropping out; and (4) delinquency, crime, and violence (Dryfoos, 1990). Clearly, participation in any one of these behaviors would diminish a youth's life chances. Indeed, engagement in some of these behaviors would eliminate the young person's chances of even having a life. Such risks to the life chances of children and adolescents are occurring, unfortunately, at historically unprecedented levels.

Consider the situation in the United States as an example. Today, in America, there are approximately 28 million children and adolescents between the ages of 10 and 17 years. About 50% of these youth engage in *two or more* of the previously noted categories of risk behaviors (Dryfoos, 1990). Moreover, 10% of America's youth engage in *all* of the four categories of risk behaviors (Dryfoos, 1990).

498

These data indicate that risk behaviors are highly interrelated in children and adolescents. Half of America's youth are at least at moderate risk as a consequence of engaging in two or more risk behaviors. One American youth in every 10 is at very high risk as a consequence of "doing it all," that is, of engaging in behaviors associated with every category of risk behavior. It is useful, we believe, to expand on the example of the problems besetting America's youth.

Illustrations of the Risk Behaviors Engaged in By Youth: The Sample Case of America

Within each of the categories of risk behavior is a burgeoning number of indications of the extensive problems besetting our nation's youth. Information derived from several recent publications – for instance, by the Center for the Study of Social Policy (e.g., the *Kids Count Data Book* from 1992 and 1993), by the Children's Defense Fund (Simons, Finlay, & Yang, 1991), by the Carnegie Corporation of New York (1992, 1994), by the Carnegie Council on Adolescent Development (1989), and by scholars such as Dryfoos (1990, 1994), Hamburg (1992), Mincy (1994), Hernandez (1993), and a committee of the National Research Council (1993) – provide several dramatic illustrations of the breadth and depth of these problems.

For example, considering the category of drug and alcohol use and abuse, it has been reported that in 1990 about 25% of 12- to 17-year-olds, and more than 50% of 18- to 25-year-olds had used illicit drugs; in addition, about 10% of sixth graders had started to use alcohol. In addition, about 25% of 12- to 14-year-olds and more than 50% of America's seventh graders were current alcohol users.

Moreover, in regard to illustrations of the behaviors involved in the risk category of unsafe sex, teenage pregnancy, and teenage childbirth, current information indicates that youth between 15 and 19 years account for 25% of the sexually transmitted disease (STD) cases each year. Moreover, 6.4% of adolescent runaways (of whom there are between 750,000 and 1,000,000 *each year* in America) have positive serum tests for the acquired immunodeficiency disease syndrome (AIDS) virus. These runaway youth often engage in unsafe sex, prostitution, and intravenous drug use. Thus, each year in America, up to 64,000 "time bombs" are going out onto the streets of our towns and cities, spreading a disease that will kill them and the people with whom they engage in unsafe sexual and drug use–related behaviors. In addition to these health risks, it should be noted that 1 million adolescents a year become pregnant; about half of them have babies. Indeed, about every minute, an American adolescent has a baby; and by age 18, 25% of American females have been pregnant at least once.

In turn, in regard to the category of school failure, underachievement, and dropping out, current information indicates that about 25% of the approximately 40 million children and adolescents enrolled in America's 82,000 public elementary and secondary schools are at risk for school failure, and each year about 700,000 youth drop out of school. About 25% of all 18- and 19-year-olds have not graduated from high school.

Finally, in regard to the risk category of delinquency, crime, and violence, information currently available indicates that youth aged 13 to 21 years accounted for 35.5% of all non-traffic-related arrests in the United States during the 1980s, although this age group was only 14.3% of the population; and in 1991, 130,000 arrests of youth aged 10 to 17 were made for rape, robbery, homicide, or aggravated assault. This figure represents an increase of 48% since 1986. Moreover, between 1980 and 1990, arrest rates of African American adolescents charged with weapons violations, with murder, and with aggravated assault increased by 102%, 145%, and 89%, respectively. However, African Americans experience rates of rape, aggravated assault, and armed robbery that are approximately 25% higher than those for European Americans, rates of motor vehicle theft that are about 70% higher, and rates of robbery victimization that are about 150% higher. Finally, rates of African American homicide are typically 600% to 700% higher.

Temporal Trends in the Risk Behaviors Engaged in by American Youth

The previously noted data regarding the prevalence of risk behaviors indicate that the current status of American youth is exceedingly problematic. Indeed, these data suggest that nothing short of a "generational time bomb" (Lerner, 1993a) is confronting American society. With so many of our nation's youth beset with so many instances of behavioral risk, America is on the verge of shortly losing much of its next generation, that is, the human capital on which the future of our nation relies (Hamburg, 1992; Lerner, 1993a, 1993b). Moreover, the "fuse" on the time bomb appears to be growing appreciably shorter: several sources of data indicate that many of the key problems of American youth are increasing at relatively rapid rates.

For instance, information from the 1993 *Kids Count Data Book*, published by the Center for the Study of Social Policy, indicates that between 1985 and 1992 many of the previously noted problems of children and youth grew substantially worse. For instance, the rate of violent deaths to 15- to 19-year-olds increased by 13%; whereas for European American youth this increased rate was 10%, for African American youth it was 78%. In addition, the percentage of youth graduating from high school decreased by 4%; the percentage of all births to single teenagers increased by 16% (involving a 26% increase among European American youth and no increase among African American youth); the arrest rate among 10- to 17-year-olds increased by 48%

(with the rate of European Americans increasing by 58% and that of African Americans by 29%); and the number of children in single-parent families increased by 9% (with the corresponding rates for European American and African American children increasing by 9% and 6%, respectively).

As noted earlier, these latter changes in family structure are associated with poverty and with the interrelation of risk behaviors among children and adolescents. As noted by Schorr (1988), childhood poverty is the single most damaging structural feature of American society affecting the quality of youth development. Accordingly, it is important to discuss the prevalence and temporal trends associated with poverty among American youth.

Youth Poverty

Youth poverty exacerbates the risk behaviors of adolescents, and poverty is a growing problem for America's youth (Huston, 1991; Lerner, 1993a). By the end of the 1980s, approximately 20% of America's children and adolescents were poor (Huston, 1991; Huston et al., 1994; Simons et al., 1991). Moreover, data in the 1992 *Kids Count Data Book* indicate that across the 1980s the percentage of youth living in poverty in the United States increased by 22%. Indeed, this trend was present in 40 states and continues to increase across the nation (Huston, 1991). Furthermore, of the 12 million American children under the age of 3 years, 25% live in poor families (Carnegie Corporation of New York, 1994). In addition, whereas the number of children under age 6 years decreased by 10% between 1971 and 1991, the number of poor children in this age group *increased by 60%* (Carnegie Corporation of New York, 1994).

Youth poverty occurs in all geographic regions of America. In fact, the rates of poverty in rural areas are as high as those in the inner cities (Huston, 1991; Jensen, 1988). Moreover, poor families in rural areas receive fewer welfare benefits and are less likely to live in states that provide Aid to Families with Dependent Children (AFDC) (Huston, 1991; Jensen, 1988).

However, it must be stressed that the probability of being a poor child is not equal across racial or ethnic groups. According to the 1993 *Kids Count Data Book*, in the 1987–1991 period the average percentage of European American, African American, and Latino children who were poor was 11.4%, 44.1%, and 37.9%, respectively. Moreover, among Latino groups, Puerto Rican children experienced the highest rate of poverty (40.4%) and Cuban children experienced the lowest rate (19.7%) (U.S. Bureau of the Census, 1991). In addition, it should be noted that, as reported in 1991 by the U.S. Bureau of the Census, Asian children and Native American youth experienced rates of poverty of 16.7% and 24.9%, respectively.

The percentages of youth living in poverty in the 1987–1991 period represent increases in the rates of poverty over the last 10 years for all racial/ethnic groups. For example, from 1979 to 1989 youth poverty grew worse by 9% for European Americans, by 5% for African Americans, and by 25% for Latinos (Center for the Study of Social Policy, 1993). In short, as noted by Huston (1991), race is the most striking and disturbing distinction between youth whose poverty is chronic and youth whose poverty is transitory.

The sequelae of poverty for youth are devastating. As Schorr (1988) stresses, poverty creates several "rotten outcomes" of youth development. For example, poverty is associated with early school failure, unemployability, long-term welfare dependency, violent crime, and feelings of hopelessness and despair (McLoyd & Wilson, 1991; Schorr, 1988, 1991). Furthermore, McLoyd and Wilson (1991) and Klerman (1991) find that poor youth arc at high risk for low self-confidence, conduct problems, depression, and peer conflict. In addition, poor youth are at risk for encountering severe health problems, such as infant mortality, lack of immunization against common childhood diseases, physical abuse, neglect, and unintended injury (Carnegie Corporation of New York, 1994; McLoyd & Wilson, 1991). Moreover, compared to their nonpoor age-mates, poor youth: are 50% more likely to have physical or mental disability; are almost twice as likely to have not visited a doctor or dentist in the most recent 2 years of their lives; are 300% more likely to be high school dropouts; and are significantly more likely to be victims of violence (Simons et al., 1991).

Addressing the Crisis of America's Children Through an Integrative Theory of Human Development

Given the number of youth who are at such profound levels of risk, our society is faced with a crisis so broad that its entire fabric is in serious jeopardy (Simons et al., 1991). With so many of our nation's communities facing the likelihood of losing much of their next generation to one or more of the several high-risk behaviors increasingly present among our nation's youth, all of our children, whether or not they themselves engage in given risk behaviors, live in risk – of experiencing the adverse economic and employment conditions associated with living in a nation that is increasingly uncompetitive globally, has a diminished pool of future leaders, offers a lowered standard of living, requires lower expectations about life chances, and provides fewer and fewer opportunities for healthy, wholesome development (Lerner, 1993a, 1995).

Simply, America is wasting its most precious resource: the human capital represented by its youth (Hamburg, 1992; Lerner, 1993a, 1993b, 1995; Lerner & Miller, 1993). This destruction of human capital is a problem that cuts across race, ethnicity, gender, and rural or urban environments (Center for the Study of Social Policy, 1992, 1993; Simons et al., 1991). Accordingly, all Americans, and certainly all of our children and adolescents, are now and for the foreseeable future confronted by this crisis of youth development. Of course, the pervasiveness of this crisis does not diminish the need to prioritize our efforts. In fact, results of evaluation studies of preventive interventions indicate that great success can occur with programs directed to youth and families most in need (Dryfoos, 1990, 1994, 1995; Hamburg, 1992; Schorr, 1988). Nevertheless, the breadth of the problems affecting our nation's youth requires us to see the issues we face as pertaining to all of us, not to only a segment or subgroup of America.

Yet, despite the magnitude of this crisis, the preponderant majority of child and adolescent development research is still not focused on the behavioral risks confronting the diverse youth of America; as a consequence, there are also relatively few developmental studies of youth poverty and its sequelae. In fact, most studies published in the leading scientific journals in child development focus on investigations of European American, middle-class children (Fisher & Brennan, 1992; Graham, 1992; Hagen, Paul, Gibb, & Wolters, 1990). Moreover, most of these studies appraise children in laboratory rather than real-life settings and do not address topics that are relevant to developing, delivering, or sustaining programs preventing risk behaviors and/or the sequelae of persistent and pervasive poverty (Fisher & Brennan, 1992; Graham, 1992; McKinney et al., 1994; McLoyd, 1994).

As a result, there is a considerable substantive distance between the work of many of America's child and adolescent developmentalists and the problems facing the youth of America (Graham, 1992; McLoyd, 1994). A similar gap exists between those who seek to develop policies and programs that will help youth lead better lives within their families and communities and the scientists who can provide the intellectual base on which to build these endeavors.

These gaps, between the major foci of contemporary child and adolescent development research and the needs of poor American youth, families, and communities (Graham, 1992; McLoyd, 1994), exist despite the presence of alternative models for science and for outreach. In a report by the Michigan State University Provost's Committee on University Outreach (1993) outreach was conceived of as a form of scholarship that involves

the generation, transmission, application, and preservation of knowledge for the direct benefit of audiences to whom and for whom the university seeks to extend itself in ways that are consistent with university and unit missions. (p. 2)

In other words, outreach involves the generation, transmission, application, or preservation of scholarship for purposes developed collaboratively with communities served by the university (Lerner & Miller, 1993; Lerner, Miller, et al., 1994). When outreach scholarship is conducted in regard to youth, their families, and/or their communities – or, more generally, in regard to human development – it may be defined as the "systematic synthesis of research and application to describe, explain, and promote optimal developmental outcomes in individuals and families as they develop along the life cycle" (Fisher & Lerner, 1994, p. 4). This instance of outreach scholarship has been termed by Fisher and Lerner *applied developmental science.*

Here, however, it is important to note that this view of outreach scholarship in the field of human development emerged within land-grant colleges of home economics, human ecology, family and consumer sciences, and human development (Lerner & Miller, 1993; Miller & Lerner, 1994). The perspectives on human development produced in these institutions have provided a vision of scholarship that integrates research and outreach (Boyer, 1990, 1994; Enarson, 1989; Lynton & Elman, 1987), a vision consistent with a 1991 statement of the National Council of Administrators of Home Economics Programs stressing the following:

The mission of the profession in higher education is to conduct research and provide education programs that are integrative and are focused on reciprocal relationships among individuals, families, and their near environments toward improvement of the human condition within a dynamic world community. (p. 5)

A theory of child and family development – *developmental contextualism* (Lerner, 1986, 1991, in press; Lerner & Kauffman, 1985; Lerner & Miller, 1993; Miller & Lerner, 1994) – has emerged within land-grant institutions promoting this home economics vision of integrative, reciprocal, and dynamic relations among developing individuals, families, and contexts (see Featherman, 1983). This theory embeds the study of children in the actual families, neighborhoods, and communities in which they live. Moreover, the model, when fully implemented, synthesizes research with policy and program design, delivery, and evaluation, and involves both multiprofessional collaboration and full partnership with the communities within which science and service are being conducted (Lerner & Miller, 1993). In other words, the people that science is intended to serve are full collaborators in the process of research and outreach.

This model may be of use in narrowing the previously noted gaps between research and the practical needs of our nation's diverse youth and families. As such, we first provide some background on this perspective and then describe the model's synthetic approach to research and application.

Developmental Contextualism: An Overview

Termed *developmental contextualism*, the theoretical perspective we employ views the basic process of human development as involving changing *relations* between developing individuals and their complex (i.e., multilevel) contexts. Because the contextual levels within which human development occurs are integrated, or "fused" (Tobach & Greenberg, 1984), and include history

(Elder, 1980; Tobach, 1981), the contexts of both humans and person–context relations involve temporality (Dixon & Lerner, 1992).

Thus, in developmental contextualism the development of youth is seen as occurring in relation to the specific features of their actual, "ecologically valid" context, that is, their specific family, neighborhood, society, culture, and physical environment, and even the point in history in which they live (Lerner, 1986, 1991, 1992, 1994, in press; McKinney et al., 1994). Moreover, because developmental contextualism sees human development as occurring within a systematically changing and complex (multilevel) system (Ford & Lerner, 1992), youth influence their contexts – for example, adolescents affect their parents – as much as their contexts (their parents) influence them (Lerner, 1982; Lerner & Busch-Rossnagel, 1981).

Developmental contextualism leads, then, to descriptions of both the problems and the potentials for healthy development associated with these bidirectional relationships between youth and their contexts (Lerner, 1994). Moreover, to explain development, one must also turn to the system of relations between youth and their contexts. In order to test these explanations, one must change something about the actual context within which youth live. These changes constitute both experimental manipulations designed to test theoretical ideas about the variables that influence the course of human development *and* interventions aimed at changing for the better the life paths of children and youth (Lerner & Miller, 1993; Lerner, Miller, et al., 1994; Lerner, Terry, et al., 1994). Depending on the level of organization involved in these contextual manipulations/interventions, we may label these planned changes of the course of human life as either policies or programs (Lerner, Miller, et al., 1994).

Thus, when we evaluate the efficacy of these interventions in regard to the changes in the human life course associated with them, we learn something about the adequacy of particular policies and programs to effect desired changes among children and youth *and* we learn something basic about how human development occurs by changing relations between the developing person and his or her actual context (Lerner, 1991, 1994, in press). In other words, within developmental contextualism there is a synthesis of basic, theory-testing research and applied scholarship (or outreach) associated with program and policy design, delivery, and evaluation (Lerner & Miller, 1993; Lerner, Miller, et al., 1994; Lerner, Terry, McKinney, & Abrams, 1994).

Building on the seminal work of Dryfoos (1990, 1994), Schorr (1988), and Hamburg (1992), we use developmental contextualism to discuss both the features of successful prevention and development-enhancing programs for youth and the principles that seem to be key in the design and implementation of such programs. In addition, we discuss how the developmental contextual approach to integrating research and outreach can be used to help universities become productive partners in community coalitions addressing the problems and potentials of children and youth; we suggest that this can be done by pursuing what Weiss and Greene (1992) term *participatory-normative evaluation* and what we term *development-in-context evaluation*.

Using Developmental Contextualism as a Framework for Preventive and Enhancement Interventions

The problems of contemporary American children and youth were not produced by a single event or from a single cause. Neither poor parenting, poverty, inappropriate media influences, inadequate health care, problems of the local, state, and federal economies, a failed educational system, racism, territoriality among social service and other youth- and family-serving agencies, nor inadequate state and federal policies alone produced the problems faced by America's children. However, all these phenomena are part of the developmental system within which America's children are embedded (Ford & Lerner, 1992), and it is this system that has produced many of the problems of our nation's youth.

Key Principles for the Design of Successful Prevention Programs

Given, then, that development in the context of this system provides the bases of these problems, this same system must be engaged in any comprehensive solution to these problems (Ford & Lerner, 1992; Lerner, 1994). As such, and as Dryfoos (1990) points out, *there is no one solution to a problem of childhood or adolescence*. The developmental system may be – and, for comprehensive and integrated solutions, must be – engaged at any of the levels of organization represented in the developmental contextual view of human development, that is, levels ranging from the biological/physiological, through the psychological, interpersonal/familial, social network/community, and institutional/societal, to the cultural, physical ecological, and historical (Lerner, 1986, 1991, 1994). Thus, for any particular problem of youth behavior and development – for example, for youth violence – solutions may be sought by, for instance, entering the system at the level of the individual, of his or her family, of the community, or of the societal/cultural context (e.g., by working to affect social policies) (Mincy, 1994; Pittman & Zeldin, 1994).

A second reason why recognition of the potential for multiple solutions to a problem is important is that *high-risk behaviors are interrelated*. As noted by Dryfoos (1990), 10% of all 10- to 17-year-olds in America engage in behaviors associated with all four major categories of high-risk behavior (i.e., unsafe sex, school failure, substance abuse, and delinquency and crime). Similarly, Schorr (1988) notes that poverty is associated with several "rotten" behavioral outcomes, for example, school failure and dropping out, unemployability, prolonged welfare dependency, and delinquency and crime.

The interrelation and systemic bases of high-risk behaviors means, then, that no one type of program is likely to be of sufficient scope to address adequately all the interconnected facets of a problem. Instead, as Dryfoos (1990) notes, *a package of services is needed within each community*. However, because of the systemic interconnections of the problems this package is to address, program comprehensiveness itself will not be adequate. Rather, *integration of services is required*.

Moreover, because of the systemic nature of the problems of children and youth, the integrated services provided to address these problems should be directed to this system, not solely at the individuals within it. In other words, the relations – among individuals, institutions, and levels of the context – provide both the bases of, and potential sources of change in, the problems of children and youth. As such, *interventions should be aimed at changing the developmental system in which people are embedded rather than at changing individuals* (Dryfoos, 1990).

Moreover, because of the systemic nature of youth problems and their potential solutions, *the timing of interventions is critical* (Dryfoos, 1990; Lerner, 1984). That is, across life the developmental system not only becomes more organized, but this organization involves, in a sense, overorganization; in other words, redundant as well as alternative portions of the system function to support developmental functioning (Hebb, 1949; Schneirla, 1957). For example, problem behaviors in adolescence may involve emotional shortcomings on the part of a youth (e.g., low self-esteem) *and* poor child-rearing skills on the part of his or her parents *and* negative appraisals about, and loss of hope for, the youth by school personnel *and* a peer group that promotes norm-breaking or even illegal behavior; each part of this system may reinforce, support, or maintain the adolescent's problem behaviors. Accordingly, problems of behavior and development, once embedded in this redundantly organized system, are more difficult to alter than they would be if these same problems were embedded in the system earlier in its development (Clarke & Clarke, 1976; Ford & Lerner, 1992; Lerner, 1984).

The developmental system remains open to intervention across the life span; that is, there is relative plasticity in human behavior and development across life (Lerner, 1984). Nevertheless, the previously noted developmental changes in the organization of a system over the course of life mean that to effect a given change in behavior or development, interventions occurring later in life require greater expenditures of effort, and require involvement of greater portions of the system, than is the case earlier in life (Baltes & Baltes, 1980; Clarke & Clarke, 1976; Ford & Lerner, 1992; Lerner, 1984).

Accordingly, preventive interventions are more economical in terms of time, scope, and other resources than ameliorative interventions. An excellent illustration of this point is provided by Hamburg (1992). Young, pregnant adolescents have a higher probability than postadolescent females of giving birth to a high-risk (e.g., a low-birth-weight and/or premature) baby. Hamburg notes that the total cost of good prenatal care for a pregnant adolescent is much less than $1,000. However, the intensive care that would be needed to keep a low-birth-weight or premature baby alive is at least $1,000 a day for many weeks or months. Often, the initial hospital cost of such care is $400,000. Thus, preventive, prenatal care for pregnant adolescents would not only save a lot of money but would also eliminate the sequelae of emotional, behavioral, social, and physical problems – for both mother and infant – associated with the birth of a high-risk baby. Yet, most pregnant adolescents, especially those under 15 years of age, receive either no prenatal care or inadequate care. Moreover, about 50% of pregnant adolescent African Americans do not receive prenatal care or receive it only in the last 3 months of pregnancy. Furthermore, poor, inner-city, and isolated rural youth are among those most likely to have no or inadequate prenatal care.

Thus, as illustrated by the information Hamburg (1992) presents about the economic and human benefits of preventing high-risk births through prenatal care, preventive interventions – although insufficiently used – seem most efficacious in the promotion of healthy youth and family development. That is, although the relative plasticity of human behavior and development across the life span means that there is always some probability that the intervention will be successful, the nature of the developmental system indicates that prevention has the best likelihood of effecting desired changes.

Of course, a system that remains open to changes for the better also remains open to changes for the worse. Thus, the interventions through which human behavior and development change are *not* akin to inoculation to disease. Accordingly, one-shot interventions in human behavior and development are unlikely to effect enduring changes. Instead, they must be designed to be longitudinal in scope (Lerner & Ryff, 1978); or, as both Dryfoos (1990) and Hamburg (1992) note, *continuity of programming must be maintained across development*. Programs conceived of as life-span "convoys of social support" (Kahn & Antonucci, 1980) should be implemented in order to protect and enhance the positive effects of preventive interventions.

Clearly, such continuity of effort is expensive. However, a commitment to life-span programming must be coupled with a commitment to *discontinue programs that have proven to be ineffective* (Dryfoos, 1990). Accountability, the requirement to deliver a high-quality program, is a necessary feature of professionally responsible, ethical, and humane programs (see Hamburg, 1992). Moreover, if only those programs that have been shown to be effective are continued, then resources devoted to poor programs may be saved. Of course, making such decisions requires appropriate evaluation information.

The Development-in-Context Evaluation (DICE) Model

Promoting positive individual and social development and change through the incorporation of participatory evaluation into program design and implementation is precisely what is considered within a developmental contextual view of evaluation. Indeed, from a developmental contextual perspective, which emphasizes a community-collaborative approach to the integration of research and outreach, *program- and community-specific evaluation is a requisite for all effective programming* (Dryfoos, 1990) *and* for an understanding of the basic processes of human development (Lerner, 1991). Accordingly, such evaluations will seek to understand how a successful program may be designed, implemented, assessed, and sustained in a specific community. To attain such knowledge, a *development-in-context evaluation (DICE)* model may be pursued (Lerner, 1995; Ostrom, Lerner, & Freel, 1995). The DICE model is an instance of the sort of community-evaluator collaborative, participatory-normative approach to evaluation promoted by Weiss and Greene (1992).

Moreover, the DICE model builds on the basic tenets of the philosophy of pragmatism in general (Dixon & Lerner, 1992), and on Charles Sanders Peirce's (1931) pragmatic maxim specifically. Pierce's conception of pragmatism focuses on the results or consequences that will occur if one accepts and acts on any idea, theory, model, policy, or innovation. Several ideas flow from this seemingly straightforward maxim. The five key ideas guiding the DICE model will now be discussed.

1. Think Holistically or Contextually

Nothing is gained by making a theoretical or practical distinction between the program/innovation and the context within which it occurs. Programs always exist within a particular community context, settings with their specific array of people, agencies, organizations, values, and history. One cannot understand or evaluate a program independent of this context. Similarly, program sustainability requires marshaling the context in support of the program.

Moreover, documentation of the program-context system will aid other communities in attempts to replicate effective programs. Understanding the contextual embeddedness of a program from another community will assist a second community in appraising not only whether a program per se has attractive components but also whether the context of the program is sufficiently similar to its own to make replication feasible.

2. Include as Many Voices or Stakeholders as Possible

To the extent that some perspectives and voices are excluded from relevant and decisive conversations, the consequences related to those points of view are silenced. As a corollary, evaluators must be competent in understanding the cultural diversity of the various stakeholders involved in the program (Dryfoos, 1990) and the different points in the life span (i.e., the different developmental levels) of the youth, families, and other community stakeholders (e.g., aged community members with no young children) with whom the evaluators work.

3. The Focus Is on the Actions Involved in Forming Effective Programs

As Jacobs (1988, pp. 49–50) noted, evaluation is best viewed as the systematic collection and analysis of program-related data that can be used to understand how a program is functioning and/or what consequences the program has for the participants. Thus, from the perspective of the DICE model, knowing after a program is completed whether some "final" outcome has been produced is less important than learning how to build an effective program over time. Although final outcomes are obviously crucial targets in program development, knowledge of whether particular outcomes occur is not useful *unless* it is coupled with knowledge of how, why, or the conditions under which a program did or did not lead to a specified outcome. Although program outcome information can be obtained from only one-time assessment, learning about program processes requires repeated assessment. Thus, the DICE model promotes a longitudinal approach to evaluation.

4. Reality Is Complex and Socially Contructed (i.e., Based on the Perspectives Present Within the Community Context)

A huge number of details may be assimilated about any program and about the context within which it is embedded. In addition, there are situations in which cause and effect are subtle; their effects over time are not obvious, and these effects may change over the course of development of a program. Thus, once again, longitudinal evaluation is necessary. Moreover, in order to construct a sufficiently rich mosaic, it is necessary to include as many of the differing perspectives, or frames of reference, present in the community as possible. In other words, it is not possible to learn about a program or its context by appraising only one or even a few variables. Accordingly, multiple variables assessed longitudinally must be appraised.

5. Evaluation Is a Core and Essential Component of Every Program and Should Be Built Into the Program's Day-to-Day Functioning

There are numerous purposes for an evaluation (Jacobs, 1988). Primary among these are that evaluations should be formative and should have a utilization focus. As Cronbach and Associates (1980) noted: "The better and more widely the workings of social programs are understood, the more rapidly policy will evolve and the more the programs will contribute to a better quality of life" (pp. 2–3). As a corollary, evaluations must not detract from the operation of the program and, in fact, should seek to form the basis of the continued functioning of the program (Weiss & Greene, 1992).

Using Asset Mapping to Launch Program and Evaluation Activities

To implement these pragmatic ideas, evaluations and the programs of which they are an inherent initial part must *build from the inside out* (McKnight & Kretzmann, 1993); that is, the initiation of programs and evaluations must involve looking for solutions or assets within the community. Kretzmann and McKnight (1993) observe that there are two paths that communities can take when seeking solutions to pressing problems. The first, and more traditional approach, begins by focusing on a community's needs, deficiencies, and problems; the second begins with a clear commitment to discovering a community's capacities and assets.

The first approach provides images of needy, problematic, and deficient communities populated by needy, problematic, and deficient people, and leads to programs that teach people about their problems and the value of "service" provided *for* them as the answer to their problems. The people begin to view themselves as people with special needs that can only be met by outsiders. Young people can begin to see themselves "as fundamentally deficient, victims incapable of taking charge of their lives or their community's future" (Kretzmann & McKnight, 1993, p. 4). Focusing only on needs or deficits leads to other problems as well: for example, fragmentation, funding going to service providers rather than to the community, undermining of the local leadership, and deepening of the cycle of dependence, all of which create a maintenance and survival strategy and thwart community development.

The second path is capacity focused and leads to the development of programs based on the capacities, skills, and assets of children, parents, and other community stakeholders. From this perspective, solutions to problems must come from the inside out. A thorough map of community assets would begin with an inventory of the capacities of the children, parents, and other residents of the community. This would be augmented with an inventory of community organizations; such formal and informal organizations are the means through which citizens assemble to solve problems or share common interests. Finally, the asset map includes the more formal institutions located in the community. Individuals, community organizations, and local institutions constitute the asset base for every community.

This second path to community problem solving is based on three straightforward and interrelated characteristics. First, the process of building programs should be asset based. The program should start with what is in the community – the capacities of the residents and of the programs, agencies, and other institutions based in the area – not with what is absent. Second, the program should be focused on building an agenda for program development based on the perspectives, values, and problem-solving capacities of local residents, associations, and institutions. Consistent with the participatory-normative approach to evaluation promoted by Weiss and Greene (1992), the internal, community-based focus stresses "the primacy of local definition, investment, creativity, hope, and control" (Kretzmann & McKnight, 1993, p. 9). Third, this path is predicated on the importance of building strong, positive relationships among local residents, associations, and institutions – on creating a collaborative, caring community.

Features of DICE

Taken together, the ideas of pragmatism and asset mapping provide an approach to evaluating how programs may enhance the development of youth and families within their community context. As an example of this approach, the Institute for Children, Youth, and Families at Michigan State University is currently using the DICE model in Flint, Michigan, involving a community-collaborative evaluation of two high school–based teen health centers, and in Lansing, Michigan, involving the development and evaluation of a youth violence prevention program at the Black Child and Family Institute (Lerner, Lerner, et al., 1994). As illustrated by these collaborations, the process of faculty–community collaboration involved in the DICE model eschews external, or outside-in, summative-, or outcome-oriented evaluations conducted by "experts" from outside of the community. Instead, the community's vision and values are seen as central in formulating the aims and indices of progress and of success for the program. Moreover, based on these community views, the community–faculty collaborative team works together to determine the information to be collected, to decide how it will be gathered, to determine how it may be analyzed, and to create a strategy for its use – both to form a better program and to leverage resources to sustain the program. Thus, as exemplified by these community-collaborative activities focused on issues of youth health, DICE evaluations have four components: (1) evaluation design, (2) data collection, (3) data analysis, and (4) using evaluation findings to promote sustained community change.

1. Evaluation Design

The hallmark of evaluation design is that it pays attention to stakeholders' perspectives (e.g., about programs and possible solutions), to assets, and to the diverse array of sound evaluation methods available to address the issues present in a community. Thus, this phase of the evaluation constitutes a key instance of the importance of a colearning model, and of the potential fruitfulness of a community–university collaboration.

University faculty may know how to identify, organize, and help deploy community-based assets; they also may know how to enable diverse stakeholders to voice their values and perspectives on community issues; finally, faculty may know about the uses and limitations of differing types of evaluation methodology and about how to develop new evaluation tools (e.g., assessment or screening instruments). However, university faculty must learn from community members about what development in the particular community context means. Faculty must learn from the community what people, agencies, programs, and institutions should be included in an asset map. Faculty must network with community members to learn (1) the issues that the community wants to address and that are seen as most salient, and thus (2) the people who must be included in the program and its evaluation. Finally, faculty must learn what specific evaluation tools are necessary and appropriate to deploy or develop in the community.

The goal of DICE, then, is to work collaboratively with the relevant stakeholders to (1) identify and describe the problem, (2) articulate program goals, and (3) identify the questions that the community wants to have answered. Within the boundaries set by the stakeholder–evaluator collaboration, the strongest and most appropriate evaluation design, for the community and for the issues it considers most vital, is formulated.

2. Data Collection

Given the array of issues that arise and methods that may need to be used in any given community, the possible methods of data collection must be similarly multifaceted. As noted previously, the range of information-gathering strategies encompasses a broad array of both qualitative and quantitative techniques (Weiss & Greene, 1992). However, the goals of any technique are (1) to provide the information that youth, families, and other community stakeholders will need to address the questions of interest; (2) to monitor (assess) the ongoing effectiveness of the program; (3) to improve the functioning of the program; and (4) to assess the extent to which program goals are being realized.

3. Data Analysis

By using both qualitative and quantitative methods, DICE can engage in "triangulation," that is, determine whether similar information is obtained by differing methods. If such "convergence" occurs, then it is more certain that the information is valid (and not just the artifactual product of a specific method).

Differing methodologies are sensitive to different aspects of program functioning. DICE is predicated on attention to the natural ecology of the community (Bronfenbrenner, 1979) and takes a developmental systems view (Ford & Lerner, 1992) of the interconnections among the levels of organization that exist within this ecology – including the relationships among youth, families, and the social and institutional networks within which they are embedded.

Accordingly, just as multiple methods must be used to ascertain the validity of information and to appraise the multiple levels of the developmental system, data analysis involves more than one computational technique or an analysis of information derived from one point in time (e.g., as might be the case if only program outcomes were of interest). Instead, data analysis is focused on the actual operations and impacts of the program as they occur longitudinally, that is, over the course of development of the program and of the participating youth and families.

A key goal here is to obtain interpretations of the day-to-day realities of the people, programs, and contexts involved in the program. Again, colearning is essential: The participants themselves are the experts about the meaning of development in their community context; they are the source of important data interpretations. Their values, and the meaning they attach to the ongoing information developed about the program, will be a critical source of community empowerment and, as a result, of the community's capacity to sustain the program (Weiss & Greene, 1992).

4. Using Evaluation Findings to Promote Sustained Community Change

Through collaborating with community stakeholders in interpreting the data obtained about the program, evaluators assist stakeholders in determining whether the findings are appropriate for the needs of the community. If so, stakeholders will be in a position to judge which features of the program should be maintained, revised, or eliminated. If not, stakeholders will be better able to clarify for the evaluator the sort of information they need in order to make such judgments. In either case, however, the capacity of the stakeholders to make better-informed decisions about their community will be enhanced.

This increased capacity constitutes a new asset for the community; it is a value-added contribution of the participatory-normative evaluation approach forwarded by Weiss and Greene (1992) and found in the DICE model. Moreover, the community's capacity to enhance the development of programs within its boundaries will be enhanced. This enhancement will occur when program-pertinent information is developed through stakeholder–evaluator collaboration. Such information will almost necessarily eventually be developed, given the increased capacity of the community and of the colearning involved in the university–community partnership. This second instance of capacity building constitutes another value-added contribution of the approach to evaluation embodied in the DICE model.

Finally, the program itself, initiated, maintained, and improved over time by an increasingly empowered community, is a third new asset introduced by the collaborative evaluation process. Accordingly, the capacity of youth, families, and other community stakeholders to enact and sustain desired programs is likely to be furthered significantly. This will occur as a consequence of (1) the community's enhanced abilities in program design, implementation, and evaluation; (2) community members' increased knowledge of themselves, gained through the data they themselves helped collect and analyze (e.g., through assessments such as asset mapping and through the ongoing data collected in the process of forming a better program); and (3) the community's increased experiences with successful decision making. Such decisions are a constant part of the process of participatory evaluation procedures such as those in the DICE model.

A Template for Creating Collaborative Communities

The DICE model represents the community-collaborative, participatory-normative approach to evaluation – *and* to program design, program development, and community empowerment – promoted by Weiss and her associates (e.g., Jacobs, 1988; Miller, 1993; Weiss, 1987a, 1987b; Weiss & Greene, 1992; Weiss & Jacobs, 1988). As such, evaluators following the DICE model do the following:

1. Work with community members to identify the problems or issues to which the program will be directed.
2. Engage the members of the community in (a) planning the evaluation; (b) deciding on the nature of any preliminary, developmental, and outcome information sought about the program; (c) collecting relevant data; and (d) documenting and interpreting the information derived from the evaluation.
3. Collaborate with the community in using the information derived from the evaluation – for example, in making any "midcourse" corrections deemed necessary to enhance program effectiveness and/or in identifying any resulting changes in the nature of the problem that led to the initiation of the program.

Moreover, evaluations using the DICE model build from a qualitative understanding of the community and of the program goals envisioned by community members; as well, evaluators collaborate with the community in the process of gaining the required knowledge. This is why such evaluations, at their core, involve *colearning* between the evaluators and the community. In addition, the community-collaborative approach develops the community's capacity to sustain the program after the evaluation is completed; indeed, the community is empowered to incorporate continued evaluations into its future plans about the program.

Finally, such evaluations are predicated on attention to the diversity that exists within the community – to the specific goals, values, and meaning systems that are present in the community and that shape the program. Recognition of the importance of such diversity appears critical in the design of effective prevention programs. As noted by Dryfoos (1990), programs that pay attention to cultural and lifestyle diversity, as well as to individual diversity, are more likely to succeed.

In sum, the concepts of developmental contextualism and the features and principles of successful prevention programs, especially when they involve a participatory, DICE approach to evaluation, appear to be highly consonant. Accordingly, the application of developmental contextual ideas and the principles of successful programs should assist in the design, implementation, evaluation, and sustainability of programs effectively addressing the problems of children and adolescents. Although, by necessity, specific features of such programs will vary with the problem(s) addressed and the community involved, it is clear from the preceding discussion that these programs will share some general features. They will involve integrated, communitywide, multiagency (or institutional) collaborations that link youth, families, and the larger community together in a sustained effort.

We believe that, in general, partnerships between the research and program professional communities are critical if integrated research and outreach – and, more specifically, the participatory approach to evaluation involved in the DICE model – are to succeed in producing effective programs for America's children and adolescents. Moreover, research and program professional partnerships will be the vital base upon which universities will be able to build effective means to respond to the problems facing America's children.

Such partnerships should begin with issues identification through broadly constituted community–university teams; these teams will be facilitated by community-based program professionals to ensure that the partnership has knowledge of, and legitimacy in, the community. University structures should then be developed to provide an integrated university capacity to work with communities on the issues raised in the identification process. Then, with community partners who invite collaboration, research and programming colleagues can join in the building of collaborative communities by doing the following:

1. Starting integrated efforts at program development, program evaluation, and community empowerment for sustainability.
2. These efforts are predicated on asset mapping for positive youth develop-

ment; this process serves to identify, organize, and deploy *integratively* the strengths of the community.

Conclusions

Ultimately, we must all continue to educate ourselves about the best means to promote enhanced life chances for *all* of our youth, but especially those whose potential contributions to our nation are most in danger of being wasted (Lerner, 1993a, 1995). As our presentation of the DICE model suggests, we believe that a collaborative, colearning system engaging the university and the community represents a key means to educate ourselves about effective programs. However, the thorough collaborations envisioned by the DICE model (Lerner, 1995; Ostrom et al., 1995), both within universities and between universities and communities, have not seriously been attempted. They may not work.

Nonetheless, the fragmented and uncoordinated current responses to the issues and needs of America's diverse children and families have not only not worked, they have failed miserably. If we are to pull our youth, and our nation, back from the precipice of generation destruction on which they now hang, we have to envision and enact new models that have reason and evidence to support their viability.

The thorough, participatory, and empowering collaboration involved in the DICE model may be such an approach, especially if it is implemented in partnership with strong, empowered communities. Policies promoting such coalitions will be an integral component of a national youth development policy aimed at creating caring communities having the capacity to nurture the healthy development of our children and youth. The future of America may hang in the balance as we test the usefulness of this model and develop policies enabling this and other community capacity-building endeavors to be developed, refined, and disseminated.

References

Baltes, P. B., & Baltes, M. M. (1980). Plasticity and variability in psychological aging: Methodological and theoretical issues. In G. E. Gurski (Ed.), *Determining the effects of aging on the central nervous system* (pp. 41–66). Berlin: Schering.

Boyer, E. L. (1990). *Scholarship reconsidered: Priorities of the professoriate.* Princeton, NJ: Carnegie Foundation for the Advancement of Teaching.

Boyer, E. L. (1994, March 9). Creating the new American college [Point of View column]. *The Chronicle of Higher Education*, p. A48.

Bronfenbrenner, U. (1979). *The ecology of human development.* Cambridge, MA: Harvard University Press.

Carnegie Corporation of New York. (1992, December). *A matter of time: Risk and opportunity in the nonschool hours.* Available from Carnegie Council on Adolescent Development, P.O. Box 753, Waldorf, MD 20604.

Carnegie Corporation of New York. (1994, April). *Starting points: Meeting the needs of our youngest children*. Available from Carnegie Corporation of New York, P.O. Box 753, Waldorf, MD 20604.

Carnegie Council on Adolescent Development (1989). *Turning points: Preparing American youth for the 21st century*. Available from Carnegie Council on Adolescent Development, 11 Dupont Circle, N.W., Washington, DC 20036.

Center for the Study of Social Policy. (1992). *Kids Count data book*. Washington, DC: Author.

Center for the Study of Social Policy. (1993). *Kids Count data book*. Washington, DC: Author.

Children's Defense Fund. (1992). *Child poverty up nationally and in 33 states*. Washington, DC: Author.

Clarke, A. M., & Clarke, A. D. B. (Eds.). (1976). *Early experience: Myth and evidence*. New York: Free Press.

Cronbach, L., & Associates (1980). *Toward reform of program evaluation*. San Francisco: Jossey-Bass.

Dixon, R. A., & Lerner, R. M. (1992). A history of systems in developmental psychology. In M. H. Bornstein & M. E. Lamb (Eds.), *Developmental psychology: An advanced textbook* (3rd ed., pp. 3–58). Hillsdale, NJ: Erlbaum.

Dryfoos, J. G. (1990). *Adolescents at risk: Prevalence and prevention*. New York: Oxford University Press.

Dryfoos, J. G. (1994). *Full service schools: A revolution in health and social services for children, youth and families*. San Francisco: Jossey-Bass.

Dryfoos, J. G. (1995). Full service schools: Revolution or fad? *Journal of Research on Adolescence, 5,* 147–172.

Elder, G. H., Jr. (1980). Adolescence in historical perspective. In J. Adelson (Ed.), *Handbook of adolescent psychology* (pp. 3–46). New York: Wiley.

Enarson, H. L. (1989). *Revitalizing the landgrant mission*. Blackburg: Virginia Polytechnic Institute and State University.

Featherman, D. L. (1983). Life-span perspectives in social science research. In P. B. Baltes & O. G. Brim, Jr. (Eds.), *Life-span development and behavior* (Vol. 5, pp. 1–57). New York: Academic.

Fisher, C. B., & Brennan, M. (1992). Application and ethics in developmental psychology. In D. L. Featherman, R. M. Lerner, & M. Perlmutter (Eds.), *Life-span development and behavior*, (Vol. 11, pp. 189–219). Hillsdale, NJ: Erlbaum.

Fisher, C. B., & Lerner, R. M. (1994). Foundations of applied developmental psychology. In C. B. Fisher & R. M. Lerner (Eds.), *Applied developmental psychology* (pp. 3–20). New York: McGraw-Hill.

Ford, D. L., & Lerner, R. M. (1992). *Developmental systems theory: An integrative approach*. Newbury Park, CA: Sage.

Graham, S. (1992). "Most of the subjects were white and middle class": Trends in published research on African Americans in selected APA journals, 1970–1989. *American Psychologist, 5,* 629–639.

Hagen, J. W., Paul, B., Gibb, S., & Wolters, C. (1990, March). *Trends in research as reflected by publications in Child Development: 1930–1989*. Paper presented at the Biennial Meeting of the Society for Research on Adolescence, Atlanta, GA.

Hamburg, D. A. (1992). *Today's children: Creating a future for a generation in crisis*. New York: Time Books.

Hebb, D. O. (1949). *The organization of behavior*. New York: Wiley.

Hernandez, D. J. (1993). *America's children: Resources from family, government, and the economy*. New York: Russell Sage Foundation.

Huston, A. C. (Ed.). (1991). *Children in poverty: Child development and public policy*. Cambridge: Cambridge University Press.

Huston, A. C., McLoyd, V. C., & Garcia Coll, C. T. (1994). Children and poverty: Issues in contemporary research. *Child Development, 65,* 275–282.

Jacobs, F. H. (1988). The five-tiered approach to evaluation: Context and implementation. In H. Weiss & F. Jacobs (Eds.), *Evaluating family programs* (pp. 37–68). Hawthorne, NY: Aldine de Gruyter.

Jensen, L. (1988). Rural–urban differences in the utilization of ameliorative effects of welfare programs. *Policy Studies Review, 7*, 782–794.

Kahn, R. L., & Antonucci, T. C. (1980). Convoys over the life course: Attachment, roles, and social support. In P. B. Baltes & O. G. Brim, Jr. (Eds.), *Life-span development and behavior* (Vol. 3, pp. 253–268). Hillsdale, NJ: Erlbaum.

Klerman, L. V. (1991). The health of poor children: Problems and programs. In A. C. Huston (Ed.), *Children in poverty: Child development and public policy* (pp. 1–22). Cambridge: Cambridge University.

Kretzmann, J. P., & McKnight, J. L. (1993). *Building communities from the inside out: A path toward finding and mobilizing a community's assets.* Available from Center for Urban Affairs and Policy research, Northwestern University, 2040 Sheridan Road, Evanston, IL 60208.

Lerner, R. M. (1982). Children and adolescents as producers of their own development. *Developmental Review, 2*, 342–370.

Lerner, R. M. (1984). *On the nature of human plasticity.* New York: Cambridge University Press.

Lerner, R. M. (1986). *Concepts and theories of human development* (2nd ed.). New York: Random House.

Lerner, R. M. (1991). Changing organism–context relations as the basic process of development: A developmental-contextual perspective. *Developmental Psychology, 27*, 27–32.

Lerner, R. M. (1992). *Final solutions: Biology, prejudice, and genocide.* University Park: Pennsylvania State University Press.

Lerner, R. M. (1993a). Investment in youth: The role of home economics in enhancing the life chances of America's children. *AHEA Monograph Series, 1*, 5–34.

Lerner, R. M. (1993b). Early adolescence: Toward an agenda for the integration of research, policy, and intervention. In R. M. Lerner (Ed.), *Early adolescence: Perspectives on research, policy, and intervention* (pp. 1–13). Hillsdale, NJ: Erlbaum.

Lerner, R. M. (1994). Schools and adolescents. In P. C. McKenry & S. M. Gavazzi (Eds.), *Visions 2010: Families and adolescents* (Vol. 2, No. 1, pp. 14–15, 42–43). Minneapolis: National Council on Family Relations.

Lerner, R. M. (1995). *America's youth in crisis: Challenges and options for programs and policies.* Thousand Oaks, CA: Sage.

Lerner, R. M. (in press). Diversity and context in research, policy, and programs for children and adolescence: A developmental contextual perspective. In G. K. Brookins & M. B. Spencer (Eds.), *Ethnicity and diversity: Implications for research policies.* Hillsdale, NJ: Erlbaum.

Lerner, R. M., & Busch-Rossnagel, N. A. (Eds.). (1981). *Individuals as producers of their development: A life-span perspective.* New York: Academic Press.

Lerner, R. M., & Kauffman, M. B. (1985). The concept of development in contextualism. *Developmental Review, 5*, 309–333.

Lerner, R. M., Lerner, J. V., Nguyen, H. X., Pease, M. L., Reiling, D. M., Firlan, U. S., White, M. D., & Freel, M. A. (1994, November 23). *Using community-collaborative evaluation research to build the capacities of youth, families, and communities to promote positive youth development: A community-university model of outreach scholarship* (Progress Report 1: A report to the Office of the Michigan State University Vice Provost for University Outreach by the Institute for Children, Youth, and Families "Evaluation Research" Group). Available from the Institute for Children, Youth, and Families, Suite 27 Kellogg Center, Michigan State University, East Lansing, MI 48824.

Lerner, R. M., & Miller, J. R. (1993). Integrating human development research and intervention for America's children: The Michigan State University model. *Journal of Applied Developmental Psychology, 14*, 347–364.

Lerner, R. M., Miller, J. R., Knott, J. H., Corey, K. E., Bynum, T. S., Hoopfer, L. C., McKinney, M. H., Abrams, L. A., Hula, R. C., & Terry, P. A. (1994). Integrating scholarship and outreach in human development research, policy, and service: A developmental perspective. In D. L. Featherman, R. M. Lerner, & M. Perlmutter (Eds.), *Life-span development and behavior* (Vol. 12, pp. 249–273). Hillsdale, NJ: Erlbaum.

Lerner, R. M., & Ryff, C. D. (1978). Implementation of the life-span view of human development: The sample case of attachment. In P. B. Baltes (Ed.), *Life-span development and behavior* (Vol. 1, pp. 1–44). New York: Academic.

Lerner, R. M., Terry, P. A., McKinney, M. H., & Abrams, L. A. (1994). Addressing child poverty within the context of a community-collaborative university: Comments on Fabes, Martin, and Smith (1994) and McLoyd (1994). *Family and Consumer Sciences Research Journal, 23*, 67–75.

Little, R. R. (1993, March). *What's working for today's youth: The issues, the programs, and the learnings*. Paper presented at an ICYF Fellows Colloquium, Michigan State University, East Lansing.

Lynton, E. A., & Elman, S. E. (1987). *New priorities for the university: Meeting society's needs for applied knowledge and competent individuals*. San Francisco: Jossey-Bass.

McKinney, M., Abrams, L. A., Terry, P. A., & Lerner, R. M. (1994). Child development research and the poor children of America: A call for a developmental contextual approach to research and outreach. *Family and Consumer Sciences Research Journal, 23*, 26–42.

McKnight, J. L., & Kretzmann, J. P. (1993). Mapping community capacity. *Michigan State University Community and Economic Development Program Community News*, pp. 1–4.

McLoyd, V. C. (1994). Research in the service of poor and ethnic/racial minority children: A moral imperative. *Family and Consumer Sciences Research Journal, 23*, 56–66.

McLoyd, V. C., & Wilson, L. (1991). The strain of living poor: Parenting, social support, and child mental health. In A. C. Huston (Ed.), *Children in poverty: Child development and public policy* (pp. 105–135). Cambridge: Cambridge University Press.

Michigan State University Provost's Committee on University Outreach. (1993). *University outreach at Michigan State University: Extending knowledge to serve society*. East Lansing: Michigan State University Press.

Miller, J. R., & Lerner, R. M. (1994). Integrating research and outreach: Developmental contextualism and the human ecological perspective. *Home Economics Forum, 7*, 21–28.

Miller, P. B. (1993). *Building villages to raise our children: Evaluation*. Cambridge, MA: Harvard Family Research Project.

Mincy, R. B. (Ed.) (1994). *Nurturing young black males: Challenges to agencies, programs, and social policy*. Washington, DC: Urban Institute Press.

National Council of Aministrators of Home Economics Programs. (1991 October). *Creating a vision: The profession for the next century*. Report of the working conference, Pine Mountain, GA.

National Research Council. (1993). *Losing generations: Adolescents in high-risk settings*. Washington, DC: National Academy Press.

Ostrom, C. W., Lerner, R. M., & Freel, M. A. (1995). Building the capacity of youth and families through university-community collaborations: The development-in-context evaluation (DICE) model. *Journal of Adolescent Research, 10*, 427–448.

Peirce, C. S. (1931). The three kinds of goodness [lecture 5]. In C. Hartshorne, P. Weiss, & A. Burks (Eds.), *Collected papers of Charles Sanders Peirce* (Vol. 5, pp. 77–93). Cambridge, MA: Harvard University Press.

Pittman, K. J., & Zeldin, S. (1994). From deterrence to development: Shifting the focus of youth programs for African-American males. In R. B. Mincy (Ed.), *Nurturing young black males: Challenges to agencies, programs, and social policy* (pp. 165–186). Washington, DC: Urban Institute Press.

Schneirla, T. C. (1957). The concept of development in comparative psychology. In D. B. Harris (Ed.), *The concept of development* (pp. 78–108). Minneapolis: University of Minnesota Press.

Schorr, L. B. (1988). *Within our reach: Breaking the cycle of disadvantage*. New York: Doubleday.

Schorr, L. B. (1991). Effective programs for children growing up in concentrated poverty. In A. C. Huston (Ed.), *Children in poverty: Child development and public policy* (pp. 260–281). Cambridge: Cambridge University Press.

Simons, J. M., Finlay, B., & Yang, A. (1991). *The adolescent and young adult fact book*. Washington, DC: Children's Defense Fund.

Tobach, E. (1981). Evolutionary aspects of the activity of the organism and its development. In R. M. Lerner & N. A. Busch-Rossnagel (Eds.), *Individuals as producers of their development: A life-span perspective* (pp. 37–68). New York: Academic Press.

Tobach, E., & Greenberg, G. (1984). The significance of T. C. Schneirla's contribution to the concept of levels of integration. In G. Greenberg & E. Tobach (Eds.), *Behavioral evolution and integrative levels* (pp. 1–7). Hillsdale, NJ: Erlbaum.

U.S. Bureau of the Census. (1991, August). *The Hispanic population in the United States: March, 1991* (Current Popualtion Reports, Series P-20, No. 455). Washington, DC: U.S. Government Printing Office.

Weiss, H. B. (1987a). Family support and education in early childhood programs. In S. Kagan, D. Powell, B. Weissbourd, & E. Zigler (Eds.), *America's family support programs* (pp. 133–160). New Haven, CT: Yale University Press.

Weiss, H. B. (1987b). Evaluating social programs: What have we learned? *Society, 25,* 40–45.

Weiss, H. B., & Greene, J. C. (1992). An empowerment partnership for family support and education programs and evaluations. *Family Science Review, 5,* 131–148.

Weiss, H. B., & Jacobs, F. (Eds.). (1988). *Evaluating family programs*. Hawthorne, NY: Aldine Press.

Wilson, W. J. (1987). *The truly disadvantaged: The inner city, the underclass, and public policy*. Chicago: University of Chicago Press.

World Health Organization. (1986). WHO study group on young people and "Health for all by the year 2000." In *Young people's health: A challenge for society* (Technical Rep. Series, No. 731). Geneva: World Health Organization.

World Health Organization. (1993). *The health of young people: A challenge and a promise*. Geneva: World Health Organization.

20   Developmental Transitions During Adolescence: Health Promotion Implications

Jennifer L. Maggs, John Schulenberg,
and Klaus Hurrelmann

Health promotion is a comprehensive and ambitious activity that entails a preventive approach to all factors that influence people's quality of life (Perry & Jessor, 1985). The World Health Organization (WHO, 1986) defines *health* comprehensively and positively as "a state of complete physical, mental, and social well-being and not merely the absence of disease or infirmity." Correspondingly, to be effective, health promotion efforts ought to be comprehensive. That is, to the extent possible, they should consider historical, ecological, cultural, political, economic, social, psychological, and biological factors, integrating aspects of public health, education, psychology, sociology, nursing, and medicine in an attempt to facilitate the optimal development and well-being of all persons. Central to this concept is the idea that healthy development can be promoted by structural and political initiatives, as well as by direct assistance to individuals and families (e.g., Feagans, 1992; Lerner, Ostrom, & Freel, chapter 19, this volume; Noack & Kracke, chapter 3, this volume; Perry, Kelder, & Komro, 1993; U.S. Congress, 1991).

The WHO (1986) charter on health promotion developed a series of basic guidelines for a comprehensive approach to health. Health is expressly understood as an essential component of daily life, with major emphasis being placed on the importance of personal and social resources. *Health promotion* is described as a process that enables individuals to acquire a greater degree of autonomy and responsibility for their own health. The aim of health promotion is to influence the social and natural environment with respect to health and at the same time to develop individual competence. To achieve a state of health and well-being, it is essential that individuals and groups be able to fulfill their needs, be aware of and achieve their hopes and wishes, and have an influence on their environments (e.g., Compas, 1993; Hurrelmann & Lasser, 1993; Millstein, Petersen, & Nightingale, 1993; Nurmi, chapter 15, this volume).

Jennifer Maggs and John Schulenberg would like to acknowledge that their efforts in preparing this chapter were supported in part by grants from the Social Sciences and Humanities Research Council of Canada and the National Institute on Alcohol Abuse and Alcoholism (AA06324).

From a developmental perspective, health promotion should involve attempts to support, alter, or redirect developmental processes that are already in motion. That is, the goal is not only to alter current attitudes and behaviors, but also to have an enduring impact on developmental trajectories (e.g., Baltes & Danish, 1980; Cairns & Cairns, 1994; Danish, Smyer, & Nowak, 1980; Vondracek, Lerner, & Schulenberg, 1986). The term *developmental intervention* has been used to describe such efforts, which may target any aspect of individuals (e.g., biochemical, cognitive, social) or their environments, and may take place at any point, or across several points, in the life span (Danish et al., 1980; Fisher et al., 1993; Vondracek et al., 1986). In this chapter, given our comprehensive definition of health, we view developmental intervention as a special case of health promotion in which the goal is to promote health as well as to facilitate optimal development.

Adolescence is a particularly important phase of life for developmental intervention for several reasons. In the domain of physical health, the primary causes of mortality and morbidity during adolescence, as in adulthood, are related to preventable social, environmental, and behavioral factors (Crockett, chapter 2, this volume; Irwin & Millstein, 1986, 1992; U.S. Congress, 1991). Many health problems of adulthood have their origin in behavioral patterns that are formed during adolescence, such as smoking, exercise, and eating habits (Friedman, 1993; Jessor, 1984). Furthermore, adolescence is a time when coping styles begin to consolidate (Compas, 1993, 1995; Kazdin, 1993; Nurmi, chapter 15, and Petersen, Leffert, Graham, Alwin, & Ding, chapter 18, this volume). Habits and lifestyles formed during these years are likely to continue throughout life (Hamburg, Millstein, Mortimer, Nightingale, & Petersen, 1993; Jessor, 1984; Susman, Dorn, Feagans, & Ray, 1992). In addition, during adolescence and young adulthood, many consequential life decisions are made concerning educational attainment, occupational choices, relationship and family formation, and lifestyle options, making adolescence an important formative period likely to yield long-term benefits of health-promoting efforts.

Clearly, it is not subjectively attractive or rewarding to behave in an objectively healthy way in every situation. In adolescence, as in adulthood, behaviors that may compromise well-being are an integral and pleasurable part of personal lifestyles. Risky behaviors such as smoking, drinking, and sexual activity can fulfill certain essential functions for adolescents such as identity exploration, coping with stress, gaining admission to or acceptance by certain peer groups, opposing adult authority, or indicating a transition to a more mature status (e.g., Chassin, Presson, & Sherman, 1989; Hurrelmann, 1990; Irwin & Millstein, 1992; Jessor, 1984; Maggs, Almeida, & Galambos, 1995; Silbereisen & Noack, 1988; Zucker, 1979). The fulfillment of these strong, immediate, and developmentally normative needs will invariably have greater valence and urgency than the much more abstract and distal goal of promoting optimal physical, emotional, or social development (e.g., Brown, Dolcini, & Leventhal, chapter 7, and Maggs, chapter 13, this volume; Millstein, 1993). This contradiction between current desires and future health is exacerbated by the inherent difficulty of understandng the probabilities of current behaviors posing threats to well-being (Beyth-Marom & Fischhoff, chapter 5, this volume). Knowledge about a health risk alone is thus unlikely to play a decisive role in the determination of adolescents' health-relevant activities (e.g., Hansen, 1992; Hawkins, Catalano, & Miller, 1992; Millstein et al., 1993).

The specific life context of adolescents, and particularly the psychosocial functions of health-damaging behaviors within that context, have received relatively little empirical attention (Franzkowiak, 1986; Irwin & Millstein, 1992; Jessor, 1984; Nordlohne, 1992; Silbereisen, Noack, & Schoenpflug, 1994). Consequently, prevention efforts based solely on knowledge acquisition and fear arousal have failed to appeal to adolescents' ways of thinking about life in general and health in particular, due to their focus on illness prevention and their neglect of much more urgent personal and social needs (Dielman, 1994; Hansen, 1992; Millstein, 1993). Health promotion efforts should assist adolescents to cope with and fulfill their normative developmental needs in a constructive manner.

The chapters in this volume have illustrated a framework that centers on the links between health risks and normative and nonnormative developmental transitions during adolescence. A central premise is that through greater understanding, facilitation, and support of these transitions, adolescents' health and well-being will be enhanced and optimal development will result. In this final chapter, we first provide a summary of the developmental transitions of adolescence and briefly discuss some of their health promotion implications, as reflected in the previous chapters. Next, basic issues concerning adolescent health promotion programs are presented, followed by a discussion of health promotion in schools and the broader community. Finally, we provide some concluding comments about adolescent health and optimal development.

Developmental Transitions of Adolescence: Health Promotion Implications

As the preceding chapters have shown, the passage toward adult roles, relationships, and responsibilities involves fundamental changes in every domain of life. Experiences and decisions during the adolescent years have the potential to build character and competence, develop skills for coping with life's challenges, and enhance health and well-being. At the same time, normative and nonnormative developmental transitions expose adolescents to many challenges and hazards that may jeopardize their optimal development and health. During the transitions into and out of adolescence, how can optimal development and health be supported and enhanced?

Adolescent Transitions in Context

As we discussed in Chapter 1 of this volume, effectively addressing this question necessitates an interdisciplinary perspective that attends to several influences ranging from sociocultural to biological ones. Sociocultural trends over the past several decades have had important implications for adolescent health and development (Brooks-Gunn & Paikoff, chapter 8, Crockett, chapter 2, and Schulenberg, Maggs, & Hurrelmann, chapter 1, this volume). How these historical changes influence adolescents' health and development depends in part on how their families interpret and cope with such changes (Galambos & Ehrenberg, chapter 6, and Noack & Kracke, chapter 3, this volume). A broad contextual perspective is essential to understanding the diversity and similarity of adolescent experience over historical time, as well as between and within cultures. In addition, a contextual perspective alerts us to the multiple levels and targets of intervention that are available. When attempting to promote optimal adolescent development, intervening only at the individual level is just one option, and often not the ideal one (Lerner et al., chapter 19, this volume).

In addition to appreciating powerful sociocultural influences when attempting to intervene in the lives of adolescents, it is equally important to understand some fundamental and nearly universal transitions that occur during adolescence, particularly pubertal and cognitive changes (Silbereisen & Kracke, chapter 4, and Beyth-Marom & Fischhoff, chapter 5, this volume). To ignore these primary transitions, particularly the individual variability in their timing, is to increase the odds that any health promotion program will be unsuccessful. Indeed, part of an effective health promotion effort might be to attempt to increase young people's knowledge of and capacity to cope with pubertal and cognitive changes, along with other normative and nonnormative transitions (e.g., Compas, 1993; Petersen et al., chapter 18, this volume). The meaning of these developmental transitions and their impact on adolescent health are heavily influenced by proximal social and educational contexts as well as distal sociocultural contexts (Beyth-Marom & Fischhoff, chapter 5, and Silbereisen, & Kracke, chapter 4, this volume). This embeddedness suggests that effective developmental intervention programs might also target the context (e.g., educating parents and teachers about pubertal and cognitive changes, reorganizing schools to be more responsive to adolescents' needs).

Affiliation Transitions

Adolescents' relationships with their families furnish a fundamental base from which they begin to launch themselves into the adult world (Galambos & Ehrenberg, chapter 6, and Noack & Kracke, chapter 3, this volume). Family relationships that balance connectedness with autonomy seem to promote optimal adolescent and young adult development. At the same time, the peer group plays a central role in socialization (Brown et al., chapter 7, this volume). Relationships with same-age friends and peers tend to be more egalitarian than relationships with adults, providing adolescents with unique and important opportunities for self-expression and leadership. Adolescence involves a series of reproductive and sexual transitions, including fundamental changes in biological, emotional, and cognitive characteristics, personal identity, and social roles (Silbereisen & Kracke, chapter 4, and Brooks-Gunn & Paikoff, chapter 8, this volume). Sexual transitions are at the same time personal and private, yet social and public, typically leading to the eventual addition of the new adult social roles of being a spouse and/or a parent (Caldwell & Antonucci, chapter 9, and Bachman, Wadsworth, O'Malley, Schulenberg, & Johnston, chapter 10, this volume). As adolescents move toward psychosocial maturity and adult relationships, experiences with their families, peers, and romantic partners have great potential to facilitate or hinder healthy development.

Attempting to intervene in affiliation transitions for the purpose of promoting health and well-being can be very difficult. By definition, affiliation transitions involve multiple individuals, which greatly increases the complexity of supporting and protecting any targeted person. Nevertheless, to the extent that the developing adolescent is adequately prepared for and supported during normative and nonnormative affiliation transitions, more successful adaptation and role functioning can be expected. At the individual level, efforts to enhance social skills and social competence (e.g., Botvin & Wills, 1985; Compas, 1993; Consortium on the School-Based Promotion of Social Competence, 1994; Weissberg, Caplan, & Harwood, 1991) can serve to increase positive social interaction. At the same time, social influence resistance skills training, typically aimed at substance abuse prevention (e.g., Dielman, 1994; Evans et al., 1978, 1981; Sussman, Dent, Burton, Stacy, & Flay, 1995), may enable adolescents to negotiate peer relations and transitions such that they can maintain health-enhancing social support without engaging in health-risk behaviors. Likewise, Brooks-Gunn and Paikoff (chapter 8, this volume) envision comprehensive, developmentally sensitive sex education efforts that aim not only to reduce unprotected sexual intercourse but also to facilitate adolescents' social negotiation skills and identity development.

At the contextual level, support from caring family members can diminish risk factors for health and optimal development that typically follow becoming an adolescent mother (e.g., Caldwell & Antonucci, chapter 9, this volume; Scott-Jones, 1991). Attempting to strengthen mesosystem links (see Bronfenbrenner, 1979) among adolescents' social contexts, such as the family and the peer group, can help young people coordinate changes in family and peer relationships. Furthermore, as we consider later in this chapter, community social and leisure contexts can provide adolescents with necessary social experiences and informal contacts with caring adults, which in turn can promote social competence and discourage problem behaviors (Hurrelmann, 1990).

Educational and Occupational Transitions

Adolescents typically face a major educational or occupational transition every few years. First, most of them move from elementary schools to larger and more impersonal intermediate or junior high schools and then again to senior high schools (Eccles et al., chapter 11, this volume). Those who continue with postsecondary education must once again adapt to a much larger institution, often in a new city away from the parental home (Maggs, chapter 13, this volume). During the high school years, the majority of adolescents also enter the labor market through part-time and summer employment (Finch, Mortimer, & Ryu, chapter 12, this volume). Once schooling is completed, most seek to find a place in the occupatonal world, a process that often takes multiple attempts to secure an acceptable and stable position (Matt, Seus, & Schumann, chapter 14, this volume).

Educational and occupational transitions represent powerful opportunities and risks for adolescents. On the one hand, successful adaptation to and performance in educational and occupational domains *is* healthy development. The acquisition of knowledge, critical thought, and practical skills are activities that define successful growth. Thus, in the ideal situation, adolescents who have the benefit of challenging, supportive, and opportunity-rich school and work environments are likely to flourish (Eccles et al., chapter 11, and Finch et al., chapter 12, this volume). For example, doing well in junior high and high school is likely to have long-term salutary effects that last at least into young adulthood (e.g., Schulenberg, Bachman, O'Malley, & Johnston, 1994). However, nearly all of the chapters in this volume have shown that many adolescents do not have the benefits of such supportive and developmentally appropriate environments. There is a great need for educational and other institutions to be more responsive to adolescents' healthy, normal desires for increasing autonomy (Beyth-Marom & Fischhoff, chapter 5, Galambos & Ehrenberg, chapter 6, Eccles et al., chapter 11, Finch et al., chapter 12, and Nurmi, chapter 15, this volume). Subgroups of adolescents, such as those who make earlier transitions into the adult roles of parent and worker, may be particularly disadvantaged in terms of transitional supports and resources (Caldwell & Antonucci, chapter 9, and Matt et al., chapter 14, this volume). In this regard, the work of Hamilton (1990, 1994) regarding the salutary effects of school-to-work apprenticeships suggests the importance of providing institutional support to help adolescents transverse the gap between formal schooling and work.

In industrialized nations, an ongoing trend can be observed toward a prolongation of time spent in school or acquiring occupational training, often lasting into the third decade of life (Crockett, chapter 2, this volume; Hurrelmann, 1984; Schulenberg & Ebata, 1994). The opportunities for achieving academic credentials are much greater for many adolescents than they were for previous generations; however, at the same time, competition for attractive entry-level positions has become fierce (Hurrelmann, 1984). In order to maintain the status and standard of living of the family of origin, adolescents today often must obtain higher educational qualifications than their parents. Furthermore, a college or university degree no longer guarantees a good job with favorable prospects for the future. Delayed entrance into the full-time labor force creates a paradoxical and potentially unhealthy situation in which many adolescents achieve financial and occupational independence relatively late in life, yet enjoy a considerable amount of freedom in social areas such as leisure (Crockett, chapter 2, this volume; Hurrelmann, 1984).

Despite the deflation of the absolute value of postsecondary education, adolescents who obtain postsecondary educational qualifications enjoy greatly enhanced occupational prospects and many other noneducational advantages (Sherrod, Haggerty, & Featherman, 1993; W. T. Grant, 1988). Attending college tends to delay significantly the entrance into adult roles (e.g., spouse, parent, worker), providing a developmental moratorium during which individuals can explore ideas, identities, and lifestyles (Marini, 1985; Nurmi, chapter 15, and Phinney & Kohatsu, chapter 16, this volume). However, this period of postponed responsibility prolongs opportunities to "sow one's wild oats," with concomitant risks for health (Bachman et al., chapter 10, and Maggs, chapter 13, this volume).

Identity Transitions

In addition to major transitions in relationships and achievement domains, there are transitions in self-definition during adolescence, with identity formation being a primary developmental task of adolescence (Erikson, 1968). Personal identity formation occurs as adolescents and young adults, through exploration and commitment, acquire a secure sense of self that encompasses an acceptance and integration of their own interests, abilities, values, and goals (Nurmi, chapter 15, and Phinney & Kohatsu, chapter 16, this volume). This process involves questioning beliefs and behaviors previously taken for granted and actively exploring alternative ideas and lifestyles (Brooks-Gunn & Paikoff, chapter 8, this volume). In particular, exploring one's vocational identity is a major "occupation" of adolescence (Vondracek, 1994; Vondracek et al., 1986). Facilitating adolescents' identity exploration and subsequent identity commitment, as well as altering self-definitions that are on an unhealthy trajectory, are likely to have short-term and long-term health benefits (e.g., Archer, 1994; Nurmi, chapter 15, this volume).

Contextual and subcultural variation in identity formation represents an important theme for health promotion (Earls, 1993; Markstrom-Adams & Spencer, 1994). In multicultural societies, the process of identity formation includes consideration of social identities related to race, ethnicity, or cultural group membership (Phinney & Kohatsu, chapter 16, this volume). For many adolescents, identity exploration and formation are closely linked with issues of religious faith and commitment (Wallace & Williams, chapter 17, this volume). Religious involvement may be an important protective factor for adolescents' health – for example, by providing a supportive community and by reducing the incidence of drug use and sexual activity. This raises several issues regarding the place of values in general, and religiosity specifically, in developmental interventions with adolescents (Thomas & Carver, 1990).

Although exploration of values, ideas, and lifestyles is normative and healthy, some experimental behaviors are likely to expose adolescents to health and developmental risks. For example, dropping out of high school or college to travel may provide invaluable life experience, but it is also likely to limit academic attainment and occupational prospects. Similarly, using substances to get high or heighten creativity may be fulfilling in the short term but may be very hazardous if it becomes chronic or is combined with other risky activities. Some have questioned the wisdom of attempting to limit experimentation in an effort to reduce health risks (e.g., substance use) because one unintended consequence may be inadequate identity exploration resulting in foreclosed identities (e.g., Baumrind, 1987). Regardless of the potential perils of identity exploration, ignoring identity concerns is far worse for one's health and well-being. Adolescents with a diffused identity (i.e., neither exploring their identity options nor making identity commitments) are more likely to experience psychosocial difficulties (e.g., Marcia, 1994) and engage in problem behaviors (e.g., Jones, 1992).

Altering Transition–Health Risk Connections

From this brief overview of major developmental transitions, it is clear that adolescents undergo pivotal changes in many domains of life. Each of these changes involves the potential for beneficial as well as harmful outcomes. The goal of developmental intervention is to encourage positive trajectories and redirect less than optimal ones. That is, as we argued in chapter 1, the goal is to influence developmental transitions in a way that facilitates continuity in health-enhancing behaviors and creates discontinuity in health-compromising behaviors.

How we can begin to accomplish this ambitious goal depends in part on the underlying model that links developmental transitions and health risks. In the introduction, we conceptualized four possible models (Schulenberg et al., chapter 1, this volume). First, if health risks result from the overwhelming

Table 20.1. *Basic issues of adolescent health promotion*

Basic issue	Examples
Goals	Reduce incidence of depression; reduce alcohol-related fatalities Abstain versus delay onset versus promote responsible behavior
Comprehensiveness	Single behavior (e.g., smoking) versus multiple behaviors Enlisting media involvement
Location	Schools, community organizations, families, workplaces

Individual centered versus
  context centered
	Social skills enhancement versus job creation or restrictions on
	  tobacco/alcohol advertising

Population versus selected
  group
	Targeting all adolescents to prevent alcohol misuse versus
	  targeting aggressive youth to prevent chronic delinquency

Timing	Before school transitions; before habits formed; after puberty
Prevention versus intervention	School dropout prevention versus smoking cessation programs

stress associated with making several simultaneous transitions (see Coleman, 1978), then effective strategies might entail rearranging the timing of the various transitions (e.g., Brooks-Gunn & Paikoff, chapter 8, and Eccles et al., chapter 11, this volume) and enhancing coping styles (e.g., Nurmi, chapter 15, Petersen et al., chapter 18, and Phinney & Kohatsu, chapter 16, this volume). Second, if health risks result from a given developmental transition contributing to an increased mismatch between the developing needs of the individual and the affordances provided by the context (e.g., Eccles et al., chapter 11, and Galambos & Ehrenberg, chapter 6, this volume), then there must be an effort to engender greater synchrony between what the developing individual needs and what the changing context provides. Operating within this model, of course, necessitates a broad interdisciplinary framework and a good knowledge base regarding person–context interactions (e.g., Lerner et al., chapter 19, this volume). Third, if health risks are viewed as *part of negotiating* a given developmental transition (e.g., Baumrind, 1987; Irwin & Millstein, 1992; Maggs, chapter 13, this volume), then effective strategies might include providing alternatives to unhealthy risk-taking that would still enable personal goal fulfillment and effective negotiation of the transition. Finally, in the model that is implicit in nearly all chapters in this volume, developmental transitions can be seen as exacerbators of previously existing health risks (e.g., Petersen, 1993), suggesting that effective strategies might involve synchronizing prevention or intervention efforts to correspond with major transitions and providing alternative contexts that serve to alter the health risk trajectory.

These four models certainly do not constitute an exhaustive list. Moreover, they should be viewed as special cases of models that emphasize reciprocal influence between developmental transitions and health across the life span (Brown et al., chapter 7, and Caldwell & Antonucci, chapter 9, this volume) and even across generations (e.g., Cairns & Cairns, 1994). We put forward these four models in the hope that they will stimulate debate concerning alternative conceptualizations of how development and health are related. In the next section, we consider basic health promotion issues.

Basic Issues Concerning Adolescent Health Promotion Programs

The creation and implementation of programs designed to promote adolescents' well-being and healthy development involve many decisions concerning priorities, goals, and strategies. This section briefly presents several basic issues that deserve careful consideration (Table 20.1). More extensive discussions of many of these issues are presented in Petersen et al. (chapter 18) and Lerner et al. (chapter 19).

Goals

Explicit consideration of the targeted goals is a critical early step in program planning. Decisions that must be made include consideration of fundamental assumptions about the concept of health (e.g., enhancing well-being versus preventing infirmity), aims for behavioral deletions or additions (e.g., quit smoking versus begin regular exercise), and targeting single versus multiple behaviors (Millstein ct al., 1993; Perry & Jessor, 1985). Particularly in the case of adolescent behavior, potentially controversial decisions must be made about whether the goal is to promote abstention (e.g., from sex or substance use), to delay onset, or to encourage responsible or non-health-damaging behavior (Brooks-Gunn & Paikoff, chapter 8, and Maggs, chapter 13, this volume). These decisions involve implicit judgments about adolescents' ability to make rational decisions as well as their right to do so (Beyth-Marom & Fischhoff, chapter 5, this volume). Program goals need to be explicit and realistic, with congruent evaluation data collected so that the success of the stated aims can be assessed (Dielman, 1994; Sussman et al., 1995).

Comprehensiveness

Recommendations for successful programs commonly call for a comprehensive approach to prevention and health promotion, whenever possible targeting individual, family, school, community, and mass media (Cairns & Cairns, 1994; Dryfoos, 1990; Perry & Jessor, 1985; Wagenaar & Perry, 1994). Evaluation research has documented the failure of knowledge acquisition and fear arousal programs to prevent or delay smoking, alcohol use, or sexual behavior (Hansen, 1992; Millstein, 1993). In contrast, successful programs often employ multiple strategies, involve multiple settings, and/or target multiple behaviors

(Botvin, Baker, Dusenbury, Tortu, & Botvin, 1990; Botvin, Dusenbury, Baker, James-Ortiz, Botvin, & Kerner, 1992; Dielman, 1994; Perry & Kelder, 1992; Perry, Klepp, & Sillers, 1989). For example, the Minnesota Heart Health Youth Program is a peer-led, school-based health promotion program embedded in a larger communitywide program of change (Perry et al., 1989; see also Perry et al., 1993). Although comprehensive, communitywide health promotion is not always feasible, it is important to recognize it as an ideal and to make cost-effective decisions about how to maximize the use of limited resources (Perry & Jessor, 1985).

Location

Schools represent a pivotal setting for health promotion, as well as possessing great untapped potential to play an even more extensive role (Cairns & Cairns, 1994; Consortium on School-Based Promotion of Social Competence, 1994; Dryfoos, 1994; Lavin, Shapiro, & Weill, 1992). Other community organizations and informal settings also have a significant positive impact on the health and well-being of adolescents (Ebata, 1995; Price, Cioci, Penner, & Trautlein, 1993; Small, 1995). Youth clubs and organizations, community sports, recreation centers, and religious organizations are just a few of the programs and settings that young people can participate in (e.g., Larson, 1994). Informal social support and encouragement from family, friends, and other significant adults also play an essential positive role in adolescents' lives (Hurrelmann, 1990). Regardless of the agency that takes the lead in providing services for youth, collaboration between organizations is essential (Dryfoos, 1994; Lerner et al., chapter 19, this volume).

Individual-Centered versus Context-Centered Approaches

Many prevention and intervention efforts have been individual centered. In other words, they have largely focused on individual behavior while ignoring or downplaying ecological and social living conditions as prerequisites of healthy development (e.g., Franzkowiak, 1993; Hurrelmann, 1990; Noack & Kracke, chapter 3, this volume; Perry & Jessor, 1985). Focusing exclusively on behavioral dimensions tends to put all of the adaptational burden on individuals; however, experience has shown that health promotion can be successful only if it is embedded in a structural context that takes into account the dependency of individual growth on environmental conditions and that aims at improving the living conditions of adolescents and their families (Anderson, Davies, Kickbusch, McQueen, & Turner, 1988; Baum, 1993; Lerner et al., chapter 19, this volume). Although changing individual behavior is a fundamental goal of most programs, it is also important to aim to effect change in other domains, including social norms (e.g., acceptability of smoking in public buildings), laws (e.g., requiring bicycle helmet use), marketing and sales (e.g., increasing the price of cigarettes, decreasing cigarette availability and advertising), environmental practices (e.g., antipollution legislation), and social-structural opportunities (e.g., access to education and health care, job creation) (Bennett, Murphy, & Bunton, 1992; Grossman, Chaloupka, Saffer, & Laixuthai, 1994; Noack, 1987).

Prevention versus Intervention

A central element in the concept of health promotion is the idea of attempting to *prevent* the emergence of disorders and impairments to health at an early stage and to improve well-being and the quality of life (Noack, 1987). The earlier such support and assistance can be introduced, the greater the chance of avoiding the development of chronic disorders, impairments, and their consequences (Hurrelmann, Kaufmann, & Lösel, 1987). Similarly, once problems arise, early and appropriate intervention greatly enhances the likelihood of positive outcomes (Noack, 1987).

Timing

A closely related issue is *when* to implement health promotion efforts, both developmentally, in terms of the age of the targeted audience, and chronologically, in terms of the natural history of a particular behavior pattern (Hansen, 1992). The difficulty of altering established habits and lifestyles suggests that the earlier the effort is made, the better (Susman et al., 1992). There is also evidence that individuals must be developmentally and experientially ready to absorb the message. For example, Dielman (1994) argues, based on an evaluation of a social influence/resistance skills intervention designed to prevent alcohol misuse, that there may be optimal ages for program implementation. Recent research from this project suggests that it is possible to intervene *too* early. Program effectiveness may be limited when the child's experience forms no basis on which to relate personally to the prevention curriculum (Schulenberg, Kloska, Zucker, Maggs, & Dielman, 1996). Factors affecting optimal windows for intervention include the timing of onset of targeted behaviors in the subgroup of interest, as well as naturally occurring transitions such as puberty or school changes.

Population versus Targeted Group

Even small decreases in the prevalence of risk factors in the population result in sizeable reductions in morbidity, mortality, and the economic costs of social programs and health care (Lilienfield & Lilienfield, 1980). Wagenaar and Perry (1994) argue that such a population-based approach to the reduction of youthful drinking is essential, because (1) such large numbers of youth are at risk that society could not afford a "cure" for adolescent alcohol use should one be available; (2) there is constant turnover in at-risk populations; and (3) the majority of alcohol-related morbidity and mortality is due to moderate drinkers who are not alcohol dependent. This argument could apply equally to other threats to adolescents' healthy development, such as accidents, precocious sexual activity, dropping out of school, and depression (Petersen et al., chapter 18, this volume).

An emphasis on supporting optimal development among the adolescent population should be recognized as an ideal, but specific efforts may be necessary for particular subgroups. Targeted interventions may be preventive, to delay or inhibit the initiation of problematic behaviors or the onset of health or social problems, or they may be corrective, to help eliminate behaviors, minimize negative consequences, or cope with chronic impairments (Hurrelmann, 1990). Different targeted risk factors, intervention strategies, and desired outcomes may be necessary, depending on the targeted group (Crockett, chapter 2, this volume; Tolan & Guerra, 1994). For example, personal and social skills enhancement training may be an appropriate primary strategy in relatively affluent suburban neighborhoods. Among the estimated one in four American youth who are at serious risk due to poverty and crime (Dryfoos, 1990), however, pressing needs will also include jobs, housing, health care, and crime prevention (Dusenbury & Botvin, 1992). In summary, population-based health promotion should improve the lifestyles and environments of the entire population, target high-risk individuals and groups for special prevention efforts, and detect and treat disorder early (WHO, 1986).

Health Promotion in Schools

Schools are a logical location for health promotion because they have regular, sustained contact with the great majority of children and younger adolescents, and they already are designed to increase knowledge, advance cognitive development, and build social skills (e.g., Consortium on the School-Based Promotion of Social Competence, 1994; Price et al., 1993). As a result of the school-based services movement, there has been an increase in the number of "full-service" schools furnishing physical and mental health care, social services, and recreational opportunities (Bond & Compas, 1989; David & Williams, 1987; Dryfoos, 1994, 1995; Lavin et al., 1992). At the same time, however, many schools have evidenced minimal change (Dryfoos, 1993). In Germany, for instance, the state ministers of education passed a resolution in 1979 to make health education a compulsory part of the school curriculum. In a representative survey of 4,000 German citizens, Arnold and Lang (1986) found that 73% considered health education in German schools to be insufficient. Similarly, a large percentage of German teachers reported feeling inadequately prepared and trained for the task of health promotion (Pfaff, Jacob, & Pötschke-Langer, 1992). In the United States, most students experience some teacher-led, classroom-based alcohol and drug prevention curriculum (Dryfoos, 1993). However, even the most intensive programs typically involve no more than a few hours a week for at most a few years (Perry & Kelder, 1992; Wagenaar & Perry, 1994). Thus, despite agreement that comprehensive health education that goes beyond substance use prevention is necessary, translating these intentions into practice has proven to be a very slow process.

School Health Promotion: Content and Strategies

For many years, hopes were high that schools could deal comprehensively with all issues of health promotion through an information-based curriculum of health education. Evaluative findings, however, have clearly indicated the limitations of such a strategy (Dryfoos, 1993; Hansen, 1992; Wagenaar & Perry, 1994). Although knowledge about healthy and unhealthy activities can be increased through fact-based programs, attitudes and behavior are much more difficult to change (Botvin, 1986; Dryfoos, 1993; Kolbe, 1985; Rundall & Bruvold, 1988; Zins, Wagner, & Maher, 1985). David and Williams (1987) argued that school health promotion should include not only the provision of health-related knowledge but should also (1) support opportunities for healthy lifestyles; (2) promote the ability to develop one's physical, psychological, and social potential; (3) develop social skills, problem-solving abilities, coping capacities, and conflict resolution strategies; and (4) encourage responsibility for individual, family, and community health. Recent prevention programs such as the "social inoculation" or the "social influence resistance" approach (c.g., Dielman, 1994; Evans et al., 1978, 1981) and the "life-skills approach" (Botvin & Eng, 1982; Botvin & Tortu, 1988; Botvin & Wills, 1985) belong to a new generation of programs that also emphasize coping strategies, such as dealing constructively with stress, as well as communication skills and assertiveness (see Consortium on the School-Based Promotion of Social Competence, 1994).

Challenges for School-Based Programs

Certain characteristics of schools and the educational system challenge their potentially beneficial impact. First, the school's primary tasks of awarding educational qualifications may create a state of tension with the goals of health promotion. The dilemma can be illustrated by a situation where an instructor teaches exercises of self-esteem enhancement but then is required to assign bad marks to some of the students, thus signaling that they failed to meet acceptable standards. As long as the selective allocation of access to society's opportunities and benefits remains a major task of schools, this inherent conflict is not likely to disappear.

Second, school itself is a major source of stress and risk to adolescents (Dryfoos, 1990; Eccles et al., chapter 11, this volume; Eccles & Midgley, 1989; Nordlohne, 1992). Increasingly, school characteristics, transitions, and practices are recognized as significant risk factors for many negative health and social outcomes.

Third, the adolescents who are most at risk may feel alienated from or may not be attending school. Children from resource-poor environments are more likely to fall behind their grade and drop out before the end of high school (Lerner et al., chapter 19, this volume). Furthermore, adolescents who make earlier transitions out of formal education and into the labor market receive far less societal support and assistance than those who go on to postsecondary education (W. T. Grant, 1988). The development, implementation, and evaluation of programs to help facilitate the transition from school to work for those who do not go to college should be given a high priority (Matt et al., chapter 14, and Nurmi, chapter 15, this volume).

Finally, even an ideal school environment cannot counteract the myriad threats to healthy development, such as poverty, parental unemployment, abusive family relationships, or inadequate housing. Especially in high-risk and resource-poor settings, school-based programs must be supported by additional community components (Dryfoos, 1994; Lerner et al., chapter 19, this volume). As Dryfoos argued, it is "unreasonable to expect that young people already disaffected with schooling will change their ways because they have learned peer resistance skills from their teachers" (1993, p. 794). For all of these reasons, health promotion efforts should include school reform, as well as being directed toward the many other areas of adolescents' daily lives (Dryfoos, 1993; Eccles & Midgley, 1989; Perry & Jessor, 1985; Wagenaar & Perry, 1994).

School as a Developmentally Appropriate, Democratic, and Health-Promoting Community

To maximize the positive impact of school on physical, psychological, and social well-being, a positive milieu that offers rich, varied opportunities and experiences is needed. Educational settings must inspire not only intellectual development, but also physical, social, and emotional growth and exploration. Optimal growth should occur when there is a good stage–environment fit, that is, a match between students' normative developmental needs and the school's environmental demands and affordances (Eccles et al., chapter 11, this volume; Eccles et al., 1993). Educational, occupational, and community policy must find answers to the question of how adolescents can satisfy their developmentally normative needs for independence, challenge, companionship, and accomplishment (Hurrelmann, 1990). One strategy is to provide adolescents with interesting, stimulating, and satisfying real-life experiences that are more appealing than problematic and health-damaging behaviors (Millstein, 1993). These could include positive forms of entertainment, sports, performance, and experiential learning.

The integration of public schools into the broader community has a great deal of potential for expanding their positive impact on adolescent and community health. The idea is to integrate adolescents and their teachers into the life of the community by utilizing existing structures as a potential for learning. For example, links between schools and the world of work can be established through visits to local companies, student volunteer programs, and internships (e.g., Finch et al., chapter 12, this volume). Schools can also serve as a resource for the community. Through active collaboration with community leaders and agencies, schools can develop a reputation for providing valuable resources, including training, exhibitions, and entertainment.

Health Promotion in a Broader Context:
Social Networks and "Free Space"

The social context and the structure of social relationships are very important aspects of health promotion. In recent years, the promotion of social networks within and between the family, neighborhood, school, employment settings, and health care institutions has increasingly become the subject of discussion (e.g., Crockett & Crouter, 1995; Silbereisen & Todt, 1994). The more adolescents are integrated into a favorable network of social relationships, the more they have the resources to deal constructively with unfavorable living conditions, critical life events, and long-term stressors and the less prone they are to engage in health-damaging behaviors (Cairns & Cairns, 1994; Noack & Kracke, chapter 3, and Wallace & Williams, chapter 17, this volume). Likewise, participating in youth organizations can have salutary effects (Larson, 1994; Quinn, 1995). Thus the social network is a powerful facilitator of coping effectively with life's difficulties (Garbarino, Schellenbach, & Sebes, 1986; Kessler, Price, & Wortman, 1985).

Hurrelmann (1990) argued that leisure situations need to be re-created that offer adolescents experiences and encounters that dissuade them from participating in health-compromising behaviors (see also Fine, Mortimer, & Roberts, 1990). Adolescents today have access to many social and material possibilities but, at the same time, they lack real challenges and means of satisfying their interests and needs beyond the superficial satisfactions offered by the consumer-oriented media and society. There exists a lack of real challenges and personal experiences that enable young people to utilize their physical abilities and social competence in a constructive manner. Herein lies a great challenge – to create "free space" that allows adolescents to explore their potential and test their limits but at the same time does not encourage health-compromising behaviors.

Promoting Adolescent Health and Development: More Research, More Education

Traditional health promotion efforts attempt to change attitudes and behaviors among targeted individuals or groups of individuals. These can range from classroom-level to national media-level strategies. Consistent with the overarching perspective put forth in this volume, however, health promotion should be viewed quite broadly as efforts aimed at helping adolescents negotiate the major developmental transitions as they move from childhood to adulthood. That is, with an expanded definition of health, the targets of health promotion efforts should also be expanded. This more indirect yet comprehensive view of health promotion should prompt the development of broader strategies that help young people not only on an individual basis but also on a family, community, and national basis.

This volume has focused on the health risks and benefits associated with normative developmental transitions during adolescence. We argue that by supporting the multiple transitions that occur during the second and third decades of life, we will increase the health and well-being of adolescents and young adults. To the extent that this premise is supported, given the importance of the adolescent years in shaping the trajectories of health across the life span, efforts to facilitate the various transitions of adolescence will yield long-term benefits. We close this volume with some thoughts on future directions for promoting optimal development and health among adolescents.

More Research

What do adolescents need? To the extent that health risks result when developmental transitions adversely affect the match between the developing person and the opportunities for growth and health provided by the context (e.g., Eccles et al., chapter 11, and Lerner et al., chapter 19, this volume), a major goal of research aimed at optimizing adolescent health and development should be to delineate the elements of a good developmental match. Among well-functioning and healthy adolescents, what are the individual characteristics and contextual affordances that engender such a developmental match or mismatch? Given that one context will not fit all adolescents and that one adolescent will not fit all contexts, what do the optimal pairings look like? Addressing these and related questions requires an unwavering commitment to focusing on the interaction of the developing adolescent in the changing context. As the present volume shows, the development of this essential groundwork for optimizing adolescent health and development is well underway (see also Cairns & Cairns, 1994; Rutter, 1995; Silbereisen & Todt, 1994), but it should be equally obvious that the bulk of the work remains to be done.

Of course, in addition to such basic research, comprehensive evaluations of developmental intervention programs are clearly needed. A student of one of the authors (J.S.) recently spoke to him regarding her new position as director of a large school enrichment program for at-risk junior high school students. She was expressing her excitement about the position but at the same time indicating her dismay over the lack of evaluation of the program. Although the program had been in existence for over a decade, and was viewed very positively by the school district and community, no formal evaluation of its effectiveness had ever been conducted. "Everyone believes that it works and that they know why it works," she said, "so maybe they think that research is not needed. I am having a hard time convincing them otherwise." One wonders how much valuable insight into how to promote adolescent health and optimal development has been lost over the years in this and countless other communities because of the lack of systematic program implementation and evaluation. As Lerner et al. (chapter 19, this volume) argue, developmental scientists are needed "in the trenches" to help design developmentally sensitive programs and conduct needed evaluation research (see Cook, Anson, & Walchli, 1993). If a program is successful, we ought to be able to know why so that we can reproduce it elsewhere. At the same time, if the program is unsuccessful, we should learn why and then alter it accordingly or discontinue it and seek other solutions.

Intervention research can offer developmental scientists much more than simply applied knowledge. Much can be learned about human development in general and about person–context interactions in particular by conducting intervention research. In a statement that places him at least a decade ahead of the majority of developmental scientists, Bronfenbrenner (1977) argued, "If you wish to understand the relation between the developing person and some aspect of his or her environment, try to budge the one, and see what happens to the other" (p. 518). Thoughtful, systematic "budging" of developing individuals and/or their changing context can yield a wealth of basic knowledge concerning developmental processes (e.g., Kellam & Rebok, 1992).

More Education

What are adolescents like? A response from a layperson will likely include an implicit or explicit reference to inherent "storm and stress." Unfortunately, many professionals would offer a similar response. A few years ago, one of the authors (J.S.) was flying home from a child development conference at which several presentations had concluded that most adolescents are well adjusted. In leafing through the airline's magazine, he came across an article entitled

"The Thunder Years." It started off with: "After the wonder years, the winds of change bring adolescence. Here's how you and your teenager can weather the storm" (Baldwin, 1993, p. 14). Much of the information presented seemed reasonable. Yet, as the title implies, the assumption throughout the article was that adolescence is inherently tumultuous: "Imagine the parent–teenager relationship in terms of a hurricane. . . . At puberty, a teenager is inexorably swept up in the swift winds of change, and parents must remain calm and aware in the eye of the hurricane" (p. 20). Hundreds of thousands of people had access to this airline magazine, another cog in the perpetuation of the "storm and stress" image of adolescents.

Parents and educators also share these beliefs and fears about adolescence. When conducting individual interviews with parents of young adolescents a few years ago, one of the authors (J.M.) was intrigued to hear parents' thoughts about the approaching adolescent years. With few exceptions, all parents indicated that they expected trouble. A common response was: "Well, she is just a wonderful child now, but we know that soon the bubble will burst and all hell will break loose when she becomes a *real* teenager." It is not difficult to imagine these parental beliefs affecting young adolescents' expectations about what looms in their immediate future. Some adolescents hold such expectations with apprehension, whereas others may view them as a challenge or a license to misbehave. Either way, it is unlikely that such expectations contribute to health and well-being.

Our two anecdotes are consistent with what studies have revealed about the negative image that teachers and other adults tend to have of adolescents and what the media portray (e.g., Eccles et al., chapter 11, this volume; Fine et al., 1990). But as developmental scientists, we know better. Evidence gathered over the past several decades is clear: Adolescence does not have to be, and usually is not, a period of storm and stress (Takanishi, 1993). In all likelihood, this large and enduring gap between what we know to be true as developmental scientists and what the general public believes has an adverse affect on young people. Thus, part of the bigger picture of promoting adolescent health and optimal development must be public policy and education.

References

Anderson, R., Davies, J. K., Kickbusch, I., McQueen, D. V., & Turner, J. (Eds.). (1988). *Health behavior research and health promotion*. Oxford: Oxford University Press.
Archer, S. L. (Ed.) (1994). *Interventions for adolescent identity development*. Thousand Oaks, CA: Sage.
Arnold, K., & Lang, E. (1986). Schule und Gesundheitserziehung. *Pädagogische Rundschau, 40*, 435–448.
Baldwin, B. A. (1993). The thunder years. *USAir Magazine, 15*, 14–20.
Baltes, P. B., & Danish, S. J. (1980). Intervention in life-span development and aging: Issues and

concepts. In R. R. Turner & H. W. Reese (Eds.), *Life-span developmental psychology: Intervention* (pp. 49–78). New York: Academic Press.

Baum, F. E. (1993). Healthy cities and change: Social movement or bureaucratic tool? *Health Promotion International, 8,* 31–40.

Baumrind, D. (1987). A developmental perspective on adolescent risk taking in contemporary America. In C. E. Irwin, Jr. (Ed.), *Adolescent social behavior and health* (pp. 93–125). San Francisco: Jossey-Bass.

Bennett, P., Murphy, S., & Bunton, R. (1992). Preventing alcohol problems using healthy public policy. *Health Promotion International, 7,* 297–306.

Bond, L. A., & Compas, B. E. (1989). *Primary prevention and promotion in the schools.* Newbury Park, CA: Sage.

Botvin, G. J. (1986). Substance abuse prevention research: Recent developments and future directions. *Journal of School Health, 56,* 369–386.

Botvin, G. J., Baker, E., Dusenbury, L., Tortu, S., & Botvin, E. M. (1990). Preventing adolescent drug abuse through a multimodal cognitive-behavioral approach: Results of a three-year study. *Journal of Consulting and Clinical Psychology, 58,* 437–446.

Botvin, G. J., Dusenbury, L., Baker, E., James-Ortiz, S., Botvin, E. M., & Kerner, J. (1992). Smoking prevention among urban minority youth: Assessing effects on outcome and mediating variables. *Health Psychology, 11,* 290–299.

Botvin, G. J., & Eng, A. (1982). The efficacy of a multicomponent approach to the prevention of cigarette smoking. *Preventive Medicine, 11,* 199–211.

Botvin, G. J., & Tortu, S. (1988). Preventing adolescent substance abuse through life skills training. In R. H. Price, E. L. Cowen, R. P. Lorion, & J. Ramos-McKay (Eds.), *Fourteen ounces of prevention* (pp. 98–110). Washington, DC: American Psychological Association.

Botvin, G. J., & Wills, T. A. (1985). *Personal and social skills training: Cognitive-behavioral approaches to substance abuse prevention.* National Institute on Drug Abuse Monograph Series 63. Rockville, MD: NIDA.

Bronfenbrenner, U. (1977). Toward an experimental ecology of human development. *American Psychologist, 32,* 513–531.

Bronfenbrenner, U. (1979). *The ecology of human development: Experiments by nature and design.* Cambridge, MA: Harvard University Press.

Cairns, R. B., & Cairns, B. D. (1994). *Lifelines and risks: Pathways of youth in our time.* New York: Cambridge University Press.

Chassin, L., Presson, C. C., & Sherman, S. J. (1989). "Constructive" vs. "destructive" deviance in adolescent health-related behaviors. *Journal of Youth and Adolescence, 18,* 245–262.

Coleman, J. (1978). Current contradictions in adolescent theory. *Journal of Youth and Adolescence, 7,* 1–11.

Compas, B. E. (1993). Promoting positive mental health during adolescence. In S. G. Millstein, A. C. Petersen, & E. O. Nightingale (Eds.), *Promoting the health of adolescents: New directions for the twenty-first century* (pp. 159–179). New York: Oxford University Press.

Consortium on the School-based Promotion of Social Competence. (1994). The school-based promotion of social competence: Theory, research, practice, and policy. In R. J. Haggerty, L. R. Sherrod, N. Garmezy, & M. Rutter (Eds.), *Stress, risk, and resilience in children and adolescents: Processes, mechanisms, and interventions* (pp. 268–316). New York: Cambridge University Press.

Cook, T. D., Anson, A. R., & Walchli, S. (1993). From causal description to causal explanation: Improving three already good evaluations of adolescent health programs. In S. G. Millstein, A. C. Petersen, & E. O. Nightingale (Eds.), *Promoting the health of adolescents: New directions for the twenty-first century* (pp. 339–374). New York: Oxford University Press.

Crockett, L. J., & Crouter, A. C. (Eds.). (1995). *Pathways through adolescence: Individual development in relation to social contexts.* Mahwah, NJ: Erlbaum.

Danish, S. J., Smyer, M. A., & Nowak, C. A. (1980). Developmental intervention: Enhancing life-event processes. In P. B. Baltes & O. G. Brim, Jr. (Eds.), *Life-span development and behavior* (Vol. 3, pp. 340–366). New York: Academic Press.

David, K., & Williams, T. (1987). *Health education in schools*. London: Harper & Row.

Dielman, T. E. (1994). School-based research on the prevention of adolescent alcohol use and misuse: Methodological issues and advances. *Journal of Research on Adolescence, 4,* 271–293.

Dryfoos, J. G. (1990). *Adolescents at risk: Prevalence and prevention*. New York: Oxford University Press.

Dryfoos, J. G. (1993). Preventing substance use: Rethinking strategies. *American Journal of Public Health, 83,* 793–795.

Dryfoos, J. G. (1994). *Full-service schools: A revolution in health and social services for children, youth, and families*. San Francisco: Jossey-Bass.

Dryfoos, J. G. (1995). Full-service schools. *Journal of Research on Adolescence, 5,* 147–172.

Dusenbury, L., & Botvin, G. J. (1992). Substance abuse prevention: Competence enhancement and the development of positive life options. *Journal of Addictive Diseases, 11,* 29–45.

Earls, F. (1993). Health promotion for minority adolescents: Cultural considerations. In S. G. Millstein, A. C. Petersen, & E. O. Nightingale (Eds.), *Promoting the health of adolescents: New directions for the twenty-first century* (pp. 58–72). New York: Oxford University Press.

Ebata, A. T. (1995). Community-based action research and adolescent development: Commentary. In L. J. Crockett & A. C. Crouter (Eds.), *Pathways through adolescence: Individual development in relation to social contexts* (pp. 235–244). Mahwah, NJ: Erlbaum.

Eccles, J. S., & Midgley, C. (1989). Stage/environment fit: Developmentally appropriate classrooms for early adolescents. In R. E. Ames & C. Ames (Eds.), *Research on motivation in education* (Vol. 3, pp. 139–186). New York: Academic Press.

Eccles, J. S., Midgley, C., Wigfield, A., Buchanan, C. M., Reuman, D., Flanagan, C., & MacIver, D. (1993). Development during adolescence: The impact of stage–environment fit on young adolescents' experiences in schools and in families. *American Psychologist, 48,* 90–101.

Erikson, E. (1968). *Identity: Youth in crisis*. New York: Norton.

Evans, R., Rozelle, R. M., Maywell, S. E., Raines, B. E., Dill, D. A., Guthrie, T. J., Henderson, A. H., & Hill, P. C. (1981). Social modeling films to deter smoking in adolescents: Results of a three-year field investigation. *Journal of Applied Psychology, 66,* 399–414.

Evans, R., Rozelle, R. M., Mittlemark, M. B., Hansen, W. B., Bane, A. L., & Havis, J. (1978). Deterring the onset of smoking in children: Knowledge of immediate physiological effects and coping with peer pressure, media pressure, and parent modeling. *Journal of Applied Social Psychology, 8,* 126–135.

Feagans, L. V. (1992). Intervention strategies to promote healthy children: Ecological perspectives and individual differences. In E. J. Susman, L. V. Feagans, & W. J. Ray (Eds.), *Emotion, cognition, health, and development in children and adolescents* (pp. 165–170). Hillsdale, NJ: Erlbaum.

Fine, G. A., Mortimer, J. T., & Roberts, D. F. (1990). Leisure, work, and the mass media. In S. Feldman & G. R. Elliott (Eds.), *At the threshold: The developing adolescent* (pp. 225–252). Cambridge, MA: Harvard University Press.

Fisher, C. B., Murray, J. P., Dill, J. R., Hagen, J. W., Hogan, M. J., Lerner, R. M., Rebok, G. W., Sigel, I., Sostek, A. M., Smyer, M. A., Spencer, M. B., & Wilcox, B. (1993). The National Conference on Graduate Education in the Applications of Developmental Sciences across the Life Span. *Journal of Applied Developmental Psychology, 14,* 1–10.

Franzkowiak, P. (1986). *Risikoverhalten und Gesundheitsbewusstsein bei Jugendlichen. [Risk behaviors and health awareness among adolescents.]* Berlin: Springer.

Friedman, H. L. (1993). Adolescent social development: A global perspective. *Journal of Adolescent Health, 14,* 588–594.

Garbarino, J., Schellenbach, C. J., & Sebes, J. M. (1986). *Troubled youth, troubled families*. Berlin: Aldine de Gruyter.

Grossman, M., Chaloupka, F. J., Saffer, H., & Laixuthai, A. (1994). Effects of alcohol price policy on youth: A summary of economic research. *Journal of Research on Adolescence, 4,* 347–364.

Hamburg, D. A., Millstein, S. G., Mortimer, A. M., Nightingale, E. O., & Petersen, A. C. (1993). Adolescent health promotion in the twenty-first century: Current frontiers and new directions. In S. G. Millstein, A. C. Petersen, & E. O. Nightingale (Eds.), *Promoting the health of adolescents: New directions for the twenty-first century* (pp. 375–388). New York: Oxford University Press.

Hamilton, S. F. (1990). *Apprenticeship for adulthood: Preparing youth for the future.* New York: Free Press.

Hamilton, S. F. (1994). Employment prospects as motivation for school achievement: Links and gaps between school and work in seven countries. In R. K. Silbereisen & E. Todt (Eds.), *Adolescence in context: The interplay of family, school, peers, and work in adjustment* (pp. 267–283). New York: Springer-Verlag.

Hansen, W. B. (1992). School-based substance abuse prevention: A review of the state of the art in curriculum, 1980–1990. *Health Education Research, 7,* 403–430.

Hawkins, J. D., Catalano, R. F., & Miller, J. (1992). Risk and protective factors for alcohol and other drug problems in adolescence and early adulthood: Implications for substance abuse prevention. *Psychological Bulletin, 112,* 64–105.

Hurrelmann, K. (1984). Societal and organizational factors of stress on students in school. *European Journal of Teacher Education, 7,* 181–190.

Hurrelmann, K. (1990). Health promotion for adolescents: Preventive and corrective strategies against problem behavior. *Journal of Adolescence, 13,* 231–250.

Hurrelmann, K., Kaufmann, F., & Lösel, F. (Eds.). (1987). *Social intervention: Potential and constraints.* Berlin: Walter de Gruyter.

Hurrelmann, K., & Lasser, K. (Eds.). (1993). *Gesundheitswissenschaften.* Weinheim: Beltz.

Irwin, C. E., & Millstein, S. G. (1986). Biopsychosocial correlates of risk-taking behaviors during adolescence. *Journal of Adolescent Health Care, 7,* 825–956.

Irwin, C. E., Jr., & Millstein, S. G. (1992). Risk-taking behaviors and biopsychosocial development during adolescence. In E. J. Susman, L. V. Feagans, & W. J. Ray (Eds.), *Emotion, cognition, health, and development in children and adolescents* (pp. 75–102). Hillsdale, NJ: Erlbaum.

Jessor, R. (1984). Adolescent development and behavioral health. In J. D. Matarazzo & C. L. Perry (Eds.), *Behavioral health: A handbook of health enhancement and disease prevention* (pp. 69–90). New York: Wiley.

Jones, R. M. (1992). Ego identity and adolescent problem behavior. In G. R. Adams, T. P. Gullotta, & R. Montemayor (Eds.), *Adolescent identity formation.* Newbury Park, CA: Sage.

Kazdin, A. E. (1993). Adolescent mental health: Prevention and treatment programs. *American Psychologist, 48,* 127–141.

Kellam, S. G., & Rebok, G. W. (1992). Building developmental and etiological theory through epidemiologically based preventive intervention trials. In J. McCord & R. E. Tremblay (Eds.), *Preventing antisocial behavior: Interventions from birth through adolescence* (pp. 162–195). New York: Guilford Press.

Kessler, R. C., Price, R. H., & Wortman, C. B. (1985). Social factors in psychopathology: Stress, social support, and coping processes. *Annual Review of Psychology, 72,* 531–572.

Kolbe, C. J. (1985). Why school health education? An empirical point of view. *Health Education, 16,* 116–120.

Larson, R. (1994). Youth organizations, hobbies and sports and developmental contexts. In R. K. Silbereisen & E. Todt (Eds.), *Adolescence in context: The interplay of family, school, peers, and work in adjustment* (pp. 46–65). New York: Springer-Verlag.

Lavin, A., Shapiro, G., & Weill, K. (1992). *Creating an agenda for school-based health promotion: A review of selected reports.* Cambridge, MA: Harvard School of Public Health.

Lilienfeld, A. M., & Lilienfeld, D. E. (1980). *Foundations of epidemiology* (2nd ed.). New York: Oxford University Press.

Maggs, J. L., Almeida, D. M., & Galambos, N. L. (1995). Risky business: The paradoxical meaning of problem behavior for young adolescents. *Journal of Early Adolescence, 15,* 339–357.

Marcia, J. (1994). Identity and psychotherapy. In S. L. Archer (Ed.), *Interventions for adolescent identity development* (pp. 29–46). Thousand Oaks, CA: Sage.

Marini, M. M. (1985). Determinants of the timing of adult role entry. *Social Science Research, 14,* 309–350.

Markstrom-Adams, C., & Spencer, M. B. (1994). A model for identity intervention with minority adolescents. In S. L. Archer (Ed.), *Interventions for adolescent identity development* (pp. 84–102). Thousand Oaks, CA: Sage.

Millstein, S. G. (1993). A view of health from the adolescent's perspective. In S. G. Millstein, A. C. Petersen, & E. O. Nightingale (Eds.), *Promoting the health of adolescents: New directions for the twenty-first century* (pp. 97–118). New York: Oxford University Press.

Millstein, S. G., Petersen, A. C., & Nightingale, E. O. (Eds.). (1993). *Promoting the health of adolescents: New directions for the twenty-first century.* New York: Oxford University Press.

Noack, H. (1987). Concepts of health and health promotion. In T. Abelin, Z. J. Brzezinski, & V. D. L. Carstairs (Eds.), *Measurement in health promotion and protection.* Copenhagen: World Health Organization.

Nordlohne, E. (1992). Die Kosten jugendlicher Problem bewältigung. *Alkohol-, Zigaretten-, und Arzneimittelkonsum in Jugendalter.* Weinheim: Juventa.

Perry, C. L., & Jessor, R. (1985). The concept of health promotion and the prevention of adolescent drug abuse. *Health Education Quarterly, 12,* 169–184.

Perry, C. L., & Kelder, S. H. (1992). Models for effective prevention. *Journal of Adolescent Health, 13,* 355–363.

Perry, C. L., Kelder, S. H., & Komro, K. A. (1993). The social world of adolescents: Families, peers, schools, and the community. In S. G. Millstein, A. C. Petersen, & E. O. Nightingale (Eds.), *Promoting the health of adolescents: New directions for the twenty-first century* (pp. 73–96). New York: Oxford University Press.

Perry, C. L., Klepp, K. -I., & Sillers, C. (1989). Community-wide strategies for cardiovascular health: The Minnesota Heart Health Program youth program. *Health Education Research, 4,* 87–101.

Perry, C. L., Williams, C. L., Forster, J. L., Wolfson, M., Wagenaar, A. C., Finnegan, J. R., McGovern, P. G., Veblen-Mortensen, S., Komro, K. A., & Anstine, P. S. (1993). Background, conceptualization and design of a community-wide research program on adolescent alcohol use: Project Northland. *Health Education Research, 8,* 125–136.

Petersen, A. C. (1993). Creating adolescents: The role of context and process in developmental trajectories. *Journal of Research on Adolescence, 3,* 1–18.

Pfaff, G., Jacob A., & Pötschke-Langer, M. (Eds.). (1992). *Gesundheitsförderung in Schulen: Ergebnisse einer Umfrage.* Bonn: Bundesvereinigung für Gesundheit.

Price, R. H., Cioci, M., Penner, W., & Trautlein, B. (1993). Webs of influence: School and community programs that enhance adolescent health and education. In R. Takanishi (Ed.), *Adolescence in the 1990s: Risk and opportunity* (pp. 29–63). New York: Teachers College Press.

Quinn, J. (1995). Positive effects of participation in youth organizations. In M. Rutter (Ed.), *Psychosocial disturbances in young people: Challenges for prevention* (pp. 274–304). New York: Cambridge University Press.

Rundall, T. G., & Bruvold, W. H. (1988). A meta-analysis of school-based smoking and alcohol use prevention programs. *Health Education Quarterly, 15,* 317–334.

Rutter, M. (Ed.). (1995). *Psychosocial disturbances in young people: Challenges for prevention.* New York: Cambridge University Press.

Schulenberg, J., Bachman, J. G., O'Malley, P. M., & Johnston, L. D. (1994). High school educational success and subsequent substance use: A panel analysis following adolescents into young adulthood. *Journal of Health and Social Behavior, 35,* 45–62.

Schulenberg, J., & Ebata, A. T. (1994). Adolescence in the United States. In K. Hurrelmann (Ed.), *International handbook of adolescence* (pp. 414–430). Westport, CT: Greenwood.

Schulenberg, J., Kloska, D., Zucker, R. A., Maggs, J., & Dielman, T. E. (1996). *Timing matters: Long-term differential effectiveness of a school-based alcohol misuse prevention program.* Unpublished manuscript, University of Michigan.

Scott-Jones, D. (1991). Adolescent child-bearing: Risks and resilience. *Education and Urban Society, 24*, 53–64.

Sherrod, L. R., Haggerty, R. J., & Featherman, D. L. (1993). Introduction: Late adolescence and the transition to adulthood. *Journal of Research on Adolescence, 3*, 217–226.

Silbereisen, R. K., & Noack, P. (1988). On the constructive role of problem behavior in adolescence. In N. Bolger, A. Caspi, G. Downey, & M. Moorehouse (Eds.), *Persons in context: Developmental processes* (pp. 152–180). Cambridge: Cambridge University Press.

Silbereisen, R. K., Noack, P., & Schoenpflug, U. (1994). Comparative analyses and beliefs, leisure contexts, and substance use in West Berlin and Warsaw. In R. K. Silbereisen & E. Todt (Eds.), *Adolescence in context: The interplay of family, school, peers, and work in adjustment* (pp. 176–198). New York: Springer-Verlag.

Silbereisen, R. K., & Todt, E. (Eds.). (1994). *Adolescence in context: The interplay of family, school, peers, and work in adjustment.* New York: Springer-Verlag.

Small, S. J. (1995). Enhancing contexts of adolescent development: The role of community-based action research. In L. J. Crockett & A. C. Crouter (Eds.), *Pathways through adolescence: Individual development in relation to social contexts* (pp. 211–234). Mahwah, NJ: Erlbaum.

Susman, E. J., Dorn, L. D., Feagans, L. V., & Ray, W. J. (1992). Historical and theoretical perspectives on behavioral health in children and adolescents: An introduction. In E. J. Susman, L. V. Feagans, & W. J. Ray (Eds.), *Emotion, cognition, health, and development in children and adolescents* (pp. 1–8). Hillsdale, NJ: Erlbaum.

Sussman, S., Dent, C. W., Burton, D., Stacy, A. W., & Flay, B. R. (1995). *Developing school-based tobacco use prevention and cessation programs.* Thousand Oaks, CA: Sage.

Takanishi, R. (1993). Changing views of adolescence in contemporary society. *Teachers College Record, 94*, 459–465.

Thomas, D. L., & Carver, C. (1990). Religion and adolescent social competence. In T. P. Gullotta, G. R. Adams, & R. Montemayor (Eds.), *Developing social competency in adolescence* (pp. 195–219). Newbury Park, CA: Sage.

Tolan, P. II., & Guerra, N. G. (1994). Prevention of delinquency: Current status and issues. *Applied and Preventive Psychology, 3*, 251–273.

U.S. Congress, Office of Technology Assessment. (1991). *Adolescent health: Volume 1. Summary and policy options.* Washington, DC: U.S. Government Printing Office.

Vondracek, F. W. (1994). Vocational identity development in adolescence. In R. K. Silbereisen and E. Todt (Eds.), *Adolescence in context: The interplay of family, school, peers, and work in adjustment* (pp. 284–303). New York: Springer-Verlag.

Vondracek, F. W., Lerner, R. M., & Schulenberg, J. E. (1986). *Career development: A life-span developmental approach.* Hillsdale, NJ: Erlbaum.

Wagenaar, A. C., & Perry, C. L. (1994). Community strategies for the reduction of youth drinking: Theory and application. *Journal of Research on Adolescence, 4*, 319–345.

Weissberg, R. P., Caplan, M., & Harwood, R. L. (1991). Promoting competent young people in competence-enhancing environments: A systems-based prospective on primary prevention. *Journal of Consulting and Clinical Psychology, 59*, 830–841.

W. T. Grant (1988). *The forgotten half: Pathways to success for America's youth and young families.* Washington, DC: Youth and America's future: The William T. Grant Commission on Work, Family, and Citizenship.

World Health Organization (WHO). (1986). *Charter der I. Internationalen Konferenz für Gesundheitsförderung.* Ottawa: Author.

Zins, J. E., Wagner, D. I., & Maher, C. A. (1985). *Health promotion in the schools: Innovative approaches to facilitating physical and emotional well-being.* New York: Haworth Press.

Zucker, R. A. (1979). Developmental aspects of drinking through the young adult years. In H. T. Blane and M. E. Chafetz (Eds.), *Youth, alcohol, and social policy* (pp. 91–146). New York: Plenum Press.

Author Index

Note: Italicized page numbers refer to citations in references

Aboud, F., 426, *440*
Abraham, C., 451, *467*
Abramowitz, R.H., 476, 484, 485, *496*
Abrams, D., 451, *467*
Abrams, L.A., 498, 503, 505, *519*, *520*
Abrams, S., 221, 236, *244*
Abramson, L.Y., 401, 402, 403, 405, 414, *415*, *419*
Achenbach, T.M., 304, *315*, 485, *493*
Adams, G., 420, *440*
Adan, A.M., 60, *81*
Adlaf, E., 453, *466*
Adler, N.E., 115, *131*, 174, 175, 179, *186*
Adler, T., 284, 285, 292, 297, *316*
Ahrendt, J.F., 101, *106*
Alan Guttmacher Institute, 190, *191*, *192*, 193, 195, *197*, *214*, 223, 224, *241*
Alba, R., 422, *440*
Albrecht, G., 376, *389*
Albrecht, H.T., 96, *109*, 350, *371*
Aldava, J.F., 27, *50*, 92, *107*
Aldous, J., 293, *315*
Alipuria, L., 420, 422, 424, *442*
Allan, E.A., 35, *52*
Allen, J.P., 143, 144, *156*
Allen, V.A., 86, 91, 100, 101, *108*
Allen, V.L., 322, *340*
Allen, W., 426, *443*
Allison, K., 39, 40, 41, *49*
Almeida, D.M., 11, *18*, 142, 144, 152, 153, 154, *156*, *158*, 308, *318*, 349, 350, 352, 355, 363, 367, *369*, 523, *544*
Alongi, C., 171, *189*
Alsaker, F.D., 56, *80*, 88, 89, 93, 96, 97, *106*
Amaro, H., 221, *241*
Amato, P.R., 146, 148, 149, 150, *156*
American Association of University Women, 296, *315*
American School Health Association, 120, *130*
Anastopoulos, A., 13, *16*
Anda, R., 247, 249, *278*

Andenas, S., 60, 61, *82*
Anderman, E.M., 284, *318*
Anderson, E.R., 148, *158*
Anderson, G.A., 403, *415*
Anderson, J.E., 448, *467*
Anderson, K.E., 225, 226, 235, *243*
Anderson, R., 532, *540*
Anderson, W.P., 401, *415*
Andersson, R.A., 100, *107*
Andrews, K., 162, 181, *187*
Anson, A.R., 539, *541*
Anstine, P.S., 532, *544*
Antonucci, T.C., 225, 227, 230, 231, 233, *241*, *242*, *243*, 246, 249, 276, 508, *519*
Anttonen, M., 414, *418*
Applegate, J.S., 236, *241*
Arce, C., 424, 435, *440*
Archer, S.L., 420, 422, 427, *441*, 528, *540*
Aries, E., 420, 422, 424, *440*
Arkes, H.R., 128, *130*
Arlin, P.K., 117, *130*
Armistead, L., 148, *158*
Armon, C., 117, *131*
Armstrong, B.G., 247, *278*
Arnett, J., 25, 27, *48*, 110, *130*
Arnold, K., 534, *540*
Aro, H., 58, *80*, 99, 101, *107*
Aronsson, G., 327, *342*
Aseltine, R.H., Jr., 2, *16*, 56, *81*, 251, 276, 347, *368*
Ashworth, C.S., 171, *186*
Asquith, P., 163, *189*
Association of the Advancement of Health Education, 120, *130*
Astone, N.M., 27, *50*, 347, *369*, 374, *390*
Atkinson, D., 422, 427, 428, 429, 431, 436, 437, *440*
Atman, C.J., 125, *134*
Attie, I., 210, *216*
Atwater, E., *191*
Austin, L., 114, 122, 129, *131*
Axinn, W.G., 250, *278*

Subject Index

abstract thought processes, 118
academic achievement
  and junior high school adjustment,
    292–313; long-term consequences,
    308–11
  and part-time work, 326–7, 333–5; selection
    argument, 326–7
  romantic relationships effect on, 172
  substance use relationship, 308–10
academic goals
  and college student drinking, 353–66
  questionnaire measures, 354–5
acculturation; *see also* ethnic identity
  definition, 423
  ethnic identity distinction, 423
achievement; *see also* school transitions;
    work transitions
  and junior high school transition,
    290–311
  and mental health, 399
achievement transitions, 5
action perspective, 349–53
adolescent fathers, 236–9
  ethnic differences in adjustment, 237–8
  psychological well-being, 236–9
adolescent mothers, 220–45
  age differences, 226–7, 232
  ethnic factors, 223–5
  family support, 225–36
  grandmother relationship, 230–1
  historical context, 36, 222–3
  intergenerational family context,
    225–36
  as life course strategy, 235
  longitudinal study, 227–9
  mental health consequences, 225–36
  "natural mentors," 234
  normative aspects, 235
  partner support, 233
  social support, 229, 232
  timing factors, 232
adolescent pregnancy; *see also* childbearing
  and cigarette smoking, 265
  epidemiologic data, 448

historical trends, 36
  and religion, 452, 465; sociocultural context,
    465
  rural–suburban differences, 43
adolescents' rights, 126–7
affect, and self-definition, 402–4
affiliative goals, 399–400
affiliative transitions, 5; *see also* divorce;
    family transitions; marriage peer
    relationships; sexual transitions
African Americans
  and adolescent fathers, 237–8
  and adolescent mothers, 223–36;
    longitudinal study, 227–36
  biculturalism, 437–8
  Black identity attitudes, 428–30
  conformity, 428–30
  identity development, 420–40; "triple
    quandary" in, 424
  identity exploration phase, 432–4
  identity internalization, 435
  inner-city: development critext,
    39–40; health, 40–1; identity
    formation, 41; subculture,
    38–41
  internalized racism, 424–5
  peer crowd influences, 180
  poverty rate, 501–2
  religion, 445
  self-disclosure, 167
  sexual choice behavior, 199–200
  unconventionality, 211–12
age at first intercourse
  and religion, 449–51
  trends, 190, 192–3
age-condensed families, 234–5
aggregate-level data, 61–2
AIDS
  cases of, trends, 448–9
  risk estimation, 120–4
alcohol use; *see also* heavy drinking
  age-related shifts, 247–8, 472
  and beliefs, 351–3, 355–66
  college students, 345–68; prevalence, 348

567